LACTOR 17

THE AGE OF AUGUSTUS

EDITED BY M.G.L. COOLEY

LITERARY TEXTS TRANSLATED BY B.W.J.G. WILSON

MAJOR CONTRIBUTIONS BY

R.A. ABDY
A.E. COOLEY
J.F. GARDNER
S.J. HARRISON
I.M.R. LEINS
B.M. LEVICK
J.W. RICH
J.H.C. WILLIAMS

THE AGE OF AUGUSTUS

First published – August 2003
Reprinted – August 2008 (with corrections and addenda)
Second Edition – August 2013 (with new translation of *Res Gestae*)

ISBN: 978 0 903625 36 4

TABLE OF CONTENTS

4

Acknowledgements

It is a great pleasure to be able to thank all those who have given generously of their time and expertise in enabling this book to appear. John Rich did much of the initial work on selecting the material; in particular the A level set passages, produced a couple of years ago, remain essentially his. Brian Wilson undertook the enormous task of translating the literary texts. I thank him not only for his translations, but for his great patience in having to put up with two different editors in turn, and for his great encouragement in the project.

Stephen Harrison helped with the selection of the poetry and provided the introduction and commentary to the poems. Jane Gardner selected, translated and commented on the legal sources: without her expertise these sources could not have been included. Barbara Levick provided the commentaries on Tacitus and Velleius. Miriam Griffin did likewise for the passages of Seneca the Younger, almost literally by return of post. Katherine Clarke provided expert guidance on Strabo; Andrew Wilson did the same for Frontinus.

Jonathan Williams, Ian Leins and Richard Abdy from the Department of Coins and Medals at the British Museum between them selected, translated, commented on and photographed the coins. The photograph of Augustus is courtesy of the British Museum non-commercial images service and the trustees of the British Museum.

Thanks are due to Cambridge University Press for permission to use Alison Cooley's translation of Augustus' *Res Gestae* from her commentary on the text (CUP 2009), and for permision to reproduce three maps from *The Cambridge Ancient History* volume X[2]; and to Oxford University Press and Amanda Claridge for allowing material from *Rome, An Oxford Archaeological Guide* (OUP 1998) to be used.

Ken Hughes' careful copy-editing greatly improved the accuracy and presentation of the text. The mistakes which remain result from my oversight, ignorance or stubbornness and for these I sincerely apologise.

Finally, greatest thanks are due to my wife, Alison, who selected, translated and commented on the inscriptions, read a draft of the entire manuscript, but more than this provided ever timely criticism, support and encouragement.

Bibliography and Abbreviations

AE	*L'Année épigraphique*
BMC	H. Mattingly, *Coins of the Roman Empire in the British Museum*, volume I: *Augustus to Vitellius*, (London 1923)
BMCRR	*Coins of the Roman Republic in the British Museum*, 3 volumes
CAH X²	A.K. Bowman, E. Champlin and A. Lintott, edd., *Cambridge Ancient History Volume X The Augustan Empire, 43 BC – AD 69* (2nd edition, Cambridge 1996)
CIL	T. Mommsen *et al*. edd., *Corpus Inscriptionum Latinarum* (Berlin 1866–)
Cooley, *RG*	A.E. Cooley, *Res Gestae Divi Augusti* (Cambridge 2009)
EJ	V. Ehrenberg and A.H.M. Jones, *Documents Illustrating the Reigns of Augustus and Tiberius*, 2nd edition (Oxford 1976)
IG	*Inscriptiones Graecae* (1873–)
IGRRP	*Inscriptiones Graecae ad Res Romanas Pertinentes* (1906–)
ILS	H. Dessau, *Inscriptiones Latinae Selectae* (1892–1916)
Inscr. It.	A. Degrassi, *Inscriptiones Italiae 13* (Rome 1947, 1963)
IRT	J.M. Reynolds and J.B. Ward-Perkins, *Inscriptions of Roman Tripolitania*
OCD	S. Hornblower and A. Spawforth, edd., *The Oxford Classical Dictionary* (3rd edition, Oxford 1996)
RIC	C.H.V. Sutherland, *The Roman Imperial Coinage, volume I from 31 BC to AD 69*, (London 1984)
Rich, *Dio*	J.W. Rich, *Cassius Dio, The Augustan Settlement (Roman History 53–55.9)* (Warminster 1990)
RPC	A. Burnett, M. Amandry and P.P. Ripollès, *Roman Provincial Coinage I: From the Death of Caesar to the Death of Vitellius* (London and Paris, 1992)
RRC	M.H. Crawford, *Roman Republican Coinage* I, (Cambridge 1974)
SEG	*Supplementum Epigraphicum Graecum*
SIG³	W. Dittenberger, *Sylloge Inscriptionum Graecarum*
Syme, *AA*	R. Syme, *The Augustan Aristocracy* (Oxford 1986)
Syme, *RR*	R. Syme, *The Roman Revolution* (Oxford 1939)
Zanker, *Power of Images*	P. Zanker, *The Power of Images in the Age of Augustus* (Ann Arbor 1988)
ZPE	*Zeitschrift für Papyrologie und Epigraphik*

Preface

The primary aim of this volume is to provide source material for the Augustus modules in Ancient History A level. It is also hoped that this selection will prove useful to undergraduates studying Augustus.

The material has been arranged in two parts. The second part consists of a thematic selection of material. The first part includes material which it was thought better to present whole rather than in pieces. I hope that cross-references and the occasional repetition of very short passages will make this the most helpful arrangement.

Much recent work on Augustus has emphasised the archaeological and visual. It is with considerable regret that this LACTOR does not include photographs (with the important exception of the coins) or architectural plans. Various practical considerations prevented this, especially the size, cost and time-scale of this volume. The gap, however, will be filled by images on the LACTOR website (address on inside front cover).

Like other LACTORs, this volume deliberately excludes some material easily available elsewhere. Therefore Cassius Dio is not included, nor is Suetonius' biography of Augustus. This volume does, however, include material which, though readily available in translation, will be far more useful in a single volume.

A reprint has allowed various minor corrections and additions to be made. I am grateful to Noreen Humble for suggesting several of these in a review. Four short passages have been added: to preserve the original numbering of pages and sources these appear as addenda.

I dedicate this volume, with great love and gratitude, to my mother and to the memory of my father.

The need for a further reprint (just in time for the bimillenary of Augustus' death), and the kind permission of Cambridge University Press has allowed this volume to make use of Alison Cooley's translation of Augustus' *Res Gestae* from her commentary on the text (CUP 2009). The previous translation of the *Res Gestae* will be freely available on the LACTOR website (see inside cover) for the lifetime of the current AS syllabus with prescribes this version. Except for this, and a couple of minor corrections, the texts, numbering and pagination of this edition remain the same as for the second edition.

May 2003, June 2008, April 2013   M.G.L. Cooley

Head of Scholars, Warwick School

Editorial Conventions for Texts of Inscriptions

[ ]   square brackets enclose words or letters which are missing in the original
             text and have been restored by the editor or translator.
[....]   dots in square brackets represent letters missing in the original text.
( )   round brackets are used to expand words abbreviated in the original text.
...   dots outside brackets mark where the translator has omitted part of the text.
[5]   Smaller font numbers inside square brackets give line numbers of the
             inscription.

Notes on Literary Sources

On poets, including **Horace, Virgil, Ovid, Propertius**, see Section **G**. On **Livy,
Velleius** and **Tacitus**, see Sections **D, E** and **F. Legal sources** translated in Section **S**
are introduced there. Minor authors are given brief introductions where passages from
their works are given, e.g. for **Zosimus,** see **L23**.

Dio (probably L. Claudius Cassius Dio Cocceianus) was born *c.* AD 163/5 into one of
     the most prominent Greek families in Bithynia (NW Turkey). He had a
     distinguished career, over about 40 years, as Roman senator and governor, retiring
     after his second consulship in AD 229. Dio's *Roman History* is written in Greek and
     covers the entire period from Rome's foundation to his own day. Dio's greatest
     value is in providing the only surviving chronological coverage of Augustus' reign,
     relying on that provided by earlier historians. His own experience offered first-hand
     experience of the governing system of the principate, but also led to anachronistic
     assumptions. Like most ancient historians, he saw no problem in effectively making
     up speeches to enliven his narrative. Dio's description of events in the age of
     Augustus needs to be treated with some caution: his interpretations and
     explanations are unreliable.
Frontinus (Sextus Iulius Frontinus) lived from about AD 30 to AD 104, and was given
     important positions by the emperors Vespasian, Domitian, Nerva and Trajan,
     including three consulships. In AD 97, Nerva appointed him Water Commissioner,
     and while in this post he wrote a book about the history, administration and
     maintenance of the aqueducts he was responsible for (*de aquis urbis Romae – The
     Aqueducts of Rome*). This book includes a wealth of technical information, facts
     and figures about the system in his day as well as exact quotations of earlier statutes.
Aulus Gellius, born between AD 125 and 128, seems to have published his *Attic Nights*
     around AD 180. He explains the title as emanating from his decision to write up
     notes he made from his reading on a great variety of subjects, during the long winter
     nights in Attica, but says he only completed the project 30 years later as an
     instructive entertainment for his children. His value lies in his repeating material
     which he read, but which is not now preserved elsewhere.
Horace: poet, 65–8 BC. See pages 97–98 for full notes.
St. Jerome's *Chronicle* is a chronological compendium of world history (Judaeo-
     Christian, Greek, Roman) from the birth of Abraham (placed in 2016 BC) to AD
     378). Based on a similar work by Eusebius, Jerome added in many facts concerned
     with Roman history, literature and scholarship. He claims as sources Suetonius and
     other (unspecified) Roman historians, but also admits it was a job done in a hurry.

He shows an 'apparent indifference to exact dating' (J.N.D. Kelly, *Jerome* 1975). Nonetheless, he also preserves many interesting snippets of information.

Josephus (Flavius Iosephus), AD 37/8–*c*.100, was a prominent Jew who, after the Jewish Revolt, gained the favour of the Flavian emperors and settled in Rome, writing books on Jewish themes in Greek. His *Jewish War* deals mainly with events he participated in, but the earlier part provides a summary of earlier Jewish conflicts. His *Jewish Antiquities* present Jewish history from the Creation to just before the revolt to non-Jewish readers.

Livy: historian, 59 BC–AD 17. See page 54 for full notes.

Macrobius was probably the praetorian prefect of Italy in AD 430. His *Saturnalia* is set as a dialogue taking place at the celebration of the festival of Saturn of AD 383 at which the greatest pagan scholars of the time discuss a variety of topics, including the calendar and famous people's jokes. Sources include other miscellanies and collections of sayings.

Cornelius Nepos, *c*.110–24 BC, lived in Rome from the 60s. Amongst various works, some of his biographies of famous men survive, including one of Atticus whom Nepos claimed to know well. Nepos published his biography before Atticus' death and then a second version afterwards.

Ovid: poet, 43 BC–AD 17. See page 99 for full notes.

Pliny the Elder (Gaius Plinius Secundus), *c*. AD 23/4–79, was a prominent equestrian, in command of the Roman fleet at Misenum, and author. His 37-book *Natural History,* in his words, 'tells the story of nature, that is to say, life.' It includes, according to his reckoning, 20,000 important facts derived from 2,000 books. He also wrote accounts of campaigns against the Germans and a history of the later Julio-Claudian period, both now lost.

Plutarch, *c*. AD 45–120, is best known for his *Parallel Lives,* biographies of Greek and Roman leaders, linking the lives of Greeks and Romans, and often drawing moral conclusions. He also wrote an unpaired biography of Augustus, which is lost. His *Moralia* includes moral and philosophical essays and literary criticism. It also includes a section on famous sayings of kings and emperors including Augustus.

Propertius: poet, born *c*. 50 BC. See page 98 for full notes.

Quintilian (Marcus Fabius Quintilianus) born *c*. AD 35 in Spain became the best known teacher of Rhetoric in Rome. In the sixth of twelve books of *The Orator's Education* (*Institutio Oratoria*), he advises on how to write the epilogue of a speech, devoting much space to laughter, including many examples of witty sayings or ripostes.

Seneca the Elder (Lucius Annaeus Seneca), *c*. 50 BC–*c*. AD 40, was born in Corduba in Spain, but seems to have spent much time in Rome. His history from the start of the civil wars almost to his death is lost. His *Controversiae* and *Suasoriae*, a collection of high points from rhetoricians he had heard, was addressed to his three sons.

Seneca the Younger (Lucius Annaeus Seneca), *c*.1 BC–AD 65, was born in Corduba in Spain. He was taken to Rome as a young child and educated under the eye of his father, the Elder Seneca. The Younger Seneca became committed to Stoic philosophy and embarked on a senatorial career, but he was sent into exile on Corsica in AD 41 under Claudius on a charge of adultery. He was recalled in AD 49 through the influence of Agrippina who wanted him to teach rhetoric to her son. When his pupil Nero became emperor, Seneca became his adviser and reached the consulship. Already in voluntary retirement, Seneca was accused of complicity in the Pisonian conspiracy and ordered to commit suicide. From the reign of Caligula on, Seneca was a successful orator and writer, composing philosophical prose works called 'dialogues' and verse tragedies on subjects from Greek tragedy.

Strabo, *c.* 64 BC–AD 21 or later, was born in Amasia in Pontus, into a family that enjoyed close involvement with the local ruling dynasty. He appears to have travelled widely, partly through his connections to members of the Roman élite, such as Aelius Gallus. His great literary achievement was a 47-book historical work, which is almost entirely lost. However, we do have his 17-book *Geography*, which was compiled during the reigns of Augustus and Tiberius, and provides an account of the entire world known to the Romans. Strabo's material came largely from older literary sources, but his mixture of Greek education, Pontic background and Roman connections, provides us with one of the most important and extensive contemporary sources on the world of Augustus.

Suetonius (Publius Suetonius Tranquillus), *c.* AD 70 – 130. Author of *The Lives of the Caesars* (biographies of Julius Caesar and the emperors from Augustus to Domitian). An equestrian, he held important posts in imperial administration under Trajan and Hadrian, including literary adviser, chief librarian, chief secretary (*a studiis, a bibliothecis* and *ab epistulis*). These posts would have given him access to official records: he says he quotes exactly from an exchange in the senate (*Aug.* 58) and from letters in Augustus' own hand (*Aug.* 71, 76). His biographies concentrate on the emperor's personality and characteristics, often conveyed by anecdote and without a chronological framework.

Tacitus: historian, born *c.* AD 56. See pages 82–83 for full notes.

Valerius Maximus compiled his book of 'memorable deeds and sayings from the City of Rome and foreign nations' in the reign of Tiberius (AD 14–37). He makes no claim to originality, merely to making a convenient selection from famous authors.

Velleius Paterculus: born 20/19 BC. See page 58 for full notes.

Virgil: poet, 70–19 BC. See pages 96–97 for full notes.

Augustus and the Coinage

Introduction

In the late 20s BC the new Roman State established by Augustus turned its attention to one of the basic concerns of good government: money and coinage. The genius of Augustus' approach to the coinage was not that it was especially innovative, but that it was systematic. It is remarkable that this important development receives almost no attention from the literary sources. Almost all the information we have about it is derived from the coins themselves.

In the Republic the Romans had produced a complex coinage in silver and bronze (gold coinage was not common). But it had rather fallen apart in the first century BC and for decades only silver coins, *denarii*, had been made. No bronze coins had been made in any quantity for years. Augustus changed all this. He introduced, and kept in fairly constant production, a coinage that was able to cover all levels of transaction. It had seven different denominations made of four metals: gold, silver, brass (zinc and copper) and copper. Large payments could be conducted in high-value gold coins; medium-value payments, such as wages, in silver or the larger base-metal coins; and small retail purchases in the lowest-value base-metal coins. Never before had the ancient world seen such a complex, inter-locking coinage suited to so many different needs.

Augustus and the small change

In the ancient world the value of a gold or silver coin was closely related to the intrinsic value of the precious metal it was made of. Base-metal coins were only of token value, as all our coins and banknotes are nowadays. Their face value was determined by their fixed 'exchange rate' with the higher-value gold and silver coins. The metal that went to make 16 copper *asses* was worth much less than the silver in one *denarius*. But that was nevertheless the official rate, and it was this relationship that gave the base-metal *as* its monetary value. Reviving the base-metal coinage also gave the state an opportunity to make a profit. Any payments which it made in token-value base-metal coins will have cost much less than ones which had to be made in 'hard' currency, gold or silver.

One constant problem in the ancient world was the provision of a sufficient amount of base-metal coinage to make the monetary system really work. Vastly greater quantities of low-denomination coins are required for general circulation than higher-value ones. In 2000, for example, the British Royal Mint had to make 869 million 1 penny coins, compared with only 84 million 1 pound coins, just to keep up with demand. The laborious, hand-held coining technology of antiquity was simply incapable of making enough small change. Ancient states often simply gave up the attempt, as the Romans themselves had for the best part of a century before Augustus. The revival of the production of a viable low-value coinage was one of his main achievements, though it is doubtful whether even he managed fully to satisfy demand.

The supply of imperial base-metal coinage was supplemented in several provinces of the Roman Empire by what are collectively known as the 'Roman provincial coinages'. City communities throughout the Empire struck base-metal coinages for local circulation. These were used alongside Roman gold and silver coins which circulated Empire-wide. The multitude of designs used on these coinages are a rich source of information on the local and provincial cultures of the Roman world.

The organisation of the imperial coinage

Augustus' new coinage began to be produced at Rome in all metals in the late 20s BC, though some 'imperial' gold and silver coins were also made at other locations outside Italy. But between about 15 and 10 BC the manufacture of all Roman gold and silver coins was gradually transferred to a new mint at Lugdunum in Gaul (Lyons, France). This was probably for reasons of ease of supply. Lugdunum was conveniently situated between the main sources of bullion supply in Spain and the military frontier on the Rhine and the Danube where were stationed the legions that formed the destination of much of the mint's output.

Base-metal coins were made in Lugdunum as well as gold and silver coins. After 12 BC, by contrast, the mint at Rome was reduced to making just base-metal coins.

At the same time as restoring the coinage to a full denominational system, Augustus also restored the old Republican monetary magistracy of the *tresviri monetales*, (the 'Three Men in charge of the Mint'). They took their title from the location of the mint of Rome which was situated close to the temple of the goddess Moneta (from which also derive the words 'mint' and 'money'). Under the Republic the names of these officials had appeared on the coins, and they reappeared under Augustus, another example of his intention to revive certain aspects of Republican constitutional tradition. It did not last long, however. The magistrates' names disappeared from the gold and silver coins with the transfer of their production to Lugdunum, and from the bronze coins made at Rome in about 4 BC.

The other major development in the coinage under Augustus was in its appearance. In the coins of the late Republic there had been no consistency in coin-design. They had depicted a wide variety of mythological and historical themes mostly connected with the families of the various monetary magistrates who were in charge of their production. Under Augustus, coin-designs continued to change year by year. But for the most part they began to refer to him and his family alone. Augustus' portrait, though not universal, became a standard design feature, accompanied by his name and titles. Though the coinage remained legally under the authority of the Senate and People of Rome, it was, like so much of the Roman constitution, to all intents and purposes dominated by the person of the emperor.

The gold *aureus* and the silver *denarius*

At the top of Augustus' new coinage was the gold coin called the *aureus* (simply Latin for 'gold coin'). It was about 18 mm across, weighed nearly 8 grams, and was made of pure gold. Gold is a soft metal, and these coins quickly became worn in circulation. The Romans had never had a regular gold coinage before. There had been quite substantial quantities of gold coins made since the 40s BC onwards, but these were unusual, prompted by the emergency conditions of the period of civil war. Augustus' gold coins were intrinsic to the coinage system as a whole. They were worth 25 *denarii*, the next denomination down.

The *denarius* was a silver coin of about the same size as the *aureus* but weighing only around 4 grams. This coin represented a continuity with the old Republican system, since it had already been in production for almost two centuries. *Denarius* literally means 'a tenner', since it was originally worth ten bronze coins (*asses*).

The base-metal coins

One of Augustus' most important innovations in the matter of the coinage was the introduction of a middle-value base-metal coin, the *sestertius*, valued at a quarter of a *denarius*. The Romans had once made tiny silver *sestertii* weighing about a gram, but these were rightly abandoned as impractical. The new version was a large, heavy coin, weighing about 28 grams and 35 mm in diameter. They were made of a brassy alloy of copper and zinc, called *oricalchum* ('mountain bronze') in Latin. This was a new metal for Roman coins, which had been only recently imported from Asia Minor. It was difficult to make and therefore slightly more valuable than bronze (copper and tin) or pure copper. It is also shiny in appearance (it is often mistaken for gold) and therefore perhaps had a superficial appearance of value.

The next coin down was called the **dupondius**, worth half a *sestertius* or two *asses*. It was also made of brass, weighed about 14 grams and was about 28 mm across.

The traditional base-unit of the whole Roman monetary system was the **as**. This was an ancient Roman denomination whose name originally came from the Greek for 'one'. From it comes our word 'ace', the name for the playing card with the value of one. The *as* had once been a large piece of bronze weighing a Roman pound (about 324 grams). Over the centuries inflation had reduced it in value till it became, under Augustus, a plain copper coin of about 10 grams in weight and the same size as a *dupondius*. There were 16 *asses* to the *denarius*, and four *asses* to the *sestertius*.

Below the *as* came two really low-value coins whose names were defined in relation to it: the brass **semis** (half-*as*) and the copper **quadrans** (quarter-*as*), both about 3 grams in weight and 17 mm in diameter. The satirist Petronius says that the measure of a really mean man was that he was prepared to pick a *quadrans* out of a dung-heap with his teeth (*Satyricon*, chapter 43). Behind the profanity is a profundity: the Roman Empire now had a full range of denominations from the highest to the lowest to cater for all its needs.

The base-metal coins tended to be simpler and less varied in design than the gold and silver. They also bore the inscription *S C* for *Senatus Consulto* ('by decree of the Senate'). It used to be thought that this referred to senatorial control of the base-metal coins as opposed to the precious metal coins that were supposedly controlled by the emperor at his mint at Lugdunum. It is just as likely that it simply refers to the senatorial decree that authorised the recommencement of base-metal coin-production in the late 20s BC. It went on to become a traditional design feature, and remained on all Roman base-metal coins until the third century AD.

Conclusion

In introducing and maintaining a multi-purpose coinage, Augustus had some real problems to overcome. Maintaining sufficient production and supply in all metals was, as we have seen, one of the biggest. It was also crucial to maintain the relative values of the different elements of the coinage system, in order to provide stability and reliability, two vital ingredients in any successful monetary system.

Why was this difficult? Because while coins made of different metals need to stand in a fixed denominational relationship to one another, the relative values of the gold, silver, and copper from which they are made may vary, perhaps considerably. This can result in the coin's official face-value actually being worth less than the bullion value of its metal. In such circumstances, coins tend to be removed from circulation and melted down, which can cause real problems for the supply of money.

Partly in response to these inevitable fluctuations, later emperors had to reduce the amount of silver in the *denarius* so much that by the reign of the emperor Septimius Severus (AD 193–211) it contained only 50% silver. Inflation also ate away at the value of the smallest denominations, the *semis* and *quadrans*, and they stopped being produced in the second century AD (much as the farthing and halfpenny disappeared from British currency in the twentieth century).

But despite these inherent problems, Augustus' coinage system was stable throughout his reign, and remained essentially intact until the mid-third century AD. The new currency system that he established was one of his most enduring reforms. This success is clear testimony to the internal stability, as much political as monetary, which he managed to introduce into the Roman Empire.

Table showing the relative values, materials and dimensions of the coins:

Coin	HS equivalent	Material	Diameter	Weight	Introduction
aureus	100 HS	gold	18mm	8g	Augustus
denarius	4 HS	silver	18mm	4g	3rd century BC
sestertius	1 HS	brass	35mm	28g	Augustus
dupondius	½ HS	brass	28mm	14g	
as	¼ HS	copper	28mm	10g	traditional unit
semis	⅛ HS	brass	17mm	3g	
quadrans	¹⁄₁₆ HS	copper	17mm	3g	

A guide to monetary values	**Sesterces**
Augustus established the property qualification for a Roman senator at	1,000,000
Augustus established the property qualification for a Roman equestrian at	400,000
The annual pay of a Roman legionary soldier was	900
In 29 BC, Augustus gave his veterans, from war booty	1,000
In 29 BC, Augustus gave every member of the Roman *plebs*	400
In AD 5, Augustus established a discharge payment for legionary veterans of	12,000
Overall, Augustus claimed to have given away	2,400,000,000
An unskilled slave seems to have cost between	200–1,000
At Rome, men received 60 *modii* (measures) of wheat annually, worth	c.300–360

Glossary

aedile: the most junior magistrate with full senatorial status.

as: the base-unit of Roman currency, a small value coin.

auctoritas: authority rather than actual power, claimed by Augustus as the basis of his rule.

augur: a priest, especially responsible for predictions based on flights of birds.

aureus: the highest value coin, made of gold.

censor: one of two senior senators, elected for eighteen months, every five years and responsible for standards in public life, especially of the senate.

cognomen: the last of a Roman's names, sometimes a type of 'nickname', but often distinguishing not just an individual, but a branch of a large family.

confiscations: refers to the seizure of land in Italy to pay off veterans who had fought for Octavian against the armies of the republican side.

consul: the highest political office in the republic. Two consuls were elected each year to serve for one year.

cursus honorum: the 'career path' involving progression through various offices of state.

denarius: a high-value, silver coin.

dictator: originally someone appointed in an emergency with wide powers. Julius Caesar usurped the post by making himself perpetual dictator, giving the term its modern use.

equestrian: a member of the class almost equal in status to a senator, but usually not involved in political life.

fasces: symbols of the power of a magistrate, carried by his retinue.

fasti: publicly inscribed lists of various sorts: dates, consuls, and triumphs.

frater arvalis: (lit. arval priest), one of 12 members of a select priesthood, all from senatorial families, and including the emperor. Members were co-opted and served until death.

freedman: a slave, formally set free by his master, automatically becoming a Roman citizen.

imperator: originally a title given by his troops to a general after a major victory, such as would eventually gain a triumph. Augustus usurps this as part of his name.

imperium: the power invested in a magistrate (e.g. a consul, praetor, or provincial governor).

imperium maius: (greater power) i.e. power greater than a normal consul, governor, etc., granted to certain members of the imperial family.

lares: guardian spirits, of households, crossroads etc.

legate: **(1)** anyone to whom authority is delegated, e.g. a military officer.

(2) *legatus Augusti propraetore* (legate of Augustus with praetorian power): the proper term for someone appointed to govern a (major) imperial province.

ludi saeculares: (Centennial Games) games held once every 100 or 110 years, to celebrate a new age.

manumission: the formal freeing of a slave, resulting in his being given Roman citizenship.

novus homo: (new man). The term applied to the first member of a family to become a senator, or to become consul.

pater patriae: (Father of the Fatherland). Title granted to Augustus in 2 BC. Though honorific, it suggested authority over the country similar to that of a father over his household.

plebs: the name given to the ordinary citizen body of Rome.

pontifex maximus: (chief priest).

praetor: elected magistrate ranking between consul and quaestor. A praetor could go on to govern certain provinces and/or stand for the consulship.

prefect: the Latin simply means 'put in charge of', and the term is applied to someone put in charge of something by someone more powerful, often the *princeps*.

princeps: the word, meaning 'leader', was Augustus' preferred designation for his position.

princeps iuventutis: (leader of the younger generation). Title of honour given to Augustus' two grandsons, suggesting that one would eventually become *princeps* proper.

proconsul: someone granted the power of a consul, usually in governing a major public province.

procurator: someone looking after possessions of the *princeps*, sometimes as governor of a (minor) imperial province.

propraetor: someone granted the power of a praetor, usually in governing a minor public province.

proscription: the procedure by which the triumvirate outlawed their enemies, making their lives and property forfeit.

quaestor: a junior magistrate and member of the senate.

quindecimvir: a member of a college of priests: the full title translates as 'Member of the Board of Fifteen for Sacrifices'. They had a particular role in celebrating the Centennial Games.

res publica: the normal Latin for 'the state'.

republic: in modern usage: a state governed by elected representatives, i.e. the opposite of monarchy or principate. The term is used to describe Rome's system of government between 510 and c.44 BC.

septemvir: a member of a college of priests: the full title translates as 'Member of the Board of Seven for Feasts'. The feasts were those in honour of Jupiter at Games.

sestertius: anglicised to **sesterce**: the unit of currency in Rome.

Salii: a college of priests.

spolia opima: (Spoils of Honour): granted to a Roman commander who killed the enemy commander in single combat, and thus a very rare and prized honour.

suffect: describes a magistrate chosen to replace the previous one. Before Augustus, this was usually only when a magistrate died in office, but under Augustus ordinary consuls regularly resigned halfway through the year to be replaced by suffect consuls.

tribe: all citizens were formally a member of one of 35 tribes. By the age of Augustus, the significance was mainly in voting administration.

tribunician power: the power of a tribune, one of ten magistrates elected annually to look after the rights of the ordinary people of Rome. Augustus adopts this power as both useful and symbolic and also grants it to assistants and successors.

triumvirate: (Board of Three): Antony, Lepidus and Octavian, who divided up the empire amongst themselves after defeating the republican armies, and ruled with special powers.

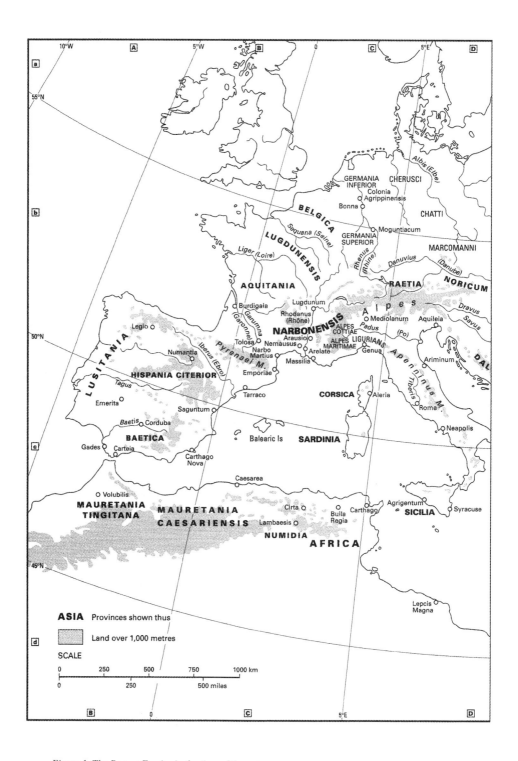

Figure 1. The Roman Empire in the time of Augustus

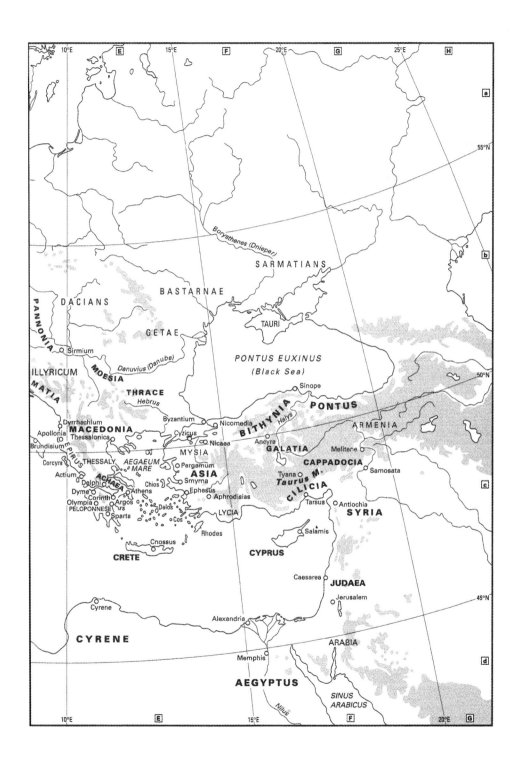

SARMATIANS

BASTARNAE

DACIANS

GETAE

TAURI

Borysthenes (Dnieper)

PANNONIA

Sirmium

ILLYRICUM

MOESIA

Danuvius (Danube)

PONTUS EUXINUS
(Black Sea)

MATIA

THRACE

Hebrus

Sinope

BITHYNIA

PONTUS

ARMENIA

Byzantium

Nicomedia

Dyrrhachium

MACEDONIA

Cyzicus

Halys

Apollonia

Thessalonica

Nicaea

Ancyra

GALATIA

Melitene

Brundisium

EPIRUS

MYSIA

CAPPADOCIA

Corcyra

THESSALY

AEGAEUM MARE

Pergamum

ASIA

Tyana

Samosata

Actium

ACHAEA

Chios

Smyrna

Taurus M.

Delphi

Ephesus

CILICIA

Dyme

Athens

Aphrodisias

Tarsus

Antiochia

Olympia

Corinth

Argos

Delos

LYCIA

SYRIA

PELOPONNESE

Sparta

Cos

Rhodes

Salamis

Cnossus

CYPRUS

CRETE

Caesarea

JUDAEA

Cyrene

Jerusalem

Alexandria

CYRENE

ARABIA

Memphis

AEGYPTUS

SINUS ARABICUS

Nilus

20

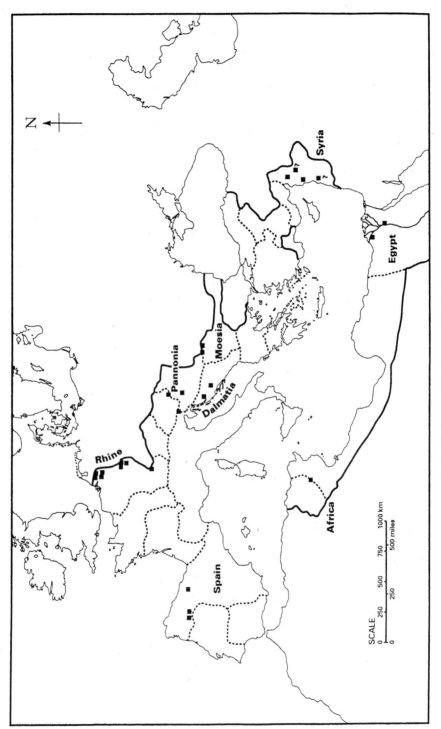

Fig. 2. Distribution of Legions, AD 14. *(After Keppie.)*

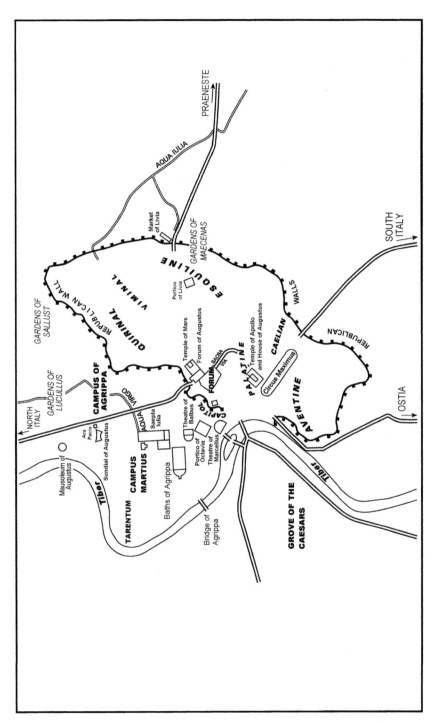

Fig. 3. Sketch map of Rome

Bronze head, 46.2 cm high, from a statue of Augustus. Found at Meroe (current North Sudan). See **N34** for the probable circumstances which make it certain that it shows Augustus in his 30s.

British Museum 1911,0901.1

SECTION A

RES GESTAE DIVI AUGUSTI
(The Achievements of the Deified Augustus)

Suetonius (*Aug*. 101.4) and Cassius Dio (56.33.1) tell us that one of the documents which Augustus deposited with the Vestal Virgins together with his will and which were read out in the senate after his death was, in Suetonius' words, 'a catalogue of his achievements, which he wished to be inscribed on bronze tablets and set up in front of the Mausoleum' (on the senate meetings of September, AD 14, see below on Tac. *Ann.* 1.8.1–5). The original outside the Mausoleum has not survived, but three copies are known, all from the province of Galatia, in central Asia Minor. The document is now normally known as *Res Gestae Divi Augusti* ('The Achievements of the Deified Augustus'), a modern title derived from Suetonius' reference and from the preface to the document.

The inscriptions. Of the three inscribed copies, the best preserved, known since the sixteenth century, is on the temple of Roma and Augustus at Ancyra (modern Ankara), the provincial capital: the Latin text is inscribed on the two inside walls of the temple porch (three columns on each wall), and a Greek version on the south external wall of the temple. Two other, more fragmentary, copies were published in the early twentieth century: one, at Apollonia in Pisidia, inscribed on a monument honouring the imperial family, gives only the Greek version; the other, at the veteran colony of Antioch in Pisidia, gives only the Latin text and is inscribed (in ten columns) in a complex dedicated to the imperial cult, with an accompanying sculptural programme celebrating Augustus' conquests and the resulting peace and prosperity (see S. Mitchell and M. Waelkens, *Pisidian Antioch* [1998]). Copies of the document were perhaps circulated to all the provinces; it is uncertain whether the decision to have it widely inscribed was a local initiative by the governor of Galatia or it is merely chance that all our copies come from there. The surviving copies enable us to restore virtually the entire text: where we do not have the Latin, it can almost always be supplied with certainty from the Greek version.

The main body of the document is written in the first person, and the Latin text must be Augustus' own words. The preface and the appendix in the form in which we have them may have been composed in Galatia, but the preface is almost certainly adapted from the original heading of the inscription outside the Mausoleum, with merely the closing words modified. The Greek version is at times close to the original, at times a free paraphrase; it is thought to have been composed in Galatia.

There are similarities in the layout of the Ancyra and Antioch copies of the Latin text which are likely to reflect the disposition of the original at Rome: each falls into two halves with the second half starting at 19.1, probably corresponding to the division of the material between the two bronze pillars; the preface is written in larger letters across several columns; the text is divided into 35 chapters, the first lines of which begin with a larger letter set a little to the left of the following lines. The section divisions within the chapters are modern, for convenience of reference.

Date of composition. Statements at 8.4 and 35.2 imply that in its present form the document dates from the last months of Augustus' life. It is usually supposed that Augustus produced a first version a good deal earlier and then revised it from time to time (Tiberius could have made a final revision after his death). This hypothesis about composition derives some support from the infrequency of references to events in Augustus' later years (though this may just reflect their relative lack of successes). E. S. Ramage, *Chiron* 18 (1988), 71 ff, argues that the whole work was composed at the end of Augustus' life cf. Cooley, *RG*, introduction section 6.

Structure. The document opens with two chapters dealing with achievements and honours of Augustus' early career, from late 44 BC to the battles of Philippi in 42. Then follows a section (chapters 3–14) recounting a selection of his achievements and honours, first military (3.1–4.3) and then civil. The next major section deals with his expenditures (chapters 15–24): it is this section which is referred to in the preface as setting out 'the expenses which he incurred for the republic and the Roman people'. This is followed by another major section recounting external successes in both war and diplomacy (chapters 25–33): it is this section in particular which purports to demonstrate how, in the words of the preface, 'he subjected the world to the empire of the Roman people'. The document closes with two chapters (34–35) which balance the two opening chapters and which deal with Augustus' position in the state after the civil wars and with associated honours to which he attached special importance.

Readership, models and purpose. As befitted its original location, the target readership of the document was clearly Roman: the citizen body in general, and in particular the inhabitants of the city of Rome. The provinces are mentioned mainly in the context of Augustus' external achievements, and only one of his many benefactions to Italian and provincial cities secures a mention (24.1). Z. Yavetz (in F. Millar and E. Segal, *Caesar Augustus: Seven Aspects* [1984], 1–36) has suggested that Augustus may have been writing particularly for the edification of the younger members of the upper orders, and this conjecture may gain some support from the subsequently discovered *Tabula Siarensis*, an inscription recording the senatorial decree prescribing honours for the dead Germanicus, which ordains that Tiberius' panegyric of Germanicus should be publicly inscribed because 'it would be useful for the youth' (see R. K. Sherk, *The Roman Empire: Augustus to Hadrian* [1988], no. 36A.II.14–17).

Inscribed records celebrating individuals' achievements were commonplace at Rome. Placards detailing victories, conquests and booty were carried in triumphs, and permanent inscriptions in this form were attached to some triumphal monuments. Inscribed accounts of individuals' honours and achievements (*elogia*) were affixed to tombs or beneath statues or other monuments in their honour. *Elogia* of this kind were set beneath the statues of the great men of the past in the Forum of Augustus (**K20–K25**). Most *elogia* are composed in the third person, but some are in the first person, like the *Res Gestae*. A number stress that the individual honoured was the first to achieve particular feats.

The *Res Gestae* thus stood in a well-established Roman tradition. But it is far longer than any other known *elogium*, just as the Mausoleum, before which it stood, was far larger than any other Roman tomb. Thus its scale was designed to emphasise the uniqueness both of Augustus' achievements and of the honours which had been accorded him in return.

In an important article ('Augustus, the *Res Gestae* and Hellenistic theories of apotheosis', *Journal of Roman Studies* 89 [1999], 1–18), A. B. Bosworth argues that one of the aims of the document may have been to justify the deification of Augustus, decreed by the senate on 17 September, AD 14, and emphasised in the opening words of the preface ('of the achievements of the *deified* Augustus ...'). Deification was believed to be the reward for wide conquests and great benefactions. A work by the

Greek writer Euhemerus (*c*. 300 BC) which represented the principal gods as deified kings was well known to Roman readers through Ennius' translation. Euhemerus described an imaginary island, Panchaia, whose central sanctuary of Zeus contained a gold inscription, set up by Zeus while he was a king and detailing his achievements and benefactions. The parallel may not have been lost on Augustus' more sophisticated readers.

Character. The document does not set out to review developments during Augustus' reign, but merely to present his personal achievements and honours, but, even within these limits, it is highly selective: Augustus practises a masterly economy with the truth. Thus he boldly opens with his controversial conduct in the period after the assassination of Caesar, but passes over his ruthless shifts of allegiance, stressing instead his extreme youth, the rapid promotion accorded by first the senate and then the people, and his claims to have acted as liberator and as avenger of his adoptive father (1–2; contrast Tac. *Ann*. 1.10.1–2). At 3.1 he boasts of his clemency to citizens; by restricting his claim to those defeated in civil war he is able to pass over his part in the proscriptions. The war with Sextus Pompeius is presented as a war against pirates (25.1). External reverses such as the loss of Germany and the failure of the Arabian expedition are passed over (26.2, 5). At 34.3 he acknowledges his primacy, but insists that it rested simply on 'authority'. The only Romans he names are members of his family and consuls for dating, and he pointedly avoids mentioning his Roman enemies by name (2, 10.2, 25). See R. Ridley, *The Emperor's Retrospect*, 2003.

One aspect of the document stresses republican tradition, Augustus' role within it and his personal modesty. The document begins with his championing of the liberty of the republic (1.1) and ends with his transference of the republic to the control of the senate and people, primacy of 'authority' and acclamation as *pater patriae* (34–35). He stresses his declining of triumphs after 29 BC, rejection of offices contrary to ancestral tradition (5–6), collegiality (6.2, 34.3) and revival of ancestral practices (8.5); he also draws attention to his converting silver statues of himself into gifts for Apollo (24.2). The roles of senate and people in conferring honours are carefully distinguished. The wish to appear modest and citizen-like may help to explain why Augustus lays such stress on his tribunician power, but never mentions the division of the provinces or the special arrangements made about his *imperium* (cf. Dio 53.32.5, 54.10.5).

That is, however, only one side of the document. As already noted, it sets out to overwhelm the reader with the scale and number of Augustus' achievements and distinctions. Numbers are constantly deployed to make this effect, and Augustus frequently draws our attention to achievements which were unique or unprecedented. His magniloquence is particularly imposing in the external section (26–33), where, by deploying the names of remote peoples and places, he seeks to convey the impression that his arms and diplomacy have brought the power of Rome to the remotest parts of the inhabited world. Here he was to some extent following in established tradition: the Romans had long claimed to rule the world, and such claims were facilitated by the slipperiness of concepts such as 'friendship', which enabled them to represent diplomatic exchanges as the acceptance of subjection; it had been claimed for Pompey and Caesar that they had brought Roman rule to the ends of the earth. See further C. Nicolet, *Space, Geography and Politics in the Early Roman Empire* (1991), chs. 1–2; Bosworth, cited above.

The physical location of the original inscription should not be forgotten: in front of Augustus' vast Mausoleum, and not far from other Augustan monuments of the northern Campus Martius which had related themes – the Altar of Augustan Peace, the Sundial, and the Porticus Vipsania, erected by Agrippa and containing a map of the world.

Influence. The document was certainly used by Suetonius for his life of Augustus: he cites it explicitly at 43.1 (quoting from *RG* 22.2), and there are a number of other passages where he is clearly drawing on it; he may have consulted the inscription itself or a text in the imperial archives. Tacitus may allude to the document at *Ann.* 1.10.1–2. Attempts to detect use of the document in other authors are inconclusive.

Further reading. P. A. Brunt and J. M. Moore, *Res Gestae Divi Augusti* (1967), and A.E. Cooley, *Res Gestae Divi Augusti* (2009) each have Latin text and translation and very helpful introduction and commentary. Besides the works cited above, see also J. Elsner, in Elsner (ed.), *Art and Text in Roman Culture* (1996), 32–53, on the monumental character and impact of the Roman original and the Galatian copies (with illustrations). E.S. Ramage, *The Nature and Purpose of Augustus' "Res Gestae"* (1987), includes a useful survey of modern research. R.Ridley, *The Emperor's Retrospect, Augustus' Res Gestae in epigraphy, historiography and commentary* (2003) challenges the view that Augustus does not lie.

Res Gestae Divi Augusti

Below is a copy of the achievements of the deified Augustus, by which he made the world subject to the rule of the Roman people, and of the expenses which he incurred for the state and people of Rome, as inscribed upon two bronze columns which have been set up at Rome.

[1.1] Aged nineteen years old I mustered an army at my personal decision and at my personal expense, and with it I liberated the state, which had been oppressed by a despotic faction.[1] [1.2] For this reason the senate passed honorific decrees admitting me to its body in the consulship of Gaius Pansa and Aulus Hirtius [43 BC], at the same time giving me consular precedence in stating my opinion, and it gave me supreme command.[2] [1.3] To prevent the state from suffering harm, it ordered me as *propraetor* to take precautions together with the consuls.[3] [1.4] In this same year [43 BC], moreover, the people appointed me consul, after both consuls had fallen in war, and *triumvir* for settling the state.[4]

[2] Those who murdered my father I drove into exile by way of the courts of law, exacting retribution for their crime and afterwards I defeated them twice in battle while they were making war upon the state.[5]

[3.1] I have often conducted wars by land and sea, civil and foreign, across the whole world, and as victor I was merciful to all citizens who asked for pardon.[6] [3.2] As for foreign peoples, those whom I could safely pardon, I preferred to preserve than to destroy.[7] [3.3] There have been roughly 500,000 Roman citizens under oath of allegiance to me. Considerably more than 300,000 of these I have settled in colonies or sent back to their towns after they had completed their terms of service, and to all of them I allotted pieces of land or else gave them money as the rewards for their service.[8] [3.4] I have captured 600 ships excluding those smaller than triremes.[9]

---

[1] In October-November 44 BC Octavian raised troops from Caesar's veteran colonies and won over two of Antony's legions. He then made common cause with Antony's opponents in the senate, led by Cicero who justified Octavian's raising of an army in terms of championing the liberty of the republic in speeches delivered on 20 December 44 (*Philippics* 3.2-5, 4.2-4).

[2] These honours were conferred in early January 43 BC, along with a gilded equestrian statue (**K16**) and the right to stand for the consulship ten years early. Augustus naturally passes over the latter grant, under which he would have had to wait until 30 BC for the consulship. Supreme command (*imperium*) was held by the higher magistrates. The anniversary of its award is recorded by the calendars, see **C2, C40**.

[3] The terms of this decree (not mentioned elsewhere) were those of the so-called 'last decree' (*senatus consultum ultimum*), frequently passed since 121 BC to provide for the restoration of order in emergencies.

[4] Both consuls were killed in defeating Antony in two battles near Mutina in April 43 BC. In early August Octavian led his army to Rome, obliging the senate to permit his election as consul (**C40**). Soon after he opened negotiations with Antony and Lepidus. They agreed that all three should be appointed 'triumvirs for settling the state' with sweeping powers, and that their enemies (including Cicero) should be proscribed and Caesar's murderers hunted down. The triumvirate was instituted, initially for five years, by a law passed in the assembly on 27 November 43 BC (see note 15).

[5] After his election as consul, Octavian had a law passed establishing a special court which tried Caesar's killers in their absence and sentenced them to exile. Antony and Octavian defeated Brutus and Cassius in two battles at Philippi in Macedonia in October 42 BC. Augustus here falsely claims sole credit for the victories (compare **C37** and note).

[6] For clemency as one of Augustus' virtues see 34.2 and Vell. 2.86.2. For less favourable versions see Suet. *Aug.* 13, 15; Dio 48.14.3-5, 49.12.4-5. Augustus' statement here is restricted to those defeated in battle, allowing him to pass over the massacre of the proscribed in late 43 BC.

[7] A traditional claim: compare Virgil, *Aen.* 6.853 (**G37**); Horace, *Carm. Saec.* 51-2 (**L28**).

[8] On Augustus' veteran settlements see further 15.3-17.2.

[9] *600 ships*: half from Sextus Pompeius in 36 BC (Appian, *Civil Wars* 5.108, 118, 121) and half at Actium (Plutarch, *Antony* 68).

[4.1] Twice I have celebrated triumphal ovations and three times I have driven triumphal chariots and I have been hailed twenty-one times as victorious general, although the senate voted me more triumphs, from all of which I abstained.[10] I deposited the laurel from my *fasces* in the Capitoline temple, in fulfilment of the vows which I had taken in each war. [4.2] On account of affairs successfully accomplished by land and sea by me or through my deputies under my auspices the senate fifty-five times decreed that thanksgiving should be offered to the immortal gods. Moreover the days during which thanksgiving has been offered by decree of the senate have amounted to 890.[11] [4.3] In my triumphs nine kings or kings' children have been led in front of my chariot. [4.4] I had been consul thirteen times at the time of writing, and I was the holder of tribunician power thirty-seven times [AD 14].[12]

[5.1] Even though the post of dictator was conferred upon me both when I was absent and when I was present by both people and senate in the consulship of Marcus Marcellus and Lucius Arruntius [22 BC], I did not accept it.[13] [5.2] I did not decline to manage the corn-supply during a very severe grain shortage, and I administered it in such a way that within a few days I freed the entire community from pressing fear and danger through my expenditure and supervision. [5.3] When the consulship too was conferred upon me at that time for a year and in perpetuity, I did not accept it.

[6.1] In the consulship of Marcus Vinicius and Quintus Lucretius [19 BC], and later of Publius Lentulus and Gnaeus Lentulus [18 BC], and thirdly of Paullus Fabius Maximus and Quintus Tubero [11 BC], even though the senate and people of Rome were in agreement that I should be appointed on my own as guardian of laws and customs with supreme power, I accepted no magistracy conferred upon me that contravened ancestral custom. [6.2] The things which the senate wanted to be accomplished by me at that time, I executed by virtue of my tribunician power, for which power I myself, of my own accord, five times demanded and received a colleague from the senate.[14]

[7.1] I was one of the triumvirs for settling the state for ten consecutive years.[15] [7.2] I have been the highest ranking member of the senate right until the very day on which I wrote this, for forty years.[16] [7.3] I have been chief priest, augur, one of the Fifteen

---

[10] *Ovations*: a minor triumph: Augustus' ovations were in 40 BC, to celebrate the reconciliation with Antony at Brundisium, and in 36 BC after the victory over Sextus Pompeius (deemed to be against pirates: 25.1). *Three times*: see **N2a**. *Hailed as victorious general*: on Octavian's first salutation as *imperator* see **H4-H5**. The first nine (down to 20 BC) were for his own successes, the rest (from 15 BC) were won by members of his family fighting under his auspices.

[11] Days of public thanksgiving were traditionally voted by the senate on receipt of a commander's report of a victory. Many of his successes will have been accorded long periods of supplications (50 days for the defeat of Antony at Mutina in 43 BC, Cicero, *Philippics* 14.29, 37) After 27 BC, Augustus also accepted supplications for victories won by his legates, e.g. **M50**.

[12] Augustus held the consulship for brief periods in 43 and 33, continuously from 31 to June/July 23, and again at the start of 5 and 2 BC. See Section **B**. On tribunician power see **H26**.

[13] *Post of dictator*: see Dio 54.1; Suet. *Aug.* 52; Vell. 2.89.5 (Section **E**).

[14] *The things which the senate wanted…*: laws on marriage, adultery, see Section **S**. *A colleague*: Agrippa (twice), see **H27**; Tiberius (thrice): see **J40**.

[15] The triumvirate (note 4), originally conferred up to 31 December 38 BC, was belatedly renewed when Antony met Octavian at Tarentum during 37. Augustus' 'ten consecutive years' makes it likely that the renewal was backdated to the start of 37 and ran until the end of 33 BC.

[16] Under the Republic the '*highest ranking member of the senate*'(*princeps senatus*) was called upon to speak first; once a senator had been appointed to the position, he held it for life. Augustus was appointed *princeps senatus* in 28 BC in connection with his first revision of the senate (Dio 53.1.3; 8.2n.). The title is not the same as *princeps* on its own, Augustus' preferred designation for his position in the state.

for conducting sacred rites, one of the Seven in charge of feasts, Arval brother, member of the fraternity of Titus, and fetial priest.[17]

[8.1] I increased the number of patricians by command of the people and senate when consul for the fifth time [29 BC].[18] [8.2] I revised the membership of the senate three times, and in my sixth consulship [28 BC] I conducted a census of the population with Marcus Agrippa as my colleague. I performed the ceremony of purification forty-two years after the last one; in this census 4,063,000 individual Roman citizens were registered.[19] [8.3] Then for a second time I conducted a census on my own with consular power in the consulship of Gaius Censorinus and Gaius Asinius [8 BC]; in this census were registered 4,233,000 individual Roman citizens. [8.4] And for a third time I conducted a census with consular power with Tiberius Caesar my son as colleague in the consulship of Sextus Pompeius and Sextus Appuleius [AD 14]; in this census were registered 4,937,000 individual Roman citizens. [8.5] By means of new laws brought in under my sponsorship I revived many exemplary ancestral practices which were by then dying out in our generation, and I myself handed down to later generations exemplary practices for them to imitate.[20]

[9.1] The senate decreed that vows for my good health be performed by consuls and priests every four years. In accordance with these vows, games have often been celebrated in my lifetime, sometimes by the four most eminent colleges of priests and sometimes by the consuls.[21] [9.2] Moreover all citizens in private and as a municipality have, with one accord, repeatedly offered prayers for my good health at all public feasts.

[10.1] My name was incorporated into the hymn of the *Salii* by decree of the senate,[22] and it was ratified by law that I should be permanently sacrosanct and that I should hold tribunician power for as long as I live.[23] [10.2] I rejected the idea that I should become chief priest as a replacement for my colleague during his lifetime, even though the people were offering me this priesthood, which my father had held. After several years, on the eventual death of the man who had taken the opportunity of civil unrest to appropriate it, I did accept this priesthood; from the whole of Italy a crowd, such as it is said had never before this time been at Rome, flooded together for my election, in the consulship of Publius Sulpicius and Gaius Valgius [12 BC].[24]

[11] The senate consecrated the altar of Fortune the Home-Bringer in front of the temple of Honour and Virtue at the Capena Gate in thanks for my return, and ordered

---

17 Augustus' priesthoods, see Introduction to Section **L**.

18 *Patricians*: see **T1**.

19 For his census of 28 BC, see List of Consuls for 28 BC (Section **B**). *A ceremony of purification* was traditionally performed at the end of the censors' term of office.

20 *New laws*: on marriage, adultery, luxury, and the freeing of slaves: see Section **S**. *Exemplary practices*: Livy expresses a similar idea as the value of history in his preface, chapter 10 (**D1**). The forum of Augustus displayed statues of Roman heroes (**K20-K25**).

21 The games were instituted by the senate in 31 BC as one of the honours for the victory at Actium (Dio 51.19.2). They may have been prompted by Augustus' upgrading of the festival held for Apollo at Actium (**H11**).

22 The Salii were an ancient priesthood (see **L2**). Augustus' name was included in the hymn of the Salii in 29 BC (Dio 51.20.1). This honour was also granted posthumously to Gaius and Lucius (**J65**).

23 *tribunician power*: see **H26**. Tribunes were traditionally sacrosanct: that is, their persons were to be regarded as sacred. This privilege was granted for life to Caesar in 44 BC, to Octavian in 36 BC after his victory over Sextus Pompey (Dio 49.15.5-6), and to his sister Octavia and his wife Livia in 35 BC (Dio 49.38.1).

24 *This priesthood (pontifex maximus)*: see **H28-H32**. Augustus avoids mentioning Lepidus by name.

the priests and Vestal Virgins to perform an annual sacrifice there on the day on which, in the consulship of Quintus Lucretius and Marcus Vinicius [19 BC], I had returned to the city from Syria, and it named the day *Augustalia* after me.[25]

[12.1] In accordance with a resolution of the senate, some of the praetors and tribunes of the people with the consul Quintus Lucretius and leading men were sent to Campania to meet me; this honour has been decreed for no one except me up to this time. [12.2] When I returned to Rome from Spain and Gaul, having settled affairs successfully in these provinces, in the consulship of Tiberius Nero and Publius Quinctilius [13 BC], the senate decreed that an altar of Augustan Peace should be consecrated in thanks for my return on the Field of Mars, and ordered magistrates and priests and Vestal Virgins to perform an annual sacrifice there.[26]

[13] Our ancestors wanted Janus Quirinus to be closed when peace had been achieved by victories on land and sea throughout the whole empire of the Roman people; whereas, before I was born, it is recorded as having been closed twice in all from the foundation of the city, the senate decreed it should be closed three times when I was leader.[27]

[14.1] My sons, whom fortune snatched away from me when young men, Gaius and Lucius Caesar, the senate and people of Rome appointed as consuls when they were fourteen years old, as a way of honouring me, on the understanding that they should enter upon the magistracy five years later; and the senate decreed that from the day on which they were brought into the forum they should take part in the councils of state. [14.2] Moreover the Roman equestrians all together presented each of them with silver shields and spears and hailed each of them as leader of the younger generation.[28]

[15.1] To the members of the Roman plebs I paid 300 sesterces each in accordance with my father's will, and in my own name I gave 400 sesterces out of the plunder from warfare when I was consul for the fifth time [29 BC], and also a second time in my tenth consulship [24 BC] out of my personal assets I paid out 400 sesterces each as a handout, and as consul for the eleventh time [23 BC] I bought up grain as a private individual and distributed twelve grain-rations, and in my twelfth year of tribunician power [12 BC] I gave 400 sesterces each for a third time. These handouts of mine never reached fewer than 250,000 men. [15.2] In my eighteenth year of tribunician power, as consul for the twelfth time {5 BC}, I gave 60 *denarii* each to 320,000 of the urban plebs. [15.3] And as consul for the fifth time [29 BC] I gave to the colonists who had been my soldiers 1,000 sesterces each out of plunder; about 120,000 men in the colonies received this handout to mark my triumphs. [15.4] As consul for the thirteenth time [2 BC] I gave 60 *denarii* each to the commoners who at that time were in receipt of public grain; these were a few more than 200,000 men.[29]

---

25 *Altar of Fortuna Redux*: celebrated on Calendars (**C35, C39, C40**) and coins (**L9**): see also the notes on the consular elections of 21 and 19 BC (Section **B**) and Horace, *Odes* 3.14 (**G29**) for the mood of joy at his earlier safe return from Spain.

26 Altar of Augustan Peace: See **K13**. Its decree and dedication are celebrated on calendars (**C12, C20, C40**).

27 Janus Quirinus: see **K47-K49** and **C4**. *Leader (princeps)*: Augustus' way of referring to himself, as at *RG* 30.1 and 32.3.

28 Gaius and Lucius: see **J56-J65**; *appointed as consuls*: **K15**; *councils of state*: **M42**. Each was 'leader of the younger generation' (*princeps iuventutis* - **J58**) just as Augustus was simply 'leader'.

29 It is impossible to give modern equivalents, but a legionary soldier's annual pay under Augustus was 900 sesterces, out of which they had to pay for food, weapons and clothing. The sums donated are therefore considerable. The dates are significant: 29 BC – return to Rome and triple triumph; 23 BC – 'constitutional settlement', recovery from illness; 12 BC – *pontifex maximus*; 5 BC – consul for the coming of age of Gaius; 2 BC – consul for coming of age of Lucius, adoption of the title *pater patriae* (see RG 35.1).

[16.1] I paid money to municipalities for the lands which in my fourth consulship [30 BC] and later in the consulship of Marcus Crassus and Gnaeus Lentulus Augur [14 BC] I allotted to soldiers; the total amount which I paid was about 600,000,000 sesterces for Italian estates, and about 260,000,000 for land in the provinces. I was the first and only one to have done this of all those who have settled colonies of soldiers in Italy or in the provinces, as far as people living in my era recall. [16.2] And later, in the consulship of Tiberius Nero and Gnaeus Piso [7 BC] and again in the consulship of Gaius Antistius and Decimus Laelius [6 BC] and in the consulship of Gaius Calvisius and Lucius Pasienus [4 BC], and in the consulship of Lucius Lentulus and Marcus Messalla [3 BC], and in the consulship of Lucius Caninius and Quintus Fabricius [2 BC], I paid cash rewards in full to the soldiers whom I settled in their own municipalities once they had completed their terms of service; for this purpose I paid out about 400,000,000 sesterces.

[17.1] Four times I assisted the treasury with my own money, transferring 150,000,000 sesterces to those who were in charge of the treasury. [17.2] And in the consulship of Marcus Lepidus and Lucius Arruntius [AD 6], I transferred 170,000,000 sesterces out of my personal assets into the military treasury, which was established on my advice, and from which rewards were given to soldiers who had completed twenty or more years of service.[30]

[18] From the year in which Gnaeus and Publius Lentulus were consuls [18 BC], whenever public revenues were lacking, I gave out distributions of grain and money from my own granary and assets, sometimes to 100,000 men, sometimes to many more.

[19.1] I built the senate-house and the *chalcidicum* adjacent to it, and the temple of Apollo on the Palatine with its porticoes, the temple of deified Julius, the *lupercal*, the portico near the Flaminian Circus, which I allowed to be called Octavian after the name of the man who had built an earlier one on the same foundation, the *pulvinar* at the *Circus Maximus*, [19.2] the temples on the Capitol of Jupiter Feretrius and of Jupiter the Thunderer, the temple of Quirinus, the temples of Minerva and of Queen Juno and of Jupiter Libertas on the Aventine, the temple of the Lares at the top of the Sacred Way, the temple of the *Penates* on the Velia, the temple of Youth and the temple of the Great Mother on the Palatine.[31]

[20.1] I restored the Capitoline temple and theatre of Pompey, incurring great expense for both buildings, without inscribing my name anywhere on them. [20.2] I restored aqueduct channels in several places which were collapsing through old age, and I doubled the capacity of the aqueduct which is called Marcian by introducing a new spring into its channel.[32] [20.3] I completed the Julian forum and the *basilica* which was between the temple of Castor and the temple of Saturn, building projects which had been started and almost finished by my father, and I started work on the same *basilica* under an inscription in the name of my sons, after it had been destroyed by fire, expanded its site, and, if I do not complete it in my lifetime, I have ordered it to be completed by my heirs. [20.4] I restored eighty-two temples of the gods in the city

---

[30] *Military treasury*: this was funded by a 5% inheritance tax, see note after **S5**.
[31] Augustus gave his building work in Rome deserved prominence: his dying words were that he had found Rome made of brick and left it made of marble, (Suet. *Aug.* 28.3 and Dio 56.30.3, though Dio interprets this as referring metaphorically to the strength of the empire. For his building in Rome, see Section **K**, especially *senate-house*: **K33-K34**; *Temple of Apollo*: **K37-K38**; *Temple of deified Julius*: **K44-K46**; *Jupiter Feretrius*: **P3**; *Jupiter the Thunderer*: **K50**.
[32] *Aqueducts*: see **K55-K57**.

as consul for the sixth time [28 BC], in accordance with a resolution of the senate, and I neglected none which needed repair at this time.[33] [20.5] In my seventh consulship [27 BC] I paved the Flaminian Way from the city to Ariminum and all the bridges expect the Mulvian and Minucian.[34]

[21.1] On private ground I built from plunder the temple of Mars the Avenger and the Augustan forum. I built the theatre which was in the name of my son-in-law Marcus Marcellus near the temple of Apollo on ground mostly bought from private individuals.[35] [21.2] I consecrated gifts out of plunder in the Capitoline temple, and in the temple of the deified Julius, and in the temple of Apollo, and in the temple of Vesta, and in the temple of Mars the Avenger, which cost me about 100,000,000 sesterces. [21.3] I remitted 35,000 pounds of crown-gold which the municipalities and colonies of Italy contributed for my triumphs in my fifth consulship [29 BC], and later, every time that I was hailed as victorious general, I refused crown-gold even though the municipalities and colonies decreed it just as generously as they had done before.

[22.1] Three times I gave gladiatorial games in my own name and five times in the name of my sons or grandsons; about 10,000 men fought in the arena in these shows.[36] Twice in my own name I presented to the people a spectacle of athletes summoned from every place and three times in the name of my grandson. [22.2] I provided games in my own name four times, and also on behalf of other magistrates twenty-three times. On behalf of the college of the Fifteen as master of the college with Marcus Agrippa as my colleague I provided centennial games in the consulship of Gaius Furnius and Gaius Silanus [17 BC]. In my thirteenth consulship [2 BC], I was the first to provide games of Mars, which after this time from then on in succeeding years the consuls provided in accordance with senatorial decree and by law.[37] [22.3] I gave to the people hunting-shows of African wild beasts in my own name or in the name of my sons and grandsons in the circus or forum or amphitheatre twenty-six times; in these around 3,500 beasts were killed.

[23] I gave to the people the spectacle of a naval battle, in the place on the other side of the Tiber which is now the grove of the Caesars, after a site 1,800 feet in length, 1,200 in width had been excavated; on it thirty warships, with three or two banks of oars, and even more of smaller size, fought against each other; in these fleets about 3,000 men fought, besides the rowers.[38]

[24.1] As victor, I replaced in the temples of all the cities in the province of Asia the ornaments which the man against whom I had waged war had held in his private possession after plundering the temples.[39] [24.2] The eighty statues or so made of silver, depicting me on foot, on horseback, and in a four-horse chariot, which stood in the city, I myself removed, and from the money realized I placed golden gifts in the temple of Apollo in my name and in the name of those who had honoured me with the statues.[40]

---

[33] *Restored 82 temples*: Livy described Augustus as 'the founder and restorer of all our temples' (**P4** section 7). Ovid also praises Augustus (**L4**) for restoring temples.

[34] *Flaminian Way*: **K68**.

[35] *Temple of Mars, Augustan forum*: **K17-K19**; *theatre of Marcellus*: **K52-K53**.

[36] *Gladiatorial games*: **K53, R24-R25**.

[37] *Centennial Games*: a great festival symbolising the start of a new age. (**L20-L28**): *Games of Mars*: **K18, C18**.

[38] *Naval battle*: **R26**.

[39] *Replaced…ornaments*: **H12-H13**.

[40] *Statues*: for the gilded equestrian statue of Octavian erected in the forum in 43 BC, see **K16**.

[25.1] I brought the sea under control from pirates. In this war I handed back to their masters for punishment almost 30,000 captured slaves who had run away from their masters and taken up arms against the state.[41] [25.2] The whole of Italy of its own accord swore an oath of allegiance to me and demanded me as its commander for the war in which I conquered at Actium. The Gallic and Spanish provinces, Africa, Sicily, and Sardinia swore the same oath of allegiance.[42] [25.3] There were more than 700 senators who served under my standards at that time, among whom there were eighty-three who either before or afterwards up until the day on which these words were written were made consuls, and about 170 priests.[43]

[26.1] I extended the territory of all those provinces of the Roman people which had neighbouring peoples who were not subject to our authority.[44] [26.2] I brought under control the Gallic and Spanish provinces, and similarly Germany, where Ocean forms a boundary from Cadiz to the mouth of the River Elbe.[45] [26.3] I brought the Alps under control from the region which is nearest to the Adriatic Sea as far as the Tyrrhenian Sea, but attacked no people unjustly.[46] [26.4] My fleet navigated through Ocean from the mouth of the Rhine to the region of the rising sun as far as the territory of the Cimbri;[47] no Roman before this time has ever approached this area by either land or sea, and the Cimbri and Charydes and Semnones and other German peoples of the same region sent envoys to request my friendship and that of the Roman people. [26.5] Under my command and auspices two armies were led at almost the same time into Aethiopia and the Arabia which is called Fortunate, and substantial enemy forces of both peoples were slaughtered in battle and many towns captured. The army reached into Aethiopia as far as the town of Nabata, to which Meroe is nearest. The army advanced into Arabia as far as the territory of the Sabaei to the town of Mariba.[48]

[27.1] I added Egypt to the empire of the Roman people.[49] [27.2] Although I could have made Greater Armenia a province, on the assassination of Artaxes its king, I preferred, in accordance with the example set by our ancestors, to hand this kingdom over to Tigranes, son of King Artavasdes, and also grandson of King Tigranes, through the agency of Tiberius Nero, who at the time was my stepson. And when the same people later revolted and rebelled, they were subdued through the agency of Gaius, my son, and I handed them over to King Ariobarzanes, son of Artabazus king of the Medes,

---

41 *Pirates…war…slaves*: the war of 36 BC was against Sextus Pompey who did use slaves to man his fleet, but had considerable support and had been officially recognised as a partner of the triumvirate in a pact of 39 BC. (see **C32**, Velleius 2.72-73, 77; Appian 5.25, 67-73, 77-122).

42 *Oath of allegiance*: for an oath taken to Augustus in 3 BC in Paphlagonia, see **H37**.

43 *Made consuls*: not surprisingly the consul lists (Section **B**) show many prominent supporters of Octavian (and sometimes their sons) being rewarded for their support.

44 *Extended the territory*: this claim could be amply justified, see Section **N** and Ovid, *Fasti* 4.487-862 (**G52**); Livy, *Preface* 7 (**D1**).

45 *Gaul*: **M15-M22**; *Spain*: **M23-M28, N47-N49, G20**; *Germany*: **N36-N38**. Gaul and Spain remained Roman provinces until the sack of Rome. The claim to Germany is far harder to justify. It could perhaps have been made before the Varus disaster, but was clearly untrue by AD 14, when Tacitus suggests campaigns in Germany were simply face-saving (*Ann.* 1.3.6) and Augustus' will advised against expansion of current boundaries (*Ann.* 1.11.4).

46 *Alps*: **N11-N17** and Horace, *Odes* 4.4 and 4.14 (**G42, G44**); *Attacked no people unjustly*: this claim is much harder to justify, but compare Suetonius, *Augustus* 21.2-3; Virgil, *Aeneid* 6.847-853 (**G37**).

47 *Through Ocean*: see **N36** and Velleius 2.106.3 (Section **E**).

48 *(A)ethiopia*: see **N33-N35**; *Arabia…Mariba*: see **N18-N22**: Augustus manages to claim a success of an expedition which clearly failed.

49 *Egypt*: see **N31-N32**. The defeat of Antony was usually presented as defeat and conquest of Egypt, as on triumphal records, **N2a**.

for him to rule, and after his death to his son, Artavasdes; on his assassination, I sent into this kingdom Tigranes, who was descended from the Armenian royal family.[50] [27.3] I regained all the provinces across the Adriatic Sea which slope down towards the east and Cyrene, which were at that stage mostly in the hands of kings, and previously Sicily and Sardinia which had been occupied at the time of the slave war.[51]

[28.1] I settled colonies of soldiers in Africa, Sicily, Macedonia, both Spains, Achaea, Asia, Syria, Gallia Narbonensis, Pisidia. [28.2] Moreover Italy has 28 colonies settled under my authority, which have been in my lifetime very busy and densely populated.[52]

[29.1] I subdued the enemy and recovered from Spain and Gaul and from the Dalmatians several military standards which had been lost by other generals. [29.2] I compelled the Parthians to give back to me spoils and standards of three Roman armies and humbly to request the friendship of the Roman people. These standards moreover I deposited in the innermost sanctum which is in the temple of Mars the Avenger.[53]

[30.1] The Pannonian peoples had never had an army of the Roman people come near them before I became leader. I made them subject to the rule of the Roman people, once they were subdued through the agency of Tiberius Nero, who at that time was my stepson and deputy, and I advanced the boundary of Illyricum to the bank of the river Danube.[54] [30.2] An army of Dacians which crossed over onto this side of that river was conquered and overwhelmed under my auspices, and afterwards my army was led across the Danube and compelled the Dacian peoples to endure the commands of the Roman people.

[31.1] Embassies of kings from India were often sent to me, such as have not ever been seen before this time in the presence of any Roman general.[55] [31.2] The Bastarnae sought our friendship through envoys, and the Scythians, and kings of the Sarmatae who are on both sides of the river Don, and the king of the Albanians and of the Iberians and of the Medes.

[32.1] Kings of the Parthians, namely Tiridates and later Phraates, son of king Phraates,[56] Artavasdes king of the Medes, Artaxares of the Adiabenians, Dumnobellaunus and Tincomarus of the Britons,[57] Maelo of the Sugambri, Segimerus of the Suebic Marcomanni fled for refuge to me as suppliants. [32.2] Phraates, son of Orodes, king of the Parthians, sent all his sons and grandsons into Italy to me, even though he had not been conquered in war, but asking for our friendship through pledging his children. [32.3] And while I have been leader very many other peoples have experienced the good faith of the Roman people; between them and the Roman people

---

50 *Armenia*: see **N23-N25**.
51 *Regained provinces…in the hands of kings*: some territories had been given to friendly kings or Antony's children by Cleopatra, but after Actium kings like Herod rushed to pledge their loyalty to Octavian (**M36**). *Siciliy and Sardinia…slave war*: taken from Sextus Pompeius in 36 BC, see note 41.
52 *Colonies*: see e.g. **N13**
53 *Parthia*: The Romans set great store by the military standards carried by each legion. Hence the (diplomatic) triumph of the recovery of the three standards lost to the Parthians after the defeat of Crassus in 53 BC. See **N41-N46** and **K14, K18-K19, G30**. By AD 14 it would have to be set against the loss of three standards in the Varus disaster.
54 *Pannonia*: see **N26-N28**.
55 *India*: see **N39 – N40**; *often* seems to mean twice.
56 *Phraates*: see **N43, N44**.
57 *Tincomarus*: appears on British gold coins of *c.* 20-10 BC (See LACTOR 4⁴, no. 1).

previously no embassies or exchange of friendship had existed.

[33] From me the Parthian and Median peoples received kings, whom they had requested through envoys drawn from their leaders: the Parthians received Vonones,[58] son of King Phrates, grandson of King Orodes, the Medes Ariobarzanes, son of King Artavazdes, grandson of King Ariobarzanes.

[34.1] In my sixth and seventh consulships [28-27 BC], after I had put an end to civil wars, although by everyone's agreement I had power over everything, I transferred the state from my power into the control of the Roman senate and people.[59] [34.2] For this service, I was named Augustus by senatorial decree, and the door-posts of my house were publicly clothed with laurels, and a civic crown was fastened above my doorway, and a golden shield was set up in the Julian senate-house; through an inscription on this shield the fact was declared that the Roman senate and people were giving it to me because of my valour, clemency, justice, and piety.[60] [34.3] After this time I excelled everyone in influence, but I had no more power than the others who were my colleagues in each magistracy.

[35.1] When I was holding my thirteenth consulship [2 BC], the Roman senate and equestrian order and people all together hailed me as father of the fatherland,[61] and decreed that this title should be inscribed in the forecourt of my house and in the Julian senate-house and in the Augustan forum under the chariot, which was set up in my honour by senatorial decree. [35.2] When I wrote this I was in my seventy-sixth year [AD 13/14].[62]

Appendix

[1] The total amount of money which he gave either to the treasury or to the commoners of Rome or to discharged soldiers: 600,000,000 *denarii* [2,400,000,000 sesterces]. [2] He built new works: the temples of Mars, Jupiter the Thunderer and Feretrius, Apollo, the deified Julius, Quirinus, Minerva, Queen Juno, Jupiter Libertas, the *Lares*, the *Penates*, Youth, the Great Mother; the *Lupercal*, pulvinar at the Circus, senate-house with the *chalcidicum*, Augustan forum, Julian *basilica*, theatre of Marcellus, Octavian portico, grove of the Caesars across the Tiber. [3] He restored the Capitoline temple and eighty-two sacred shrines, the theatre of Pompey, aqueducts, Flaminian Way. [4] Expenses supplied for theatrical shows and gladiatorial games and for athletes and hunting-shows and the mock sea-fight, and money given to colonies, municipalities, and towns destroyed by earthquake or by fire, or individually to friends and senators, whose census qualification he topped up: too many to count.

---

58 *Vonones*: see **N46**.
59 *Sixth and seventh consulships*: Augustus is clear about his constitutional settlement belonging to 28 and 27 BC: on all the reforms and honours see **H18-H25**.
60 *Golden shield*: the *clupeus virtutis* (Shield of Virtue). See **H24, H25**.
61 *Father of the Fatherland (pater patriae)*: see **H38**.
62 *Seventy-sixth year*: Augustus was 76 on 23 September, AD 13 and died on 19 August, AD 14.

SECTION B

The *FASTI CONSULARES* (LIST OF CONSULS)

The consulship. The consuls were the two joint chief magistrates, elected by the people from amongst the senate for a single year, by a complicated electoral process. In the Republic, the consuls had supreme power (*imperium*) which included military, political and legal authority. Powers of a consul were limited by his fixed period of office and the presence of a colleague with the same supreme power. If a consul died during his year of office, a suffect consul was elected.

The consulship might seem an anomaly under the principate. In fact consuls continue not only under Augustus, but as long as the Western Roman Empire. Various reasons can be found. Initially the *imperium* possessed by a consul was of real value to Octavian/Augustus. The consulship symbolised the traditional method of Roman government, which Augustus was keen to be seen as preserving. The consulships provided a useful way of rewarding friends, and encouraging others; in particular, suffect consulships come into use as a way of sharing around the honour of a consulship. Furthermore, the administration of provinces had come to rely on ex-consuls going out to govern provinces as proconsuls.

The consular elections. Sources on whether elections under Augustus were real contests are somewhat contradictory: Tacitus, *Annals* 1.15.1 implies not: but Suetonius, *Augustus* 40 speaks of Augustan legislation to suppress bribery, mentioned occasionally by Dio (see below under **8 BC**). Dio 53.21.6–7 writes 'In the case of those who were to hold office, for example, he selected some himself and nominated them; and, although he left the choice of the rest to the people and plebs in the traditional way, he took care that no one should be appointed who was unsuitable or as a result of faction or bribery.' The *tabula Hebana* gives a great deal of information about electoral procedure but tells us nothing about the elections as contests (honours for Gaius and Lucius **J65**: the whole document translated in Sherk, *The Roman Empire: Augustus to Hadrian*, Cambridge 1988, no. 36B).

The Fasti Consulares. The normal method of dating a year was by giving the names of the consuls elected for the start of the year (*consules ordinarii* – regular consuls). Lists of consuls, the *fasti consulares*, were displayed publicly at Rome and elsewhere. Considerable fragments of these *fasti* have survived, notably the *Fasti Capitolini*, inscribed on an arch in the forum (see note on Triumphal *Fasti*, **N2**). From these and other fragments of consular *fasti*, together with other inscriptions and literary sources, a list of consuls can confidently be established for the Augustan period (though it remains possible that one or two suffect consuls have not been recorded).

Bibliography: The *Fasti* are published in Degrassi *Inscriptiones Italiae* 13.1 (1947 – Commentary in Latin); EJ gives a conflated Latin text; Syme, *Roman Revolution*, a list of names.

Prosopographia Imperii Romani (ed. E. Klebs *et al*. Berlin 1897–8; 2nd edition 1933 onwards) gives biographical details and sources for all the consuls: text in Latin; some parts of the alphabet are very out of date. Syme, *Augustan Aristocracy*, gives information on most of the Augustan consuls.

[In the list below, the names of regular consuls appear in bold, with suffect consuls appearing beneath the consul they replaced (e.g. in 31 BC, Octavian/Caesar was consul for the whole year, while his initial colleague, Messalla Corvinus, was replaced by Titius, who was himself replaced by Pompeius.]

31 BC   Imp. Caesar Divi f. III

M. Valerius Messalla Corvinus
M. Titius
Cn. Pompeius

Imperator Caesar Divi filius III: Octavian's two previous consulships were in 43 BC, when only 19 years old, and 33 BC. Even at the time of this his third consulship, he was only 31. The minimum legal age for a consul was 42 years old, making Octavian ineligible until 20 BC, by which time he had been consul 11 times.

Augustus' proper name at birth and until 44 BC was Gaius Octavius. On his adoption by the will of his great-uncle, Gaius Julius Caesar, he took the *nomen* (family name) of his adopted family. He also took the name 'Caesar' apparently as a condition of Julius Caesar's will. Thus as consul in 43 BC he appears on the *Fasti* as Gaius Iulius Caesar, son of Gaius. According to usual practice, however, his old family name, 'Octavius' would have been used as the *cognomen* 'Octavianus', and this is how he is initially referred to by Cicero. (Cicero later calls him Caesar, but usually 'the boy Caesar'; C. Matius, a supporter of Julius Caesar, refers to him as 'the young Caesar'; M. Brutus, refusing to acknowledge the adoption, calls him Octavius). In Britain he is usually referred to (until 27 BC) as 'Octavian', the anglicised version used by Shakespeare amongst others.

Julius Caesar was officially deified after his death. The Latin word *divus* was used to describe such gods: thus Caesar was known as 'Divus Julius'. Official Roman titles would include the first name of a man's father. Octavian manipulated this tradition to include in his name the fact that his adoptive father had been deified. Thus he added to his name 'Divi f[ilius]' (son of the Deified), treating 'Divus' as if it were his father's first name!

In 38 BC Agrippa declined a triumph for victories won by him under Octavian's supreme command. From this point, Octavian began to use the title 'Imperator' as a *praenomen* (first name). This was properly a form of address given by soldiers to their general after a victory, as Octavian was saluted after the battle of Mutina in 43 BC (see **H4–H5**). Julius Caesar used the title permanently.

Finally, on 16 January, 27 BC he adopted the word '*augustus*' (the meanings given for this adjective in the *Oxford Latin Dictionary* are 'solemn, venerable, worthy of honour, august, majestic, dignified in appearance'; see also Suet. *Aug*. 7) as the name 'Augustus'.

Marcus Valerius Messalla Corvinus: fought for the republicans at Philippi, but transferred his allegiance first to Antony, then to Octavian. He wrote pamphlets against Antony and fought at Actium. He was *praefectus urbi* (City Prefect) for a few days in 26/25 BC (**P7, P8, K7**). Tacitus describes him as 'crammed with the spoils of the war between Antony and Augustus' (Tac. *Ann* 11.7).

Marcus Titius: a turncoat: a prominent supporter of Mark Antony; in 35 BC he murdered Sextus Pompeius who had earlier spared his life. Years later a popular demonstration ejected him from games he was staging in the Theatre of Pompey in Rome (Velleius 2.79.5–6). In 32 BC, he deserted Antony for Octavian, (Plutarch, *Antony* 58), passing on details of Antony's will which Octavian published.

Gnaeus Pompeius: probably a great-grandson of the dictator Sulla; not the same branch of the family as Pompey the Great. He was *quindecimvir* (**L27r**) and Arval priest (**L7**).

30 BC   Imp. Caesar IV

M. Licinius Crassus
C. Antistius Vetus
M. Tullius Cicero
L. Saenius

Marcus Licinius Crassus: his grandfather of the same name had been one of the leading politicians in the first half of the first century BC, defeated by the Parthians at Carrhae in 53 BC. The grandson was initially a supporter of Sextus Pompey, then Mark Antony. The date of his defection to Octavian is not recorded. For his military success and claim to *spolia opima*, see **D3–4, N2c, P3–P4**.

Gaius Antistius Vetus: served under Julius Caesar, but joined the liberators in 44 BC, before serving as legate of Octavian against the Salassi. Suffect consul 1 July – 13 September 30 BC. As legate of Augustus, he led successful campaigns against the Cantabri in Spain in 26–25 BC. See Velleius 2.90.4 (Section **E**) and **N48**.

Marcus Tullius Cicero: the son of the orator and politician murdered by Mark Antony in the proscriptions in 43 BC. He became governor of Syria.

Lucius Saenius: unknown.

29 BC   Imp. Caesar V   **Sex. Appuleius**
                                                   Potitus Valerius Messalla

Sextus Appuleius: the elder son of Octavian's step-sister Octavia, thus one of his closest relatives (see family tree 1). Proconsul of Nearer Spain, he celebrated a triumph in 26 BC (**N2d**); proconsul of Asia, and legate of Illyricum in 8 BC.

Potitus Valerius Messalla: probably a cousin of Valerius Messalla Corvinus, consul in 31 BC; governor (proconsul) of Asia for two years, *quindecimvir* for the *ludi saeculares* in 17 BC (**L27r–s**).

28 BC   Imp. Caesar VI   **M. Agrippa II**

The same with censorial power conducted a census.

Marcus Agrippa: consul for the first time in 37 BC. During the year of his second consulship, he married Octavian's niece, Marcella.

census: censors were traditionally appointed every 5 years, to serve for 18 months. Their main function was to carry out the census, but they were also responsible for the morals of the state and could throw people out of the senate. It was symptomatic of the confusion of the late Republic that since 70 BC no censors had completed their tasks. Without formally being censor, Augustus effected the functions of a censor at various points, revising the senatorial roll three times (*RG* 8.2): in 29/28 BC (Dio 52.42.1–4, 53.1.3); in 18 BC (Dio 54.13–14) and probably AD 4. He carried out further censuses in 8 BC and AD 14 (*RG* 8). He was given power over public laws and morals akin to those of a censor in 19 BC, 18 BC, and 11 BC (*RG* 6). His moral legislation (see Section **S**) was enacted through tribunician power (*RG* 6.2).

27 BC   Imp. Caesar VII   **M. Agrippa III**

26 BC   Imp. Caesar VIII   **T. Statilius Taurus II**

Titus Statilius Taurus had been suffect consul in 37 BC. Velleius, writing about the helpers of eminent men, speaks of Augustus having Agrippa, 'and next to him Statilius Taurus, whose lack of distinguished ancestry did not prevent his being nominated for several consulships, triumphs and priesthoods' (2.127.1). He had commanded Octavian's army at Actium (Plutarch, *Antony* 65). After his consulship, he was legate in Spain and prefect of the city in 16 BC (see **T16, K5, K7**).

25 BC   Imp. Caesar VIIII   **M. Iunius Silanus**

Marcus Iunius Silanus supported his brother-in-law, Lepidus, then Antony, but defected to Octavian before Actium (Plutarch, *Antony* 59).

24 BC   Imp. Caesar X   **C. Norbanus Flaccus**

Gaius Norbanus Flaccus: his father had been general of the triumviral forces in the Civil War and consul in 38 BC. He himself was later governor (proconsul) of Asia, probably 18/17 or 17/16 BC.

23 BC   Imp. Caesar, son of the Deified, Augustus XI abdicated and in his place, L. Sestius Quirinalis Albinianus was made consul.

A. T[erentius Var]ro Murena [...] and in his place Cn. Calpurnius Piso was made consul. After Imp. Caesar Augustus abdicated from the consulship he received tribunician power.

Augustus had held the consulship each year since 31 BC. Thereafter he held the consulship only twice more, in 5 BC and 2 BC, on each occasion when his grandsons, and designated successors, Gaius and Lucius Caesar, came of age (Suet. *Aug*. 26.2).

Lucius Sestius Quirinalis Albinianus joined the tyrannicides in 44 BC as quaestor to Marcus Brutus. He was proscribed, but later pardoned. He is not heard of again until his consulship, after which he governed Spain (**M27**).

Aulus Terentius Varro Murena: other versions simply treat Piso as *consul ordinarius* (regular consul), but the *Fasti Capitolini*, probably the most important, give the text above. However the crucial part of the text explaining why a replacement was needed for Murena is missing. A brother-in-law of Maecenas, variously named as Licinius, Varro and Murena, was involved in a conspiracy against Augustus, almost every aspect of which has provoked great disagreement (see **E91.2** with note 28 and **P9–P10**). The man named on the *Fasti* has been claimed as the conspirator himself or a close relation and the text can be restored as 'condemned during his magistracy' or 'died before taking office' to support different views.

Gnaeus Calpurnius Piso: on the man and his consulship see **H42**.

22 BC   M. Claudius Marcellus Aeserninus   L. Arruntius

Marcus Claudius Marcellus Aeserninus: an aristocrat, but unusually old as a consul. He is mentioned in the *ludi saeculares* **L27r** (as Marcus Marcellus).

Lucius Arruntius was proscribed and fled to Sextus Pompey, but was restored and commanded part of Octavian's fleet at Actium. (Velleius 2.85.2; Plutarch, *Antony* 66). He was the first of his family to be a senator and served as *quindecimvir* at the Centennial Games (see **L27f**, **L27r**). His son is mentioned by Tacitus as a notable heir to a wealthy family (*Annals* 11.7).

21 BC   M. Lollius   Q. Aemilius Lepidus

21 BC: consular elections for this year caused considerable unrest, according to Dio (54.6.1–4), as Augustus, who was in the East and not standing for election, was initially elected together with Lollius.

Marcus Lollius: came from a non-senatorial family: he was a partisan of Augustus (Hor. *Odes* 4.9.33ff). He annexed Galatia and became its first governor in 24 BC (**N1**). He was a member of the *quindecimviri* involved in celebrating the *ludi saeculares* (**L27r**). For his military disaster in 16 BC see Velleius 2.97.1 with note (Section **E**). He was nonetheless appointed in 1 BC as mentor to Gaius Caesar in the East where he fell into disfavour with Augustus and died, see **P17** and **T19**.

Quintus Aemilius Lepidus: eventually elected after a fierce contest. His father had been consul in 66 BC and he was a distant relation of the triumvir. He was governor (proconsul) of Asia and *quindecimvir* at the Centennial Games (**L27r**).

20 BC   M. Appuleius   P. Silius Nerva

Marcus Appuleius: probably a younger son of Augustus' step-sister, Octavia. (Syme, *The Augustan Aristocracy*, 316–7).

Publius Silius Nerva: the first of a senatorial family to reach the consulship. A companion of Augustus at the dice-table (Suetonius, *Augustus* 71.2). Governed Tarraconensis c.19–17 BC (Velleius 2.90.4) and Illyricum c. 16 BC, fighting in the Alps (Dio 54.20.1–2). His three sons all became consuls (AD 3, 7, 13).

19 BC   C. Sentius Saturninus   Q. Lucretius Vespillo
          M. Vinicius

19 BC: Dio 54.10.1–3: 'Gaius Sentius was consul for that year. When it became necessary to elect a colleague for him, since Augustus again declined the place which had been kept for him, strife broke out once more [*i.e. as in 21 BC (above)*] at Rome and murders occurred, so that the senators voted a guard for Sentius. Since he did not wish to use it, they sent envoys to Augustus, each with two lictors. When he was informed of what had happened, recognising that there would be no end to the evil, he did not treat them in the same way as before but appointed as consul one of the envoys themselves, Quintus Lucretius, although he had been listed among the proscribed, and hastened to Rome himself.'

Gaius Sentius Saturninus: the first of a senatorial family to become consul: a kinsman of Scribonia, first wife of Octavian. He was *quindecimvir* at the Centennial Games and was later given a succession of important military commands, see Velleius 2.91.3 – 2.92.5 and 2.105.1–2 with notes (Section **E**).

Quintus Lucretius Vespillo: commander of Pompey's fleet in 48 BC; proscribed in 43 BC, but safely concealed by his wife in their house.

Marcus Vinicius: another dice-playing friend of Augustus (Suetonius, *Augustus* 71.2). He was one of the *quindecimviri* for the *ludi saeculares* and held a series of military commands (Velleius 2.96.2, 2.104.2).

18 BC   P. Cornelius Lentulus Marcellinus   Cn. Cornelius Lentulus

Both consuls were members of the distinguished and extensive Cornelius Lentulus family and both are extremely difficult to identify with certainty: see Syme, *The Augustan Aristocracy*, chapters 18 & 21.

Publius Cornelius Lentulus Marcellinus: perhaps a son or close connection of Scribonia, first wife of Octavian, by her first marriage, thus step-brother of Julia.

Gnaeus Cornelius Lentulus: easily confused with his homonymous relation, the consul of 14 BC: currently most references to Cornelius Lentulus are thought to refer to the augur (see below).

17 BC   C. Furnius   C. Iunius Silanus

Gaius Furnius obtained mercy for his father who had fought for Antony at Actium. Successful as legate of Augustus in Tarraconensis (see **N48**) and known as an orator.

Gaius Iunius Silanus: not from the same branch of the family as M. Iunius Silanus (cos 25 BC). Nothing significant is known about him.

16 BC   L. Domitius Ahenobarbus   P. Cornelius Scipio
                                                                   L. Tarius Rufus

Lucius Domitius Ahenobarbus: son of the consul of 32 BC; his family were made 'patrician' by Octavian in 29 BC (*RG* 8) and he married Antonia, elder daughter of Mark Antony and Octavia, around 25 BC; governor (proconsul) of Africa in 12 BC; legate of Augustus in Illyricum some time between 6 and 1 BC. A member of the Arval Priesthood in AD 14 (**L7**) and named in Augustus' will. The emperor Nero was his grandson. For more on his career and character, see Tacitus, *Annals* 4.44 and Suetonius, *Nero* 4.

Publius Cornelius Scipio: a member of one of the most distinguished Roman families, son of Scribonia, first wife of Octavian by her second marriage, thus step-brother to Julia. At some point governor (proconsul) of Asia.

Lucius Tarius Rufus: of humble origin, he served as an officer at Actium (**T17**) and governor (proconsul) of Cyprus and of Macedonia, around 27 BC. A friend of Augustus (**H48**).

15 BC   M. Livius Drusus Libo   L. Calpurnius Piso

Marcus Livius Drusus Libo: perhaps a brother of Scribonia, Octavian's first wife, adopted by the father of Livia.

Lucius Calpurnius Piso: his father (L. Calpurnius Piso Caesoninus) had been consul and censor. His own career was equally distinguished: see Velleius 2.98.3 with note (Section **E**) and **D7, K7, K8, M50**.

14 BC   M. Licinius Crassus Frugi   Cn. Cornelius Lentulus Augur

Marcus Licinius Crassus Frugi: adopted son of the consul of 30 BC. Governor (proconsul) of Africa 9/8 BC.

Gnaeus Cornelius Lentulus Augur: member of a very noble family, he received a large grant of money from Augustus (**T18**). Governed Asia 3–2 BC and a Balkan province at some point under Augustus.

13 BC   Ti. Claudius Nero   P. Quinctilius Varus

Tiberius Claudius Nero: The future emperor Tiberius.

Publius Quinctilius Varus: married a daughter of Agrippa (**T14**) perhaps around the time of his consulship. Later married Claudia Pulchra, the daughter of Augustus' niece, Marcella. Though a patrician, his family had been in obscurity for centuries and he owed his career to the favour of Augustus. Governor (proconsul) of Africa and legate in Syria, he was later responsible (or blamed) for the disastrous loss of three legions in Germany in AD 9. (See Vell. 2.117–120, Section **E** and Index of Names under Varus).

12 BC   M. Valerius Messalla Appianus   P. Sulpicius Quirinius
                C. Valgius Rufus
                C. Caninius Rebilus   L. Volusius Saturninus

Marcus Valerius Messalla Appianus: husband of the younger Marcella (Augustus' niece). Born into the patrician Claudius Pulcher family, adopted by the patrician M. Valerius Messalla (consul 32 BC), he died before 6 March.

Publius Sulpicius Quirinius: the first member of his family to be consul, honoured for his military ability. Tacitus gives an obituary, *Annals* 3.48 (**T19**). As governor of Judaea he conducted the census in the nativity story (**M47 – M49**).

Gaius Valgius Rufus: a literary figure, not from a consular family. Seems to have been part of the literary circle of Valerius Messalla Corvinus (consul 31 BC).

Gaius Caninius Rebilus: son of a suffect consul of 45 BC, a member of the *quindecimviri* at the celebration of the *ludi saeculares* (**L27r**). He died in office.

Lucius Volusius Saturninus: first cousin of Ti. Claudius Nero, Livia's first husband. Tacitus (*Annals* 3.30.1) gives a brief obituary.

11 BC   Paullus Fabius Maximus   Q. Aelius Tubero

Paullus Fabius Maximus: son of the consul of 45 BC; an intimate friend of Augustus (**J22, L7**), from a distinguished family. See **H34** for his proposal for honouring Augustus while governor (proconsul) of Asia. Ovid addresses several poems *Ex Ponto* to him. Involved in some scandal involving the imperial house in AD 14 – see **P18**.

Quintus Aelius Tubero: son of a prominent historian and lawyer, and maternal grandson of an extremely famous lawyer and jurist. *Quindecimvir* at the *ludi saeculares* (**L27r**).

10 BC   Iullus Antonius   Africanus Fabius Maximus

Iullus Antonius: son of Mark Antony by his first wife Fulvia. Brought up by Octavia. For his career and marriage to Marcella (Augustus' niece) see Velleius 2.100.4 (Section **E**). He committed suicide in 2 BC when accused of adultery with Julia and designs on the principate (**P13**). Tiberius cited Augustus allowing Antonius' name to remain on the *Fasti* as an example of his clemency, according to Tacitus (*Ann* 3.18).

Africanus Fabius Maximus: younger brother of the consul of the previous year; governor (proconsul) of Africa 6/5 BC.

9 BC   Nero Claudius Drusus   T. Quinctius Crispinus Sulpicianus

Nero Claudius Drusus: Drusus – younger brother of Tiberius (see **J43–J47**). He was not replaced as consul after his death late in the year.

Titus Quinctius Crispinus Sulpicianus: from a patrician family, the Sulpicii, adopted by another patrician family, the Quinctii, though both families had been without recent consuls. Little is known of the consul himself, except that he is associated in the scandal of the Younger Julia (Velleius 2.100.5).

8 BC   C. Marcius Censorinus   C. Asinius Gallus

8 BC: Dio records that the elected consuls for this year both had to resort to bribery to secure their election. Augustus declined to investigate (Dio 55. 5).

Gaius Marcius Censorinus: from a family claiming descent from one of the ancient kings of Rome. See Velleius 2.102.1 with note (Section **E**).

Gaius Asinius Gallus: son of C. Asinius Pollio, friend of Augustus; married Vipsania when Tiberius had to divorce her to marry Julia. He was *quindecimvir* at the Centennial Games (**L27r**) and proconsul of Asia 6/5 BC. Augustus judged him 'ambitious enough to aim at principate, though not equal to it' according to Tacitus (*Annals* 1.12.4 and note Section **F**).

7 BC   Ti. Claudius Nero II   Cn. Calpurnius Piso

Tiberius Claudius Nero: The future emperor Tiberius.

Gnaeus Calpurnius Piso: elder son of the consul of 23 BC. Governor of Africa some time between 5 BC and AD 2. He was later put on trial in AD 20 for having poisoned Germanicus (Tacitus, *Annals* 2.43ff).

6 BC   C. Antistius Vetus   D. Laelius Balbus

Gaius Antistius Vetus, son of the suffect consul of 30 BC. Later proconsul of Asia (**M56**).

Decimus Laelius Balbus: first of his family to be consul. *Quindecimvir* at the *ludi saeculares* (**N27r**).

5 BC   Imp. Caesar Augustus XII   **L. Cornelius Sulla**

                                                      L. Vinicius

              Q. Haterius   C. Sulpicius Galba

Augustus: consul for the year in which Gaius Caesar assumed the *toga virilis* (came of age).

Lucius Cornelius Sulla: a member of the family of Sulla the Dictator. 'The choice of L. Sulla appears peculiar' according to Syme, *Augustan Aristocracy*, 86.

Lucius Vinicius: a relation of the suffect consul Vinicius of 19 BC, Augustus rebuked him for visiting his daughter Julia (Suet, *Aug* 64). Possibly the son of the suffect consul of 33 BC.

Quintus Haterius: first of his family to be consul; well known as an orator, married a daughter of Agrippa.

Sulpicius Galba: from a patrician family, but the first consul for several generations: a hunchback and poor but indefatigable pleader! (Suet. *Galba* 3)

4 BC   C. Calvisius Sabinus   **L. Passienus Rufus**

              C. Caelius Rufus   Galus Sulpicius

Gaius Calvisius Sabinus: son of father of the same name who was consul in 39 BC and held important commands under Octavian in the 30s BC and held a triumph in 28 BC (**N2b**).

Lucius Passienus Rufus: first of his family to be consul; son of a famous orator. See Velleius 2.116.2 with note (Section **E**).

Gaius Caelius Rufus: not otherwise known.

Galus Sulpicius: from the same *gens* (family) as Sulpicius Galba, consul the previous year, but nothing else is known.

3 BC   L. Cornelius Lentulus   **M. Valerius Messalla Messallinus**

Lucius Cornelius Lentulus: a member of the very distinguished family, the Cornelii Lentuli. Probably proconsul of Africa AD 3/4 or 4/5.

Marcus Valerius Messalla Messallinus: elder son of M. Valerius Messalla Corvinus, consul of 31 BC. *Quindecimvir* at the Centennial Games (**L27r**).

2 BC   Imp. Caesar Augustus XIII   **M. Plautius Silvanus**

                                                      L. Caninius Gallus

              C. Fufius Geminus

              Q. Fabricius

Augustus XIII: Augustus consul for the year in which Lucius Caesar assumed the *toga virilis* (as in 5 BC for Gaius Caesar).

Marcus Plautius Silvanus: his mother Urgulania was a very good friend of Livia (Tac. *Ann*. 2.34). He led several military campaigns AD 7–9, see Velleius 2.112.4 (Section **E**).

Lucius Caninius Gallus: son or grandson of the consul of 37 BC.

Gaius Fufius Geminus: son of Octavian's legate in Pannonia in 35–34 BC who recovered the area. His own achievements, if any, are unknown.

Quintus Fabricius: otherwise unknown.

1 BC   Cossus Cornelius Lentulus   **L. Calpurnius Piso**

              A. Plautius   A. Caecina Severus

Cossus Cornelius Lentulus: a member of the very distinguished family, the Cornelii Lentuli, see Velleius 2.116.2 with note (Section **E**), **M4, N10**.

Lucius Calpurnius Piso (the Augur): younger son of the consul of 23 BC. Governor (Proconsul) of Asia AD 3–5. Arval priest, **L7**.

Aulus Plautius: presumed first cousin to the consul of the previous year.

Aulus Caecina Severus: an experienced military officer, the first of his family to be consul. See also Velleius 2.112.4 with note (Section **E**).

AD 1   C. Caesar   **L. Aemilius Paullus**

                                                      M. Herennius Picens

Gaius Caesar: the heir apparent, designated as consul for AD 1 from his coming of age in 5 BC, away in Syria for the whole year of his consulship.

Lucius Aemilius Paullus: son of Paullus Aemilius Lepidus (consul 34 BC, censor 22 BC); grandson of Scribonia (first wife of Octavian); by birth related to several of the most noble families of Rome; chosen as husband for Julia, daughter of Agrippa, he conspired against Augustus in AD 8. He was probably the Arval priest being replaced in AD 14 (**L7**) and so may not have died until shortly before then.

Marcus Herennius Picens: son of a suffect consul of 34 BC. Apparently insignificant.

AD 2   **P. Vinicius**   **P. Alfenus Varus**
        P. Cornelius Lentulus Scipio   T. Quinctius Crispinus Valerianus

Publius Vinicius: son of M. Vinicius, suffect consul in 19 BC. Velleius served as tribune under him in the Balkans a little before AD 1 (Vell. 2.101). Proconsul of Asia. Known as an orator.

Publius Alfenus Varus: son or grandson of a father of the same name, consul in 39 BC. Little else is known.

Publius Cornelius Lentulus Scipio: a member of the very distinguished family, the Cornelii Lentuli, (consuls 3 BC, 1 BC) about whom little else is known for certain.

Titus Quinctius Crispinus Valerianus: presumed the adopted brother of the consul of 9 BC. An Arval priest in AD 14 (**L7**).

AD 3   **L. Aelius Lamia**   **M. Servilius**
        P. Silius   L. Volusius Saturninus

Lucius Aelius Lamia: see Vell. 2.116.3 and note (Section **E**). His father had been legate of Tarraconensis in 24 BC.

Marcus Servilius: from a noble family without a consul for many generations.

Publius Silius: elder son of P. Silius Nerva, consul 20 BC. Velleius served as tribune under him in the Balkans a little before AD 1, (Vell. 2.101, Section **E**).

Lucius Volusius Saturninus: son of L. Volusius Saturninus (consul 12 BC) who was first cousin of Livia's first husband, Ti. Claudius Nero. Obituary in Tacitus, *Annals* 13.30.2.

AD 4   **Sex. Aelius Catus**   **C. Sentius Saturninus**
        Cn. Sentius Saturninus   C. Clodius Licinus

Sextus Aelius Catus: younger brother of the consul of 11 BC. His daughter, Aelia Plautina, married the future emperor Claudius.

Gaius and **Gnaeus Sentius Saturninus**: sons of the consul of 19 BC. Not otherwise prominent under Augustus.

Gaius Clodius Licinus: an historian, see **R17**.

AD 5   **L. Valerius Messalla Volesus**   **Cn. Cornelius Cinna Magnus**
        C. Vibius Postumus   C. Ateius Capito

Lucius Valerius Messalla Volesus: son of Potitus Valerius Messalla, suffect consul 29 BC. For his cruelty as governor (proconsul) of Asia, see **M76 – M77**.

Gnaeus Cornelius Cinna Magnus: grandson of Pompey the Great. Pardoned by Augustus despite conspiring against him, according to Seneca (**P11**).

Gaius Vibius Postumus: see Velleius 2.116.2 with note (Section **E**). He went on to serve as governor (proconsul) of Asia from AD 12 to 15.

Gaius Ateius Capito: a prominent lawyer (**T21**) who also interpreted the rite for the *ludi saeculares*.

AD 6   **M. Aemilius Lepidus**   **L. Arruntius**
                                 L. Nonius Asprenas

Marcus Aemilius Lepidus: grandson of Scribonia, first wife of Octavian, and elder brother of L. Aemilius Lepidus (consul AD 1, see above). Augustus judged him 'capable of becoming emperor but disdaining it', according to Tacitus, *Annals* 1.13.2 and note, with details of his career (Section **F**).

Lucius Arruntius: an orator, son of the consul of 22 BC. Augustus judged him to have 'both the ability and the nerve to make a bid' for the principate, according to Tacitus, *Annals* 1.13.1–2 and note (Section **F**).

Lucius Nonius Asprenas: closely connected to Augustus: a Nonius Asprenas is described by Suetonius (*Augustus* 56) as being a close friend of Augustus, though this was more probably his father. The consul of AD 6 was a nephew of Quinctilius Varus, the son-in-law of Augustus. He was a legate of Varus at the time of the Varian disaster (see Vell. 2.120.3). In AD 14 he was governor (proconsul) of Africa (Tacitus, *Annals* 1.53.6) as part of a 3-year term: an unusual honour. His brother was consul in AD 8.

AD 7   Q. Caecilius Metellus Creticus Silanus   A. Licinius Nerva Silianus
                                                     Lucilius Longus

Quintus Caecilius Metellus: adopted son of a famous family. Governor of Syria in AD 14.

Aulus Licinius Nerva Silianus: younger son of Silius Nerva (consul 20 BC), adopted by the Licinii family. See Velleius 2.116.4 (Section **E**) for his character and early death.

Lucilius Longus: a close friend of Tiberius and the only senator to accompany him in his retirement on Rhodes (Tac. *Ann.* 4.15).

AD 8   M. Furius Camillus   Sex. Nonius Quinctilianus
            L. Apronius   A. Vibius Habitus

Marcus Furius Camillus: from a famous family, long absent from consulship. Later governor (proconsul) of Africa in AD 17 (see Tacitus, *Annals* 2.52).

Sextus Nonius Quinctilianus: a younger brother of Nonius Asprenas, consul two years previously; governor (proconsul) of Asia in the early years of Tiberius.

Lucius Apronius: see Velleius 2.116.3 and note (Section **E**).

Aulus Vibius Habitus: brother of Vibius Postumus (consul AD 5): not otherwise known.

AD 9   C. Poppaeus Sabinus   Q. Sulpicius Camerinus
            M. Papius Mutilus   Q. Poppaeus Secundus

Gaius Poppaeus Sabinus: governor of Moesia AD 12–35. See **T22** for Tacitus' assessment.

Quintus Sulpicius Camerinus: from a famous family, long absent from the consulship but recently prominent (consuls 5 BC, 4 BC). Possibly an epic poet who wrote a sequel to Homer's *Iliad*.

Marcus Papius Mutilus: from a noble Samnite (Italian) family. The Samnite leader C. Papius Mutilus, who led the Samnites against the Romans in the Social War was certainly an ancestor, perhaps his great-grandfather. His grandfather received the citizenship; he was a *novus homo* who reached the consulate.

Quintus Poppaeus Secundus: from the area of Picenum, north-east Italy, not from a senatorial family. He and Papius gave their names as consuls to family legislation, though both remained unmarried (Dio 56.10).

AD 10   P. Cornelius Dolabella   C. Iunius Silanus
            Ser. Cornelius Lentulus Maluginensis   Q. Iunius Blaesus

Publius Cornelius Dolabella: grandson of the consul of 44 BC. Married a sister of Quinctilius Varus.

Gaius Iunius Silanus (priest of Mars): son of father of the same name, consul 17 BC. Condemned in AD 22 for corrupt governorship of Asia – see **M77**.

Servius Cornelius Lentulus Maluginensis: from the distinguished Cornelius Lentulus family, but otherwise obscure.

Quintus Iunius Blaesus: not from the same family as the other Iunii and the first of his family to be consul. As uncle of Sejanus, prominent under Tiberius.

AD 11   M' Aemilius Lepidus   T. Statilius Taurus
            L. Cassius Longinus

Manius Aemilius Lepidus: grandson of the triumvir, great-grandson of both Sulla and Pompey (Tacitus, *Annals* 3.22).

Titus Statilius Taurus: son of the consul of 26 BC.

Lucius Cassius Longinus: a distant relation of C. Cassius the tyrannicide; his wife was the sister of two consuls, Q. Aelius Tubero (cos. 11 BC) and Sextus Aelius Catus (cos. AD 4).

AD 12   Germanicus Caesar   C. Fonteius Capito
C. Visellius Varro

Germanicus Caesar: born in 15 or 16 BC. The elder son of Drusus and Antonia, thus grandson of Livia, and adopted by his uncle Tiberius in AD 4 at the same time as Augustus adopted Tiberius. His consulship was around 15 years before the official age and held without the usual experience of having been praetor (Dio 56.26.1).

Gaius Fonteius Capito: probably the son of the consul of 33 BC who was a close friend of Antony. According to Dio (56.26.1), Germanicus' colleague was 'considered a nonentity'.

AD 13   C. Silius A. Caecina Largus   L. Munatius Plancus

Gaius Silius Aulus Caecina Largus: a friend of Germanicus: their respective wives were also friends. He received triumphal ornaments in AD 15 for actions with Germanicus (Tacitus, *Annals* 4.18).

Lucius Munatius Plancus: grandson of the consul of 42 BC.

AD 14   Sex. Pompeius   Sex. Appuleius

Sextus Pompeius: somehow related to Augustus, according to Dio 56.29.5. Also distantly related to Pompey the Great.

Sextus Appuleius: son of the consul of 29 BC and therefore Augustus' (step) great-nephew.

SECTION C

THE CALENDARS

Fasti anni Juliani (Calendars of the Julian year)

Many inscribed stone calendars, showing days and months of the calendar reformed by Julius Caesar, were displayed publicly in Rome and various other Italian cities. These calendars also gave details of which days were officially regarded as lucky or unlucky days for business, and of public holidays. Parts of over twenty such calendars have been found. These mainly date from the time of Augustus and Tiberius and include dates and sometimes details of traditional games and festivals, but also of a large number of festivals which relate specifically to the imperial family. The *fasti* survive in various portions, and give varying amounts of detail (see below).

These *Fasti* are collected (with Italian commentary) in *Inscriptiones Italiae, XIII – Fasti et Elogia: Fasciculus II – Fasti anni Numani et Juliani,* ed. Degrassi, 1963, and a calendar is conflated from various individual calendars in EJ, pages 44–55.

The Sources – abbreviations used below and brief description.

Amit. *Fasti Amiternini* [*Inscr. It.* 13.2.25]: found at ancient Amiternum (60 miles north-east of Rome). Preserve parts of March and June and roughly the first twenty days of each of the last six months of the year.

Ant. *Fasti Antiates* [*Inscr. It.* 13.1.3]: found at Antium (30 miles south of Rome). Preserve roughly the first eighteen days of each month between July and November.

Arv. *Acta Arvalium* [*Inscr. It.* 13.2.2]: a calendar used by the Arval Brethren, see **L7**.

Maf. *Fasti Maffeiani* [*Inscr. It.* 13.2.10]: recorded and transcribed by the antiquary Maffei (1675–1755) when in the Farnese collection in Rome. Then almost complete, now mostly lost.

Opp. *Fasti Oppiani* [*Inscr. It.* 13.2.13]: found in 1894, on the north side of the Flavian Amphitheatre (Colosseum) in Rome, under the Oppian hill.

Prae. *Fasti Praenestini* [*Inscr. It.* 13.2.17]: found at Praeneste (modern Palestrina, 20 miles east of Rome). See **C1**. Much of January, March and April survive, together with other fragments. It gives a great deal of detail.

Val. *Fasti Vallenses* [*Inscr. It.* 13.2.18]: found at Rome and in possession of the della Valle family. Preserve most of August.

Vat. *Fasti Vaticani* [*Inscr. It.* 13.2.23]: found in Rome, now in the Vatican Museum. The middle of March survives.

Ver. *Fasti Verulani* [*Inscr. It.* 13.2.22]: found at Verulae (50 miles east of Rome). Preserve the second half of January.

[Modern dates are used, and years are added where they can be deduced either from the consular dates or other sources. These years refer to the event described, not the year in which the event was first celebrated, which cannot be established from the calendars. In some cases we cannot even tell whether an event was first commemorated under Augustus or Tiberius.]

C1 Praeneste Calendar set up by a freedman

The freedman, Marcus Verrius Flaccus, won a particular reputation for his teaching methods. For in order to stretch the abilities of his pupils, he used to hold contests between those of similar standard and not only laid down the subject matter on which they were to write but also offered a prize for the winner to take away, usually a book which was either beautiful or rare. For this reason he was selected by Augustus as tutor for his grandsons and transferred to the palace along with his whole school, but on the condition that he should accept no more pupils. He taught in the hall of Catulus' house, which at that time was part of the palace, and was paid 100,000 sesterces per annum. He died at a ripe old age in the reign of Tiberius. There is a statue to him in Praeneste in the lower part of the forum facing the hemicycle, where he had displayed the Calendar of Praeneste, which he had personally revised and had engraved on its marble walls.

[Suetonius, *Grammarians* 17]

C2   January 7   [43 BC]
Prae: Imperator Caesar Augustus [first took the *fasces*] when Hirtius and Pansa were
consuls.

The *fasces* were a bundle of rods (usually with an axe blade) carried in public by assistants of magistrates.
They could be used to inflict punishment and thus were a symbol of the magistrates' authority. (The symbol
of the *fasces* was revived by Mussolini and thus created the word 'fascist'). The occasion of Octavian taking
the *fasces* was when he was granted *imperium* by the senate and made *propraetor* [*RG* 1.2–3]. Aulus Hirtius
and Gaius Vibius Pansa were both killed leading the Republican armies against Mark Antony at Mutina in
April 43 BC.

C3   January 8   [AD 13]
Prae: A statue of *Iustitia Augusta* (Augustan Justice) [was dedicated when Plancus]
and Silius were consuls.

C4   January 11   [29 BC]
Prae: [Imperator Augustus Caesar ....for the third time] since Romulus, closed
Janus [when he himself for the fifth time, and Appuleius, were consuls].

For the Temple of Janus, **K47 – K49**.

C5   January 13   [27 BC]
Prae: [The Senate decreed that] a crown of oak-leaves be placed [above the door of
the house of Imperator Caesar] Augustus [because] he restored to the Roman
people [the republic].

crown of oak-leaves: awarded traditionally for saving the lives of citizens: see **H14; H20; H21**. The crucial
words '[the republic]' appear in square brackets because the relevant Latin expression can no longer be read
on the inscription. What can be read is *....p. R. restituit* – (Augustus) restored to the Roman people ... The
gap could be filled by *'rem publicam'*, though it is a matter of dispute whether this can mean 'Republic' in
a constitutional sense. A recent gold *aureus* of 28 BC (**H18**), showing a figure kneeling in front of a seated
figure with a scroll, carried the legend *'leges et iura p. R. restituit'* – '(Octavian) restored to the Roman
people laws and rules' – which suggests an alternative text here.

C6   January 14
Ver: [Day] unfit for public business by decree of the senate. Birthday of Antony.
Opp: Unfit for public business.
Prae: [Day] unfit for public business by decree of the senate.

According to Dio (51.19) the senate made this decree, along with others in honour of Octavian before his
return to Rome in 30 BC.

C7   January 16   [27 BC]
Prae: Imperator Caesar was called [Augustus] when he himself, for the 7th time, and
Agrippa [for the 3rd time were consuls].

See **H22– H23**.

C8   January 16   [9 BC]
Prae: Ti(berius) Caesar [...] from Pan[nonia].

See Velleius 2.96.2 (Section **E**).

C9 **January 16** [AD 10]

Ver: Public Holiday by decree of the senate because on this day the Temple of Concord was dedicated in the forum.

Prae: [The temple of] Au[gustan] Concord was [dedicated] when P. Dolabella and C. Silanus were consuls.

See **K40**, **K41**.

C10 **January 17** [probably AD 5 or 9]

Prae: Priests, a[ugurs, *quindecimviri*, *septemviri*] for banquets burnt victims [to the divinity of Augustus at the altar] which Tiberius Caesar dedicated. Public Holiday [by decree of the senate because on this day Tiberius Caesar] dedicated [an altar] to his father Augustus.

Augurs, quindecimviri, septemviri *for banquets*: various priesthoods (to all of which Augustus belonged), see **L1**.

C11 **January 27** [AD 6]

Prae: Temple [of Castor and] Pollux was dedicated.

See **K39**.

C12 **January 30** [9 BC]

Prae: Public Holiday by decree of the senate because on this day the altar of Augustan Peace [in the Campus] Martius was dedicated when Drusus and Crispinus [were consuls].

See **A12.2**, **K13** and **C20**.

C13 **February 5** [2 BC]

Prae: Public Holiday by decree of the senate because on this day Imperator Caesar Augustus, chief priest, holder of tribunician power 21 times, consul for the 13th time, was named *pater patriae* (Father of his Fatherland) by the senate and people of Rome.

pater patriae: see **H38**, **M20** and *RG* 35.1.

C14 **February 21 or 22** [AD 4]

Ver: [Offerings to the spirit] of Gaius Caesar.

On Gaius Caesar and his death, see **J56–J62**.

C15 **March 6** [12 BC]

Prae: Public Holiday [by decree of the senate because on this day I]mperator Caesar Augustus [was made] chief priest when [Quir]inius and Valgius were consuls. Because of [this] the *duumviri* offered sacrifice and the people, wearing garlands, had a public holiday.

On Augustus being made *pontifex maximus* (chief priest) see **H28–H32** and **C17**. The *duumviri* were local magistrates.

C16   April 24   [27 BC]
Prae: Tiberius Caesar put on the *toga virilis,* when Imperator Caesar for the 7th time and Marcus Agrippa for the 3rd time, were consuls.

Putting on the *toga virilis* (a man's toga) symbolised for Romans a boy's coming of age at around 16. It is not clear when this date was marked down in the calendars.

C17   April 28   [12 BC]
Cae: Public Holiday because on this day a statue of Vesta was dedicated in the Palatine House.
Prae: Public Holiday by decree of the senate because on this day a statue and [altar] to Vesta was dedicated in the house of Imperator Caesar Augustus, *pontifex maximus,* when Quirinius and Valgius were consuls.

See **C15** above and **H31, H32** for the altar to Vesta in Augustus' house.

C18   May 12   [2 BC]
Maf: Games of Mars in the Circus.

The games celebrated the dedication of the Temple of Mars Ultor in the Forum of Augustus, see below, **C40** and **K17–K19**.

C19   June 26   [AD 4]
Amit: Public Holiday by decree of the senate because on this day Imperator Augustus adopted as [his] son [Tiberius Caesar] when Aelius [and Sentius were consuls].

On Augustus' adoption of Tiberius, see **J41–J42**. Velleius Paterculus (2.103.3 – Section **E**) gives the date as 27 June.

C20   July 4   [13 BC]
Amit: Public Holiday by decree of the senate because on this day the altar of Augustan Peace in the Campus Martius was begun, when Nero and Varus were consuls.

On the altar see **A12.2, K13** and **C12** above.

C21   August 1   [30 BC]
Prae: [Egypt returned] to the power of the people of Rome. To the Virgin Victory on the Palatine. To Hope in the Forum Holitorium. Public Holiday by decree of the senate because on this day Imperator Caes[ar Augustus freed the state from the most terrible danger.]
Amit: Public Holiday by decree of the senate because on this day Imperator Caesar, son of the Deified, frees the state from the most terrible danger.
Ant: To Hope. Augustus recaptured Alexandria.

The Battle of Actium was fought on 2 September, 31 BC (see **C31**). Antony and Cleopatra made good their escape to Alexandria. Octavian paid more immediate attention to the settlement of his own army and that left behind by Antony. Agrippa returned to Italy and Octavian, with a brief return to Brundisium to deal with discontented veterans, toured the Eastern provinces, which had been part of Antony's command (Suet. *Aug.* 17.3). It was not until the summer of 30 BC that Octavian approached Egypt from Syria. On Egypt's capture, see **N31, N32**.

C22   August 2   [probably 26 BC]
Val: Public Holiday because on this day Imperator Caesar defeated *Hispania Citerior* (Nearer Spain).

On the campaigns of Augustus and his deputies in Spain, between 26 and 19 BC, see **N47–N49**. Officially the campaign was won in 26 BC.

C23   August 3   [probably AD 8]
Ant: Tiberius Augustus won a victory in Illyricum.

On Tiberius' campaigns in Illyricum, see **N26** and Velleius 2.110 – 114 (Section **E**).

C24   August 10   [AD 7]
Amit: Public Holiday because on this day altars to Mother Ceres and Augustan Ops were established in fulfilment of a vow, when Creticus and Longus were consuls.
Ant: Public Holiday in honour of Ceres and Augustan Ops.

Ops was the personification of Abundance, Ceres the goddess of Corn. This entry is probably to be explained by Dio (55.31.6), mentioning unrest amongst the people caused by food shortage. Dio tells us that two former consuls were appointed to oversee the corn supply.

C25   August 14   [29 BC]
Ant: Augustus triumphed.

The Antiates calendar only gives a single date (August 14), but Augustus' three consecutive triumphs (13–15 August) are well attested, see **H16**.

C26   August 18   [29 BC]
Amit: To the deified Julius at the forum.
Ant: The temple of the deified Julius was dedicated.

Octavian built a temple to his deified adoptive father at the site in the forum where Julius Caesar's body had been (illegally) cremated (see **K45**). The dedication was celebrated with games of various sorts, including the first appearances in Rome of a hippopotamus and a rhinoceros (Dio 51.22).

C27   August 19   [AD 14]
Amit: The most mournful day.
Ant: Augustus died.

This was also the day on which Octavian first became consul in 43 BC (see below, **C40**). Dio 56.30.5 remarks on the coincidence.

C28   August 20   [AD 2]
Ant: Offerings to the spirit of Lucius Caesar.

See **J63–J65** for Lucius Caesar, Augustus' grandson, and his premature death.

C29   August 28   [29 BC]
Maf: On this day the altar of Victory in the Senate House was dedicated.
Vat: Public Holiday [on this day] because [an altar of] the goddess [Victory] was dedicated.

A statue of Victory had been taken from Tarentum in Sicily (Dio 51.22). For a coin showing the Senate House, see **K33**.

C30   **September 1**   [22 BC]

Arv: To Jupiter *Tonans* (Thunderer) on the Capitol. To Jupiter *Liber*, to Queen Juno on the Aventine.

Amit: To Jupiter *Tonans* (Thunderer) on the Capitol.

Ant: Holiday in honour of Jupiter.

See **K50**.

C31   **September 2**   [31 BC]

Amit: Public Holiday by decree of the senate because on this day Imperator Caesar Augustus, son of the Deified, won at Actium when he and Titius were consuls.

The Senate decreed this holiday before Octavian's return to Rome in 30 BC (Dio 51.19).

C32   **September 3**   [36 BC]

Arv: Holiday and supplications at all couches of the gods (*pulvinaria*) because on this day Caesar Augustus won in Sicily.

The victory in Sicily was over Sextus Pompey. Given command of the navy in April 43 BC, but then outlawed, Sextus Pompey had used his power to rescue fugitives from the proscriptions, occupy Sicily and blockade Italy. His position of strength was recognised by the triumvirs in the Pact of Misenum in 39 BC. But he favoured Antony and threatened Octavian's position. The dangers Octavian faced were more severe and more numerous than in any other war (Suet. *Aug.* 16.3). 20,000 slaves were freed and recruited to row Pompey's ships (Suet. *Aug.* 16.1). Agrippa was largely responsible for the defeat of Sextus Pompey in battle at Naulochus. Octavian's reputation as a commander was not helped by his apparently being asleep when he should have been giving the battle-signal (Suet. *Aug.* 16.2). Octavian celebrated a triumphal ovation on 13 November, 36 BC. The *Res Gestae* 25.1, 27.3 describes his victory as over pirates and slaves.

C33   **September 23 and 24**   [63 BC]

Arv: Public Holiday by decree of the senate because on this day Imperator Caesar Augustus, *pontifex maximus* (chief priest) was born. To Mars, Neptune in the Campus Martius, to Apollo at the Theatre of Marcellus.

Maf: This day is Augustus' birthday. Circus Games.

Val: Birthday of Imperator Caesar.

The Senate decreed this holiday before Octavian's return to Rome in 30 BC (Dio 51.19). Suetonius tells us that the *equites* always celebrated Augustus' birthday over two days, voluntarily and unanimously (*Aug.* 57.1).

C34   **October 9**   [28 BC]

Amit: To the *genius publicus*, to favourable Fortune, to Venus *Victrix* on the Capitol, Games in honour of Apollo on the Palatine.

Ant: Games. Augustus dedicated the temple of Apollo.

For Augustus' Temple of Apollo on the Palatine, see **K37–K38, G19**.

C35   **October 12**   [19 BC]

Amit: Public Holiday by decree of the senate because on this day Imperator Caesar Augustus came into the city from overseas provinces and established an altar to *Fortuna Redux* (Fortune the Restorer).

Maf: *Augustales.*

Dio 54.10.1–3 describes unrest in Rome in 19 BC after the consular elections. Augustus nominated a consul and returned from the Greek island of Samos. Dio continues 'For this and his other achievements during his absence many honours of all kinds were voted him. He accepted none of them, except that an altar should be erected to Fortuna Redux (this was the title they gave the goddess) and that the day of his return should be entered among the festivals and called *Augustalia*.'

C36   **October 19**   [Probably 48 BC]
Ant: *Divus* Augustus put on the *toga virilis*.

The *toga virilis* (man's toga) was assumed at a Roman's coming of age, at around 16.

C37   **October 23**   [42 BC]
Prae: [Imperator Caesa]r Augustus won at Philippi. Brutus killed in the later battle.

The battle of Philippi was fought between Republicans (led by Brutus and Cassius) and 'Caesarians' (led by Antony and Octavian). Octavian ran away from the battle (Pliny, *NH* 7.148) or was providentially warned to be absent (Appian, *Civil Wars* 4.110, citing Augustus' own autobiography), but Antony defeated Cassius.

C38   **October 23**   [AD 12 (or possibly AD 11 or AD 13)]
Prae: Tiberius Caesar triumphed over Illyricum.

See Velleius 2.121.2 (Section **E**). The campaign had ended in AD 9, but was overshadowed by the Varus disaster.

C39   **December 16**   [19 BC]
Amit: Altar to Fortuna Redux was dedicated.

See above, **C35**.

C40   **The Calendar at Cumae**   (AD 4–14)

This fragmentary stone calendar was not (unlike all the examples extracted above) a complete almanac, listing all the days of the year and giving dates for public business and traditional and Augustan festivals. Instead it recorded only events from the career of Augustus (here known as 'Caesar') and birthdays of members of his family. It also starts not on January 1, but at some point in July or August, perhaps August 1. It can probably be dated to AD 4 – 14 through its lack of references to Gaius and Lucius Caesar or the death of Augustus.

Aug. 19   [On this day Caesar] first entered the consulship. [...]

Sep. 4–22 [On this day] the army of Lepidus went over to Caesar.

Sep. 23   Birthday of Caesar. Sacrificial victims to Caesar, supplication.

Oct. 7   Birthday of Drusus Caesar. Supplication to Vesta.

Oct. 18   On this day Caesar put on the *toga virilis*. Supplication to Hope and Youth.

Dec. 15   On this day the altar to Fortuna Redux, which brought Caesar Augustus back [from overseas] provinces, was dedicated. Supplication to Fortuna Redux.

Jan. 7   [On this day] Caesar first took the *fasces*. Thanksgiving to eternal Jupiter.

Jan. 16   On this day [Caesar] was called [Augustus]. Thanksgiving to Augustus.

Jan. 30   [On this day the altar of Augustan Peace was dedicated]. Thanksgiving for the power of Caesar Augustus, guardian [of Roman citizens and the whole world?].

Mar. 6   [On this day Caesar] was made [chief] priest. Thanksgiving to Vesta, to the Penates of the Roman people.

Apr. 14   On this day Caesar was victorious for the first time. Supplication to Augustan Victory.

Apr. 16   [On this day Caesar was first] hailed ['imperator']. Supplication to *Felicitas imperii*. (Prosperity of empire).

May 12 [On this day the temple of Mars was dedicated. Supplicat]ion to the Might of Mars.

May 24 [Birthday of Germanicus Caesar]. Supplication to Vesta.

Aug. 19: Octavian's first, suffect, consulship followed the deaths of both consuls of 43 BC, Aulus Hirtius and Vibius Pansa, fighting at Mutina. It was in every respect unconstitutional – Octavian was only 19 at the time and the minimum age laid down by law was 42, nor had Octavian served previously as *quaestor*. But as a centurion remarked in the senate, his sword would make Octavian consul if the Senate did not (Suet. *Aug.* 26.1). On Octavian's first consulship, see also Tac. *Ann.* 1.9.

Sep. 4–22: This was in 36 BC, after Agrippa's defeat of Sextus Pompey (see note on **C32** above). Lepidus tried to take over possession of Sicily but his troops defected to Octavian who deposed Lepidus as triumvir (Appian, *Civil Wars* 4.123–126). The exact date is lost in the calendar, but must be between the defeat of Sextus Pompey (September 3) and the following entry.

Oct. 7: On Drusus Caesar, step-son of Augustus, brother of Tiberius, see **J43 – J47**.

Apr. 14: The first battle of Mutina, 43 BC, was fought between the forces of the Republic and Mark Antony. The consuls Hirtius and Pansa led the republican army. Octavian successfully defended the republican camp against Lucius Antonius. See **H4**. Suetonius (*Aug.* 11) reports unchallenged Antony's claim that Octavian ran away.

Apr. 16: This salutation took place after the first battle of Mutina (see above and **H4**). Octavian began to use *imperator* as his *praenomen* (first name) as Julius Caesar had latterly done.

May 24: The birthday of Germanicus is recorded on other calendars. For Germanicus, son of Drusus, step-great-nephew of Augustus, see **J66**.

SECTION D

LIVY

Livy (Titus Livius, 59 BC – AD 17) wrote a history of Rome from its foundation in 753 BC to 9 BC. This was divided into 142 books (from the length of the surviving books, this would represent about 8,000 pages of a modern paperback). Livy's History (*Ab Urbe Condita – From the Foundation of the City*) was easily the most detailed contemporary history of the Augustan period and will have been the single most important source for most later Roman historians writing about Augustus. However of his 142 books, only books on Rome's earlier history (books 1–10 and 21–45) survive.

Of the other books only short summaries remain. These were probably made in the fourth century, and may even be summaries of summaries. Where we can compare Livy's work with the summary version, it is clear that the summaries are not always reliable. For the Augustan period (books 133–142) the summaries are extremely short, missing entirely for books 136 and 137, and only really provide a few 'headings' from Livy's treatment of Augustus' reign.

However, we do have Livy's preface to his history, in which, writing between 27 and 25 BC, he sets out the reasons for starting his huge historical work. From this it seems that Livy's work had certain points in common with Augustan ideology: a patriotic conviction in the righteousness of the Roman Empire and its moral integrity; a glorification of traditional values; and, of course, an interest in Rome's past. But Livy's preface also shows an ambivalent attitude to Augustus' creation of a principate, though recognising that desperate measures are needed to restore Rome.

D1   The preface to Livy's History

[1] Whether I shall produce anything worthwhile in recording the achievements of the Roman People from their city's first beginnings, I have no idea, nor if I did would I dare assert it. [2] For myself, I am very well aware that my choice of subject lacks both novelty and originality. New writers are always convinced that they are going to improve upon the primitive endeavours of their predecessors by bringing greater certainty to the facts or a more sophisticated treatment to their subject. [3] Be that as it may, it will be a source of real satisfaction to myself at least, if I succeed as far as I can in adding something to the record of the achievements of the greatest nation in the world. And should my own reputation be obscured by the large number of previous writers on this topic, I shall derive consolation from the nobility and distinction of those whose reputations will eclipse my own.

[4] For this is a massive undertaking. It involves research across a span of some seven hundred years. From small beginnings the material has grown and grown until it now seems liable to collapse beneath its own weight. I am fully reconciled to the fact that most of my readers will find my account of Rome's early origins and the period immediately following somewhat tedious; they will be hurrying forward to these more recent times when our nation's long-established predominance seems to be bringing about its own collapse. [5] By contrast, from this aspect of my researches I myself shall seek satisfaction, since it will allow me to turn my attention away from the evils that my own generation has witnessed for so many years, at least for as long as I keep my mind's eye fixed upon our glorious past. I shall thus spare myself the anxieties which may well distract the historian of contemporary events, even if they fail to divert him from the truth.

[6] The events before, or rather leading up to, the foundation of the city belong rather to the realm of poetic legend than uncontaminated historical documentation. It is, therefore, not my intention to assert or deny their accuracy. [7] It is a concession we must allow to antiquity that it be permitted to surround the origins of Rome with a

certain aura of the supernatural by mingling human with divine activity. And if it is appropriate to allow any nation to see its foundation as divine and the hand of heaven in its origins, then surely Rome's military achievements are so glorious that when they claim that Mars himself was the Father of their nation and of its Founder, Romulus, then every nation upon earth should accept the claim with as little protest as they accept Rome's secular domination.

[8] But whatever comments or criticisms readers may make of them, I do not intend to waste my energies in evaluating legends such as these. [9] The central question, to which I would ask each of my readers to give the most careful consideration, is this: what were the characteristics of the way of life and moral code of those early Romans, their leadership, and that genius for politics and warfare which underpinned the acquisition and expansion of their empire? And then let him observe how, as inherited values gradually collapsed, traditional morality was first undermined and then like a house of cards collapsed with ever-increasing rapidity, until the headlong plunge towards disaster brought us to our present state, in which we find our vices intolerable and their necessary remedies no less so.

[10] The study of history is salutary as well as useful, particularly for the way in which it confronts the student with the records of every sort of experience, and by setting them upon a conspicuous pedestal, as it were, holds them up for close examination. He can then select for himself, and his society, what to imitate for its virtues and what to avoid for its disreputable motivation and deplorable consequences. [11] It is possible, of course, that enthusiasm for my subject has made me a prejudiced witness, but I genuinely believe that Rome, as a state, has achieved unprecedented greatness, unparalleled respect for religion, unrivalled wealth of noble exemplars. Far more slowly than in any other city have avarice and luxury found a foothold here; for far longer than in any other city has honour been paid to modesty of life-style and habits of thrift. So very true is it that poverty makes the finest antidote to avarice. [12] Only in recent times has wealth introduced us to avarice and an extravagance of pleasures created a lust for self-indulgence and licentious living, which threatens to destroy us and the whole of our civilisation.

[Livy, *preface* 1–12]

[1] Books 1–5 seem to have been completed between 27–25 BC (see **K47** and note on the Temple of Janus). The preface was presumably added at this time.

[5] *Turn my attention away from the evils that my own generation has witnessed for so many years*: Livy, born in 59 BC, would have lived through the period of political chaos in Rome in the 50s; the civil war between Julius Caesar and Pompey (49–48); Caesar's dictatorship and assassination (44); civil war and the triumvirate; the battle of Actium. Despite his statement, however, he wrote in great detail about this period: 24 books (109–132) deal with 51–31 BC. In contrast, the first 5 books take Rome from 753 – 390 BC.

[9] *Our vices intolerable and their necessary remedies no less so*: seems to suggest a very ambivalent attitude to the new Augustan order being established. Augustus referred to Livy as a 'Pompeian' (**P21**), perhaps indicating that Livy's sympathies were with Pompey and against Julius Caesar in their conflict. Certainly in the early books of his history, Livy shows a great liking for the traditions and institutions of Rome under republican government.

[10] *upon a conspicuous pedestal*: Livy likens his written history to monuments recalling famous figures. It is hard not to associate this idea with the statues and inscriptions relating to the greatest Romans which Augustus arranged in his forum (see **K20–K25**), being built at the same time as Livy's history.

Livy's History: The Summaries of Books 133–142

D2   Summary of Book 133   (31–29 BC)

After the defeat of his fleet at the battle of Actium, Mark Antony escaped to Alexandria. There, besieged by Caesar and reduced to the utmost despair, above all by the false rumour of the death of Cleopatra, he was driven to commit suicide. Caesar himself captured Alexandria and then, with Cleopatra preferring death by suicide to the prospect of falling into the hands of her conqueror, he returned to Rome and celebrated three triumphs – the first for his campaign in Illyricum, the second for his victory at Actium, and the third for his defeat of Cleopatra. Thus after twenty years he brought the civil wars to an end. Marcus Lepidus, son of Lepidus the Triumvir, launched a conspiracy against Caesar, and while trying to start a new war was captured and killed.

Battle of Actium: 2 September, 31 BC. An ancient commentator on Horace *Odes* 1.37 (see **G24**) says 'Livy tells us that Cleopatra, when she was being deliberately treated with great generosity as a prisoner of Augustus, repeatedly said "I will not be part of a triumph."'

After twenty years: from January 49 when Julius Caesar crossed the Rubicon to start his civil war against Pompey to August 30, the close of Octavian's Alexandrian campaign or possibly the closing of the gates of the Temple of Janus (11 January, 29 BC).

D3   Summary of Book 134   (29–27 BC)

When Gaius Caesar had established the peace and re-imposed order in the provinces, he was given the *cognomen* Augustus. The sixth month, Sextilis, was re-named August in his honour. While he held an Assembly at Narbo, a census was carried out in the Three Gauls, which his father, Caesar, had conquered. Also recorded are the wars waged by Marcus Crassus against the Bastarnae, the Moesians, and other tribes.

The name 'Augustus' was decreed in January 27 BC (**H22–H23**). On the month August, see **H35–H36**: the summary is probably wrong about the date. The census in Gaul (see Dio 53.22.5) was the first known census conducted in a province. The principal purpose was to facilitate the collection of tribute. On the administration of Gaul, see **M15–M22**. Crassus' campaigns against the Bastarnae were in 29 BC.

D4   Summary of Book 135   (28–26 BC)

This is the record of the wars waged by Marcus Crassus against the Thracians, and by Caesar against the Spaniards, together with the final defeat of the Salassi, an Alpine tribe.

If the summary of books 134 and 135 is accurate, Livy seems to have treated the Augustan settlement of 27 BC immediately after his account of the civil war, and thus out of the annalistic (year-by-year) order he usually seems to employ.

On Thrace, Spain and the Alpine tribes, see **N50–N51**, **N47–N48**, and **N13–N16** respectively.

Summaries of Books 136–137 are not preserved

D5   Summary of Book 138   (15–13 BC)

The Raeti were defeated by Caesar's stepsons, Tiberius Nero and Drusus. Agrippa, Caesar's son-in-law, died. A census was conducted by Drusus.

On the Raeti, see **N11**, **N14–N16**. The census of Drusus was in Gaul in 13 BC (see **D6**).

D6   Summary of Book 139   (12 BC)

The states of Germany on both sides of the Rhine were attacked by Drusus, and a revolt which arose in Gaul over the census was settled. An altar to the god Caesar was dedicated at the confluence of the Arar and the Rhône, with an Aeduan named Gaius Julius Vercondaridubnus being instituted as its priest.

On the revolt, see Dio 54.32.1. On the Pan-Gallic altar at Lugdunum (Lyons), see **M18–M21**.

D7   Summary of Book 140   (13–11 BC)

The Thracians were brought to heel by Lucius Piso. The defeat of the Cherusci, Tencteri, Chauci, and other German tribes across the Rhine by Drusus is also recorded. Augustus' sister Octavia died, having already lost her son Marcellus. He is commemorated by a theatre and a portico named after him.

On the Thracians, see **N50–N51**. *Marcellus*: died in 23 BC. The summariser presumably digresses onto buildings named after him, not through following Livy, but because the buildings were still well known in the summariser's own day.

D8   Summary of Book 141   (11–10 BC)

This contains the record of Drusus' war against the tribes on the further side of the Rhine, whose most conspicuous warriors were Chumstinctus and Avectius, two tribunes from the state of the Nervii. Drusus' brother, Nero, subdued the Dalmatians and the Pannonians. Peace was made with the Parthians, and the standards lost both by Crassus and later by Antony were handed back by their king.

On Drusus' campaigns against the Germans, see Dio 54.33 and 54.36. On Tiberius Nero's campaigns against Dalmatia and Pannonia, see Dio 54.34.3; 54.36.3; Vell. 2.96.2.

Crassus' standards were recovered from the Parthians in 20 BC (see e.g. **N42**), so it is not clear why Livy, or more likely the summariser, placed it here.

D9   Summary of Book 142   (9 BC)

Here we have the record of the war waged by Drusus against the German states across the Rhine. He himself died of a broken leg thirty days after an accident in which his horse fell on it. His brother Nero, who had rushed to his side on hearing the news of his illness, brought his body back to Rome, and it was interred in the tomb of Gaius Julius. The encomium was spoken by his stepfather, Caesar Augustus, and further honours were bestowed upon him at his funeral. Disaster to Quinctilius Varus.

The death of Drusus occurred in 9 BC, the end point of Livy's history. However the disaster to Varus took place in AD 9. Presumably some allusion to the disaster by Livy in describing Drusus' German campaign has been garbled by the summariser into being part of the narrative of the book.

SECTION E

VELLEIUS PATERCULUS, *HISTORY OF ROME* (2, 88–124)

Velleius Paterculus

Velleius' forbears came from south of Rome, winning citizenship in the Social War (90–88 BC). His grandfather served with Pompey, Brutus, and the father of Emperor Tiberius. He was born in 20 or 19 BC, went with Gaius Caesar to the East, then served under Tiberius in Germany and the Balkans. He entered the senate in AD 7, and reached the praetorship of AD 15. His Greek and Roman *History*, in two books, is summary, becoming fuller with the Augustan and especially the Tiberian periods. It was written *c*.AD 30 and dedicated to M. Vinicius, consul that year. Velleius as a contemporary and eye-witness was ideally placed to write Augustan political and military history, but his conventional patriotism and bias towards the official point of view, particularly his fawning on Tiberius (typical of the senate of his day, as its decree on Cn. Piso the Elder shows) though excusable in a subordinate loyal to his commander, vitiate his work for some scholars. But he is a valuable foil to the hostile Tacitus, Dio, and Suetonius.

Velleius Paterculus, *History of Rome* 2.88–124

[88.1] While Caesar was finishing off his campaigns at Actium and around Alexandria,[1] Marcus Lepidus launched a plot to assassinate him as soon as he returned to Rome. The young man, distinguished more for his good looks than any natural intelligence, was the son of Lepidus, the former Triumvir for setting the republic in order, and Brutus' sister, Junia.[2] [88.2] At that time Gaius Maecenas, of an equestrian but distinguished family, was commander of the city guards.[3] With his inexhaustible reserves of energy he could tolerate sleepless nights when a crisis required it and combined shrewdness of calculation with practicality in action. Yet if he ever could snatch time from the affairs of state, he showed a more than feminine inclination for a life of luxurious ease. He was as close to Caesar as Agrippa was, but received from him rather less public recognition. Yet he gave all the signs of being satisfied with the narrow stripe, though he could have had honours as great as Agrippa, if he had so desired.[4] [88.3] Working under cover and with the utmost discretion, Maecenas uncovered the plans of this impetuous youth and, without raising any general alarm, arrested him and thus speedily put an end to a plot which had threatened to resurrect the horrors of a renewed civil war. Lepidus paid the penalty for his abominable conspiracy, while his wife, Servilia, whose suicide gained her an immortality which compensated for her premature death, deserves respect similar to that accorded to Antistius' wife, mentioned above.[5]

---

[1] *Actium, Alexandria*: these campaigns of 31 and 30 BC led to the defeat and death of Antony and Cleopatra.

[2] *Marcus Lepidus*: the distinction of his father made him ambitious, and having Caesar's assassin Brutus as an uncle made him intolerant of autocrats. He had also been betrothed, if not married, to one of Mark Antony's daughters (Appian, *Civil Wars* 5.93).

[3] *Maecenas*: see **R1–R13**.

[4] *The narrow stripe*: this band of purple on the tunic was the mark of the equestrian order. Maecenas was not the only man to prefer the lower (and safer) rank, which avoided open participation in politics; see **R27**.

[5] *Servilia*: she belonged to a family famous for its devotion to senatorial government, the Servilii Caepiones, whose *cognomen* Brutus had taken. The wife of P. Antistius, who died equally heroically in the massacres of pro-senatorial politicians in 82 BC, was Calpurnia, mentioned in Vell. 2.26.3.

[89.1] Caesar returned to Italy and Rome to be greeted by huge crowds and universal acclaim from young and old, rich and poor alike. The magnificence of his triumph and the public games he provided could hardly be adequately described within the scope of a full-scale work, let alone one as restricted as this.[6] [89.2] There was nothing, thereafter, which men could hope for from the gods, nor the gods provide to men, no blessings which in their wildest imaginings men could pray for nor good fortune bring to pass, which Augustus on his return to Rome did not restore to the republic, the Roman people, and the world at large. [89.3] Twenty years of civil strife were ended, foreign wars laid to rest, peace restored, and man's crazed lust for warfare everywhere dead and buried.[7] Force was restored to the laws, authority to the courts, majesty to the senate;[8] the power of the magistrates was reduced to its former limits, except that two praetors were added to the eight;[9] the ancient, traditional form of the republic was brought back.[10] [89.4] Fields were cultivated once again, religious rites observed;[11] men felt safe at last, with their property rights secured. Existing laws were revised and improved; new ones passed to the general advantage.[12] The senatorial lists were revised strictly, but not unkindly;[13] leading citizens who had earned triumphs and other civic distinctions were encouraged by the *princeps* to contribute to the adornment of the city.[14] [89.5] Only the office of consul was Caesar prevailed upon to hold successively, despite his frequent protestations, until his eleventh election.[15] Later he was to refuse it vigorously. His rejection of the dictatorship was as obstinate as the people's determination to offer it to him.[16] [89.6] As for the wars he waged as victorious

6   *Triumph*: Octavian on entering Rome celebrated a triple triumph 13–15 August, over Dalmatians, for Actium, and for Alexandria/Cleopatra/Egypt (not Antony!); see *RG* 4.1; **H16**; Dio 51.21.5–9. *Games:* Dio 51.22.4–9; *RG* 22.

7   *Twenty years of civil strife*: Caesar had crossed the River Rubicon, initiating the Civil Wars, on 10 January, 49 BC; Octavian closed the Temple of Janus on 11 January, 29 BC (**C4**); it signified that *foreign wars were laid to rest* (see **K47–K49**). *Peace restored*: for the 'Augustan Peace' (imposed by conquest), see *RG* 12.2.

8   *Majesty to the senate*: this was a new idea of the Principate, first found in Livy; majesty properly belonged to the Roman People as a whole.

9   *The power of the magistrates was reduced*: traditional limits had been exceeded in the years of crisis: the Triumvirs themselves exercised powers that were equivalent to a triple Dictatorship. *Two praetors were added to the eight*: that was in 23 BC (Dio 53.32.2). There had been eight since the reforms of Sulla (81 BC), who had made the number of consuls plus praetors coincide with the number of provinces at the time. But pressure of work (at home praetors presided over the state Treasury and over courts, and abroad they governed provinces) and the ambitions of politicians led to occasional increases (to 16 in 44 BC, Dio 43.49.1). For the twelve reached and exceeded by AD 11 see note on Tac, *Ann.* 1.14.4).

10 *The ancient, traditional form of the republic was brought back*: Velleius' meaning has been intensively discussed; the most convincing interpretation is that all the machinery of state as it had been known before the civil wars was set going again; that did not mean that Emperors could not tinker with it.

11 *Fields were cultivated*: by 31 BC there were 60 legions in the field, mostly recruited from Italy; Virgil, *Georgics* 1.505–8 (**G9**) complains of its agricultural desolation. *Religious rites*: see *RG* 20.4; 22.2; Suet. *Aug.* 30f; **L1**.

12 *Existing laws were revised ... new ones passed:* see *RG* 8.5; Section **S**. Suet. *Aug.* 34.1, mentions legislation on adultery, electoral bribery and sumptuary.

13 *The senatorial lists were revised*: in 29, 18, 11 BC: see *Res Gestae* 8.2; Suet., *Aug.* 35 (showing how ill received Augustus' activity was) and *Aug.* 54; Dio 52.42; 54.13f.; 54.35.1.

14 *To contribute to the adornment of the city*: see **K5** for three individuals, named by Tacitus; Suet. *Aug.* 29.5 for a further four; Dio 54.18.2.

15 *Only the office of consul was Caesar prevailed upon to hold successively*: Augustus held the consulship (see Section **B**) in 43, 33, from 31–23 BC (the eleventh), and in 5 and 2 BC to introduce Gaius and Lucius Caesars to public life. Refusals came in 22, 21 and 19 BC (*RG* 5.3; Suet. *Aug.* 26.2; Dio 54.10.1).

16 *Rejection of the dictatorship*: see *RG* 5.1 (22 BC); Suet. *Aug.* 52 (on his knees, with breast bared); Dio 54.1.4.

commander, the universal peace his victories imposed upon the world,[17] the innumerable achievements inside and outside Italy, these would tax the energies of a writer prepared to spend the whole of his life describing them alone. But mindful of the declared objective of my work, I have laid before the eyes and minds of my readers a broad overall picture of his principate.

[90.1] As I have observed above, the civil wars were now dead and buried, and the limbs of the body politic torn apart by the wounds inflicted by so long a series of conflicts were healing back together. Dalmatia, after 220 years of armed rebellion, was brought to a firm acknowledgement of Roman rule;[18] the Alps, teeming with wild and barbarous tribes, were subdued;[19] the Spanish provinces were pacified after numerous campaigns, some successful, some less so, some conducted by Augustus himself, others by Agrippa,[20] whom the friendship of the *princeps* had advanced to a third consulship and then to a share of his tribunician power. [90.2] Roman armies had originally been sent to these provinces 250 years ago, during the consulship of Scipio and Sempronius Longus, in the first year of the second Punic War, under the command of Gnaeus Scipio, Africanus' uncle.[21] For the next 200 years warfare continued there, with such massive casualties on both sides that through the loss of generals and armies Rome suffered regular disgrace and sometimes even threats to her imperial power. [90.3] Those Spanish provinces cost both Scipios their lives; those provinces strained the resources of our ancestors in a humiliating 15-year campaign under Viriathus;[22] they caused panic among the Roman populace during the war in Numantia;[23] they were the scene of the disgraceful surrender of Quintus Pompeius and of Mancinus' even more despicable capitulation, which was repudiated by the senate when they handed over their disgraced general to the enemy; Spain's armies, too, destroyed so many of our commanders, both consular and praetorian, and in our fathers' time made Sertorius so powerful, that for some five years it was impossible to decide whether the armies of Rome or Spain were more likely to prevail and which nation would yield obedience to the other.[24] [90.4] These, then, were the provinces – so vast, so densely populated, so ferocious – that some 50 years ago Caesar Augustus pacified so effectively that, where previously there had been no respite from the most devastating wars, now under the legate Gaius Antistius, then under Publius Silius, and others after him, there was no room even for brigandage.[25]

---

17 *Waged as victorious commander*: Augustus campaigned in Spain, 27–24 BC (**N47–N48**), and oversaw operations in Gaul, 16–13, and Germany 11–10 and 8 BC. *Universal peace his victories imposed*: see *RG* 13.

18 *Dalmatia*: in 9 BC, the first conflict having started in 229 BC; compare *Res Gestae* 30.1. A three-year rebellion broke out in AD 6.

19 *The Alps*: Tiberius and Nero Drusus campaigned there in 15–14 BC: *Res Gestae* 26.3; **N14–N15**; Dio 53.25.3–5. The triumphal monument erected listed 48 tribes (**N16**).

20 *The Spanish provinces*: Baetica ('Further'), Tarraconensis ('Nearer'), and Lusitania; the division was probably made in 27 BC (**M23**). After Augustus' campaigns (above, 89.6) rebellion broke out in the North-West and was repressed by Agrippa in 19 BC (See **N47–N49**; Dio 53.25.5–8; 54.11.2–6).

21 *250 years ago*: the prime object then had been to attack the basis of Hannibal's power. Velleius was writing in AD 30; he uses a round number. *(Cornelius) Scipio*: this man, consul 222 BC, and his brother Publius, consul 218, were killed in 211, and replaced by Publius' son (consul 205 BC), who finished the second Punic War at Zama in 202 and was given the name *Africanus*.

22 *Viriathus*: Spanish hero of the 'Lusitanian' war, 154–139 BC.

23 *Numantia*: the Numantine war was the final major struggle, 143–133 BC, during which the surrenders of Q. Pompeius and C. Hostilius Mancinus took place.

24 *Sertorius*: an able follower of the popular politician Marius, he held out in Spain against the restored senatorial government 80–72 BC, but never posed a real threat to Italy.

25 *Gaius Antistius (Vetus)*: suffect consul, 30 BC; governor of Tarraconensis 26–25 BC, he defeated the Cantabri (**N48**). *P. Silius (Nerva)*: consul 20 BC, governor in 19 BC.

[91.1] While peace was being imposed in the West, in the East the Parthian king handed back to Augustus the Roman standards lost to Orodes when Crassus was crushed, and those yielded to his son Phraates when Antony's army was repelled.[26] This *cognomen*, Augustus, was conferred on him on the proposal of Plancus with the unanimous support of the senate and people of Rome.[27] [91.2] But to some the supreme felicity of the current order was intolerable. Two men of widely differing character launched a conspiracy to assassinate Caesar. Lucius Murena might have seemed a honourable man, had he not become involved in this crime; Fannius Caepio, his accomplice, had long since proved a villain. They were arrested by the authorities and suffered by law the same violent death which they had planned for Caesar.[28] [91.3] Soon afterwards Egnatius Rufus, who was in every respect more a gangster than a senator, acquired such ever-increasing popularity as aedile by using his own slaves as a public fire-brigade that he was elected praetor for the following year. Soon after he even dared to stand for the consulship; but the widespread notoriety of his criminal activities and the fact that his finances were as impoverished as his character encouraged him to gather together a band of like-minded villains and plot Caesar's assassination, doubtless with the intention that, since his own safety was incompatible with Caesar's, he would eliminate him before his own death.[29] [91.4] Certainly it seems to be characteristic of the outlook of such men that, rather than die alone, they prefer that their deaths should bring down the state as well. The result would be the same, but the publicity rather less. In this respect Egnatius proved no more successful a conspirator than the previous two. He was consigned to prison with his accomplices and met the death his life so richly deserved.

[92.1] We should not allow the remarkable actions of a distinguished consul of the time, Gaius Sentius Saturninus, to be robbed of due recognition.[30] [92.2] Caesar was abroad, reorganising the affairs of Asia and the East, thus personally bringing to the world at large the blessings of his peace. In Caesar's absence Sentius happened to be sole consul and dealt with a number of matters like a stern consul of olden times, showing a traditional severity and admirable firmness of purpose. In particular, he

---

26 *Handed back ... the Roman standards*: this event, in 20 BC, was intensively celebrated (see **N42**) and the standards were eventually deposited in the Temple of Mars Ultor (**K19**); it concealed the fact that Augustus had avoided dangerous war with the people who had defeated and killed M. Licinius *Crassus* (53 BC – **N41**) and defeated *Antony* (36 BC), and whom he was expected to conquer (Horace, *Odes* 1.12,53–54 (**G23**)).

27 *This* cognomen, *Augustus, was conferred on the proposal of Plancus*: the date was 16 Jan. 27 BC (see **C7**, **H22**–**H23**), and the new name distanced its holder from his Triumviral personality. The proposer, L. Munatius Plancus (consul 42 BC) had earned himself a reputation as a turncoat.

28 *A conspiracy to assassinate Caesar*: one of the most discussed episodes in Roman history. First the men involved: *Lucius Murena*: even this man's name is controversial, like his consulship for 23 BC (see Section **B**). *Fannius Caepio*: his name is certain, and shows that he belonged to a family, the Fannii, ever loyal to senatorial government; Caepio had been a *cognomen* of the assassin of Caesar, Brutus. Second, the date of the conspiracy is in doubt, 24, 23, or 22 BC. Third, some scholars have denied that there was a conspiracy, holding that Augustus framed two inconvenient politicians. Fourth, and most important, since the conspiracy came close to Augustus' abdication of the consulship and assumption of the tribunician power in mid-23 BC, it is possible that the two events were connected, although many scholars regard the constitutional change as part of the evolution of Augustus' principate, or due to an illness. However, it is hard to sever Fannius Caepio from the political change, and to believe in a tranquil abdication in mid-consulship. *Arrested by the authorities*: the conspirators were caught at Naples but were condemned *in absentia* (Dio 54.3.5; **P9**–**P10**).

29 *(Marcus) Egnatius Rufus*: see also Dio 53.24.4–6. He was aedile probably in 22 BC, (Dio says 26 BC), praetor in 21, and stood for the consulship in 19. This opportunistic behaviour, possible during Augustus' absence, may have been driven by need for money (to be obtained from governing a province).

30 *Gaius Sentius Saturninus*: the consul of 19 later served with distinction in Africa, Syria, and Germany against Maroboduus, winning triumphal ornaments in AD 6. See Consular *Fasti* for 19 BC (Section **B**).

exposed the fraudulent practices of the tax-collectors, punished their greed, and recovered revenues to the public treasury.[31] But it was in the conduct of the elections that he really showed his true mettle.[32] [92.3] Where he felt candidates for the quaestorship unworthy, he blocked their candidature;[33] when they persisted, he threatened to exercise his consular prerogatives if they appeared in the Campus Martius for the elections.[34] [92.4] He even vetoed the candidature of Egnatius, who was at the height of his popularity at that point and hoping to match his successful capture of the praetorship after his aedileship by adding the consulship to his praetor's office. Sentius swore that even if Egnatius was chosen by popular mandate, he would refuse to declare him duly elected. [92.5] In my opinion that glorious action is comparable to any of the legendary achievements of the consuls of old. Sadly, we are naturally inclined to be more generous in our praise of what we learn by hearsay than of what we actually see with our own eyes. Contemporary achievement we invest with envy; the past with admiration. We learn from the past; we feel diminished by the present.

[93.1] Roughly three years before the plots of Egnatius exploded on the public scene and at about the time of the conspiracy of Murena and Caepio, exactly 52 years ago from now,[35] Marcus Marcellus, son of Augustus' sister, Octavia, died while still a young man, after celebrating his appointment as aedile with a most magnificent public spectacle.[36] It had been generally assumed that if anything happened to Augustus, Marcellus would succeed him, though Marcus Agrippa would be unlikely to acquiesce too readily in such an appointment.[37] Certainly, if reports are to be believed, the lad was endowed with great natural abilities, high spirits, and a cheerful disposition, with talents to match the heavy responsibilities for which he was being groomed. [93.2] After his death, Agrippa returned from Asia and married Caesar's daughter, Julia, Marcellus' widow.[38] He had withdrawn temporarily from the limelight and set out, ostensibly on a special mission for the *princeps*, but in reality (so it was rumoured) because of his private dislike of Marcellus. Julia's record as a mother proved unfortunate, both for herself and for Rome.[39]

---

31 *Fraudulent practices of the tax-collectors*: these had been notorious for more than a century and a half (Livy 25.3.8–5.1), and continued so. There is no trace of Saturninus on the Customs Law of Asia (*SEG* 39, 1189, lines 88–102, with translation) but significantly many new regulations were drawn up in 17 BC. *Recovered revenues to the public treasury*: evidently the amounts that tax collectors had succeeded in extracting were disproportionately larger than what they had undertaken to pay the state; or contractors had overcharged for supplies delivered to the State.

32 *Conduct of the elections*: as sole consul, Saturninus presided over the elections, and in the following sections he exercises his right of keeping out unsuitable candidates by forbidding them to stand and undertaking not to allow any votes cast for them to be nominations, as if there were papers handed in to him by candidates; there was nothing so formal.

33 *Candidates for the quaestorship*: this magistracy carried with it membership of the senate, and could be held at the age of 24; there were twenty posts available.

34 *Campus Martius*: the open area in which elections were held; see **K4**.

35 *Exactly 52 years ago from now*: the year is 23 BC.

36 *Marcus (Claudius) Marcellus*: died as aedile after 1 August. *Young man*: he was in his twentieth year according to Propertius 3.18.15 (**G33**). For his prospects, involving the consulship ten years before the legal age, see note on **J29**. *Magnificent public spectacle*: perhaps the *Ludi Magni* of 4–19 September.

37 *Marcus Agrippa*: a repeat of the civil wars, with Agrippa in Antony's role and Marcellus in Octavian's, was probably expected (see note [28] on Augustus' illness of 23 BC).

38 *Returned from Asia*: Agrippa had gone to Lesbos, probably not to show disapproval of Marcellus' advancement (compare Tiberius in 6 BC) but to be close to Balkan and eastern armies if Augustus were assassinated, i.e., as an insurance for him. *Julia*: married to Marcellus in 25 BC; five children by Agrippa. See **J48–J54**.

39 *Record as a mother*: her children were Gaius and Lucius, who died prematurely; the younger Julia, exiled in AD 8 and died in AD 28 (**J55**); Agrippina the Elder, who died in custody in AD 33 (Tac. *Ann.* 6.25), and Agrippa Postumus, exiled in AD 5 and killed in AD 14 (see note [147] and Tac. *Ann.* 1.6.1).

[94.1] At this period Tiberius Claudius Nero, now in his nineteenth year, entered public life as quaestor.[40] He was only three years old when, as I have already recorded, his mother Livia, the daughter of Drusus Claudianus, had been given in marriage to Caesar by her own former husband, Tiberius Nero.[41] [94.2] Thus the young man enjoyed an upbringing and training fit for a god. Since he was also blessed with a distinguished lineage, good looks,[42] and formidable physique, and had been educated to the highest level that study and his own outstanding ability could achieve, he gave early promise of the greatness to come. His very looks foreshadowed the future *princeps*. [94.3] The shortage of grain posed major problems to the new quaestor, but under his stepfather's instruction he managed the task so skilfully both in Ostia and in Rome that his performance revealed the great potential which was later to be so fully realised.[43]

[94.4] Soon after, he was given another commission by his stepfather, to make a tour of inspection of the eastern provinces with an army and then to reorganise them.[44] There, too, he gave ample evidence of his varied abilities, when he marched into Armenia with his legions and brought it back into the control of the Roman people, before appointing Tigranes, son of Artavasdes, as its ruler. His name and reputation so alarmed the Parthian king that he sent his own children to Caesar as hostages.[45]

[95.1] When Tiberius Nero returned home, Caesar decided to test him in a war of considerable importance,[46] appointing, as his coadjutor, his brother Drusus Claudius, born to Livia when she was already a member of his own household.[47] Together they launched a two-pronged attack upon the Raeti and Vindelici, [95.2] successfully storming a large number of cities and fortresses, and winning a number of pitched battles. The enemy tribes held very powerful defensive positions which were hard to approach; their numbers were considerable and their natural ferocity was a greater threat to the Roman army than their actual casualties, sustained in inflicting a total and bloody defeat upon the enemy, would suggest.

[95.3] The censorship of Plancus and Paulus preceded these events and, being conducted with mutual acrimony, it brought neither honour to the incumbents themselves nor benefit to the republic.[48] One lacked the force of personality for the office, the other the strength of character. Paulus was too slight a man for the censor's role; Plancus should have feared it, since there were no charges he could lay or hear laid against younger men that he could fail to recognise in his own conduct, old though he was.[49]

---

40 *Entered public life as quaestor:* [24/3 BC] he was allowed five years' remission (note [33]).
41 *Given in marriage to Caesar:* see **J26**. Tiberius Nero had been praetor in 41 BC and was a partisan of Antony: the new marriage damaged Octavian's relations with the family of his former wife, including Sextus Pompey, and so was useful to Antony.
42 *Good looks:* Suet. *Tib.* 68.1–3 gives a less idealised portrait.
43 *Shortage of grain:* see Suet. *Tib.* 8; another problem of 23–22 BC. (*Res Gestae* 15.1; 5.2).
44 *Another commission:* 20–19 BC: it seems that Tiberius found the new king of Armenia already in possession and had only to crown him: **N23** and Dio 54.9.4f.
45 *Sent his own children…as hostages:* this was more probably a response to the presence of Augustus himself in the East when the standards were handed back; see **N43–N44** and 91.1. They were not really 'hostages'.
46 *A war of considerable importance:* the brothers subdued the Alpine regions: see note [19] and **N14–N15**.
47 *(Nero) Drusus Claudius:* usually called (Nero) Drusus. His birth in 38 BC, three months after the marriage of Octavian and Livia was a source of speculation (Suet. *Claud.* 1.1; Dio 48.44.4), encouraged by his popularity; he had dash and affability. Hopes were crushed on his death on campaign in Germany, 9 BC (**J43–J47**).
48 *Censorship:* held in 22 BC, it was an instant failure: the very platform on which the censors sat collapsed: Dio 54.2.2. On the censorship see Section **B**, under 28 BC.
49 *Paulus (Aemilius Lepidus):* suffect consul 34 BC, after having been proscribed by the Triumvirs (Suet. *Aug.* 16.3) and having changed sides from the Liberators. *(Lucius Munatius) Plancus:* see note [27]. After his daughter Plancina's disgrace in AD 20 (Tac. *Ann.* 3.17), Velleius was free to attack Plancus.

[96.1] Then came the death of Agrippa, a *novus homo* whose innumerable achievements had won him nobility and elevated him to a position in which he was Tiberius Nero's father-in-law.[50] Indeed, Augustus had adopted Agrippa's children, his own grandchildren, under the names of Gaius and Lucius.[51] The death brought Nero and Caesar closer together, since his daughter Julia, previously married to Agrippa, now married Nero.[52]

[96.2] The war in Pannonia followed soon after.[53] First undertaken by Agrippa and Marcus Vinicius, your grandfather, consul, and then carried on by Nero, it proved to be a major campaign, ferocious, and – because it was so close – a threat to Italy.[54] [96.3] The tribes of Pannonia and the peoples of Dalmatia, the geography of the area and its rivers, the size and disposition of its forces, the superb and innumerable victories of our glorious general in this war – all this I shall unfold elsewhere. My present work must adhere to its overall design. With victory assured, Nero celebrated an ovation.[55]

[97.1] But while everything was going so very well in this part of the empire, in Germany a major disaster was sustained under the legate, Marcus Lollius, a man whose whole life had been devoted to the pursuit of profit rather than honourable conduct, and whose extreme depravity was matched only by his skill in concealing it.[56] The Fifth Legion lost its standard and this brought Caesar out to the Gallic provinces from Rome.[57] [97.2] The full weight of responsibility for the war in Germany was then transferred to Drusus Claudius, Nero's brother, a young man endowed with as many remarkable qualities as human nature can inherit or human effort develop to perfection.[58] [97.3] Whether his talents were better suited to military action or the subtler skills of peacetime is hard to say; what can be said for certain is that his sweet nature, charm, and easy-going lack of superiority towards his friends were, reportedly, inimitable, while his good looks almost matched his brother's. Alas, though he had conquered much of Germany and shed much German blood on many a different battlefield, while he was still consul the cruel Fates snatched him away in his thirtieth year.[59] [97.4] Thereafter the whole burden of the war devolved upon Nero, and he bore it with characteristic courage and success. He conducted a victorious campaign all over

---

50 *Death of Agrippa*: March 12 BC: on Agrippa, see **R6–R7**; **T2–T14**, note [37] and notes on Tac. *Ann*. 1.11.1; **J33**. *Novus homo ... nobility*: 'new men' were, strictly, those who had not held curule office (aedileship, praetorship, consulship; more commonly the phrase is used of those who were the first in their family to enter the senate, as Agrippa was (**T2**). Nobility is a rank, hereditary in the male line, won under the Republic by all who attained the consulship; but real achievements ennobled Agrippa. *Nero's father-in-law*: Velleius' loyalty to Tiberius is showing! Tiberius married Vipsania in about 19 BC (**J35**; Suet. *Tib*. 7.2).

51 *Adopted Agrippa's children*: in 17 BC (Dio 54.18.1).

52 *Julia ... married Nero*: see on Tac. *Ann*. 1.12.4; **J48**.

53 *The war in Pannonia*: 13–9 BC. See *Res Gestae* 30.1, and note [18].

54 *Agrippa*: he went to the Balkans in 12 BC: Dio 54.28.1f. *Marcus Vinicius*: suffect consul in 19 BC; *consul*: Velleius is addressing his grandson during his consulship of AD 30. *A threat to Italy*: see 111.1.

55 *Superb and innumerable victories*: see Dio 54.31.2–4; 54.34.3; 54.36.3; 55.2.4. *Ovation*: on 16 Jan., 9 BC (**C8**). It was a minor form of triumph, in which the victor entered Rome on horseback instead of in a chariot.

56 *A major disaster*: 16 BC, but not now thought to be major. *Marcus Lollius*: consul 21 BC, he died in the East while acting as adviser to Gaius Caesar (**T19**; Tac. *Ann*. 1.10.4; Suet. *Aug*. 23.1; Dio 54.20.4f.; Obsequens 71); that left his entire reputation vulnerable (**P17, T19**; Suet. *Tib*. 13.2). In any case the contrast with the successes of Tiberius and Drusus was valuable.

57 *Brought Caesar out*: see note [17].

58 *Drusus Claudius*: see **J43**, note [19] and [47] and on **J26, J34**.

59 *Had conquered much of Germany*: Dio 54.32f.; 55.1.2–5. He reached the Elbe, but permanent occupation was another matter; thoroughness as well as geographical scope are in question. *Snatched him away*: by a fall from his horse, 9 BC. See **J36**; **J45**; Dio 55.1.4–2.3 and note on **J46**.

Germany without loss to the army in his care – as a general he was always particularly concerned to avoid casualties – and his conquest was so complete that he reduced the country almost to the status of a tributary province. He was then accorded a second triumph and a second consulship.[60]

[98.1] While the events described above were going on in Pannonia and Germany, a ferocious war broke out in Thrace, with all the tribes of that nation erupting into rebellion.[61] Lucius Piso suppressed the revolt with great courage, though today (as city prefect) we see him rather as a conscientious and supremely gentle guardian of our civic order and security.[62] [98.2] As Caesar's legate he waged a three-year campaign and by a combination of pitched battles and sieges, in which he slaughtered vast numbers of the enemy, he returned these ferocious tribesmen to their previously peaceful state. By this achievement he restored security to Asia and peace to Macedonia. [98.3] Of this man it must be generally agreed and stated that his character is a remarkable blend of energy and gentleness, and that it would be almost impossible to find anyone more dedicated to the cause of civil peace yet more capable of action, and when action was needed more capable of undertaking it with the utmost discretion.

[99.1] Shortly afterwards Tiberius Nero, having held two consulships and enjoyed two triumphs, having been made the equal of Augustus by sharing with him the tribunician power, being now the foremost citizen of the state save only one (and that because he wished it so),[63] our greatest general, blessed above all by fame and fortune, a second guiding light and leader of our nation, [99.2] sought from his father-in-law, who was also his stepfather, leave of absence for a period of rest after the relentless labours of recent years. It was an act of remarkable, incredible, indescribable loyalty to Caesar and though he concealed his real motives, they were soon apparent.[64] Gaius Caesar had already assumed the toga of manhood; Lucius, too, was approaching maturity and Tiberius did not want his own distinction to rob the youngsters of the limelight at the beginning of their public careers.[65] [99.3] An account of public reaction at the time to this proposal, the individual feelings, the tears of all who bade farewell to a great man, and how nearly the state imposed the claims of duty upon him – all this must be reserved for proper treatment elsewhere. [99.4] What I must record even in this brief summary about his seven-year sojourn in Rhodes is this: it was of such a character that all who set out for the overseas provinces, whether as proconsuls or imperial legates, interrupted their journeys to visit him; and though he was always only a private citizen (if such majesty can ever be called "private"), on meeting him they saluted him formally by lowering their *fasces*, thus declaring that his status in retirement was more

---

60   *The whole burden ... devolved upon Nero*: see Dio 55.6.2–5. *Reduced.. almost to the status of a tributary province*: this shows Roman aims between the Rhine and Elbe. *Second triumph*: Dio 55.6.5. The consulship was for 7 BC.

61   *War broke out in Thrace*: Dio 54.34.5–7 (under 11 BC, probably the last year of the war).

62   *Lucius (Calpurnius) Piso (the Pontifex)*: consul 15 BC, and one of the most consistently successful men in Augustan and Tiberian public life (portrait: frontispiece of R. Syme, *The Augustan Aristocracy* (Oxford, 1986)). He died in AD 32 as Prefect of the city (**K7–K8**), so was still alive when Velleius was writing.

63   *The foremost citizen of the state*: Velleius is correct: Tiberius now had tribunician power, see note on **J40**.

64   *Sought...leave of absence*: see Suet. *Tib.* 10f.; Dio 55.9.5–8. *His real motives ... were soon apparent*: they are still hotly debated. Velleius relates Tiberius' public explanation. It is possible that Tiberius took offence at the mistrust of him shown by supporters of Gaius and Lucius Caesars (compare Dio 55.9.2).

65   *Gaius Caesar had already assumed the toga of manhood*: 5 BC: **J56**; Dio 55.9.9. *Lucius too was approaching maturity*: he took the toga in 2 BC: Dio 55.9.10.

distinguished than their official rank.[66] [100.1] The whole world soon realised that Nero was no longer the city's guardian – the Parthians broke off their alliance with us and seized Armenia; Germany rebelled, now that its conqueror's eyes were turned elsewhere.[67]

[100.2] But in Rome in the selfsame year (thirty-one years ago), when the deified Augustus was sharing the consulship with Gallus Caninius [2 BC] and dedicating the temple of Mars, feasting the hearts and eyes of the Roman people on the most splendid and spectacular gladiatorial show and a mock naval battle,[68] within the emperor's own household a disaster struck which is abominable to relate and appalling to recall.[69] [100.3] His own daughter, Julia, as ever indifferent to her father's position and her husband's, set out on a way of life which explored to the utmost all the extremes of extravagance and lechery that a degraded woman could initiate or experience, equating the magnitude of her good fortune only with the extent of the licence it afforded to her vices, and the legitimacy of that licence only with her own caprice.[70] [100.4] It was at that point that Iullus Antonius, the outstanding example of Caesar's clemency but then the violator of his household, avenged with his own hand the crime which he had committed.[71] (After his father's defeat not only had Augustus given Iullus immunity, but also made him a priest, praetor, consul, and governor of a province, and even admitted him to the closest ties of kinship by marriage to his sister's daughter, Marcella.) [100.5] In addition, Quintius Crispinus, who concealed an extreme depravity behind a mask of unbending superciliousness, together with Appius Claudius, Sempronius Gracchus and Scipio, as well as others of lesser family from both orders, paid the penalty they would have paid for violating any man's wife for their crime of violating the daughter of Caesar and the wife of Tiberius Nero.[72] Julia herself was banished to the island of Pandataria and thus removed from the eyes of her parents and her countrymen, though Scribonia her natural mother voluntarily accompanied her and remained to share her exile.[73]

[101.1] Soon after this Gaius Caesar, whose previous visits to other provinces had only been of a temporary nature, was sent to Syria and paid a visit en route to Tiberius

---

66   *Status in retirement*: Tiberius possessed *imperium maius* in the east (he had been commissioned to deal with Armenia again: Dio 55.9.4) and tribunician power until 1 BC; regular governors were subject to his commands. Suet. *Tib*. 11.5 –13.1 distinguishes earlier and later periods of exile, but stresses that the courtesies continued, though Tiberius tried to avoid them, but see **J37**.

67   *The Parthians broke off their alliance*: the trouble had begun by 6 BC, see **N25**. *Germany rebelled*: see Dio 55.10a.2–3. Little is known of campaigns between 7 BC and AD 4.

68   *Dedicating the Temple of Mars* ...*gladiatorial show* ...*naval battle*: on 12 May 2 BC (**C18**); see *RG* 21.1; Suet. *Aug*. 29.1; Dio 55.10.6–8; **K18** and note [26].

69   *A disaster struck*: even if this was not part of an on-going feud between sections of the imperial family, as has been argued (were Gaius and Lucius, sons of the adulteress, legitimate?), the involvement of the Emperor's daughter was bound to give it a political dimension, see (**P12–P16**).

70   *(The Emperor's) daughter Julia*: Dio 55.10.12–14. Her alleged licence made a mockery of the Augustan laws on adultery (**S10–S27**); and he had just been given the title *pater patriae* (Father of the Fatherland).

71   *Iullus Antonius*: Dio 55.10.15. The most dangerous of Julia's alleged lovers, as the son of Mark Antony. See **P13**.

72   *(Titus) Quintius Crispinus (Sulpicianus)* ... *Appius Claudius (Pulcher)* ... *(Tiberius) Sempronius Gracchus* ... *(Cornelius) Scipio*: all were members of the nobility; the last three of the highest distinction. Gracchus' ultimate fate: **J48**. *Paid the penalty*: but Augustus treated the affair as treasonable, rather than as mere adultery, and Antonius killed himself (**P13**).

73   *Julia herself was banished*: public demonstrations achieved her return to Rhegium on the mainland: Dio 55.13.1a. *Scribonia*: see Dio 55.10.14. She was the wife that Augustus discarded in favour of Livia, and her behaviour supports the view that Julia's fall was a political affair.

Nero, who accorded him all the respect due to a superior.[74] The quality of his performance in Syria proved somewhat mixed, affording ample material for his admirers and sufficient for his critics. He held a conference with the youthful and talented king of the Parthians on an island formed by the embrace of the Euphrates' waters, each accompanied by equivalent retinues.[75] [101.2] This spectacle, as splendid as it was memorable, with the two armies, Roman on one side, Parthian on the other, drawn up on opposite banks of the river while the two outstanding leaders of their empires and peoples held their discussions, I was lucky enough to see with my own eyes, while serving as military tribune in the early days of my military service. (In fact, Marcus Vinicius, I had already attained this rank under your father and his colleague, Publius Silius, in Thrace and Macedonia.[76] Having later visited Achaea, Asia, and all the eastern provinces, together with the mouth and both coastlines of the Black Sea, it gives me great pleasure to recall my many happy experiences of all the events, peoples, nations and cities I saw there).[77] On this occasion the Parthian king first dined with Gaius on the Roman bank of the Euphrates; then Gaius dined with him on enemy soil. [102.1] At this time rumour spread abroad the news of the conspiracy of Marcus Lollius, which had already reached Caesar through the Parthian king. They revealed the treacherous, twisted, and deceitful character of a man whom Caesar had hoped would prove a mentor to his own youthful son. In a few days he was dead, though I do not know whether that death was fortuitous or voluntary.[78] But popular delight at the death of this man was as intense as the distress felt throughout those provinces soon after at the death of Censorinus, a man born to earn men's admiration.[79]

[102.2] Gaius then marched into Armenia and at first this foray proved successful. Later, in the area of Artagera, in the course of negotiations in which he rashly allowed himself to be personally involved, he was seriously wounded by a certain Adduus, as a result of which he became somewhat incapacitated mentally as well as physically, and proved less capable of service to his country.[80] [102.3] He had a plentiful supply of companions ready to pander to his weaknesses through flattery – for flattery always walks hand in hand with greatness – and this led to his desire to grow old in that most distant and remote corner of the world rather than return to Rome. Finally, reluctantly and under protest, he was on his way back to Italy when he fell ill and died in a Lycian city called Limyra, only about a year after his brother Lucius Caesar had died in Marseilles on his way to Spain.[81]

[103.1] But Fortune, who had robbed us of our hopes of Caesar's mighty line, had already restored to the republic her own favourite champion.[82] Indeed Tiberius Nero's

---

74 *Gaius Caesar ... was sent to Syria*: in 1 BC, replacing Tiberius: Dio 55.10.17–21. *Paid a visit en route to Tiberius Nero*: Suet. *Tib.* 12. 2; Dio 55.10.19. Now it was Gaius with *imperium maius* (see note [66]).

75 The king was Phraataces (Phraates V). This and the following section suggest that the Euphrates was to be recognised as a boundary between the two empires. In fact the Romans had protectorates such as Osroene east of the river, and were maintaining their right to appoint the king of Armenia.

76 *your father and ...Publius Silius*: consuls in AD 2 and 3, they probably served in the Balkans in 1 BC and AD 1.

77 *Having visited Achaea*: Velleius' career is an example of the extensive travel that Roman military service entailed. It is possible that he accompanied Gaius Caesar on his journey from Athens to Asia Minor.

78 *Conspiracy of ... Lollius*: see **T19**; note [56] and **P17**.

79 *(Gaius Marcius) Censorinus*: he was consul 8 BC and currently proconsul of Asia, dying in AD 3.

80 *He was seriously wounded*: 9 Sept., AD 3: **J59**; Dio 55.10a.4–8. He was taking over Armenia for its Roman appointee. He died on the following 21 or 22 February: **J60–J61**; Dio 55.10.9.

81 *Lucius Caesar had died*: on 20 Aug., AD 2: **J64**; Dio 55.10a.9.

82 *Fortune, who had robbed us*: compare the language of Augustus' will, wrongly reported by Suet. *Tib.* 23 as showing his reluctance to make Tiberius his heir. *Champion*: similar phraseology was used by Augustus himself: Suet. *Tib.* 21.3.

return from Rhodes, in the year of your father Publius Vinicius' consulship [AD 2] and before the deaths of either Gaius or Lucius, had led to an incredible outpouring of national rejoicing.[83] [103.2] Caesar Augustus did not hesitate for long. There was no need to search for a successor; simply to choose the outstanding candidate. [103.3] And so, following the death of both young men, he now insisted on doing what he had wanted to do after the death of Lucius, but had been prevented by Nero's own vigorous opposition because Gaius was still alive.[84] He appointed him a partner in the tribunician power, despite his repeated objections both in private and in the senate. Then, on 27 June, in the consulship of Aelius Cato and Gaius Sentius [AD 4], in the 755th year of Rome's foundation, twenty-six years ago, he adopted him.[85]

[103.4] The joy Rome knew that day, the crowds of citizens, the prayers poured out from hands raised almost into heaven, the general hope of permanent security and of an empire that would endure for ever, all these I shall hardly be able to describe even in my substantive work, let alone do justice to in this brief account. Sufficient here to have described what a blessed day it was for all. [103.5] On that day the light of hope assured shone like a beacon upon parents for their children, husbands for their marriages, on landowners for their inheritance, and all men for their future security, for peace at home and abroad, and for a tranquil civic order which exceeded men's aspirations and was fulfilled beyond their wildest dreams. [104.1] On that same day Marcus Agrippa, the son born to Julia after Agrippa's death, was also adopted. But in Nero's adoption ceremony the following words, Caesar's own, were specifically added to the standard formula: "I make this adoption for the sake of Rome".[86]

[104.2] Not for long did Rome detain at home her champion and the guardian of her empire. She quickly despatched him to Germany, where three years previously when your very distinguished grandfather, Marcus Vinicius, was governor, a vast war had broken out.[87] He conducted the campaign in a number of theatres, in some with considerable success, and for that reason was awarded by decree the decorations of a triumph together with an inscription describing his achievements in fulsome terms.[88] [104.3] Having previously discharged my duties as military tribune, at this period I was serving as a soldier with Tiberius. Immediately after his adoption, I was sent out to Germany with him as prefect of the cavalry, taking over my own father's position. Thereafter, for nine successive years, whether as prefect or legate, I was the observer, and, even within my modest capabilities, the adjutant of his heroic achievements.[89] Nor do I think it probable that humanity will ever see the like of it again, that spectacle which I was so privileged to enjoy, when throughout the most crowded parts of Italy

---

[83]   *Tiberius Nero's return from Rhodes*: perhaps early Aug. AD 2. See Suet. *Tib.* 13.2–14.1, a less rosy picture; Dio 55.10a.10.

[84]   *Nero's own vigorous opposition*: if Tiberius' 'exile' had been due to the resentment of Gaius and Lucius in the first place, his unwillingness to become Gaius' partner can be understood.

[85]   *Adopted*: **C19**; Suet. *Aug*. 65.1; *Tib*. 15. 2; Dio 55.13.2.

[86]   *Marcus Agrippa ... was also adopted*: Agrippa Postumus, born in 12 BC, was an incongruous 'brother' to Tiberius, but both branches of the family obtained something. *'I make this adoption for the sake of Rome'*: so Suet. *Tib*. 21.3; two adoptions, one of a man of 45, required justification. The crucial tone of this phrase cannot be recaptured.

[87]   *She quickly despatched him to Germany*: his arrival in Gaul is recorded on an inscription, (*CIL* 13.3570.) *A vast war had broken out*: AD 1. See note [67]. *Marcus Vinicius*: consul 19 BC, probably remained until AD 4.

[88]   *Decorations of a triumph*: this award (special dress, statue) took the place of the triumph proper for private individuals under the Principate; the first known to accept it after Tiberius and Nero Drusus was L. Piso in 11 BC (98.1; Dio 54.34.6–7). For Piso, see **K7**.

[89]   *For nine successive years*: AD 4–12: Velleius was praetor in AD 15.

and the whole extent of the Gallic provinces, men flocked to see their old commander once again, a Caesar by his deserts and courage long before he gained the title,[90] each congratulating himself more fully for the association than Tiberius on his preferment. [104.4] At the sight of him tears of joy welled up in his old soldiers' eyes; with an unfamiliar fervour they rushed to greet him, longing to shake his hand and wholly unable to refrain from cries like "Is it really you, Commander? Have we got you back, safe and sound?" or, "I served with you in Armenia; I was in Raetia". "You decorated me in Vindelicia"; "me in Pannonia"; "me in Germany". Words cannot describe the feelings, and in doing so I may well strain the credulity of my readers.[91]

[105.1] He marched straight into Germany, subdued the Canninefates, the Attuarii, and the Bructeri, recovered the Cherusci (a tribe for whom our disaster, alas! would soon earn a regrettable notoriety), crossed the Weser, and penetrated its hinterland. Caesar insisted on taking personal charge of all the most difficult and dangerous parts of that campaign, giving command of the less risky sections to Sentius Saturninus, his father's former legate in Germany.[92] [105.2] Sentius was a man of many outstanding qualities, conscientious, energetic and far-sighted; in the performance of his military duties he showed stamina as well as skill; yet when his duties left him room for leisure, he enjoyed it with an open-handed elegance that would lead one to describe him as generous and very good company, rather than extravagant or effete. I have already given an account in preceding chapters of this man's remarkable abilities and distinguished consulship. [105.3] The year's campaigning season, extended right up to December, added to the fruits of that amazing victory. His own devotion to duty dragged Caesar back to Rome,[93] even though the midwinter Alps raised a mighty barrier in his way; but at the beginning of spring his guardianship of the empire brought him back to Germany, in whose heartlands before departing he had been the first to pitch his winter camp, on the headwaters of the Lippe.[94]

[106.1] Ye gods, what we achieved that following summer under Tiberius Caesar's leadership would fill a vast book! Our armies crossed and re-crossed the whole of Germany, we conquered tribes almost unknown to man, we recovered the revolted tribes of the Cauchi. All their young warriors, countless in number, magnificent in physique, though securely defended by their own terrain, threw down their arms, and surrounded by the shining ranks of our soldiers under arms, along with their generals cast themselves before the tribunal of our commander-in-chief. [106.2] We broke the power of the Langobardi – a tribe yet more ferocious than the fearsome Germans. Finally, we did what had never before been even contemplated in our wildest dreams, let alone actually attempted: up to four hundred miles beyond the Rhine, as far as the river Elbe which flows between the lands of the Semnones and the Hermunduri, a Roman army marched with its

---

90 *A Caesar by his deserts and courage*: on adoption Tiberius became Tiberius Julius Caesar (Claudianus); Velleius has both Augustus and Julius Caesar in mind, the latter a formidable soldier.

91 *I may well strain the credulity of my readers*: he does not: Tiberius was a cautious general, very careful of his men (see 97.4; 114.2; 115. 5), and not known to have suffered any serious reverse.

92 *He marched straight into Germany*: for the campaigns see also Dio 55.28.5–7. *Cherusci*: on the middle Weser. Under Arminius they were to destroy P. Quinctilius Varus and his three legions in AD 9, see Vell. 117–119. *(Gaius) Sentius Saturninus*: see 92.1–3 and notes 31–33. He too received triumphal honours: Dio 55.28.6.

93 *Dragged Caesar back to Rome*: according to Dio 55.27.5 such visits to Rome were due to Tiberius' fear of Palace intrigue.

94 *On the headwaters of the Lippe*: the Romans were over-wintering in Germany, confirming their control.

standards,[95] [106.3] while at the same time our fleet, thanks to the remarkable good fortune and meticulous planning of our leader, combined with his accurate observation of the seasons, sailed along the shores of the Atlantic Ocean and up the river Elbe from a sea unheard of and unknown to man.[96] They conquered innumerable tribes and achieved their rendezvous with Caesar and his army, bringing with them an abundance of supplies of every kind.

[107.1] I cannot resist a small – perhaps even trivial – interpolation at this point in the midst of the great events I am describing. We had secured the nearer bank of the above river with our encampments, while the further gleamed with the armed warriors of the enemy, who would constantly shrink back through profound terror at the sight of our ships. One of the barbarians, advanced in years, magnificent in physique, and of high status, as his dress made clear, climbed into his dug-out canoe (made from a log, as usual there), and alone controlling this bizarre vessel he advanced into the middle of the stream and enquired whether he might be allowed to disembark safely upon the bank held by our soldiery and behold Caesar. [107.2] Permission was granted. He beached the canoe and having gazed upon Caesar in silence for a considerable time, declared, "Our young warriors are mad to worship your divinity when you are absent and yet, when you are present, to fear your army more than they trust your good faith. But I, Caesar, by your gracious consent, have this day beheld the gods of whom I had hitherto only heard tell; and for me this is the most blessed day I had ever hoped to see." Granted his request to clasp Caesar's hand, he returned to his canoe and looking back constantly over his shoulder at Caesar, he paddled it back to his own bank of the river.

[107.3] Having defeated every nation and country he had entered, Caesar marched his army back into winter quarters, safe and unharmed. Indeed it had only once been challenged to battle, and that was as a result of treachery which resulted in a disastrous defeat for the enemy. He then left for Rome with the same haste as in the previous year.[97]

[108.1] There was nothing left to conquer in Germany except the people of the Marcomanni, who had been summoned from their tribal lands by their leader Maroboduus and then retreated into the hinterland, where they occupied the plains surrounded by the Hercynian forest.[98] [108.2] However brief my narrative, I must not fail to mention Maroboduus.[99] He was of noble birth and powerfully built, ferocious by temperament, yet a barbarian by origin rather than education, exercising a dominion over his subjects that owed nothing to internal feuds, or chance, or temporary security dependent on the inclinations of his subjects. Rather his aspiration for a stable regime and royal power made him determined to move his tribe far away from Roman influence and to migrate to an area where, having recoiled before superior forces, he could make his own kingdom as powerful as possible. So having seized the lands

---

[95]   *Langobardi*: located near the Elbe. *As far as the river Elbe*: Tiberius was emulating Nero Drusus (9 BC) and L. Domitius Ahenobarbus (AD 1): Florus 2.30.26; Tac. *Ann*. 4.44.3; Dio 55.10a.2. But this was a joint operation, later emulated by Germanicus. *Semnones*: they were subject to Maroboduus. *Hermunduri*: dealt with by Ahenobarbus (Dio 55.10a.2); they were now on the upper Main.

[96]   *Sailed along the shores of the Atlantic*: see *RG* 26.4, **N36**.

[97]   *He then left for Rome*: see note [93].

[98]   *Marcomanni*: they too ('Marchmen') belonged to the Elbe group of tribes. After the 9 BC campaign of Nero Drusus (Florus 2.30.2) they left the upper Main for Bohemia.

[99]   *Maroboduus*: the great, perhaps Roman-trained, leader of the Marcomanni, who built up suzerainty over the Semnones, Lugii, and Langobardi.

already described, he brought all his neighbours under control either by war or by treaties of alliance.

[109.1] As for the body of men who guarded his kingdom, he trained them up to almost Roman standards of discipline by incessant armed forays, so that they soon became a force of the highest quality which constituted a threat even to our own empire. His policy towards Rome was to avoid provoking us to war, while making it clear that if we were so provoked, he had both the resources and the will to resist. [109.2] His emissaries to the various Caesars sometimes commended him to them as a suppliant, sometimes professed to speak as the representatives of an equal. Tribes and individuals in revolt from Rome found sanctuary with him, and at all times he played the role of Rome's rival with little attempt at concealment. By training his army in regular wars against his neighbours, he had built up its numbers to 60,000 infantry and 4,000 cavalry and was preparing it for a greater undertaking than any which he had currently in hand. [109.3] He was rendered the more formidable by his location: he had Germany to the north and west of him, Pannonia to the east, and Noricum to the south. As a result he was feared by all, because they all constantly expected to be attacked by him. [109.4] Nor did he allow Italy to feel safe from the threat of his growing empire, since his own borders were not much more than 200 miles from the summit of the Alps, which marked the frontiers of Italy.[100]

[109.5] Such was the man, such the region against which Tiberius Caesar resolved to launch a two-pronged attack in the following year. Sentius Saturninus was instructed to lead his legions through the Chatti and into Bohemia (which is the name of the region occupied by Maroboduus), cutting his way through the Hercynian forests which enclosed the area. From the other side he himself intended to lead against the Marcomanni the Roman army currently serving in Illyricum, starting from Carnuntum, which is the nearest point in Noricum.[101]

[110.1] Man proposes, Fortune disposes of his plans, sometimes by disruption, sometimes by delay. Caesar had already prepared his winter quarters on the Danube and moved his army up to within some five days' march from the enemy, and had already decided that Saturninus should advance as well. [110.2] The forces of the latter, almost equidistant from the enemy but separated by them, were due to unite with Caesar's in a few days at the specified rendezvous, when the whole of Pannonia – together with Dalmatia and all the tribes of that area who had been drawn into alliance with them – broke out in revolt, with an arrogant over-confidence born of the blessings of a protracted peace and their now fully developed resources.[102] [110.3] Necessity took priority over glory; it did not seem safe to leave Italy exposed to an enemy so close at hand, while the army was buried in the remote hinterland. The full number of the peoples and tribes that had revolted came to more than 800,000. Of these about 200,000 battle-trained infantry and about 8,000 cavalry were being mustered. [110.4] Of this vast array, led by highly skilled and energetic generals, one section decided to attack Italy, which was linked to them by the direct route through Nauportus and

---

[100] *Nor did he allow Italy to feel safe*: since the capture of Rome in the early fourth century BC and the invasions by the Cimbri and Teutones in the last years of the second (Tacitus, *Germania* 37), the Romans were permanently afraid of Gauls and Germans.

[101] *In the following year*: AD 6. Twelve legions were involved. *Hercynian forests*: ancient writers were vague about the location. *Carnuntum*: A Roman base near present-day Vienna.

[102] *The whole of Pannonia ... broke out in revolt*: for the course of these campaigns, see Dio 55.28–34. Both parts of Illyricum, in the later provinces of Pannonia and Dalmatia, were involved. *Protracted peace*: they had been pacified since 9 BC.

Tergeste;[103] some had erupted into Macedonia; some remained to defend their homelands. The supreme command rested with the two Batones and Pinnes.[104] [110.5] All the Pannonians were familiar not only with Roman discipline, but also with the Roman language; the majority even had some familiarity with literature and other intellectual pursuits. Heaven knows, no nation ever planned a war and then acted so quickly in declaring it, nor put that declaration into effect so decisively. [110.6] Roman citizens were overwhelmed, merchants butchered, while in the area furthest removed from the commander-in-chief a large number of veterans were cut to pieces;[105] Macedonia was seized by armed insurrectionists and total devastation by fire and sword prevailed everywhere.

So great was the terror inspired by this war that even Caesar Augustus was shaken and alarmed, despite his well-known composure under pressure, derived from his long experience of major wars. [111.1] So levies were raised, and everywhere all the veterans were also recalled to the standards, while men and women were compelled to supply freedmen as soldiers in proportion to their census rating.[106] The emperor was heard to remark in the senate that, if they were not careful, enemy forces could be within sight of Rome in ten days. Senators and Roman equestrians were required to contribute their best endeavours to the war effort, and duly promised them. [111.2] Yet all these preparations would have been in vain without the guiding hand of the emperor. And so, just as the republic sought from Augustus the protection of his armies, so it demanded of him for this war the leadership of Tiberius.

[111.3] My own modest talents also enjoyed an opportunity for notable service in this campaign. Having completed my equestrian service, I was now quaestor-designate, not yet a senator but accorded equivalent status to both senators and even tribunes of the people.[107] As such I was entrusted by Augustus with a section of the army which I took out to his son in the field. [111.4] Then as quaestor I surrendered my right to be allotted a province and was despatched instead to Tiberius as his legate (staff officer).

In the course of that first year we saw some amazing enemy orders of battle. But thanks to the strategic insight of our general, we used every opportunity to avoid action against the full fury of their united forces, while contriving to wear them out by piecemeal engagements. We watched with admiration as Tiberius, with the full authority of a commander-in-chief, conducted this campaign with a remarkable blend of moderation and practical good sense. He showed shrewd judgement in the location of his winter quarters; he ensured that the enemy was thoroughly hemmed in by our outposts, so as to prevent any break-out and ensure that the resulting lack of supplies and internal frustrations gradually sapped their strength.

[112.1] I must now record for posterity the achievement of Messalinus in that first summer of the war, which proved as fortunate in its outcome as it was daring in its conception. [112.2] He was a man whose spirit more than matched his breeding, a son entirely worthy of his father, Corvinus, and one who fully deserved to bequeath his

---

[103] *Nauportus and Tergeste*: Vrhnika, near Ljubljana; Trieste.
[104] *Batones and Pinnes*: two Pannonians (Bato was a Breucian), one Dalmatian (a Bato of the Desidiates).
[105] *Merchants butchered*: like the veterans (often brutal land-grabbers), merchants (often greedy) were favourite targets for rebels.
[106] *Levies were raised*: for Augustus' measures, see **N27–N28**; Dio 55.31.1.
[107] *Having completed my equestrian service*: young men were supposed to serve as commanders of auxiliary troops and as tribunes of the soldiers in a legion before they stood for the quaestorship (on which see notes on **J34** and note [33]); Velleius was thoroughly qualified.

cognomen to his brother Cotta.[108] He was in command in Illyricum when, together with his seriously depleted Twentieth Legion, he was caught and surrounded by a sudden uprising. He routed and put to flight more than 20,000 enemy troops, and for this deed was decorated with triumphal honours.[109]

[112.3] The barbarians placed so little faith in their numbers and had such little confidence in their own strength that wherever Caesar was they soon lost hope. Indeed, the section of their army which was facing Tiberius found itself harassed at will as opportunity offered and brought to the point of destruction by famine, to such an extent that it no longer dared to face his attacks nor to join battle with our men when they offered battle and deployed for action. So they occupied Mount Claudius and took refuge behind a line of defences.[110] [112.4] But the division which had poured out to confront the army from the transmarine provinces, led by the consulars Aulus Caecina and Silvanus Plautius, surrounded our five legions, together with their auxiliaries and a large force of royal cavalry which Rhoemetalces, king of Thrace, was bringing to our support, having joined up with the two generals mentioned above. On them they inflicted a devastating defeat, which nearly proved fatal.[111] [112.5] The king's cavalry was routed; the cavalry units put to flight; the cohorts were wavering; there were signs of panic in the legions. But that day the courage of the Roman soldier claimed more glory than he left to his generals, who had singularly failed to follow the example of their commander and had blundered into the enemy by chance, before finding out from their scouts his exact position. [112.6] At this moment when the fortunes of battle were so evenly poised, it was the legions who found strength within themselves to rally the line. Some of their officers had had their throats cut; the camp prefect and a number of prefects of the cohorts were cut off; centurions were wounded; some of the senior centurions were dead; with no interest in mere defence, they engaged the enemy ferociously, burst through their line, and from the jaws of apparent defeat snatched victory.

[112.7] Agrippa, who had been adopted by his natural grandfather at the same time as Tiberius, had for the last two years begun to show evidence of his real character. Now, at about this time, he revealed a strange depravity of mind and an impetuosity of temperament which cost him the affection of the one who was both his father and grandfather. His vicious habits grew daily more deplorable until he died the death which his madness deserved.[112]

[113.1] Let me now show you, Marcus Vinicius, the extent to which Tiberius proved himself as great a war leader as you can see he is a peacetime emperor. With the two armies now united – his own and those who had come to him as reinforcements – he now had in one camp ten legions, more than seventy cohorts, fourteen cavalry units

---

108 *(Marcus Valerius Messala) Messalinus*: consul 3 BC. *(Marcus Valerius Messala) Corvinus*: consul 31 BC (see Section **B**); also a celebrated orator. *(Marcus Aurelius) Cotta (Maximus Messalinus)*: consul AD 20. See Dio 55. 29.1; 30.1–2 for a variant account.

109 *Triumphal honours*: see note [88].

110 *Mount Claudius*: Dio 55.30.2 mentions a Mt. Alma; scholars prefer a site east of Siscia (Sisak) in the Papuk range, good country for partisans.

111 *Aulus Caecina (Severus)*: consul 1 BC, governor of Moesia. *(Marcus) Plautius Silvanus*: he had been consul in 2 BC (see Section **B**) and came from Galatia. *Rhoemetalces*: running a troubled dependent kingdom for Rome (**M34**), he naturally had forces of his own. *A devastating defeat*: the battle of the Volcaean marshes. The generals were bringing reinforcements to Tiberius at Siscia.

112 *Agrippa (Postumus)*: he fell into deeper and deeper disgrace, increased no doubt as he protested: relegated to Sorrento and dismissed from the family in AD 5, exiled to Elba by senatorial decree in AD 7; killed on Augustus' death in AD 14.

and more than ten thousand veterans, together with a large body of volunteers and the considerable forces of the royal cavalry, all of which together constituted the largest force ever seen anywhere since the days of the civil wars. For this reason morale was naturally very high and their numbers gave them the highest possible expectation of victory. [113.2] But our commander knew exactly what he was doing and preferred functional efficiency to public display – as we have always seen in all his campaigns, where he followed the course of action which would win subsequent approval rather than immediate popularity. So, realising that his force was too big to be easily controlled or effectively co-ordinated, he waited a few days to allow the newly-arrived army to revitalise its energies after its long march, and then decided to send them away, [113.3] ordering them to return whence they came.[113] The route back was long and exceedingly arduous, its difficulties almost defying description; but he escorted them with his own army in order to deter attacks on his united forces, while at the same time ensuring that the enemy, each fearing for their own territories, should not combine to attack the separated section of his departing army. He then returned to Siscia at the beginning of a very severe winter and put his legates in charge of the divisions of his winter quarters.

[114.1] Here is another detail, hardly one of the great peaks of human endeavour yet important as evidence of real and substantial merit as well as practical utility, which was certainly a delight to experience and a mark of our general's remarkable human qualities. Throughout the whole period of the German and Pannonian rebellion, none of us, whether of higher or lesser rank, fell ill without finding our health and welfare a matter of personal concern to Caesar, as though he had all the time in the world to give this single problem his undivided attention, despite being preoccupied with a mass of important responsibilities.[114] [114.2] For those who needed it, there was his carriage and pair; his litter was generally available, and like others I enjoyed the use of it; his doctors, his field kitchen, and now even his bath were there to help alleviate the suffering of the sick, as if brought along solely for that purpose; all they lacked were their home and servants, but nothing that could be provided by servants or desired by the sick. [114.3] Let me add one other item which anyone who was there at the time will immediately recognise, as they will all my other details. He was the only general always to ride on horseback, not in a carriage; and throughout the greater part of his summer campaigns the only one who sat to dine with his invited guests, instead of reclining. He forgave those who failed to follow his practice, provided that their example did no harm. He often admonished; sometimes reprimanded; rarely punished; seeking the middle way by pretending not to see most peccadilloes, while curbing some more significant faults.

[114.4] Winter brought its reward in the shape of an end to the war, and in the following summer the whole of Pannonia sought peace, though remnants of warfare continued in Dalmatia. I shall, I hope, give a full description in the appropriate volumes of my history of how that savage army, so many thousand strong, which had so recently threatened Italy with slavery, surrendered the weapons which they had so recently deployed at the river Bathinus,[115] and to a man made obeisance at the knees of our

---

[113] *He decided to send them away*: the problems of deploying and supplying the enormous force in the difficult terrain must have determined this decision.

[114] The Romans were beginning to find themselves short of men willing to undertake military service; and Tiberius' concern boosted morale. Compare 115. 5.

[115] *The river Bathinus*: the river is the Bosut or the Bosna. *Captured or gave up*: see Dio 55.34.4–6.

victorious commander, while their two formidable generals, Bato and Pinnes, were respectively captured or gave themselves up.

[114.5] At the beginning of autumn the victorious army retired to winter quarters and Caesar gave command of the whole force to Marcus Lepidus, a man whose fame and fortune is second only to that of our two Caesars.[116] The more one got to know and understand him, the more one admired and felt real affection for him, recognising that he was indeed an adornment to the great family from which he sprang. [115.1] Caesar now focused his attention and his forces on the second phase of the campaign, the war in Dalmatia. Here he enjoyed outstanding support from his legate, my brother Magius Celer Velleianus, and this is attested both by the words of Tiberius himself, and of his father, and by the generous decorations with which Caesar presented him at his triumph.

[115.2] At the start of summer Lepidus took his army out of winter quarters, making his way to a rendezvous with Tiberius through tribes that were savage and dangerous, because still at full strength and as yet untouched by defeat.[117] He had to contend with ferocious terrain and enemy forces who barred his way at great cost to themselves; but having destroyed their crops, fired their homes, and slaughtered their warriors, delighted with his success and loaded with booty he fought his way through to Caesar. [115.3] For this action he should have been granted a triumph, had it been conducted under his own auspices; as it was he was presented with triumphal ornaments on the recommendation of the senate, who thus concurred with the judgement of the two *principes*.[118]

[115.4] That summer brought this very dangerous war to an end. The Perustae and the Desidiates, Dalmatian tribes whose mountain strongholds, ferocious character, extraordinary military skill, and locations in narrow mountain passes rendered them well-nigh impregnable, were finally brought to heel not so much by Caesar's leadership as by his own personal involvement in the hand to hand fighting, and then only after they had been almost wiped out. [115.5] Nothing in his conduct of this formidable war or his German campaigns did I see that was more impressive or more admirable than the fact that our commander never regarded the possibility of victory as desirable, if it was to be paid for by the loss of his soldiers' lives; to him the most glorious course of action was that which was the safest; he put conscience first and fame second; his strategy owed nothing to his army's opinions; his army everything to their general's foresight.

[116.1] In the Dalmatian war Germanicus gave signal proof of his courage when he was sent ahead of his commander into many difficult locations.[119] [116.2] Vibius Postumus, a consular, as governor of Dalmatia earned triumphal decorations in a considerable number of efficiently conducted operations; Passienus and Cossus, men in some respects of very different character, but famed for their courage, had earned similar decorations for their campaigns in Africa a few years earlier. But Cossus also bequeathed to his son a *cognomen* which is testimony to his victory, and the young

---

116 *Marcus (Aemilius) Lepidus*: consul AD 6, and Tacitus' model senator; see on *Ann*. 1.13.2. *Second only to that of our two Caesars*: Lepidus was connected with the imperial family by kinship and several marriages.

117 *Start of summer*: AD 9.

118 *He should have been granted a triumph*: see note [88].

119 *Germanicus (Julius Caesar)*: adopted by Tiberius in AD 4, he was sent to the field in AD 7, implausibly, according to Dio 55.31.1, because Augustus did not trust Tiberius. For his achievements, see Dio 56.11; 56.15.

man is himself born to be a model of every virtue.[120] [116.3] Lucius Apronius took part in Postumus' operations and for his efforts in that campaign deserved the honours which his outstanding qualities later brought him.[121] Luck always plays a large part in all these matters, and, I am sad to say, we can find yet greater proofs of its power than these. But in this field too we can recognise abundant evidence of its effects. Aelius Lamia, for example, was a man of old fashioned qualities, who always tempered a traditional severity with a general kindliness to all. In Germany and Illyricum, later in Africa, he performed outstandingly, but was deprived of triumphal decorations not by lack of merit but by lack of opportunity.[122] [116.4] As for Aulus Licinius Nerva Silianus, son of Publius Silius, not even the man who knew him best could find sufficient words to express his admiration when he declared that he had all the virtues of an admirable citizen and a straightforward leader of men. He was robbed by an early death both of the fruits of his very close friendship with the *princeps* and of crowning his career by matching the heights of his father's own achievements.[123] [116.5] If anyone claims that I have contrived an excuse to mention these men, I shall concede the point. Among good men such justifiable candour is hardly a crime, as long as there is no misrepresentation.

[117.1] Scarcely had Caesar put the finishing touches to the war in Pannonia and Dalmatia than, within five days of the completion of his great achievement, dire news arrived from Germany of the death of Varus and the slaughter of three legions, three cavalry units, and six cohorts – as though Fate had granted us at least this one modest kindness, that the disaster should not strike while the general was still pre-occupied. Its cause and the chief actor require a brief digression.[124]

[117.2] Quinctilius Varus was born of a distinguished though not noble family, a man of gentle disposition and placid character, mentally lethargic as well as physically, and better accustomed to the leisure of barrack life than active service.[125] He was not averse to wealth, as his governorship of Syria made clear, for when he entered that province he was poor, and Syria rich; when he left he was rich, and Syria poor.[126] [117.3] While he was in command of the army stationed in Germany, he took it into his head that this people, who were impossible to subdue by force and whose only human characteristics were the possession of human limbs and voices, could be civilised by

---

[120] *(Gaius) Vibius Postumus*: suffect consul AD 5, he belonged to a new family supported by Tiberius and Germanicus, and his brother was suffect in AD 8. *(Lucius) Passienus (Rufus)*: consul 4 BC, who campaigned in Africa as proconsul a little before AD 9. *Cossus (Cornelius Lentulus) Gaetulicus*: consul 1 BC and governor of Africa probably in AD 5–7, defeating the Gaetulians and Musulamii: Dio 55.28.3–4; (**M4, N10**). *Bequeathed to his son*: this was the consul of AD 26, who inherited the name Gaetulicus and governed Germany for many years.

[121] *Lucius Apronius*: consul AD 8, he became a legate of Germanicus in Germany, AD 15 (Tac. *Ann.* 1.56.1), and proconsul in Africa, AD 18–21 (Tac. *Ann* 4.13). He was connected by marriage with the Lentuli.

[122] *(Lucius) Aelius Lamia*: a brilliant career: consul AD 3, legate of Tiberius in Germany AD 4–6 and perhaps AD 10–11, proconsul of Africa before AD 17/18 (Tac. *Ann*. 4.13.5), he was later allowed to govern Spain in absence (6.27.2), dying as prefect of the City.

[123] *Aulus Licinius Nerva Silianus*: consul AD 7 and perhaps died that year. For his father see 90.4.

[124] *The death of (P. Quinctilius) Varus and the slaughter of three legions*: one of the most famous and costly Roman defeats (cf. 119.1). Another account: Dio 56.18.1– 22.2. Arguably this was a main cause of a change of policy in Germany, from immediate conquest to preliminary softening up by punitive raids and diplomatic methods. Varus, consul with Tiberius in 13 BC, like him was a son-in-law of Agrippa (**T14**) and later married Augustus' great-niece, Marcella.

[125] *Distinguished though not noble*: he was, like Tiberius, of a patrician family that had not won a consulship for centuries.

[126] *Governorship of Syria*: 7/6–5/4 BC.

the rule of law.[127] [117.4] With this fixed purpose he advanced into the heart of Germany, as if into the midst of a people who delighted in the pleasures of peace, and wasted the summer campaigning season giving judgements and pursuing the niceties of judicial procedure. [118.1] But, to a degree that must be seen to be believed, the Germans are immensely cunning and supremely savage, a nation born for deceit. They trumped up a series of fictitious lawsuits, challenging one another in violent disagreements at one moment, and the next offering thanks to the Romans for the fact that their system of justice was putting an end to such disputes, adding that their own savage natures were being civilised by this new and unfamiliar procedure in that they were settling by law what used to be settled by brute force. All this made Quinctilius so thoroughly complacent that he came to see himself as an urban praetor, dispensing justice in the forum, not an army commander in the heart of German enemy territory.

[118.2] His opponent was a young man of noble birth called Arminius, the son of Sigimerus, their tribal chieftain; physically strong, mentally agile, with natural abilities unusual in a barbarian, his eyes and looks betrayed the fiery ambition that burned within him. On previous campaigns he had always fought with us, attaining by virtue of his Roman citizenship the status of an equestrian.[128] He took full advantage of our general's carelessness as an opportunity for treachery, shrewdly calculating that no one could be more quickly defeated than one who feared nothing, and that complacency was the most common source of calamity. [118.3] So he began by recruiting a small band of conspirators and soon increased their numbers. He insisted convincingly that the Romans could be defeated, and allied action to decision by setting a date for the uprising. [118.4] The plot was reported to Varus by a loyal German with a famous name, Segestes;[129] he demanded action, but the Fates had by now blinded Varus' every mental faculty to what was afoot. It is indeed a truism to observe that whom the gods plan to destroy they first make mad, thus ensuring (tragically) that what happens to their victim seems to have happened deservedly, and that chance disaster comes to appear culpable. And so Varus refused to believe the report and claimed that Arminius' goodwill towards him could be relied upon as being no more than he deserved. After that first warning there was no time left for a second.

[119.1] The pattern of events which marked that appalling catastrophe, the most grievous disaster suffered abroad by Rome since that of Crassus in Parthia,[130] I shall attempt to describe, as others have done, in my full history. The present summary is sufficient cause for tears. [119.2] This was the finest army of them all, the élite of Roman soldiery in its discipline, skill, and military experience. Thanks to its general's indolence, its enemy's treachery, and Fate's iniquity, it was surrounded, denied an opportunity either to make a fight of it – or to break out, as some wished – without risk of punishment. Indeed some were even severely disciplined for showing a characteristically Roman spirit of resistance. Now, hemmed in by forests, marshes,

---

[127] *In command of the army stationed in Germany*: he succeeded Saturninus in AD 7. *Civilised by the rule of law*: Varus began organising parts of Germany on provincial lines, behaving like a proconsul on circuit. Hence the common modern misapprehension that Varus was a lawyer.

[128] *Arminius*: for his obituary, see Tac. *Ann*. 2.88 (AD 19) recording his age as 37 and his years in power as twelve. *The status of an equestrian*: that must have been the case with many enfranchised Gauls, if they possessed the requisite 400,000 sesterces.

[129] *Segestes*: he was Arminius' uncle, a close relationship in German society, but often fraught with rivalry; so Segestes was steadfastly loyal to Rome, and claimed Roman protection when worsted in AD 15: Tac. *Ann*. 1.55.

[130] *Crassus*: see **N41** and note [26].

and ambushes, they were cut down and annihilated by the very enemy whom they had previously slaughtered like cattle, whose life or death depended on their momentary inclination to rage or compassion.[131] [119.3] The general preferred to die rather than make a fight of it. Like his father and grandfather before him, he killed himself.[132] [119.4] Of the two camp prefects, however, one, Lucius Eggius, set an example as glorious as that of the other, Ceionius, was despicable. The latter, with the bulk of his army destroyed, proposed surrender, preferring death by execution rather than in battle. As for Vala Numonius, Varus' legate, in most respects a quietly honourable gentleman, he set the most appalling example by leaving the infantry deprived of cavalry support and fleeing for the Rhine along with the rest of the fugitives. Fate avenged his deed: he lived no longer than those he had abandoned, and died a deserter. [119.5] Varus' half-burnt body was mutilated by his barbarous opponents; his head was cut off and brought to Maroboduus, who sent it to Caesar; but in the end it was given an honourable burial in the family tomb.

[120.1] The news brought Caesar hurrying back to his father. Ever the protecting *patronus* of the Roman empire, he took upon his shoulders the traditional role of a patron.[133] He was sent to Germany, steadied the Gallic provinces, distributed his armies, reinforced his garrisons, fully confident in his own great abilities rather than fearful of an over-confident enemy who was threatening to launch a second invasion of Italy like that of the Cimbri and Teutones.[134] [120.2] He seized the initiative, took his army across the Rhine, and carried to the enemy the war which his father and Rome would have been happy to prevent. He penetrated deep into enemy territory, opened up roads, devastated crops, burned houses, routed any that dared to face him, and made a glorious return to winter quarters, without loss of any of the troops with which he originally crossed the Rhine.

[120.3] Credit is due to Lucius Asprenas, who was serving as legate under his uncle Varus.[135] Thanks to the strenuous and courageous efforts of the two legions under his command, he saved his army from the great disaster and, by a rapid march to the winter quarters of the Lower Rhine army, he steadied the resolve of the tribes on the Gallic bank of the river who were already wavering in their loyalty. There are, however, some who believe that though the survivors owed their lives to him, those who were butchered under Varus had their properties seized by him, and that the inheritances of the butchered army were appropriated by him at will and made his own. [120.4] Great praise is due also to the courage of Lucius Caedicius, the camp prefect, and those with him at Aliso, who were surrounded and besieged by a vast army of Germans.[136] Having surmounted all the problems which shortage of supplies was making intolerable and an abundance of enemy insurmountable, they gave way neither to risky initiatives nor feeble caution, but awaited their opportunity and forced their way back to the main army with the sword. [120.5] All this shows that Varus, assuredly a man of high principle and excellent intentions, lost his life and that of his magnificent army more through his

---

131 *Hemmed in by forests*: the site of the disaster (compare Tac. *Ann*. 1.60.3), long debated, seems from archaeological discoveries to have been at Kalkriese, 16 km. north of Osnabrück.

132 Varus' Republican father Sextus had killed himself after the defeat at Philippi (Vell. 2.71.3).

133 Patronus: Velleius writes metaphorically of Tiberius as a defending counsel.

134 *Cimbri and Teutones*: see note [100].

135 *Lucius (Nonius) Asprenas*: consul AD 6. (See Section **B**, also Dio 56.22.2ᵃ –4).

136 *Aliso*: a fort on the Lippe, established by Drusus in 11 BC, perhaps at Haltern (compare Dio 54.33.3f.; Tac. *Ann*. 2.7).

own deficiencies as a commander than any lack of courage in his soldiers. [120.6] While the Germans were inflicting every savagery upon their captives, Caldus Coelius, admirable scion of a long line of ancestors, performed a memorable action.[137] He seized the links of the chains with which he was bound and struck them so violently against his own head that his blood and his brains immediately gushed out and he died.

[121.1] No less courage and success than at the start marked the later campaigns of Tiberius in Germany in subsequent years. He shattered the enemy's power by means of land and sea expeditions, settled major issues in the Gallic provinces, and by enforcement rather than penalties calmed the disputes that had inflamed the people of Vienne.[138] At this point the senate and people of Rome responded to his father's request that Caesar should enjoy equal power to himself over all the armies and provinces by decreeing that it should be so,[139] since it was manifestly absurd that what was defended by him should not be subject to his authority, [121.2] and that he who was the first to the rescue should not be recognised as having first claim to the honours that might accrue.

Returning to the city he celebrated a long overdue triumph for his victories in Pannonia and Dalmatia, necessarily postponed by the succession of wars.[140] [121.3] Its magnificence was hardly remarkable, for it was Caesar's triumph. But remarkable indeed had been Fortune's generosity to him. All those pre-eminent enemy commanders were on display, not reported dead in despatches but shown alive in chains – and it was my good fortune and that of my brother to march in that triumph in the company of outstanding heroes, decorated with outstanding honours.

[122.1] There are many other shining and outstanding examples of Tiberius Caesar's moderation, amongst which one that must command universal admiration is the fact that, though he had without question earned the right to seven triumphs, he was content with three. No one can doubt, for example, that the recovery of Armenia and the installation of a client king, on whose head he had personally placed the royal insignia, together with his settlement of the East, deserved a triumphal ovation, and that as victor over the Vindelici and Raeti he had earned the right to enter the city in a triumphal chariot;[141] [122.2] similarly after his adoption, having broken the power of the Germans in three years of continuous campaigning, that he was entitled to, and was right to accept, the same honour; and that following Varus' disaster, after the most successful outcome of his whole military career with the elimination of the Germans, a triumph should have been arranged for our greatest general.[142] But with Tiberius one finds it hard to decide whether to admire more his limitless acceptance of toil and danger or his limited acceptance of honours.

[123.1] We come now to the moment which all Rome dreaded. Caesar Augustus had sent his grandson Germanicus to Germany to complete the final stages of the campaign,

---

137 *Every savagery*: see Tac. *Ann.* 1.61.4–6.

138 *Settled major issues in the Gallic provinces*: for later troubles in Gaul, dealt with by Germanicus in AD 13, see the *Tabula Siarensis*, lines 12–15 (R. Sherk, *Trans. Docs. of Greece and Rome* 6 (Cambridge, 1988) 64 no. 36).

139 See also Suet. *Tib.* 21.1. His *imperium* was made equal to that of Augustus over the entire Empire.

140 *He celebrated a long overdue triumph*: 23 Oct., AD 12: **C38**. See also Suet. *Tib.* 20. The victory had been won in AD 9.

141 *Moderation*: Tiberius' cardinal virtue: see on Tac. *Ann.* 1.14.1. *he was content with three (triumphs)*: the other two were over the Pannonians in 9 BC (an ovation: **C8**) and the Germans in 7 BC. *The recovery of Armenia*: 20–19 BC. See **N23–N24** and 94.4. *The Vindelici and Raeti*: 15–14 BC. See note [19] and **N14–N15**.

142 *A triumph should have been arranged*: but the war was still going on.

and was about to despatch his son, Tiberius, to Illyricum to reinforce the peace imposed by war.[143] He set off for Campania with the intention of seeing Tiberius on his way and at the same time attending an athletics festival dedicated in his honour by the people of Naples. He was already aware of the advance of decrepitude and the early symptoms of declining health, but with his indomitable will he persisted in escorting his son; and having left him at Beneventum, he himself made for Nola.[144] His health deteriorated daily and knowing very well whom he must send for if he wished to leave matters in safe hands after his death, he hurriedly recalled his son, Tiberius, who reached the side of the father of his country even sooner than expected.[145] [123.2] Only then did Augustus declare that his anxieties were over; and reclining in the embrace of his beloved Tiberius, he commended to his care their joint endeavours and announced that he was ready for the end, if so the Fates demanded. Augustus' breathing became less laboured when Tiberius first appeared and when he heard the voice of him that was most dear to him. But soon, since the Fates defeat all human solicitude, at the age of seventy-six, in the consulship of Pompeius and Apuleius, he returned to the elements from which he came, and gave his divine soul back to heaven.[146]

[124.1] I have not the time, for I must hasten on, nor (were time available) would any man have the capacity to describe the general anxiety of those times, the senate's alarm, the popular turmoil, the universal fear, and how narrow was the boundary upon which we stood between safety and destruction.[147] Suffice to have said only what was said by all: "We feared the ruin of the world; we found it not even stirred. So great was the majesty of one man that there was no need of arms to defend the good or to resist the bad". [124.2] But there was one battle, metaphorically speaking: the state's battle with Caesar, as the senate and people of Rome sought to persuade him to succeed to his father's post, and his with them as he strove for his right to be the equal of others as a citizen rather than as emperor to stand above them. At last, reason not ambition won the day, once he realised that whatever he refused to guard must necessarily perish. He is the only man whose lot it has been to refuse the principate for longer, almost, than others fought to usurp it.[148]

---

143   *The moment which all Rome dreaded*: there were real dangers, from foreign enemies (Germans; Parthia), discontented armies (Germany and Pannonia), and rival claimants, real (Postumus) or suspected (Germanicus). *Had sent ... Germanicus to Germany*: see on 121.1; also Tac. *Ann.* 1.31.2. *Despatch Tiberius to Illyricum*: see Suet. *Tib.* 21; Dio 56.31.1.

144   *Made for Nola*: see Dio 56.29.2.

145   *Tiberius ... reached the side of the father of his country even sooner than expected*: see Suet. *Tib.* 21. Too late to find Augustus alive, however, according to Dio 56.31.1.

146   *Gave his divine soul back to heaven*: Velleius alludes to the deification, see 124.3.

147   *Universal fear*: See note [143]. For the precautions that Tiberius took at Augustus' funeral, see Tac. *Ann.*1.8.6f. Postumus was immediately killed: Tac. *Ann.* 1.6.1; Suet. *Tib.* 22; Dio 57.3.5; **J48**; Vell. 93.2 and 112.7.

148   *There was one battle*: Velleius' presentation of what scholars have misleadingly called the 'hesitation' of Tiberius to take over the Principate; compare Tac. *Ann.* 1.11f., which looks more like an inconclusive debate between Tiberius and the senate on the form that his principate was to take, and Dio 57.3.3. *Succeed to his father's post*: the military metaphor that Velleius uses here of the Principate ('post') is repeated in the official decree on Cn. Piso the Elder (M. T. Griffin, *JRS* 87 (1997) 249–63, at 252, line 130), as well as informally by Augustus himself in his letter to Gaius about the succession (**J57**) and by Ovid ironically of Augustus leaving his post to read Ovid's verses (**G56**, line 219). Metaphor was necessary because there was no single position to take over. *The only man ... to refuse the principate for longer ... than others fought to usurp it*: rhetoric. Velleius, like most senators, and Augustus, but not Tiberius, regarded the position necessarily as one of dominance, with the Emperor taking the initiative; for Tiberius' view, see Suet. *Tib.* 27–9.

[124.3] Once his father had been restored to heaven,[149] his body adorned with human honours, his name with the title of divinity, the first duty of the new *princeps* was to organise the voting assemblies along the lines recorded by the deified Augustus in his own hand.[150] [124.4] On this occasion my brother and I were lucky enough, as Caesar's candidates, to be nominated for the praetorship immediately after the noblest of candidates and those who had held priesthoods, thus acquiring the unique privilege of being the last of the candidates recommended by the deified Augustus and the first of those by Tiberius Caesar.[151]

---

149 Death and deification: 17 Sept; Tac. *Ann*. 1.10.8; Dio 56.46. The ascent was witnessed: Dio 56.42.3; 56.46.2.

150 *Voting assemblies*: this is the transfer of elections to the senate recommended by Augustus in his political testament: see on Tac. *Ann*. 1.11.3 and 15.1, with Dio 56.33.

151 *Caesar's candidates*: politicians canvassed for candidates they supported; the emperor did likewise, and those candidates he supported were called 'Caesar's candidates'. See Suet. *Aug*. 56. *Immediately after the noblest of candidates and those who had held priesthoods*: there were twelve places available, and since Tiberius undertook not to support more than four candidates (see Tac. *Ann*. 1.15.2), who would have been sure of election, there should have been two nobles in front of Velleius and his brother (another useful military man: see 115.1). For nobility see note [50]; nobles would win prestigious priesthoods, such as the pontificate and augurate, at an early age; new men, such as Cicero and Pliny the Younger, became augurs after holding the consulship. *Last of the candidates recommended by the deified Augustus*: the consular elections were over when Augustus died; the praetorian and others followed the 'accession' of Tiberius, but besides drawing up his political testament, Augustus had decided which candidates he wished to support, and Tiberius kept the same list.

SECTION F

TACITUS, *ANNALS* 1.1–15

Cornelius Tacitus was born, probably in southern Gaul or northern Italy, *c.* AD 56. He pursued a successful senatorial career, beginning under the Flavian emperors and culminating under Trajan in a consulship in AD 97 and the proconsulship of Asia in AD 112/3. Tacitus began his literary career, around AD 98, with various minor works: *Agricola* (a laudatory biography of his father-in-law, Gnaeus Iulius Agricola, governor of Britain around AD 77–84, which includes bitter criticisms of Domitian), the *Germania* (an ethnographic account of the Germans) and the *Dialogus* (a work in dialogue form discussing the reasons for the decline of oratory). He followed these with two more extended historical works, now always known as the *Histories* (Latin: *Historiae*) and the *Annals* (Latin: *Annales*). The *Histories* was the first to be written and covered the period AD 69–96, that is, from soon after the death of Nero to the death of Domitian; only the first five books are extant, covering the years 69–70 and dominated by the succession wars which followed Nero's death. The *Annals* covered the period AD 14–68, that is, from the accession of Tiberius to the death of Nero; the extant portions are Books 1–6 (covering AD 14–37, the reign of Tiberius, although most of Book 5 is lost) and Books 11–16 (covering the years AD 47–66). Both the *Histories* and the *Annals* were written in the annalistic format traditional in Roman historical writing, that is, with events arranged by the consular year and subdivided into domestic and external (largely military) sections, but Tacitus adapted this format freely for his own purposes.

A brilliant stylist, Tacitus wrote with mordant wit and lapidary concision. He hardly observed his own claim to impartiality (*Histories* 1.1; *Annals* 1.1.3). Although he was ready to concede that monarchy was inevitable and recognised the excellence of Nerva and Trajan as rulers, his historical works are a devastating critique not only of the failings of individual emperors, but of the principate as an institution. In his hostile accounts of Augustus' successors he was following and building upon a tradition established by earlier imperial historians, but it is unlikely that any of his predecessors took as cynical a view of Augustus himself. Sparing in his direct observations, Tacitus builds up much of his picture by innuendo and the reporting of rumour and hostile views.

Tacitus declared his intention to write an account of the reign of Augustus (*Annals* 3.24.3), but no trace of such a work survives. For his view of Augustus and his reign we are thus dependent on the opening chapters of the *Annals* and incidental remarks later in the work. The *Annals* open with a brief preface and introductory observations on Augustus' establishment of the principate (1.1–3); Tacitus then turns to Augustus' death (1.4–5) and Tiberius' accession (1.6–15). At the outset Tacitus brilliantly sketches the means by which Augustus established monarchical power, and he returns at 1.9–10 to the evaluation of Augustus. Here he avoids passing his own judgement, but merely presents contrasting views which he attributes to contemporaries, one partial, the other hostile. Tacitus does not expect us to adopt either view: each has features which we are clearly intended to recognise as unconvincing; however, he places the hostile view second and gives it much more space, and it is evident that it is with this view that he has the greater sympathy.

The other theme of these chapters is Tiberius' rise to the succession. His emergence as heir apparent is tautly sketched in 1.3, and the manner in which his succession was secured in Augustus' last years and after his death is described in the following chapters.

By a wealth of innuendo and lavish use of reported rumour, Tacitus contrives to suggest that Tiberius' succession was the result of intrigue in which Livia played a dominant part. This is a heavily distorted interpretation: despite their breach over Tiberius' withdrawal to Rhodes in 6 BC, the death of Gaius Caesar in AD 4 left Augustus with no real alternative to Tiberius, and the disgrace of Agrippa Postumus in AD 6–7 made his position as Augustus' heir apparent impregnable. Controls on Tacitus' version of Augustus' death and Tiberius' accession are supplied by the parallel and sometimes less hostile accounts of Suetonius (especially *Aug.* 97–101; *Tib.*15–25) and Cassius Dio (especially 56.29–57.7). Some or all of the earlier historical accounts available to Tacitus were used by these writers, and each may have consulted Tacitus himself (Suetonius wrote a few years after Tacitus, Dio in the early third century). Like Tacitus, Dio reports views of Augustus allegedly exchanged by contemporaries after his death (56.43–45). There are a number of points of contact between this passage and *Annals* 1.9–10, but, unlike Tacitus, Dio gives only views favourable to Augustus and explicitly states his agreement. Most scholars suppose that Tacitus and Dio were here following a common source, though there is no agreement on which may have been closer to the original; it is possible that Dio was drawing on Tacitus himself and remoulding what he found.

R. H. Martin, *Tacitus* (1981) is an excellent introduction to Tacitus and his work, with good discussion of the present passage at pp.108–14. There are good treatments of Augustus' death and Tiberius' accession at R. Seager, *Tiberius* (1972), 48ff, and B. M. Levick, *Tiberius the Politician* (1976), 47ff. There is a very detailed commentary on this section of the *Annals* by F. R. D. Goodyear (1972).

Tacitus, *Annals* 1, 1–15

[1.1] At the beginning kings held the city of Rome.[1] Liberty and the consulship were established by Lucius Brutus.[2] Dictatorships were resorted to when occasion required.[3] The power of the *decemviri* lasted only two years; the consular authority of the military tribunes was short-lived.[4] Cinna's despotism was brief, as was Sulla's.[5] The sway of Pompey and Crassus quickly yielded to Caesar, and the armed might of Lepidus and Antony to Augustus, who, under the name of *princeps*, took the whole state, exhausted by civil discords, into his rule.[6] [1.2] The successes and reverses of the ancient Roman

---

1   This sentence locates the period which Tacitus is to write of in the whole context of Roman history, and sketches the history of Roman monarchy: Rome had begun with monarchy under the kings and reverted to it under Augustus; individuals had held more or less autocratic power at times in the intervening period, but none for long.

2   *Lucius Brutus*: see on Virgil, *Aeneid* 6.817–823 (**G37**).

3   *Dictatorships*: in the early Republic it was common for a dictator to be appointed in a military crisis or for some other special purpose. A dictator outranked the consuls and held office without a colleague.

4   *Decemviri*: 'board of ten men', appointed in 451 BC to draw up a law code, the Twelve Tables. According to tradition, a second such board had been appointed in 450 to complete the work, and had attempted to continue in power, but had then been ousted. *Consular ... tribunes*: boards of between three and eight 'military tribunes with consular power' (in modern works usually known as consular tribunes) were elected in place of consuls in many years between 444 and 367 BC, exercising the same powers as the consuls. The reasons for this innovation and for its abandonment are obscure. See T. J. Cornell, *The Beginnings of Rome* (1995), 334–7.

5   *Cinna*: associate of Marius and opponent of Sulla, in effective control at Rome from late 87 BC to his death in 84 BC. *Sulla*: victor in civil war in 82 and dictator from 82 to *c*. 80 BC.

6   *Under the name of princeps, took the whole state ... into his rule*: Tacitus acknowledges that Augustus preferred to be known as *princeps*, 'leading citizen', but insists that his power was in reality monarchical. Contrast the formulation in the pro-Augustan view reported at 1.9.5: 'he had ordered the republic ... under the name of *princeps*'.

people have been recorded by distinguished historians, and talented authors were not lacking to describe the times of Augustus, until they were deterred by the growth of flattery.[7] The reigns of Tiberius, Gaius, Claudius, and Nero have been recounted either during their lifetime in terms which fear made false, or after their death when loathing was still fresh. [1.3] Accordingly my purpose is to say a little about Augustus and his final years and then to treat the principate of Tiberius and the subsequent period, writing dispassionately, since I am remote from any motive for bias, hostile or favourable.[8]

[2.1] After the deaths of Brutus and Cassius, the republic no longer had an army. Pompey had been defeated in Sicily, Lepidus disposed of, and Antony killed.[9] As a result even the Julian faction had only Caesar left to lead them. He laid aside the title of triumvir and presented himself as a consul, content to defend the people by virtue of the tribunician power.[10] Thereafter, once he had seduced the soldiery with gifts, the people with corn, and everyone with the delights of peace, he gradually increased his power, arrogating to himself the functions of the senate, the magistrates, and the law. He faced no opposition, since the bravest souls had died in battle or fallen victim to proscription, while the surviving nobles enjoyed a wealth and status which increased in proportion to their servility; and having profited by revolution, they preferred present safety to the insecurity of the past. [2.2] The provinces too had little objection to the prevailing state of affairs. They had lost faith in the rule of the senate and people, having suffered at the hands of rival governors and avaricious magistrates, and having been denied the protection of the laws, which were constantly subverted by violence, intrigue, and finally corruption.[11]

[3.1] Augustus, however, took various reinforcements for his despotism: he raised Claudius Marcellus, his sister's son, to the pontificate and the curule aedileship while he was still a youth;[12] he promoted Marcus Agrippa, of undistinguished origins but a good soldier who had helped him to victory, to a double consulship, and then on the death of Marcellus made him his son-in-law;[13] he granted imperatorial titles to Tiberius Nero and Claudius Drusus, his step-sons, his own family being then still alive.[14] [3.2]

---

7   Livy's history continued down to 9 BC. Other writers who dealt with the Augustan period, but whose histories have not survived, included Cremutius Cordus (**P21**), Asinius Pollio (**R18–R19**), Aufidius Bassus, the Elder Seneca and the Elder Pliny.

8   Ancient historical writers customarily indicated the subject of the work and justified its choice in their prefaces, often adding observations on predecessors (compare Livy, **D1**). They also commonly proclaimed their own freedom from bias. Tacitus makes similar points at *Histories* 1.1.

9   *Pompey ... defeated*: at Naulochus in 36 BC. He escaped, but was soon captured and put to death. *Lepidus*: attempted to intervene in the war in Sicily with Sextus Pompeius in 36 BC, but Octavian took over his army. He was allowed to live on in disgrace, dying in 13 BC.

10   *Triumvir*: Octavian, Antony and Lepidus were appointed 'triumvirs for setting the republic in order' with sweeping powers in November 43 BC. They were initially appointed for five years, and in 37 BC secured a belated extension, to run probably to the end of 33 BC. After his breach with Antony *c.* 32 BC Octavian ceased to use the title. *Consul, ... tribunician power*: Tacitus here indicates the ways in which Augustus chose to present himself, contrasted with what he perceives as the realities of power. In fact Augustus resigned the consulship in 23 BC and the tribunician power took its place, but from Tacitus' present perspective the chronological sequence appears a trivial detail, which he chooses to disregard.

11   *The provinces*: on administration of the empire, see Section **M**. For imperial edicts, see **M60–M67** and for controls on provincial governors, see **M76–M79**.

12   *Marcellus*: born 42 BC; married Augustus' daughter Julia in 25; died in 23 BC while aedile.

13   *Agrippa*: see **T2–T14**.

14   *Tiberius ... Drusus*: Tiberius Claudius Nero (born 42 BC) and Nero Claudius Drusus (born 38 BC), sons of Livia by her first husband Tiberius Claudius Nero. Augustus employed them as commanders in the Alps in 15 BC and in central Europe from 12. In 11 BC they were given independent grants of *imperium*, and thereafter their successes were recognised by salutations as *imperator*, held jointly with Augustus (compare *RG* 4.1). For the members of Augustus' family mentioned here, see Section **J**, with family trees.

For he had adopted Agrippa's sons, Gaius and Lucius, into the family of the Caesars, and, before they had even laid aside their boys' togas, he had been shamelessly eager, despite a parade of refusal, for them to be named *principes iuventutis* and to be designated consuls.[15] [3.3] Agrippa died, and both Lucius Caesar, on his way to join the army in Spain, and Gaius, on his way home from Armenia while still weakened by a wound, were carried off either by a death fated to be premature or by the treachery of their step-mother, Livia. With Drusus long since dead, Nero was Augustus' only surviving step-son, and everything now converged upon him.[16] He was adopted as Augustus' son, his colleague in *imperium*,[17] and partner in the tribunician power, and was paraded before all the armies, with his mother no longer scheming behind the scenes, but giving open encouragement.[18] [3.4] For now that Augustus was an old man, she had come to exercise such domination over him that he banished to the island of Planasia his only grandson, Agrippa Postumus, who, though he certainly lacked good qualities and his powerful physique inclined him to a brutish ferocity, had nonetheless been found guilty of no crime.[19] [3.5] By contrast, he had given Drusus' son, Germanicus, command of the eight legions of the Rhine and ordered Tiberius to adopt him, although he had a grown son of his own who was now approaching maturity, doing so in order to increase the number of safeguards he could rely on.[20] [3.6] No war remained in progress at that time, except that against the Germans, whose purpose was rather to obliterate the disgrace of Varus' loss of an army than to extend the empire or extract any worthy reward.[21] [3.7] At home all was quiet and the magistrates enjoyed their traditional titles. The younger generation had been born after the victory at Actium, and most of their elders during the civil wars. How many remained who had seen the republic?

---

15   Augustus adopted his grandsons Gaius (born 20) and Lucius (born 17) as his sons in 17 BC. In respectively 5 and 2 BC, immediately after taking the toga of manhood, each was declared *princeps iuventutis* ('leader of the younger generation') and designated to hold the consulship in five years' time (*RG* 14). Augustus had declined such a designation for Gaius in 6 BC (Dio 5.9.2, confused), but his clear intention to advance Gaius rapidly seems to have provoked Tiberius' withdrawal to Rhodes in that year.

16   Agrippa died in 12 BC, Drusus in 9 BC, Lucius Caesar in AD 2, Gaius Caesar in AD 4. The implausible allegation that Livia was responsible for the deaths of Gaius and Lucius is also reported at Dio 55.10a.10. Following Gaius' death, Tiberius and Agrippa Postumus were adopted as Augustus' sons, and Tiberius was granted tribunician power and *imperium*. For Tiberius' powers, see **J40**; Dio 55.13.2, 56.28.1; Suet. *Tib.* 16.1, 21.1; Vell. 2.121.1.

17   *Imperium*: the supreme administrative power at Rome, held by the higher magistrates (normally, consuls and praetors) and by promagistrates; only its holders could levy and command armies and exercise the highest jurisdiction. The symbol of *imperium* was the *fasces*, bundles of rods with (outside Rome) an axe, which were carried by lictors (six for a praetor, twelve for a consul). Octavian assumed *imperium* on 7 January 43 (note [48]; **C2**), and retained it for the rest of his life. In June-July 23 when he resigned the consulship, adjustments were made to his *imperium* to ensure that it remained life-long and was greater than that of the proconsuls (Dio 53.32.5). Augustus also had special grants of *imperium* conferred on various members of his family, beginning with Agrippa in 23 BC.

18   *Paraded before all the armies*: exaggerated – Tiberius was occupied in AD 4–14 with the Balkans and the German frontier.

19   *Agrippa Postumus*: son of Agrippa and Julia, born in 12 BC after his father's death. He was adopted by Augustus in AD 4, but, on the grounds of his bad character, in AD 6 the adoption was cancelled and Agrippa confined at Surrentum, and in AD 7 he was formally exiled by decree of the senate to Planasia (a tiny island a short distance SW of Elba). Compare 1.6.2; Suet. *Aug.* 65.1, 4; Vell. 2.112.7; Dio 55.32; **J67**. Only Tacitus ascribes his fall to Livia.

20   *Germanicus*: born 15 BC; adopted by Tiberius in AD 4 when he himself was adopted by Augustus; given command of the Rhine army in AD 13. Augustus may have intended to mark out Germanicus as the ultimate successor (**J66**). More probably he envisaged him and Tiberius' son Drusus as a pair.

21   The loss of three legions by Publius Quinctilius Varus in AD 9 led to the abandonment of the conquests in Germany which had been made since 12 BC and Roman withdrawal west of the Rhine. Between then and Augustus' death only short raids were launched across the Rhine.

[4.1] The revolution was complete; nothing remained of the old sound ways. Equality had been abandoned and all looked only to the commands of the *princeps*, fearing nothing for the present while Augustus remained in good health and so could sustain his own position, that of his house, and the general peace. [4.2] But as advanced old age took its toll of health and vigour and death drew near, together with the expectation of change, a few began to talk vainly about the blessings of liberty, many to dread the possibility of war, and some to desire it. The vast majority began to gossip about the failings of their prospective masters. [4.3] Agrippa, they said, was savage, embittered by disgrace and lacking both the age and experience to shoulder so great a burden.[22] Tiberius Nero had maturity and was well tried in war; but he had the old, ingrained arrogance of the Claudian family and a sadistic streak whose symptoms, though suppressed, often manifested themselves.[23] [4.4] From early childhood he had been brought up in the ruling family; as a young man he had been loaded with consulships and triumphs; and even in those years which he had spent as an exile in Rhodes under the appearance of withdrawal from public life, he had had no thoughts in his mind save resentment, hypocrisy and secret lusts. [4.5] On top of all that, there was his mother, endowed with all of a woman's lack of self-restraint. In fact, they said, they were doomed to be slaves to a woman and a couple of adolescents, who would trouble the state while Tiberius lived and one day tear it apart.[24]

[5.1] While this sort of talk continued, Augustus' health deteriorated and some suspected his wife of plotting his death. The rumour spread that a few months earlier Augustus had sailed to Planasia to visit Agrippa, with the knowledge of a chosen few and accompanied only by Fabius Maximus;[25] that many tears were shed and signs of affection exchanged there by both parties; and that this gave grounds for hope that the young man would be restored to the home of his grandfather. [5.2] It was further said that Maximus had revealed all this to his wife, Marcia, and she to Livia; that Caesar had learned of it; and that, when soon afterwards Maximus died, possibly by his own hand, at his funeral Marcia was heard lamenting and denouncing herself for being the cause of her husband's death. [5.3] Whatever the truth of the matter, Tiberius had scarcely entered Illyricum before he was summoned back by an urgent letter from his mother; and it is uncertain whether on reaching the city of Nola he found Augustus still alive or already dead.[26] [5.4] Livia had established a tight cordon of guards round the house and approach roads; optimistic reports were issued from time to time, until all the appropriate preparations were complete; finally a single bulletin declared that Augustus was dead and Nero was in charge.[27]

---

22   *Agrippa*: few, if any, can have deluded themselves that there was any prospect of Agrippa succeeding.
23   *Arrogance of the Claudian family*: both Tiberius' parents were Claudians by descent, see **J26**. The historical tradition records numerous instances of arrogant Claudii, mainly invented.
24   *Adolescents*: Germanicus and Tiberius' son, Drusus. In the event they remained on good terms.
25   *Fabius*: Paullus Fabius Maximus, a leading senator from an old patrician family. For essentially the same story reported by Plutarch, see **P18**.
26   *Nola*: in Campania, 18 miles east of Naples.
27   Augustus died on 19 August, AD 14. For other accounts of his death see Suet. *Aug*. 98.5–99, *Tib*. 21; Vell. 2.123; Dio 56.30–31. Of these only Dio mentions the allegations that Augustus had visited Agrippa, that Livia poisoned him, and that Tiberius did not arrive back until after his death (accepting the last of these). Suetonius and Velleius both assert that Tiberius returned before his death, and Suetonius' circumstantial details make this more likely. The stories of the visit to Agrippa and the poisoning are surely false. Tacitus appears to be drawing a deliberate parallel (with some verbal correspondences) with his account of the murder of Claudius by his wife at the end of *Annals* book 12 (it may not be accident that he uses the name Nero for Tiberius here). His account at 5.4 of the steps taken by Livia to manage the news (not in any of the other sources) may draw on Livy's story of the way in which Queen Tanaquil secured the succession for King Servius Tullius (Livy 1.41).

[6.1] The first act of the new principate was the murder of Agrippa Postumus.[28] Although Agrippa had suspected nothing and was unarmed and he himself was resolute in his intention, the centurion who did the deed had the greatest difficulty in despatching him. Tiberius said nothing to the senate about the matter; he was pretending that his father had left orders which instructed the military tribune responsible for his custody to put Agrippa to death without delay when he himself had breathed his last. [6.2] Augustus had certainly uttered many harsh criticisms of the young man's character and had thus ensured that his exile was sanctioned by decree of the senate; but he never steeled himself to have any of his relatives killed, nor was it credible that he would have had his grandson put to death to ensure his stepson's peace of mind; more likely, Tiberius and Livia, he through fear and she with a step-mother's malice, had moved swiftly to eliminate a young man whom they suspected and hated.[29] [6.3] When the centurion reported, after military custom, that his order had been carried out, Tiberius replied that he had given no order and that a formal report must be laid before the senate. When this was discovered by Sallustius Crispus who was party to the secret dealings (it was he who had sent the note to the tribune), he was afraid that he would be personally held accountable for the deed and that he was equally at risk whether he lied or told the truth.[30] So he warned Livia that the secrets of the household, the advice of friends, and the services of soldiers should not be made public and that Tiberius should not undermine the power of the principate by referring everything to the senate, since it was of the very essence of ruling that accounts would only balance if they were rendered to a single individual.[31]

[7.1] At Rome there was a headlong rush to servitude. Consuls, senators, equestrians – the higher their status the greater the haste, the greater the hypocrisy, as each composed his expression so as to appear neither delighted at the death of one *princeps* nor distressed at the accession of another, carefully blending tears with joy, flattery with lamentation. [7.2] Sextus Pompeius and Sextus Appuleius, the consuls, were the first to take the oath of allegiance to Tiberius Caesar,[32] and in their presence Seius Strabo and Gaius Turranius did likewise, prefects both, the former of the praetorian cohorts, the latter of the corn supply.[33] Soon senate, soldiery, and people followed

---

28 *The first act of the new principate*: these words are echoed at 13.1.1 'the first death in the new principate', pointing up the parallel between the accessions of Tiberius and Nero (see note [27]).

29 *Nor was it credible*: not asserting Tacitus' own view, but reporting what men thought at the time. *More likely ... :* again best taken as reporting the contemporary view.

30 *Sallustius*: Gaius Sallustius Crispus was a wealthy intimate of both Augustus and Tiberius, **R27**.

31 For the execution of Agrippa Postumus see also Suet. *Tib*. 22 and Dio 57.3.5–6. All three accounts agree that, when the officer responsible reported the execution, Tiberius denied knowledge of the order and threatened to take the matter further, but in the event took no action (Suetonius' language is very close to Tacitus' here). Only Tacitus reports the involvement of Sallustius Crispus. Dio asserts that the order was issued by Tiberius after Augustus' death; Suetonius declares himself undecided whether it was issued by Augustus or by Livia, and, if the latter, whether she acted with Tiberius' knowledge. Tacitus evokes a murky world of court intrigue with an account left deliberately opaque: 6.1–2 suggests Tiberius' guilt, but stops short of asserting it, and the tale of Sallustius' approach to Livia may suggest Tiberius' innocence. The order to the guard was surely sent in Augustus' name, but who issued it cannot be determined.

32 *Oath*: the inhabitants of the western provinces had taken an oath of allegiance to Octavian and his family in 32 BC, and this had been subsequently extended to the rest of the empire. It now became a standard feature of the accession procedure. See *RG* 25.2 and **H37**.

33 *Seius Strabo and Gaius Turranius*: holders of the important equestrian prefectures in Rome (it is not clear why Tacitus omits the prefect of the *vigiles* (the watchmen or fire brigade)). Seius Strabo was then sole praetorian prefect, but his son, the infamous Sejanus, was made his colleague later in the year, and in AD 17 Strabo was transferred to the prefecture of Egypt. The prefecture of the corn supply (*annona*) had been created at some point after AD 7 (cf. Dio 55.31.4).

suit.[34] [7.3] For Tiberius initiated all business through the consuls, as though the old republic still existed and he himself had doubts about ruling.[35] Even the edict by which the senators were called to the senate-house was issued by virtue of the tribunician power, which he had received under Augustus. [7.4] The edict itself was brief and its tone very modest, to the effect that he would consult about the honours due to his father, that he was remaining with the corpse, and that this was the only public duty which he was discharging. [7.5] But in fact, on the death of Augustus, he had given the password of the day to the praetorian cohorts, as commander; the armed guards and other appurtenances of the court were his; soldiers escorted him to the forum and the senate-house. He sent dispatches to the army as though the principate had already been conferred upon him, and acted decisively in every sphere, except when addressing the senate.[36] [7.6] All this stemmed primarily from his fear that Germanicus, with so many legions and a swarm of allied auxiliaries at his disposal, and remarkable popular support, might prefer the reality of power to its expectation. [7.7] He had an eye to public opinion also, since he wished to appear to have been summoned and elected by the republic, rather than to have infiltrated his way to power through a wife's scheming and a senile old man's adoption. Later it became clear that he had affected this hesitant manner as a way of testing the inclinations of the leading men.[37] For he distorted men's words and expressions into proofs of treachery, and he never forgot them.

[8.1] At the senate's first meeting he allowed no business to be transacted except matters pertaining to the funeral of Augustus, whose will, brought in by the Vestal Virgins, named Tiberius and Livia as his heirs.[38] Livia was adopted into the Julian family and the Augustan name. In default his grandsons and great-grandsons were nominated heirs, followed in third position by the leading citizens, most of whom he loathed; but he had named them out of ostentation and in order to win the admiration of posterity. [8.2] His bequests were appropriate to the means of a private citizen, except

---

34   *Soldiery*: deliberately intruded by Tacitus into the traditional formula 'senate and people'.

35   *As though ... he himself had doubts about ruling*: Tacitus implies that in reality Tiberius had no doubts. Augustus' body was carried in solemn procession from Nola to Rome, with Tiberius in attendance; the body was borne by the leading men of the local towns and for the final stage by the *equites* (Suet. *Aug.* 100.2; Dio 56.31.2). On the way Tiberius issued the edict summoning the senate meeting which Tacitus goes on to report at 8.1–5. Tiberius already possessed Augustus' chief constitutional powers, since he held the tribunician power and *imperium* equal with Augustus' (note [17]), and no-one doubted that he would take Augustus' position as *princeps*, but propriety required that this be formally confirmed by the senate. Tiberius refused to allow the senate to discuss the matter until after the funeral, and, when it was raised, probably on 17 September (note [58]), he expressed marked reluctance to accept the principate (11–13). Like the other sources, Tacitus treats all this as a charade, whose hypocrisy is brought out by Tiberius' dealings with the soldiers, and offers reasons for Tiberius' delays and hesitations (7.5–7). Some modern writers hold that his reluctance to assume the principate was genuine. More probably, he was simply observing the proprieties, both in delaying the discussion until after Augustus' funeral and in then putting on a show of reluctance not unlike those which Augustus himself had made in 27 BC and at subsequent renewals of his powers (Dio 53.11; 55.6.1, 55.12.3; 56.28.1). His tenure of *imperium* made him quite within his rights in issuing orders to the troops.

36   The same contrast is made by Suet. *Tib.* 24 and Dio 57.2.1–3.

37   For other ancient explanations of Tiberius' delay see Suet. *Tib.* 25; Dio 57.3.1–4. Both cite fear of Germanicus; Dio also gives Tacitus' second explanation.

38   This senate meeting was held on the day after Augustus' cortège arrived in Rome, probably about 4 September (Dio 56.31.2; Levick, *Tiberius* 70). For other accounts of the meeting and of Augustus' will, giving additional details, see Suet. *Aug.* 100.2–3, 101, *Tib.* 23; Dio 56.31.2–33.6. Besides the will, Augustus left other documents, including a summary (*breviarium*) of the state of the empire and the *Res Gestae*. According to Dio 56.33 these were all read at this meeting; Tacitus mentions only the *breviarium* and claims that it was read at the later meeting after the funeral (1.11.3–4). *Tiberius and Livia*: Tiberius received two-thirds of the estate after legacies, Livia one-third. She was henceforth known as Julia Augusta.

that he left 43,500,000 sesterces to the people and *plebs*, to the soldiers of the praetorian cohorts 1,000 sesterces, and to Roman citizens serving as legionaries or in cohorts 300 sesterces each.[39] [8.3] Next, the senate was consulted about Augustus' honours, of which the following were the most important: that the funeral procession should pass through the triumphal gate (proposed by Asinius Gallus); that the titles of the laws he had carried and the names of the peoples he had conquered should be paraded before him (proposed by Lucius Arruntius).[40] [8.4] Valerius Messala proposed that the oath of allegiance to Tiberius should be renewed annually;[41] and when Tiberius asked him if he had suggested this in response to any prompting from himself, he replied that it was entirely on his own initiative, and that in all matters pertaining to the safety of the state he would be influenced only by his personal judgement, even at the risk of giving offence. This represented the only form of flattery which remained available. [8.5] The senate declared with one voice that the corpse should be carried on the shoulders of senators to the funeral pyre. Caesar excused them with haughty moderation, and issued a warning to the people by edict that they should not seek to have Augustus cremated in the forum rather than, as planned, in the Campus Martius, as once before the funeral of the deified Julius had been turned into a riot by excessive zeal.

[8.6] On the day of the funeral,[42] the soldiery stood around the corpse like a bodyguard, eliciting much mockery from those who had witnessed in person or heard from their parents of that day when servitude was still fresh and liberty had been reclaimed with no happy outcome, when the assassination of the dictator Caesar seemed to some the vilest of deeds, but to others the most glorious. But now, they said, it seems that the aged *princeps,* with long years of power behind him and abundant resources left to his heirs with which to coerce the state, actually needs a bodyguard to guarantee himself a quiet funeral.

[9.1] After this there was much discussion about Augustus. Most people wondered at such trifles as the coincidence that the day on which he had once assumed *imperium* was the same as that on which he had died;[43] and that he had departed this life at Nola in the same house and bedroom as his father Octavius. [9.2] They remarked also on the number of his consulships, which matched the combined totals of Valerius Corvus and Gaius Marius; on the thirty-seven consecutive years of his tribunician power; on the title of *imperator* gained on twenty-one occasions; and on the other honours, multiple or novel.[44] [9.3] Among those of a more thoughtful turn of mind, however, his life was either extolled or criticised. One school of thought argued that duty to his father and the needs of the republic, in which there was then no place for law, had driven him to civil war, a course which none could prepare for or execute by honourable means.[45]

---

[39]   The bequest to the people would have amounted to a donative of about 200 sesterces each for the urban *plebs* (compare *RG* 15). Suetonius and Dio also mention a donative of 500 sesterces each for the urban cohorts, omitted by Tacitus or a scribe.

[40]   Both these proposals were carried out: Dio 56.34.2, 56.42.1. Triumphing commanders passed through the gate from the Campus Martius into the city, and Augustus now made the reverse journey.

[41]   Yearly renewal of the oath became normal from the time of Gaius on.

[42]   Here and at 10.8 Tacitus pointedly refrains from giving any details about Augustus' funeral, on which earlier historians will have dilated. For accounts see Suet. *Aug.* 100.2–3; Dio 56.34, 56.42. The funeral was probably held about 8 September (Levick, *Tiberius* 70).

[43]   *Day on which he had once assumed imperium*: Augustus assumed his first consulship on 19 August, 43 BC, (**C40**) but had held *imperium* since 7 January (**C2, C40**).

[44]   Augustus himself proclaims these honours at *RG* 4.1, 4. Marcus Valerius Maximus Corvus was consul six times between 348 and 299 BC ; Marius was consul in 107, 104–100 and 86 BC.

[45]   *Duty: pietas* – claimed as one of Augustus' cardinal virtues on his golden shield (*RG* 34.2).

[9.4] While seeking vengeance on his father's murderers, he had indeed made many concessions to Antony, many to Lepidus. Once the latter had lapsed into the inertia of senility and the former become corrupted by his own vices, there remained no other solution to the discords of the fatherland than that it should be ruled by one man. [9.5] Yet he had ordered the republic not as a kingdom, nor as a dictatorship, but under the name of *princeps*; the boundaries of the empire were now defended by the Ocean and by mighty rivers; legions, provinces, fleets and the general administration were all now • co-ordinated; towards citizens the law was observed, restraint towards allies. The city itself was now magnificently adorned; only on a few occasions had force been used, to guarantee peace and quiet for the rest.

    [10.1] Others argued to the contrary.[46] Duty to his father and the crisis of the republic, they said, were simply convenient pretexts. His lust for despotic power had led him to incite the veterans by bribery, to raise an army when a young man and a private citizen, to corrupt the consular legions, and to feign support for the Pompeian faction.[47] [10.2] Soon, having by senatorial decree seized the *fasces* and status of praetor, he took possession of both their armies after the deaths of Hirtius and Pansa, whether these were due to enemy action, or Pansa's to the application of poison to his wounds and Hirtius' to his own mutinous soldiery and Caesar's machinations.[48] He had then extorted the consulship from a reluctant senate and turned against the republic the very forces which he had received for the campaign against Antony.[49] Proscriptions of citizens and land confiscations had followed, of which not even the perpetrators approved. [10.3] It might be granted[50] that the deaths of Brutus and Cassius were a debt he owed to an inherited enmity (though it is right for private feuds to be waived in the public interest), but Pompeius had been duped by a spurious peace and Lepidus by the pretence of friendship; later Antony, seduced by the treaties of Tarentum and Brundisium and by marriage to Octavian's sister, had paid with his life for a spurious kinship.[51] [10.4] That peace had followed could not be denied; but it was a peace stained with blood – the military disasters of Lollius and Varus, and at Rome the killings of such as Varro, Egnatius and Iullus.[52] [10.5] Nor was Augustus' household spared. There was the abduction of Nero's wife and

---

46   This passage may be intended to evoke and rebut the account given at *RG* 1.

47   Relations between Octavian and the consul Antony broke down in October-November 44 BC, when Octavian raised troops from Caesar's veteran colonies and won over two of Antony's legions. He then made common cause with Antony's opponents in the senate. *Lust for despotic power* (*cupido dominandi*): Augustus claimed that he had raised the army to free the republic from 'the despotism (*dominatio*) of a faction' (*RG* 1.1).

48   *Seized the fasces*: Octavian's command was made official in early January 43 by a decree of the senate voting him praetorian *imperium*. Octavian took up his *imperium* on 7 January. *Deaths of Hirtius and Pansa*: at the battles of Mutina in April 43. The allegation that Octavian was responsible for their deaths is also reported by Suet. *Aug.* 11.

49   *Extorted the consulship*: after Hirtius' and Pansa's deaths relations between Octavian and the senate deteriorated. In early August he led his army to Rome, obliging the senate to permit his election as consul. *Turned against the republic*: soon after becoming consul, Octavian opened negotiations with Antony and Lepidus and reached the agreement under which they were appointed triumvirs (note 10).

50   Tacitus (10.3–7) continues to put the case against Augustus. He does not explicitly take either this side or the pro-Augustan version put forward in section 9.

51   *Spurious peace*: the Peace of Misenum, 39 BC, between the allies Antony and Octavian and Sextus Pompeius, was observed by neither side. *Treaties*: Tacitus reverses their order: the Brundisium agreement, under which Antony married Octavia, was concluded in 40, that at Tarentum in 37 BC.

52   *Lollius*: defeated in Gaul by German invaders in 16 BC. *Varro*: Licinius Varro Murena, who conspired and was put to death, with his accomplice Fannius Caepio, see **P9–P10** and note on Vell 2.91.2 (Section E). *Egnatius*: Marcus Egnatius Rufus. See Vell. 2.91.3 (Section E). *Iullus*: Iullus Antonius, son of Antony by an earlier marriage, but brought up by Augustus' sister Octavia and married to one of her daughters, Fulvia. The most conspicuous and potentially dangerous of Julia's lovers, he was suspected of treason and compelled to commit suicide, see **P13**.

that ludicrous consultation with the priests as to whether she could legally marry while pregnant but not yet delivered of her child;[53] the extravagant lifestyle of .... Vedius Pollio;[54] and finally there was Livia, an oppressive mother to the state and an oppressive stepmother to the house of the Caesars. [10.6] There were no honours left for the gods, now that Augustus chose to be worshipped with temples and godlike images by *flamines* and priests.[55] [10.7] He had not even appointed Tiberius as his successor from affection or from concern for the republic but because, when he looked at his arrogance and cruelty, he hoped that the odious comparison would redound to his own greater glory.[56] Only a few years before,[57] when Augustus had been requesting from the senate a renewal of the tribunician power for Tiberius, in the midst of a complimentary speech he had included, as if to excuse them, certain criticisms of his deportment, style of dress, and way of life.

[10.8] However, once the funeral rites were duly completed, a temple and divine cult were decreed.[58] [11.1] But it was Tiberius who was now the focus of men's prayers. He dilated upon the massive burden of empire and his own modest capacities.[59] Only the genius of an Augustus, now deified, was equal to such a mighty task. He himself, having been summoned by Augustus to share his labours,[60] had learned by experience how arduous a task it was to be ruler of the world, and how subject to the vagaries of fortune. For that reason, in a state which could depend on the talents of so many distinguished men, all the burdens should not fall upon the shoulders of one.[61] The task of government would be more readily discharged through the co-operative efforts of a greater number. [11.2] This speech lacked the conviction appropriate to such worthy sentiments.[62] Tiberius' words, whether by nature or habit, were always hesitantly and ambiguously expressed, even when he was not trying to mask his intentions. On this occasion, however, when he was doing his utmost to conceal his most secret ambitions, they became all the more convoluted, ambiguous, and capable of several interpretations. [11.3] For the senators, by contrast, there was only one anxiety – to avoid being seen to understand him all too well.[63] They were in the midst of a flood of protestations, lamentations and supplications, stretching out their arms to

---

53   *Nero*: Livia's first husband Tiberius Claudius Nero. Octavian married her on 17 January 38 (see **J26**).
54   *Vedius Pollio*: a wealthy equestrian friend of Augustus (whom he made his heir, **K30**), most notorious for feeding clumsy slaves to his lampreys (**H40**; Dio 54.23). The words before Vedius Pollio's name are corrupt and another name may have been lost.
55   Augustus sought to avoid direct cult in Rome or cult except in conjunction with other gods outside Rome, see **L8–L18**. At *Ann.* 4.38.4–5 Tacitus reports criticisms of Tiberius for refusing cult. *flamines*: priests responsible for the cult of an individual god.
56   The absurd allegation that Augustus only made Tiberius his successor so that he might benefit from the comparison is also mentioned by Dio 56.45.3 and is noted and refuted at Suet. *Tib.* 21.2–3. *Concern for the republic*: Augustus declared when adopting Tiberius that he was doing so 'for the sake of the republic' (Vell. 2.104.1 (Section **E**); Suet. *Tib.* 21.3).
57   *A few years before*: in fact presumably in AD 13 (see 3.3 and **J40–J41**).
58   Calendars show that the senate decreed divine cult for Augustus on 17 September. The conferment of the principate on Tiberius was probably considered at the same meeting (reported by Tacitus at 1.11–13).
59   *Burden*: Suetonius is even more graphic: according to him (*Tib.* 25.1) Tiberius said that he was 'holding a wolf by the ears'.
60   *To share his labours*: phrases of this kind were often applied to men associated with the emperor in power, notably Agrippa and Sejanus (Tac. *Ann.* 4.2.2, cf. Vell. Pat. 2.127.1).
61   *So many distinguished men*: this phrase shows that Tiberius was not thinking of devolving power on his sons Germanicus and Drusus but was asking senators to share the responsibility of directing policy.
62   *Conviction*: it is not clear whether Tacitus means that Tiberius was insincere or whether he failed to convince his hearers. Tiberius' hesitant speech is noticed elsewhere (*Ann.* 4.31.1); Tacitus claims that it was due to artifice and remarks that he could be forceful enough when he chose (*Ann.* 13.3.5).
63   *Understand him ... too well*: this must mean that they were avoiding letting Tiberius become aware that they saw through his pretence of not wishing to rule; so they stepped up their prayers to match his (pretended) resolution.

the gods, the statue of Augustus, and the knees of Tiberius himself when he gave orders for a document to be produced and read out.[64]

[11.4] It contained a list of all public resources – the numbers of citizens and allied auxiliaries in the army, the fleets, the client kingdoms and provinces, together with the tributes and taxes they paid, and the essential expenditure and optional grants they received. Augustus had recorded all this in his own hand, adding the recommendation (whether through motives of jealousy or genuine anxiety) that the empire should not be extended beyond its current boundaries.[65]

[12.1] With the senate now reduced to the most grovelling entreaties, Tiberius happened to remark that, though he did not feel equal to the task of ruling the whole republic, he would accept the guardianship of whichever part was entrusted to him. [12.2] At this point Asinius Gallus interjected,[66] "What I want to know, Caesar, is this: which part of the republic would you like to have entrusted to you?" Disconcerted by the unexpected question, Tiberius was silent for a moment.[67] But he recovered his poise and replied that, given his feelings of inadequacy, it would be entirely inappropriate to make or avoid any particular choice, since his preference was for total exemption. [12.3] Gallus guessed from Tiberius' expression that he had given offence, so he now explained that his intention in putting the question had not been to recommend the dividing of what was indivisible, but to demonstrate from Tiberius' own acknowledgement that the republic constituted a single body which must be governed by the will of a single ruler.[68] He also praised Augustus and reminded Tiberius of his own victories and many outstanding achievements over his long years in public life. [12.4] This did nothing to mollify the emperor. He had long hated Gallus for marrying his own former wife, Vipsania, Marcus Agrippa's daughter, and thereby revealing a degree of ambition inappropriate to an ordinary citizen, and for inheriting a censoriousness worthy of his father, Asinius Pollio.[69]

[13.1] Lucius Arruntius then spoke in very similar terms and gave no less offence, though Tiberius lacked any long-standing animosity towards him. But he was a rich man with a high public profile whose public reputation matched his remarkable talents, and he was therefore suspect.[70] [13.2] Indeed during one of their last conversations

---

64   *Document*: this is Augustus' 'political testament'. Dio 56.32.1a–33.6 mentions four documents left by Augustus besides his will: instructions for his funeral, his account of his achievements, the account of imperial resources (which shows the grip that Augustus had on the Empire); and the advice; Vell. 2.124.3 mentions the management of the elections as another item. Both items were helpful to Tiberius, but it is gratuitous to claim that they were added by him.

65   *The Empire should not be extended*: the cost of the war in Germany (three legions lost in AD 9) was a factor behind this advice; but creeping imperialism continued elsewhere, with advances in Africa in AD 14 and the annexation of Cappadocia and Commagene in AD 17.

66   *(Gaius) Asinius Gallus*: a prominent senator, consul 8 BC, eventually accused of adultery with the Elder Agrippina, he was imprisoned and starved to death in AD 33 (Tac. *Ann*. 6. 23.1–3).

67   *Tiberius was silent*: such phrases show that Tacitus was not entirely dependent on the senatorial record for his account of debates.

68   *The will of a single ruler*: this was unlikely to placate Tiberius, who had been arguing for collective decision-making.

69   Asinius' marriage will have taken place after 11 BC, when Tiberius divorced Vipsania to marry Augustus' daughter Julia (Dio 54.35.4). Asinius is often found urging Tiberius to assert himself, no doubt because the more power the *princeps* had the more his relatives would benefit: the sons he fathered reached the consulship in the twenties. Gallus' father was Asinius Pollio the historian, who did not accept the conventional, pro-Augustan interpretation of late Republican history.

70   *Lucius Arruntius*: consul AD 6, was a distinguished orator. For his death in AD 37 see *Ann*. 6.48, where he famously describes Tiberius as 'torn apart by the constraints of power'. But it was not Tiberius, on Tacitus' showing, who was responsible for his death.

Augustus, in discussing the principate, had distinguished between those who had the capacity to fill the office but would refuse it, those who desired it but lacked the capacity, and those who had both the capacity and the desire.[71] He had suggested that Marcus Lepidus had the ability but would reject the principate with contempt;[72] Gallus Asinius coveted it but was inadequate to the task; while Lucius Arruntius had both the ability and the nerve to make a bid for it, if the chance was offered. [13.3] Of the three names mentioned, our sources are agreed upon the first two; but an alternative tradition reads Gnaeus Piso for Arruntius.[73] Lepidus apart, all of them were soon disposed of at Tiberius' instigation under varying criminal charges.[74] [13.4] Quintus Haterius and Mamercus Scaurus also inflamed his inherently suspicious temperament, Haterius by asking how long he proposed to allow the state to be without its head; Scaurus by saying that there were grounds for optimism that the senate's prayers would soon be answered in the fact that he had not used his tribunician powers to veto the consuls' proposals. Tiberius promptly launched a tirade against Haterius; but the remarks of Scaurus, against whom his anger was the more implacable, he passed over in silence.[75]

[13.5] In the end, exhausted by the general clamour and the individual protestations, he began to give way little by little, to the point of ceasing to provoke continuing demands by his persistent refusal, without actually acknowledging that he had now accepted the principate.[76] [13.6] The sources record that Haterius later went into the palace to offer his apologies and, as Tiberius walked past, he clasped his knees in supplication – an act which brought Tiberius crashing to the ground, either by a mishap or because he had tripped him. This nearly led to his own death at the hands of the bodyguards. Despite his efforts, the threat to this distinguished senator's life remained undiminished until he appealed to Augusta (Livia), and gained protection through her zealous intervention.[77]

[14.1] She too became the object of widespread flattery by the senate.[78] Some proposed that she be given the title of "parent" or "mother" of her country; very many that the title "son of Julia" be added to Caesar's formal designation. [14.2] Tiberius, however, repeatedly insisted that honours for women should be strictly curtailed and that he personally would display the same moderation over honours offered to himself. Nevertheless, jealousy made him anxious; and because he regarded elevation in status for a woman as a diminution of his own, he refused to allow her to be voted even a

---

71 The different personalities of this fictional conversation reveal likely occasions for the creation of each version. Since Arruntius comes as the climax of the present version, it is likely to belong to the tittle-tattle that followed his death (immediately before Tiberius' own).

72 *Marcus Lepidus*: consul AD 6, was a distinguished soldier honoured with the triumphal ornaments and closely connected with the imperial family. He is presented as a self-respecting senator who spoke his mind and died naturally in AD 33 (*Ann.* 6.27.4).

73 *Gnaeus Piso*: consul 7 BC, is the outspoken son of a Republican and a friend of Tiberius, who was governor of Syria during Germanicus' mission, AD 17–19, and who in 20 was accused of murdering him and forced to suicide (*Ann.* 2.43; 55–58; 69–82; 3.7–19).

74 *All were ... soon disposed of at Tiberius' instigation*: clearly inaccurate in substance and chronology.

75 *Quintus Haterius*: a servile orator (*Ann.* 4.61) whose question also implied that Tiberius should be sole ruler (head). *Mamercus Aemilius Scaurus*: a raffish playwright and orator who survived political attacks until AD 34, when he and his wife committed suicide (*Ann.* 6.29.4–7). *Launched a tirade*: Scaurus' comment implied that the senate was already undertaking the responsibilities that Tiberius offered. That was why only Haterius was attacked.

76 What happened to the motion before the senate is unclear. Tiberius already had enough official powers to make him emperor. It looks as if the debate petered out.

77 Livia was known for the help she gave to ambitious or endangered politicians: see the senatorial decree on Cn. Piso the Elder (M.T. Griffin, 'The Senate's Story', *JRS* 87 (1997) 251); Vell. 2.130.5; Tac. *Ann.* 5.3.1.

78 See preceding note; it is hard not to believe that there was irony in these proposals for a woman, especially that the solecism of identifying a man by his mother should be applied to the old-fashioned Tiberius.

single lictor, and also vetoed an altar of Adoption and other such honours.[79] [14.3] But for Germanicus Caesar he requested proconsular *imperium*,[80] and a special delegation was despatched to confer it on him and at the same time to offer condolences on the death of Augustus. The reason he did not seek similar distinctions for Drusus was that he was consul-designate and already present in Rome.[81] [14.4] For the praetorship he nominated twelve candidates, which was the traditional number established by Augustus. When the senate urged him to increase the number, he bound himself by a strict oath not to do so.[82]

[15.1] That was the first time, too, that elections were transferred from the citizens' assemblies (held in the Campus Martius) to the senate.[83] Hitherto, though the most important were settled by decision of the *princeps*, some were still left to the wishes of the assembly of the tribes. The people raised no objection to the loss of this prerogative, except perhaps in casual conversation,[84] while the senate gladly acquiesced, since it was consequently spared the need for expense and undignified solicitation of votes, as Tiberius guaranteed that he would not recommend more than four candidates, who would have to be appointed without rejection or canvass.[85] [15.2] At the same time the tribunes sought permission to celebrate at their own expense games which would be added to the official calendar and be known as the Augustales (derived from the name of Augustus).[86] But it was decided that they should be financed by the state treasury, and that the tribunes should be allowed to wear triumphal dress in the Circus Maximus but not to ride in a triumphal chariot.[87] [15.3] The conduct of this annual celebration was soon transferred to the praetor, to whom fell responsibility for civil suits between citizens and foreigners.

---

79 His response was negative in the long as well as the short term: she lost much of the influence she had enjoyed under Augustus (*Ann*. 3.64.2). *Honours for women*: women could not vote, let alone hold official powers; they had only influence, religious functions, and ornamental honours. In an oligarchy or monarchy that could mean much indirect power. Conservatives disapproved of that too. *Moderation*: this was one of Tiberius' 'virtues', advertised on his coinage along with clemency, and guyed by Tacitus (*Ann*. 1.8.5). *Lictor*: attendants carrying bundles of rods and axes graded magistrates' power: a consul had twelve. Livia *was* allowed one when she functioned as priestess of Augustus (Dio 56.46.2).

80 *Proconsular* imperium: Presumably Germanicus had been only a legate of Augustus; now he acquired independent military powers.

81 *Drusus ... consul designate and already present in Rome*: a power intended for use abroad would be inappropriate to a consul, who was supposed to be in Rome during his term of office; and in any case had power there; 'present' probably refers to that year of office: Drusus was about to go to Pannonia (*Ann* 1.24.1).

82 *He nominated twelve candidates*: as elections were now transferred to the senate, Tiberius probably read out the names of the twelve candidates who had come out top in the senatorial vote for the twelve places. Augustus had sometimes allowed more praetorships (sixteen in AD 11 (Dio 56.25.4)). Tiberius exploits his devotion to the memory of Augustus, successfully resisting ambitious senators struggling for office.

83 *Elections were transferred*: this disputed sentence probably means simply that preliminary elections were held in the senate, so that only the same number of candidates as places were presented to the citizens' assemblies for their vote.

84 *Casual conversation*: the people had lost not only the excitement of voting but the bribes that went with it.

85 *He would not recommend more than four candidates*: there was no legal reason why the Emperor (or anyone else) should not recommend up to the full number of places, but such blanket imperial recommendations would destroy the chances of other candidates. *Who would have to be appointed*: this probably refers to the actual future effect of the recommendation rather than to any legal obligation on senators voting or on the citizens' assemblies.

86 *Augustales*: the calendars show them celebrated on 9 or 12 October.

87 *Triumphal chariot*: this was unsuitable for wholly civil officers of the Roman plebs such as tribunes.

SECTION G

AUGUSTAN POETRY

Poetry as Historical Source Material

Ezra Pound once famously remarked that "poets are the antennae of the race". Such an assertion, if true, would be sufficient to justify the inclusion of poetry in a volume of source material for the history of any period. But it is not the function of the poet to deal in facts, to record information, nor (usually) to report events. That is the task of journalism – an altogether humbler trade.

Poets deal in perceptions, moods, emotions, responses, desires, hopes, fears. Historical virtues such as accuracy, objectivity, comprehensiveness, balance, exactness (save of language) are not for them. Ambiguities, suggestiveness, compression to the point of obscurity, image and association, echo and overtone, implication not explication, metaphor, simile, symbol, intensity of feeling – these are the poet's virtues and the would-be historian must be aware of them before he can use such material effectively.

If, then, the reader seeks to know not so much what happened or even why, but rather what it felt like at the time, what were the responses and perceptions of sensitive and articulate contemporaries (the "antennae people") to the events in which their lives were inextricably entangled, then the poet's value is considerable. Could we, for example, fully understand the enormity of the suffering of the First World War without the War Poets? Or the intensity of the feelings of Irish Nationalism without Yeats?

But always we must read with care. The Roman Poets were, after all, what we would now call the "spin-doctors" of their time. They identified themselves with the regime of Augustus and wrote in part at least to serve its purposes. But they were also great artists and no great artist can be entirely constrained by the wishes of his patron – his integrity will prevail and he will exploit constraints to enhance his creation by transcending the limitations imposed upon him. So it was with the Roman "court poets", most notably Virgil. We must take the poets in the context of their time – a time in which men had grown tired of civil war and turned to Octavian/Augustus as to a god in gratitude for the gift of peace and as the source of inspiration for old values restored and new ideals espoused. To such feeling the poets helped to give expression.

What then is the translator's task? This is a sourcebook, not a work of art. Should he not, therefore, seek simply to convey meaning as accurately as possible, without regard for that inexpressible element which distinguishes poetry from prose? There, alas, is the problem. Meaning in poetry is not like meaning in prose; poetry is many-faceted, subtle, inapprehensible. Prose conveys information; poetry suggests response. The translator cannot himself write poetry – those who think they can nearly all conspicuously fail. The best a translator can do is to seek to convey something of the meaning and feeling of his original in a form which, while seeking to convey the poet's perceived intention, at the same time declares to the reader "this was not prose and should not be read as prose". This is the primary justification for translations which retain the poetic format and such devices as rhythm and metre, assonance, alliteration, and rhyme, metaphor and enriched language, and other "poetic" features. The translator is saying, simply: "my poet once sought to convey to you a range of ideas, emotions, responses, aspirations in the most moving, beautiful and persuasive way he could. Do not therefore read my piece as prose; do not imagine either that I think I am a poet. But by poetic devices I hope to remind you constantly that once, long ago, a great poet was at work and is speaking to you now. Your analytical skills as an historian are not enough. You must bring to bear on your material sensitivity, empathy, imagination and insight – and, if you can spare it, just a touch of sympathy for your humble servant, the translator".

Introduction to Virgil, Horace, Propertius, Ovid and the Greek Anthology

Virgil: According to the surviving ancient biographies (**R15**), Publius Vergilius Maro (generally known in English as Virgil, though some prefer the spelling 'Vergil') was born near Mantua in northern Italy in 70 BC, and educated first at nearby Cremona and Mantua and then at Rome. His father is said to have lost property in the confiscations of 42–41, but by the time of his death Virgil had become wealthy through gifts from friends (he is said to have left 10,000,000 sesterces). His first poems, the pastoral *Eclogues*, were probably published around 39–38, and shortly after this he entered the circle of Augustus' friend Maecenas. His next major work, the four books of the *Georgics*, dealing with agriculture, was probably published in 29; Virgil is said to have read this poem to Octavian after his return from defeating Antony and Cleopatra, and it includes laudatory references to Octavian and to his ending of civil war (see **G8–G12**). Virgil then began work on the *Aeneid*. When he died in 19 BC, the poem was complete but unrevised. Augustus overruled Virgil's instruction to his executors that the poem should be destroyed.

The *Aeneid* is an epic poem in twelve books. The first six deal with Aeneas' flight from Troy and the wanderings which brought him and his companions to Italy: the narrative starts with the Trojans' shipwreck on the African coast and reception by Dido, queen of Carthage (Book 1); the earlier part of the story is then narrated by Aeneas to Dido (Books 2–3). Books 7–12 recount Aeneas' wars in Italy against Turnus and the Latins. The poem's principal theme is the founding of what was to become the Roman nation: Aeneas is constantly presented as fulfilling the Trojans' destiny, and in the three passages given below Virgil explicitly looks forward to future history culminating in Augustus. His portrayal of *pius Aeneas*, outstanding for his dutifulness (*pietas*) to the gods, his family and his nation, is evidently intended to evoke Augustus. Thus, although the poem dealt with the remote (in fact legendary) past, it also served to celebrate Augustus and his achievements.

Virgil's principal literary model in the *Aeneid* was Homer, both the *Odyssey* (especially in the first part of the poem) and the *Iliad* (in the war narrative of the second part). He was also indebted to numerous other writers, many of which now survive only in fragments, for example the *Annales* of Ennius, which recounted Roman history down to the early second century, when the poem was composed, and which the *Aeneid* supplanted as the Roman national epic.

The *Aeneid* is not a work of simplistic propaganda, but a complex and subtle masterpiece, and modern interpretations vary widely. Many see Virgil as taking an unequivocally positive view of Roman, and Augustan, imperial ideology. Others interpret him as taking a more pessimistic view, with 'a private voice of regret' alongside the 'public voice of triumph' (in the formulation of A. Parry, in S. Commager (ed.), *Virgil: A Collection of Critical Essays* [1966], 121).

W. A. Camps, *An Introduction to Virgil's Aeneid* (1969), is a good introductory study. Recent work is surveyed by P. Hardie, *Virgil* (*Greece and Rome New Surveys in the Classics* no. 28, 1998) and may be sampled in the essays collected in S. J. Harrison (ed.), *Oxford Readings in Vergil's Aeneid* (1990), and C. Martindale (ed.), *The Cambridge Companion to Virgil* (1997).

Horace (Quintus Horatius Flaccus) was born in 65 BC, the son of a freedman, whose auctioneering business made him wealthy enough to give his son an upper-class education at Rome and Athens. While at Athens, the young Horace joined the army of Brutus as a military tribune and fought at Philippi (42 BC). Horace's family lost its property in the ensuing confiscations, but he obtained remunerative employment as a public scribe, and began to write poetry. From 38 BC he enjoyed the friendship of Maecenas, who in due course made him secure with the gift of an estate in the Sabine district. Later in his career, Horace was on friendly terms with Augustus himself. Horace died in 8 BC, shortly after Maecenas.

Horace's first works, composed in the thirties, were the *Satires* and *Epodes*. He then produced the first three books of *Odes*, composed on Greek models in a variety of lyric metres *c*. 30–23. Next came the first book of *Epistles* (c. 21–20). In 17 Horace wrote, on Augustus' commission, the *Carmen Saeculare* (*Centennial Hymn*), sung at the Centennial Games. He then produced the fourth book of *Odes* (*c*. 17–13), and the remaining *Epistles* were composed towards the end of his life.

The *Odes* vary greatly in tone and persona between poems and sometimes (e.g. **G29**) within individual poems. Many are light-hearted, dealing with erotic themes, drinking-parties and the like, but Horace can also assume a solemn, even prophetic voice. Moral reflections abound. Many of the poems are addressed to Maecenas or other great men of the period. Only a minority of the poems refer directly to Augustus and his achievements, but it is from these that the present selection is drawn.

Horace often claims that his talents and/or his metrical forms are too modest for grand themes such as war (so in this selection *Odes* 1.6 (**G22**) and 4.2 (**G41**)), and sometimes he represents himself as declining invitations to write on such themes. In some of these cases he will have been responding to genuine requests, but he is also adopting and turning to his own purposes a literary motif deriving from Greek court poets of the Hellenistic period.

The *Odes* referring to Augustus repeatedly touch on his present or future divinity. The doctrine that a man might become a god after his death through outstanding services to humanity had become widely accepted long before Augustus' day: on this view, Hercules, the twins Castor and Pollux, and Dionysus (Bacchus) were held to have become gods in this way, and so too was the legendary first king of Rome, Romulus, identified with the god Quirinus. In 42 BC, two years after his death, Julius Caesar was officially declared by the senate and Roman people to be a god, Divus Julius, and since that time Octavian/Augustus had been 'Divi filius', 'son of the deified'. From the time of his victory over Antony it will have been universally recognised that on his death Augustus too would be deemed to have become a god, and this expectation is reflected in Horace and the other Augustan poets (e.g. *Odes* 3.3.11–12 (**G26**); Virgil, *Aeneid* 1.289–90 (**G36**)). In the Greek East, cults to living men had been well established since the time of Alexander the Great, and from 29 BC Augustus accepted cult in the eastern provinces, though stipulating that his cult should be linked with that of the goddess Roma. No doubt mindful of Julius Caesar's excesses in his last months, Augustus sought to avoid being openly worshipped during his lifetime in Rome, but he did receive many near-divine honours, such as the pouring of libations to his *genius* (divine spirit) at banquets, evoked at *Odes* 4.5.29–36 (**G43**, see also **L8–L18**). The poets did not scruple to refer openly to him as a god (e.g. *Odes* 1.2.41–52 (**G21**); 4.5.32 (**G43**); cf. 3.5.2–4 (**G27**)).

In the first three books of the *Odes* Horace's references to Augustus celebrate his ending of civil war and look forward to further successes, notably anticipated victories against the Parthians and Britons. Augustus, however, left Britain alone and preferred to employ diplomacy rather than war to resolve the Parthian problem: in 20 BC the Parthians were induced to hand over the captured Roman soldiers and standards as a condition of Roman friendship. In the later poems composed after this settlement, Horace celebrates Augustus' achievements: his successes in war and diplomacy are represented as having brought the whole world into obedience to Rome (thus *Centennial Hymn,* 53–6 (**L28**); *Odes* 4.5.25–8 (**G43**); 4.15.6–8, 21–4 (**G45**); cf. *RG* 26–33), while at home Augustus has, Horace assures us, brought prosperity and, through the marriage legislation of 18 BC, the restoration of traditional morality (thus *Centennial Hymn* 17–20, 57–60 (**L28**); *Odes* 4.5.17–24 (**G43**)). The manner in which Horace praises Augustus may owe something to orators' conventions for praising rulers.

G. W. Williams, *Horace* (*Greece and Rome New Surveys in the Classics* no. 6, 1972) is a good short introduction. For more recent work see, e.g., the essays collected in N. Rudd (ed.), *Horace 2000: A Celebration* (1993), and S. J. Harrison (ed.), *Homage to Horace: A Bimillenary Celebration* (1995). There are good, brief commentaries on the *Odes* by K. Quinn; D. A. West (Book 1); G. W. Williams (Book 3). P. White, *Promised Verse: Poets in the Society of Augustan Rome* (1993), is an important study of Augustus' relationship with Horace and his fellow poets, setting it in the context of contemporary social and literary relationships and arguing cogently against the view that Augustus and his associates pressed the poets to produce propaganda for the regime; on Horace's handling of the relationship see also R. O. A. M. Lyne, *Horace: Behind the Public Poetry* (1995).

Propertius (Sextus Propertius), born perhaps around 50 BC (his death-date is unknown), came of a local élite family from Assisi in Umbria, who seem to have lost some of their property in the land-confiscations of 41 BC (Propertius 4.1.130; for the confiscations see on Virgil, *Eclogue* 1, **G1**). Four books of his *elegies* are preserved, though many scholars think the extant second book contains poems from two different books. The first book was probably published about 28 BC, the last perhaps some fifteen years later. The first book pursues the topics of love-elegy as established by the poet Gallus, the private life of love as an alternative to a public career, and its comparison with slavery and warfare; it shows less interest in conformist politics and 'Augustan' issues than the extant Books 2 and 3, in which several poems to Maecenas (e.g 2.1, **G15**), suggest that, as in the cases of Horace and Virgil, Propertius was 'spotted' by Maecenas and at least partly influenced by his patronage towards more patriotic themes. This is clear by the time of Book 4, where the poet claims (at least in part) to be returning to the Hellenistic poetic tradition of Callimachus in writing nationalistic elegies of an aetiological character, i.e. which give the mythical or historical origin of a modern phenomenon (a religious ritual, building or other cultural feature); to some degree this gave the sanction of literary history to political convenience, since ideologically significant or even propagandistic phenomena (such as the cult of Actian Apollo in 4.6, **G39**) could be selected for such treatment.

Further reading: M. Hubbard, *Propertius* (1974); H-P. Stahl, *Propertius: 'Love' and War* (1985).

Ovid (P. Ovidius Naso; 43 BC – AD 17) was born of an élite family in Sulmo, modern Sulmona in the Abruzzi. After an education which involved substantial training in rhetoric, he began his poetical career as an elegist from the late 20s BC with the *Amores* (a somewhat comic take on the usual themes of love-elegy, originally in five books; only the three-book second edition is extant), the *Heroides* (three books (probably) of elegiac letters of lament from mythological heroines, followed, probably much later, by a single book of three pairs of wooing poems from heroes followed by the relevant heroines' replies; all four books are extant) and a lost tragedy, *Medea*. The *Ars Amatoria* (published in its current form about 1 BC) is a didactic poem in three books which addresses first the young men of Rome (Books 1–2) and then the young women (Book 3) with advice on how to conduct love-affairs.

This poem, which was in clear contradiction to the moral reforms of Augustus which included legislation against adultery, was to get Ovid into trouble later. Perhaps sensing this, in the next ten years he turned to ostensibly more serious subjects: the *Fasti*, a poem on the religious calendar with a book on each month, of which only the first half (six books) seems to have been written, and the hexameter *Metamorphoses*, his only extant work not in elegiac couplets, which showed epic scale and ambition in tracing the history of metamorphoses from the world's beginning to the poet's own time. Both poems present a combination of mythological learning, continuing erotic interests, verbal and other wit, and encomium of Augustus and his family.

In AD 8 Ovid was banished from Rome to the distant city of Tomis on the Black Sea (in modern Romania). His extensive exile poetry, mainly consisting of various types of letter home (five books of *Tristia*, four *Ex Ponto*) written over the next decade before his death, tries to argue (unsuccessfully, as far as we know) for his return from banishment, which he ascribes (especially in *Tristia* 2 – **G56**) to the (long published) *Ars Amatoria* and to a (more recent) unspecified 'error' which seems to have involved unwitting knowledge of some high political secret. Two millennia later, scholars are still unclear precisely what this 'error' was, though it may have been connected with the disgrace of Augustus' grand-daughter Iulia who was exiled at the same time as Ovid.

Ovid's political attitudes are not easy to pin down. He is not a poet who naturally turns to political themes, and when he touches them he often seems either to be going through the required propagandistic motions or to be mischievously destabilising cherished Augustan ideas. But 'subversive' appears to be too strong. For Ovid, aged 11 at the Battle of Actium, Augustus (whom Ovid survived by only a few years) was a political institution with which he had grown up, at which he could poke fun while assuming it is the *status quo*, and this, together with his literary (and perhaps temperamental) bias to lighter and less conformist themes, may underlie his apparent combination of irreverence towards and acceptance of the Augustan order.

Further reading : J. Barsby, *Ovid* (*Greece and Rome New Surveys in the Classics 12*, 2nd edition, Oxford, 1991), R. Syme, *History in Ovid* (Oxford, 1978), A. Barchiesi, *The Poet and the Prince* (Berkeley, 1994).

Greek Anthology. These poems remind us that not all the poets praising Augustus and his family were Italian or wrote in Latin, and sometimes give a slightly different perspective. They are selected from the vast and various body of Greek epigram known as the *Greek Anthology*. Antipater of Thessalonica was patronised by the aristocratic Piso family and wrote between c.11 BC and AD 12, while Crinagoras, an aristocrat from Mytilene, seems to have been patronised directly by the imperial family during his long writing career (c.45 BC to AD 11).

Principles of selection and presentation

The poems included here have been arranged as far as possible in chronological order. This selection of poetry includes the triumviral period, unlike the rest of the book. Most of the poetry is presented in this section, but Horace's *Carmen Saeculare*, written to celebrate the *ludi saeculares* of 17 BC is presented in the context of the other documents relating to the games (**L28**) and passages from Ovid, *Fasti* are generally presented with the people, places or events to which they relate.

G1　Virgil, *Eclogue* 1

In this Eclogue some believe that Tityrus represents Virgil, who may have appealed successfully to Octavian against the confiscation of his farm in the land confiscations of 41 BC, imposed to pension off with small farms the soldiers who had fought for Octavian at Philippi in 42 BC. Others deny this, on the grounds that each name in the poems represents one person, and since in *Eclogues* 3, 5 and 9 Menalcas clearly represents Virgil, Tityrus cannot. Coleman (*Vergil Eclogues*) suggests that the poem is not autobiographical at all, though it may reflect personal experience, and that Virgil is simply depicting the contrasting situations of two typical Italian countrymen at a time of crisis.

MELIBOEUS:
Tityrus, beneath the spreading shade of a mighty beech you lie,
Composing upon your slender pipe a melody for the woodland Muse.
But we are now forced to leave the confines of our country, the landscape we love.
For we are refugees, while you, friend Tityrus, lie back beneath the leaves
And teach the whole woodland to echo with the name of lovely Amaryllis.　　　5

TITYRUS:
Ah Meliboeus, my friend, it is a god who has blessed us with this time of peace.
For to me that man shall be a god for ever; and often at his altars
A tender lamb from my fold shall pour out his blood in sacrifice.
For he it is that has allowed my cattle to wander at their own free will,
As you can see, and me to play what songs I choose upon my rustic flute.　　　10

MELIBOEUS:
It's not that I begrudge you your good fortune; rather I marvel, when on every side
In all the countryside I see such chaos. See how I drive my goats onwards
And ever onwards – it breaks my heart. My she-goat, here, can barely follow me.
She's just given birth to twins, after hard labour, in the dense shelter of this hazel
Thicket – the flock's one hope, but she's abandoned them on the naked rock.　　　15
I must have been blind not to foresee disaster – for I remember how
The oak trees, lightning-struck from heaven, often told of evils yet to come.
Enough of that! Come tell me, Tityrus, this "god" of yours, who is he?

TITYRUS:
There is a great city, Meliboeus, which men call Rome. Heavens, what a fool I was!
I thought it was like that little town of ours, to which our shepherds go　　　20
So often, when we drive our tender lambs to market. There's no comparison,
No more than puppies are like full grown hounds, or kids like nanny goats.
Those were the images I always used, to make comparison of great with small.
But Rome is different. She is so vast, she's raised her head as far above
All other cities as over the wild brier-rose the cypress towers.　　　25

MELIBOEUS:
What cause could there be so powerful as to make you visit Rome?

TITYRUS:
Freedom, my friend! At long, long last she saw my enforced idleness,

Though by then my beard fell whitening before the barber's shears.
See me she did, at last, and after the long years came to me. By then
I was a slave to Amaryllis, for my Galatea had left me. And yet   30
I must confess, for all the time I was in thrall to Galatea,
There was no hope of Freedom, and no chance to earn my living.
Victims innumerable left my folds for sacrifice; great cheeses
In countless numbers were pressed out to feed a thankless town, but still,
Never would I return from town again with money in my hand.   35

MELIBOEUS:
So that's the reason, Amaryllis, why you called so sadly on the gods;
That's the love for whom you left their apples hanging from the trees.
Your Tityrus had gone, gone far from home. Even the pines, my Tityrus,
The fountains too, and all these lovely orchards here were calling you home.

TITYRUS:
What could I do? Neither from slavery could I find escape, nor yet   40
Elsewhere seek gods to offer their present help in trouble.
But, Meliboeus, there in Rome I saw that youth, the youth for whom
My altars smoke for twelve whole days in each and every year. He
Was the first to give the answer to my prayer: "Go, feed your flocks,
Herdsmen, go feed your oxen as you did before; go raise your bulls."   45

MELIBOEUS:
My aged friend, Fortune has blessed you, so these lands
Are yours for ever, sufficient for your needs, though naked rocks
Obscure them, while with mud and reeds the marshland chokes your pasture.
Yet they know their own fields; no unfamiliar grazing will torment
Your breeding flocks, nor vile contagion from a neighbour's herd   50
Bring sickness to them. My aged friend, Fortune indeed has blessed you.
Here 'mid familiar streams and holy springs you'll revel in cooling shade.
On one side, as always, by your neighbour's fence, the hedgerow hums
With willow blossoms plundered by the bees of Hybla, while for you
Their gentle murmur's soft seduction ushers in sweet slumbers.   55
Across the way, beneath that beetling crag, the woodman's serenade
Beguiles the breezes, while your noisy favourites, pigeons and turtle-doves,
Coo unrelentingly on high upon the airy summits of the elm.

TITYRUS:
The bounding stags shall graze upon the air; the seas retreat and leave
Their fishes stranded on the open shore; Parthians shall drink   60
The River Arar, Germans the Tigris, nomadic exiles both
Who stray across each other's frontiers – all this shall happen first,
Before the memory of his kindly gaze fades from my heart.

MELIBOEUS:
As for us, we're forced to leave home – scattered abroad, some to thirsty Africa,
Some till they reach the Scythians, or the chalk-rich waters of swift Oaxes, some   65
Even as far as the Britons, they who dwell out on the distant edges of the world.
Alas! Shall I ever see again, long years from now, the borders of my country,
My humble homestead with its turf-clad roof? Shall I see again
In later years my erstwhile kingdom and the modest harvest of its fields?

Will some blaspheming soldier now possess my fallow fields, once lovingly tilled?   70
Or some barbarian harvest my crops? That's the price we pay, we wretched citizens,
For civil discord. Ours was the labour sowing in the fields; theirs the reward.
Now graft your pear trees, Meliboeus, set your vines in rows – and all for nothing.
Up now, my goats; away, once happy flock. Never again shall I
Lie stretched at leisure in some mossy cave, watching you from afar   75
Suspended on the heights of some thorn-clad precipice.
Songs shall I never sing again; and you, my goats, under my shepherd's care
Shall never more go grazing on the clover-blossom or the shoots of bitter willow.

TITYRUS:
You could at least have rested here with me this night, stretched
On a mattress of green leafage. Here I have ripened apples, here   80
Sweet chestnuts and abundant quantity of new pressed cheeses.
See how from chimneys on the distant roofs the smoke curls upwards,
And far above long shadows stretch and tumble from hills.

7   *that man shall be a god*: various hints in the poem (especially 42–45) indicate that this benefactor
        is the young Caesar (later Augustus), in his early twenties at the time of the land-confiscations of
        41 BC, his responsibility as the triumvir in charge of the main part of Italy.
40–45   Tityrus' legal status and that of his property (slave or free? whose flocks ?) is notoriously obscure.
        This poem (like *Eclogue* 9) alludes vaguely to the land-confiscations and to reprieves received by
        some owners (perhaps Virgil himself) but avoids undiplomatic specificity.

G2   Virgil, *Eclogue* 4

This "Messianic" Eclogue is so called because of its perceived similarities with Judaeo-Christian prophecy
foretelling the coming of the Messiah. Resemblances between Virgil and Isaiah are probably due to the
Sibylline prophecies he uses here, which are likely to have been influenced by the environment of Jewish
Alexandria in the Hellenistic period. Certainly its tone is messianic, in that it foresees the coming of a new
golden age under Octavian (later Augustus), which Virgil associates with the birth of a child. The child's
identity is debated endlessly. Suggestions have included the infant son of Asinius Pollio, the friend of Virgil
who was consul in 40 BC, when the poem was written, and who introduced him to Octavian; a hoped-for
child of Mark Antony and Octavia, sister of Octavian, whose marriage sealed the treaty of Brundisium in
40 BC, reconciling Octavian and Antony, an event which seems to be reflected in the poem's prophecies of
peace; a child of Octavian himself (his only daughter, Julia, was born in 39 BC); Marcellus, born to Octavia
and M. Claudius Marcellus in 42 BC and later adopted as Augustus' heir; or even Jesus Christ himself, as
suggested by St Augustine on the grounds that it was a Sibylline prophecy adopted by Virgil. However, it
is not necessary to believe that any specific child is referred to. Indeed in the political uncertainties of the
period, it was prudent not to be specific. For the most important modern treatment of this poem, see R. G.
M. Nisbet, *Collected Papers on Latin Literature* (1995), 47–75.

Come, Muses of Sicily, and let us sing a somewhat nobler song.
Orchards and humble tamarisks do not afford delight to everyone.
If woods are to be our song, those woods must match a consul's dignity.

Already the final age, the Age of Iron, has come – as was foretold
By Cumae's Sibyl. Now the great cycle of the centuries begins again.   5
Justice, the maiden goddess, now returns; and now returns the golden realm
Of Saturn; while from the heavens above there is sent down a new,
Untainted race of men. Holy Lucina, goddess of childbirth, look with favour
We beseech you upon this son now being born to us, beneath whose rule

The Iron Age shall cease and a new nation, a golden generation, shall rise up 10
Throughout the world. Your own Apollo is already King.

And in your consulship, Asinius Pollio, (yes yours!) there shall begin
This age of glory, and the majestic march of time commence once more.
Under your leadership all last remaining vestige of our guilt is purged,
Its taint removed and all the earth released from everlasting dread. And he 15
Shall live for ever with the gods; he shall behold the heroes
Who dwell among them, and shall himself be seen by them. His rule
Shall compass all the earth with peace won by his father's virtues.

And for you, my child, shall all the earth un-tilled pour forth
Her first fruits, dainty gifts, of all-embracing ivy fronds, valerian, 20
And arum lilies blended with smiling blossom of the acanthus tree.
Goats of their own free will shall homeward come, their udders filled
To bursting, from the fields; mighty lions will hold no terrors for them.
Of its own free will, your cradle, too, shall bloom with flowered loveliness;
Serpents shall be no more, and treacherous herbs whose poisons deal in death 25
Shall die themselves; and in their stead Assyrian balsam everywhere shall grow.

But when you can read the tales of glorious heroes' and your father's deeds,
And from them first learn to understand the nature of true valour,
Then shall the fields slowly grow golden with the waving corn,
Then shall the blushing grape hang from untended brambles, while the oak 30
From its tough branches shall distil the fragrant honey dew.
Yet even then shall there still remain some trace of man's primeval sin,
Bidding him still to venture on Thetis' seas, and to surround with walls
His fortress cities, and cleave his mother earth with furrows. Then shall we see
Another Argo (with a second Tiphys at the helm) bearing its chosen heroes, 35
Also another mighty war, with great Achilles sent a second time to Troy.

But after, when strengthening years have brought you now to manhood,
Traders at last shall even quit the oceans, and pine-built ships
Their merchandise; for now all lands shall bear the fruits of all the world.
Earth shall no more endure the harrow's tooth nor vines the pruning shears; 40
The tough ploughman too shall for ever loose his oxen from their harness;
Wool shall no more discover the deceit of varied dyes whose colours trick the eyes;
But in the meadows, of his own free will, the ram shall change his fleece's hue
Now to a sweetly blushing purple, now to saffron yellow of the crocus bloom;
Meanwhile spontaneous scarlet shall adorn the fleece of grazing lambs. 45
"Let centuries such as these run on for ever," cried the concordant Fates
To their turning spindles, expressive of Destiny's firm-fixed purposes.

The time draws nearer. Enter upon your lofty honours now,
Beloved offspring of the gods, O mighty progeny of Jupiter.
See how the world with mighty globe bows down and makes obeisance, 50
With lands and vast expanses of the sea, and all the heights of heaven.
See the rejoicing of our whole creation as the new age dawns. This I pray:

May there remain for me of my long life one final part, with breath
And inspiration sufficient to hymn the praises of your glorious deeds.
My songs shall yield to none; neither shall Thracian Orpheus conquer me   55
Nor Linus, though his mother brings her aid to one, his father to the other,
To Orpheus Calliope, the Epic Muse, to Linus lovely Apollo;
Great Pan himself, were Arcady the judge, could not contend with me;
Great Pan himself, were Arcady the judge, must needs confess defeat.

Come then, my infant child, begin to know your mother with a smile,   60
For her ten months have brought the lengthy pangs of travail;
Come then, my infant child, for those who at their birth deny a smile
To parents no god shall honour with festal board, nor goddess with her bed.

1   *Muses of Sicily*: a reference to Theocritus, Virgil's Greek pastoral predecessor; the elevated and
        symbolic content of this poem is indeed unlike Theocritus.
5   *Cumae's Sibyl*: the most famous Italian member of the supposed group of Sibyls (female prophets)
        in the ancient world; this phrase also suggests that this poem uses the famous Sibylline prophecies,
        of which later versions are extant.
12   *Asinius Pollio*: consul in 40, when the poem was clearly written (line 3), and negotiator of the Treaty
        of Brundisium (autumn 40 BC), the poem's background (see introduction).
18   *peace won by his father's virtues*: could refer ambiguously to either Octavian or Antony (most
        likely) or even to the peace-maker Pollio (see introduction).
55–59   Orpheus appears here as a poet of wisdom with country connections, Linus as a famed pastoral
        singer, and Pan as the presiding god of pastoral poetry.

G3   Horace, *Epode* 7   The cycle of violence

This poem, along with the related *Epode* 16, is one of the most pessimistic of the *Epodes*, seeing no exit
from Rome's cycle of civil war in the early 30's BC, which the poet ironically traces back to the similarly
fratricidal killing of Remus by Romulus at the foundation of Rome. Scholars tend to think that this dark
poem was written before Horace was drawn into the circle of Maecenas in c.38 BC; poems after that date
(e.g. *Epode* 9 below) certainly suggest that there is indeed a solution to Rome's problems – in the person of
Caesar/Augustus.

Madmen, rushing to ruin, you know not where. Why lay
Your hands again on swords once sheathed?
Have you not drunk your fill of Latin blood, spilled
On the battlefields of land and sea?
And to what purpose? Not that the overweening towers   5
Of jealous Carthage should be burnt by Rome;
Nor that the Briton, yet unconquered, might be marched
Along the Sacred Way in shackles;
Rather that Parthia's prayers might find fulfilment, and Rome
Should perish at the hand of Romans.   10
This is not nature's way: never against its own does wolf
Or lion think to bare its fangs.
Comes the blind Fury? Or does some greater force consume us?
Is it blood guilt? Come – answer me!
No answer comes. With faces pale as death and faculties   15
All numbed, they gawp dumbfounded.
Face the truth: Romans are playthings of a bitter Fate, punished
For fratricidal murder by association,

Since that first day when blameless Remus' blood was spilt
Upon the earth, leaving posterity accursed.   20

4   *battlefields of land and sea*: a reference to the civil wars since the death of Julius Caesar in 44 BC;
     'sea' probably refers to the campaigns against Sextus Pompey in the late 40's and early 30's (see
     note on *Epode* 9.7 = **G5**).
6   *Carthage*: destroyed by Rome in 146 BC after a century of Punic Wars.
7   *Briton*: for Britain as a target for Roman imperial conquest, at least in poetry, see **N29–N30**.
8   *Sacred Way*: the road from the Forum to the Capitoline hill in Rome, the traditional route for a
     triumphal procession.
9   *Parthia*: seen as Rome's greatest enemy in the period between the Parthian annihilation of a Roman
     army under Crassus at the battle of Carrhae (53 BC) and the Roman settlement with Parthia achieved
     in 20 BC (see **G34** below).
13   *blind Fury*: the personification of punishment for previous crime.
19   *Remus*: a reference to the version of Rome's foundation legend in which Romulus killed his twin
     brother Remus in a dispute over which of them was to have precedence as founder.

G4   Horace, *Satires* 1.5.27–33   A journey from Rome to Brundisium

This satire (published c.35 BC) records one of Horace's roles as a dependent of Maecenas, acting as his
travelling companion. The journey is politically important: Maecenas and Cocceius are going to Brindisi in
37 BC on a diplomatic mission to sort out differences between their leader Octavian (in Italy) and his
colleague Antony (visiting from his Eastern powerbase).

Noble Maecenas was due to meet us here, at Anxur,
Together with Cocceius, both sent as emissaries upon affairs
Of national importance, and both skilled at reconciling friends
Who've quarrelled. Here I was spreading black collyrium salve   30
On my bloodshot eyes when they arrived, Maecenas and Cocceius,
With them Fonteius Capito, a gentleman of polished charm,
And one of the closest friends of Antony.

G5   Horace, *Epode* 9   Rejoice for victory at Actium

This poem, addressed to Maecenas, looks forward to the celebration at Rome of Octavian's victory at Actium
in NW Greece (2 September 31 BC). The poem takes the form of reportage in the manner of a war-
correspondent, which has led many to believe that Horace witnessed the battle himself. It follows the
standard Augustan propaganda version of the battle (also found in *Odes* 1.37 = **G24**, and in Virgil's treatment
in *Aeneid* 8, discussed in **G38**), playing up the unnamed Cleopatra's suspect gender and supposed Eastern
vices, and playing down the role of the Roman Antony (here only named as 'our enemy'); Actium is thus
presented as largely a war against foreigners rather than what it was, the climactic battle of a civil war.

Maecenas, friend of the gods, you've got some Caecuban from long ago,
Laid down for feasts and festivals,
Name the day when in your lofty mansion I shall drink with you
– Jove willing – in celebration of
Our Caesar's victory, while Dorian lyre and wild barbarian   5
Flutes make melody together.
Let's celebrate again, as once we did when Neptune's admiral
Was driven from the seas, his vessels burnt,
Sextus, that friend to treacherous slaves, who threatened Rome
With those same manacles he freed them from.   10
Meanwhile, for very shame, (deny it if you can, incredulous Posterity!)
In service to a woman, Roman soldiery
Bears stake and weapons, and can bring itself to yield obedience

To wrinkled eunuchs, while the sun itself
Looks down upon that foul and curtained tent set up amidst   15
The standards of our Roman legionaries.
This was the target of two thousand Gauls who charged their steeds
Foaming against it, ("Caesar" their battle-cry),
While ships of our enemies lurked in their harbour-lairs,
Deaf to the order for a left deployment.   20
Hail, Victory! Can you longer delay the golden chariots and oxen
Unblemished for the sacrifice?
Hail Victory! Goddess, who never brought us home so great
A general from the Jugurthine wars,
Not even Africanus, whose courage built for him a sepulchre upon   25
The ruins of a conquered Carthage.
Conquered by land and sea, our enemy has exchanged his Punic
Purple cloak for lamentation's black.
Where is he now? Fighting the head-winds, setting his course, perhaps,
For Crete, famed for her hundred cities,   30
Or seeking the Syrtes' sand-banks, tossed by southern gales, or else
Borne far away on perilous seas unknown.
Slave-boy, come here, bring out the larger goblets and pour out
The Chian or the Lesbian vintage,
Or better still a goodly measure of that Caecuban – to check those qualms   35
I feel from all this talk of ocean waves.
What joy it is to drive away our fearful care for Caesar's fortunes
With Bacchus' own sweet vintage.

1	*Caecuban*: a high-class Italian wine
7, 9	*Neptune's admiral …*: Sextus Pompeius, son of Pompey the Great, defeated eventually by Octavian and Agrippa at the sea-battle of Naulochus in 36 BC. He claimed to be under Neptune's particular protection.
9	*that friend to treacherous slaves*: Sextus enlisted runaway slaves in his navy, a fundamental threat to Roman social order.
15	*that foul and curtained tent*: a mosquito-netted enclosure, symbolic of Eastern luxury and effeminacy.
17	*Gauls*: Galatians from Asia Minor (Turkey), but of Celtic ancestry. Their king, Amyntas deserted Antony shortly before the battle.
21	*golden chariots and oxen*: part of the ritual of the triumphal procession in Rome
24	*Jugurthine wars*: campaigns against the African King Jugurtha, in the late second century BC; the conquering general was the great Marius.
25	*Africanus*: Scipio Africanus the younger, the final conqueror of Carthage in 146 BC.
31	*Syrtes*: notorious sandbanks off the coast of North Africa.
34	*Chian … Lesbian*: two high-class Greek wines.

G6   Horace, *Satires* 2.1.1–20   A satirist's lot is not a happy one

Published c.30 BC and addressed to Trebatius, a distinguished lawyer. Horace suggests that his first book of satires has been criticised, and asks Trebatius whether he should continue in the same vein (ironically, given that this is the opening of a new book!). Trebatius suggests writing about Octavian, as Horace's satiric predecessor Lucilius had written about the great general Scipio a hundred years before, but Horace declines, while complimenting Octavian, suggesting that there is a right and a wrong time to approach him with poetry, and implying some intimacy with him.

Horace:	Some people say they think my satire is too cutting,	
	That it goes far beyond convention's bounds; others complain	
	That all my compositions are so flabby, so devoid of muscle;	
	Others again that any hack could turn out lines like mine	
	By the thousand every day. Come on, Trebatius, tell me what to do.	
Trebatius:	Take a break.	5
Horace:	You mean, give up my writing altogether?	
Trebatius:	Yes.	
Horace:	Dammit, you're right. That's the best answer. But,	
	What about my insomnia?	
Trebatius:	Anyone that needs deep sleep	
	Should lubricate himself with oil and swim three times across the Tiber,	
	Then towards nightfall keep his system pickled in undiluted wine.	
	But if your urge to write is a raging obsession, take a risk and tell	
	Of unconquered Caesar's deeds of derring-do. I promise you	10
	You'll reap a rich reward.	
Horace:	Good father T, I'd love to, but willing	
	Though my spirit is, yet flesh is weak. Not everyone can sing	
	Of pikes and bristling battle lines, or dying Gauls who fall	
	With spear points shattered, or the wounded Parthian	
	Slipping from his horse.	15
Trebatius:	But surely you could write of Caesar himself, so just,	
	So brave, as old Lucilius had the sense to write of Scipio.	
Horace:	Give me the opportunity and then I'll show what I can do.	
	But if the moment is inopportune, then Flaccus' flattery	
	Will never find an entrance to the ears of a distracted Caesar.	
	Always be careful how you stroke the mule. He's on his guard	
	At all four corners and his hooves are lethal.	20

G7   Horace, *Satires* 2.6.29–59 Miseries of city life

This passage describes a stressful day in Rome for Horace, attending to his business affairs and to his duties as a dependent of Maecenas (see on *Satires* 1.5 = **G4**). There is a vignette of Horace's relationship with Maecenas: though the latter is a great politician, Horace claims to talk to him about trivialities and not to be privy to secrets of state. We may suspect that Horace is advertising both his closeness to the great man and his discretion about his affairs; he may well have known more than he lets on here. On Maecenas, see **R1–R13**, on Horace and Maecenas, see **R14**.

"What's all this about, you mad idiot? What are you playing at?"
So speaks some bloody-minded passer-by, cursing me to high heaven.
"You trample on everything and everyone in your way; you'd think   30
Your business with Maecenas was the only thing that mattered."
I love the implicit compliment. It's milk and honey to my ears, I swear.

But then, when I reach the dreary Esquiline, at once another hundred
Bits of other people's business buzz about my head, worrying at me
Like dogs. "Roscius wants you to join him at Libo's Wall, the Puteal,   35
To-morrow, before seven." "The Secretariat would be most grateful,
Quintus, if you could remember to look in today about a matter of major
Public importance which has just come up." "Could you get Maecenas
To sign these documents?" And if you say, "OK, I'll try", at once the speaker
Turns the screws by adding, "I know you'll manage it – if you *really* care."   40

Time flies – it's now seven, nearly eight years actually, since Maecenas
Began to number me among his friends – to the extent at least
Of consenting to share his carriage with me on a journey, and confiding
Such portentous trivialities to me as: "What's the time?" or "Which fighter
Would you put your money on – the Thracian Chicken or the Syrian?"   45
Or "There's a real nip in the air now – people need to be careful;" and all
The sort of rubbish that can safely be deposited in a leaky ear.
For all this time yours truly has become increasingly from day to day,
From hour to hour, the object of men's envy. If Maecenas went
To the games or exercised with me in the Campus Martius, up would go   50
The universal cry, "That lucky bastard!" If some blood-curdling rumour
Leaked round the streets from the speakers' Rostra, everyone I met
Wanted my opinion. "Come on, there's a good chap, you must know the answer;
You're close to the powers that be, the official channels. Is there some news
About the Dacians?" "Not that I've heard." "You're pulling my leg, as usual." 55
"Not a word, I promise. So help me god." "Come on! Is Caesar going to give
The army their promised pensions, farms in Sicily or even Italy perhaps?"
I protest, swearing that I know nothing, leaving them utterly amazed
That any man alive can really be the soul of such incredible discretion.

G8   Virgil, *Georgics* 1.24–42

This is the climax of the formal opening of the *Georgics*, in which Caesar (the future Augustus) is invoked at the climax of a list of agricultural deities as a future astral god and a sponsor of this poem, overtly about farming but symbolically about the morality of hard work and Roman citizenship.

Caesar, above all others you I invoke, though yet
We cannot know which heavenly hierarchy will speed
To claim you as its own, whether you choose to be   25
Guardian of cities, Land's custodian, whom the earth's
Great globe proclaims as author of its fruitful crops,
Giver of increase, lord of the seasons, decking your brow
With mother Venus' myrtle; whether you come as lord
Of the vast Ocean, sole recipient of sailors' prayers,   30
Honoured by farthest Thule as liege, while Tethys seeks
With all her waves to buy you for son-in-law;
Whether instead to slow summer's months you add yourself,
Another constellation, where space opens up between
Virgin Erigone and fiery Scorpio's claws – who now retracts   35
His arms, to leave you more than your due share of heaven.
Take any form – though Tartarus expects you not as king,
Nor may you of that dread kingdom feel desire,
Much though the Greeks admired Elysium, and Proserpine
Reclaimed cared not to follow Ceres back to earth –
Take any form, but grant me easy passage, and graciously   40
Incline your head to bless my audacious enterprise; with me
Pity the ignorance of country-folk who've lost their way.
Enter upon your destiny, learning even now
To answer prayer.

31   *Thule*: an island traditionally seen as the northern limit of the known world, commonly identified
        as Iceland, while *Tethys* is a sea-goddess.

G9   Virgil, *Georgics* 1.498–514

This is the end of Book 1, which concludes with a prayer that Caesar (Augustus) will save Rome from its
current troubles. This is clearly written before the decisive battle of Actium (31 BC), perhaps in the mid or
late 30's.

> Gods of our country, heroes of our land,
> Romulus, Mother Vesta, who protects our Tuscan Tiber
> And Roman Palatine, grant us at least this boon:
> Thwart not our youthful prince who comes to save   500
> Our shipwrecked century. Long since and enough
> Our blood has repaid the perjury of Troy's Laomedon;
> Enough have the halls of heaven begrudged you to us,
> Complaining you care too much for mortal glory.
> Reversed on earth are good and evil now; so many wars   505
> Rack the great globe, while crime wears many masks;
> Lost is all honour for the ploughman's trade; our fields
> Squalid, bereft of farmers, lie un-tilled; into straight swords
> Are melted all our rounded pruning hooks. Eastward
> Euphrates moves to war, northward Germania; neighbour cities   510
> Break their confederate leagues to take up arms; the while
> An impious Mars runs riot through the world.
> Just so the chariot teams burst from their starting gates
> And lap by lap gain speed, and all the while
> Their driver, helpless to hold them back, is borne along   515
> By horses heedless of the rein.

500   *youthful prince*: Caesar's youth (about 30 by now) is still remarkable for a Roman leader, and can
        serve to identify him without naming (see *Eclogue* 1.42–5 = **G1** above).
502   *the perjury of Troy's Laomedon*: Laomedon's deception of the gods when building Troy is here
        represented as a mythically distant and therefore politically unproblematic cause of Rome's
        suffering in the civil wars (compare the use of Romulus and Remus in Horace, *Epode* 7 = **G3**).
509–10 the references to unrest in East (the Euphrates represents Parthia) and North (Germany) express
        universal disruption as well as specific trouble-spots of the 30's BC.
515   *Their driver*: the image is taken from chariot-racing, a favourite Roman sport. The driver who is
        carried along may suggest the young Caesar himself, who needs the help of the gods to bring Rome
        and the world under control.

G10   Virgil, *Georgics* 2.167–176

These lines are the climax of Virgil's 'praise of Italy', bringing together a patriotic encomium of Italian
landscape, praise of Caesar, and poetic programmatic statements about the *Georgics*. They appear to date
from the period 30–29 BC (see note on line 170).

> Vigorous the line of manhood born of Italy,
> Marsians and Sabine stock, and tough Ligurians,
> So tolerant of hardship, men of the javelin, the Volscians,
> The Decius family, men like Camillus, aye, and Marius too,
> Both Scipios, those iron men of war, and mightiest of all,
> You, Caesar, who now on Asia's furthest shores   170

Already victor turn the pathetic Indians from our walls.
Hail, great mother of harvests, golden land of Saturn,
Mighty mother of heroes – for you I enter upon a theme
Ancient in honour and art, for you I dare
Unseal the Muses' holy fountain and to sing   175
Old Hesiod's Ascran song through Roman towns.

168–9 A list of old Roman heroes culminating in the great contemporary figure of Caesar (for this
       encomiastic technique see Horace *Odes* 1.12 = **G23**); these are precisely saving military heroes –
       the Decii were self-sacrificing Roman heroes in the fourth and third centuries BC (cf. note on
       Propertius 3.11.61–4, = **G31**), Camillus saved Rome in the 390's, Marius in the last decade of the
       second century BC, while the Scipios (father Africanus and adopted son Aemilianus) won the Second
       and Third Punic Wars respectively.
170–1 *Asia's furthest shores*: the geography and triumphal tone here suggest that these are the clear-up
       campaigns after Actium in 30–29 BC.
171   *pathetic Indians*: rhetorical exaggeration (Indians never threatened Rome, see **N39–N40**).
176   *Old Hesiod's Ascran song*: the first explicit statement in the poem that it is (partly) a Latin adaptation
       of the *Works and Days* of Hesiod from Ascra in Boeotia, an archaic Greek poem which like the
       Georgics combines agricultural and moral instruction.

G11   Virgil, *Georgics* 3.8–48

These lines introduce the second half of this four-book poem and look forward to the next step in Virgil's
poetic career after the *Georgics*. The symbolic marble temple with Caesar in the middle and decorated with
his current victories might look forward in some degree to the poetic artefact of the *Aeneid*, which has Caesar
near its centre (in Book 6: see **G37**) and praise of his victories on the prophetic Shield of Aeneas (in Book
8; **G38**); but in general these lines seem to promise a poem devoted to Caesar's own recent achievements
(see especially lines 46–8) rather than the *Aeneid*, which though it gave Caesar and his victories a cameo
role naturally focussed largely on the mythical deeds of his ancestor Aeneas. This passage appears to belong
to the period 30–29 BC, when the triumphant return of Caesar from the East is soon expected (his triumph
was in fact celebrated in August 29 BC).

For I must find a theme by which I too may rise
To higher things, and there my name shall dance
Victorious ever on the lips of men. If life allow,   10
I shall be first to bring the Muses home to Italy,
Down from the heights of Helicon; I shall be first
To claim the victor's Idumaean palm for you, my Mantua.
By your still waters, in your pastures green I'll build
A marble temple there, where mighty Mincius winds
His stream's slow coils, and wreathes with tender reeds   15
His banks. There in the midst shall Caesar's statue stand
And hold for me his temple. In his honour I,
In Tyrian purple, focus of all eyes, along the stream
Shall drive one hundred four-horsed chariots.
At my behest all Greece shall leave their games,
Alpheus' river and Nemea's groves, with chariot   20
To compete and cruel boxing glove. I myself,
With brows bedecked with close-clipped olive wreath,
Shall bring my gifts. Now, even now, what joy it is to lead
Solemn processions to the holy shrine and there
To see the bullocks sacrificed; or on the stage to watch
The changing scene, the sets divide, and how

Woven in fabric Britons raise the purple curtains up. 25
Then on the doors I'll set a battle, wrought in gold
And solid ivory, between the armies of the Ganges' tribes
And Quirinus, the victor; there I'll show the Nile,
His mighty waters billowing with war, while decked
With warships' brazen beaks great columns rise.
Then shall I add the cities of Asia tamed, Niphates' rout, 30
The fleeing Parthians' final fusillade; two trophies
Won from far-separated foes, twin triumphs too
For victories gained on widely-distant shores.

Fashioned of Parian marble there shall stand
Statues which seem to breathe, Assaracus' descendants,
That clan whose origins derive from Jove himself, 35
Tros, our great ancestor, and Troy's co-founder
Cynthian Apollo. Then shall accursed Envy hide her head
For fear of Furies and Cocytus' stream implacable,
Ixion's writhing snakes, his monstrous wheel, and Sisyphus'
Unconquerable rock.
                                    Meanwhile let me pursue
My songs of Dryad groves and virgin glades, obedient, 40
Maecenas, to your arduous commands. No lofty theme
My spirit may address without your aid. Come then,
Away with dull delay, urgent Cithaeron summons
With mighty voice, hounds of Taygetus call
And Epidaurus, too, tamer of horses, while the woodlands' roar 45
Redoubled, bellows its assent.
                                    But soon I shall gird
Myself to tell the tale of Caesar's blazing wars, and bear
The glory of his name down the long years, no less far
Than is Tithonus' birth, from Caesar's, his kinsman.

13   *My Mantua*: the region of Virgil's birth.
27–31   These lines refer to potential and imagined victories of Caesar in the East, invoking Quirinus, the
        divine name of Romulus, as patron of Roman arms: the Ganges exaggeratedly claims victory in
        India (paralleling Alexander the Great), the Nile refers to the conquest of Alexandria (see on
        Horace *Odes* 4.14 = **G44**) and the 'cities of Asia' to the clear-up operations after Actium, while
        the Armenian river Niphates and the Parthians present as conquered areas which were yet to be
        tackled.
32   *twin triumphs*: Caesar actually celebrated three simultaneous triumphs in August 29 BC, see **H16**.
        This reference perhaps envisages the conjunction of the last two as one continuous campaign and
        was clearly written before August 29 BC.
34   *Assaracus*: one of Aeneas' Trojan ancestors.
43–5   Cithaeron in Boeotia and Taygetus near Sparta are both great mountains and prime sites for hunting;
        Epidaurus near Argos was famed for horse-breeding.
48   *Tithonus*: another distant Trojan ancestor (in mythology, the consort of the dawn-goddess Aurora,
        who gave him eternal life but not eternal youth).

G12   Virgil, *Georgics* 4.559–62

These lines come almost at the end of the *Georgics*. Here the poet juxtaposes his peaceful composition of
the *Georgics* (now concluded) with the current military achievements of Caesar in the East (30–29 BC).

Such were the songs I sang of the farmers' care
Of fields and herds and orchards, while on the banks
Of deep Euphrates mighty Caesar thundered in war,   560
And after victory gave the rule of law
To willing subjects, setting his sights on heaven.

560–1   *On the banks of deep Euphrates*: clearly a reference to the post-Actium eastern campaigns of 30–29
         BC, though these are unlikely to have gone as far as the River Euphrates, which here represents (as
         at 1.509–10 above) the (in fact undefeated) Parthians.
562   *setting his sights on heaven*: here as in 1.24–42 (above) Caesar's future deification is envisaged as
         earned by his great deeds.

Propertius 1.21 and 1.22   Elegies on the Perusine War

These two poems, the first a form of sepulchral epigram, the second an autobiography in a traditional position
at the end of the poetic book, evoke in poems published around 28 BC, at least a decade after the event, the
bloody episode of the siege of Perusia (Perugia) in 41 BC, where Propertius' relatives clearly fought against
Caesar (Augustus). These laments for an unfortunate relative are not highly subversive or anti-Caesarian;
note that in 1.21 Gallus' death is pointedly not ascribed to Caesar's forces, and that 1.22 contains a very
generalised and non-partisan lament for the madness of civil war (cf. Horace *Epode* 7 = **G3**). Nevertheless,
these poems clearly show more political independence than the nationalistic Augustan poetry written under
Maecenas' patronage in Books 3 and 4 (see below).

G13   Propertius 1.21   Lament for a relative killed in the battle of Perusia
My fellow-soldier, wounded upon the ramparts of Perusia,
Fleeing disaster such as overtook your friends, those groans
Are mine. No need to force your haunted eyes to look.
I am the closest of your comrades, one tiny remnant of our soldiery.
Fly for your life and give your parents something to be glad for;   5
But never let your sister learn from your tears the truth
Of my death, how Gallus fought his way safe through Caesar's lines,
But random death at some stranger's hands he could not flee.
Bones she will find in plenty scattered on the hills
Of Tuscany. Never let her know that they are mine.   10

G14   Propertius 1.22.   Perusia
Tullus, for our long friendship's sake, you ask me constantly
What is my status, what my family, where dwell my household gods.
You surely know our country's war-graves, Perusia's cemeteries,
Where in our darkest hours perished the flower of Italy,
When civil wars of Rome had driven her people mad.   5
That is for me the reason why the dust of Tuscany is above all
The bitterest, for it received my kinsman's scattered limbs,
Poor soul, without the funeral offering of earth outpoured.
Close by, where rich in her fertile fields adjacent Umbria
Stretches her arms to touch the plains below – there was I born.   10

G15   Propertius 2.1   Dedication to Maecenas

This poem to Maecenas sets out in the traditional *recusatio* or refusal (see on Horace Odes 1.6 = **G22**) the
poet's incapacity (but importantly, not his lack of will) to pursue a more serious or political type of poetry
than erotic elegy; its praise of Maecenas (see esp. lines 36–37) suggests a patron-type relationship, even if
Propertius politely declines the topic of Caesar's victories as too great for his own powers. This poem may
date to before 27 BC since Caesar is not yet called Augustus (contrast Propertius 2.10.15, **G17**).

You ask me, Maecenas, whence the inspiration of my many songs
Of love, and whence this book so honey-sweet upon a poet's lips.
Neither the epic Muse, Calliope, nor yet Apollo, Lord of song
Arouse my genius – rather my own true love, my Cynthia.
If glorious in the silks of Cos you should command her go,   5
Why then from Coan fashions will this volume all be made;
Suppose I behold her once, locks blown awry across her brow,
And praise her so; then proudly she walks rejoicing in my praise;
If with those ivory fingers she should caress her lyre into song, then I
Will wonder to behold her hands' dexterity and easy grace;   10
But if she should close her eyes and summon up sweet sleep,
Then will I find a thousand novel themes for poet's melody;
But when, as for action stripped, she casts away her dress
And wrestles with me, then I compose vast Iliads of song.
Whatever my mistress does, whatever she may say,   15
From tiniest trifles are derived my mightiest melodies.

Had but the Fates once granted me, Maecenas, the power
To march heroic armies into war, then would I sing
Not of the Titans warring on the gods, nor Ossa heaped
Upon Olympus, that Pelion might make a highway into heaven;   20
Neither of ancient Thebes, nor Troy (the source of Homer's fame)
Nor yet of Xerxes, whose command made two seas one;
Not Remus' first kingdoms, nor lofty Carthage lusting after war,
Not menacing Cimbric tribes, nor Marius' martial deeds.
Rather my song would be of Caesar's wars, great Caesar's works,   25
Caesar, your friend, and after him, Maecenas, you yourself
Would be my theme. As often as I sang of Mutina, and of Philippi
With her war-cemeteries, Roman all, of wars at sea and of the rout
Of foes about the shores of Sicily, of shattered homesteads
In Etruria's antique land, the captured coasts of Egypt, where still stands   30
The Pharos built by Ptolemy; even as oft as I sang of Egypt and the Nile
Marching in mourning raiment into Rome, a captive now
And helpless with all his seven streams; of kings with chains of gold
About their necks, and ships' beaks rolling up the Sacred Way,
The trophies of Actium – even so often these would be my song,   35
Into their tapestry of warlike deeds the Muse would weave
Your name for ever and your loyal heart, steadfast in peace or war.
<For always at his side steadfast you stood; and here on earth
You show to men proof of that friendship, even as >
To the shades below Theseus shows proof of friendship for Ixion's son,
Pirithous, or to the gods on high Achilles for Menoetius' son, Patroclus.

Callimachus with his attenuated breath could ne'er declaim
The wars of Jupiter and Enceladus on the Phlegrean fields;   40
Nor yet can my heart's inspiration trace with mighty verse
The lineage of Caesar back to his ancient ancestors in Troy.
Sailors of storm and tempest spin their yarns; ploughmen of bulls;
Soldiers the tally of their wounds; the shepherd counts his flock.

The wars I tell, by contrast, are confined all to one narrow bed;   45
Each to his own profession; there let each live out his little day.
Fame is the guerdon of a lover's death; a different fame attends
On him that lives in joy of just one love. May such be my Love to me!
For she is wont, as I remember it, to call anathemas upon inconstancy;
The whole of Homer's *Iliad* she excoriates, and all for Helen alone.   50
It may be of Phaedra's poisoned cup I'll drink, a stepmother
Whose cup could bring Hippolytus no harm; or else my destiny
Is death by Circe's herbs, unless for me Medea, witch of Colchis, heats
In brazen cauldron on an Iolcan hearth some poisoned brew.
But no! My only Love has all my senses plundered; she alone.   55
Hers is the house from where my funeral procession shall depart.

Medicine can offer cures for every sickness known to man;
Love, and love only, hates its pain's physician.
Machaon could heal the limping feet of Philoctetes;
Chiron, Phillyra's son, restored his sight to Phoenix;   60
Asclepius, god of Epidaurus, gave the dead Androgeos back
To his father, Minos', hearth through use of Cretan herbs;
The Mysian youth who felt the biting wound of Haemon's spear
By that same spear point gained relief once more.
If there were any man alive that could relieve my sickness, such a one   65
Could offer apples to the hands of Tantalus himself; he alone
Could with their punctured pitchers for the Danaids fill up those casks,
And spare those dainty necks from watery torment everlasting.
Why, he could loose from their Caucasian crag Prometheus' pinioned arms
And from the caverns of his inmost breast expel the vulture.   70

And so, when finally the Fates call in the life I owe, and I
Am nothing more than one short name upon some tiny tomb,
Maecenas, the envied hope of all our youth, the one true source
Of all my glory, whether in life or death, grant me I pray but this:
If as you journey chance should bring you near this tomb of mine,   75
Halt for a moment in your British chariot with ornamented yoke,
And shed a tear, and to my silent ashes say these words:
"Poor man, a cruel mistress brought about his death."

19–24   The poet here rejects the traditional topics of epic, both Greek (battles of gods, Titans and Giants,
        Thebes, Troy, the Persian Wars) and Roman (earlier Roman military history).
25–38   Here the poet claims that were he capable of epic, Caesar's wars (and Maecenas' loyalty to Caesar)
        would be his prime topic. The list he gives begins with the victories of Mutina (43 BC, Caesar's
        earliest military victory, against Antony) and includes Philippi (42, Caesar's victory against Brutus
        and Cassius), the sea-campaigns around Sicily (43–36) against Sextus Pompeius, and the victories
        of Actium and Alexandria (31–30). It also adds in the siege of Perugia (30, *Etruria's antique land*),
        for which see on **G13** and **G14**.
38–39   These lines are not part of the existing Latin text of the poem. But the sense requires an insertion
        of some kind and the two lines in italics serve simply to preserve the train of thought.
41–2   Very likely an allusion to the *Aeneid*, which Propertius clearly knew about before its publication
        (Propertius 2.34.61–6, and see **R15**.30).

G16   Propertius 2.7   On marriage legislation?

This poem seems to refer to a failed attempt by Caesar in the 20's BC (probably before 27, as he is not called Augustus) to introduce the kind of marriage-legislation successfully implemented by him in the law of 17 BC which forced bachelors to marry on pain of various penalties (*Lex Iulia de maritandis ordinibus* – see S3–S6). This failed legislation is otherwise unrecorded, and scholars have sometimes doubted its historicity.

> My Cynthia for sure rejoiced to have that law repealed
> Whose promulgation drove us once to tears of bitterness,
> For fear it might part us both for ever. And yet, to separate
> Against their will a pair of lovers is beyond the power
> Of Jupiter himself. "And of mighty Caesar too?"   5
> I hear you ask. Aye, Caesar too. Mighty in war
> He may be; but conquered nations count for nought
> In lovers' warfare. For sooner would I have my head
> Dismembered from my neck than, like some newly-wed,
> Let passion's fires die; or, as a married man and traitor
> To our love, pass by your bolted door and gaze thereon   10
> My eyes awash with tears. And then, what kind of dreams
> Would those my wedding flutes sing out, with notes
> More dismal than the funeral trumpet? And if you ask
> How then shall I get sons to win my country glory, I reply
> That I shall not – of my blood no soldier shall be born.
> Love's warfare is the only war for me; and if I served   15
> Beneath the colours of my one true love,
> Great Castor's steed would scarce suffice to bear me.
> Love's were the wars in which I won so great a name
> and stretched my fame far as the ice-capped Russian Steppes.
> You are my sole delight, my Cynthia; god grant that I am yours
> Alone! Such love to me counts more than fatherhood.   20

G17   Propertius 2.10   The poet turns from love to epic themes

Apparently with greater political commitment than poem 2.1 (above) and perhaps written somewhat later (see on lines 15–16), this poem promises to engage in epic about Caesar's battles now that the material of erotic elegy has been exhausted (lines 7–8). But once again there are reservations. This epic enterprise is still in the future (lines 19–20), and the familiar protestations of poetic incapacity for such a great task are again raised; lines 23–26 suggest that the poet still belongs to the lower world of love-elegy.

> Now comes the time to dance to a different tune across
> The hills of Helicon; now is the time to gallop o'er the plain
> My steeds of Thessaly. Now my delight is telling tales of war,
> Brave squadrons and my Leader's Roman camp.
> And though my strength may fail, yet will I win the praise   5
> Of my audacity; in great endeavours, endeavour will suffice.
> Youth sings the songs of love; maturity of tumult and battle-din.
> Wars now shall be my song; my darling's script is written out.
> Now with severer mien and graver pace I seek to make my way;
> Now my Muse teaches me to play upon a different lyre.   10
> My Genius, arise! Ye Muses of Pieria, forget your humble lays;
> Your powers re-invigorate. A mighty work calls for a mighty voice.

No more can Euphrates claim that her Parthian cavalry defends her
In retreat; rather she regrets that once she denied the Crassi homecoming.
Great Augustus, to your triumph even India now offers up her neck,   15
While far Arabia's un-ravished home trembles to see you come.
If there be any land concealed upon Earth's furthest shores,
Captive, in time to come may it too feel the power of your hands.
Such is the camp to which I play camp-follower; yours the campaigns
Whose songs shall make me great. May Fate preserve that day for me.   20
Just as before a mighty statue, when we cannot reach to lay our wreathes
Upon its brow, we place them upon the ground before its feet,
So now, unable to ascend the heights of glory's hymnody,
We offer to you our modest frankincense, a pauper's sacrifice.
I am no Hesiod; unfamiliar to my songs are Ascra's fountains;   25
For Love has dipped them only in Permessus' humbler streams.

4   *my Leader's Roman camp*: an expression of political enthusiasm.
13–14   A reference to the defeat of Crassus and his son by the Parthians at Carrhae in 53 BC, an ignominy
         which Augustan policy sought to erase (cf. **G30**, **N41**).
15–16   India and Arabia here again seem to represent distant lands witnessing Augustus' greatness rather
         than realistic military targets (though there was an unsuccessful Roman expedition to Arabia in
         26–25 BC, probably after this was written, and India is mentioned hyperbolically as a target in
         Propertius 3.4 = **G30**). See **N39–N40**.

G18   Propertius 2.15   Love song for Cynthia

This poem is more typical of the general run of material in the first two extant books of Propertius, narrating
as it does an erotic episode in the life of love with Cynthia. It is less politically conformist than either 2.1 or
2.10; lines 41–6 suggest that the world would be a better place if everyone made love and not war, and seem
to refer to the Battle of Actium as a civil conflict, in opposition to the pro-Caesarian presentation of it as a
foreign war against Cleopatra (see e.g. Virgil *Aeneid* 8.675–713, **G38**; Horace *Epode* 9 = **G5** and *Odes* 1.37
= **G24**).

I'm the luckiest man alive! It was a night lit up with ecstasy.
My bed became the gift of heaven with the delights of making love.
What thousands of sweet nothings did we whisper in the lamplight!
What wars of love we waged when once the lights were out.
One moment with naked breasts she wrestled with me; and the next   5
Discreetly covered, with her tunic down, she played so hard to get.
Exhausted I closed my eyes for sleep; she opened and unsealed them
With loving kisses, crying, "Have you no stamina, lying there like that?"
How we embraced and rang the changes too on all the ways of making love!
How often my kisses lingered so long upon those lips of yours!   10
There is no pleasure if you close your eyes when making love, and blindly
Thrash around; did you not know, it is the eyes that lead the way to love.
Paris himself, they say, fell victim to the naked charms of Spartan Helen,
When first he saw her rising from Menelaus' bed-chamber. Naked too,
They say, Endymion was when the Moon goddess, Phoebus' sister,   15
Fell for him once and man with naked goddess lay upon their bed of love.
But if, my Cynthia, with obdurate heart you still insist on lying clothed,
Torn clothes will quickly teach you what my rough handling means.
And then, if my anger drives me to inflict still further punishment,
You'll show your mother the bruises on your arms in evidence.   20

Your youthful breasts are firm; no sagging shape as yet forbids our sport;
Leave such concerns to mothers who feel shamed by their children's birth.
While still the Fates allow us, let us feast our eyes on love; soon enough
The long night comes for you when morning breaks no more.
Would that your heart's desire led you now to bind us both in chains   25
So strong that no day's breaking ever could set us free again.
Take as exemplars now the turtle-doves, linked by the chains of love,
Where in totality of conjoined bliss both male and female meet.
The man has lost his wits who seeks an end to love's insanity;
Wholly bereft of sense is moderation to all who truly love.   30
Earth will first mock the ploughman with false fruit born out of season;
Sooner the Sun-God harness to his chariot black horses of the night;
Rivers will first back to their fountain-heads recall their waters;
Oceans will turn to deserts and fishes first gasp for water
Before I shall ever shift elsewhere my love with all the pain it brings.   35
Hers shall I be in life, in death I shall remain her love.
If she consents from time to time to grant such nights like that which last
We had, then one single year will count for me a veritable lifetime.
But if she will grant me many of the same, I shall become immortal.
For any man one single such night would make him a god.   40
If only such a way of life could be the object of desire for all men,
Reclining on couches with their limbs relaxed by undiluted vintage,
Then there would be no weapons of savage steel, nor ships of war,
Nor Roman bones all tossed upon the waves of Actium;
Then Rome herself, so oft assailed by triumphs of Roman over Roman,   45
Rome would in weariness soon cease to tear her hair lamenting for her own.
This at least, and rightly, will our children's children find to praise in us:
Our wine cups never gave the gods offence nor did them any hurt.
My Cynthia, while yet bright are the lights of life, do not desert life's joys;
If every kiss you have you give to me, yet will it not suffice.   50
Just as the tired leaves fall from the withered garlands on your brow,
And you may watch them everywhere afloat within the wine-cups' pools,
So we, who as lovers dream the high dreams of hope, may find perchance
That to-morrow's dawning will close up our destiny's account.

G19   Propertius 2.31   The opening of Phoebus' Portico

This poem celebrates the opening in 28 BC of the portico to Augustus' temple of Palatine Apollo (see
K37–K38 for this key Augustan monument and its association with the battle of Actium).

You ask me why I come so late today? The fault was Phoebus',
For on this day his golden portico was opened by mighty Caesar.
It was so vast to gaze upon, a mighty spread of Punic marble columns;
Between the columns stood, in statuary, the Danaids,
Offspring of aged Danaus. Then, from the midst there rose   5
The gleaming marble temple, shrine more dear to Phoebus
Than his Ortygian homeland. Next, upon the pediment appear
Twin chariots of the Sun; below twin doors, a noble work
Of Libyan ivory, telling their tale, the one of Gauls

From high Parnassus hurled; the other mourning the death   10
Of Niobe, child of Tantalus. Then, finally, the Pythian God himself,
Standing between his mother and sister, clad in priestly robes
Declaimed his prophecies. Marble he was, yet fairer did he seem
Than Phoebus' self, singing from open lips on silent lyre.
There round the altar Myron's oxen stood, statues that seemed alive.   15

4   *The Danaids*: fifty mythological sisters who (all except one) murdered their cousin-husbands on
         their wedding-night as the result of a family feud and then took refuge in Egypt; a possible symbolic
         reference to the husband-murdering Egyptian Cleopatra, defeated at the battle the Palatine complex
         celebrates.
9–11   The story of the repulse of the Gauls from Parnassus (278 BC) and of the mythological vengeance
         of Apollo and his sister Diana on Niobe who insulted their mother Latona both illustrate the power
         of Apollo to defend his own, as Augustan propaganda implied that he did at Actium (see Propertius
         4.6 = **G39**).

G20   Crinagoras 29 (*Greek Anthology* 9.419)   **Augustus in Spain**

This poem seems to refer to Augustus' campaigns in 26–25 BC against the Cantabrians in northern Spain
(cf. 4 'Pyrenean waters'). Line 6 'two continents' seems to imply Roman mastery of Europe and Asia.

Though to Hercynia's forest depths he goes, or far Soloeis
Near Libya's lovely gardens, the Hesperides, the fame
Of Caesar, the Most August, goes with him everywhere.
The Pyrenean waters as my witnesses I claim.
To wash there once the local woodcutters were loth;
We have two continents; they'll be baths for both.

G21   Horace, *Odes* 1.2

This poem, prominently placed second in the collection after the dedicatory poem to Maecenas, offers
extravagant praise of Octavian/Augustus, relieved by some touches of light humour: recent bad weather is
a menacing portent and linked with the recent civil war; Rome needs, and has in him, a divine saviour.

   Tiber floods were frequent. The only flood known to have occurred about the time this poem may have
been composed was in January 27, on the night after the conferment of the name Augustus (Dio 53.20.1).
Scholars differ on whether the settlement of 27 is a likely occasion for the poem; the use of the title '*princeps*'
at line 50 may be an indication in favour of this context.

   This is the only contemporary poem which suggests that Augustus may be an Olympian god disguised
as a man. There is little other evidence for association of Augustus with Mercury.

Enough for now has Father Jupiter poured out
Upon the earth in snow and biting hail, while with his red
Right hand he smote our holy citadels and brought
   Dread to the city,

Dread to the nations, that the grim time might return   5
When Pyrrha bewailed portents not seen before,
When Proteus drove all his seals to visit
   The high mountains,

Shoals of fishes stuck in the tops of elms,
Habitations formerly familiar to doves,   10
And panic-stricken deer swam in the flood
   That covered the land.

We have seen yellow Tiber, his waves
Repulsed with violence from his Tuscan shore,
Rush to hurl down the king's memorial   15
   And Vesta's temple,

Boasting of vengeance won for his spouse,
Importunate Ilia, as his vagrant waters spread,
Against Jupiter's will, beyond his left bank,
   Wife-besotted river.   20

Of citizens sharpening swords against citizens,
By which grim Persians better would have perished,
And of their battles the youth shall learn, made few
   By their parents' vice.

Which god shall the people call to aid the crumbling   25
Empire? With what prayers shall the holy virgins
Weary the ears of Vesta, now less inclined
   To hear their hymns?

To whom shall Jupiter assign the task of sin's
Atonement? Come at last, we pray you, adorned   30
With clouds to cloak your radiant shoulders,
   Prophet Apollo.

Or, if you prefer, come Venus, smiling Queen
Of Eryx, round whom hover Laughter and Longing.
Or, if you care for your neglected race and offspring,   35
   Come founder Mars,

Glutted, alas, with too long drawn-out sport,
Delighting in battle-cries and helmets polished smooth,
And in the fierce gaze of Marsian infantry
   Against their bloodied foe.   40

Or Mercury, winged son of bountiful Maia,
If you have changed your form and on earth
Are imitating a youth and willing to be called
   Caesar's avenger,

Return late to heaven and long be pleased   45
To dwell amongst the people of Quirinus,
And may no wind bear you off too soon,
   Angry at our sins.

Remain here rather, delighting in great triumphs,
And in being called Father and *Princeps*,   50
And do not permit the Medes to ride unpunished,
   While you are leader, Caesar.

6   *Pyrrha*: wife of Deucalion, the Greek Noah: the couple were the sole human survivors in the Greek
           version of the flood legend.
7   *Proteus*: a minor sea-god, herdsman of seals.
15   *the king's memorial*: the Regia, the headquarters of the *pontifex maximus*. This building and the
           adjacent temple of Vesta were ascribed to Numa, the legendary second king of Rome.
18   *Ilia*: otherwise known as Rhea Silvia, mother of Romulus and Remus. After her seduction by Mars,
           her father had her thrown into the Tiber, and she was thus deemed the Tiber's bride. Horace here
           seems to have substituted the Tiber for its tributary the Anio, which plays this role in other versions
           of the Romulus story.
22   *Persians*: the Parthians. The Parthian empire occupied the eastern part of the former Persian empire.
           The Augustan poets regularly refer to the Parthians as Persians or Medes to evoke the famous Greek
           conflicts with the Persians.
34   *Eryx*: in western Sicily (modern Erice), seat of a famous temple of Venus.
39   *Marsian*: the Marsi, in the central Apennines, were important contributors of soldiers to Roman
           armies, and played a leading part in the rebellion of the Social War (91–87 BC).
46   *Quirinus*: Romulus.
51   *Medes*: Parthians.

G22   Horace, *Odes* 1.6.   **Praises of Agrippa**

This poem, addressed to Agrippa (?63–12 BC), Octavian's military right-hand man, is a *recusatio* or
complimentary 'refusal' poem. Horace cannot write on Homeric-type epic topics such as the deeds of
Agrippa or Augustus which need an epic poet such as Varius: the battles he treats in his lighter lyrics are
the battles of lovers. But while gracefully declining to write about Agrippa's deeds, this poem in fact manages
to praise his distinguished military career and to compare him implicitly with the great heroes of Homer.

> Varius, our eagle of Homeric verse, will hymn
> Your courage and conquest of our enemies,
> Glorying in every deed our soldiers, under your command,
> Performed, savage with ship and steed.
>
> But I, Agrippa, cannot essay such heights, to tell the deadly   5
> Wrath of Peleus' son, Achilles, never known to yield,
> Or sing the sea-borne wanderings of devious Ulysses,
> Or Agamemnon's savage lineage,
>
> The House of Pelops. My skill's too slight for greatness;
> Modesty and my feeble lyric Muse forbid me to detract   10
> Through poverty of inspiration from the glories of
> Great Caesar and yourself.
>
> What poet in song could ever justly hymn great Mars, clad
> In his adamantine tunic, or Meriones, black with the dust
> Of Trojan plains, or Tydeus' son, who proved with Pallas' aid   15
> Himself the equal of the gods in war?
>
> Not I. Whether in sportive mood or all aflame, I sing of feasts
> And savage maidens' wars against their boy-friends,
> Waged with their weaponry well-manicured – their finger-nails.
> As usual – I'm the joker in the pack.   20

1   *Varius*: elsewhere paired by Horace with Virgil as a poet who praised Augustus; here seen as an
           epic poet in Homeric style. Varius helped prepare the *Aeneid* for publication, see **R15**.41.
4   *ship and steed*: points to Agrippa's key role in Augustus' victories by sea (Naulochus, Actium) and
           land (Philippi).

5–9 these lines suggest that Horace cannot reach the heights of epic or tragedy (6–7 allude to Homer's
     Iliad and *Odyssey*, lines 8–9 to the tragic story of Pelops and the house of Agamemnon, a key topic
     of Greek tragedy but also treated by Varius (see line 1) in a lost tragedy *Thyestes*.

13–16 these lines allude to particular episodes in the battles of Homer's *Iliad*.

G23 Horace, *Odes* 1.12

This ode uses a framework from the Greek lyric poet Pindar to praise Augustus, invoking first gods and then
heroes who achieved deification (with some implication that Augustus will in time belong to these classes)
before turning to the great men of Roman history and climactically to Augustus himself. The twelfth stanza
(45–48) seems to refer to the wedding of Julia and Marcellus in 25 BC (see commentary), giving a rough
date for the poem. For a fuller discussion of the poem, see G.Williams, *Tradition and Originality in Roman
Poetry* (1968) 270–4.

> Goddess of History, tell us the man, the hero whom
> You choose to celebrate on lyre or high-pitched flute;
> The god, perhaps? Whose is the name that laughter-loving
> Echo returns
>
> Upon the long-shadowed slopes of Helicon,   5
> High on Mount Pindus, or the snows of Haemus
> Whence the wild woodlands followed the golden
> Voice of Orpheus?
>
> By his mother's arts he could delay the tumbling
> Rivers' rage, the wild winds' courses, gently he   10
> Could entrance with tuneful strings to follow him
> The listening oaks.
>
> But where shall I begin, save as custom commands, with Jove
> The Father's praise, who rules the worlds of men and gods,
> Tempering the sea and earth and sky with the   15
> Cycle of the seasons.
>
> He, from whom is begotten nothing greater than he;
> He, to whom nothing exists alike or approximate.
> Yet second to him in honour Pallas asserts her claim,
> Pallas, mighty in battle,   20
>
> Nor shall I pass you in silence, Bacchus, the freedom-god,
> Nor Virgin Diana, hound of the wildest beasts;
> Nor you, terror of all with your arrows infallible,
> Phoebus Apollo.
>
> Heracles too shall I sing, and the children of Leda,   25
> Both famous for victories, one with his horses, in boxing
> The other. As soon as their star shines out on high
> Bright for the sailor
>
> Down from the cliffs sink the waves whipped up by the gale;
> Submissive the winds, and the storm-clouds scatter in fear;   30
> At their command the menacing waves sink back to the depths
> Of the ocean's embrace.

Romulus next after these shall I name – or the quiet kingdom of
Numa Pompilius? Tarquin perhaps, lord of the proud *fasces*?
Hesitation abounds. Shall I tell, perhaps, of Cato's   35
Illustrious death?

Regulus, the Scaurus family, and Paullus so prodigal
Of his great spirit at Cannae, when Hannibal triumphed –
These with my far-famed native Muse I shall honour
With gratitude – Fabricius also,   40

Whom cruel poverty reared for war, Camillus, and Curius, too,
With his un-barbered hair – poverty and the hard life
On old ancestral farms, with life's exigencies,
Gave him the skills.

Tree-like and imperceptible as age, the glory grows   45
Of the Marcelli; conspicuous among them all the star
Of Julius shines, like the moon's light among
Heaven's lesser fires.

Father and Guardian of the human race,
Offspring of Saturn, into your care the Fates   50
Have given great Caesar. Long may you reign
With Caesar as lieutenant.

Whether the conquered Parthians, who threaten even now
Our Latium, he leads in deserving triumph,
Whether the peoples of the eastern shores,   55
Chinese and Indians,

As adjutant of Jove with equity he'll rule the earth's
Wide bounds, while you, with mighty chariot, shake
All Olympus, and on the sacred groves of godlessness
Discharge avenging thunderbolts.   60

1   *Goddess of History*: Clio, one of the Muses.
5–6   *Helicon*: a mountain in Boeotia, traditional home of the Muses. *Pindus* and *Haemus* are famed
         mountains in N. Greece.
9   *his mother's arts*: the mother of the poet Orpheus was Calliope, another of the Muses.
25   *the children of Leda*: Castor and Pollux, sometimes collectively called the Dioscuri, great semi-
         divine heroes of Greek mythology and athletics, protectors of sailors.
33–4   *Romulus … Numa*: the founder and the religious-minded second king of Rome respectively.
         Tarquin's proud fasces: a reference to Tarquin the Proud, the last Roman king, ejected in 510 BC
         for tyrannical abuse of power (hence the reference to the *fasces*, the bundle of rods symbolising the
         royal power to punish subjects, inherited by the consuls of the Republic).
36   *Cato's illustrious death*: Cato the Younger, who fought for the Republican side against Julius Caesar
         in the Civil War and committed suicide after defeat at the battle of Thapsus in 46 BC, a death which
         was the subject of much contemporary encomium. He was praised by Augustus (see **H43**). Cato's
         anomalous inclusion here in a list of much earlier Romans has been seen as an allusion to Horace's
         own youthful Republicanism (see on **G25** below).
37–44   More Republican heroes: Horace himself narrates the story (possibly fictional) of M. Atilius
         Regulus in *Odes* 3.5 = **G27**; *the Scauri* probably refers to two members of the noble Aemilii Scauri
         who were prominent in Roman politics about 100 BC; *Paullus* is L. Aemilius Paullus, killed fighting

against Hannibal in the great Roman defeat at Cannae (216 BC), while C. *Fabricius* Luscinius and
M.*Curius* Dentatus were notable generals and politicians of the first half of the third century BC,
both often seen as types of antique virtue, and M. Furius *Camillus* saved Rome in the 390's BC,
first by defeating Veii and then by ensuring the resettlement of Rome after its sack by the Gauls.

45–46 *The glory of the Marcelli*: a reference to a family distinguished in Roman history (esp. through M.
Claudius Marcellus, a great general in the Second Punic War), and in particular to the contemporary
M. Claudius Marcellus, nephew and designated heir of Augustus, who married Augustus' daughter
Julia in 25 BC (he died in 23 BC – see Virgil *Aeneid* 6.854ff, **G37**, and Propertius 3.18 = **G33** for
poetic obituaries; and **J29**–**J32** for Marcellus generally).

46–47 *The star of Julius*: the comet seen at Julius Caesar's funeral and thought to represent his divinity;
see **H3**, **K45**; here it symbolises the Julian family in the context of Julia's marriage to Marcellus.

53–56 *Parthians …Chinese …Indians*: the Parthians represent a propaganda target under Augustus (see
on *Epode* 7.9 = **G3** and **N41**–**N46**), while the even more distant Chinese and Indians (the latter sent
ambassadors to Augustus – **N39**–**N40**) are included to stress the worldwide potential of Augustus'
military power (cf. the similar list of conquered peoples at Virgil *Aeneid* 8.720–28, **G38**).

G24 Horace, *Odes* 1.37 Suicide of Cleopatra

This poem celebrates the news of Cleopatra's suicide on 10 August 30 BC. Horace had already celebrated
her defeat at Actium (2 September 31) in *Epode* 9 = **G5**. Both poems follow the official line, playing down
the role of Antony to present the conflict as a foreign rather than civil war, and exploiting Roman prejudices
against female rulers and orientals to present Cleopatra as a monster. On her death Horace is more
magnanimous: some interpreters see this as striking an independent note, others as again following
Augustus' lead.

> Come now, my boon companions, now's the time
> To drink, to dance, beating the earth with foot
> Unfettered, and with feasts worthy of the Salii to deck
> The couches of our gods – aye, now's the time!
>
> For it were sacrilege before to draw up Caecuban   5
> From ancestral cellars, while that queen
> Was plotting demented ruin for the Capitol,
> Planning our empire's funeral rites
>
> With her contaminated crew of men
> Diseased by vice, herself without restraint   10
> In hoping for what she fancied and drunk
> With fortune's sweetness. But she came to her senses
>
> When scarcely one ship survived the fire,
> And her mind crazed on Mareotic wine
> Was brought back to real terrors, when Caesar   15
> Pursued her as she flew from Italy,
>
> Pressing on with his oars, like a hawk
> Against gentle doves or a swift hunter
> Against a hare in the snowy plains
> Of Thessaly, his aim to load with chains   20
>
> The doom-laden monster. Seeking
> A nobler death, she did not in woman's fashion
> Tremble at the sword, nor with her swift fleet
> Reach secret coasts for safety.

She dared to gaze with face serene on her   25
Fallen palace, and bravely grasped
Savage serpents, to drain their dark
Venom through her body's veins.

Determined on death, she grew fiercer yet,
Disdaining to be brought, a queen no more,   30
By harsh Liburnian galleys to be paraded,
No humble woman, in a proud triumph.

3–4	At *supplicationes* (days of public rejoicing after victories etc.: cf. *RG* 4.2), temples were opened and images of the gods placed on couches, where ordinary citizens placed offerings. Horace suggests that this time the gods should get especially lavish offerings: the Salii were priests (cf. on *Aeneid* 8.663–4 and **L2**) who were renowned for their splendid dinners.
5	*Caecuban*: from Fundi, in southern Latium, one of the most highly prized wines of Italy.
13	*scarcely one ship*: greatly exaggerated – Octavian's forces did use fire at Actium, but Antony and Cleopatra escaped with over sixty ships (Plutarch, *Antony* 66–68), and most of the rest of their fleet surrendered intact.
14	*Mareotic*: a sweet wine, the most famous wine of Egypt.
16	*from Italy*: another exaggeration: in the war Cleopatra remained on the east side of the Adriatic.
17ff	Horace glosses over the eleven-month gap between the Actium battle and Cleopatra's death.
31	*Liburnian galleys*: small galleys, used to decisive effect at Actium because of their greater manoeuvrability.

G25   Horace, *Odes* 2.7.   **After the amnesty**

This ode greets the return to Italy of Pompeius, an otherwise obscure old friend of Horace, with whom he had fought against Octavian at Philippi. But this recall of youthful opposition is no statement of present political independence; the initial question 'who has now restored you to citizenship?' praises the amnesty of Octavian which allowed such former enemies to return, and after nearly twenty years Horace is amusingly ironic about his lack of military success in the long-distant Republican defeat.

My friend, together we often risked our very lives,
When Brutus led our armies – who has now restored
You to citizenship, to your ancestral gods,
And to the skies of Italy?

Pompey, oldest of all my friends, with whom so oft   5
I drank away the dilatory day with undiluted vintages,
And garlands in my hair, gleaming with scented oils
Of Syrian cinnamon.

Together at Philippi we fought and routed fled in panic,
When, coward that I was, I threw away my shield;   10
Courage was broken there and menaces proved empty
Bluster, where our soldiers bit the dust.

Terror took hold of me, but Mercury swiftly concealed me
In the dense fog of war and through the enemy bore me away;
But battle's retreating breakers sucked you back   15
And tossed you on the stormy waves of war.

So now, in thanks to Jupiter, we pay the banquet pledged
So long ago; weary with war's long rigours lay your limbs
Beneath my laurel tree, and show no mercy to those
Captive wine-jars laid by for this day.   20

Pack up your troubles in our shining drinking-cups
To overflowing filled with best Massic vintage; pour
Perfumes in plenty from enormous conch-shells;
Whose is the task to hasten to prepare

Coronals of myrtle and green parsley sprays? Whom   25
Will the dice of Venus declare master of revelry?
Madder than wild Bacchanals I shall rave. Such ecstasy
Is sweet, when friends come home again.

G26   Horace, *Odes* 3.3

This and the two following poems belong to the group of six solemn 'Roman Odes' (*Odes* 3.1–6) which form a distinct group. They are all in the same metre, and deal with solemn moral themes; a number of them make reference to Augustus and current political circumstances.

   This poem opens with a statement of the doctrine that a man may attain divinity by exceptional services, with an apparently incidental reference to Augustus (see general introduction to Horace). The case of Romulus-Quirinus leads on to the speech of Juno permitting his deification. In Juno's speech he develops the Virgilian theme of Rome's imperial destiny. The final stanza (lines 69–72) provides an ironic and distancing conclusion, repeating the familiar disclaimer of lyric poetry's suitability for epic themes.

   Suetonius (*Julius* 79.3) reports a rumour (doubtless false) that Julius Caesar contemplated moving the capital of the empire from Rome to Alexandria or Ilium (the former Troy). The stress which Horace places on the danger of refounding Troy probably relates not to this rumour, but to Antony's supposed eastern designs. Horace will have been well aware that Augustus had no intention of moving the capital. The use of the name Augustus shows that the poem was written after January 27 BC.

A man who is just and tenacious of purpose
Is not shaken from his firm resolve
By inflamed citizens urging wrong courses, nor
By the oppressive tyrant's frown, nor by the South Wind,

Turbulent lord of the storm-tossed Adriatic,   5
Nor by the mighty hand of thundering Jupiter.
If the universe should fall shattered,
The ruins will strike him undismayed.

By this virtue Pollux and the wandering Hercules
Strove and attained the stars' fiery heights,   10
By whose side Augustus shall recline
Imbibing nectar through radiant lips.

By this you earned the same reward, Father Bacchus,
Borne by your tigers, dragging the chariot-yoke
On untamed necks. By this Quirinus escaped   15
Acheron, brought by the horses of Mars,

While Juno spoke these welcome words to
The gods gathered in council: 'Ilium, Ilium,
A doom-laden, unchaste judge and a foreign woman
Have brought you down to dust.   20

From the day Laomedon broke contract and denied
The gods their covenanted wages, you were condemned –
You and your people and your fraudster leader,
Forfeit to chaste Minerva and to me.

No more does Paris, her infamous guest, shine   25
For the Spartan adulteress; no more does
Priam's perjured house with Hector's help
Break back the waves of warrior Achaeans.

The war, prolonged by our disputes, now
Is over. Forthwith I lay my grievous   30
Wrath aside. My hated grandson, whom
That Trojan priestess bore, I give back

To Mars. I shall suffer him to enter
The abodes of light and there to sip
Sweet draughts of nectar and to be   35
Enrolled among the gods' calm ranks.

As long as the broad seas rage between Ilium
And Rome, then let her exiles reign
In happiness wheresoever they wish;
As long as the cattle-herds trample the tombs   40

Of Priam and Paris and wild beasts hide
Their cubs unharmed among them, then let
The gleaming Capitol stand, and the Medes,
Triumphed over, get laws from fierce Rome.

Feared far and wide, may Rome extend her name   45
To earth's farthest boundaries, where
The midway sea divides Europe from Africa,
And where brimming Nile waters his fields.

Stronger to spurn the lure of gold,
Buried (and better so when earth conceals it),   50
Rather than harvest it for human use, with hands
Greedy to plunder every sacred thing,

With her armies she will reach whatever boundaries
Constrain the world, eager to view
Where noonday sun-fire dances with the heat,   55
Or where clouds and rainstorms swirl in manic rout.

Such are the fates I tell for warlike Quirites,
But on these terms: let them not seek
Through too much piety or confidence in power,
To build again the roofs of ancestral Troy.   60

Fraught with ill-omen shall be Troy's re-birth;
Troy's destiny re-born shall repeat her doom;
And I myself shall lead her conquerors,
I, sister of Jupiter, and his consort too.

And if a third time the brazen walls should arise   65
With Phoebus' help, then thrice again should Troy
Perish at my Argive warriors' hands, thrice should its wives
As captives lament their husbands lost and sons.'

This will not suit my playful lyre. Where
Are you heading, Muse? Cease wilfully   70
To report the speeches of the gods and
Diminish great themes with little metres.

16   *Acheron*: one of the rivers of Hades.
18ff   According to legend Troy was captured by two successive Greek forces: the first was led by
        Heracles (Hercules) against King Laomedon, the second by Agamemnon against Priam.
32   *Trojan priestess*: Ilia or Rhea Silvia, a Vestal Virgin, who gave birth to Romulus after being seduced
        by the god Mars, son of Jupiter and Juno.
47   *midway sea*: the Straits of Gibraltar.
57   *Quirites*: Romans.

G27   Horace, *Odes* 3.5

In this poem (written after January 27: line 2) Horace opens by anticipating military victory against the Britons
and Parthians and then passes to a re-telling of the Regulus story, with a speech for Regulus matching that
for Juno in *Odes* 3.3. Marcus Atilius Regulus, consul in 256 BC, had taken the war to the Carthaginians by
invading Africa; he won an initial victory, but was then defeated and captured. The story of his return home
is legendary, but was in circulation at least by the later second century. In the event Augustus left Britain
alone and struck a deal with Parthia under which the prisoners were returned, without payment of ransom.

In heaven his thunder taught us Jupiter
Is king. Augustus will be held a god
Amongst us, when to the empire
He adds the Britons and grim Persians.

Have Crassus' soldiers lived on,   5
Disgraced husbands to barbarian wives?
Woe for the senate, for tradition overturned!
Have Marsians and Apulians grown old

Under a Median king, bearing arms for in-laws,
Forgetting the sacred shields, the Roman name,   10
The toga and eternal Vesta, while Jupiter's
Temple and the city of Rome still stand?

He saw it all, prophetic Regulus,
When he refused disgraceful terms
And feared pernicious precedent,   15
Bringing ruin upon the coming age,

Unless the captive youths should die
Unpitied. 'With my own eyes,' he cried,
'I saw standards fixed to Punic shrines
As trophies, and weapons seized from soldiers   20

Without bloodshed. With my own eyes I saw
Wrists pinned behind the free backs of citizens,
And the gates of Carthage standing open, and their fields,
Once wasted by our warfare, under plough.

No doubt a ransomed soldier, bought with gold,   25
Returns to fight more fiercely! Expense you
Add to shame. Once doctored with dye,
Wool never reclaims its lost colours.

True manhood, once lost, does not care
To be restored to decadents. If a doe   30
Fights who slips the tightened toils
Of hunters' nets, then will a soldier prove brave

Who trusted himself to treacherous enemies,
And the Carthaginians will be crushed in a second
War by him who tamely once felt straps   35
On his bound back arms, fearing to die.

Not knowing whence he takes his life,
Such a man has mixed peace with war.
For shame! O mighty Carthage, towering
Over Italy's ruins of disgrace!'   40

Men tell the story still: of how he deemed
Himself disfranchised, spurned his chaste wife's kiss;
Moved his own children off; and fiercely
Turned his manly gaze upon the ground,

Until with advice never elsewhere given   45
He strengthened the senate's wavering resolve,
And amid his weeping friends
Hastened away, a peerless exile.

Too well he knew what horrors were prepared
By his barbarian torturer. Yet he brushed off   50
Kinsmen who blocked his way, and the Roman
People delaying his return,

As though leaving behind the lengthy dealings
Of his clients, with a lawsuit settled,
Heading off for rustic Venafrum   55
Or Lacedaemonian Tarentum.

4, 9   *Persians ... Median*: Parthian(s).
5   *Crassus' soldiers*: defeated by the Parthians at Carrhae in 53 BC.
8   *Marsians and Apulians*: Italian peoples (cf. *Odes* 1.2.39).
10   *sacred shields*: see on *Aeneid* 8.664, **G38**.
53 ff The comparison is with a senator of Horace's own day, leaving his business in the city for a period
       of leisure on a country estate or in one of the Greek cities of southern Italy. Venafrum was in
       Campania; Tarentum, on the instep of Italy, had been founded from Sparta (in antiquity usually
       known as Lacedaemon).

G28   Horace, *Odes* 3.6

As often in contemporary literature, the civil wars are here presented as divine punishment. Horace suggests that the gods sent the wars as requital for ancestors' offences (line 1), for neglect of their temples and worship (lines 2–4, 7–8), and for sexual licence (lines 17 ff). Lines 2–4 must be an implicit allusion to the restoration of the temples in 28 BC (*Res Gestae* 20.4), and the poem may have been composed about that time. However, its tone is largely pessimistic, particularly from lines 17 ff on. It is unlikely that (as has often been supposed) Augustus made a first, unsuccessful attempt to pass laws about sexual morality about 28 BC (See **G16**).

Ancestral crimes, though innocent, you'll pay
The gods for, Roman, till you restore
Their temples, their crumbling shrines,
And images with black smoke besmirched.

Because you hold yourself less than the gods, you rule.   5
Hence your beginning; to this ascribe your end.
Neglected, the gods have visited many
Woes upon grief-stricken Italy.

Already twice Monaeses' and Pacorus'
Band have suppressed our unhallowed   10
Onslaughts and grin at having added
Our booty to their scanty ornaments.

Almost, pre-occupied with civil strife,
By Dacian and Ethiopian was our Rome
Destroyed – the latter fearsome with his fleet,   15
More skilled the Dacian with his arrow-flight.

Fertile in sin our times stained first
The marriage-bed, the family, the home.
Sprung from this fount, disaster's flood has rolled
Across our fatherland and populace.   20

The maiden ready for marriage delights
To learn Ionic dances and acquires
Accomplishments. To her very fingertips
Her thoughts run all on unchaste love.

Soon she's hunting younger adulterers   25
At her husband's parties, not choosing
Partners for forbidden pleasures
Snatched in haste with the lights away,

But going openly with whoever asks
With her husband in the know,   30
Whether it's a salesman or a Spanish ship's
Captain, big spender purchasing her shame.

Not from such parents sprang the youths
Who stained the sea with Punic blood,
Smote Pyrrhus, mighty Antiochus   35
And dread Hannibal. For these

Were manly offspring of a rustic stock,
The sons of soldiers, taught to turn the soil
With Sabellian mattocks, homeward then return
Obeying their strict mother's call,   40

Bearing their load of timber for the fire,
While waning Sun shifts shadows on the hills,
Frees up the oxen's yoke, and brings the happy hour
Behind his own departing chariot wheels.

What has destructive Time not rendered worse?   45
Our parents, more degenerate than their sires,
In us have fathered still more rotten stock –
And yet more prone to vice will be our heirs.

5–6   The Romans traditionally regarded their empire as reward for their piety to the gods.
9   *Already twice* ...: apparently referring to Parthian victories over L. Decidius Saxa in 40 BC (won by
       Pacorus, son of King Orodes) and over some of Antony's forces in 36 BC (in which the Parthian
       noble Monaeses may have played a part).
13   *civil strife*: the Actium war.
14   *Dacian*: this people beyond the Danube was commonly regarded as a threat at this period. *Ethiopian*:
       poetic licence for Egyptians (the Ethiopians' northern neighbours).
34   *stained the sea*: in the naval victories of the First Punic War (264–241 BC).
35   *Pyrrhus*: this Greek king came to the aid of Tarentum in 280 BC and won victories over the Romans;
       but he himself suffered heavy losses, and he withdrew after a defeat in 275 BC. *Antiochus*: Antiochus
       III, king of Syria defeated by the Romans in Greece and Asia Minor in 191–189 BC.
39   *Sabellian*: the Roman name for the Oscan-speaking peoples of the central Apennines.

G29   Horace, *Odes* 3.14

Augustus was absent from Rome from summer 27 to 24 BC, chiefly in Spain. During this period he began
the conquest of north-west Spain and suffered a serious illness. Here Horace celebrates his return, first in
the manner of a herald proclaiming a public rejoicing (1–12) and then as though organising a private party
of his own (13–28).

Like Hercules, People of Rome, Caesar, lately said
To have sought the laurel whose price is death,
Now seeks home and hearth again, a conqueror
    From the Spanish shore.

Rejoicing in her unique husband, let his wife   5
Make sacrifice to the just gods and come forth,
And our glorious leader's sister, and, seemly
    With suppliant headbands,

The mothers of maidens and young men lately
Made safe. And you, lads, and lasses who've yet   10
To wed, from evil-omened words keep
    Clean your lips.

Truly this festal day will banish for me
Anxiety's black clouds; rebellion or violent
Death I need not fear while Caesar   15
    Holds the earth.

Go fetch me perfumes, slave, and garlands too,
And a jar of wine that can remember
The Marsian War, if there's a flask that escaped
    Marauding Spartacus. 20

A word as well to lovely-voiced Neaera,
Bid her come quickly, bunching her chestnut hair,
But if the spoil-sport doorman makes delay,
    Take yourself off.

Greying hair soothes spirits once 25
Eager for quarrels and violent brawling.
I'd not have stood for this in the heat of my youth,
    When Plancus was consul.

1   *Hercules*: said to have visited Rome on his way back from defeating the monster Geryon in Spain.
9–10   *lately made safe*: by Augustus' ending of civil war.
15–16   *Caesar holds the earth*: the phrase probably carries two meanings – Augustus' world rule and his remaining on earth until (like Hercules) he eventually becomes a god.
19ff   *Marsian War ... Spartacus ... Plancus was consul*: Horace slips in allusions to past upheavals which contrast with the peace enjoyed after Augustus' ending of civil war. The Marsian War is the Social War (91–87 BC); Spartacus led the slave rebellion of 73–71 BC; Plancus was consul in 42 BC, when Antony and Octavian defeated Brutus and Cassius at Philippi (with Horace fighting on the losing side).

G30   **Propertius 3.4**   **Expedition to Parthia (20 BC)**

This poem marks the Eastern campaign of 21–20 BC led by Tiberius, Augustus' stepson, though Augustus himself was technically supreme commander. This campaign was much anticipated as an Augustan project and was presented as long-postponed retribution for the Roman defeat by the Parthians at Carrhae in 53 BC (see lines 10–11 and note on 2.10.13–14, **G17**); its diplomatic success in obtaining the legionary standards lost by Crassus was proclaimed as a great military victory (**K14, N42**). Though making the right patriotic noises, Propertius' poem avoids simple propaganda by two means: the stress on the material gains to be got from this expedition (lines 1–3), and the picture of the poet himself as an inactive observer couched in his mistress' lap (lines 14–17). Lines 14–24 give a vivid imagined picture of a Roman triumph.

Caesar, our god, is meditating war on India's wealth; he plans
To plough the waters of the pearl-rich sea with his armadas.
Men of Rome, mighty will be the profit; Tiber, the furthest bounds
Of earth will now provide fresh triumphs for you, and Euphrates' streams
Shall flow beneath your laws. Too late a province, Parthia 5
Shall yield to civic order and Italian lictors' rods,
And Parthian spoils shall come to know Jupiter, Latium's god.
Forward! Away! Vessels well-tried in war, unfurl your sails!
You steeds of war, bend to the task you know so well!
All omens smile upon you – such is my song. Take your revenge 10
For Crassus and his slaughtered soldiery! Write a new page of glory
For the history books of Rome!

O Father Mars, and Sacred Vesta's flames of destiny,
Hearken to this my prayer: grant that before I die the day may come
When I shall see Caesar's chariots weighted down with spoils, 15
His horses shying back and shying back again before
The People's cheers, while cushioned in my darling's soft embrace

I turn to gaze, and from their placards read of captured cities,
See the arrows fired in retreat by Parthians, see the bows
Of trousered soldiers, see their captive kings seated below their weaponry.   20
O Venus, guard your children: grant that the head and offspring
Of Aeneas' line whom you now see alive may live for ever.
Theirs be the booty earned by their labours; for me it is enough
To live to cheer them onward down the Sacred Way.

G31   Propertius 3.11   Cleopatra

This poem integrates Propertius' depiction of the life of love, and of the lover's 'enslavement' by his mistress
with political concerns: this framework is used to give the standard Augustan propaganda version of the
battle of Actium (foreign war against weird and evil Orientals) by suggesting that Antony was another lover
enslaved by a mistress (Cleopatra).

Why so surprised to find my life turned upside down by woman? Why surprised
That I, though man, am subject to woman's laws, and captive dragged behind
Her chariot wheels? Your charge is cowardice; the charge is base and false.
Her yoke I cannot shatter nor can I break the chains of bondage.
Who better than the sailor knows his doom is coming on the wind?   5
Who better than the soldier learns from his wounds to be afraid?
Gone are my careless days of youth when I too loved to boast
Like you. Learn now from this my catalogue – and be afraid.

Medea, witch of Colchis, beneath the yoke of adamant once drove
Those fire-breathing bulls, and sowed in the warrior-bearing earth   10
The seeds of battle. She closed the guardian serpent's fearsome jaws
That so to Aeson's palace might be carried off the fleece of gold.
Penthesilea, a Maeotian, dared once to assault the navy of the Greeks,
A savage archer queen fighting from horseback against ships with arrows.
But when from her brow her conqueror stripped her golden helmet,   15
Victor was vanquished, man was overcome by woman's lovely form.
Omphale, lovely queen of Lydia, who in the waters of Lake Gyges bathed,
Gained beauty's fair renown to such degree that Heracles, whose might
Established pillars at the confines of a world he pacified, for her
Performed with rough hands a woman's work, carding her task of wool.   20
Queen Semiramis founded Babylon, the Persians' capital, and raised
On high its massive walls, solid with brick, and built so wide
That on those rampart-walks twin chariots opposed could drive
Towards each other, yet their sides not graze nor axles touch.
Euphrates' stream she led right through the heart of her own citadel,   25
Bactra she did command to bow the knee in homage to her rule.
Why should I tell of heroes? Why convict the very gods of infamy?
Even great Jove has brought disgrace upon himself and on his household.

Why should I tell of her that lately brought disgrace on Roman arms,
Sampled the sexual favours of her household slaves, and then   30
Issued the price and invoice of her shameful marriage:
The walls of Rome and Senate cowed to her royal command?
O guilty Alexandria! Egypt, a land most aptly shaped for treachery;
Memphis, by Rome's disasters so often stained in blood,

Whose sands robbed Pompey of three triumphs due.   35
O Rome, from your great name no day can ever wipe this blemish out.
Better for you by far, great Pompey, if your funeral had gone out
From Naples on Phlegrean fields, or destiny decreed submission to a father-in-law.
To think that the harlot queen of cursed Canopus, born of the blood
Of Philip, whose mark of shame is for ever branded on the Roman's brow,   40
Should dare to match against our Jupiter her barking Anubis,
Should dare to force our Tiber to endure the threats of Egypt's Nile,
And with her rattling castanets should dare to drown out Roman trumpets,
Or with her puny rowing boats to chase Rome's great Illyrian galleys,
Or dare to stretch her foul mosquito nets across Tarpeia's rock   45
And issue judgements from the place where Marius' arms and statues stand.
What profit is there now that once we broke the axes of Tarquinius,
Whose life of arrogance once earned for him a name to match his pride,
If we must then endure a woman's rule? Enjoy your triumph, Rome,
And in your safety pray the gods to grant Augustus length of days.   50
But yet back to the wandering streams of trembling Nile you fled,
And soon, O Queen, upon your hands you felt the chains of Romulus.
I saw those arms which felt the deadly bite of sacred serpents,
Those limbs I saw as they embraced death's hidden paths of sleep.
"Rome, you had naught to fear with such a citizen to guard you",   55
She cried, her speech confused by endless draughts of undiluted wine.
Our city, high upon her seven hills, ruler of all the world,
Cringed at the fear of war and shook to hear a woman's threats.
Where now the spoils of Hannibal, where now the monuments
Of conquered Syphax, and the fame of Pyrrhus crushed beneath our feet?   60
Curtius filled the Lake to earn his monument of fame;
Decius upon his charger riding to death broke through the battle lines;
Horatius' path, the Track of Cocles, tells of demolished bridges;
And one there is, Corvinus, to whom the raven gave his name.
Our walls by gods were founded and by gods will always be defended.   65
While Caesar lives our Rome need scarcely fear great Jupiter himself.
Where now the navies of the Scipios? Where now Camillus' standards?
Where now the Bosporus, so lately captured by the might of Pompey?
Apollo, Lord of Leucas, will relate how all our enemies were put to flight,
And how one single day could overturn a mighty armament of war.   70
Sailor, remember Caesar, whether your course be outward bound
Or homeward; aye, in every corner of the Ionian sea, remember Caesar!

29   *lately*: in fact some years before (this poem may have been published as much as a decade after
      Actium), but much more recently than the mythological examples given in lines 9–26.
31   *shameful marriage*: note that Antony is invidiously unnamed here.
35   *sands*: refers to Pompey's notorious murder on the shores of Egypt in 48 BC on the orders of Ptolemy
      XIII, Cleopatra's brother and then consort. *His three triumphs*: Pompey's remarkable military
      record (triumphs in 81, 71 and 62 BC) was of course matched by the three simultaneous triumphs
      celebrated by Caesar in 29 BC, including one for the battle of Actium narrated in this poem.
39–40 Cleopatra (like Antony in 31) is invidiously unnamed. The phrase 'blood of Philip' refers to the
      Macedonian origin of her Ptolemaic Egyptian dynasty.
45–6 *Tarpeia's rock...the place where …*: the Capitol.
55   Cleopatra's supposed last words are improbably pro-Augustan.

60   *Syphax*: a Numidian ally of Hannibal conquered by Rome in the Second Punic war; *Pyrrhus* – the
        king of Epirus, who invaded Italy in the 270's BC and was defeated by Rome after much difficulty.
61–4   Another catalogue of early Roman heroes, this time celebrated by monuments in the Forum
        Romanum. Curtius, probably 5C BC, was supposed to have ridden his horse into a chasm in the
        Forum (the *lacus Curtius*) in order to save Rome, while various members of the Decii were supposed
        to have sacrificed themselves by riding alone at the enemy after vowing their lives in exchange for
        Roman victory. Horatius Cocles was supposed to have held a bridge across the Tiber to prevent the
        Etruscan Porsenna from capturing Rome at the end of the 6C BC, and M.Valerius Corvinus was
        supposed to have enjoyed the help of a raven in fighting the Gauls in 390 BC (see **K22**).
67   For Camillus and the Scipios see note on Virgil, *Georgics* 2.168–9, **G10**.
68   *Bosporus, so lately captured*: a reference to Pompey's victory against Mithridates in 63 BC, only
        relatively recently compared with the long-ago events of the previous line.

G32   Propertius 3.12   To Postumus 'On going to the wars'

This poem suggests the emotional cost of the Parthian expedition of 21–20 BC mentioned in 3.4 = **G30**, once
again raising the issue of material gain, and again showing some ambivalence about this particular Augustan
military enterprise. The rest of the poem praises Galla's fidelity, comparing it to that of Penelope to Odysseus.

> Postumus, how could you bear to leave your Galla all alone
> Lamenting, and ride off to war behind the gallant standards of Augustus?
> Was glory from the spoils of Parthia worth so much more
> Against your Galla's constant prayers for you to stay with her?
> May God forgive me, but I call a curse on all such avaricious men
> And all who choose a soldier's arms before the arms of their true loves.

G33   Propertius 3.18   Death of Marcellus

This poem laments the death at the sea-resort of Baiae in 23 BC of Marcellus, son of Augustus' sister Octavia
and the aristocrat M. Claudius Marcellus, married in 25 to Augustus' daughter Julia (celebrated in Horace
Odes 1.12; see **G23**) and Augustus' intended heir. For Virgil's parallel lament in *Aeneid* 6 see **G37**.

> Here, where the sea is barricaded from the black waters of Avernus
> And plays instead among the stagnant pools of Baiae's balmy waters,
> Here where the Trojan trumpeter, the dead Misenus, lies in the sands,
> And Hercules' highway, arduously built, re-echoes to the sea-roar;
> Here where that Theban-born divinity once came as benefactor   5
> And visited the cities of mankind, whose cymbals clashed to honour him;
> Here …. But alas, abominable Baiae, profoundly guilty to the very core,
> Which hostile god has taken his abode within your waters? For it was here
> Marcellus died, here he bent his gaze to view the hellish waters
> Of Styx, and here around the infernal waters of the lake   10
> His sad ghost wanders now. Futile his pedigree; useless his virtues; wasted
> His mother's goodness, and his own close kinship with the house of Caesar.
> What profit now the crowds that flocked but yesterday to honour him
> Beneath the theatre's waving awnings, what profit all his mother's tender care?
> Marcellus is dead. Poor lad, he stood only within the twentieth year of life.   15
> So many virtues in so small a space as life's last tally closes his account.
> Go now; lift up your heart with pride; revel in your triumphant fantasies
> With the whole theatre rising to its feet and ringing your applause.
> Go deck yourself in finery which Attalus of Pergamum might envy; go
> And at the Great Games glitter with your gems. Your funeral pyre   20
> Will have them all. For to those flames, whether of high estate or low,
> We all shall come. Dark is death's road, but down that road must go

All men, and all must seek to bribe the triple barking throats of Cerberus;
All men must board the universal barge of Charon, grim ferryman of Styx.
Though fearful man may make a hiding place of brass or iron, Death   25
Will always find him out and head first drag him from his hiding place.
Good looks could not preserve Nireus, nor strength Achilles; nor his wealth
Born of the golden streams of Pactolus sufficed to save rich Croesus.
Into your hands, grim ferryman, whose vessel bears the souls of pious men,
Into your hands let them commend this corpse now emptied of life's breath.   30
Where once went Claudius, Sicily's conqueror, and by the road
That Caesar went, far from the ways of men Marcellus' soul has gone.

19   *Attalus of Pergamum*: the name of several Hellensitic kings of a rich state in Asia Minor.
20   *Great Games*: the *Ludi Romani*, celebrated by Marcellus as aedile in 23 BC.
31–2 These lines refer to the great forebears of Marcellus, his paternal ancestor C. Claudius Marcellus
      (see note on Virgil *Aeneid* 6.855, **G37**) and his maternal ancestor Julius Caesar, with some
      suggestion of apotheosis to match Caesar.

G34   Horace, *Epistles* 1.12.25–29   To Iccius – count your blessings

This epistle is addressed to Iccius, agent in charge of the estates of Agrippa (see on *Odes* 1.6 = **G22**) on the
rich island of Sicily. The news bulletin from Rome at the poem's end praises the victories of Agrippa himself
in Spain (**N48**) and of Tiberius, Caesar/Augustus' stepson, in the East (**N24**), about the time of the poem's
publication (20–19 BC).

Now, in case you do not know how things are at Rome: the Cantabrians
Have surrendered to Agrippa, while Armenia has fallen to the valour
Of Claudius Nero. Phraates of Parthia, acknowledging defeat
On bended knee, has now accepted Caesar's imperial power. Golden Plenty
From her abundant horn has poured out her harvest riches upon Italy.

G35   Horace, *Epistles* 1.16.27–9   Compliment to Augustus by Varius

The safety of Rome and of Caesar/Augustus are seen as indissolubly connected; both are under divine
protection. An ancient commentator on this poem tells us that Horace is here quoting from Varius' panegyric
to Augustus. On Varius see Horace *Odes* 1.6.1, **G22** and note.

Does Rome desire your safety, Caesar, more
Than you desire hers? We cannot know.
Jupiter knows the answer, He who cares for both alike;
It is his secret; may he always keep it so.

G36   Virgil, *Aeneid* 1.257–296   Jupiter's prophecy

The *Aeneid* opens with the shipwreck of Aeneas and his companions by a storm summoned by their enemy
Juno. The scene then passes to heaven, where Venus, Aeneas' mother, complains to Jupiter that his destiny
is not being fulfilled (1.229–53). Jupiter reassures her with the speech which forms this extract.

The Romans had two foundation legends, that of the Trojan Aeneas and that of Romulus, the founder of
the city of Rome. Although there were variant accounts (thus Ennius and others held Romulus to have been
Aeneas' grandson), the version followed by Virgil here had taken shape by the late third century BC when
the first histories of Rome were written, and became orthodox. According to this Aeneas founded Lavinium;
one of his sons founded Alba Longa and his descendants ruled there as kings; in due course one of Aeneas'
descendants, Romulus, founded Rome. The town of Lavinium, about fifteen miles south-west of Rome,
survived to Virgil's own day. Alba Longa, the supposed mother-city of the Latins in the Alban Hills south
of Rome, was believed to have been destroyed by Tullus Hostilius, the third king of Rome, but was in fact
legendary. The line of kings of Alba (see *Aeneid* 6.767–70, **G37**) was invented to bridge the gap between
the estimated dates of the destruction of Troy and the foundation of Rome. On the origins of these foundation
legends see T. J. Cornell, *The Beginnings of Rome* (1995), 57–73.

'Come lay your fears aside, Cytherea, for yet unchanged
And fixed stands your people's destiny. You shall see the city
And the promised walls of Lavinium; and high to the stars of heaven
You shall transport great-hearted Aeneas. My resolve does not change.   260
But now, since these fears gnaw at your heart, yet more shall I show you,
Unrolling the scroll of the fates to reveal their mysteries.
Aeneas shall wage a vast war in Italy, shall crush fearsome
Peoples, and shall establish for his men civil traditions
And city walls for their safeguard, until three summers   265
Have seen him reigning in Latium, and three winters have passed
Since he conquered the Rutulians. Thereafter, the boy,
Ascanius, bearing also now the name Iulus (Ilus it was
While Ilium stood), shall complete in rule each circling
Month for thirty long years. From its seat at Lavinium   270
He shall transfer his kingdom, building with mighty ramparts
The city of Alba Longa. Here for three hundred years
Shall endure the rule of Hector's race, till a priestess of royal blood
Named Ilia, pregnant by Mars, shall bring her twin sons to birth.
Then, prospering under the tawny cover of the wolf his nurse,   275
Romulus shall take over his nation, shall build city-walls
Of Mars, and from his own name shall call his people Romans.
No limits of space or time do I place upon them; to them I have given
An empire without bounds. Savage Juno, moreover,
Who now troubles with her terrors land, sea and heaven,   280
Shall alter her plans for the better, and with me shall nurture
The Romans, lords of the world, the race of the toga.
Such is my will. And, as centuries roll by, a time will come
When Assaracus' house shall bring to servitude Phthia
And famous Mycenae and lord it in conquered Argos.   285
There shall be born a Trojan of noble stock, Caesar,
Who shall extend empire to the Ocean and fame to the stars,
Julius his name, passed down from great Iulus.
One day, free from care, you shall welcome him, heaped
With the Orient's spoils, and he too shall be called upon in prayer.   290
Then shall the savage centuries lay wars aside and turn
To gentleness. Grey-haired Faith and Vesta, and Quirinus
With his brother Remus shall give laws. Then shall be closed
The gates of War, grim with their close-bolted bars of iron;
Within, unholy Rage shall sit on cruel weaponry,   295
Wrists pinioned behind back by a hundred knots
Of brass, roaring hideously from bloody mouth.'

257   *Cytherea*: 'of Cythera', a common epithet of Aphrodite/Venus, after her temple on this island off
      the south-east coast of the Peloponnese.
268   *Iulus*: for Virgil (as for the Elder Cato, cited by Servius, the ancient commentator on Virgil) the
      names Ascanius and Iulus were both borne by the son of Aeneas' Trojan wife Creusa. For Livy
      (1.3.1) Iulus was Creusa's son, and Ascanius was Aeneas' son by his Italian wife Lavinia, while
      others make Iulus the son of Ascanius (e.g. Dionysius 1.70).
273 ff The famous legend of the Wolf and the Twins. The virgin priestess of Vesta, Ilia, (also known as
      Rhea Silvia) was seduced by Mars. Her wicked uncle Amulius, king of Alba, set her twin infant
      sons Romulus and Remus adrift on the Tiber, but they were swept ashore and suckled by a wolf.

279 ff   *Juno ... shall alter*: Juno is reconciled to Aeneas and his destiny at the end of the *Aeneid* (12.791–842), but the reconciliation was not final, since her hostility was held to have continued until the Punic Wars. See also Horace, *Odes* 3.3 = **G26**.

283–5   Rome was effectively the dominant power in Greece from her victory in the Second Macedonian War (200–196 BC). From 146, when Macedonia was made a province, most of Greece was subject to the jurisdiction of its governor. The province of Achaea, comprising most of mainland Greece, was established by Augustus, probably in 27 BC. The Roman defeat of Greece is also anticipated at *Aeneid* 6.836–40, **G37**.

284   *Assaracus*: Aeneas' great-grandfather.
      Phthia: home of Achilles.

286   It is disputed whether the initial reference is to Julius Caesar, with a later switch of subject, or that there is deliberate ambiguity, or whether Virgil refers throughout to Octavian/Augustus.

290   The allusion to the '*Orient's spoils*' surely refers to the profits of the latter's war with Antony and Cleopatra (and probably also to an expected Parthian war). Thus 289–90 anticipate Augustus' deification, while 291ff go on to celebrate his ending of civil war.

292   *Quirinus*: a god early identified with Romulus.

293   *Remus*: said to have been killed in a dispute with his twin Romulus over the founding of Rome; his death is often taken as symbolic of Roman civil strife.

293–4   *closed the gates of War*: alludes to the closure of the gates of the shrine of Janus in 29 BC after Octavian's ending of civil war (cf. *RG* 13; Horace, *Odes* 4.15.8–9 = **G45**, **K47–K49**).

295–6   These lines evoke Apelles' painting of War later installed in the Forum of Augustus, (**K27**).

G37   Virgil, *Aeneid* 6.752–892   Pageant of Roman heroes

In Book 6 Aeneas visits the Underworld, accompanied by the Sibyl of Cumae. There he sees the souls of the dead and meets his father Anchises. In the final section of the book, Anchises sets out to inspire Aeneas to his remaining task by showing him souls waiting to be reborn – his own descendants and the future great men of Rome.

In this parade of what, apart from Augustus, were for his readers the great men of the Roman past, Virgil was clearly influenced by the Roman practice at funeral processions, when the deceased was accompanied by men impersonating his ancestors and wearing their death-masks. Praise of these ancestors was included in funeral orations, and such displays were regarded as inspiring contemporaries to emulate their achievements. Augustus was accompanied by such a parade of all the great men of the Roman past at his funeral in AD 14 (Dio 56.34.2). A similar parade in stone form was to be seen in the statues erected in the colonnades of the Forum of Augustus, opened in 2 BC, see **K20–K25**.

As at funerals, the great men are here grouped by families. First come Aeneas' own descendants, and here Virgil passes from Romulus via a celebration of the city of Rome to a panegyric of Augustus, in which he celebrates Augustus as destined to bring back a golden age and extend Roman power to the ends of the earth, and by implication looks forward to his deification. Next come men of other families: first the other kings, then the great men of the Republic, grouped by family and without any chronological order: great achievements are celebrated, but darker elements also intrude such as the Decii's self-sacrifice, the harsh punishments inflicted by Brutus and Torquatus, and the civil war between Caesar and Pompey. This section culminates in the second climax, the ringing declaration of the Romans' imperial mission (847–853). One family remains, the Marcelli, and the pageant ends with a poignant tribute to Augustus' nephew and intended heir Marcus Claudius Marcellus, who died in 23 BC. Later tradition relates the effect of Virgil reciting the passage to Augustus and his sister Octavia, mother of Marcellus, see **R15**, section 32.

Many scholars regard the overall tone and import of this passage as consistently upbeat and panegyrical. Others interpret it as more qualified, stressing pessimistic aspects.

Anchises ceased speaking, and drew his son, and with him
The Sibyl, into the midst of that noisy throng of souls.
Climbing a hillock whence he could see them all spread
In a long line before him, and could thus pick out
And identify each face as it came, he began once again.   755
'Come now, I shall speak of the glory due to fall to the Dardanian
Stock, and of the descendants from the Italian race
Which await, illustrious souls destined to enter

Our name. All this I'll tell you, and your own fate.
Look, there, you see the young man who leans on his unmetalled spear   760
And by lot has drawn the next place in the light. He is the first
To share Italian blood and ascend to the breezes above:
Silvius, an Alban name, your son to be born after your death,
Whom, the late child of your old age, your wife Lavinia
Shall rear in the woods, a king and a father of kings.   765
Through his offspring our line shall rule in Alba Longa.
Next to him, there, is Procas, glory of Troy's people, and Capys,
Numitor, too, and he whose name will renew yours,
Silvius Aeneas, your peer alike in piety and in arms
If ever he takes his place to reign in Alba.   770
What youths! Look at the strength they show and at
The civic crowns of oak which shade their brows!
These are the men to set citadels on the hilltops for you –
Nomentum and Gabii, Fidenae and Collatia's fortress,
Pometia and the castle of Inuus, Bola, and Cora too –   775
These will then be names, but now are nameless places.
Moreover, in time, a child of Mars shall join his grandfather,
Romulus, whom his mother Ilia shall bear, of Assaracus' line.
See how the twin crests stand so proudly over his helmet, and
How the father of the gods now marks him out with his own honour.   780
His, my son, his are the auspices under which that famous Rome
Shall match her empire to the bounds of earth, her spirit to Olympus,
And enclose by a wall seven citadels as one city, blessed
In the abundance of her sons, like the Berecyntian mother,
When she rides her chariot through Phrygia's cities,   785
Wearing her turret-crown, happy to be mother of gods, and clasping
To her embrace her hundred grandsons, all divinities, and tenants all
Of the high halls of heaven. Hither now turn your twin eye-beams
And see this race, your Romans. Here is Caesar and all
Iulus' offspring, destined to pass beneath the great vault of heaven.   790
This is the man, this is he whom so often you hear promised to you,
Augustus Caesar, son of a god, who shall bring back again
The age of gold to Latium, the very land where once
Old Saturn ruled, and shall spread our empire's bounds
Beyond the Garamantes and Indians, whose countries lie   795
Beyond the stars and the courses of time, and beyond
The highway of the sun, where Atlas, pillar of heaven, wheels
The firmament on his shoulders, studded with blazing stars.
Already now the Caspian kingdoms and the lands
Of Lake Maeotis tremble at oracles foretelling his coming,   800
And terror-struck the sevenfold estuaries of Nile are all astir.
Hercules, indeed, did not traverse the world so far, although he slew
The bronze-footed hind, and brought peace to the forests
Of Erymanthus, making all Lerna tremble at his bow. Nor did
Bacchus, who in triumph guides his chariot with vine-stem   805
Reins, driving his tigers down from Nysa's lofty crest.

Do we then hesitate still to enlarge our valour with deeds?
Does fear still deter us from setting our feet on Italian soil?
Who then is he, far off, marked out by his olive-branch
And bearing sacred emblems? I recognise the locks, the greybeard chin   810
Of the Roman king, who shall first found the city on laws,
Sent from tiny Cures and its poor land to mighty empire.
Next will follow one who shall shatter the nation's peace,
Tullus, who shall stir to arms men sunk in sloth and troops
No longer used to triumphs. Ancus is next, too boastful   815
And even now delighting too much in popular favour's breezes.
Do you now wish to see the Tarquin kings and the proud soul
Of Brutus the avenger, and the recovered *fasces*?
He shall be the first to take the consul's power and the savage axes,
And, when his sons stir up new wars, shall summon them   820
To punishment, though their father, for fair liberty's sake.
Unhappy man, however posterity shall judge that deed: for him
Love of his country and limitless desire for praise shall prevail.
See, the Decii, too, and far off the Drusi, and Torquatus, savage
With the axe, and Camillus, bringing back the standards.   825
As for those souls you see there, equal in their armour's brightness,
In concord are they now, for as long as they are kept within the night,
But alas, what a war they will rouse should they ever attain
To the daylight of life, what battles and slaughter together they'll raise,
The father-in-law descending from the towering Alps and Monaco's citadel,   830
And the son-in-law arrayed against him with the forces of the East.
O my children, do not let your hearts grow accustomed to such wars;
Do not twist the sword of her strength so supreme in your fatherland's heart.
Be first to show mercy, you who derive from Olympus your descent.
Throw down the weapons from your hands, O my blood.   835
That one, over there, shall drive his chariot to the Capitol
In triumph over Corinth, renowned for smiting the Achaeans.
And that one shall uproot Argos and Agamemnon's Mycenae,
And the Aeacid himself, the descendant of Achilles, great in arms,
And shall avenge the Trojan ancestors and Minerva's desecrated temples.   840
Great Cato, and Cossus, who could leave your praises unsung?
Who could omit the Gracchi, or the two Scipios, thunderbolts
Of war and bane of Libya, or Fabricius, powerful
In poverty, or you, Serranus, sowing seed in your furrow?
Where, Fabii, are you taking me, now weary? You are that Maximus,   845
The one man who by delaying restores our state.
Others, I do believe, will mould bronze more delicately
Into breathing statues, or fashion living faces from marble,
Will plead cases better, or plot with a pointer the movements
Of the heavens and expound the risings of the stars.   850
Roman, remember to rule the peoples by your empire
(These shall be your arts), to impose civilisation upon peace,
To spare those made subject and to war down the proud.'
So spoke Anchises, and as they were marvelling, added these words:

'See how Marcellus advances, conspicuous with his Rich Spoils,   855
A victor towering over all other men. Riding into battle,
He shall restore Roman fortunes, quelling a great uprising,
Shall lay low Carthaginians and rebel Gauls, and shall be
The third to hang up captured arms for father Quirinus.'

To this Aeneas replied, for another he saw walking alongside,   860
A youth, noble in appearance and in glittering armour,
But his brow was forlorn and downcast were his eyes.
'Who, father, is that, accompanying the man as he passes?
Is it his son or descendant, born of that same mighty line?   865
Why round him the buzzing throng? His is an air of greatness within.
Yet black night encircles his brow with the shadows of sorrow.'
As tears swelled in his eyes, father Anchises began once more.
'Son, seek not to know this mighty source of your people's distress.
Him the Fates will barely show to the world, and then permit him no more.   870
O Gods above, too mighty would the stock of Rome have seemed,
If this gift of yours had endured to be theirs. What a noise
Of the mourning of men shall come from that Field to Mars' great city!
What funeral rites will Tiber behold, flowing past the new-built burial-mound!
No youth of Trojan blood shall ever by promise so high   875
Raise the hopes of his Latin forebears. Nor, in the days to come,
Shall Romulus' land ever take such pride in its offspring.
Alas for his piety to gods and men! Alas for his old-fashioned faithfulness
And his right arm unbeaten in war! For none would have faced
Him in battle and lived, whether on foot he had confronted   880
The foe, or with his spurs he had scoured the flanks
Of his foam-spattered steed. Alas, poor boy, if only you could
Break fate's harsh decrees! You shall be Marcellus.
Give lilies from full hands. Let me scatter bright flowers and heap up
At least these offerings for my descendant's soul and so perform   885
Vain service.'

Thus they wandered far and wide throughout that region
And visited all that the broad plains of nether air had to show.
Having guided his son through each individual sight,
Anchises fired his heart with a yearning for the glory to follow,
Spoke of the wars which remained for him to fight,   890
Of the Laurentine peoples and Latinus' city, and taught him
How he might avoid or how endure each toil to come.

756   *Dardanian*: Trojan.
760   *unmetalled spear*: a spear without a metal tip was awarded as a Roman military distinction.
761–5   In the version followed by Virgil, Alba Longa was founded by Ascanius-Iulus, but after his death
        his half-brother Silvius took his place as its king. See further above, introduction to *Aeneid*
        1.257–296 = **G36** and note on 1.268.
772   *civic crowns of oak*: awarded to soldiers who saved citizens. See **H14, H20–H21**.
779   *twin crests*: obscure, but compare the 'twin flames' on Augustus' head at *Aeneid* 8.681.
784   *Berecyntian mother*: Cybele, the Great Mother, named here after her cult site at Mt Berecyntus.
        Her cult was brought from Asia Minor to Rome in 205 BC, and Augustus' house was close to her
        temple on the Palatine.

789   *Caesar*: perhaps deliberately ambiguous between Julius Caesar and his adopted son.

790   *Iulus' offspring*: the Iulii Caesares claimed descent from Aeneas' son Iulus.

793–4   *age of gold ... Saturn*: a Greek myth of the ages of man asserted that man had declined progressively from the first Golden Race. Here, as at *Georgics* 2.536–540 and *Aeneid* 8.319–327, Virgil combines this with the legend that Saturn, when expelled from heaven by his son Jupiter, became king in Latium, introduced agriculture and reigned in peace and prosperity.

795   *Garamantes*: a people dwelling on the edge of the Sahara. Virgil alludes to the recent campaign of the proconsul Lucius Cornelius Balbus, who triumphed in 19 BC. See **N9, N2f**.
        Indians: an allusion to the embassies they had sent to Augustus in 25, when he was in Spain, and in 20, when he was in the East. See **N39–N40**.

799   *Caspian kingdoms*: Augustus received embassies from the Iberians and Albanians to the west and the Medes to the south of the Caspian Sea (*RG* 31). Virgil may allude to them here.

800   *Lake Maeotis*: the Sea of Azov. The Scythians, who inhabited the region north of the Black Sea, sent an embassy to Augustus in 25, and at some point he received an embassy from 'Sarmatian kings from both sides of the river Tanais' (*RG* 31: the Tanais, the modern Don, flows into the Sea of Azov). Virgil may intend an allusion to these embassies here.

801   *Nile*: alluding to Augustus' conquest of Egypt. See **N31–N32**.

802 ff   Hercules and Dionysus/Bacchus were widely held to have been heroes who won divinity as a result of their achievements: Hercules' wide travels and benefactions, and Dionysus' eastern conquests as far as India (these were a new myth developed at the time of Alexander). Virgil thus implicitly alludes to Augustus' future deification (as also by placing Augustus immediately after Romulus, who was deified, and by referring to his divine adoptive father at line 792 and perhaps at line 789). See further the introduction to Horace and *Odes* 3.3.9 ff (**G26**).

809–17   Virgil refers to several of the kings of Rome: Numa Pompilius, Tullus Hostilius, Ancus Marcius, Tarquinius Priscus and Tarquinius Superbus. All of these would have been familiar to Virgil's readers from the first book of Livy's history, (see **D1**) published a few years before the *Aeneid*.

817–23   *Brutus*: L. Iunius Brutus, first consul in 509 BC, who was said to have played a leading part in the expulsion of Tarquin the Proud after his son's rape of Lucretia (whence '*avenger*') and to have put his own sons to death for conspiracy. His descendant, the assassin of Caesar, is inevitably called to mind.

818   *fasces*: bundles consisting of rods and an axe carried by attendants (lictors) as symbols of the power (*imperium*) of the principal magistrates of the Republic, as formerly of the kings. Later, when Roman citizens achieved the right to appeal to the people, the axes were left out within the city of Rome.

824   *Decii*: Publius Decius Mus, as consul in 340 BC, and his son of the same name as consul in 295 BC, were believed to have 'devoted' themselves to death in battle and so won the day for the Romans. They were regularly included in lists of exemplary feats by great Romans (as in Propertius 3.11.62 – **G31**).
        Drusi: a more surprising inclusion, possibly in compliment to Livia, who came from the family of the Livii Drusi (see **J26**). The best known member of the family was Marcus Livius Drusus, whose unsuccessful attempt to enfranchise the Italian allies during his tribunate in 91 led to the outbreak of the Social War.
        Torquatus: Titus Manlius Torquatus, one of the great commanders of the later fourth century, who had initially made his name by winning a duel with a Gaul. *Savage with the axe*: like Brutus, he executed his own son (in 340 BC, for disobeying his ban on single combat).

825   *Camillus*: Marcus Furius Camillus conquered Veii in 396 BC, and it was believed that in 390 BC, after the Gauls had sacked Rome, he attacked them as they withdrew and recovered the gold which had been paid to induce them to leave. Virgil's substitution of standards for gold here probably alludes to Augustus' recovery of standards from the Parthians (long expected, and finally achieved in 20 BC, see **N42**).

826–35   This passage refers, without naming them, to the civil war between Caesar and Pompey (who from 59 BC until her death in 54 BC had been married to Caesar's daughter Julia). Caesar might have been referred to with the Julii at 789, but is brought in here, out of family order.

834–5   Here Virgil alludes to the clemency which Caesar famously showed to the defeated Pompeians, but also appears to suggest that Caesar ought not to have begun the civil war.

836–40   For the Roman conquest of Greece presented as revenge for Troy see *Aeneid* 1.283–5, **G36**.

836   *That one*: Lucius Mummius, who, as consul in 146 BC, defeated the rebellious Achaean League (comprising most of southern Greece) and sacked Corinth.

838   *That one*: Lucius Aemilius Paullus, who, as consul in 168 BC, defeated Perseus, the last king of Macedon, at Pydna. Perseus claimed descent from Achilles through his mother. Argos and Mycenae were not directly affected by this war, but the Macedonian kings claimed to be of Argive origin.

841   *Cato*: the Elder, famous for his censorship of 184–183 BC and one of the great figures of the first half of the second century.
       Cossus: Aulus Cornelius Cossus, the second winner of the *spolia opima* (see below on line 855).

842   *Gracchi*: successive members of this family, all bearing the name Tiberius Sempronius Gracchus, had been outstanding commanders and senators. However, the best known members of the family were the controversial tribunes, Tiberius and Gaius, both of whom died in civil strife.
       Scipios: Scipio Africanus the elder, whose defeat of Hannibal at Zama in 202 BC ended the Second Punic War, and his grandson by adoption, Scipio Africanus the younger (Aemilianus), who captured and destroyed Carthage in 146 BC.

843   *Fabricius*: Gaius Fabricius Luscinus, consul in 282 BC and 278 BC during the war against Pyrrhus, often cited as an exemplar of the supposed frugality of Roman leaders in early times.

844   *Serranus*: Gaius Atilius Regulus, consul in 267 BC and 256 BC.

845   *Maximus*: Quintus Fabius Maximus Cunctator ('the Delayer'). One of the principal commanders of the Second Punic War, Fabius successfully implemented the strategy of avoiding battle with Hannibal, first during his dictatorship in 217 BC after the disastrous defeat at Lake Trasimene.

846   This line is a quotation, slightly adapted, of a celebrated line of Ennius about Fabius.

847–53 The classic statement of the Roman imperial mission. Virgil concedes superiority in the arts to the (unnamed) Greeks, but asserts Roman military pre-eminence.

853   Romans had traditionally claimed to observe this principle. Compare *RG* 3.2; Horace, *Carmen Saeculare* 51–2 (**L28**).

855   *Marcellus*: Marcus Claudius Marcellus defeated the Gauls in the Po valley in 222 BC and was one of the chief Roman commanders in the Second Punic War.
       Rich Spoils: *spolia opima*, spoils taken from an enemy commander and dedicated by the Roman who had killed him. Such spoils were reputed to have been dedicated only three times: by Romulus, by Cossus in the later fifth century (see line 841), and by Marcellus in 222. But see **P3–P4** for a claim in 29 BC, disingenuously denied by Augustus.

859   *Quirinus*: Virgil here follows a variant tradition. Other authorities hold that *spolia opima* were always dedicated in the small temple of Jupiter Feretrius on the Capitol, see **P3** and **K21**.

873   *Field*: the Campus Martius ('Field of Mars'), where the imperial dead were cremated.

874   *burial mound*: the huge Mausoleum of Augustus, in the Campus Martius, completed in 28, the regular burial place of members of Augustus' family. His nephew Marcellus was the first to be buried there: for his funerary inscription, see **J32**.

891   *Laurentine ... Latinus*: in Book 7, on arrival at the Tiber mouth, Aeneas encounters the Laurentes, dwelling south of the Tiber, and their king Latinus.

G38   Virgil, *Aeneid* 8.626–731   The shield of Aeneas

In Book 8 Aeneas conducts a successful search for allies in the forthcoming war, during which he visits Evander and the future site of Rome. Meanwhile, among the gods, his mother Venus persuades her husband Vulcan to make Aeneas new armour (370–453). The book ends with the delivery of the armour and a detailed description of the decoration on the shield.

This episode is modelled on Homer, *Iliad* 18.428–617, where Achilles' mother Thetis persuades Hephaestus (Vulcan's Greek equivalent) to make him new armour, and the shield is described in detail as showing a variety of natural and human scenes, including two cities, one at peace and the other at war.

Virgil tells us that Aeneas' shield (obviously not envisaged as an object which it would be feasible to manufacture, but as supernatural) displayed all Roman and Italian history (626–9) and that he merely selects episodes for description. Those he selects illustrate Roman history up to his own day in a fashion which complements the accounts given in the two earlier passages reproduced above. As with 1.257–96 and by contrast with the parade at 6.756 ff, this account culminates with Augustus, and here Augustus is given the lion's share of attention: the earlier scenes are accorded a mere 41 lines (630–70), whereas the Augustan section gets 54 lines (675–728).

Virgil vividly evokes the appearance of the shield, with much reference to the metals and colours used, and most of the scenes are described in highly pictorial terms, as is shown by D. A. West, in Harrison (ed.), *Oxford Readings in Vergil's Aeneid* 295–304. The decoration is envisaged as comprising three bands. The outer band shows earlier Roman history, from which Virgil selects just a few scenes: first, various events from the origin of the city down to the Gauls' assault on the Capitol, and then two scenes of a different kind, an evocation of Rome's religious rituals (663–6) and a glimpse of the Underworld (666–70). Next comes a decorative middle band showing the sea encircled by dolphins (671–4). The inner band shows the battle of Actium and its sequel.

   Recent views include Hardie, *Virgil's Aeneid* 97–110, 120–5, 336–76, interpreting the shield as a cosmic icon of Rome's universal dominance, and R. A. Gurval, *Actium and Augustus* (1995), 209–47, arguing that the tone is not unequivocally pro-Augustan.

   On the shield the fire-god, not ignorant of the prophets
   Or unaware of ages to come, had engraved the fortunes of Italy
   And the Romans' triumphs; there too he had shown all the future line
   Of Ascanius' stock, and the wars which they fought, in due order.
   There he had fashioned a wolf, new-littered, who lay   630
   In Mars' green cave, and twin boys, who hung at her nipples
   And played without fear, as they sucked on their mother
   And she bent her sleek neck back to groom them in turn
   And licked them each into shape. Close by the god had added
   Rome and the rape of the Sabine women, seized in defiance of custom   635
   From the audience sitting assembled and celebrating great circus-games,
   And of an instant a fresh war erupting between Romulus' offspring
   And aged Tatius and the austere people of Cures. Next, the self-same kings
   Had laid their quarrels aside, and now at the altar of Jupiter, armed,
   They were standing with bowls in their hands concluding   640
   A treaty by the sacrifice of a pig. Close by, two chariots
   Launched in opposite directions had torn Mettus apart
   (But you should have kept your word, man of Alba!),
   And Tullus was dragging the treacherous warrior's guts
   Through a forest, where brambles were sprinkled with blood   645
   Like the dew. Porsenna next was portrayed, commanding Rome
   To restore Tarquinius from exile, harassing the city by powerful siege,
   While Aeneas' offspring in liberty's name were rushing to arms.
   There you could see him, the picture of indignation and of menace,
   Furious that Cocles had dared to tear down the bridge, while Cloelia   650
   Had broken her bonds and was swimming the river.
   At the top of the shield Manlius, the Tarpeian citadel's guardian,
   Was standing in front of the temple and holding the Capitol's heights,
   Where with fresh new thatch the palace of Romulus bristled.
   And here, flying through the gilded colonnades, a goose,   655
   Of silver, sang out that the Gauls were at the threshold.
   The Gauls, close by, among thorn bushes, had the citadel
   In their grasp, protected by the dark and the gift
   Of a moonless night. Their hair was fashioned in gold,
   And gold were their garments, and gleaming the stripes of their cloaks;   660
   With gold their milk-white necks were circled; twin Alpine javelins
   They each of them brandished, and long shields protected their bodies.
   Here he had fashioned the Salii leaping, the naked Luperci,
   Wool-bearing caps and the sacred shields fallen from heaven,
   While chaste matrons led sacred processions through the city   665
   In their soft-cushioned carriages. Far off from here he added
   Tartarus' habitations and the towering doorways of Dis,

And the torments of criminals, and you, Catiline, suspended
High on a menacing crag and shrinking from the face of the Furies,
And, set apart, the righteous, with Cato laying down their laws.   670
Between these scenes was a depiction of a broad swelling sea,
Waves wrought in gold, all flecked with white foam. Circling
Around it in silver, bright dolphins were churning the waters
With tail-fins and cleaving a way through the surf.
At the centre you could see the fleets, wrought in bronze,   675
And the Actian war, there see the battle-lines drawn,
And all Leucate boiling with war, and the waves sparkling with gold.
On one side was Augustus Caesar, leading the Italians
To battle together with Senate and People, the Penates
And the great gods, standing on the high poop, while from his brow   680
Twin flames shot joyfully upward, and on his helmet his father's star appeared.
On the other wing, Agrippa, with the winds and the gods on his side,
Stood aloft, leading his line, and – that proud badge of war –
His temples adorned with the ships' beaks of the naval crown.
On the other side, with barbarous arms and a motley array,   685
Antony, returned in conquest from the eastern peoples and the Red Sea,
Brought Egypt into the battle, the might of the Orient, far-away Bactria,
While (for shame!) an Egyptian wife followed behind.
The fleets charged into battle; the whole sea foamed,
Shattered with oar strokes and the bow-waves of three-toothed prows.   690
They made for open water. Now you would think that the isles of the Cyclades,
Torn loose, were sailing the seas or mountains colliding in battle
With towering mountains – so vast were the turreted decks of the ships,
On which men hastened to battle. Blazing tow and flying steel
Were scattered everywhere by hands and weapons, while with fresh   695
Slaughter Neptune's fields grew red. In the midst the queen summoned
Her squadrons with the Egyptian rattle, but failed even yet
To see the twin snakes waiting at her back. Her gods, misbegotten,
Of every kind, even barking Anubis, ranged against Neptune,
Minerva, and Venus, brandished their armaments. At the heart   700
Of the struggle, engraved in iron, Mars raged, and
From the skies the grim Furies, and Discord, delighting
In her garment divided, ran riot; behind her Bellona
Followed, bloodily flailing. Above and surveying it all,
Actian Apollo was drawing his bow. For terror of this, all,   705
Egyptian and Indian, Arab and Sabaean, were turning to flight.
The queen herself could be seen, having summoned the winds,
To be opening her sails and now, even now, to have loosened the ropes.
Amid carnage, and pale at the prospect of death, the fire-god
Had portrayed her carried along by the waves and the north-west wind.   710
Opposite, the Nile, grieving with his mighty body, was stretching out
His folds and with all his robes was calling back the defeated
To his watery bosom and the secret retreats of his streams.
But now Caesar was riding in triple triumph through the walls
Of Rome, and was making to Italy's gods his vow everlasting,   715

Three hundred great shrines, all through the city. Now resounding
With joy and games and applause were the streets. At each temple
Was a chorus of matrons, at each an altar; before the altars
The sacrificed bullocks lay strewn upon the ground.
He himself, seated on the snow-white threshold of shining Apollo,   720
Told over the gifts of the nations, and high on the proud portals
He displayed them, while rank upon rank the vanquished nations passed by,
As varied in their tongues as in their garb and arms.
Here Mulciber had moulded the Nomads and the Africans
In their loose-flowing robes; here the Lelegae, the Carians   725
And the Gelonian archers. The river Euphrates passed (now gentler
In its flow), and the Morini (most distant of men), the twin-horned Rhine,
The Dahae unconquered before, and Araxes outraged at his bridge.
All this on Vulcan's shield, the gift of his mother, Aeneas wondered at.
Ignorant of what they portrayed, he rejoiced in the images,   730
Raising on his shoulders the fame and fate of his offspring.

634–41   *The rape of the Sabine women.* According to the legend, Romulus' new settlers, lacking wives, invited neighbouring peoples to a new festival with horse-races (the *Consualia*), and then seized women during the show; the subsequent war was ended by the women's intervention, and by treaty the Romans then formed a new state with their Sabine neighbours. See Ovid, *Ars Am.* 1.101–134 (**G47**) and Livy 1.9–13.

639–41   The standard Roman ritual for concluding treaties was carried out by the fetial priests and involved the sacrifice of a pig.

641–6   According to legend, Mettus Fufetius, dictator of Alba, concluded a treaty with King Tullus Hostilius by which Alba accepted Roman supremacy, but subsequently went back on it (Livy 1.23–29); Tullus punished him and destroyed Alba Longa, transferring its citizens to Rome.

646–51   Roman tradition had it that, after the expulsion of Tarquin, Lars Porsenna, king of the Etruscan city of Clusium, attacked Rome on his behalf, but eventually withdrew. Horatius Cocles was believed to have held the Etruscans at bay single-handed while the Tiber bridge was destroyed, and Cloelia to have escaped with her fellow hostages by swimming the Tiber (see Livy 2.9–13). Both are frequently mentioned as exemplary Roman feats (e.g. Propertius 3.11.63, **G31**).

652–62   When the Gauls sacked Rome *c.* 390, the rest of the city was abandoned as they approached, but the Capitol was defended, and a Gallic assault on the Capitol was said to have been thwarted when the geese gave the alarm and by the prompt action of Marcus Manlius Capitolinus (Livy 5.47).

654   *thatch ... palace*: thatched huts, supposedly the residence of Romulus, were preserved and regularly restored on both the Capitol and the Palatine Hill down to Augustus' day.

663–6   A puzzling passage: the only part of the description of the Shield not explicitly linked to a specific event or individual.

663   *Salii*: an ancient association of priests (see **L2**).
       Luperci: another ancient priesthood. On 15 February they ran naked round the Palatine, whipping bystanders.

664   *caps ... shields*: part of the equipment of the Salii (see **L2**).

665–6   Roman matrons were said to have contributed generously to the dedication at Delphi after the capture of Veii in 396 BC and to the ransom paid to the Gauls, and to have been rewarded with the right to ride in a carriage in the city (Livy 5.25.9, 50.7).

667   *Tartarus*: the part of the Underworld where the worst criminals were punished (described at *Aeneid* 6.548–627).
       Dis: the ruler of the Underworld.

668   *Catiline*: conspired to create civil unrest in 63 BC.

670   *righteous*: in Elysium, described at *Aeneid* 6.637–702. *Cato*: the Younger. Although a bitter opponent of Julius Caesar, even Augustus praised Cato (**H43**).

677   *Leucate*: a promontory on the south of the island of Leucas. The battle was in fact fought some thirty miles to the north.

679   *Penates*: the tutelary gods of the Roman state. These cult objects, reputed to have been brought from Troy, were kept in the temple near the Roman forum.

680   *standing on the high poop*: the same Latin phrase is used of Aeneas returning to the beleaguered
        Trojans at *Aeneid* 10.261.
681   *flames*: as also from Aeneas' helmet (8.620; 10.270).
684   *naval crown*: a gold crown decorated with miniature ships' beaks, a unique distinction awarded to
        Agrippa for his command in the naval victory over Sextus Pompeius in 36 BC, see **T13**.
686   *Antony*: mentioned only here by name in the various Augustan poetical accounts of the battle of
        Actium (Horace, *Epodes* 9 = **G5**, *Odes* 1.37 = **G24**; Propertius 4.6 = **G39**), and presented as leading
        the East against Rome.
        in conquest: in fact Antony's eastern expedition of 36 BC had not been conspicuously successful.
698   *snakes*: the asps which Cleopatra used to commit suicide.
705   *Actian Apollo*: the promontory of Actium, off which the battle was fought, was the site of a sanctuary
        of Apollo, a fortunate coincidence since Octavian had already formed a close link with this god and
        had decided in 36 to build a temple to him next to his house on the Palatine.
707–8   Cleopatra's withdrawal was the turning-point in the battle (Plutarch, *Antony* 66; Dio 50.33).
714   *triple triumph*: Octavian triumphed on three successive days 13–15 August 29 BC (*RG* 4.1, **H16**),
        for his Balkan wars of 35–33 BC; victories at Actium (31 BC); and Alexandria (30 BC).
716   *three hundred great shrines*: presumably referring primarily to the temple restoration of 28 BC, but
        the number is exaggerated – only 82 temples were restored then (*RG* 20.4).
717–28 The final scene is an imaginary celebration, with Augustus himself located at his new white marble
        temple to Apollo on the Palatine, which had been dedicated on 9 October 28 BC. All of the listed
        conquered nations, except for the Geloni and the Dahae, could be regarded as brought under
        Augustus' control by or at the same time as the defeat of Antony and Cleopatra, but the parade
        clearly also points, with poetical exaggeration, to expectations of further far-flung conquest,
        extending to the borders of Ocean. See also **N8b** in Addenda, page 415.
724   *Mulciber*: Vulcan.
725   *Lelegae ... Carians*: ancient pre-Greek peoples of western Asia Minor, brought under Augustus'
        control through his defeat of Antony.
726   *Gelonian(s)*: from the Ukraine.
        Euphrates: defeat of Antony had extended Augustus' control to the Euphrates, but expected victory
        over the Parthians beyond this river is no doubt also suggested.
727   *Morini*: in northern Gaul. Gaius Carrinas celebrated a triumph over them in 28 BC (see **N2b**).
728   *Dahae*: east of the Caspian Sea.
        Araxes: this river flowed from Armenia (which Antony had subjugated, but was out of Augustus'
        control until the settlement of 20 BC) to the Caspian, which was believed to be a gulf of Ocean.

Horace, *Carmen Saeculare* (Centennial Hymn), 17 BC: see L28.

G39   Propertius 4.6   Temple of Apollo of Actium

This poem celebrates the Palatine temple of Apollo, tracing its origin to the battle of Actium (31 BC), after
which it was vowed by Augustus (see **K37** and **K37b** in Addenda page 415). The poem's apparent ritual
setting is a framework taken from the Hellenistic poet Callimachus, a proclaimed model for Propertius'
fourth book; it has been suggested that the poem may be connected with the Actian Games of 16 BC, its
approximate date of composition. As in 3.11 (**G31**), the narrative of Actium which occupies most of the
poem follows the traditional and propagandistic Augustan line (as in Horace *Epode* 9 = **G5**, and Virgil,
Aeneid 8 = **G38**), even to the extent of omitting entirely any reference to Antony, supporting the Augustan
line that Actium was a battle against a foreign enemy. The prominence of Apollo is natural given the poem's
fundamental connection with a temple of Apollo.

> The priest is making sacrifice. Now for the sacrifice's sake keep
> Holy silence. May the stricken heifer fall before my sacred hearth.
> Let there now be joined the battle of the poets, my Roman garlands set
> Against Philetas' ivy-wreaths; now from the urn be poured for me
> The waters of Cyrene, for Callimachus his source of holy inspiration.
> Give me soft Grecian unguents, spices give of sweetest frankincense,   5

And three times weave the woollen wreaths about my hearth.
With waters sprinkle me, while from Mygdonian flasks beside
The new-built altars ivory flutes make music's sweet libation to the gods.
Stand afar off, Deceit; let Evil dwell beneath some distant sky.
Made smooth with purest laurel branches is the priest's new highway.   10

Come then, my Muse! For now I sing of Palatine Apollo's temple. Come,
Calliope, Queen of the Muses, for my tale is worthy of your favour too.
For Caesar's glory I compose my songs; and while I sing of Caesar
Even you, Great Jupiter, I pray, pause briefly now and hearken to my tale.

A bay there is, beloved of Phoebus, which runs back towards Epirus' shores,   15
And there a secluded harbour dims the soft murmur of the Ionian sea,
Whose waters guard the monuments of Actium and of the Julian fleet.
The harbour itself affords an easy passage to mariners' prayers. Here
There joined in battle all the armies of the world. Vast upon the sea
Lay pine-built warships; mixed were the omens which Fate gave their oars.   20
To one side was the fleet which Trojan Quirinus doomed, disgraced
By the woman who brandished Roman spears. On the other side
Augustus' flagship swelled its sails with Jove's omens on its side,
Its standards long familiar with their country's victories. Now at last
Nereus had marshalled their formations into twin crescents, while   25
His waters trembled, lit by the flashes of bright armaments.
Then Phoebus left the isle of Delos, fixed for ever under his protection,
Though once alone of isles it floated free, the angry South Wind's plaything.
He stood above Augustus' ship, his hair bound up not loose,
Falling across his neck, and thrice his unfamiliar fires blazed, twisting   30
Their slanting torch-like flames; he brought no peacetime music for his lyre
Of tortoise-shell; rather he glared as once he glowered on Agamemnon,
Son of Pelops, when with his plague he carried off the Greeks from camp
To greedy funeral pyre; or as when once he slew the serpent, Python,
Which terrorised those goddesses of peace, the gentle Muses.   35

Then spoke Apollo thus: "Scion of Alba Longa, Saviour of the World,
Augustus, acknowledged greater than your great Trojan ancestors,
Conquer now by sea; already the land is yours. My bow fights for you,
And the whole burden of the quiver on my shoulders fights on your side.
Set your country free from fear; you are its champion; on you it depends   40
And on your ship it lays the cargo and mighty burden of its people's prayers.
If your defence should fail, ill-omened were the birds that Romulus
Saw flying from the Palatine when seeking auguries wherewith to found
The walls of Rome. And now they dare too much and row too close; for shame
That while you rule an alien queen should sail the seas of Latium.   45
Fear not, for though the oarage of their fleet is swift as a hundred wings,
They have no welcome from the seas they sail. And though
Their figureheads are monsters armed with missiles such as Centaurs bear,
Try them and you will find their timbers are but hollow planks,
Their demons but painted terrors. It is the cause that makes or mars   50

The courage of a soldier. For if he has no justice at his side,
Shame strikes his weapons down. The hour has come. Commit your fleet
To battle. I am the master of the hour. I shall be helmsman
To Caesar's Julian ships, with hands that bear the laurel wreaths of victory."
He spoke, and from his bow discharged the full salvo of his weighty quiver;   55
Then closest and next behind his bow was Caesar's spear. Rome was the victor;
Apollo proved true. The woman paid the price. Her broken sceptres float
On the Ionian waters while from Mount Ida's star his father Julius
Gazed down in wonder. "I am a god," he said, "and there I see
Proof that he is my offspring, sprung from my blood."   60
With hymns of triumph Triton escorted him; and every goddess of the sea
Clustered about our freedom's standards clapped her hands with joy.
But she fled for the Nile, putting her faith too blindly in
Her fleeing craft. One thing alone she gained: she did not die
When Fate decreed. Heaven found a better way. One woman would have made   65
A paltry triumph, when she was marched through streets where once Jugurtha
Was led prisoner. Such was the way Apollo of Actium gained his monument,
For every arrow fired from his bow destroyed ten warships of our enemies.

Of wars I have sung sufficient. Now the Lord of Victory, Apollo,
Demands my lyre, laying aside his armour for the dance   70
Of peacetime celebration. Now let banquets all in white proceed
Amid soft woodlands; garlands of roses pour their blandishments
About my neck; let wine crushed from Falernian vine-presses be poured;
And now three times let strands of spices from Cilicia suffuse my hair.
Now in their cups let poets find inspiration from the Muse; Bacchus,   75
It is your wont to give of your rich abundance to your own Apollo.
Now let one poet tell of the Sygambri, marsh-men reduced to servitude;
Now let another sing of Ethiopian Meroe and her dark kingdoms;
Yet another celebrate the Parthian, bound by a treaty, signal of defeat,
Though late in time. "Let him restore the standards of Remus, for soon   80
His own he will surrender. Yet if, for a while, Augustus shall spare
The archers of the East, let him but delay until his grandsons may redeem
Such trophies. Crassus, rejoice! if you have understanding 'mid the sands
Of darkness where you lie. For now, men may traverse Euphrates to your tomb."

Such is my prayer. And so shall I spend my nights with drink and song,
Until the new day casts his beams upon my wine.

22   *the woman*: Cleopatra, invidiously unnamed as at line 57 and 3.11.39–40 (**G31**); here there is an
        implication that she is inappropriately performing a male military role.
32–3   the reference is to the first book of Homer's *Iliad*.
77–81   references to Augustan victories against the German Sygambri (16–13 BC), Ethiopia (expeditions
        of mid 20's **N33–N35**), and Parthia (diplomatic settlement of 20 BC, which crucially involved the
        return of the standards, **N41–N42**).
82   *his grandsons*: Gaius and Lucius Caesar, sons of Agrippa (see on Horace Odes 1.6 = **G22**) and
        Julia, who were adopted by Augustus as his heirs in 17 BC at infant age.
83   *Crassus*: the standards (see on 78–81 above) were lost in his defeat at Carrhae in 53 BC.

G40   Crinagoras 27 (*Palatine Anthology* 9.291)   Have faith – in Caesar

This poem, while praising Caesar (Augustus) in the conventional way, plainly refers to Roman reverses against German tribes – perhaps the defeat of Lollius in 17–16 BC, or that of Varus in AD 9. Admission of even temporary military setbacks is unusual in Latin poetry after Actium.

> What though the Ocean hoists her floods on high,
> Or German armies drink Rhine's waters dry;
> Never shall they do harm to Roman might,
> If Rome has faith that Caesar rules aright.
> So Zeus' sacred oaks endure, their roots unshaken,
> Whose withered leaves are by the storm winds taken.

G41   Horace, *Odes* 4.2

This ode is addressed to Iullus Antonius, son of Mark Antony, probably in 16 BC, the year he was aedile (a junior magistrate), and looks forward to the expected return of Augustus from campaigning in Gaul and Germany (a return which actually happened in 13 BC, the publication date of the fourth book of *Odes*). The warning against the imitation of Pindar, the loftiest of the Greek lyric poets, is partly ironic: though Horace presents himself as less ambitious than Pindar, his poetry in praise of victories both here and in *Odes* 4.4 = **G42** and *Odes* 4.14 = **G44** puts him firmly in the Pindaric tradition. Iullus Antonius was at this point in high favour with Augustus, whose sister Octavia (previously married to Antony as his second wife) had brought him up, though he was Antony's son by his first marriage to Fulvia; he had married Octavia's daughter Marcella (brother of Marcellus, see on *Odes* 1.12 = **G23**) in 21 BC, and was to be consul in 10 BC, but he was disgraced and committed suicide as a result of the scandal associated with Augustus' daughter Julia in 2 BC. He is reported to have written an epic on Diomedes; hence perhaps Horace's implication here that Iullus is a more appropriate encomiast of Augustus than himself (cf. lines 33–4). For a fuller discussion of this poem see S.J. Harrison in ed. Harrison, *Homage to Horace* (1995) 108–27.

> Iullus Antonius, the man who tries to rival Pindar,
> Might as well strive by Daedalean art
> To fly on waxen wings, giving his name
> To some glassy sea.
>
> Like mountain torrent raging from the hills,   5
> Which cloudbursts swell to burst familiar banks,
> Boiling, immense, the voice of Pindar roars
> *Basso profundo*.
>
> His are Apollo's laurels, well-deserved,
> Whether in dithyrambs audacious he deploys   10
> New language, born aloft on lines set free
> From metre's laws;
>
> Whether he sings of gods and kings, or heroes
> Born of gods, such as laid low the Centaurs
> In well-deserved death, or damped the flames   15
> Of the dread Chimaera;
>
> Whether he sings of those the Olympic palm
> Brings home exalted to the skies, singing
> Of boxer or steed, to honour them with greater gifts
> Than statues by the hundred;   20

Whether for youthful hero he laments, lost
To a weeping bride, praising to the stars
Their strength, their spirit and their golden virtues,
Robbing of prey black Orcus.

A great wind helps the swan of Dirce's fount   25
To soar, Antonius, often as he seeks the high
Cloud kingdoms; but in mode and manner
Like Mount Matinus' bee,

Which by hard labour harvests the sweet thyme
Along the woods and banks of spray-soaked Tiber,   30
A lesser poet, I fashion laboured verse
To make my songs.

A poet of loftier powers, Antonius, you shall sing
Of Caesar, when along the Sacred Way
Adorned with triumphal laurel, well-deserved,   35
He drags Sygambrian savages.

No better gift or greater than him to earth
The Fates have given and the kindly gods,
Nor could they give, if back to the age of gold
The centuries should roll.   40

Of Rome's high holidays shall you sing, and of the
Public games, prayers answered, welcome-home
For brave Augustus, and of the Forum too
On holiday – from lawyers.

I, too, if I can have my little say, shall add   45
To yours my best endeavours, a hymn to the Sun,
Lovely and worthy to be praised, for joy
That Caesar's home again.

And while you lead the way, we'll all be shouting
Not once, but again and again, "Triumph! Hurrah!",   50
"Hurrah!" and "Triumph!", Romans in unison, as we burn
Incense to the kindly gods.

Ten bulls, ten cows, no less will pay your debts
To heaven; one little calf for me, new-weaned
And fattening on the green sward, will suffice   55
For my vows,

Its brow like the crescent moon's horned fires
On the third day of its new arising; and
Where it bears a mark, a splash of white,
The rest is tawny-red.   60

1–4   *Daedalean art*: Daedalus made artificial wings for his son Icarus, but the latter flew too high and
        crashed into the sea below, which was then named Icarian after him.

5–24   These stanzas survey the various types of Greek lyric poetry written by Pindar in the fifth century
        BC; his metrical structures (actually complex and intricate) were sometimes seen as formless, hence
        lines 11–12.
25   *Dirce's swan*: Pindar, here linked with the river Dirce of his native Thebes, just as Horace is linked
        in 28 with Mount Matinus near his own birthplace in S. Italy.
34   *Sacred Way*: the traditional route of the Roman triumph.
35   *Sygambrian savages*: German opponents defeated by Augustus in 16–13 BC.
39–40   *age of gold*: this claim that Augustus has caused the mythical Golden Age to return is made
        elsewhere in contemporary poetry, e.g. Virgil *Aeneid* 6.792–3 (**G37**).

G42   Horace, *Odes* 4.4

This ode and *Odes* 4.14 below celebrate the achievements of Augustus' two stepsons, Nero Claudius Drusus
and his elder brother the future emperor Tiberius (Ti. Claudius Nero) in their victories of 15–14 BC against
tribes in the German and Swiss Alps, see **N14–N15**. The two poems are clearly an important structural pair
within the book (each precedes a poem addressed to Augustus himself), and Suetonius' biography of Horace
(**R14**) claims that Augustus encouraged Horace to write the fourth book of Odes in order to praise his
stepsons. Both poems also recall the victory poems of Pindar in technique (despite *Odes* 4.2, **G41**); Horace
thus turns Pindar's celebrations of Greek athletic victories into celebrations of Roman military victories. In
4.4 the defeat of Hannibal's brother Hasdrubal by the brothers' ancestor (see on 37–40) is seen as parallel
to his descendants' achievements, fitting Roman ideas of family continuity; in 4.14 the victories of the
brothers are seen as the ultimate achievements of the supervising Augustus himself, reflecting the formal
situation by which the *princeps* was technically the supreme commander of most Roman armies and hence
the official recipient of all military glory, as clearly depicted on a coin celebrating the victories, **N15**.

> Like Jove's winged minister of lightning fire
> Whom heaven's king made king of all the birds
> That wander the air, when he had proved him
> Trusty with gold-haired Ganymede –
>
> Youth and his natural power at first despatch him   5
> Out from the nest, an untrained labourer; but when
> The storms are gone and the spring breezes
> Teach ambition how to soar,
>
> Forgetting his first fears, soon his eager swoop
> Sends him a terrorist against the sheepfold;   10
> Then love of banquets and battle drives him
> To feast on wrestling snakes;
>
> Or like a lion whelp, new-weaned from his tawny
> Mother's milk, whom a roe-deer greedy for
> Rich pasture spies, but only in time   15
> To die, providing a first kill –
>
> Such was the Drusus whom the Vindelici saw
> Waging his war beneath the Raetian Alps.
> I ask not whence came their ancient custom
> To arm their right hands   20
>
> With the Amazonian battle-axe, for omniscience
> Is heaven's prerogative. But those same hordes,
> Widely victorious over many years were vanquished
> By youthful stratagem.

Thus they discovered to their cost the power   25
Of mind and natural talent, properly brought up
In god-fearing home, the power of paternal love,
Augustus', for Nero's two sons.

To strong and noble only are strong sons born.
Heredity in bulls and champion steeds declares   30
The father's quality; nor can the fearsome eagle
Beget the timid dove.

Training holds the key to release inherent powers;
In moral education conscience learns strength;
When moral principle declines, defects   35
Mar nature's best handiwork.

Rome, what a debt you owe to Nero's clan. I cite
As witnesses Metaurus' stream, Hasdrubal vanquished,
And that glorious day when the darkness
Was driven from Latium,   40

The day which gave us victory's sweet smiles, the first
Since the savage African tore through Italia's towns
Like fire through pinewoods, or like Easterly
Storms on Sicilian waters.

From then, as victory followed victory, our young   45
Heroes blossomed, our ruined shrines defiled
By violence and blaspheming Punic hands
Had upright gods once more.

Perfidious Hannibal declared at last: "Like deer,
Hunted for plunder by the ravening wolves, we madly   50
Play the hunter, though for us triumph at best
Must be escape and evasion.

A nation, undaunted by the fiery sack of Troy,
Tossed on the seas of Tuscany, has endured to bring
Its holy relics, children, and venerable fathers   55
Safe to Ausonia's cities,

Just as an oak, lopped by the toughened axe
On Mount Algidus, rich with its shadowing leaves,
From every stroke and murderous cut discovers
New strength and resource within.   60

Against a Hercules, who loathed defeat, even the hydra
Failed to renew its strength as Rome renews hers.
The guardians of the golden fleece or Cadmus could not
Bring forth from the earth as many new warriors.

Drown it in the sea, and up it comes more beautiful. 65
Wrestle, and to ringing cheers it throws each new
Victorious opponent, and wages wars for
Mothers to tell their children.

To Carthage no more shall I send messengers
Proclaiming proud victories. Dead, dead, dead 70
Is all hope; fortune and family name all died
When Hasdrubal was slain."

Nothing there is that Claudian hands cannot accomplish,
So long as kindly Jupiter defends those hands,
And wisdom's counsels guide our footsteps through 75
War's sharpest hazards.

37–40 *Metaurus' stream*: in Umbria, scene of a major battle in 207 in the Second Punic War in which the brothers' ancestor, C. Claudius Nero, defeated and killed Hannibal's brother Hasdrubal. In lines 52–72 Hannibal is imagined as speaking at that time.
63–4 The earth-generated bulls defeated by Jason in the Argonaut saga and the men who sprang from the earth at Cadmus' foundation of Thebes are seen as parallel to Rome's capacity continuously to produce formidable warriors.

G43   Horace, *Odes* **4.5**

Augustus was away from Rome, in Gaul and Spain, in 16–13 BC; this poem calling on him to return was perhaps written around 14 BC. As in the Centennial Hymn, Horace takes the opportunity to celebrate Augustus' recent achievements, including the law carried by Augustus in 18 BC making adultery a crime (lines 21–4: on the law, see **S10–S27**), the Parthian settlement and the Scythian embassy (lines 25–6), and the conquest of north-western Spain by Augustus and Agrippa (lines 27–8: on Spain, see **N47–N49**). At lines 30–36 Horace evokes the practice of pouring a libation for Augustus at dinners, both public and private, instituted in 30 BC by decree of the senate (Dio 51.19.7). For a full discussion of this poem see I. Duquesnay, in S. J. Harrison (ed.), *Homage to Horace* (1995), 128–187.

Sprung from the kindly gods, best guardian
Of Romulus' people, too long you've been away.
To the holy council of senators you promised an early return –
    So come home.

Show to your country, kindly leader, the light 5
Of your presence. When your smile, like the spring, shines out
On your nation, the passing day is fairer, and the sun
    Shines more warmly.

As a mother yearns for her youth, now absent for more
Than a year, detained by the malice of southerly gales 10
Across the Carpathian sea as he lingers far off from his
    Own sweet home,

Calling him with vows, prayers, and consulting of omens,
Never lifting her gaze from the curving shore;
Even so, smitten by loyalty's longing, his country 15
    Yearns for its Caesar.

For cattle safely roam the pastures;
Ceres and kind Prosperity feed the countryside;
Mariners sail the seas made peaceful; and
    Good faith fears blame.   20

The chaste home is not stained by lechery;
Custom and law have tamed besmirching vice;
Mothers are honoured in children like their fathers;
    Penalty presses hard on crime.

With Caesar safe, who'd fear the Parthian, who   25
The ice-bound Scythian or the brood that rough
Germany bears? Who would fret over wars
    In savage Spain?

Each on his own hillside ends the day, and gives
His vines in marriage to the lovelorn trees; and happy then   30
Back to his wine he goes, and at the second course
    Invokes you as god.

With many a prayer, with unmixed wine poured out
From bowls he calls upon you, and with his household gods
He links your godhead, like Greece remembering   35
    Castor and great Hercules.

'Long holidays, O kindly Leader, grant
To Italy', we say with dry lips
As day begins, and say again when full of wine
    When the sun is under the Ocean.   40

1   The opening lines echo a famous passage from Ennius' *Annals*, in which the Roman people lament the death of Romulus (106–9 Skutsch).

11   *Carpathian sea*: between Crete and Rhodes. Horace may envisage the youth as having gone from Italy to Asia, but the image may not be intended to be so specific.

27   *Germany*: an invasion of Gaul by the Sygambri, a German tribe, had provided the immediate occasion for Augustus' departure from Rome in 16 BC. The Sygambri came to terms before Augustus' arrival in Gaul, but Augustus must already have been planning the advance into Germany which began in 12 BC.

35   *godhead*: the libation was properly to Augustus' *genius*, his guardian divinity, but here Horace uses the related term *numen*, which properly denotes his innate 'divine power'.

G44 Horace, *Odes* 4.14.

For the context of this poem, see the introduction to *Odes* 4.4 above.

How shall the Senate, how the Quirites too,
Be diligent to immortalise your virtues
With full entitlement of civic rank, with titles
And memorial calendars,

Augustus, first of all First Citizens   5
Wherever suns shine on the shores of men,
Whose martial valour the Vindelici, untouched
As yet by Rome's rule of law,

Lately discovered? Yours was the army, too,
Which eager Drusus led, when he cast down   10
The implacable Genauni, the swift Breuni,
And their high citadels

Which crown the awful Alps, in grisly retribution.
Then did the elder Nero launch his grim assault
Beneath your favouring auspices, putting to flight   15
The savage Raetians.

You should have seen him in that mortal strife,
With what prodigious slaughter he destroyed
Hearts to death and freedom sacrificed; no less
Indomitable than the South Wind,   20

Who whips the waves, while all the clouds are rent
By the storm-dancing chorus of the Pleiades.
So eager he to hound the hostile ranks, through fire
Spurring his foaming steed

Like Aufidus, who bull-like rolls his stream   25
Across Apulian Daunus' domains, and in his rage
He meditates destruction ineluctable
For the well-farmed fields.

Just so did Claudius, charging in massed assault,
Tear open the barbarians' iron ranks, harvesting   30
Van and rearguard, strewed upon the ground;
A victor without losses.

Yours were the soldiery, your the master-plan,
Yours the benign divinities, Augustus. For this day
A suppliant Alexandria surrendered, opening up   35
Harbours and empty palace;

And, after thrice five years, on this same day,
A kindly Fortune brought a successful end
To war, adding her meed of praise and glory sought
To your completed task.   40

You are the wonder of the world – Indian and Persian,
Cantabrian unconquered before, and nomad Scythian –
All marvel at you, Italy's present guardian,
Imperial Rome's protector.

All hearken to your word, even Nile who hides   45
His secret springs and sources, Danube too,
And boiling Tigris, monster-bearing Ocean, who roars
Around far Britain's coasts;

Land of the Gauls, reckless of death, and Spain,
That stubborn country, and the Sygambri too,   50
Lovers of slaughter, all have laid arms aside
To do you honour.

25–28   The simile of a river in spate is traditional for a raging epic warrior in Homer, but the river chosen
        (Aufidus) comes from Horace's own home region of Apulia.
29   *Claudius*: Tiberius (Tiberius Claudius Nero).
34–40   These lines imply that the victories of the brothers took place or were reported on 1 August 15 BC,
        exactly 15 years after the official date of Augustus' own victory against Antony and Cleopatra
        at Alexandria (cf. *Odes* 1.37, **G24**). The supposed coincidence is likely to be a flattering
        contrivance.
41–52   These three stanzas allude to various actual or potential triumphs of Augustus, giving an impression
        of world domination. The Spanish Cantabrians gave much trouble in the 20's (cf. *Odes* 3.14 = **G29**)
        but were finally defeated in 19 BC; for Indians and Medes (= Parthians) see on 1.12.54–6, **G23**; the
        Scythians are another expression of geographical extent rather than an actual conquest. The Nile
        was the scene of the victory at Alexandria (see on 34–40 above), the Tigris looks again to Parthia,
        while for Britain see on *Epode* 7.7 = **G3**. Augustus campaigned in Gaul in 16–13 BC (see
        introduction to *Odes* 4.2 = **G41**), and against the German Sygambrians in the same period (see on
        Odes 4.2.35 above). See further in Section **N**.

G45   Horace, *Odes* 4.15

The opening motif is traditional: the young Virgil had represented Apollo in *Eclogue* 6.1–12 as warning him
to stick to pastoral poetry, and was himself there following the Hellenistic poet Callimachus (*Aetia* fragment
1). However, Horace gives the old theme a new twist: war poetry is redundant now that Augustus has
established both civil peace and prosperity and universal obedience to Rome.

   As with *Odes* 4.5, the heart of the poem consists of praises of Augustus' achievements. While that poem
ended with the new custom of pouring libations for Augustus, this poem (the last in the book) closes (lines
25–32) by proposing the revival of an old practice: the Romans believed that it had once been their custom
for songs in praise of famous men of the past to be sung at banquets, accompanied on the flute, but already
in the early second century the Elder Cato had recorded the practice as long obsolete. Horace also works in
here an allusion to the recently published *Aeneid*.

I wished to tell of battles and of conquered towns,
But Phoebus rebuked me with his lyre,
Warning against venturing with
My tiny sails on the wide Tyrrhenian sea.

Your time, Caesar, has restored rich harvests   5
To the fields, and to our Jupiter the standards
Stripped from the Parthians' insolent porches;
Has closed the shrine, vacated by wars,

Of Janus Quirinus; has thrown a bridle on
Licence, wandering from right order;   10
Has banished crime, and has summoned
Back the ancient ways

By which the Latin race and Italian
Might grew great, and fame and majesty
Of empire stretched to the lands of morning   15
From the couch of the setting sun.

While Caesar guards our state, no madness
Between citizens or violence will drive out
Peace, nor rage, that anvil of swords,
And foe to wretched cities.   20

Those who drink Danube's deep waters will
Break no Julian edict; nor will the Getae,
Nor the Seres, nor the treacherous Persians,
Nor those who dwell by Tanais' stream.

And we, on work days and on holidays,   25
Amid the gifts of joyous Bacchus,
Our wives and offspring at our sides,
Having first prayed to the gods in proper form,

Shall sing, after our father's fashion,
To the strains of Lydian flutes, of leaders   30
Who did deeds of valour, and of Troy, Anchises,
And kindly Venus' progeny.

6   *to our Jupiter the standards*: the Parthian standards were eventually deposited in the temple of Mars Ultor (see *RG* 29.2, **K19**, **N42**).

8–9   *shrine ... of Janus Quirinus*: near the Forum, traditionally closed when Rome was nowhere at war. See further *RG* 13, **K47**–**K49** with notes.

21–4   Horace's claim that the most remote peoples now accepted Roman authority is largely without foundation. The Persians (i.e. Parthians) had agreed to the settlement of 20 BC, and embassies had been received from peoples living near the Tanais (the modern Don: see on Virgil, *Aeneid* 6.800, **G37**), but in neither case did this amount to submission to Roman rule. Despite expeditions from Macedonia, the lower Danube peoples, the Getae, Dacians and Sarmatae were not brought firmly under Roman control until the campaigns of Lucius Calpurnius Piso, around 12–10 BC. The Seres (Chinese) had no dealings with the Romans in Augustus' day.

32   *Venus' progeny*: deliberately ambiguous, indicating both her son Aeneas and his supposed descendant Augustus.

G46   Horace, *Epistles* 2.1. 1–4 and 245–270   The Epistle to Augustus

The opening of this poem (published after 12 BC) addresses Caesar/Augustus as the benevolent sole ruler of Rome and as the guardian of its morals. Its close compliments the poets who have written about Augustus, while again using the convention of the *recusatio* (see on *Odes* 1.6 = **G22**) to praise the great leader's achievements while professing that his own poetic capacity is in fact insufficient to do them justice. For the composition of this poem being prompted by Augustus, see *Life of Horace* **R14**.

Caesar, upon your shoulders all alone you bear the burden
Of so many and such cares: with arms you guard our state,
With morals enhance it, and with laws improve it. Too much
Would I offend against the public good were I to steal your time
With my too lengthy conversation.   4

...... They do no dishonour to your judgement of them, nor to the gifts   245
Which (amid universal approbation) you have heaped upon them,
Those poets whom you love so much, Virgil and Varius.
Statues of brass cannot express more truthfully the features of a man
Than do the works of poets which describe the characters and minds
Of famous men. As for myself, never would I prefer to be

The author of those little talks that crawl along the ground,   250
When I might tell the tale of your achievements, singing aloud
Of foreign landscapes, courses of mighty rivers, and great citadels
Set high upon mountain tops, or of the realms of wild, barbaric kings,
And all the wars which under your auspices throughout the world
Have now been ended, while the great bars upon the temple doors   255
Clang shut on Janus, Guardian of the peace, and through your leadership
Rome is even feared by Parthia. If but capacity could match desire,
All these would be my song. But alas, such is your majesty
That no slight song of mine is equal to the task, nor for very shame
Would modesty permit me to attempt a task my powers must refuse.   260
A conscientious zeal may urge to action those it loves – but it's foolishness;
The more so if the action it commends depends upon the poet's art.
For men are far more quick to learn and happy to remember what inspires
Contempt than what they hold in honour and esteem. I know how you'll reply:
"I have no interest in courtiers' obsequiousness, to me it's burdensome.
I do not desire my likeness, caricatured in wax, to be displayed for sale,   265
Not anywhere; nor would I wish my praises to be sung in poet's
Ill-constructed verses – such idiotic gifts would bring the blushes to my face,
When in a coffin with my poet's works I find myself dumped
In some refuse cart and carried off to the market, where as waste paper
It's sold to incense sellers, perfume vendors, pepper merchants,
And whoever else can find a use for it to wrap their wares in."   270

247   On Varius, see Horace *Odes* 1.6.1 and note (**G22**).

G47   Ovid, *Ars Amatoria* (The Art of Love) 1.1–228

This is the opening section of Book 1 of the *Ars Amatoria*, which deals with how to pick up girls. The frivolous subject matter is amusingly set in tension with Ovid's apparently grand claims for his work, which suggest analogies with heroic epic (note the allusions to the *Iliad* and the Argonaut saga, 6–8, and again to Achilles, 11–17) as well as with more 'serious' didactic works such as Virgil's *Georgics*. The passage includes an irreverent account of the Rape of the Sabines as a model for picking up girls at the theatre, but concludes with an encomiastic set piece, celebrating the departure in 1 BC on Eastern campaign of Augustus' young grandson and designated successor, the short-lived Gaius Caesar (cf. note on Propertius 4.6.82, **G39**).

If any of our people lacks the skill of making love, then
Let him read this book; he'll soon make love like an expert.
It takes skill as well as oars and sails to make a ship go fast;
To drive a racing chariot takes skill; and skill to make good love.
Automedon was a born charioteer, lord of the pliant reins;   5
Tiphys the master helmsman of the Haemonian *Argo*. But I
Am sweet Love's own supreme artificer; Venus made me his master.
I shall be called the Tiphys and Automedon of Love.
Love is no push-over; he can fight like a tom-cat – and he does.
But he's only a boy; still wet behind the ears; and I can handle him.   10
Chiron, son of Philyra, made Achilles a maestro on the lyre,
Crushing that vile bad-temper by his soothing arts. Achilles,
Who scared the living daylights out of friends and enemies alike,
Was himself scared witless, so they say, of that ancient sage.
The hands at which Hector was condemned one day to die   15

Were held out to the cane when "Sir" commanded. Chiron
Was tutor to Achilles, son of Aeacus; I tutor Love. Both of them
Are nasty little swine; well, look at their mums – both goddesses!
Still, in the end, the bull's neck bows to the yoke
Of the ploughman; high-mettled stallions are broken to the bit;   20
Love will surrender to me in the end, though I bear in my heart
The wounds of his arrows, the scars of his brandished fires.
The fiercer Love's arrows wound, the more savage his blows,
The richer the vengeance I'll take for the pains I've endured.
I cannot tell a lie: Phoebus Apollo, my art is no gift of yours;   25
No arts of prophecy are mine, gifts of the birds of the air;
Clio and all her sister Muses didn't appear to me (as to Hesiod once),
While in your vales, sweet Ascra, I watched my sheep. Hard practice
Is my inspiration here; this poet knows his stuff. So, pay attention;
I'll tell the truth. Venus, mother of Love, my enterprise bless!   30
Away, pretty ribbons, away, you symbols of maiden's modesty;
Be off, long skirts, that hide those pairs of pretty ankles.
I sing of naught forbidden by the law, connived-at fornication.
Nothing, of course, to make my songs ripe for prosecution.

Let's make a start. *Identify, pull, protract.* Identify the target; not easy;   35
Work at it. You're still a raw recruit to this war's weaponry.
You've found her? Now you must pull her. Seductive language needed,
Yes, lots of it. Next, protract – make the affair go on – spin it out.
That's all there is to it, the Lovemakers' Handicap race. And my chariot
Will mark out the course, the limits, the finishing line – our objective.   40

While you're still free to play the field, free to play fast and loose –
The target identify for your opening ploy: "You're the only one for me".
She won't come easy, floating down some misty evening breeze; so,
You must keep looking if you want to find the girl you fancy.
Know-how is critical. Hunters know just where to stretch out the nets   45
For the stag, or where in the valley is lurking the boar with his tusks;
The fowler's familiar with orchards; the angler with hook and line
Knows his waters, and just where they teem with uncountable fish.
You too, who hunt your quarry as fuel for a towering passion,
You too must master your hunting grounds, where all the girls hang out.   50
It's not some great expedition with sails spread to the ocean winds
That I'm suggesting; the journey is short; if you seek, you shall find.
Perseus, of course, had a long way to go to save Andromeda from
Dark-skinned Indians; Phrygian Paris, too, when he kidnapped that Greek.
But Rome herself has countless pretty girls to offer you. "Here,"   55
You will say, "I shall find the gathered beauty of the world."
Countless as all the corn in Gargara, or as Methymna's grapes,
As fishes in the seas, as leaves that shelter all the airborne birds,
Countless indeed as all the stars of heaven are the girls
That Rome provides. Venus, Aeneas' mother, still is queen   60
Of her son's own city. How do you fancy them? Young and fresh,

And not yet ripe for plucking? Right before your eyes the perfect one
Will soon appear. Rather the bloom of youth? Thousands there are
To suit your fancy. You'll confess defeat – you cannot choose.
But if your pleasure is maturity, a measure of experience, why then   65
They come, I promise, not just single spies but in battalions.

Just take a gentle stroll beneath the shade of Pompey's Portico,
When the declining sun is drawing near the tawny Lion's pelt
Of Hercules; or in Octavia's Portico, gift that a grieving mother
Once added to her son's, a rich work cloaked in marble.   70
Keep your eyes open too for Livia's Colonnade, richly adorned
With ancient paintings, memorial to its builder's famous name;
Watch too the Danaid Portico, where Belus' daughters dared to plot
Death for their hapless cousins, where savage with drawn sword
Their father stands. Don't miss Adonis' festival whom Venus lamented;   75
Let not the seventh day, which Syrian Jews hold sacred, pass you by.
Shun not the temple of Memphitic Io, the heifer dressed in linen;
Many the convert maidens she supplies to offer what she gave to Jupiter.
Try for the law-courts too; they're good for love. (Would you believe it?)
There in the noisy forum you'll light up the fires of passion.   80
Then, too, where now the shade of Venus' marble temple falls
And Appius' nymph assaults the air with compressed waters,
There will you often find an advocate, victim of Love's deceit,
Who caution preached to others but himself threw caution to the winds.
There he is, lost for the words of which he once was prodigal. The world's   85
Turned upside down when for themselves our lawyers have to plead.
And Venus mocks him meanwhile from her next door shrine;
The erstwhile Counsel is her client now, and seeks a consultation.

But above all go to the theatres, hunting in the round.
These are places where your prayers are generously answered.   90
There you will find your object of desire, or just a little bit
Of sporting slap and tickle; a one night stand perhaps or, if you prefer,
A keepsake for the longer term. Just as the crowding ants in long array
Coming and going carry in their mouths the grain that is their food;
Or as the bees head for their woodland bowers and scented fields   95
Flitting among the flowers and ravishing the wild thyme's blossoms,
So do the female smart set rush to join the crowds that watch
The games in numbers that overwhelm my powers of calculation. They
Have come there to see the sport – and to be seen. That is the place
Which, like a croupier, rakes in the losses made by chastity.   100
Romulus, you first brought Roman games into disrepute, when you
Sanctioned for Roman widowers the rape of the Sabine women.
Those were the days when awnings were not spread to overhang
The marble theatre seats; nor did our stages blush with crocus-spray;
Our floral decorations were the leaves which shady Palatine produced,   105
Crudely distributed, while the stage itself lacked all adornment.

The seats where people sat were simple sods of turf, and leaves
Not wreaths gave random cover for their unkempt hair.
On that day, expressive glances dart; each marks with a look
The woman of his choice; wild passions stir in secret hearts.　　　　110
And while the Tuscan flautist played some rough and ready tune
And the dancer tapped with his foot the triple beat, and the crowd
Kept cheering (for applause in olden times was all pretty crude),
The King gave the long-awaited signal for rape to begin.
Up they all leapt, straight away, their shouts betraying intention,　　　115
Their lecherous hands grabbing the innocent girls.
As doves, the most timid of birds, take flight from the eagle;
As newly-born lambs take flight at the sight of the wolf;
So did those terrified girls flee the men in panic disorder.
Bright cheeks lost their glow; all colour fled from their faces.　　　　120
Though one was the terror, the forms that it took were diverse:
For some tore their hair; and some simply sat, just frozen in panic;
One calls all in vain for her mother; another stays silent in sorrow;
One howls while another is dumb-struck; one stays while another
Takes flight. They are taken, led off to the rape, as loot　　　　125
For begetting of children. Yet for many their fear did them honour.
And if any resisted too much and rejected advances, on high
In the arms of her passionate partner she was lifted and carried away,
With these words, "Come, why do you ruin those delicate eyes
With such tears? As your father was once to your mother; so shall I　　130
Be to you." So, Romulus, that was the bonus you gave to your soldiers!
If you give it to me, I'm your soldier for ever, I promise.
As you see, our solemn theatricals stick to tradition and still
Present to the fairer sex the permanent threat of an ambush.

Don't miss the races either, those noble equestrian contests.　　　　135
The Circus, so packed with people, provides such good possibilities.
No need for secret signals with fingers to pass on your messages;
No need for nods to get your answer back. Just sit down
Right next to your mistress; for no-one will try to prevent you.
Get as close as you can, sit thigh to thigh; it's so easy. The rows　　140
Compel you; you cannot avoid it, even if she doesn't like it. The force
Of circumstance, the law of place, means you must touch the girl.
Find an excuse to make pleasant conversation; let your words,
Your opening words that is, be clear for all to hear. "Those horses
Approaching the starting gate – who's the owner?" Go on; do it. Ask it　145
Eagerly; then, whomever she favours, be certain to back him at once.
And while the mighty procession of youthful contestants passes by
Reserve your greatest applause for the statue of Venus, your mistress.
Next, if by luck a small speck of dust should fall on the lap
Of your lady – it happens – then with the tips of your fingers just brush it　150
Away; and if not, why then, with your finger-tips brush away – nothing.
Any excuse will suffice you to serve her ladyship.

Then if her cloak is too low slung and trails on the ground, you must
Gather it in, take infinite pains to hold it up – clear of the filth. A reward
For such services rendered will immediately come; for if she allows it,   155
You'll be given a chance to ogle her legs and give them the once over.
But take your precautions as well, just in case the man sitting
Behind you is using his knees for massage on her delicate back.
Little things please fickle minds. Many find that a cushion
Is helpful, if skilfully placed by a crafty, solicitous hand.   160
Some more helpful hints: fold a programme and fan her discreetly,
And set a light stool for support for that delicate foot.

Such are the openings the Circus will offer the lover's apprentice.
Now for the Forum, where they scatter the sands of disaster.
For there on that sand has Cupid, the offspring of Venus, fought many   165
A battle, and suffered the wounds which he watched others suffer.
For just as he speaks, holds her hand, and asks for a book, and enquires
"Who's winning?" and places his bet, he is wounded and groans
As he feels Cupid's dart and perceives the swift-flying dart, and himself
Becomes part of the tournament which he is watching.   170

Caesar lately put on a show, representing a sea-battle, bringing a fleet
Of the Persians on stage and ranged it against the might of Athens' navy.
From seas to the east and west the boys flocked in; from east and west
The girls came crowding; into Rome poured the whole wide world.
In those crowds who could fail to discover an object of love? How sad   175
That many young Romans should fall to defeat by the love of a foreigner.

But see how Caesar prepares to add what remains of the unconquered
World to his previous conquests. The utmost Orient soon shall be ours;
Parthia shall pay the penalty, bringing delight to all Crassus' sons
In their graves, and the standards so shamed by barbarian hands.   180
He comes, the Avenger, a manifest leader, young though in years.
A boy, wars he wages no boy should engage in. Let all coward souls
Cease to number the birthdays of gods. To the household of Caesar
It falls, and to Caesar himself, to learn prematurely what true valour is.
Genius, gift of the gods, grows swifter than years in the passage of time;   185
Losses it cannot bear, those penalties of cowardly procrastination.
Small though he was, Tirynthian Hercules throttled twin snakes
And thereby in his cradle proved himself a worthy scion
Of his father Jove. Bacchus, a lad you are still, but great you were
When conquered India grovelled beneath your wands.   190
O noble Youth, under your sire's experience and auspices
You shall conduct your war; under his experience and auspices
The victory shall be yours. Such a beginning, bearing such a name,
Makes victory yours by right. First of our Youth you are; but you shall be
The First of Senators. Brothers you have; avenge your brothers' wrongs.   195
A father you have; defend your father's rights. For arms you bear –

Your father's arms, arms of your fatherland; its enemies aspire
Against your father's will to seek to seize his dominions.
Holy your weapons borne in duty's cause; cursed are their arrows.
Duty and Righteousness will take their stand before your standards.   200
The Parthians have lost the argument; in battle too they must endure defeat;
My general must add to Latium the riches of the kingdoms of the East.
Great Father Mars; Caesar, our father too: grant blessings as he goes;
Gods are you both – the one already, now; the other a god to be.
Hear me – I prophesy! Victory shall be yours; I shall sing hymns   205
To pay my vows; great shouts of praise shall echo from my lips.
There shall you stand and with my words inspire your battle-line;
Heaven grant those words prove worthy of the task, a match for courage.
Mine is no song of Roman hearts that face the Parthian backs,
A foe that fires arrows from his steeds already turned to flight.   210
You flee to conquer, Parthian? What will you do when conquered?
Already ill-omened, Parthian, is the god for whom you fight.
Loveliest of all our leaders, Caesar, soon shall come the day
When you shall march in triumph, decked in gold, with four white steeds
To draw your chariot. War-lords shall go before you, bound in chains   215
About their necks, lest flight may save them now as once it did.
Young men and maidens crowding together shall with joy behold
A day of inspiration for the hearts and minds of all that see it.
And if amid the crowd some girl should ask the names of kings,
Or countries, mountains or seas, carried in the procession,   220
Answer everything – it matters not whether she asked or no.
If you don't know the answer, pretend you know it well.
This is Euphrates – his forehead is fringed with reeds;
That'll be Tigris, see how his hair hangs down all blue cerulean;
These are Armenians – let's say; this is Persia, child of Danae;   225
That was a city in the valleys of Achaemenia. There's a war-lord,
There's another; make sure you have their names, if you can;
And if you can't, pick anything that is appropriate.

5–6   *Automedon* was the charioteer of Achilles in the *Iliad*, while the helmsman *Tiphys* belongs to the
      epic Argonaut story.
27–8 A comic allusion to Hesiod's *Theogony*, where the archaic Greek poet recounts an inspirational
      meeting with the Muses at the beginning of his (very different) didactic poem about gods and heroes.
31–2 *pretty ribbons … long skirts*: the dress of respectable unmarried girls and married women
      respectively. The warning against forbidden sexual dalliance for respectable women constitutes
      technical compliance with Augustan legislation on adultery, but is of dubious sincerity (note that
      Augustus himself seems to have thought the *Ars* socially subversive – see introduction above and
      Tristia 2 = **G56**).
58   The agricultural comparisons specifically and amusingly recall details from Virgil's *Georgics*.
67–88 Here famous Roman landmarks are entertainingly described as places of assignation. These include
      (69–73) significant Augustan monuments, with some irreverence in this context as they have
      particular links with imperial ladies: the Portico of Octavia, Augustus' sister, and the colonnade
      named after Augustus' consort Livia (for the actual buildings, see **K30–K32**). For the Danaid
      portico (73), used here for its wicked women rather than its Actium associations, see on Propertius
      2.31.3, **G19** and **K38**.
93–8 A comic parody of an epic simile of Virgil's (*Aeneid* 4.402–7).

101   *Romulus*: an irreverent use of Rome's founder, with whom the 'refounder' Augustus could be compared (e.g. in the parade of great Romans in Virgil, *Aeneid* 6 = **G37**).

131–2   Possibly a comic allusion to contemporary difficulties of recruitment in the Roman army.

164   *Forum*: It was still used for some gladiatorial contests in the Augustan period.

171   *lately*: 2 BC; this mock sea-battle (see **R26**, Dio 55.10.7) celebrated the dedication of the temple of Mars Ultor in the Forum of Augustus (for which see **K17–K28**).

177   *Caesar*: ambiguous between Gaius (the leader) and Augustus (technically in charge).

178–9   *the utmost Orient … Parthia*: Gaius' expedition was clearly presented as another episode of vengeance against Parthia for the defeat of Crassus (see on Horace *Epode* 7.9, **G3**).

179–180 The legionary standards shamefully lost by Crassus in 53 BC were returned in the settlement of 20 BC and placed in the temple of Mars Ultor on its dedication in 2 BC (hence their mention here). On the standards, see **K19**, **N41–N42**.

183–4   Gaius was 19, the same age at which Augustus himself had commanded his first army at Mutina (for which see on Propertius 1.21 and 22, **G13–G14**).

194   *First of our youth*: translates the title *princeps iuventutis*, given to Gaius and his brother Lucius in 5 BC, see **J58**.

195–6   Combines complimentary allusions to Gaius' regard for his own younger brothers (Lucius and Agrippa Postumus) and for his adoptive father Augustus with allusions to the infighting in the Parthian royal family which was the technical pretext for Roman intervention in Parthia and Armenia in 1 BC (see **N25**).

G48   Antipater 47 (*Greek Anthology* 9.297)
To Gaius, setting out for Parthia in 1 BC.

This poem may be fruitfully set alongside Ovid *Ars Amatoria* 1.177–216 = **G47**, which treats the same event, the Eastern expedition of Gaius in 1 BC, with even greater flattery of Gaius.

> Set out for the Euphrates, son of Zeus. Already in haste
> The eastern Parthians are deserting to you now.
> Set out, great prince, you'll find their very bows unstrung
> For fear of you. Rule, Caesar, as your father taught you how.
> Earth's boundary, the Ocean, now alone defines the Roman nation;
> To the rising Sun yourself be first to make this declaration.

4   *Caesar … your father*: Gaius and his adoptive father Augustus.

G49   Ovid, *Fasti* 1. 1–14 (Introduction and dedication to Germanicus)

This is the introduction to Ovid's poem on the Roman calendar. It indicates that the *Fasti*, even in its half-completed state, was revised in exile after the death of Augustus, the address to whom at the beginning of Book 2 (see below) was very likely the original beginning (see *Tristia* 2.552, **G56**); Augustus was the obvious original addressee, not least because of his role as *pontifex maximus* (head of the state religion). This revised proem addresses Germanicus (16/15 BC – AD 19), grandson of Livia, probably after the death of Augustus in AD 14, when Germanicus was the adopted son of and obvious heir apparent to Augustus' successor Tiberius. Germanicus is also chosen as a suitable dedicatee since he is the likely author of an extant Latin translation of a Greek poem on astronomy (Aratus' *Phaenomena*); Aratus was used by Ovid in the astronomical parts of the *Fasti*.

   Most extracts from Ovid's *Fasti* are presented in this book in Sections **H** to **N**, with the various people, places and events they describe. For particular passages of the *Fasti*, see the concordance of passages.

> Latium's annual calendar, its times and seasons and their source,
> The signs celestial that rise and sink below the earth – these are my song.
> Caesar Germanicus, look kindly on my labour and receive
> This dedication, playing the helmsman to my timid craft.
> Though slight my compliment, turn not away; it is a gift   5

Of obligation vowed to yourself; approach and bless it with divinity.
Here you will read of holy rituals dredged from the annals of the past,
And how by its own peculiar circumstance each day is marked.
Here too you will find your family's own domestic festivals;
Oft of your father will you read, oft of your grandsire too. 10
Their ornaments triumphal which adorn my painted calendar,
These will be yours one day – your brother Drusus' too.
Let others sing of Caesar and his wars; Caesar's altars rather
Are my theme, and all the days he added to the sacred calendar.

9–10   Germanicus' father here is his adoptive father Tiberius, his grandfather Tiberius' adoptive father Augustus.

12   *Drusus*: Germanicus' adoptive brother and son of Tiberius; Germanicus held a German triumph in AD 17 which was decreed two years before (about the time of this passage), while Drusus held an ovation (lesser triumph) in AD 20.

13   *Caesar*: here Augustus, who established many of the politically significant festivals highlighted in the *Fasti*.

G50   Ovid, *Fasti* 1. 529–536   The principate foretold

This passage is spoken by the prophetic nymph Carmentis and 'foretells' the future rule of the imperial house.

"The time will come when he that guards the world will guard
You also, and the worshipper lead worship of himself. 530
Safe in Augustus' hands and of his offspring shall lie Rome's destiny;
His house shall hold the reins of empire. Thus it is decreed.
Then shall the son of this reluctant god, his grandson too,
Sustain with resolution born of heaven the burdens of their father.
And just as upon undying altars I, one day, shall honoured be 535
By sacrifice, so shall Augusta Julia be our new divinity".
Thus spoke the nymph Carmentis.

532   The *reluctant god* is Julius Caesar, his (adoptive) son Augustus (dead at the time of writing) and his (adoptive) grandson the current emperor Tiberius.

536   Augustus' widow Livia was adopted by his will into the Julian family with the name Livia Augusta (AD 14). Ovid correctly predicts her deification (by Claudius).

G51   Ovid, *Fasti* 2. 3–18   The theme of the poem and dedication to Augustus

From the probable original dedication of the *Fasti* to Augustus (see on 1.1–14 above), stressing the poet's literary ambition, relinquishing of earlier frivolity (e.g. the *Ars Amatoria*) and intent to praise Augustus.

My poems, now for the first time your sails swell to the breeze;
Not so long ago, I well remember, you were a slender work.
For me you were accomplices in love, ready for anything, as I 5
A stripling poet in the flush of youth made sport with my verses.
Now I am one that sings of holy things, the fixed seasons of the calendar.
From that to this could any man believe the poet's pathway runs?
This is my soldiering; for the arms I bear are all the arms I can. And yet
My strong right arm is not so feeble that it cannot do some service. 10

I have no strength to hurl a javelin from muscled shoulders;
I am no cavalier to ride high on the backs of mighty stallions;
Helmet I lack to guard me; girt with no sharpened sword;
(With weapons such as these a nobody can win the argument).
Your titles rather, Caesar, are my theme, which I pursue with all   15
My heart's enthusing; your lofty honours my march's destination.
Therefore draw near and with your kindly gaze behold my gifts,
If from the task of pacifying foes you find a brief respite.

15   *titles*: in the sense of commemorations of Augustus' victories in the Roman calendar, of which
        many had been inserted by him.

G52   Ovid, *Fasti* 4. 857–862   Rome's universal rule

A general encomium of Rome's worldwide supremacy, following an account of its foundation celebrated at the *Parilia* (21 April). The mention of several Caesars may allude to the situation after AD 4 when Augustus had adopted Tiberius and Tiberius had adopted Germanicus, setting up two generations of successor Caesars.

A city there arose (could any then such prophecy have credited?)
Destined to set on every land on earth a conqueror's foot.
Rome, may a universal rule be yours for ever, and for ever
Yours the rule of Caesar; may you oft possess not one but several Caesars;   860
And when you tower o'er a conquered world, I pray that you
May stand for ever head and shoulders over lesser men.

Ovid's *Metamorphoses*

The subject-matter of the *Metamorphoses* (mythological and often erotic changes of shape) allowed little opportunity for political material except at its end when the poem came to the present day in its overtly chronological structure (see on 15.812–879 = **G55**), but it is notable that two Augustan encomia are improbably and prominently inserted in mythological contexts in Book 1.

G53   Ovid, *Metamorphoses* 1.199–205

This passage (the first simile in the poem) encomiastically compares the gods' outraged reaction to the wicked Lycaon's plot against Jupiter with Rome's reaction to one of the conspiracies to assassinate Augustus.

The speech of Zeus set the high Council of the Gods a-buzzing,
All agog to know what mortal could have dared Lycaon's crime.   200
So too, when that sacrilegious gang went mad and sought
With Caesar's blood to wipe from earth the very name of Rome,
Dazed and amazed by terror at destruction's sudden menace
All humanity and all the whole wide world shrank back in horror.
And just as great Jove rejoiced to find the gods of heaven loyal,   205
So you, Augustus, did rejoice to see your nation's true fidelity.

G54   Ovid, *Metamorphoses* 1. 557–566

This conclusion of the story of the nymph Daphne (pursued erotically by Apollo) relates how she is turned into the bay-tree which then provides the garlands which famously decorated Augustus' house (along with the oak wreath, the highest Roman decoration for valour). The poet's location of the origin of these bay garlands in a failed mythological rape has been thought by some to compromise the overtly pro-Augustan effect of this passage.

Apollo cried to Daphne, "Since metamorphosed thus you can never be
My bride, yet as a tree for ever, mine you shall ever be.
My locks with your laurel always shall be decked; adorned my lyre;
My quiver also; laurel shall grace the brows of Roman generals,   560
When shouts of joy shall sing their triumphs home, and Capitol
Behold their long processions. You at Augustus' gates shall always stand,
Trustiest of guardians watching the oak-wreath of his civic crown
That hangs before his doors. And, as my head for ever keeps
Its youthful locks un-barbered, so shall you always wear   565
The springtime glory of your foliage.

G55   Ovid, *Metamorphoses* 15. 812–879

This is the conclusion of the *Metamorphoses*, which seems to have been revised by Ovid in exile (see on line 871). Apart from the final immortalisation of Ovid himself through his poetry (871–9), which might be taken as the defiant voice of the exiled poet, this passage presents two climactic and seemingly complimentary metamorphoses – that of Julius Caesar into a god, and that of Augustus into a god, the second of these being of course a future and prospective event. In 845–51, as in *Fasti* 3.697–710, **K43**, we are given the euphemistic version of the end of Caesar by which Venus snatches his soul at the moment of assassination and at once effects his apotheosis.

And thus to his daughter, Venus, Father Jupiter replied:
"On the fixed tablets of the Fates I've read your children's destiny;
I marked it well and now, dispelling your ignorance, I reveal it to you.
Caesar, the son for whom you grieve, my Cytherean goddess, has fulfilled   815
His time on earth, the cycle of his years owed to mortality is now complete.
Yours is now the task, assisted by his son, to bring him to his place as god
Among the gods of heaven, now to be worshipped in his earthly shrines.
That son, alone inheriting his father's name, shall bear alone
The burden of his destiny, and as the bravest of avengers   820
Of his father's death, shall for his wars have Jupiter himself as ally.
Under his auspices the conquered walls of Mutina besieged shall beg
For peace; Pharsalia shall know his might; while the Emathian fields
Of Macedonian Philippi shall again run wet with slaughter.
Sextus Pompeius, too, of mighty name, shall taste surrender on Sicilian waves,   825
And the Egyptian consort of Rome's general, shall find her foolish hopes
Of marriage quickly confounded by her own defeat. Empty will prove
Her threats that Rome's own Capitol shall be a slave to her Canopus.
Why should I speak of lands barbarian? Why list the nations on the furthest coasts
Of both our oceans? Name for me any corner of the inhabited world –   830
It shall be Caesar's. To him no less the seas shall also owe obedience.

But when he has given to earth the gift of peace, then shall he turn his mind
To civil jurisprudence, and as a paragon of justice pass new laws,
Establishing by force of his example a new morality for all mankind.
Scanning Time's far horizons he shall provide for ages yet to come,   835
And generations all as yet unborn, bidding his son, the offspring born
To his blessed wife, to bear his name and carry on the burden of his care.
Not till old age and length of days has to his merits matched his years
Shall he ascend to take his heavenly throne and kiss the stars, his brethren.

But now, take up this spirit from its slaughtered corpse; make of him   840
A constellation; that so for evermore our Julius, deified, may gaze
In benediction on the Capitol and Forum from his lofty shrine above."

Scarce had he finished speaking when, in the Senate's midst,
All-mothering Venus had assumed her place, invisible to all.
Then from the limbs of her beloved Caesar she caught his departing spirit,   845
Nor would she suffer it to be dissolved and scattered through the air.
Up to the stars of heaven she carried it, and as she went felt it take fire
And quicken into light. Freed from her bosom, higher than the moon
It flew, trailing its flaming tresses all along its boundless course.
His star shines out, and when he sees his offspring's mighty works   850
He owns them greater than his, and in his owned defeat rejoices.
The son forbids his deeds to be afforded precedence over his father's;
But fame, free from convention's bonds and yielding obedience to none,
Grants him the palm against his will, and in this alone is disobedient.
So too to Agamemnon, his greater son, great Atreus gives the precedence;   855
So Theseus surpasses Aegeus, and his father Peleus Achilles. So, finally,
(To cite in evidence a paradigm which honours both), his father Saturn
Proved a lesser god than Jupiter, he who in moderation rules the citadels
Of heaven, and all the kingdoms of the tripartite universe.
As Jupiter in heaven, so Augustus rules the earth, each as both Lord and Father. 860

Ye Gods above, companions of Aeneas, to whom both sword and fire
Gave way, to you I make my prayer. Ye native Gods of Italy, and thou,
Quirinus, Father of our city, Gradivus, too, father of Quirinus
The unconquerable; Vesta, revered among the household gods of Caesar;
Phoebus Apollo, who with Caesarean Vesta art Caesar's familial god;   865
And lofty Jupiter who sits on high upon Tarpeia's rock, and all such
Other gods as it is meet and right for poets to invoke, grant this my prayer:
Late be that day, far later than our time, on which the spirit of Augustus leaves
This world, where he is lord and governor, and makes its way to heaven
Where, though removed from sight, he graciously will hearken to our prayers.   870

And now my work, my monument, is done. Neither the wrath of Jupiter,
Nor fire, nor sword, nor all-devouring age can ever blot it out.
Let that last day come which has no mastery of me, save only of my body;
Come when it will and end for me the brief span of life's lottery.
My soul, my better part, shall live for ever, carried far beyond the furthest stars, 875
And there indelible on Time's memorials my name shall stand for ever.
And wheresoever Roman power spreads among its subject peoples,
There shall my name for ever flourish on the lips of men. And if
The prophecies of holy seers prove true, through all succeeding centuries
My fame shall live.

815   *Caesar*: Julius Caesar.
817   *his son*: Augustus.
820   *bravest of avengers*: see on *Fasti* 3.697–710 (**K43**).
822   *Mutina*: see on *Fasti* 4.625–8 (**H4**).

821–8   a swift summary of Augustus' military career. 823–4 repeat the strictly misleading Virgilian idea (cf. *Georgics* 1.489–92) that the battle of Pharsalus won by Julius Caesar in 48 BC and the battle of Philippi won in 42 BC by Augustus were in the same place, 825 refers to the wars against Sextus Pompey in the early 30's BC (see on Propertius 2.1.25–8, **G15**) and 826–8 to Cleopatra and Actium.

836   *his son*: Tiberius, Livia's son, adopted by Augustus in AD 4.

852   *the son*: Augustus. The comparison which follows seems to be encomiastic of Augustus rather than denigratory of Julius Caesar.

868–70   These lines represent the general approach of the Augustan poets to the status of Augustus, arguing that he will be a god after his death.

871   *Neither the wrath of Jupiter*: a reference to thunder and lightning, but also matching closely the language used by Ovid of the anger of Augustus which led to his exile. These final lines seem to be written from a post-exilic perspective: Ovid's poetry will outlive his miserable physical existence and be independent of political control (cf. line 873).

G56   Ovid, *Tristia* 2.1–360 and 2.497–578: The Poet's Lament

This, the longest of the exile poems at 578 lines, occupying a whole book of the *Tristia*, is Ovid's major plea to Augustus for clemency, written early in his exile (AD 9). In it the poet blames his poetry and his mysterious 'error' (see Introduction, page 99) for his situation; the 'error' is clearly so sensitive as to be unmentionable, but the poetry and especially the *Ars Amatoria* (see **G47**) is vigorously defended, along with much flattery of Augustus. As often in the exile poetry, Ovid pleads for a better place of exile than the distant and uncultured Tomis, rather than actual return to Italy (181–6, 573–8).

My books, why should I waste my time on you? You've brought me nothing
    But hard labour and bad luck. I'm in despair – and ruined by my talent.
Damnation to the Muses! Why then go straight back to them? They caused
    Your condemnation – you got what you deserved. Isn't one penalty enough?
Ah, but it was my poems that made both men and women want to know me;   5
    But alas! I wrote them when omens were unfavourable.
It was my poems that had me branded for depravity by Caesar, and placed
    My *Art of Love* upon the Index of forbidden books.
Take poetry from my life, and from my life you take away the grounds
    Of condemnation; on the debit side of my account I place my guilty verses.   10
Such is the profit of my toil and all my late night labours, such
    My reward – talent has brought me only punishment.
If I were wise I'd hate those learned sister-Muses – justly so, because
    To us their devotees they are divinities who bring disaster.

But such is the insanity that plays companion to my illness, now I've stubbed   15
    My toe, I'm here again kicking the very rock I kicked before,
Like some defeated come-back gladiator who can't resist the arena's lure,
    Or shipwrecked vessel putting out to sea again to face the storm.
As Telephus, Teuthrania's sometime lord, found in the spear that wounded him
    The cure; so too perhaps my wound will find its source also the cure.   20
My Muse may find the means to still the rage that once she stirred in Caesar;
    Often to song's persuasion are the gods susceptible, for all their power.
Caesar himself commanded once mothers and daughters of Ausonia to sing
    A hymn to Ops, the turret-crowned, the Goddess of Abundance;
For Phoebus, too, he ordered hymns upon that day when once he held   25
    The Centennial Games, which every generation sees but once.
Caesar, Most Merciful, these are my precedents, through these I pray to you,
    Grant that your anger may grow soft before my inspiration's prayer.
Your wrath indeed was righteous; nor can I still deny I got my just deserts –
    Nor yet so brazen am I still that shame no longer sits upon my lips –   30

But, if I had not sinned, what scope could then be found to show your mercy?
  In this my fate your mercy may find material and scope.

If every time humanity had sinned Jupiter had hurled his thunderbolts,
  How soon would he have emptied all his armoury.
Now when he thunders down and makes the wide world cringe before his roar,   35
  He puts to flight the rain-clouds and once more makes pure the air.
Rightly, then, is he called the Father of gods, their only Governor;
  Rightly the whole wide firmament believes that none is mightier than Jove;
You likewise, Augustus, are proclaimed your country's Father and its Governor;
  Model your action, therefore, on the god with whom you share those titles.   40
Indeed you do so; nor did anyone that laid his hands upon the reins of empire
  Ever display so great capacity for moderation.
To conquered foes how often you gave pardon, pardon the like of which
  To you no victor would have granted were the roles reversed.
How many have I seen promoted to riches and high offices,   45
  Who once took arms against your very life.
And yet the day that saw their warfare end, ended your anger too; and so
  Together to the temples friend and foe brought out their offerings.
Just as your soldiery rejoice to see the conquest of their enemies, so too
  Your enemies have reason to rejoice at their own downfall.   50
Mine is a better cause, for none can say that I bore arms against you;
  None can say I followed the armies of your enemies.
By sea, and land, and all divinities invisible I swear; I swear
  By your own self, your godhead present, manifest to all:
This heart of mine was always on your side, O Mightiest of men;   55
  My mind was yours I swear, for there alone my loyalties abide.
I prayed that you would find your way to join the stars of heaven, but late
  In time; I was a humble member of a mighty congregation
Which made that self-same prayer; incense of loyalty I burned for you, as one
  Among the multitude, who with my prayers assisted public prayer.   60

Need I remind you that my books are full to overflowing with your name,
  And even those that damned me hold a thousand references.
Inspect my greater work, my *Metamorphoses*, still left unfinished – there
  I tell the tale of forms transformed in ways incredible.
There you will find my public proclamations of your name,   65
  There you will find my sure and certain proofs of loyalty.
No song can make your glory greater than it is, nor find a space
  In which by growing it could greater be.
Great Jove has fame enough; and yet it pleases him to hear his deeds
  Become the stuff of legend, and himself material for song,   70
And when men tell of battles in his wars against the Giants, we must believe
  He takes delight to hear his praises sung.
Your praises others sing in lofty tone, as fits the theme; with genius
  Far more copious than mine they hymn your glory.
But still, though heaven's favour may be won with outpoured blood of hecatombs 75
  Of oxen, yet 'tis won no less by tiny offerings of incense.

It was some savage enemy, alas!, un-named and all too cruel, that read to you
   Those verses which I light-heartedly composed.
He could instead have read you from my books poems which sang your praises,
   And earned from you for me a kinder judgement.   80
I lost all my friends, for Caesar's enmity meant none could be my friend,
   And at such a time I to myself was all but enemy.
Just as when once an earthquake-stricken house begins to fall, and all
   Its weight leans in upon its weakened elements,
If by some chance a tiny crack appears, then the whole edifice gapes open wide, 85
   And crumbling falls in ruins beneath its weight; so I,
Thanks to my songs, received the enmity of men – and justly so; but yours,
   Yours was the countenance which to the crowd gave leadership.

Yet I remember that there was a time when my life and character received
   Your approbation, as in the Knights' parade I rode my steed, your gift.   90
But if that cannot stand to my advantage, if I can gain no credit for my merits,
   Remember this at least: there was a time when I was free from censure.
I held within my hands the fate of men accused; and my performance justified
   That trust; for those same cases passed the scrutiny of *centumvirs*.
In private cases too, as sole Adjudicator, my judgements were received   95
   Without complaint, and even losing parties found me fair.
Ah, woe is me – my blighted recent past has ruined me, though ten times over
   I could have summoned your own judgements then to my defence.
One final slip spelled ruin, my frail craft, survivor of so many raging seas,
   Deep in the ocean depths now lies, wrecked by a single storm.   100
I am destroyed, not by some single particle of sea; rather the total force
   Of every wave and all great ocean's might have fallen upon my head.

Something I saw – why did I choose to see? Why did I make my eyes accomplices?
   I knew the fault – why then did I fail to recognise its true significance?
Actaeon unwitting once beheld Diana naked – yet, for all his innocence   105
   He fell a prey to his own hunting dogs.
Even among the gods on high it seems bad luck demands a recompense;
   No accident brings pardon when a god is wronged.
On that same day when my accursed error led me astray, my house,
   My modest house was utterly destroyed, though faultless utterly.   110
Modest it was indeed – and yet they say as famous in our fathers' time
   And no less illustrious than any other,
Famous it was neither for too much wealth nor poverty; rather a fount
   Of knights famed for their lack of fame in wealth or poverty.
Granted my house is modest in its wealth, its origins obscure, yet still   115
   Thanks to my genius its fame will know no bounds.
And though I misused that genius with all the excess frivolity of youth,
   Yet have I won myself a name whose greatness the whole world knows.
Vast schools of learned doctors know my name, and none would dare
   To number among their objects of contempt Ovidius Naso's name.   120
And so my house, though favoured by the Muses, has tumbled to its ruin
   Fallen beneath the weight of one severe indictment.

But yet its fall is such that it can rise again – it only needs that time
    May ripen Caesar's wrath into forgiveness.
Great was your clemency when you chose my punishment, which proved   125
    Kinder than apprehension's expectation.
You gave me back my life; your anger's march was halted short of death.
    Great prince, how sparingly you used your power!
And yet a further gift you gave me – as if my life were never gift enough:
    The wealth of my inheritance was spared from confiscation.   130
As for my deeds, you spared them senatorial condemnation;
    No special court imposed my banishment.
Savage invective, worthy of a prince, became the medium by which
    You took your own reprisal for your injuries.
Harsh was your edict, gravely threatening, and yet the terms   135
    In which my penalty was named were mild:
For I was described as "relegated", "absent by compulsion", but not "exiled";
    Specific to my fate and mine alone the terms of that decree.

Only a witless madman could conceive a punishment more dire than thus
    To find himself the source of anger to so great a potentate.   140
But sometimes it can happen that a god allows his divinity to be appeased;
    Sometimes the storm-clouds flee and the bright day returns.
I have seen an elm tree burgeon with its load of vine leaves,
    Even when smitten by the bolt of savage Jupiter.
Though you may bid me banish all my hopes, hope I shall always hold;   145
    Though you forbid it, hope alone and always stays alive.
My hopes greatly revive, gentlest of princes, when I turn my thoughts to you;
    My hopes die back when those same thoughts return to what I did.
For I am like the seas tossed by the winds, whose anger ever lacks consistency;
    Their madness is uneven and their rage rises and falls;   150
Sometimes their wild crescendo dies away, and for a while they fall
    So silent one would think that they had lost their forces.
So too my fears – they vanish, they return; they chop and change,
    Giving me hope that I may soften you, and then destroying it.

Therefore by all the gods, to whom I pray with confidence that they   155
    Will grant you length of days, if they but love the name of Rome;
By this our native land, whose safety and security depend on you, our Father,
    This land of which I recently was part, one of its people –
By these I pray: that all the debt your thoughts and actions have well merited
    Our grateful city will repay to you for ever;   160
I pray that Livia may long be spared to share with you companionable years;
    No other husband ever could deserve a wife so noble;
Had she not been born, unmarried life would best have suited you;
    No other woman was there so fitted to take you as her spouse;
I pray that, like you, your son Tiberius may safely live to rule one day   165
    In his old age, with you beside him as senior colleague;
I pray your grandsons, Drusus and Germanicus, bright lights of youth, may emulate
    And then surpass the deeds alike of father and grandfather;

I pray that Victory, never a stranger to Augustus' camp, may now be present
    To your aid, and visit the standards that she knows so well,   170
And round Ausonia's general hovering now on her familiar wings,
    Place on his shining locks the victor's laurel wreath;
He is the one through whom you wage your wars; through his right arm you fight;
    To him you delegate your mighty auspices and all your gods;
Divided, in half your person you are present here to guard your city;   175
    In him the other half is far away waging Rome's savage wars;
I pray for you that he comes back to Rome a victor over conquered enemies,
    Shining on high on his triumphal charger, decked with garlands.
For these my prayers, I pray you in return to spare me, bury your thunderbolts,
    That savage weaponry which, to my cost, I know too well.   180
Spare me, I pray you, Father of our Country, and as this name suggests,
    Be merciful and do not deny to me some hope of your forgiveness.
I pray not for return, though we can believe that the mighty gods
    Have oft vouchsafed us greater than we asked.
If you but grant my prayer a gentler exile, nearer to Rome, the greater part   185
    Of this my punishment is lifted from my shoulders.

In sufferings I now endure the ultimate – thrust out among the enemies of Rome,
    To where no exile could be further from his homeland.
Alone I am cast out, sent to the Danube's seven estuaries, where I am crushed
    Beneath the frozen pole-star of Parrhasian Callisto.   190
Here the Ciziges and the Colchians, the Teretean hordes, the Getan tribes,
    Are scarcely warded off by Danube's stream which flows between.
Others have been expelled for graver misdemeanours; none has received
    A land than mine more distant as his place of exile.
No land there is so distant, save the homes of ice and cold and enemies;   195
    And the unfathomable sea with waters gripped in iron bonds of ice.
Here on the left, ill-omened Euxine coast, is Rome's last outpost of dominion;
    Beyond, the Bastarnae and Sauromatians hold the land.
Here is the last extremity of Rome's Ausonian law, which barely clings
    As if by fingertips upon the very edge and margins of your rule.   200

These are the reasons for my prayer, that you will banish me to some safe spot,
    That losing my native land I may not also lose my peace of mind:
Spare me the fear of native tribesmen, to whom the Danube is no barrier,
    That I, your citizen, may live beyond the reach of captors.
It is the sacred right of those who spring from Latin ancestry, that while   205
    The Caesars live, they never should be bondsmen to barbarians.

Two crimes proved my undoing: first a poem; then a misjudgement.
    About the charge and fault in one I must not speak –
My insignificance is such I dare not open up again the wounds I caused
    To Caesar; it is enough that once I pained him to excess.   210
The other charge remains: that by a filthy poem I have become
    To all instructor in obscene adultery.
Even the hearts of heavenly beings must sometimes fall into error;
    Many the trivia which must be too small for your attention.

Just as great Jupiter, who guards the gods and all the heavens on high,   215
   Has not the time to turn his mind to unimportant trifles,
So too while you survey the mighty globe which now on you depends,
   These lesser things should not to you be matters of concern.
It is absurd to think the ruler of the world should leave his post
   To read my little ditties set to uneven measures.   220
The weighty circumstance of Rome's prestige makes no such demands;
   Nor does its burden on your shoulders lie so light that you
Can turn your godhead to take note of silly, sportive trifles, censoring
   With your own eyes my casual scribblings.
Now there is Pannonia to subdue; and now the coastline of Illyria;   225
   Raetia now alarms us; now the Thracians are up in arms.
Armenia sues for peace; and now with timid hand the Parthian horseman
   Surrenders to you his bow and Crassus' captured standards.
Now through your son the Germans feel the vigour of your prime,
   As now a Caesar on behalf of mighty Caesar wages war.   230
In short, greater than ever in all our history extends our empire, yet
   No single part of it is subject to the weakness of decay.

The city also wearies you, your guardianship of laws, and your concern
   For morals, which you long to see matching your own.
The peace you bring to all the nations can never be your lot, because   235
   You wage an unrelenting war against men's vices.
How then can it surprise me that amidst this weight of overwhelming cares
   You lacked the time to read my scrolls of sportive verses?
How I could wish that you had had the time – for if you had, never
   In all my *Art* would you have found the grounds for accusation.   240
That poem, I confess it, wears no mask of due solemnity, nor yet
   Does it possess such qualities as make it worthy of a prince's eye.
Yet are its contents not of such a kind as are forbidden by the law's command,
   Nor does it offer education to Rome's young wives.
And lest you doubt for whom I write my books, four lines of verse   245
   In one of its three volumes can be found, as follows:
"Away pretty ribbons, away you symbols of a maiden's modesty;
   Be off long skirts that hide those pairs of pretty ankles.
I sing of naught forbidden by the law, permitted fornication,
   Nothing, of course, to make my songs ripe for prosecution."   250
Is it not true that from this work of *Art* I have strictly removed all women
   Whom robe and marriage-garland declare protected persons?

"But", you reply, "even a matron has the power to use forbidden wiles;
   And gain the know-how to enable her to tempt untaught."
Well then, you must deny our Roman matrons opportunity to read. From any poem
   They'll find material enough to enhance delinquency.
If they be but disposed to viciousness, they'll find – whate'er they touch –
   Material with which to train their morals for depravity.
Let her peruse old Ennius' *Annals* – crudest tale of all – and there she'll learn
   Just how it was that Trojan Ilia became a mother.   260

Lucretius' opening line, "Mother of all Aeneas' lineage", will surely make her ask
    By whom sweet Venus once became progenitor of the Aeneadae.
If in due order I may bring my evidence, then I shall later show
    That every kind of poem may corrupt man's tender soul.
Yet that is no reason, surely, why all books should be condemned? Nothing   265
    Of benefit there is that lacks concomitant capacity for harm.
What greater benefit has man than fire? But if some criminal prepares
    To burn your thatches, then with fire he arms his evil hands.
Medicines will sometimes remove, sometimes restore a patient's health;
    Thus it teaches us which herbs are beneficial, which are dangerous.   270
The robber and the cautious traveller alike gird on their swords, the one
    To lay an ambush, but the traveller for self-defence.
Men learn the art of eloquence that they may plead the cause of innocence;
    Yet sometimes it condemns the innocent, the guilty it protects.
So too with poetry: provided it is read with upright mind, it's clear   275
    Poems can do no harm to anyone – not even mine!
If anyone believes that from such source vices arise, he is mistaken
    And exaggerates the influence of my writings.
Suppose, however, I admit the charge – are not the games as much the source
    Of wickedness? As for the theatres – you'd better close the lot.   280
Many are led astray where in the Campus Martius they set up the voting pens –
    When sands of martial contests strew the hard earth.
Abolish the Circus – its licentiousness is hardly safe for any one; for here
    The maiden sits in close proximity to men she does not know.
Why are the colonnades still open? Here women of a certain kind parade   285
    In hopes that there they'll meet their customers.

What places are more august than our temples? Of these as well beware,
    If you're a woman with a temperament for vice.
When woman stands within the shrine of Jupiter, the thought may well occur
    How many of her kind have Jupiter to thank for their maternity.   290
But if she slips next door to make her prayer at Juno's temple, she will think
    Of all the bitter grudges Juno bore towards her husband's paramours.
Let her but look on Pallas' statue and straightway she'll ask how it could be
    That virgin goddess brought up Erichthonius, born of sin.
Suppose she enters mighty Mars' temple, your gift to Rome, there Venus stands   295
    United by Cupid to the Avenger god, her husband locked outside.
But if she sits in Isis' temple, then she will ask why Juno, Saturnian queen,
    Hounded her over the Ionian sea and out beyond the Bosphorus.
Anchises will ever keep alive the memory of Venus; and Endymion
    Hero of Latmos the memory of the Moon; Iasion of Ceres.   300
Anything can corrupt the minds of those whose minds are ready for depravity.
    Everything has its place, and if retained therein can do no harm.

My *Art* was written solely for courtesans; as for our well-bred ladies,
    Its opening page commands them to keep their hands well off.
When women rush to trespass on forbidden ground, the priest who denied   305
    Them entry is cleared of blame; theirs is the culpability.

But yet it cannot be a crime to read sweet songs of love; for much there is
    The chaste and good may read about and yet refrain from imitation.
Our matrons of severest mien behold the naked shapes of women
    As they stand ready for every kind of lechery;   310
Our Vestals' eyes must gaze upon the forms of prostitutes; but yet
    The owner of those eyes has not been deemed deserving of penalty.

So why then is my Muse too frivolous by half? And for what reason does
    My book provide for men incitement to make love?
There's nothing for it – transgression I must confess; my sin is ever before me. 315
    I am ashamed of my misjudgement and misuse of talent.
Why rather did my poems not torture Troy once again and tell,
    How once it fell before the armoured ranks of Argives?
Why was Thebes not my song, its seven gates each manned by a chosen general,
    Where two brothers mortal wounds inflicted each on the other?   320
Rome, the embodiment of war, herself did not deny material, and to sing
    The story of one's native land indeed is patriotic labour.
And finally, great Caesar, you have filled the whole world with your deeds;
    Surely I should have found a voice to sing of one small part of them?
Just as the sun with all its radiant beams attracts the eye, so too   325
    Your deeds should surely have aroused my dormant muse.
I stand accused; yet is it not deserved. I plough a narrow furrow in my fields;
    For me the theme of Caesar is too great, its harvest too abundant.
 The skiff that dares the dangers of the boating lake on holiday should not
    Imagine it is therefore fit to trust itself to life on the ocean wave.   330
It may be that I (though even this I doubt) am better suited to the lighter vein,
    Able enough to turn my hand to unpretentious verses.
Were you to bid me tell the tale of Giants tamed by the lightning stroke
    Of Jupiter, the burden would overwhelm me, I would fail.
Imagination's riches are required to recount our Caesar's mighty deeds;   335
    Without it, the poet's labour would be swamped by his material.
But still I dared the attempt; but in attempting I detracted from my theme,
    And – which was tantamount to blasphemy – damaged your majesty.

Hence to my lesser task did I return, the trivial songs of youth, and stirred
    The heart within my breast with love's romantic fictions.   340
Would God I had not done so, but my fates impelled me forward twisting
    To my own detriment the ingenuity that nature gave me.
Alas for my learning! Woe for my parents' gift of education! Why
    Did my eyes enjoy delight of dalliance with letters?
Such literary lechery was the cause you hated me; I told of arts   345
    By which you feared lest dangerous liaisons be aroused.
Yet from my pedagogy have no brides yet learned deception's arts.
    How could they? None can instruct where they are ignorant.
Such were the gentle songs of love's delights which I devised,
    That never did breath of scandal even whisper across my name.   350
Nor is there even among the common herd a single husband who
    Can doubt through fault of mine his claim to fatherhood.

Trust me, my character is different far from what my songs suggest –
  My life is modesty itself, my Muse merely a jester –
Of my work the greater part is pure romantic fiction, quite untrue to life;   355
  For itself it claims more licence than to its humble author is allowed.
For the construction of a writer's mind no book reveals; its aim is pure delight.
  Innumerable pleasures it deploys to charm the hearer's ear.
Were it not so, Accius would be a monster, Terence a dissolute,
  And bellicose would every poet seem that sang of savage wars…..   360

….. And what if I had written mimes, with all their filthy jokes? For they
  Are always guilty of incitement to forbidden lecheries.
In them the smooth adulterer figures constantly, while the crafty wife
  Spins cunning stories to deceive her simple-minded husband.   500
And who are the spectators? The nubile maid, the matron, and her husband,
  Her son, and nearly all the members of the Senate.
Nor does it suffice to have their ears assaulted with abominable language,
  But they must also make their eyes familiar with a host of shameful deeds.   504
And when the seducer has deceived the husband by some novel trickery, the cheers
  Ring out and gifts of garlands greet the author's popularity.
The more debased the drama of our stage, the higher grows the profit, while the fees
  The hapless praetor pays grow greater in proportion.
Look at your own expenses for your Games, Augustus, you will find
  Expenses innumerable like these, all costing you a fortune.   510
You've seen such things yourself; you've often given us such spectacles –
  Such is the kindly nature of your all-pervading majesty –
And with your eyes, whose beams shed light on every corner of the globe,
  You've watched with equanimity such staged adulteries.
If it is right and proper to create these mimes which mimic filthy lechery,   515
  Surely some lesser penalty is due to my material?

Can it be perhaps the stage itself that makes this sort of writing safe for authors?
  Has theatre's licence been conceded also to staged mimes?
My poems also often have been set to dancing for the people; often too
  They've even offered entertainment, Caesar, to your eyes.   520
Surely you must admit that, as in our homes the ancient portraits gleam
  With forms of heroes painted by artists' hands, so too
There is some spot in which at least some miniature resides, which shows
  The many forms of Venus and the varied acts of love?
One shows a seated Ajax, son of Telamon, with rage transparent on his face;   525
  Another Medea, the barbarian mother, with murder in her eyes;
But there's a Venus, too, who through her fingers wrings her sea-drenched hair,
  Her modesty scarce veiled by the waves that gave her birth.

Some make their songs of warfare to resound with clash of bloody weapons,
  Some sing the glories of your lineage, some hymn your deeds.   530
But nature through envy has begrudged me this, and hemmed me within
  A narrow compass, granting but slender powers to my muse.
And yet the blessed author of your own beloved *Aeneid* was allowed to get

His *"Arms and a Hero"* into Dido's Carthaginian bed;
Nor is there any section of that mighty work more read than this, the tale   535
    Of illegitimate liaison in a bond of consummated love.
Its youthful author, Virgil, once before described the fiery loves of Phyllis
    And the gentle Amaryllis, all in the sportive strains of pastoral.
I also long ago wrote pastoral; I too was guilty of that same offence;
    My fault was hardly novel, yet my penalty is novelty indeed.   540
I wrote my songs in days when you were censorious of our misdemeanours.
    Yet as a Knight I passed you on the street often, but always un-rebuked.
Such were the reasons why in my youthful folly careless, I believed
    My words would bring no harm; now I am old they have.
For late in time the waves of retribution have submerged that book   545
    From long ago; far distant from past crime is present penalty.

And yet I beg you, do not imagine all my work is frivolous; for I
    Upon my vessel often have unfurled some splendid sails.
Six books of the Calendar, and six again, have I composed; each book
    With month coincident, its ending shared by month and book alike.   550
This is the work I recently composed under your patronage, O Caesar,
    This the work to you I dedicated – but my fate has now disrupted it.
Then, to the tyrants of the tragic stage I gave their royal sceptres, and speech
    Grandiloquent, well suited to the mighty buskin's themes.
I sang no less of metamorphoses and those whose forms took on new shapes,   555
    Though at the last my hands lacked the final touch.
Would that you might but briefly turn your mind from anger, and command
    At your leisure but a few short lines from this to be declaimed,
Those lines in which, beginning from the world's first origins, I took
    My tale down to these present times of yours, great Caesar.   560
Then will you see how great has been your heart's own gift to me,
    And with what heartfelt love I sing of you and yours.

None have I injured with the destructive malice of my song;
    None by my verses stood accused of crime.
My wit is innocent; always I shunned a bitter, gall-doused humour;   565
    No jokes of mine are scripted with letters from a poisoned pen.
Among so many thousands of our citizens and all my myriad writings, I –
    And I alone – am wounded by my Muse, Calliope.
So, for this reason, I believe no Roman citizen rejoices at my downfall;
    Many I think are grieved by my misfortunes.   570
It is incredible that any should mock and kick me when I'm down, if they
    Can feel one spark of generosity towards my verses' lack of inhibition.

These are my prayers. May they and others like them bend your holy will,
    O Father, your country's saviour and protector.
I ask not to return to Italy's Ausonian shores, unless perhaps one day
    For the long tedium of my punishment compassion conquers you;   575
Only a safer exile and a quieter place of sojourn is my plea,
    That so my penalty may better match the scale of my offence.

21   the reference is clearly to the *Ars Amatoria*.

23–7   a reference to Horace's *Centennial Hymn* (**L28**).

39   *your country's father*: Augustus' highest honour – cf. on *Fasti* 2.119–44, **H38**.

41–8   These lines stress Augustus' vaunted mercy to opponents (*clementia* – see **H24**).

62   A reference to the propagandistic parts of the *Ars Amatoria* (see on Ars 1.1–228, **G47**).

63   *my Metamorphoses, still left unfinished* : the incomplete state of the *Metamorphoses* is stressed by Ovid early in exile (e.g. *Tristia* 1.7); it must have been all but complete, but seems to have been edited in exile (see on *Met*.15.871, **G55**). The claim that the *Metamorphoses* includes praise of Augustus is true (see **G53–G55**).

79   *poems which sang your praises* : esp. the *Fasti* (see **G49**).

90   *Knight's parade* : Ovid belonged to the élite equestrian class, who were technically supplied with their formal parade horses by the emperor (see **T30**).

93–6   An allusion to Ovid's career as a minor magistrate.

103–9   These obscure lines are the clearest hint as to Ovid's unmentionable 'error', suggesting via the Actaeon myth that he witnessed (and failed to reveal?) something politically sensitive (e.g. the adulteries of the younger Julia; cf. introduction above).

161–68 Flattery of the imperial house is here added to flattery of Augustus himself.

181   *Father of our Country*: see on 39 above.

207–10 see on 103–9 above.

211   *filthy poem* : the *Ars Amatoria*.

229   *your son*: Tiberius, campaigning in Germany.

242–52 see on *Ars Amatoria* 1.31–2, **G47**.

260   *Ilia*: she was raped by Mars and became the mother of Romulus and Remus.

294   *born of sin*: Ericthonius in myth sprang from the ground and the sperm of Hephaestus, spilt as he attempted to rape Athene.

297–8   Isis as the heroine Io was one of Jupiter's many conquests and hounded by Juno.

335–8   The claim to have written on Augustus' deeds appears to be unfounded, unless it alludes to *Amores* 1.1, where Ovid represents Cupid as interrupting his epic poem and turning him to love-elegy.

353–60 A key argument: immoral poetry does not mean an immoral author.

359   *Accius ... Terence*: leading tragic and comic playwrights.

487   *mimes*: a very popular form of performance in the Augustan period, with scripts, music and slapstick action.

533   *your own beloved Aeneid*: Virgil's undeniably Augustan epic is wittily argued to have improper elements.

549   Ovid's apparent claim here to have written all twelve books of the *Fasti* when only six are extant is highly problematic (unless Books 7–12 were indeed written but have since been lost). Since he here argues (justifiably) that this is his most Augustan work, he may be misleadingly suggesting that he has the other six flattering books ready and that their publication would be a *quid pro quo* for the emperor's mercy.

553–4   A reference to Ovid's lost tragedy *Medea* (see Introduction).

556   see on 63 above.

558–60 The reference appears to be to the flattering conclusion to the *Metamorphoses* (translated above, *Met*.15.812–879 = **G55**).

FROM TRIUMVIRATE TO PRINCIPATE

This section contains sources relating to the establishment of the principate, the term used to describe Augustus' position as *princeps*. Full consideration of the period of the triumvirate, November 43 BC to 33/32 BC, lies outside the scope of this book. Nonetheless, since putting 'Octavian' behind him was a crucial part of the 'Settlement of 28/27 BC' some sources dating to the triumviral period are included. The sources are arranged by the chronology of the events described.

Triumvir (H1–H8)

H1   Augustus' signet ring

Initially the deified Augustus used a signet ring engraved with a sphinx. He had found two such rings in his mother's collection, so alike as to be indistinguishable. During the civil wars, when he was away from Rome, his friends used one of them to sign letters and decrees which the exigencies of the moment required to be issued in his name. His correspondents used to make a nice little quip to the effect that "the sphinx is riddling again." Later Augustus sought to avoid the sphinx's unpleasant associations by signing documents with an image of Alexander the Great.

[Pliny, *Natural History* 37.10]

Sphinx: the mythical riddler appears also on coins from Pergamum under the legend 'AUGUSTUS'. Suetonius (*Augustus* 50) adds that later still, the seal with Alexander the Great was replaced by one with his own head. Augustus deliberately associated himself with Alexander the Great: see **Index** 'Alexander'.

H2   Caesar's heir, *aureus*, 43 BC

Obv.:   Bare head of Octavian right, bearded.
      C CAESAR COS PONT AVG (Gaius Caesar, *consul, pontifex, augur*)
Rev.:   Head of Julius Caesar, wearing laurel wreath, right.
      C CAESAR DICT PERP PONT MAX (Gaius Caesar, perpetual dictator, *pontifex maximus*)

[*RRC* 490/2, *BMCRR* Gaul 74]

This coin is dated to late 43 BC, when at the age of nineteen Octavian became consul for the first time on 19 August, after his march on Rome in July. It is one of his earliest portraits. The twin busts of Octavian and Julius Caesar and the shared name emphasise the close connection between them on which Octavian was trying to capitalise. He wears a beard as a sign of mourning for his adoptive father. His name on the obverse reveals the important point that in the 40s he styled himself Gaius Caesar. He was well aware of the talismanic value of this adopted name in securing the support he needed to succeed to Julius Caesar's inheritance.

H3   Octavian's delight at a comet appearing after Julius Caesar's assassination

His own words are evidence of his delight: "Coincident with the very days in which I was celebrating my games," he wrote, "a comet shone for a whole week in the northern sky.

It rose about an hour before sunset, shining brightly and clearly visible in all lands. The common people believed it was a sign that Caesar's spirit had been received into the conclave of the immortal gods, and as a symbol of that event the likeness of a star was added to the bust of Caesar, which we shortly after dedicated in the Forum". So much for his public sentiments. Privately, however, he had a different interpretation and rejoiced to think that the birth of the comet referred to himself and that he had been born under its protection. Certainly, to tell the truth, it did appear to have a salutary effect everywhere.

[Pliny, *Natural History*, 2.94]

Presumably Pliny quotes here from Augustus' (lost) autobiography. The games (between 20 and 30 July, 44 BC) were in honour of Venus *Genetrix* (Venus the Ancestress, that is the claimed ancestress of the Julian family). After Julius Caesar's official deification in 42 BC Octavian used 'Divi filius' (son of the Deified), as part of his official title (see e.g **H18** and note on Section **B** –31 BC).

H4   The battle of Mutina in Ovid, *Fasti*

On the next day, the fourteenth, mariner, head for the harbour   625
And safety. Storms from the west are coming, mixed with hail.
Yet come what may, this is the self-same day that Caesar struck
The armies of Mutina with a hail-storm of his own – his soldiery.

[Ovid, *Fasti* 4. 625–628]

This passage and (**H5**) from Ovid's poem on the Roman calendar mark the anniversary on 14 April of the battle of Mutina (43 BC), the occasion when the 19-year old future Augustus won his first military victory (see also Propertius' poem **G15.27**), and the official proclamation two days later of his title of *imperator*, 'Commander'. Both dates are marked on the Augustan calendar at Cumae (**C40**).

H5   Octavian hailed as *imperator* in Ovid, *Fasti*

This fifteenth day is that which Cytherean Venus once commanded
To speed more quickly, hurrying her horses on a looser rein downhill
To sunset, that the more quickly should the next day dawn and bring   675
To young Augustus victory and the accolade of *imperator*.

[Ovid, *Fasti* 4. 673–676]

H6   Law and morality during the Civil Wars

Gnaeus Pompeius was then elected consul for the third time with a programme for the reform of public morality, but the remedies proved worse than the disease they were designed to eliminate. He turned out to be both author and subverter of his own legislation, losing by force of arms what by force of arms he had sought to impose. This was immediately followed by twenty years of constant civil war with the total breakdown of law and order. The most abominable crimes went unpunished; the most admirable deeds proved a recipe for disaster. At long last, in his sixth consulship [28 BC], Caesar Augustus felt his position to be sufficiently secure to revoke the laws he had introduced as Triumvir and to introduce the new constitution which we now enjoy in peace under the principate.

But the result was that our slavery intensified. We lived under constant surveillance by informers, for whom the rewards available under the legislation of Papius and Poppaeus proved a great incentive. As a result, anyone who failed to win the privileges of parenthood found his property deemed vacant and forfeit to the state in its capacity as the parent of all its citizens. The corrosive effects of this evil and its disastrous consequences for so many estates came to afflict the life of the whole community, whether in Rome, Italy, or elsewhere.

[Tacitus, *Annals* 3.28]

Tacitus is led to digress on law and morality in relating a proposal to amend legislation on family matters, *Annals* 3.25: see **S9**.

Gnaeus Pompey: Pompey the Great was consul for the third time in 52 BC: he legislated against bribery and violence and regulated judicial procedure and rules on the election and tenure of officials. The legislation was severe, but for his friends' benefit he ignored these restraints.

Force of arms: civil war broke out at the beginning of 49 BC, when Julius Caesar crossed the Rubicon and invaded Italy, and ended with the capture of Alexandria in August 30 BC.

Revoke the laws: see Dio 53.2.5: the revocation probably consisted in his proclaiming that laws might be challenged in the courts: outright blanket revocation would have meant invalidating acts on which the careers and fortunes of survivors depended.

Triumvir: see *RG* 1.4 and 7.1 with notes (Section **A**).

New constitution: the settlement of 28–27 BC: see **H18–H25**.

Informers: they both supplied information to prosecutors and brought their own prosecutions.

H7   The change in Augustus

The deified Augustus was a mild *princeps*, as long as you judge him from the beginning of his principate. When, as Triumvir, he shared the state with others, he could kill with the best of them. When he was eighteen years old, the same age as you are now, he had already buried his dagger in his friends' hearts; he had already plotted to assassinate Mark Antony, the consul; he had already been party to the proscriptions.

[Younger Seneca, *Concerning Clemency* 1.9.1]

H7 and **H8** introduce and conclude Seneca's explanation of the clemency shown by Augustus towards a would-be assassin, Cinna (see **P11**). Seneca seeks to furnish a good example to his addressee and former pupil, the emperor Nero, but also to flatter him by insisting that Nero's behaviour has already surpassed that of the young Augustus/Octavian. He is inaccurate about Nero, who is portrayed as innocent of bloodshed when he had already murdered Britannicus early in AD 55, and also about Augustus, who at 18 (Sept 45 to Sept 44 BC) had not yet betrayed friends, not plotted to assassinate Antony, nor taken part in the proscriptions of 43–42 BC. Seneca has backdated Octavian's crimes to show that Nero has already shown himself superior to Augustus in clemency.

H8   The change in Augustus (continued)

That was Augustus in his old age, or rather as he stood upon the threshold of old age. As a young man he was hot-blooded, quick tempered, guilty of many deeds which he was reluctant to remember. No one will dare to compare your own mild nature with that of the deified Augustus, even if a competition between the years of youth and of advanced old age were appropriate. So his conduct was restrained and merciful? Of course it was! But only after the seas of Actium had been stained with Roman blood, after his own fleet as well as that of his enemies had been wrecked off Sicily, after the bloody sacrifices at Perusia and all those proscriptions.

[Younger Seneca, *Concerning Clemency* 1.11.1]

Seas of Actium stained with Roman blood: Seneca, writing almost a century after the event, clearly presents Actium as a battle between Romans, rather than the war against foreigners which Octavian and the poets presented (see below **H9–H11**).

Sicily: Sextus Pompey had established a power base in Sicily from 44 BC and posed a real threat to Octavian. Octavian was twice defeated by him in naval battles in 38 BC, but Agrippa's campaign of 36 BC defeated Sextus Pompey and he was killed. Augustus presented Sicily as a war against slaves and pirates (*RG* 25.1, 27.3).

Perusia: this town in Umbria (modern Perugia) was besieged, captured and plundered by Octavian in 41 BC. See Appian *Civil Wars* 5.32–49 and Propertius' poems in this selection, **G13** and **G14**.

Actium and aftermath (H9–H17)

H9   Battle of Actium (31 BC): dedication to Apollo of Actium

Here, too, near the mouth (of the Ambracian Gulf) is the sacred site of the temple of Apollo of Actium. There is a ridge of high ground, at the summit of which is set the temple itself; below it a plain with a sacred grove, and a dockyard where Caesar dedicated as the first fruits of his naval victory an offering of ten ships, a representative sample of each type from those with a single bank of oars right up to a ten-banker.

[Strabo, *Geography* 7.7.6]

H10   Victory monument celebrating Actium, 29 BC, Nikopolis in Epirus (NW Greece)

[Imperator] Caesar, son of the deified [Julius, having won] a naval victory in the war which he waged on behalf of the state in this region, [dedicated] to Neptune [and] Mars the camp, decorated with spoils, [from] which he set out to pursue [the enemy], as consul for the fifth time and hailed *imperator* seven times, once peace had been achieved by land [and sea].

[EJ 12, updated *AE* 1977.778]

In order to celebrate his victory at Actium, Octavian created a new city, Nikopolis ('Victory City'), near the site of the battle, one of two towns of this name (the other near Alexandria) which he founded in memory of his victories over Antony and Cleopatra, in emulation of similar city-foundations by Alexander the Great. He also established the prestigious quadrennial Actian games and enlarged the temple of Apollo, which stood where Antony's camp had been. This inscription, engraved on the frieze of a portico, commemorates his victory monument, decorated with the prows of ships captured from Antony, set up on the hill where his own camp had been. It illustrates the common theme of universal peace by land and sea, and represents the victory as being won on behalf of the state (cf *RG* 25.2–3).

H11   Ambracia and other cities re-founded as Nikopolis: the Actian Games

In antiquity Ambracia enjoyed a quite exceptional prosperity and was chosen as his royal residence by Pyrrhus, who did much to grace the city architecturally. But more recently, thanks to their record of constant insurrection and the endless warfare between the Macedonians and the Romans, Ambracia and all the other cities of the region have suffered general devastation. As a result, Augustus recognised in the end that these cities had no future, so he brought the remaining inhabitants into a single new foundation situated on the Gulf of Ambracia. He named it Nikopolis in honour of his victory in the naval battle fought at the mouth of the gulf against Mark Antony and Cleopatra, the Egyptian Queen, who personally took part in the battle.

Nikopolis now enjoys a flourishing population which is increasing daily; it has extensive territory and is splendidly adorned with the spoils of the Actian campaign. In addition, the sacred precinct of Actian Apollo which stands in its suburbs is lavishly equipped, with a gymnasium and stadium for the quadrennial games in its sacred grove, and the sacred hill of Apollo rising above. The Actian games, dedicated to Apollo of Actium, have been given Olympic status and are managed by the Spartans. The other settlements in the area are satellites of Nikopolis. In days gone by the Actian games were celebrated in honour of the god by the people of the locality and the prize for each contest was a wreath. But Caesar's patronage has greatly enhanced their prestige.

[Strabo, *Geography* 7.7.6]

Strabo is interested in the creation and destruction of cities, which alters the landscape of the empire. Here the city is highly symbolic as a reminder of the victory over Antony, and thus it has an important history attached. *endless warfare*: Rome and Macedonia fought three major wars in 214–205 BC; 200–188 BC; 171–167 BC and forcibly made Macedonia a province in 146 BC after further violence.

H12   Augustus returns works of art plundered by Antony

Then there is the city of Rhoeteium standing upon a hill, and contiguous with it a low-lying shoreline on which stand the tomb and temple of Ajax together with a statue of

him, which Antony seized and carried off to Egypt, though it was returned to the people
of Rhoeteium by Caesar Augustus together with a number of other works of art. In fact,
where Antony carried off the finest of dedicated offerings from the most famous of
temples to give to his Egyptian woman, Augustus gave them all back again to the gods.

[Strabo, *Geography*, 13.1.30]

Augustus *RG* 24.1 boasts of his return of works of art plundered by Antony.

H13   Statues restored to the Temple of Hera at Samos

The temple of Hera is open to the sky and also full of the finest statues, among them
three colossal works of Myron set on one base, which Antony took away. Augustus
Caesar put two of them back on the same base, Athene and Heracles, but moved the
Zeus to the Capitol, having built a shrine for it there.

[Strabo, *Geography*, 14.1.14]

Myron: famous Greek sculptor, active 470–440 BC. Originals and copies of his work were very popular with
Romans. Augustus also returned to Ephesus a statue of Apollo by Myron, taken by Antony (Pliny, *NH* 34.58).

H14   Octavian awarded the siege crown (30 BC)

During the consulship of Marcus Cicero's son, on 13 September, the senate made a
presentation to Augustus himself of the siege crown, since the civic crown was deemed
so very inadequate.

[Pliny, *Natural History* 22.13]

13 September: Octavian captured Alexandria on 1 August 30 BC, Cleopatra committed suicide on 10 August.
Despite what Pliny implies, the crown must have been voted rather than presented on this date as Octavian
did not return to Rome until the following year. Dio 51.19 gives details of this and other honours voted to
Octavian at around this time.

siege crown, civic crown: Pliny explains (*Natural History* 22.6–8) 'there is no greater honour than the
grass crown, only awarded by a whole army to a single person who has rescued them from a desperate situation.
The same crown is called a siege crown when a whole camp is relieved and saved from dreadful destruction.
The civic crown (of oak leaves) was awarded for saving the life of a citizen in war.' Pliny's roll of honour
culminates with Scipio Africanus (**K24**) and Augustus, *RG* 34.2 mentions the civic, but not the siege crown.

H15   Backing a winner – a talking raven

Returning in high spirits from the Actium campaign, Caesar was greeted among the
cheering crowds by a man with a raven which he had taught to say: "Hail, Caesar, our
victorious commander-in-chief." Caesar was delighted by the bird's punctilious
courtesy and bought it for twenty thousand sesterces. The owner's colleague, who had
not been allowed a share of the emperor's generosity, told Caesar that the man had
another raven and suggested that he be asked to demonstrate its talents also. The bird
was duly brought out and spoke the words which it had been taught: "Hail, Antony,
our victorious commander-in-chief." Caesar was not at all put out, and contented
himself with telling the owner to share the reward with his colleague.

[Macrobius, *Saturnalia* 2.4.29]

This amusing anecdote shows clearly that what mattered in the war between Antony and Octavian was
backing the winner, and that Octavian might, at least after his victory, be prepared tacitly to admit it.

H16   Octavian's triple triumph

He returned to Rome and celebrated three triumphs – the first for his campaign in
Illyricum, the second for his victory at Actium, and the third for his defeat of Cleopatra.
Thus after twenty years he brought the civil wars to an end.

[Summary of Livy book 133]

Octavian celebrated three triumphs on three successive days, 13, 14, 15 August 29 BC. Various sources name the triumphs: the official record (see **N2c**) actually omits the middle triumph. Virgil (**G38**, line 714) has Octavian's triple triumph depicted amongst scenes from Roman history on Aeneas' mythical shield. *RG* 4.1 mentions the triple triumph and the refusal of further triumphs. Suetonius describes the triumphs as being for Dalmatia, Actium, Alexandria (*Augustus* 22.1). *Twenty years*: Livy counts from January 49 BC when Julius Caesar crossed the Rubicon to Octavian's capture of Alexandria in August 30 BC.

H17   Triumphal arch?, 29 BC, Rome, Roman Forum

The Senate and People of Rome (set this up) in honour of Imperator Caesar, son of the Deified, consul five times, designated consul for a sixth time, *imperator* seven times, to commemorate the preservation of the state.

[EJ 17 = *ILS* 81]

This large inscription (9 ft long, 2 ft high, and 3 ft deep, found in the 16th century near the temple of Castor, but subsequently lost) may come from the triple arch to the south of the temple of the Deified Julius (See **K14**). This probably celebrated Octavian's triple triumph (see **H16**) but was perhaps subsequently modified to commemorate his recovery of the legionary standards from the Parthians too.

The settlement of 28–27 BC (H18–H25)

This has been widely discussed, both in terms of what exact powers Augustus relinquished and assumed, and in terms of what he wished to present as taking place. See for example, Syme, *Roman Revolution* 313–330; Brunt & Moore, *Res Gestae Divi Augusti* 8–10, 75–77; *CAH* X² 76–79, 113–117. The most important source is, of course, what Augustus himself wrote at *Res Gestae* 34. Dio 53.1–20 gives a narrative account, but one inevitably influenced by over 200 years of hindsight. His conclusions are more or less the opposite to the picture presented by Augustus of giving back power. 'In this way all the power of the people and senate passed to Augustus and from then was established what, to speak accurately, is monarchy.' Two main points should be noted. Firstly that Augustus was in reality no less 'master of everything' after 27 BC than before. Secondly, that despite this reality, Augustus felt that presentation mattered: the wish to draw a line under the triumvirate, civil war, and Octavian is clear; but equally the fate of Julius Caesar, who had seemed not even to think the façade of traditional government worth preserving (see, for example, Suetonius *Julius* 76–79) must have made Augustus realise that a republican spin was worthwhile, not least perhaps in allowing members of the governing class to feel they could continue to serve the *princeps* with honour (see, for example, **H42**).

H18   New *aureus* 28 BC

Obv.:   Head of Octavian right, wearing laurel wreath.

IMP CAESAR DIVI F COS VI (Commander Caesar, Son of the Deified, consul for the sixth time)

Rev.:   Octavian, seated left on magistrate's chair (*sella curulis*) wearing toga, holding out scroll in right hand; magistrate's document container (*scrinium*) on ground to left.

LEGES ET IVRA P R RESTITVIT (He has restored to the Roman People their laws and rights)

[BM CM 1995.4–1.1]

This unique coin is one of the most important new pieces of evidence relating to Octavian's rise to supreme power. Probably made in the province of Asia, it shows Octavian wearing the laurel wreath awarded to him for his triple triumph of 29 BC. The reverse legend proclaims his restoration of the laws and the constitutional rights of the Roman People. He is depicted as consul, handing over a document scroll to an unseen recipient, perhaps in the very act of restoration. This coin reveals that the constitutional settlement was already being proclaimed as complete in 28 BC.

H19 Division of Empire into two

This passage is continued in **M2**.

For when his country entrusted him with the pre-eminent position in its governance and he became supreme ruler for life in war and in peace, he divided the whole empire into two parts. One he assigned to himself, the other to the people of Rome. For himself he took all those areas that still needed a military garrison.

[Strabo, *Geography*, 17.3.25]

H20 The civic crown (27 BC)

(In civil wars) The Senate has made no grant of a laurel wreath to anyone, nor indeed has anyone desired it when a section of the state was in mourning. But the grant of the civic crown of oak-leaves is a different matter. Then hands are eagerly stretched out to receive an honour which is awarded for saving the lives of fellow-citizens. Thus the door-posts of the house of Augustus triumphantly declare his glory for ever.

[Valerius Maximus, 2.8.7]

laurel wreath: symbolised a triumph (see note on **H21**).

civic crown: on this award, see note on **H14**. Augustus was given this award, widely commemorated (e.g. **A34.2, C5, G54, H21, H23, H32, J23, L10, T28**) for saving the lives of fellow-citizens in general by bringing an end to civil war.

H21 Civic crown: *aureus*, 27 BC

Obv.:   Bare head of Augustus right.

CAESAR COS VII CIVIBVS SERVATEIS (Caesar, consul for the seventh time, for saving the citizens)

Rev.:   Eagle, wings spread, standing on oak-wreath; two laurel branches behind.

AVGVSTVS / S C (Augustus, by decree of the Senate)

[*RIC* Augustus 277, BMC Augustus 656]

In one symbolically packed design centred on the eagle, the bird of Jupiter, a powerful allusion to Augustus' position of supremacy, the reverse of this coin refers to many of the privileges granted in January 27 BC: the name Augustus; the civic crown; the right to have laurel branches (associated with victory and the god Apollo) before the entrance to his house. The letters S C (by decree of the senate) refer to the Senate's grant of these exceptional honours, not to the issue of the coin.

H22   'Augustus' 27 BC

When Gaius Caesar had established the peace and re-imposed order in the provinces, he was given the *cognomen* Augustus. The sixth month, Sextilis, was re-named August in his honour.

[Summary of Livy 134]

The name 'Augustus' was decreed 16 January 27 BC according to the calendars (**C7**; **C40** and *RG* 34.2; Suetonius, *Augustus* 7.2; Velleius 2.91.1). On the naming of the month, Dio 55.6.6 agrees with Censorinus (**H36**) in giving the year as 8 BC. Presumably the summariser mistook a digression by Livy for notice of the actual event.

H23   Ovid, *Fasti* on the name 'Augustus'

Upon the Ides in great Jove's shrine the priest, well-purified,
Offers the entrails of a gelded ram upon the flames. For on that day
Was restitution made of every province to Rome's sovereign people;
Then was your grandsire honoured by the holy name "Augustus".   590
Read all the titles on the waxen images that deck our nobles' *atria*;
Never were titles heaped upon a single man as great as these.
Africa proclaims one victor by her name; another witness bears
To Cretan power subdued; another the bandits of Isauria. This
From Numidian conquest gained his glory, that from Messana,   595
A third at the city of Numantia once made his mark. But Drusus
Gained death as well as glory from his conquered Germany.
Alas that virtue such as his should gain in recompense so short a span.
But if from his conquests Caesar should gain his titles, his would be
Honours as many as the wide world holds the names of nations.   600
Some from a single enemy have titles won, Torquatus from his foe
Despoiled of necklace; Corvinus from the raven, his strange auxiliary.
Pompeius Magnus, Great is your name, and great the measure of your deeds;
But greater yet, greater than any name, is he that conquered you.
Fabius is the name that holds fame's highest rung; and theirs   605
The Greatest house, claiming the well-earned name of "*Maximus*".
Yet mortal only are the honours earned by these; Augustus alone,
Our Caesar, bears a name worthy to partner mighty Jove himself.
"Revered" (or "august") do the Fathers call our holy things; august
The temples consecrated with due ritual and priestly hands to heaven.   610
From that same *august* stem derives the craft of *augury*; thence too
The increase, or *augment*, to mortal men which comes as gift of Jove.
May he augment our Leader's empire, may he augment his years;
Long may the oak-leaf crown protect your doors. May the inheritor
Of that great name shoulder the burden of the wide world's rule,   615
Blessed by heaven's auspices and those same omens as blessed his father.

[Ovid, *Fasti* 1. 587–616]

587   *Ides*: 13 January. Ovid thus dates both the division of provinces and the award of the name 'Augustus'.
593–6   These lines refer to the assumption after the relevant conquests of the extra names of Africanus, Creticus, Isauricus, Numidicus, Messanicus and Numantinus by various great Roman generals in the Republic, thus implying that 'Augustus' has some precedent.
596–8   These lines lament the loss of Drusus, brother of Tiberius and father of Germanicus, who died in 9 BC after victories in Germany, for which he received the title 'Germanicus' which was passed on to his son.
601–6   More Roman names deriving from military achievements (Torquatus from despoiling a Gaul of his torque or necklace in the 4C BC; for Corvinus see **K22**.

611   *August...augury*: Munatius Plancus who formally proposed the name in the Senate quoted a famous
        line from Ennius, 'After famous Rome was founded by augury august' as evidence for the
        suitablility of the name, 'Augustus' (Suet. *Aug.* 7.2).

616   *His father*: Augustus' adoptive father Julius Caesar, see **J4**.

H24   Shield of Virtue, Arles (26 BC)

The Senate and People of Rome gave to Imperator Caesar Augustus, consul eight times,
a shield of valour, clemency, justice, and piety towards gods and country.

[EJ 22 = *AE* 1952.165]

A large marble copy from Arelate (Arles in Provence) of the golden shield set up in Augustus' honour in
the Senate House in Rome, near the Altar of Victory, probably in 26 BC. See *RG* 34.2.

H25   Shield of Virtue, *denarius, c.* 19 BC

Obv.:   Bare head of Augustus left.

            CAESAR AVGVSTVS

Rev.:   Round shield.

            S P Q R / CL V (The Senate and People of Rome [dedicated the] Shield of
            Virtue)

[*RIC* Augustus 42b, *BMC* Augustus 335]

See **H24** above.

The settlement of 23 BC (H26–H27)

Like the settlement of 28/27, this has been widely argued about (see, for example, Syme, *Roman Revolution*
331–348; Brunt & Moore, *Res Gestae Divi Augusti* 10–12; *CAH* X² 84–87, 113–117). The issues
here concern what prompted this constitutional settlement (Marcellus' death; Augustus' illness; a
conspiracy; or some combination) as well as the technicalities of his powers – *tribunicia potestas*
(tribunician power) and *imperium maius* (greater executive power). Augustus does not include this
settlement in his *Res Gestae*.

H26   Tribunician power (23 BC)

The tribunician power was a term formulated by Augustus to express the supremacy
of his own position. It allowed him to avoid the title of king or dictator, while giving
a title to his predominant position in all the highest offices of state. He then selected
Marcus Agrippa to share this title with him as colleague and, after his death, Tiberius
Nero, thus ensuring that there could be no doubt about his intended successor. Since
he had complete confidence in Tiberius' lack of ambition as well as his own pre-
eminence, he hoped that this would prevent others from developing unhealthy
ambitions for the throne.

[Tacitus *Annals* 3.56]

Tribunician power: Augustus took this power, or activated power he already had, in mid-23 BC during a political crisis in which he gave up the consulship. Besides the powers it conferred within the City it stood for Augustus' championship of the people (traditionally the role of the tribunes). But he soon exploited it as a means of indicating his partner in power and so, if Augustus died first, his successor. Tribunician power always appears as one of the titles of the emperor. Dio explains the powers as 'giving them the right to stop measures taken by anyone else if they disapprove, protecting them from maltreatment and permitting them, if they think that they have been injured in some way, however trivial, not only in deed, but also in word, to execute the person responsible without trial as accursed.' (Dio 53.17.9). 'Protection from maltreatment' (sacrosanctity) is mentioned specifically alongside the tribunician power by Augustus, *Res Gestae* 10.1.

Marcus Agrippa: he held it 18–12 BC (**H27**); Tiberius 6–1 BC and from AD 4 onwards (**J40**).

H27   Augustus and Agrippa as Tribunes, *denarius*, 13 BC

Obv.:   Bare head of Augustus right.
         CAESAR AVGVSTVS
Rev.:   Augustus and Agrippa wearing togas seated on a tribune's bench.
         C SVLPICIVS PLATORIN (name of monetary magistrate)

[*RIC* Augustus 407, *BMC* Augustus 115]

Agrippa was granted tribunician power in 18 BC, renewed in 13 BC, and he and Augustus appear together on this coin as fellow-tribunes. This image reinforced the important illusion that Augustus did not exercise a monopoly on executive power, but that he shared it with colleagues in the proper Republican manner.

Pontifex Maximus (12 BC) (H28–H32)

The *pontifex maximus* was the chief priest. Priesthoods in Rome were usually occupied by public figures. The *pontifex maximus* was elected by popular vote. Julius Caesar was elected (through bribery) in 63 BC. After his death, Lepidus the triumvir became *pontifex*, perhaps irregularly. Augustus ostentatiously allowed Lepidus to remain *pontifex maximus* after his deposition in 36 BC and boasted about his moderation and regard for legality in his *Res Gestae* 10.2. The pontificate is recorded on Augustus' titles and all emperors after Augustus adopted the office. The technical requirement for the *pontifex maximus* to live in quarters adjoining Vesta's temple in the Roman forum was satisfied by Augustus dedicating a shrine to Vesta in his house on the Palatine.

H28   Calendar at Cupra, 12 BC

Caesar was made *pontifex maximus* and gave a donation to the people.

[*Inscr. It.* 13.1.7 – *Fasti Cuprenses*]

Other calendars mark Augustus being made *pontifex maximus* on 6 March. See **C15**, **C40**.

H29   Lepidus allowed to remain *pontifex maximus* until his death

Even to Lepidus he allowed an unconscionable time in which to die. For long years he tolerated his wearing the regalia of a ruler, and only after his death did he allow the office of *pontifex maximus* to be transferred to himself, preferring the office to be regarded as an honour rather than the spoils of victory.

[Younger Seneca, *Concerning Clemency* 1.10.1]

H30   Augustus *pontifex maximus*, Ovid, *Fasti*

In March, when for the sixth time Phoebus has climbed from Ocean   415
Up steep Olympus' slopes, cleaving the ether with his winged stallions,
You who draw near to worship at chaste Vesta's holy shrine
Wish her all joy, and lay your incense offering on her Trojan hearth.
This was the day when to our Caesar's countless titles, granted for merit
As he preferred not flattery, was added the honour of the Pontificate.   420
Now over Vesta's everlasting flames Caesar's abiding presence will preside.
Now you behold united heaven's twin guarantees of empire.
Ye Gods of antique Troy, the noblest prize of him who rescued you,
Gods, the protecting burden by whose aid Aeneas eluded all his enemies,
Now behold, a priest sprung from Aeneas' line raises in his hands   425
His kindred gods; Vesta be guardian to his kindred head.
You fires, well nurtured by his holy hand, live on and flourish,
Live on for ever inextinguishable fire and leader alike. Such is my prayer.

[Ovid, *Fasti* 3. 415–428]

417   *Vesta:* as *pontifex maximus* he was in charge of the shrine of Vesta, see **H31**.
426   *kindred head* : Augustus, supposed descendant of Venus, is thus related to Vesta, Venus' great-aunt.

H31   A shrine to Vesta dedicated in Augustus' house

Vesta, claim your day, the twenty-eighth of April. Vesta is now received
Within her kinsman's house. The holy fathers of the senate have   950
So ordained it. Now of that house Phoebus holds a part, another
To Vesta is conceded, while the remaining third belongs to Caesar.
Long live the laurels of the Palatine; long live Caesar's house adorned
With oak leaves. One habitation holds three everlasting gods.

[Ovid, *Fasti* 4.949–954]

These lines record the dedication of a shrine of Vesta in Augustus' own house on the Palatine on 28 April 12 BC (cf. **C17**). This 'privatisation' of Vesta is typical of Augustus' manipulation of Roman tradition.

950   *kinsman* : Augustus, supposed descendant of Venus, is thus related to Vesta, Venus' great-aunt.
951   *Phoebus*: the Temple of Apollo adjoined Augustus' house (**K37–K38**).
953–4   *laurels*: laurel wreaths were worn by generals celebrating a triumph: the oak leaves were those of
         the civic crown (see **H20**). *Three gods*: Apollo, Vesta and Augustus himself.

H32   *Aureus,* 12 BC

Obv.:   (Not illustrated) Bare head of Augustus right.
           AVGVSTVS DIVI F (Augustus, son of the deified)

Rev.:   Closed door between two laurel-branches; above, a wreath.
           OB C S (For having saved the citizens) /
           L CANINIVS GALLVS (name of moneyer)

[*RIC* Augustus 419, *BMC* Augustus 126]

This coin depicts the front door of Augustus' house, decorated with the honours granted to him by the Senate in January 27 BC: the right to have an oak-wreath permanently fixed above his doorway and laurel branches either side (see **H21**). Laurel boughs adorned the houses of important Roman priests, the *pontifex maximus* and the *flamines*. They were also symbolic of the god Apollo, Augustus' patron deity, to whom he had attributed the victory of Actium and whose temple was directly adjacent to his house (**K37–K38**).

In 12 BC, the year in which this coin was made, Augustus became *pontifex maximus,* the senior priestly office at Rome.

Augustus, 11 BC–AD 14 (H33–H43)

H33 Coin showing Augustus raising fallen *Res Publica* to her feet, *aureus*, 12 BC

Obv.: Bare head of Augustus right.

AVGVSTVS

Rev.: Augustus wearing toga extending his right hand to a personification of the Roman State (*Res Publica*) who kneels before him.

COSSVS LENTVLVS (name of monetary magistrate); RES PVB (The State); AVGVSTVS

[*RIC* Augustus 413]

Only one specimen of this coin type is known, but is now lost. It is illustrated in Zanker, *Power of Images*, (fig. 74). It shows a remarkable scene, of Augustus raising the personification of the Roman State from her knees as her saviour. It is often taken to refer to Augustus' pretended restoration of the old Roman Republic in the constitutional sense. But Augustus never actually claimed to do this in so many words. *Res Publica* does not mean 'republic' in the modern sense, but something more neutral like State or Commonwealth. Romans still thought they were living in a *Res Publica* throughout the imperial period.

The calendar at Amiternum celebrated 1 August, when in 30 BC he had captured Cleopatra's capital of Alexandria, as the day when Augustus freed the *Res Publica* from the most terrible danger (**C21**). It is the general restoration of peace and stability which followed on from the victory at Actium that is being depicted here, rather than anything specifically constitutional.

H34 New calendar for Asia, based on Augustus' birthday, *c.*9 BC

H34a Edict of the proconsul, Paullus Fabius Maximus

[.............] we have inherited from our predecessors [.......] of the gods favourable and [.........] whether the birthday of the most divine Caesar is more pleasurable or more advantageous, we would rightly suppose it is the same as the beginning of everything, even if not by nature, at any rate in terms of being useful, inasmuch as he put right everything which is falling to pieces and has passed into poor condition, and he gave a new look to the whole world, which would have embraced ruin most cheerfully, had not Caesar's birth supervened for the common good fortune of everything. Consequently, someone would rightly suppose that this is the beginning of life and existence for himself, the end and limit of regret that he has been born. [11] And since one could take a starting-point from no day more fortunate for both the public and the private advantage than one which has been the good fortune for all, and since it more or less happens that magisterial office is taken up at the same time in cities in Asia, quite clearly an arrangement predestined in this way according to some divine plan, so that it might become the starting-point for honours towards Augustus, and since it is difficult to give adequate thanks for his great benefactions, unless on account of each and every one of them we were to plan some way of repaying, and also since men would celebrate a birthday more pleasurably if it were shared by all, and if some particular pleasure too because of office-holding were added for them, it seems right to me that for all states there is one and the same New Year's day, the birthday of the most divine Caesar, and that on that day everyone enters magisterial office, that day being 23 September, so that it may be honoured more extraordinarily by taking on as well some extra religious ceremonial and so that it may become more familiar to everyone, which I think will also provide the most benefit for the province. [26] But it will be necessary to write a decree by the assembly of Asia which has encompassed all his virtues, so that what has been planned by us for the honour of Augustus may remain in perpetuity. And I shall order the decree inscribed upon a slab to be set up in the temple, having ordered that the edict be written in both languages.

[There is also a fragmentary appendix to the proconsul's edict in Greek.]

H34b Decree by the Assembly of Asia

[30] It was decreed by the Hellenes in Asia, on the motion of the chief priest Apollonios, the son of Menophilos, from Aezani: since providence which has divinely arranged our life has eagerly and zealously mustered the most perfect [good] for life, having borne Augustus, whom she filled with virtue for the benefit of mankind, [having freely given] to us and to our descendants, as it were, [a saviour] who stopped warfare, [and] who will arrange [peace; and since having come into being] Caesar surpassed the hopes of [all] those who anticipated [good news], not only outdoing those who had been [benefactors] before him, but [leaving] those yet to be born with no hope of [outdoing him]; [40] and since [the birthday] of the god made a beginning for the world of the good news brought about by him, and once Asia had passed a decree in Smyrna during the governorship of Lucius Volcacius Tullus, whilst Papion, [from Dios Hieron,] was secretary, that the person inventing the greatest honours for the god would be crowned, Paullus Fabius Maximus, the proconsul of the province and benefactor, sent out from that god's right hand and judgement with the others through whom he has benefited the province, the size of whose benefactions no words might successfully express, invented for Augustus' honour what even until now had been unknown to the Hellenes, namely to begin the time for life from his birthday: therefore with good fortune and for our deliverance it was decreed by the Hellenes in Asia, that the New Year for all cities begins on 23 September, which is the birthday of Augustus. [52] But so that the day may always correspond in each city, that the Hellenic date too be used along with the Roman. And that the first month 'Caesar', just as has also been decreed earlier, be reckoned beginning from 23 September, the birthday of Caesar, and that the crown voted to the inventor of the greatest honours for Caesar be given to Maximus the proconsul, and that in addition the proclamation be made in perpetuity at the gymnastic contest of Rome and Augustus at Pergamon, that 'Asia crowns Paullus Fabius Maximus, who invented with the utmost reverence honours for Caesar'. [60] And that in the same way the proclamation be made also in the contests held in each city for Caesar. And that the official rescript of the proconsul and the decree of Asia be inscribed on a slab of white marble, and that this be set up in the sanctuary of Rome and Augustus. And also that the public advocates for the year take care that both the official rescript of Maximus and the decree of Asia be inscribed on white marble slabs in the main cities of the assize-districts, and that these slabs be set up in the shrines of Caesar. The months will be reckoned as follows: 'Caesar' 31 days; Apellaios 30 days; Audnaios 31 days; Peritios 31 days; Dystros 28 days; Xandikos 31 days; Artemision 30 days; Daisios 31; Panemos 30; Loos 31; Gorpiaios 31; Hyperberetaios 30. In all 365 days. [71] In a leap-year Xandikos will be reckoned 32 days. And so that the months and days may correspond from the present moment, the current month Peritios will be reckoned up until the 14th, and on 24 January we will reckon the first day of the month

Dystros, and for each month the start of the new month will be the ninth day before the first day of the Roman month. And the intercalated day will always be of the intercalated first of the month Xandikos, every three years.

[Greek, fragments of Fabius' decree also in Latin. EJ 98 = SEG 4.490]

In c.26/5 BC the general Assembly of the province of Asia offered a crown to anyone who could propose the most striking means of honouring Augustus. Slightly oddly, it appears that the prize was not won until almost two decades later, by the Roman governor proposing to honour Augustus by introducing a new calendar into the province of Asia, beginning on Augustus' birthday. Apart from the first month, 'Caesar', the rest of the months retain their Macedonian names. A dossier of inscriptions was published in many cities. The edict of the governor (proconsul) was inscribed in both Greek and Latin, and it was accompanied by two decrees issued by the provincial assembly (*koinon*), which consisted of representatives from the province's communities, one of whose tasks was to organise emperor-worship, but who were also concerned with representing their local interests at Rome.

Fragments of different sections of the texts survive from Priene, Apamea Kibotos, Eumeneia, Maionia, and Dorylaeum, allowing a fair reconstruction of the whole to be achieved. The fragment from Maionia shows that the decision was published not only in the province's major towns, but also in less populated areas.

The tone and substance of these documents honouring the emperor mark a shift in emphasis from previous ruler cults. Augustus' birth is celebrated as heralding a new era of peace and prosperity, and Augustus is honoured simply for existing and for his benefits in general, rather than for specific acts of generosity.

Bibliography: R.K. Sherk, *Roman Documents from the Greek East* (John Hopkins Press, 1969) no.65.

H35   August renamed (8 BC)

August is the next month. It used to be called Sextilis, the Sixth, until it was re-named in honour of Augustus by a decree of the senate, whose terms I give below:

> "Whereas it was in the Sixth Month that our supreme Leader, Caesar Augustus, both entered upon his first consulship and three times marched in triumph into the city, and led his legions down from the Janiculum in loyal obedience to his auspices; and whereas it was in this same month that Egypt was brought under the power of the Roman People; and whereas it was in this month that an end was brought to our civil wars; and whereas for all these reasons this month is and has been the most felicitous for our empire; now therefore it is resolved by the senate that this month shall be named August."

On the same grounds a similar resolution of the people was passed, proposed by the tribune, Sextus Pacuvius.

[Macrobius, Saturnalia 1.12.35]

The decree followed the precedent set in 44 BC, by the renaming of *Quinctilis* as *Julius*, after Julius Caesar. Dio 55.6.6 has Augustus preferring August to September, the month of his birth.

H36   August renamed (2)

The month which had been *Sextilis* was named *August* in honour of Augustus, by decree of the senate in the consulship of Marcius Censorinus and Asinius Gallus, the twentieth year of Augustus' reign.

[Censorinus, On the Birthday 22]

H37   Oath of loyalty to Augustus, 3 BC, Paphlagonia

In the 3rd year from Imperator Caesar Augustus, son of a god, when he was consul for the 12th time, on 6 March at Gangra in the [market-place], oath taken by the inhabitants of Paphlagonia and of the Romans engaged in business among them.

[8] I swear by Zeus, Earth, Sun, all the gods and goddesses, and by Augustus himself

that I will be well-disposed towards Caesar Augustus, his children and descendants for the whole period of my [life] in word, deed, and thought, considering as friends those whom they consider as friends, and regarding as enemies those whom they judge to be enemies, and that I shall spare neither my body nor soul, life nor children, on behalf of their interests but in every way on behalf of their affairs I shall face every danger. [18] I shall disclose whatever I perceive or hear being spoken or plotted or performed against them, and I shall be hostile towards anyone who speaks or plots or performs any of these things; I shall pursue and ward off by land and sea, with weapons and steel, any whom they judge to be enemies. [26] And if I do anything contrary to this [oath] or anything not conforming with what I have sworn, I myself swear complete and utter destruction against myself, my body and soul, life and children, my whole family and interests as far as my whole succession [and] all born from me, and let neither land nor sea receive the bodies of my family or of my descendants, or produce fruits [for them].

[36] All those in [the land] also swore in the same terms in the temples of Augustus throughout the [districts] at the altars [of Augustus]. Similarly the Phazimonites who inhabit what is now called Neapolis all [swore] in the temple of Augustus at [the altar] of Augustus.

[Greek: EJ 315 = *ILS* 8781]

This oath (one of several loyalty oaths found in the Greek East) was found engraved upon a sandstone slab found at Phazimon, a minor city in Paphlagonia (northern Turkey), whose capital was Gangra. The dating system used here ('in the 3rd year from Imperator Caesar Augustus') alludes to the incorporation of Paphlagonia into the province of Galatia in 6/5 BC.

Pater Patriae (Father of the Fatherland) 2 BC

The grant of this title, 'Father of the Fatherland' is given as the culminating honour in the *Res Gestae* (35.1) It is celebrated on the Calendar (**C13**), appeared on the base of a golden statue in the Forum of Augustus (**K28**), and appeared regularly on coinage after 2 BC (see **M20**). Dio (55.10) notes that this represented only the formal offering of a title by which he had previously been addressed. Suetonius records Augustus' tearful response (Suet. *Aug*. 58.2). The title referred to Augustus' role as saviour of the Roman people: Cicero had been hailed as Father of the Fatherland (*Parens Patriae*) after the defeat of the rebel Catiline in 63 BC, as was Caesar after his death (Suet. *Julius* 85). It also suggested the close, familial relationship between Augustus and the people, as well as his paternal authority over them.

H38   Ovid, *Fasti* on Augustus as *pater patriae*

O that I had a thousand voices, and such a spirit in my breast as that
By which you told the tale of great Achilles, Homer of Maeonia,   120
That I might sing with alternating line the holy Nones:
This is the highest honour yet bestowed upon my Calendar.
My inspiration fails; my strength crumples beneath the load; for this
Above all other days is that which these my songs must celebrate.
Madman I was. How could I think to lay such awesome weight upon   125
Frail elegiacs? This was a theme for high heroic verse.
Pater Patriae, your Country's Holy Father, such is the name and title
Conferred upon you by People, Senate, and my own Equestrians.
Events preceded us. Late though it was, your title merely matched
The achievement; for long since have you been Father of the World.   130
Yours is the title here on earth which high in heaven is that of Jupiter;
Father you are of men on earth, as of gods in heaven is Jupiter.
Romulus, yield pride of place: mighty the walls Augustus' guardianship

Has given to Rome, while yours were such that Remus lightly leaped across.
Tatius and tiny Sabine Cures felt your power; Caenina too. But Roman   135
From furthest east to utmost west have Caesar's conquests made
All that the sun beholds. You, Romulus, held some tiny stretch
Of conquered land. Caesar controls all that there is beneath the gaze
Of lofty Jupiter. You raped, where Caesar commanded sacrosanctity
For wives; your grove played host to wickedness, Caesar repulsed it.   140
Violence you ever loved; while Caesar cherishes the rule of law.
You were Rome's lord and master – he simply *princeps*, our first citizen.
Remus denounced you; Caesar forgave his enemies. You to the heavens
Were by your father raised; Caesar raised his father.

[Ovid, *Fasti* 2. 119–144]

133–144 This contrast between Augustus and Romulus has been seen as subversive given that the two are
often equated, but the comparison surely reflects praise on Augustus as moral reformer rather than
anything else.

H39   The succession

"I have now been summoned to the imperial throne by the unanimous desire of gods
and men alike. Your remarkable abilities and my own love for my country have
encouraged me to offer you a peaceful transfer of the principate, for which our
ancestors fought civil wars and which I myself gained by force of arms. In this I am
following the example of the deified Augustus, who raised to a pre-eminence second
only to himself first his nephew, Marcellus, then his son-in-law, Agrippa, then his two
grandsons, and finally Tiberius Nero, his step-son. Augustus sought a successor from
within his own household; I seek mine from the whole state."

[Tacitus, *Histories,* 1.15]

The context is the emperor Galba (AD 69) speaking to Piso on his adoption into the imperial family. He cites
as precedent for this adoption similar action by Augustus in the case of Marcellus, Agrippa, Gaius and Lucius
Caesar, and Tiberius. Galba's addressee was Lucius Calpurnius Piso Frugi Licinianus, of high descent and
exemplary character. Potential threats from the German legions (Vitellius) and the Praetorian Guard (Otho)
forced him to act quickly. Piso was to have powers second to those of Galba which would have made him
sole emperor as soon as Galba died.
Marcellus: see **J29–J32**.
Agrippa: see **H26, H27,** and *Annals* 1.3.1 (Section **F**).
Two grandsons: Gaius and Lucius Caesars; see **J56–J65**.
Tiberius Nero: see **J40**; *Annals* 1.11–13 (Section **F**); Suet. *Tib.* 15.2 –16.1; Dio 55.13.1ᵃ–2.
Within his own household: with the exception of Agrippa, the relatives named were substitutes for a non-
existent son, made sons by adoption. Galba was in the same situation but made a virtue of choosing outside
his family: the Julio-Claudian method had been disastrous, producing Gaius Caligula and Nero.

H40   Augustus prevents cruelty towards a slave

[1] Shouting abuse at an angry man only serves to make matters worse – you get angry
yourself, quite unnecessarily. [2] There are many different approaches to such a man,
including sweet reason. But you need to be someone of formidable personality if you
are going to use the same tactics as the deified Augustus once used at dinner on Vedius
Pollio to suppress his anger. One of his slaves had broken a crystal goblet, so Vedius
ordered him to be seized and put to death in a cruelly unusual manner. He had a fishpond
full of enormous lampreys and he ordered him to be thrown into it. Anyone can see
that he was trying to show off. It was sheer barbarity. [3] The slave boy escaped from
his captors and flung himself at Caesar's feet, begging only that he should be allowed
to die in some other way, and not as an *hors d'oeuvre* for the lampreys. The sheer

novelty of the cruelty shocked Caesar and he ordered the lad to be released, every crystal goblet to be broken in front of him, and the fish pond to be filled in. [4] Only a Caesar could reprimand a friend in such a fashion and he put his power to admirable use. "Do you make a habit of ordering men to be dragged away from your dinner table and torn to pieces in such novel forms of punishment?" he asked. "Are men to be disembowelled because one of your goblets has been broken? Are you so profoundly arrogant as to order a man to be marched to his death in the very presence of Caesar?"

[Younger Seneca, *On Anger* 3.40.1–4]

On the treatise of Seneca *On Anger*, see the note on **P20**.

Vedius Pollio was a friend and supporter of Augustus (see **K66**). On his death in 15 BC he left his luxurious villas to Augustus, who tore down the one in Rome to build the portico of Livia (**K30**). The story shows, incidentally, how the power imbalance, masked by the apparent equality of social relations between the *princeps* and his friends, could suddenly be exposed.

H41   Augustus' wish to lay aside his position

[4.2] The deified Augustus, on whom the gods heaped more gifts than any other man, never ceased to pray for peace and quiet, a release from the affairs of state. His conversation always reverted to this topic – how much he longed for leisure. This was the source of consolation, false perhaps but none the less sweet for that, with which he would lighten his labours: that one day he would be able to live for himself. [4.3] In a letter which he sent to the senate assuring them that in his retirement his position would be preserved in a manner consistent with his former distinction, I found the following passage: "However, in such matters actions speak louder than promises. But I have so longed for such a time that, since I am still denied its realisation, I have anticipated something of its pleasures in the delights of conversation." [4.4] Leisure seemed to him so great a blessing that he relished it in imagination because he was denied it in reality. He realised that everything depended on himself alone, for he was the source of happiness for men and nations. As a result he derived the greatest joy from imagining the day on which he would be able to lay aside his greatness. He fully understood the price he paid in sheer sweat for all those blessings which shone so brightly all across the world, the unseen fears they masked.

[Younger Seneca, *On the Shortness of Life* 4.2–5]

The dialogue *On the Shortness of Life* is addressed to Seneca's father-in-law. It argues that life only appears to be short because we use time so badly and suggests that the only truly profitable way of spending one's life is on the acquisition and application of philosophical wisdom. Augustus serves as an example of someone in the highest position in public life who really longed to give it up. In fact, the notion of serving reluctantly for the public good had been established as the proper pose for emperors since 27 BC when Augustus offered to surrender his powers. Suetonius, *Augustus* 28 offers an elaborate defence of Augustus' decision not to return to private life after Actium and again in 23 BC.

H42   Augustus encourages a republican stalwart to become consul

Piso had given enthusiastic help to the re-invigorated republican faction in Africa against Julius Caesar. He then became a supporter of Brutus and Cassius. When he was permitted to return to Rome, he made no attempt to seek political advancement, until Augustus went out of his way to encourage him to take on the consulship – which he accepted.

[Tacitus, *Annals,* 2.43]

(*Gnaeus Calpurnius*) *Piso*: he fought in Africa in 46 BC (Caesar? *African War* 3.2; 18.1). That he accepted the consulship from Augustus in 23 BC, when another republican, C. Sestius, was also consul, was a triumph for Augustus' diplomacy – or a necessary concession at a crisis (see Section **B** – 23 BC). Piso was the father of the man accused of murdering Germanicus in AD 19.

H43 Two-edged riposte

I must mention a remark he made as a compliment to Cato. He happened to be visiting a house where Cato had once lived. In an effort to ingratiate himself with Caesar, Strabo made some derogatory comment about Cato's obstinacy. Augustus replied that "any man who is eager to preserve the constitutional *status quo* must be both a good citizen and a good man." This profound comment served two purposes: it both paid a handsome compliment to Cato and served Augustus' own interests in discouraging would-be revolutionaries.

[Macrobius, *Saturnalia* 2.4.18]

Marcus Porcius Cato (Uticensis) the great-grandson of the famous censor, adopted a similarly reactionary approach to politics. With Pompey, he fought against Julius Caesar in the civil war, committing suicide in April 46 BC in Utica (N. Africa) after the Battle of Thapsus. He came to stand for republicanism and liberty. Virgil depicts him on the Shield of Aeneas administering justice in the Elysian fields of the underworld (**G38**, line 670).

Augustus as Judge (H44–H52)

In AD 13 a statue of *Iustitia Augusta* (Augustan Justice) was dedicated (**C3**). Suetonius implies (*Aug*. 33.1) that personal jurisdiction was an important part of Augustus' role, as it certainly was by Suetonius' own time, under Trajan and Hadrian. For various edicts concerning provincial administration, see **M53–M68**. The cases below show Augustus as a judge in private cases. The anecdotes tell us more about Augustus' reputation than about legal procedure.

H44 Verdict on a murder trial: letter of Augustus to Knidos, 6 BC, Astypalaea

....[When] Kairogenes son of Leu[ka]theos was the magistrate.

Imperator Caesar Augustus, son of a god, chief priest, consul designate for the 12th time, in his 18th year of tribunician power, sends greetings to the magistrates, council, and people of the Knidians. Your envoys Dionysios son of Dionysios, and Dionysios son of Dionysios son of Dionysios, met with me at Rome, and, having given me a decree, accused Euboulos son of Anaxandridas who is already dead, and his wife Tryphera who was present, concerning the death of Euboulos the son of Chrysippos. [10] Having instructed Asinius Gallus my friend to scrutinise by torture those of the household slaves liable to the charge, I learnt that Philinos son of Chrysippos had attacked the house of Euboulos and Tryphera for three nights in succession with violence and in the manner of a siege, and that on the third night his brother Euboulos too had been brought along to join in the attack. The householders Euboulos and Tryphera, since they could not achieve safety in their own house, either by negotiating with Philinos or by barricading themselves against the attacks, ordered one of their household slaves not to kill, as perhaps someone might have been provoked to do by quite justifiable anger, but to force them back by pouring their excrement over them. [23] But the household slave whether by design or by accident – for he himself persisted in denying it – let go of the chamber pot together with what was being poured down, and Euboulos fell under it, though it would have been fairer if he rather than his brother had been saved. I have sent to you the actual interrogations too. I would have been surprised at how much the defendants feared the examination of the slaves at your hands, had you not seemed to have been excessively harsh against them, and tough on crime in all the wrong respects, being angry not with those who deserved to suffer everything whatever, since they had launched an attack against someone else's house at night with violence and force three times and destroyed the common safety of you all, but with those who were unfortunate even at the time when they defended themselves, and had done nothing whatever wrong. But now you would seem to me to act correctly if you take care that the records in your public archive also agree with my opinion regarding these matters. Farewell.

[Greek: EJ 312 = *SIG*³ 780]

Along with another imperial letter, from the emperor Hadrian to the Astypalaeans, this letter from Augustus to the Knidians was found engraved upon a marble slab, on the Greek island of Astypalaea. In it, Augustus responds to a case of alleged murder referred to him by envoys from the free city of Knidos (on a peninsula of the coast of modern Turkey, 60 miles east of Astypalaea). We do not know what prompted the Astypalaeans to have the letter engraved, although perhaps it may be because Knidos does not emerge in an entirely favourable light. It opens by naming the eponymous magistrate at Astypalaea.

H45   Augustus shamed into appearing in court
A retired soldier who had been summoned to court and looked like losing his case marched up to Caesar in a public place and asked him to appear on his behalf. He immediately chose one of his entourage to act on the man's behalf and warmly recommended him to the litigant. The veteran rolled up his tunic to display his scars and bellowed at the top of his voice: "When you were in danger during the Actium campaign, I didn't look for a substitute; I fought for you in person." Caesar blushed and appeared in person at the trial on the man's behalf, since he did not want to be thought too proud or ungrateful.

[Macrobius, *Saturnalia* 2.4.27]

H46   A fable about Augustus
You may be inclined to dismiss traditional tales as airy-fairy nonsense, so let me tell you about an event that happened within my own living memory.

Once upon a time there was a married man who loved his wife very dearly. He was just about to present his son with the white toga of manhood when his freedman took him on one side into a quiet corner where he told him a string of lies about the lad and even more about the shocking misdemeanours of his wife, a lady of exemplary chastity. He was in fact hoping to supplant the boy as his father's heir. Finally he added what he knew would prove to be for such a devoted husband the unkindest cut of all, the allegation that an adulterer was paying regular visits to his house and that its reputation was being polluted by the basest lechery.

The husband was outraged by these foul slanders about his wife. So he pretended that he was going to make a visit to his country estate, but in fact he remained secretly in town. That night he suddenly returned to his house and headed straight for his wife's bedroom. Showing an almost excessive desire to defend his young manhood, his wife had in fact instructed their son to sleep there. While the household slaves were rushing about looking for lights the husband, unable to contain the force of his blazing sense of outrage, went to the bed and groping about in the darkness felt a head and realised that the hair was short. With no thought but to avenge his injured pride he plunged a sword into the sleeper's breast.

The lights arrived and at once he saw his son and there, sleeping beside him, his innocent wife who had heard nothing, since she was sunk in the first stages of a profound slumber. Thereupon he sentenced himself to a fitting penalty for his own crime and fell upon the sword which his own credulity had unsheathed.

The prosecutors laid an accusation against the woman and haled her off to Rome to the Centumviral Court. Innocent though she undoubtedly was she became the victim of malicious suspicion by reason of the fact that she inherited her husband's property. Her supporters nevertheless stood up for her and boldly defended the cause of this innocent lady. In the end the judges sought the help of the deified Augustus in the discharge of their juror's oaths, since they were puzzled by the complexities of the accusation.

He quickly disposed of the obscurities surrounding the slanders and laid bare their true source. "The freedman was the cause of the disaster," he declared. "The freedman should pay the penalty. As for the woman, who has been bereaved of her son and widowed of her husband, in my opinion she deserves our sympathy rather than our condemnation. If the father and head of the family had thoroughly investigated the charges laid against her and meticulously examined the slanders, he would not have destroyed his whole family line root and branch by this terrible crime."

The lesson is clear: let your ears hear everything but take nothing for granted on first impulse, since those of whom you would least expect it may be the guilty ones; and those who are entirely innocent may be the victims of malicious accusation.

[Phaedrus, *Fables* 3.10]

Gaius Julius Phaedrus (c. 15 BC – AD 50) was a freedman of Augustus. He composed five books of verse fables in Latin, modelled on the collection of Aesop, but also including instructive stories based on later collections and from his own experience as in this example.

H47   Augustus takes the law into his own hands
Having drafted a law on adultery (the *lex Julia*), in which regulations were established for the trial of those charged and the punishment of those convicted, he happened one day to meet a young man whose name had been slanderously linked with his daughter Julia. When he attacked him with his fists, the young man cried out, "But Caesar, you have established a legal procedure." Augustus was so ashamed of himself that he refused to eat for the rest of that day.

[Plutarch, *Moralia* 207.9]

H48   The trial of Tarius for attempted patricide, with Augustus on the jury
[15.2] By contrast, everyone admired Tarius, whose son was caught plotting to kill his own father. He heard the evidence and found him guilty, but was content to sentence him to exile. And a very comfortable exile it was, too. This would-be parricide was required to live in Marseilles, and given the same annual allowance as he had received before his crime. The result of all this was that everyone (remarkably, in a city where even the most villainous scoundrel can be sure to find someone to defend him) was convinced that the accused had been rightly condemned, since his own father who could not hate him had found it in him to pronounce him guilty.

[3] This will allow me to present you with an excellent example of a noble ruler whom you may compare with an equally admirable father. When he was ready to begin the trial of his son, Tarius invited Caesar Augustus to attend the hearing. This he did, entering the sanctuary of a private citizen's home, sitting beside him, and sharing in the discussions of a family not his own. He did not suggest that they came to his house instead, for then the trial would have been Caesar's hearing, not the father's. [4] The case was concluded; all the evidence thoroughly examined, both that of the young man, delivered in his own defence, and that of the prosecution. At this point Caesar asked that each person present should record his verdict in writing, in case his own verdict influenced that of all the others. Then, before the voting tablets were opened, he

declared on oath that he was not prepared to accept an inheritance from Tarius, rich man though he was. [5] Some might argue that in this he showed a degree of moral cowardice in revealing a concern that public opinion might suspect him of improving his own chances of inheritance by clearing away the competition in finding the son guilty. My own view is diametrically the opposite. Each one of us should be perfectly confident of facing down the malicious comments of our critics by relying on his own clear conscience. But a ruler must pay constant attention to public opinion. So Caesar took an oath that he would not receive an inheritance.

[6] As a result Tarius lost a second heir on that same day, but Caesar preserved the independence of his judgement. And having demonstrated that his severity was free of external influence – as any ruler must always be careful to do – he declared that the boy should be banished and his father should decide the location of that banishment. [7] His sentence was not the sack, the snakes, nor even prison; his concern was not for the guilty man, but for him to whom he acted as adviser. He stated, in effect, that a father should be satisfied with the mildest form of punishment when his son was young and had acted on impulse in a crime where his participation had been half-hearted, which was almost the same as innocence. Sufficient then that he should leave the city and remove himself from his father's sight. [16.1] No wonder Caesar was invited to participate in family councils. No wonder he was made a joint heir with children who were blameless. Such is the quality of mercy that adorns a ruler. Wherever he goes, gentleness and mercy follow in his train...

[Younger Seneca, *Concerning Clemency* 1.15.2 – 1.16.1]

On Seneca's treatise *On Clemency* see **H7**. Seneca's point here is that showing clemency can be a way for an emperor to gain popularity.

The story about Tarius reminds us that the Roman *paterfamilias* (father of the family) had the power of life and death over his children, as well as over his slaves, but he was expected to hold proper judicial enquiry, as did Tarius, before exacting punishment. Augustus is shown as participating in this domestic trial on equal terms with others, but, after the condemnation, his view of the penalty clearly prevails. The acceptance of inheritances from private citizens was a delicate issue, see **T34–T36** and note.

H49   Augustus overrules a will (1)

Gaius Tettius was disinherited in infancy by his father, even though his father, Tettius, had lived in lawful wedlock with his mother, Petronia, until she died. The deified Augustus, acting in his capacity as *pater patriae* (Father of the Fatherland), personally issued a decree instructing him to enter upon the possession of his father's property, on the grounds that it was wholly unjust of Tettius to deny his paternity to a son whom he had legitimately begotten of his own free will.

[Valerius Maximus, 7.7.3]

On the cases in this anecdote, and **H50–H51**, see F. Millar, *The Emperor in the Roman World*[2] pp.529–530.

H50   Augustus overrules a will (2)

The case of Septica, mother of the Trachali brothers of Ariminum, was similar. In a fit of pique and as an insult to her sons, she married a relatively elderly husband named Publicius when she was past the age of child-bearing. She too made no mention of them in her will. The sons appealed to Augustus. He regarded as invalid both the marriage and the woman's testamentary dispositions as evidenced by the fact that he instructed the sons to retain possession of their mother's estate and forbade her new husband to keep her dowry, on the grounds that he had not entered upon the marriage in order to procreate children.

[Valerius Maximus, 7.7.4]

H51 A case of impersonation

While Augustus was the guardian of our commonwealth a similar act of duplicity, on this occasion illustrative of feminine audacity, was suppressed at Mediolanum (Milan). The woman was trying to pass herself off as a certain Rubria, who was falsely believed to have perished in a fire, and thus to insinuate herself into a property which was nothing to do with her. She had plenty of distinguished witnesses from her district as well as support from members of Augustus' own circle, but thanks to Caesar's own resolute integrity she left empty-handed, foiled of her despicable intentions.

[Valerius Maximus, 9.15. ext. 1]

H52 Law on the power of Vespasian, AD 69/70, Rome

[................] or that it be lawful to make a treaty with whomever he wishes, just as it was lawful for the deified Augustus, Tiberius Julius Caesar Augustus, and for Tiberius Claudius Caesar Augustus Germanicus.

[3] And that it be lawful for him to convene the senate, to introduce or send back a motion, and to pass senatorial decrees by motion and by voting, just as it was lawful for the deified Augustus, Tiberius Julius Caesar Augustus, and Tiberius Claudius Caesar Augustus Germanicus.

[7] And that, when the senate is convened by his will or authority, order or command, or when he is present, the legality of everything be regarded and preserved just as if the senate had been declared and convened as the result of a statute.

[10] And that all candidates for a magistracy, power, post, or curatorship of anything whom he recommends to the senate and people of Rome, and to whom he gives and promises his support, an extraordinary reckoning is to be held for them at their elections.

[14] And that it be lawful for him to advance and enlarge the city's sacred boundary, when he judges it to be in the state's interest, just as it was lawful for Tiberius Claudius Caesar Augustus Germanicus.

[17] And that whatever he judges to be to the state's advantage and in keeping with the majesty of things divine and human, public and private, let him have the legal power to perform and do this, just as it was for the deified Augustus, Tiberius Julius Caesar Augustus, and Tiberius Claudius Caesar Augustus Germanicus.

[22] And that in those statutes or plebiscites it has been written, that the deified Augustus, or Tiberius Julius Caesar Augustus and Tiberius Claudius Caesar Augustus Germanicus are exempt, let Imperator Caesar Vespasianus be released from those statutes and plebiscites, and whatever in accordance with any statute or bill the deified Augustus or Tiberius Julius Caesar Augustus or Tiberius Claudius Caesar Augustus Germanicus had to do, all these things it be lawful for Imperator Caesar Vespasianus Augustus to do.

[29] And that whatever has been performed, accomplished, decreed or commanded by Imperator Caesar Vespasian Augustus before this statute was proposed or by anyone commanded acting by his order or command, these things are to be lawful and binding just as if they had been performed by command of the people or commoners.

Sanction

[33] If anyone in consequence of this statute has acted or will act contrary to the statutes, bills, plebiscites or senatorial decrees, or if in consequence of this statute he does not do what he ought to do in accordance with a statute, bill, plebiscite or senatorial decree,

let him not be liable for this, nor because of this is he to be obliged to give anything to the people, nor is there to be a legal process or settlement concerning this against him, nor is anyone to allow a case to be pleaded before him concerning this matter.

[EJ 364 = *ILS* 244]

A large bronze tablet, displaying the final section of the bill put before the people of Rome granting powers to Vespasian on his accession as emperor following the civil wars of AD 68/9. The first part must have appeared on a separate tablet. In the extant text, Augustus is repeatedly cited as the first precedent for the powers being granted, followed by Tiberius and Claudius, the other 'good' Julio-Claudians (omitting the 'bad' Gaius Caligula and Nero). Despite this, the inscription does not provide incontrovertible evidence that Augustus did actually possess these powers. For further discussion of the problems inherent in this inscription for understanding the formal constitution of the Principate, see works listed below.

Bibliography: P.A. Brunt, 'Lex de imperio Vespasiani', *JRS* 67 (1977) 95–116; M.H. Crawford, ed., *Roman Statutes* I (London 1996) no. 39.

SECTION J

THE IMPERIAL FAMILY

This section arranges members of Augustus' family in roughly chronological order. Agrippa is not included (see **T2–T14**). Suetonius devotes a section of his biography of Augustus to his family: *Augustus* 61–65. Four family trees, given at intervals through Augustus' reign (31 BC; 17 BC; AD 1; AD 14) give ages of the members of the family and appear on pages 411–414.

Augustus' family: general (J1–J3)

J1   Childless marriage to Livia

There is such a thing as a specific physical incompatibility and a sterile couple can procreate when they have intercourse with others, as was the case with Augustus and Livia.

[Pliny, *Natural History*, 7.57]

Augustus' first wife, Scribonia, bore him Julia during their only year of marriage. Livia had two sons by her first husband. At the time of their marriage in 39 BC, Augustus was 23/24, Livia 18/19.

J2   Family deaths

I would not wish to list his sorrows individually, but in summary he lost his sons-in-law, his children, and his grandchildren, and while he lived on earth no man could have been more aware of his mortality.

[Younger Seneca, *To Polybius, On Consolation*, 15.3]

J3   His large family

In the year in which he died, Augustus saw the birth of his grand-daughter's grandson, Marcus Silanus.

[Pliny, *Natural History*, 7.58]

GAIUS JULIUS CAESAR (100 – 44 BC) (J4)

Antony (as quoted by Cicero, *Philippics* 13.24), famously addressed the young heir of Julius Caesar as 'you, boy, who owe everything to your name.' At the time (44/43 BC) the remark was hardly an exaggeration, and the importance of Julius Caesar's legacy was shown by the nomenclature of members of Augustus' family.

J4   Julius Caesar / Augustus, *denarius* 17 BC

Obv: Augustus, head bare, right.
     AVGVSTVS DIVI F (Augustus, Son of the Deified)

Rev: Youthful laureate head of Julius Caesar, right, above four-rayed comet.
     M SANQVINIVS IIIVIR (M Sanquinius, moneyer)

[*RIC* Augustus 338 / *BMC* Augustus 71]

The reverse design of this coin of Augustus includes a representation of a youthful Julius Caesar. The four-rayed, tailed comet seen above the head recalls the appearance of the comet hailed the *Sidus Iulium* (star of Julius) in 44 BC, which came to symbolise the divinity of Julius Caesar, and which identifies his portrait here. Although Caesar had been dead almost thirty years by this time, his important position within the imperial family was preserved, no doubt largely because his divine status afforded Augustus the claim to be *Divi filius* ('Son of the Deified), as reflected by the inscription on the obverse of this coin.

GAIUS OCTAVIUS (father of Augustus) (J5–J7)

Gaius Octavius was the original name of Augustus (and his natural father). Suetonius, *Augustus* 1–4 and 8, gives more details about Augustus' family, derived, he tells us, not from Augustus' autobiography, but from other sources, including ones hostile to Augustus.

J5   Octavian's family background

[1] Then Caesar's will was opened. In it he adopted Gaius Octavius, the grandson of his sister Julia. A few things should be said about his background, even if it comes ahead of its proper place. [2] Gaius Octavius, his father, was born into a family which though not patrician was equestrian and very distinguished and was himself well-respected, upright, honourable and wealthy. He was chosen as praetor at the top of a list of candidates of noble birth. This distinction led to his marrying Atia, a daughter of Julia. After his praetorship he obtained by lot the province of Macedonia and was there acclaimed *imperator*. While returning to stand for consul he died, leaving a son not of age. [3] He was brought up in the house of his step-father, Philippus, but Gaius Caesar, his great-uncle, loved him as his own son, and at eighteen Octavius followed him on campaign in Spain and afterwards accompanied him, always staying in the same place and travelling in the same vehicle, and he honoured him, while still a boy, with the office of a priest. [4] At the end of the civil war Caesar sent him to study in Apollonia to train with a liberal education the talents of this remarkable young man; after that he had intended Octavius to accompany him on wars against the Getae and Parthians.

[Velleius Paterculus, *History of Rome*, 2.59]

a son not of age: the young Octavius was four when his father died (Suet. *Aug.* 8.1).
Apollonia: in Macedonia (now Albania), immediately opposite the heel of Italy. In 45–44 BC, Julius Caesar was gathering an army there for the campaigns in the East.

J6   The career of Octavius

Gaius Octavius, son of Gaius, grandson of Gaius, great-grandson of Gaius, father of Augustus, twice military tribune, quaestor, plebeian aedile with Gaius Toranius, president of the judicial commission, praetor with proconsular power, hailed as victorious general from the province of Macedonia.

[*ILS* 47 = *CIL* 6.1311]

This is inscribed upon a marble plaque of unknown provenance within Rome, probably originally displayed on a statue base. Other letters partially survive on its left side, perhaps from an inscription concerning Julius Caesar. The dynastic character of the inscription is clear from the extended formula of filiation. This can be paralleled for non-imperial families, but clearly seeks to emphasise the family's longevity. The use of the name 'Augustus' shows that the monument was erected at least a generation after Octavius' death in 59 BC.

J7   A statue group dedicated by Augustus to his father, Octavius

Its honorific position is clear evidence of the prestige accorded to a work of Lysias, which the deified Augustus dedicated in honour of his father Octavius, in a niche adorned with columns above the arch on the Palatine. It shows a *Chariot and Four horses with Apollo and Diana* – all carved from a single block.

[Pliny, *Natural History* 36.36]

This statue group formed part of the sanctuary to Apollo on the Palatine, officially dedicated on 9 October 28 BC (see **K37–K38**).

AUGUSTUS (23 September 63 BC – 19 August AD 14) (J8–J24)

The passages in this section cover Augustus as a person, a topic to which Suetonius devotes a considerable part of his biography (*Augustus* 66–92). Many anecdotes about Augustus were recorded: many ancient collections of sayings of famous people survive. On Augustus' nomenclature, see note on his consulship of 31 BC (Section **B**).

J8   Augustus' eyes

The deified Augustus had grey eyes, like those of a horse, and the whites of his eyes were abnormally large for a human being. For this reason it used to irritate him if people scrutinised his face too closely.

[Pliny, *Natural History*, 11.143]

Suetonius, *Augustus* 79.2 provides a different view: 'he had clear, bright eyes and liked to believe that there was some divine spirit in them: he was pleased if anyone he gazed at keenly dropped their glance as if looking at the bright sun.'

J9   Augustus' illnesses recorded on *Fasti* of Latin Holidays

27 BC: Imperator Caesar affected by illness.
24 BC: Imperator Caesar affected by illness.

[*Inscr. It.* 13.1.2]

Augustus' poor health was well known (Suet. *Aug.* 81.1 and **P1**). An illness in 23 BC was apparently almost fatal (Dio 53.30) and perhaps partly prompted the settlement of that year (see introduction to **H26–H27**). Dio also records Augustus falling ill while campaigning in Spain in 25 BC (53.25.7).

J10   Augustus successfully treated by Musa

It is certainly claimed that when the deified Augustus was ill he was cured by lettuce, thanks to the skill of his doctor, Musa, even though Gaius Aemilius, his previous doctor, had refused to prescribe it for superstitious reasons.

[Pliny, *Natural History* 19.128]

Antonius Musa achieved great fame (Suet. *Aug.* 59). Dio (53.30.3) says that the successful treatment was cold drinks and cold baths; Suetonius (81.1) that the treatment was cold poultices instead of the hot ones previously prescribed. Pliny later states that Musa saved Augustus from a dangerous illness by using a treatment diametrically opposed to that of his mentor (*Natural History* 29.6).

J11   'Festina lente'

They say that both in conversation and in his letters Augustus habitually commended the Greek proverbial expression "make haste slowly".

[Aulus Gellius, *Attic Nights* 10.11.5]

This is also mentioned as one of Augustus' favourite expressions by Macrobius, *Saturnalia* 6.8.9 and Suetonius, *Augustus* 25.4, who puts the advice in the context of military command.

J12   'Count to ten first'

Athenodorus, the philosopher, begged Augustus' permission to return home on grounds of old age. Augustus agreed, but as he was saying "goodbye" Athenodorus offered one final word of advice. "Remember, Caesar, whenever you are angry, do not say or do anything until you have repeated to yourself the twenty-four letters of the (Greek) alphabet." Augustus grabbed him by the hand exclaiming, "I still have need of you here." He would not let him go for another whole year, quoting the old saying that "Silence is also golden and pays a safer dividend".

[Plutarch, *Sayings of Kings and Commanders, Moralia* 207.7]

Athenodorus: from Tarsus in Cilicia. He probably came to Rome with Octavian in 44 BC, staying as a court philosopher.

whenever you are angry: Dio in his 'obituary' on Maecenas, 55.7.1 wrote 'Maecenas had proved especially valuable when Augustus lost his temper, for he would always soothe him down and bring him to a calmer frame of mind.' He then quotes an anecdote of how Maecenas prevented Augustus from hastily condemning a group to death.

'The wit of Augustus' in Macrobius, *Saturnalia* (J13–J19)

These anecdotes about Augustus are amongst those reported by one of the characters, Avienus, in Macrobius' *Saturnalia*. One of the topics covered in the wide-ranging dialogue, set over the period of the Saturnalia festival of AD 383?, is witty sayings of and about famous people, taken from earlier authors.

J13   The wit of Augustus
Avienus remarked that "Augustus Caesar certainly had a well developed sense of humour, but was always careful to preserve the dignity of his office and proper standards of decency, and would never allow any lapse into mere vulgarity."

[Macrobius, *Saturnalia* 2.4.1]

J14   The wit of Augustus (2)
He had written a tragedy called *Ajax* but was unhappy with the result and destroyed it. Later, the tragedian Lucius Varus asked him how his Ajax was progressing and he replied: "he has fallen upon his sponge."

[Macrobius, *Saturnalia* 2.4.2]

The same anecdote is reported by Suetonius, *Augustus* 85.2. Ajax in the Trojan War committed suicide by falling on his sword.

J15   The wit of Augustus (3)
There was an ex-soldier who had been struck on the head with a stone while on campaign and had a conspicuous and unsightly scar on his forehead. He was boasting somewhat extravagantly about his military exploits when he was gently rebuked by Augustus' comment: "You really must remember not to look round when you are running away."

[Macrobius, *Saturnalia* 2.4.7]

J16   The wit of Augustus (4) – Herod's pigs
When he heard that among the two-year-old boys in Syria whom Herod, King of the Jews, had ordered to be put to death was his own son, he remarked that "it would be better to be one of Herod's pigs than his own son."

[Macrobius, *Saturnalia* 2.4.11]

Macrobius wrote in Latin, but part of the point of the original joke may have been a pun in Greek ('hus' = pig; 'huios' = son). The 'Massacre of the Innocents' is attested elsewhere only in Matthew 2.16. Herod did execute three of his sons: on his family see **M42**.

J17   The wit of Augustus (5) – a mean host

Someone once asked him to dinner and offered a menu that was extremely economical – everyday fare, you might call it. Augustus almost never refused an invitation, so after this inadequate and rather unpretentious meal he whispered to his host as he was saying goodbye: "I had no idea that I was such a *very* close friend of yours."

[Macrobius, *Saturnalia* 2.4.13]

J18   The wit of Augustus (6)

I have always admired Augustus' ability to take a joke against himself even more than his capacity for witty repartee. After all, good-natured tolerance is a more admirable quality than the gift of a quick tongue, especially when it extends to putting up with gibes that border on the malicious.

[Macrobius, *Saturnalia* 2.4.19]

Suetonius (*Augustus* 51 and 55) comments on Augustus accepting jests against himself. See also **J19**.

J19   The wit of Augustus (7)

A man from the provinces who bore a remarkable resemblance to Augustus was visiting Rome and his likeness became the focus of attention everywhere. Augustus ordered him to be brought to see him and having observed the likeness asked whether his mother had ever come to Rome at any time. "No, Sir," came the reply, but then, determined to push his luck, he added: "But my father did – often!"

[Macrobius, *Saturnalia* 2.4.20]

J20   Augustus' good fortune

When he sent his grandson, Gaius, out to campaign in Armenia, he prayed to the gods that they should give him Pompey's popularity, Alexander's boldness, and his own good luck.

[Plutarch, *Sayings of Kings and Commanders, Moralia* 207.10]

J21   Augustus' rhetorical style

As a speaker Augustus possessed a spontaneity and grace of expression appropriate to the dignity of his position as *princeps*.

[Tacitus, *Annals*, 13.3]

Roman politicians were educated in rhetoric; Augustus' skills (praised for elegance and restraint by Suet. *Aug.* 86) were achieved in spite of the early interruption of his education (Julius Caesar was killed when he was eighteen). The context of the passage above is Tacitus' scrutiny of the skills of later emperors; in AD 54, Nero, aged sixteen, was reduced to reading Seneca's script.

J22   A joke about Augustus' meanness

Fabius Maximus, complaining of the smallness of the 'presents' which Augustus used to give his friends, called them 'imperfects'.

[Quintilian, *The Orator's Education*, 6.3.52]

In Latin Fabius changed the word *congiarium*, meaning 'gift', but also 'a large vessel' for *heminarium*, meaning 'small vessel'.

J23   Evading a joke by a joke

When Augustus was being presented by the Gauls with a golden collar weighing a hundred pounds, Dolabella said jokingly, but hoping to get what he said in jest,

"Imperator, present me with a collar". Augustus replied, "I would rather present you with a civic crown."

[Quintilian, *The Orator's Education*, 6.3.79]

On the civic crown, see **H14**, **H20**. The point of the joke here is that it was made of oak leaves.

J24   Coin portrait of Augustus, aged 73: *as*, AD 11–12

Obv: Augustus, head bare, left.

       IMP CAESAR DIVI F AVGVSTVS IMP XX (Imperator Caesar Augustus, Son of the Deified, hailed victorious general twenty times)

Rev: S C (Senatus Consulto (by decree of the Senate)) large, in centre.

       PONTIF MAXIM TRIBVN POT XXXIIII (*Pontifex Maximus*, Tribunician power for the thirty-fourth time)

[*RIC* Augustus 471 / *BMC* Augustus 275]

By the time this coin was struck Augustus was in his seventies. Despite this, all late coin issues exhibit a relatively youthful portrait of the Emperor, a tendency which can be seen from his depiction in other media. The image is a sharp contrast to Suetonius' description of the ageing *princeps* (Suetonius, *Augustus* 79–80: compare also coins of Queen Elizabeth II who turned 73 in 1999). On gold, silver and brass coinage alike, Augustus' image varies little, showing his distinctive hair and features (reminiscent of Alexander the Great) with or without the laurel-wreath that becomes such a familiar symbol of the emperor on Roman coinage. The predisposition to display Augustus' continued youth on his coinage may reflect the unique position Augustus had obtained. His image was depicted on a complex tri-metallic coinage system for over forty years – there was clearly no Roman precedent for such continued representation. The persistence of this image was, however, surely conscious and reflected the lifelong links he had established between his own image and that of Alexander the Great, as well as his association with Apollo and indeed his semi-divine status as the son of the god Julius Caesar. Features of the imagery of all these figures can be identified in the portraiture of Augustus.

OCTAVIA (c. 70? –11 BC) (J25)

Octavia, Augustus' only sibling, married C. Claudius Marcellus by 54 BC and had a son, Marcellus, and two daughters by him. After his death in 40 BC, she married Mark Antony as part of the Treaty of Brundisium. Though he divorced her in 32 BC, she brought up all of Antony's surviving children, including those by Cleopatra, their own two daughters and the three children of her first marriage. Her ashes were placed alongside Marcellus' in Augustus' Mausoleum, see **J32**.

J25   Octavia's grief at the death of Marcellus

[2.2] Let me set out for your inspection two examples, the finest of your sex and of this century – the one a woman who surrendered to her grief and was overwhelmed by it; the other whose misfortune was no less, her loss still greater, but who refused to allow her sorrows to hold dominion over her for long but quickly recovered her equanimity. [2.3] Octavia and Livia, the one Augustus' sister, the other his wife, both lost their sons while they were still young men – and both would have been certain to become emperor in due course...

*(For the rest of section 2.3 see **J29**)*

[2.4] For the whole of the rest of her life Octavia never put an end to her tears and lamentations, refusing to accept words of consolation from any source. She would tolerate no distraction; her whole mind and body were focused on and obsessed with that one subject. As she was at his funeral, so she remained for the rest of her life: I do not mean that she lacked the will to rise above her grief; rather that she refused to be helped to rise above it – as if she felt that to lose her grief would be to lose a second child. He had been her beloved son – yet she refused to have his portrait anywhere, refused to hear his name even mentioned. She hated all mothers, particularly Livia for whom she conceived a particular loathing, because the joy that had seemed destined to be her own had now transferred to Livia's son. She espoused the darkness of solitude, sparing no thought even for her brother, rejecting the poems and other compositions designed to honour Marcellus' memory, and closing her ears to every source of comfort. She withdrew from all official ceremonial, hated even any exposure to the reflected glory of her brother's high position, and buried herself in the life of a recluse. Even in the company of her children and grandchildren she refused to abandon her mourning garments, declaring herself totally bereaved, despite the implied insult to her many surviving relatives.

*(for the continuation of this passage, see **J28** and **J45**)*

[Younger Seneca, *To Marcia – On Consolation* 2.2 – 2.4]

Probably Seneca's earliest surviving work, this consolation was written in the reign of Gaius (AD 37–41). Marcia had lost her young son: Seneca confronts Marcia with a bad example in Augustus' sister Octavia, and a good one in his wife Livia (**J28**), who was Marcia's friend; on Marcellus, see **J29–J32**.

LIVIA DRUSILLA (58 BC – AD 29) (J26–J28)

Livia's father was M. Livius Drusus Claudianus, a member, by birth, of the Claudius family, then adopted. He was proscribed by the triumvirs, and died at Philippi.

J26 Livia's 'obituary'

In the following year, in the consulship of Gaius Fufius and Lucius Rubellius (both with the *cognomen* Geminus), Julia Augusta (Livia) died at an advanced old age. Her lineage was of the most distinguished in Rome: herself a member of the Claudian family, she was by adoption a member of the Livian and Julian families also. Her first marriage was to Tiberius Claudius Nero, to whom she bore children. He had gone into exile during the Perusian War, but returned to Rome once peace was established between the Triumvirs and Sextus Pompeius. But then Caesar (Octavian) became infatuated by her beauty and carried her off, though history does not relate whether this was against her will. Indeed he introduced her to his household while she was still pregnant without even allowing her time to give birth. She produced no more children, but the marriage of Agrippina to Germanicus gave her a link with Augustus' own blood line, with the result that they shared great-grandchildren. She maintained an old-fashioned morality in her domestic life, though she was more approachable than ancient custom would have deemed fitting for a Roman matron. As a mother she was domineering, as a wife amiable; she was more than a match for her husband's wiles and her son's deviousness. Her funeral was modest; the implementation of her will the subject of long delays. Her great-grandson, Gaius Caesar, soon to be emperor, delivered her panegyric from the Rostra.

[Tacitus, *Annals,* 5.1]

Advanced old age: Livia was born on 30 January, 58 BC and died in AD 29.

Her first marriage: her second marriage to Octavian, on 17 January, 38 BC, when she was six months pregnant with Nero Drusus, caused scandal (Tacitus, *Annals* 1.10.5, Dio 48.34.3; 48.44.2–5).

Sextus Pompeius: he was related to Octavian's previous wife, Scribonia, and when Octavian divorced her to marry Livia, it led to a rift, and to a long-standing feud in the imperial family between Scribonia's descendants, beginning with her daughter, Julia, and those of Livia, beginning with Tiberius. The failed marriage of Julia and Tiberius of 11 BC was the first link between Livia and the bloodline of Augustus.

Marriage of Agrippina to Germanicus: took place in about AD 5 and was intended to unite the two branches of the family.

Domineering: Tiberius curbed her influence: Tacitus, *Annals* 1.14.1–2 (Section **F**) also Suetonius, *Tiberius* 26.2; Dio 57.12.4.

J27   Livia on leaded bronze coin of Clazomenae, Asia

Obv: Augustus, laureate, right
         ΚΛΑΖΟΜ ΚΤΙΣΤΗΣ ((coin) of the Clazomenians, Our founder
         (Augustus))
Rev: Bust of Livia, right
         ΘΕΑ ΛΙΒΙΑ (Livia, the goddess)

[*RPC* 1, no.2496]

Although Livia is often thought to be an exceptionally influential member of the Augustan household, her portrait is curiously absent from the denominations of the Roman Imperial coinage system, though the elder Julia is depicted. However, Livia's portrait does appear on several of the autonomous city coinages. This coin was produced by the city of Clazomenae (west coast of Modern Turkey) after its re-foundation by Augustus, which is often thought to have occurred after an earthquake in 12 BC. Livia is interestingly described as a goddess, reflecting the tendency for imperial cult in the provinces.

J28   Livia's reaction to the death of her son, Drusus

[3.2] His mother, Livia, had not been able to snatch a last kiss from her son nor enjoy the consolation of hearing his dying words. Over the long journey in which she followed Drusus' last remains she was tormented by the innumerable funeral pyres burning across the whole of Italy – as if time and again she were losing the son she loved. But as soon as she had laid him in his tomb, along with his body she laid aside her sorrow and made no further display of grief than was appropriate while Caesar was alive or fair to Tiberius, her surviving son. Finally, she never ceased to honour the name of her beloved Drusus, displaying his likeness everywhere in public and in private, and deriving the greatest pleasure from talking about him and hearing of his exploits. She lived constantly with his memory. But when someone has made a memory a source of misery, he cannot bear to hold onto it or constantly return to it as she did.

[4.1] I have no doubt that you will find more to admire in the example of your close personal friend, Julia Augusta (Livia). She it is that invites you now to be advised by her. [4.2] In the first paroxysm of her grief, a time when all those in distress are at their most inconsolable and inclined to anger, she gave an audience to Areus, her husband's philosopher friend, and acknowledged that he did a great deal to help her, much more indeed than the Roman people, whom she was reluctant to inflict with her own sorrows; more than Augustus who, having lost one of his two main sources of support, was himself shattered and unable to endure the further burden of his relatives' distress; more than her son, Tiberius, whose devotion ensured that at that bitterly lamented funeral which the whole world mourned she felt that her only loss had been in the number of her children.

[Younger Seneca, *To Marcia – On Consolation* 3.2–4.2]

For the context of this passage, see the note to **J25**. On Drusus, see **J43–J47**.

MARCUS CLAUDIUS **MARCELLUS** (42–23 BC) (**J29–J32**)

The son of Octavia and C. Claudius Marcellus, Marcus Claudius Marcellus was Augustus' nephew. He married Julia, Augustus' daughter, in 25 BC. He died before he had been firmly established as Augustus' heir, but his early death only enhanced his reputation, notably with the poets: see **G33**, **G37** (*Aeneid* 6.860–886) and **R15**.32.

J29   Marcellus' character

Octavia lost Marcellus. Augustus, his uncle and father-in-law, had already begun to depend on him and to lay upon his shoulders the burden of empire. He was a young man of quick intelligence and great abilities, blessed with a truly remarkable degree of self-restraint and moderation for one of his years and wealth. He had great powers of endurance, an indifference to pleasure, and a willingness to undertake whatever burdens his uncle chose to lay upon him – or, metaphorically speaking, whatever edifice he chose to build upon him. He chose well; those foundations would not sink beneath any weight.

[Younger Seneca, *To Marcia – On Consolation* 2.3]

For the context of this assessment of Marcellus, see note on **J25**.

father-in-law: Marcellus married Julia in 25 BC (Dio 53.27.5).

had begun to depend on him: this cautious assessment is right: Seneca has immediately before this passage asserted that Marcellus 'would have been certain to become emperor in due course', but when Augustus was gravely ill, shortly before Marcellus' illness and death, he preferred Agrippa. (Dio 53.30–31).

great abilities: Velleius, 2.93.1 (Section **E**) gives a similar assessment.

J30   Marcellus as aedile [23 BC]

Then, while Marcellus, the son of Octavia, Augustus' sister, was aedile during his uncle's eleventh consulate, he stretched awnings across the forum from the first of August onwards, even though no games were being held, in order to improve conditions for those engaged in litigation.

[Pliny, *Natural History* 19.24]

J31   Marcellus' death and funeral [23 BC]

Virgil refers to Marcellus, the son of Augustus' sister, Octavia, whom Augustus adopted. Marcellus fell ill at fifteen and died aged seventeen at Baiae, while he was aedile. The state mourned his death greatly, because of his affability, and because he was Augustus' son. In his honour, Augustus ordered that 600 chosen citizens should take part in the funeral procession. Therefore he was conveyed in great state and laid to rest in the Campus Martius.

[Servius, *Commentary on Aeneid*, 6.861]

Servius is commenting on Marcellus' appearance in the pageant of Roman heroes in the *Aeneid* (**G37**.861). He is probably wrong about Marcellus' age: Propertius 3.18 15 (**G33**) gives his age as 19.

J32   Epitaph of Marcellus and Octavia, Mausoleum of Augustus

Marcellus, son of Gaius,	Octavia, daughter of Gaius,
son-in-law of	sister of
Augustus Caesar	Augustus Caesar

[*AE* 1928, no. 2]

This inscription, carved on a single stone, was found in the Mausoleum in 1927. Marcellus died in 23 BC, his mother, Octavia, in 11 BC.

TIBERIUS CLAUDIUS NERO (16 November 42 BC – 16 March AD 37) (J33–J42)

On Tiberius' career under Augustus, see Suetonius, *Tiberius* 6–21, and Levick, *Tiberius the Politician* (London 1976) pages 11–81.

J33   Tacitus' 'obituary' on Tiberius

Tiberius died in his seventy-eighth year. His father was Tiberius Claudius Nero and he was a member of the Claudian family on both sides, though his mother was subsequently adopted also into the Livian and then the Julian families. From earliest infancy he was the victim of ever-changing fortunes. He followed his proscribed father into exile; then, as Augustus' step-son, he became a member of his household; there he faced a struggle with a number of rivals – as long as they lived – notably Marcellus and Agrippa, followed by Gaius and Lucius Caesar; even his own brother, Drusus, enjoyed a higher level of general popularity. But he found himself on far more dangerous ground when he married Julia, since he had to decide between tolerating or repudiating his wife's adulteries. On his return from Rhodes he was for twelve years heir to the emperor's household, and for twenty-three more the absolute master of the Roman empire.

His character likewise passed through a number of distinct stages: for as long as he was a private citizen or holding high office under Augustus his conduct and reputation were impeccable; while Germanicus and Drusus remained alive he concealed a cunning and devious nature behind a mask of affected virtue; and again, while his mother Livia was still alive he retained a mixture of good and bad qualities; as long as Sejanus remained his favourite (or, later, the object of his suspicions) though loathed for his cruelty, he still concealed his vices; but with this final restraint eliminated, he lost all sense of shame and degenerated into a monster of criminality and perversion and thus revealed at last his essential character.

[Tacitus, *Annals* 6.51]

Tiberius died: on 16 March, AD 37, aged 78. He was born on 16 November, 42 BC.

Rivals...popularity: for the consequences of Tiberius' mother's marriage to Augustus, see **J26** above.

(Marcus Claudius) Marcellus: see **J29–J32**.

Agrippa: see **T2–T14**. He was never Tiberius' rival, but belonged to the previous generation and was Augustus' partner in power when Tiberius was a youthful military commander.

(Nero) Drusus: see **J43–J47**.

Married Julia: see **J48**.

Return from Rhodes: AD 2; and Tiberius lived at Rome in retirement until Gaius Caesar died in AD 4.

Distinct stages: Tacitus' scheme of conduct declining as restraints were removed is a desperate remedy for the historian's problem of explaining the failure of a Principate that began with high promise. Behind it lies the fact that when his last heir apparent died (Drusus Caesar in AD 23) it left the urgent question of the succession open to a struggle that Tiberius did little to repress.

J34 Imperial nepotism

At about this time Tiberius commended Germanicus' son, Nero, to the favour of the senate when he had only just come of age and asked that he be exempt from service on the Board of Twenty (*vigintiviri*) and allowed to stand for the quaestorship five years earlier than the law allowed. The request was greeted with a degree of mockery, but Tiberius cited as a precedent the similar concession gained by Augustus for himself and his brother. Yet even in those days I have little doubt that such a request would have met with ridicule, albeit concealed. But those at least were the early days of the Caesars' imperial power, when tradition and precedent carried rather more weight; Augustus' ties of kinship, furthermore, as stepfather to Tiberius, had been significantly less close than those of Tiberius, as grandfather, to his grandson Nero.

[Tacitus, *Annals* 3.29]

The context is a speech of Tiberius to the senate in AD 20, seeking for Nero Drusus an age concession for entry to the quaestorship similar to that which he (and his brother Drusus) had received from Augustus.

Commended Germanicus' son Nero: Tiberius kept to the comparatively modest precedents set by Augustus when advancing Tiberius and his brother Nero Drusus in 24 BC; he avoided the extravagant privileges granted in 6 BC to Gaius and Lucius Caesar (consulships at the age of 19).

The law: it prescribed the order and age for the holding of offices, and the intervals between them; the quaestorship (the first senatorial office) might be taken at the age of 24.

J35 His marriage to Vipsania (probably 20 or 19 BC)

Atticus had a grand-daughter by Agrippa, the first husband of his own young daughter. Before she was more than a year old Caesar betrothed her to his step-son, Tiberius Claudius Nero, son of Drusilla [Livia], and this union confirmed their relationship and led to increasing familiarity.

[Nepos, *Life of Atticus* 19.4]

Nepos wrote a biography of Pomponius Atticus (110–32 BC), see on **P3**.

J36 Tiberius' journey to Drusus' death-bed

The longest known vehicular journey in twenty-four hours was that accomplished by Tiberius Nero when racing to his brother's sick-bed in Germany. On that journey he covered nearly two hundred miles.

[Pliny, *Natural History* 7.84]

This journey is described with more dramatic detail by Valerius Maximus, 5.5.3, possibly Pliny's source. On Drusus' death, see **J43–J47**.

J37 Archelaus of Cappadocia snubs Tiberius in retirement

King Archelaus had ruled Cappadocia for fifty years. Tiberius hated him, because during his 'retirement' to Rhodes Archelaus had made no effort to pay his respects. This deficiency was not due to any arrogance on the part of Archelaus, but simply because he had been advised by sources close to Augustus that as long as Gaius Caesar was in favour and responsible for affairs in the East, too close a friendship with Tiberius would be inadvisable.

[Tacitus, *Annals* 2.42]

Archelaus: Antony appointed him in 36 BC; Augustus extended his kingdom to include Rough Cilicia (see **M30**). He belonged to a nexus of dependent royal families deployed in Rome's imperial interests; he established connexions with such dynasts as Herod the Great of Judaea and married a member of the Pontic dynasty. His debt to Tiberius for defending him in a court case was not well repaid: Dio 57.7.4–7, from which it seems that he was no longer fit to rule. During his retirement, Tiberius was still courted by some, but felt the neglect of others (see **T19**).

J38   Tiberius on Rhodes, 6 BC – AD 2

The people of Rhodes (set this up) on behalf of Tiberius Claudius Nero.

[Greek: EJ 77b]

This inscribed statue base probably dates from the period of Tiberius' presence in retirement on the island of Rhodes.

J39   Tiberius, victor at Olympic Games, AD 1 or earlier, Olympia

Tiberius Claudius Nero, son of Tiberius, victor at the Olympic games with the four-horse chariot… Apollonios, son of Apollonios, the Eleian, who is also Tiberius Claudius (honours) his patron and benefactor. To Olympian Zeus.

[Greek: EJ 78 = *SIG³* 782]

The dedicator of this monument (Tiberius Claudius Apollonios) is eager to retain both his Greek and Roman identities, describing himself both as 'Eleian' (a native of the district where Olympia is situated) and as Roman citizen, having presumably received a grant of Roman citizenship from Tiberius.

J40   The succession and the award of tribunician power

(In a letter to the senate) Tiberius pointed out that Drusus had a wife and three children and that he had now reached the same age as that at which he himself had been summoned by the deified Augustus to accept a similar responsibility (i.e. *tribunicia potestas* – tribunician power).

[Tacitus, *Annals* 3.56]

In AD 22, Tiberius, then 62, gave his son, Drusus, who was around 35, tribunician power (see **H26**), following the example of Augustus. In 6 BC, Augustus, then aged 56, had needed a partner in power old enough to take over instantly the incumbent emperor died, and so awarded Tiberius, then 35, tribunician power for 5 years. After his retirement and return, Tiberius received further ten-year grants in AD 4 and AD 13.

Augustus adopts Tiberius

See *Fasti* (**C19**) and Velleius 2.103.3–104.1 with note (Section **E**). The adoption of Tiberius (Livia's son by her first marriage) in AD 4 followed the death of Gaius Caesar. Augustus also adopted Agrippa Postumus at the same time and made Tiberius adopt his nephew Germanicus.

J41   Tiberius, *aureus* of AD 13–14

Obv: Augustus, laureate, right.
          CAESAR AVGVSTVS DIVI F PATER PATRIAE (Caesar Augustus, Son of the Deified, Father of the Fatherland)
Rev: Tiberius, head bare, right.
          TI CAESAR AVG F TR POT XV (Tiberius Caesar, Son of Augustus, Tribunician power for the fifteenth time)

[*RIC* Augustus 225 / *BMC* Augustus 506]

The rather late elevation of Tiberius as the principal successor of Augustus is reflected in the coin evidence. This *aureus* showing Tiberius' portrait coupled with that of Augustus can be dated to the last year of the *princeps*' life, while other portrait coins date from AD 9. Tiberius was only adopted by Augustus late in AD 4, receiving at the same time the tribunician power that marked the principal successor.

J42   Augustus on Tiberius

He said that he would leave to the Romans as his imperial successor a man who had never had second thoughts on any single matter. By this he meant Tiberius.

[Plutarch, *Sayings of Kings and Commanders, Moralia* 207.11]

There is no context given for this remark: Plutarch simply repeats it as one of fifteen sayings of Augustus in a work collecting sayings of famous people.

NERO CLAUDIUS **DRUSUS** (38 BC – 9 BC) (**J43–J47**)

Drusus was the son of Livia by her first husband, Tiberius Claudius Nero. However she divorced him to marry Octavian while pregnant, and Drusus was therefore born into Octavian's household. He married Antonia, younger daughter of Octavia and Mark Antony.

J43   Drusus' career

The father of Claudius Caesar was Drusus, initially given the first name Decimus, later Nero. Livia, after marrying Augustus while pregnant, gave birth to him within three months, and there was suspicion that he was the product of adultery with his stepfather. Certainly the Greek verse 'Lucky the parents of a child of three months' was quickly quoted everywhere. During his quaestorship and praetorship, Drusus commanded wars against the Raetians and against the Germans. He was the first Roman general to navigate the North Sea and achieved the huge task of creating ship canals beyond the Rhine, which are still known as Drusus' canals. The enemy was frequently beaten and driven deep into remote wilds: Drusus did not leave off the pursuit until the figure of a barbarian woman of superhuman size forbade him stretch further his conquest.

His victories earned him an ovation and triumphal ornaments, and his consulship followed straight on from his praetorship. On resuming his campaign he died of disease in his summer camp, known thereafter as the Cursed Camp. His body was carried to Rome by the leading citizens of towns and colonies and met by a group of officials and laid to rest in the Campus Martius. The army raised a burial mound in his honour, for a soldier to run round in an annual ceremony, when the communities of Gaul would make public prayers and offerings. In addition, the Senate, amongst many other honours, decreed an arch decorated with trophies on the Appian Way and that he and his descendants should be given the *cognomen* 'Germanicus'.

[Suetonius, *Claudius* 1.2–3]

Suetonius begins his *Life of Claudius* with a brief account of the career of his father, Drusus. For the continuation of this passage, see **J47**.

J44   *Elogium* for Drusus, c.2 BC, Forum of Augustus

[Nero] Claudius Drusus Germanicus, son of Tiberius, consul, urban praetor, quaestor, *augur*, [was hailed as/died while] *imperator* in Germany.

[EJ 80 = *AE* 1934.151]

This *elogium* from the Forum of Augustus (see **K20–K25**) honours Drusus (Augustus' stepson and younger brother of the future emperor Tiberius) who receives his statue for his victories in Germany (12–9 BC), in virtue of which he received the honorific name 'Germanicus', an ovation, and triumphal decorations.

J45 Livia's grief at the death of Drusus

Livia lost Drusus, who would surely have been a great emperor, having already proved himself a great military leader. He had already taken his army deep into German territory and planted his standards in places where it was scarcely known that Rome existed. He died on active service and in his final illness even his enemies respected his condition by honouring the mutually agreed peace terms and not daring to hope for what was clearly to their advantage. He died in the service of his country. His death was attended by a profound sense of loss in Rome, the provinces, and throughout Italy where townships and colonies poured out to pay their last respects, escorting his cortège all the way to the city for all the world like a triumph rather than a funeral.

[Younger Seneca, *To Marcia – On Consolation* 3.1]

On the context of this passage, see introduction to **J25**; for its continuation, see **J28**.
a great military leader: see Velleius 2.97 and notes (Section **E**).

J46 Funeral honours for Drusus

There were some who missed the pomp and circumstance of a state funeral and drew unfavourable comparisons between the funeral of Germanicus and the splendour and magnificence of the honours paid by Augustus to Germanicus' father, Drusus. They remarked that in the dead of a bitter winter Augustus had personally travelled as far as Ticinum and had escorted the cortège all the way back to Rome; the family statues of the Claudian and Julian families had surrounded the bier; there had been lamentation in the forum and a panegyric from the rostrum; every kind of honour, whether handed down by ancestral custom or devised by subsequent generations, had been heaped upon him.

[Tacitus, *Annals* 3.5]

Tacitus' context is the death in suspicious circumstances in AD 19 of Germanicus, Drusus' son, and Tiberius' heir-apparent. Popular disquiet was increased by an apparent lack of public mourning on the part of the imperial family. Drusus' body had come from Germany in 9 BC for a full state funeral at Rome (see **D9** and Dio 55.2.1–3); the funeral of Germanicus had taken place at Antioch, leaving only an urn of ashes (Tacitus, *Annals* 2.83.3) to be deposited in Augustus' Mausoleum; that was why the ceremonies differed.

J47 Drusus' character

(This passage continues J43)

[1.4] It is generally believed that his keen public spirit was matched by a thirst for personal glory. For as well as seeking victory over our enemies in battle, he longed also to capture the *spolia opima*. And so, often at great risk to himself, he would pursue the German commanders all over the battlefield. But he also made no secret of his intention to restore the traditional constitution. This, I imagine, is the reason that some authorities have dared to suggest that Augustus harboured suspicions against him and recalled him from his province, and then had him poisoned for a somewhat dilatory response. [1.5] I mention this simply to avoid any sin of omission rather than because I believe there is any truth or probability in the story. For Augustus so loved him while he was alive that he always nominated him as a co-heir along with his own sons, and even acknowledged it once in a public statement to the senate; and after his death he made a fulsome public funeral oration over him, praying to the gods that they would make his own Caesars, Gaius and Lucius, like Drusus and grant to himself in due course as noble a death as they had given him. Not content with inscribing an elegy upon his tomb in verses which he himself composed, he also published a short biography in prose.

[Suetonius, *Claudius* 1.4–5]

Spolia opima (Spoils of Honour): for their importance and prestige, see introduction to **P3–P4**.

JULIA (The Elder) (39 BC – AD 14) (J48–J54)

Julia was Augustus' only child. Her mother, Scribonia, was divorced by Augustus immediately after Julia's birth. Julia was married three times: to Marcellus in 25 BC; after his death, to Agrippa, in 21 BC, by whom she produced five children; finally, after Agrippa's death, to Tiberius in 12/11 BC. Many references to her concern her adulterous behaviour for which she was eventually exiled, see below and **P12**.

J48 Tacitus' 'obituary' of Julia (AD 14)

The same year marked the death of Julia. Originally she had been exiled by her father, Augustus, to the island of Pandataria for her flagrant sexual extravagances, and later to the town of the Regini (Reggio), which stands on the shores of the Straits of Sicily (Straits of Messina). While Gaius and Lucius Caesar were still in their prime she had been married to Tiberius, but had regarded him with contempt as being beneath her. This was the real reason why Tiberius 'retired' to the island of Rhodes. Once he became emperor Tiberius kept her isolated, exiled, and in disgrace, and bereft of hope following the murder of Postumus Agrippa. He allowed her to die a lingering death through destitution and prolonged decrepitude, calculating that the sheer length of her exile would guarantee its obscurity. A similar motive accounts for his savage treatment of Sempronius Gracchus. He was a man of noble family, highly intelligent and blessed with a gift for eloquence which he did not always put to the best of uses. He seduced Julia while she was still married to Marcus Agrippa; but that was not the end of the affair. When she was 'transferred' to Tiberius, this serial adulterer stoked the fires of her contempt and loathing for her new husband to the extent that it was widely believed that the letter she wrote to her father Augustus inveighing against Tiberius was in fact composed by Sempronius. As a result, he was banished to the island of Cercina (Kerkenna) in the African Gulf (Gulf of Gabes) where he endured fourteen years in exile. Soldiers were then sent to murder him ....

[Tacitus, *Annals* 1.53]

Julia: had been exiled in 2 BC (see **P12** and Dio 55.10–16); her return to the mainland had been due to demonstrations made on her behalf by the populace (Dio 55.13.1).
married to Tiberius: 11 BC, see note on Tacitus, *Annals* 1.12.4, Section **F**.
why Tiberius retired: Tiberius retired to Rhodes in 6 BC (Dio 55.9.5, where the behaviour of his step-sons Gaius and Lucius Caesar is given as the reason).
Postumus Agrippa: for the killing of Julia's son, see note on Tacitus, *Annals* 1.3.4, Section **F**.
Sempronius Gracchus: a kinsman of the famous tribunes of the second century BC. He may himself have been tribune when Augustus exiled him (Dio 55.10.15).
married to Agrippa: after the death of Marcellus in 23 BC, Julia was married to Agrippa between 21 BC (Dio 54.6.5) and Agrippa's death in 12 BC.

J49 Dynastic plans: Julia

Sejanus wrote that he had heard that Augustus, in planning his daughter's marriage, had even had some thoughts of seeking a husband from the equestrian order.

Tiberius replied: "You say that Augustus thought of marrying his daughter to a member of the equestrian order. His own life was so distracted by all the cares of state that he must have realised that any man chosen for such a marriage alliance would be seen to have been elevated far above all others. So it is hardly surprising that in his discussions he mentioned men such as Gaius Proculeius who lived conspicuously quiet lives and avoided any entanglement in public life."

[Tacitus, *Annals* 4.39–40]

Tacitus reports that in AD 25, Sejanus, an equestrian, though Tiberius' partner in power, wrote to ask to marry Tiberius' daughter, Livilla. The authenticity of these letters is questionable, but Suetonius had similar evidence available to him, and states that Augustus considered equestrians as potential new husband for

Julia after Agrippa's death (Suetonius, *Augustus* 63.2). Gaius Proculeius was a reputable equestrian, connected with Maecenas (Dio 54.3.5).

J50   The wit of Julia (1): Julia's character and popularity
[2] She was now thirty-eight and had reached a stage of life at which, if she had had any sense, she would have realised that she was on the threshold of old age. But she continued to abuse the generosity of both Fortune and her own father. Yet she was a lover of literature and widely read – not difficult in a home like hers – and was blessed in addition with a gentle good nature and capable of great kindness. As a result she was regarded with enormous affection on all sides, though those who were aware of her more depraved predilections could not but be amazed at the apparent contradictions in her character.

[Macrobius, *Saturnalia* 2.5.2]

Macrobius follows his selection of anecdotes about Augustus (see above, **J13–J19**) with a series about Julia. *Threshold of old age*: Roman men were either 'young men' (under 40) or 'old men' (over 40), the threshold being the usual retirement age for soldiers.

J51   The wit of Julia (2): Augustus' relations with Julia
[3] Not once, but many times, her father had advised her in terms that were a mixture of parental affection and serious admonition that she should exercise restraint in the extravagance of her dress and her scandalous choice of friends. Yet when he looked at his flock of grandchildren and their undoubted resemblance to their father, Agrippa, he could not bring himself to entertain doubts about her virtue. [4] As a result, he fondly imagined that his daughter was blessed with a character so naturally extrovert that it conveyed an impression of lasciviousness which was in fact entirely false; indeed, he confidently persuaded himself that it was a family trait which she shared with her ancestor, Claudia. As a result, in his private conversations with friends, he remarked that he was forced to put up with two spoilt children, Rome and Julia.

[Macrobius, *Saturnalia* 2.5.3–4]

J52   The wit of Julia (3): Julia's entourage contrasted with Livia's
Here is another famous remark of Julia's. At a gladiatorial show people could not help noticing the difference between Livia's entourage and that of Julia. Round Livia were gathered men of maturity and distinction; round Julia sat members of the extravagant younger set. Her father suggested to her in a letter that she should take note of the difference between the demeanour of the state's two leading ladies. She penned this neat retort: "Yes, and we too will all be old one day."

[Macrobius, *Saturnalia* 2.5.6]

J53   The wit of Julia (4): life-styles
Similarly, having had a lecture from one of her more serious friends about the importance of modelling her life-style more closely on the frugal simplicity of her father, she commented: "He seems to forget that he is Caesar; I never forget that I am Caesar's daughter."

[Macrobius, *Saturnalia* 2.5.8]

Frugal simplicity: Augustus claimed this traditional virtue, see, for example **S30**, **K30** and Suet. *Aug.* 72–73.

J54   Julia's behaviour
In Rome, an example of such licentious behaviour *(the wearing of ceremonial floral wreaths)* is provided by none other than the deified Augustus' daughter, Julia: during

one of her nocturnal escapades, she placed a floral wreath on the statue of Marsyas – he complains about it in one of his letters.

[Pliny, *Natural History* 21.9]

Statue of Marsyas: also mentioned **P12**.

One of his letters: a plausible change to the Latin makes the letter not Augustus', but simply a letter of that period.

JULIA (The Younger) (c. 19 BC – AD 28) (J55)

Julia was the daughter of Agrippa and Julia, thus the granddaughter of Augustus. She is usually referred to as the Younger Julia to avoid confusion with her mother. she was married to Aemilius Paullus in 4 BC but (like her mother) was convicted of adultery and exiled by Augustus in AD 8, to the island of Trimerus, see **P16**.

J55   Death of Augustus' granddaughter, Julia (AD 28)

At about this time Julia, Augustus' granddaughter, died. She had been convicted of adultery and banished to the island of Trimerus off the coast of Apulia. There she endured twenty years of exile, alleviated only by the support of Livia, the Augusta, who had secretly contrived to ruin her step-children when they prospered, only to make an ostentatious display of pity for them when disaster struck.

[Tacitus, *Annals* 4.71]

Ostentatious display of pity: this feminine quality is certainly insisted on in sources favourable to Livia: see note on Tacitus, *Annals* 1.13.6 (Section **F**).

GAIUS JULIUS CAESAR (20 BC – AD 4) (J56–J62)

Gaius Caesar was the eldest child of Agrippa and Julia, thus Augustus' first grandchild and his first male descendant. He was adopted by Augustus in 17 BC after the birth of his brother and given a series of exceptional honours, which marked him out as Augustus' chosen successor. Chief of these was the title *princeps iuventutis* (roughly 'Leader of the Younger Generation') awarded by the equestrian order in 5 BC, and deliberately evoking the idea of *princeps*. Gaius married Livilla before his departure for the East in 1 BC (Tacitus, *Annals* 4.40; Dio 55.10). Livilla was perhaps 13. The marriage between Augustus' grandson and Livia's granddaughter linked the two branches of the family. On Gaius, see also **M42** (part of Augustus' council) and **K11** and **M84** (honours from Rome and Athens).

J56   Celebrations for Gaius Caesar's coming of age, about April 5 BC, Sardis

The Assembly of the Hellenes in Asia and the people and council of the Sardians honoured Menogenes, the son of Isidoros, the son of Menogenes, as follows:

Metrodoros, the son of Konon, Kleinias, Mousaios and Dionysios, the chief magistrates, made their report: [7] since Gaius Julius Caesar, the oldest of the sons of Augustus, has assumed the most prayed-for bright white toga with all its honour after his purple-bordered one, and all men rejoice on seeing Augustus' prayers for his children fulfilled; and since in view of such great good fortune our city judged to be sacred the day of his coming-of-age, on which each year everyone in bright white clothing wears a wreath, and the magistrates each year carry out sacrifices to the gods and make prayers through the sacred heralds on behalf of his welfare, and join in dedicating his statue setting it in the temple of his father; [14] and on the day on which the city received the good news and the decree was ratified to wear wreaths during this day too and perform most splendid sacrifices to the gods, and to send an embassy concerning these matters to go to Rome and to rejoice together both with Gaius himself and Augustus; the council and people decided to send envoys chosen from the best men to give greetings from the city and to present to him a copy of this decree sealed with the public seal, and to discuss with Augustus about what is expedient for the Assembly of Asia and the city, and they chose as envoys Iollas the son of Metrodoros and Menogenes the son of Isidoros the son of Menogenes.

[Greek: EJ 99 = *IGRRP* 4.1756, lines 1–21]

This is the first of twelve documents in honour of a local citizen, Menogenes, on a tall pedimented marble plaque (2.24 m. high), found near the temple of Artemis at Sardis. He had acted as envoy to convey the city's congratulations to Augustus on the occasion of Gaius Caesar ceremonially putting aside his *toga praetexta* in favour of the *toga virilis* to mark his coming of age (early Jan 5 BC). For the other documents, see **M85**.

For the first time since 23 BC, Augustus was consul, to celebrate Gaius' coming of age. He also gave 240 sesterces to 320,000 members of the urban plebs (*RG* 15.2). In this same year Gaius was decreed *princeps iuventutis* (leader of the youth) and was elected to the consulship for five years' time.

J57   Augustus' letter to Gaius

The other night I was reading a volume of the letters of the deified Augustus, which he had written to his grandson, Gaius. It was all so elegantly expressed that I could not put it down. The style was neither ponderous nor fussy, but remarkably fluent and unaffected. In one of the letters I found a reference to the nature of the so-called 'climacteric', this very year of life that we have been discussing. Here is a transcript: *23 September*.

My dear Gaius, most beloved of little donkeys, greetings. I swear I always miss you so much when you are away from me. But on days like today I miss you most of all, and my eyes yearn for a glimpse of my darling Gaius. So wherever you are on this special day, I hope you are happy and in good health and celebrating my sixty-fourth birthday. From this you can see that I have "passed the grand climacteric", which is the common lot of all elderly gentlemen – my sixty-third year is now complete. So I pray to the gods that I may be allowed to spend whatever span of life remains to me in good health and with our country enjoying its current prosperity, while I watch you and your brother proving your mettle as you wait to take over my post.

[Aulus Gellius, *Attic Nights* 15.7.3]

all so elegantly expressed: see **J21**. Suetonius, who had access to Augustus' own copies of his letters, and quotes frequently from them, also describes his style as 'elegant' (Suet. *Aug*. 86).
I swear I always miss you: in 1 BC, after his marriage to Livia Julia, daughter of Drusus, Gaius had been sent to the East with proconsular *imperium* (the power of a proconsul), Dio 55.10.18.
celebrating my 64th birthday: 23 September, AD 1.
take over my post: Augustus uses a military metaphor.

J58   Gaius and Lucius as *principes iuventutis*, *aureus* 2 BC to AD 11

Obv: Augustus, head laureate, right.

CAESAR AVGVSTVS DIVI F PATER PATRIAE (Caesar Augustus, Son of the Deified, Father of the Fatherland)

Rev: Gaius and Lucius Caesar, standing, veiled, with shields, spears and priestly symbols between them.

C L CAESARES AVGVSTI F COS DESIG PRINC IVVENT (Gaius and Lucius Caesar, Sons of Augustus, Consuls designate, Leaders of the Younger Generation)

[*RIC* Augustus 205 / *BMC* Augustus 513]

This coin design of the mint of Lyons, produced sometime after 2 BC, shows Augustus' grandsons Gaius and Lucius as *principes iuventutis*, a title first awarded to Gaius Caesar by the equestrian order in 5 BC, at the same time as he was named consul designate for AD 1. Although this title did not give the holder any official power, it became an unofficial designation of the imperial successor.

J59   Wounding and death of Gaius

[42] In the East the Armenians were causing further problems. Caesar therefore sent out there one of his two grandsons, the Caesars. Both were destined to die young, one of them without opportunity for distinction. For Lucius died of disease in Marseilles, while Gaius succumbed to wounds in Syria while fighting to recover Armenia, which was seeking to defect to Parthia. [43] Pompey had originally defeated King Tigranes and conditioned the Armenians to tolerate a form of subject status whose only condition was that they should accept Rome's choice of ruler. This condition had been in abeyance for some time, but was now re-imposed by Gaius after a minor campaign, which nevertheless involved a certain number of casualties. [44] The king had appointed a certain Dones as governor of the Artagerae. He pretended to betray his master by handing to Gaius a document which purported to contain an account of the royal treasures, and while he was studying it Dones suddenly drew his sword and attacked him. Caesar was wounded but recovered temporarily <....................>.

[Florus: *Two Hundred Years of War – A Summary* 2.32.42–44]

Tigranes was defeated by Pompey in 66 BC.

wounded but recovered temporarily: a gap follows in the text. Velleius, perhaps influenced by his loyalty to Tiberius describes Gaius as incapacitated mentally as well as physically, 2.102.2 (Section **E**).

J60   Notice of Gaius' death on *Fasti* at Cupra in Picenum

21 February, Gaius Caesar, son of Augustus, died in Lycia, aged 22. At Rome legal proceedings were suspended until his bones were placed in the Mausoleum. On 9 September he had been injured waging war in Armenia, while besieging the town of Artagira.

[*Inscr. It.* 13.1.7]

Other calendars mention offerings to Gaius' spirit being made on this day (**C14**).

J61   Decree honouring Gaius Caesar, AD 4, Pisa

[….at Pisa in the forum in the Augusteum, the following were present at the drafting:] Quintus Sertorius Atilius Tacitus son of Quintus, Publius Rasinius Bassus son of Lucius, Lucius Lappius Gallus [son of Lucius], Quintus Sertorius Alpius Pica son of Quintus, Gaius Vettius Virgula son of Lucius, Marcus Herius Priscus [son] of Marcus, Aulus Albius Gutta son of Aulus, Titus Petronius Pollio son of Titus, Lucius Fabius Bassus son of Lucius, Sextus Aponius Creticus son of Sextus, Gaius Canius Saturninus [son] of Gaius, Lucius Otacilius Panthera son of Quintus.

[5] Seeing as a statement was made, although there were no magistrates in our colony because of disputes concerning the candidates, and these things had been done which have been written below: since on 2 April the message had been brought that Gaius Caesar, the son of Augustus who is Father of the Fatherland, chief priest, protector of the Roman empire, and guardian of the whole world, and the grandson of the Deified, after a consulship which he had completed while successfully waging war beyond the furthest boundaries of the Roman people, after he had carried out his state duties properly, with the most warlike and greatest peoples subdued or brought into alliance, had received wounds in service of his country and as a result of this disaster had been snatched away from the Roman people by the cruel fates, when already designated a leader who was most just and most like his father in his virtues, and the one defence of our colony. [14] This event came at a time when the grief had not yet abated which the whole colony had felt at the death of [Lucius] Caesar his brother, consul designate, augur, our patron, and leader of the younger generation, and it had renewed and multiplied the sorrow of everyone individually and collectively. Therefore all the town councillors and colonists, since as it happened there were in the colony neither chief magistrates nor prefects nor anyone in charge of the administration of justice, agreed amongst themselves, in view of the importance of such a great and so unexpected a calamity, that, from the day on which his death had been announced right up until the day on which his bones will be brought back and buried and his spirit duly laid to rest, everyone, dressed in mourning, with the temples of the immortal gods, the public baths, and all shops closed, ought to abstain from banquets; and that the married women who are in our colony ought to be assistant mourners; [25] and that the day on which Gaius Caesar passed away, namely 21 February, ought to be handed down to memory as one of mourning, equivalent to the day of the Allia, and be marked in the presence of all by regulation and by desire; and that care be taken that no public sacrifice nor any offerings nor betrothals nor public banquets be held, undertaken, or proclaimed hereafter for that day or on that day which will be 21 February, and that no theatrical or circus shows be held or watched on that day; and it was agreed that on that day each year rites be performed publicly to his spirit by the magistrates and by those who are in charge of the administration of justice at Pisa, in the same place and in the same way as it has been established rites be performed for Lucius Caesar; [34] and it was agreed that an arch be set up in the most frequented place of our colony decorated with the spoils of peoples subdued or brought into alliance by him, and that on top of it should be placed a statue of him on foot in triumphal dress, and on either side of this statue two gilded equestrian statues of Gaius and Lucius Caesars: and it was agreed that as soon as we will be able to appoint and have chief magistrates in accordance with the colony's law, those two chief magistrates first appointed are to bring before the town councillors this matter which has been agreed by the councillors and all colonists, and that this be legally taken care of by invoking the councillors' public authority, and at their instigation be entered into the public records; [42] meanwhile Titus Statulenus Iuncus, priest of Augustus, lesser priest of the public rites of the Roman people, should be asked to explain with the envoys the present difficulty faced by the colony, and to declare the public duty and wish of all in a dispatch delivered to Imperator Caesar Augustus, who is Father of the Fatherland, chief priest, in his 26th year of tribunician power; and Titus Statulenus Iuncus, leader of our colony, priest of Augustus, lesser priest of the public rites of the Roman people, did this, with a dispatch such as is described above delivered to Imperator Caesar Augustus, chief priest, in his 26th year of tribunician power, Father of the Fatherland.

[51] The councillors decided that whatever had been done, performed, and resolved upon by general assent of all social classes on 2 April in the consulship of Sextus Aelius Catus and Gaius Sentius Saturninus, should in its entirety thus be done, performed, observed, and adhered to by Lucius Titius son of Aulus and Titus Allius Rufus son of Titus, joint chief magistrates, and by those whoever hereafter will be joint chief magistrates or prefects or any other magistrates in our colony, and that all these things be thus done, performed, observed, and adhered to in perpetuity; and that Lucius Titius son of Aulus and Titus Allius Rufus son of Titus, joint chief magistrates, see to it that all these things written above in accordance with our decree be entered into the public records by the public scribe in the presence of the proquaestors at the earliest possible opportunity. Decreed.

[*EJ* 69 = *ILS* 140]

Gaius Caesar had been sent from Rome to the East in 1 BC in order to settle turbulent affairs in Armenia. His sudden death on 21 February AD 4 whilst on active service in the East (having been wounded at the siege of Artagira (**J59**)) provoked the town of Pisa to respond even more fulsomely than it had done to the death of Lucius just two years earlier (see below **J64**). This decree is more detailed in its praise of Gaius' achievements, celebrating his foreign conquests and echoing the almost poetic language ('snatched away from the Roman people by the cruel fates') with which Augustus described the same tragedy in *RG* 14. The decree includes detailed specification for his honorific monuments, down to the sculptural programme on the arch. It also sets Gaius' death on a par with what was regarded as one of the worst disasters suffered by Rome, the defeat by the Gauls at the river Allia on 18 July 390 BC, which led to the sack of Rome. The Pisans thus mourn Gaius as having been heir presumptive to Augustus.

The passing of this decree in spite of the lack of local magistrates in post, due to problems surrounding the elections, shows the town's anxiety not to seem slow in responding to the crisis. Once again, envoys are to be sent to Augustus, led by a local dignitary whose priesthoods link him with Rome, in order to draw his attention to the loyal sentiments of the colony. As with Lucius, the town is eager to stress the unanimity of all ranks of society in mourning Gaius.

Gaius still remains in the family group of statues (**J68**), in AD 7–8, 3 or 4 years after his death.

J62 Augustus' grief at the death of Gaius Caesar

When Gaius Caesar died in Syria, the deified Augustus complained in a letter couched in restrained and amicable terms (as you would expect from that most kindly of souls) that despite his severe recent loss one of his dearest friends had gone to a most sumptuous dinner party. Pollio wrote to him in reply, "On the very day that I lost my son Herius I too had dinner."

[Elder Seneca *Controversies* 4 preface 5]

Seneca recalls that Asinius Pollio (see Index of Persons) made a speech within three days of the death of his son and maintained his usual routine. At Pisa, banquets were forbidden as part of official mourning for Gaius Caesar (**J61** line 24).

LUCIUS JULIUS CAESAR (17 BC–AD 2) (**J63–J65**)

Lucius Caesar was the second son of Agrippa and Julia, thus Augustus' grandson. Like his brother, he was marked out as a potential successor to Augustus by being adopted as his son, and being made a *princeps iuventutis* (Leader of the Younger Generation – see above, **J58**) and made consul designate when only 14 (**K15**).

J63 Aemilia Lepida once betrothed to Lucius Caesar

[22] Aemilia Lepida had a family background of great distinction, being a member of the Aemilian family and the great-granddaughter of Lucius Sulla and Gnaeus Pompey…..

[23] …. She had at one time been betrothed to Lucius Caesar and thus destined to become the daughter-in-law of the deified Augustus.

[Tacitus, *Annals* 3.22–23]

Aemilia Lepida: one of the high-born women who were intended to form a link with the ruling dynasty, so drawing their families within Augustus' orbit.

J64   Decree honouring Lucius Caesar, AD 2, Pisa

On 19 September at Pisa in the forum in the Augusteum, the following were present at the drafting: Quintus Petillius son of Quintus, Publius Rasinius Bassus son of Lucius, Marcus Puppius son of Marcus, Quintus Sertorius Pica son of Quintus, Gnaeus Octavius Rufus son of Gnaeus, Aulus Albius Gutta son of Aulus.

Seeing as Gaius Canius Saturninus son of Gaius, joint chief magistrate, made a statement concerning increasing the honours of Lucius Caesar, the son of Augustus Caesar who is Father of the Fatherland and chief priest and in his 25th year of tribunician power, an augur, consul designate, leader of the younger generation, and patron of our colony, and seeing that he asked them what they wished to be done concerning this matter, they decreed on this matter as follows:

[9] Since the senate of the Roman people, among the other very many and very great honours of Lucius Caesar, the son of Augustus Caesar who is Father of the Fatherland and chief priest and in his 25th year of tribunician power, an augur and consul designate, by general assent of all social classes, with eagerness […], the task was given to Gaius Canius Saturninus, joint chief magistrate, and to the ten leading men of choosing and investigating which place of theirs seems more suitable, or of buying with public money from private individuals the place of which they approved more; and that at this altar each year on 20 [August] offerings be publicly made to his departed spirit by the magistrates or by those who are in charge of jurisdiction at that time, with those for whom it shall be right and proper to wear the garment clothed in dark togas; [20] and that a black bull and ram adorned with dark woollen headbands be sacrificed to his departed spirit, and that these victims be burnt in this place, and that over them individual urns of milk, honey, and oil be poured; and then finally that the right be granted to the rest, if any should wish as a private individual to make offerings to his departed spirit [provided that no one] offer more than one wax taper or one torch or wreath, while those who have performed the sacrifice dressed in the Gabine manner kindle the pile of wood and also tend it; [and that] the place in front of this altar, where that pile is gathered together and arranged, lie open to a distance of 40 feet, and be enclosed by oak stakes and for this purpose heaps of wood each year be set there, and that this decree together with the earlier decrees relating to his honours be inscribed or engraved upon a large pillar fixed in the ground next to this altar; for as regards the rest of the formalities which they will have decided and will decide should be avoided or guarded against on that same day, what the senate of the Roman people will decree about these things should be followed; [33] and that at the first possible moment envoys from our social class approach Imperator Caesar Augustus, Father of the Fatherland, chief priest, in his 25th year of tribunician power, and ask him that it be allowed to the Julian colonists of the Loyal Julian Colony of Pisa to do and carry out all these things in accordance with this decree.

[EJ 68 = *ILS* 139]

This decree granting honours to the lately deceased Lucius Caesar shows the council and inhabitants of Pisa expressing their feelings of loyalty towards Augustus and his family. In part, this may be due to the town's status as a recent colony: Pisa had been refounded by either Julius Caesar or Augustus with the introduction of veteran soldiers from a legion with the honorific name 'Loyal'. Above all, however, Lucius Caesar had been its patron, so it was natural for honours to be heaped on him following his sudden death on 20 August AD 2 in the south of France. The speed with which the council acted, though, is noteworthy, passing this decree less than a month later, even before the Senate at Rome had finalised all its plans for his honours. The council emphasises its respect for Augustus: it meets in the Augusteum, a building named in his honour; Lucius' relationship to Augustus and Augustus' titles are given more prominence than Lucius' own official posts; and it sends envoys directly to Augustus himself to seek his approval for its decree. This would also, of course, have drawn his attention to its loyal actions. The council also models itself upon the Roman Senate, both in terms of its language and procedure (compare the senatorial decrees relating to the Centennial Games – **L27**) and in imitating the honours granted to Lucius by the Senate. The council is anxious to allow private citizens to honour Lucius themselves as well, but also takes pains to ensure that no individual can upstage the public ceremonies, by limiting the nature of the offerings anyone may make.

On the death of Lucius, see also **C28**; Tacitus, *Annals* 1.3.3 (Section **F**); Velleius 2.102.3 (Section **E**); Dio 55.10A. Lucius still remains in the family group of statues (**J68**), in AD 7–8, 5 or 6 years after his death.

J65 Posthumous honours for Gaius and Lucius (*Tabula Hebana*, Heba in Etruria)

And (it has pleased the senate) that the Salii should insert into their hymn the name of Germanicus Caesar, to honour his memory, an honour also given to Gaius and Lucius Caesar, brothers of Tiberius.

And (it has pleased the senate) that to the 10 centuries of the Caesars, which usually cast their votes for the *destinatio* of praetors and consuls, be added 5 centuries. Since the first 10 are named after Gaius and Lucius Caesar, the next 5 shall be named after Germanicus Caesar. In all these centuries the senators and equestrians of the jury-panels which have been, or will be, drawn up for public cases, shall cast their votes. One of the magistrates, for the purpose of carrying out the *destinatio*, shall summon to the voting area the senators, and those permitted to speak in the senate and the equestrians, in accordance with the law passed by the consuls, Lucius Valerius Messalla Volesus and Gnaeus Cornelius Cinna Magnus, to cast their votes.

[*Tabula Hebana* = EJ 94a lines 4–12]

The passage above comes from a bill honouring Germanicus, AD 19–20. He is awarded honours previously given to Gaius and Lucius Caesar by a law of AD 5. The first honour is that his name is to be included in the archaic hymn of the Salii, an honour also granted to Augustus in his lifetime (see *RG* 10.1 and note).

The other honours concern the election of praetors and consuls. It seems that the law of AD 5 created additional centuries ('electoral colleges') made up of senators and equestrians and named after the grandsons of Augustus. The law was clearly intended to honour the recently dead Caesars. Its permanence, intention and effect on the electoral procedure are more contentious. It seems that these centuries voted on the candidates (the procedure being the *destinatio*), and that those selected (*destinati*) would probably go forward to the final general vote with the endorsement and the combined votes of the Centuries of Gaius and Lucius. The general assembly (in which the voting system always favoured the choice of the upper classes) was presumably expected to follow the example set by the new Centuries of Gaius and Lucius. However nothing can be deduced for certain from this document about the reality or unreality of elections under Augustus.

Bibliography: *OCD*[2] entry '*destinatio*'. Full text, translation and commentary in M. H. Crawford (ed.), *Roman Statutes* (London 1996) no. 37–38.

NERO CLAUDIUS DRUSUS **GERMANICUS** (15 or 16 BC – AD 19) (**J66**)

Germanicus was the son of Drusus (son of Livia and Tiberius Claudius Nero) and Antonia (younger daughter of Octavia and Mark Antony). Thus he was, on his father's side, Augustus' step-grandson and on his mother's side, Augustus' great-nephew. His family connexion to Augustus was further strengthened in AD 4 when Augustus adopted Tiberius who in turn adopted Germanicus (his nephew) and again by his marriage in AD 5 to Agrippina (daughter of Julia and Agrippa).

J66 Germanicus considered as Augustus' heir

Germanicus, Augustus' great-nephew, was universally admired and Augustus had toyed with the idea of making him the ruler of the empire. But he was dissuaded by the entreaties of his wife, Livia, and instead adopted Tiberius, while Tiberius adopted Germanicus.

[Tacitus, *Annals* 4.57]

This assertion can certainly not be disproved, and it is repeated by Suetonius, *Gaius* 4; but Augustus could see for himself the advantages of having a tried general, previous holder of tribunician power, as his successor in AD 4, when he had just lost two young heirs and Germanicus was not yet twenty and without military experience. *Tiberius adopted Germanicus*: Suetonius, *Tiberius* 15.2 and Dio 55.13.2, going further, have Tiberius 'forced' to adopt Germanicus.

Germanicus is positioned prominently in the Pavia Imperial family group, see **J68**.

AGRIPPA POSTUMUS (12 BC – AD 14) (**J67**)

As his name implies, Agrippa Postumus was born to Julia after the death of his father Agrippa. He was Augustus' grandson, but unlike his brothers Gaius and Lucius was not given accelerated promotion or early adoption into Augustus' family. He was adopted, along with Tiberius, in AD 4, after the death of his brothers, but was 'abdicated' in AD 6 and was exiled to Planasia. He was killed immediately after the death of Augustus. It is not clear who ordered his death. See Tacitus, *Annals* 1.3.4 – 6.3 (Section **F**); the 'official' version in Velleius 2.112.7 (Section **E**); and rumours of a reconciliation shortly before Augustus' death (**P18**).

J67   Agrippa on leaded bronze coin of Corinth, Achaea, AD 4–5

Obv: Agrippa Postumus, head bare, right.
CORINTHI AGRIPPA CAESAR ((coin) of the Corinthians, Agrippa Caesar)

Rev: Legend within decorated circle.
C HEIO POLLIONE ITER C MVSSIO PRISCO IIVIR (C Heius Pollio, Magistrate for the second time. C Mussius Priscus, Magistrate)

[*RPC* 1, no.1141]

His period of favour was short-lived and although he appears on the provincial coinage, such as this coin from Corinth, he was never depicted on the imperial coinage.

J68   Statue group honouring members of the imperial family, past and present, AD 7–8, North Italy

To Imperator Caesar Augustus, son of the Deified, chief priest, Father of the Fatherland, augur, one of the Fifteen in charge of sacrifices, one of the Seven in charge of feasting, consul 13 times, hailed as *imperator* 17 times, in his 30th year of tribunician power.

To Livia, daughter of Drusus, wife of Caesar Augustus.

To [Gaius] Caesar, son of Augustus, grandson of the Deified, priest, consul, hailed as *imperator*.

To [Lucius] Caesar, son of Augustus, grandson of the Deified, augur, consul designate, leader of the younger generation.

To Tiberius Caesar, son of Augustus, grandson of the Deified, priest, twice consul, hailed as *imperator* three times, augur, holder of tribunician power 9 times.

To Germanicus Julius Caesar, son of Tiberius, grandson of Augustus, great-grandson of the Deified.

To Drusus [Julius] Caesar, son [of Tiberius], grandson of Augustus, great-grandson of the Deified.

To Nero Julius Caesar, [son] of Germanicus, great-grandson of Augustus.

To Drusus Julius Germanicus, son of Germanicus, great-grandson of Augustus.

To Tiberius Claudius Nero Germanicus, son of Drusus Germanicus.

[EJ 61]

Preserved only in a manuscript, this series of inscriptions from northern Italy (Ticinum?) may have belonged to a large statue base or to an arch, supporting portrait statues in honour of members of the imperial family. The following reconstruction of the group is suggested (numbers beneath indicate their approximate age in AD 7–8):

NERO	DRUS.	GERM.	TIB.	AUG.	LIV.	GAIUS	LUC.	DRUS.	CLAUD.
(2)	(20)	(23)	(48)	(69)	(64)	(dead)	(dead)	(1)	(17)

It is interesting to note the relative prominence of the family members, as reflected in their juxtaposition with each other. Gaius and Lucius Caesars are included, despite being dead, whilst Tiberius' position at Augustus' right hand suggests his new prominence as heir. Germanicus' name and position next to Tiberius reflect his adoption by him, and his role as future heir presumptive. The future emperor Claudius occupies only a marginal place. Agrippa Postumus, then aged 18 and Augustus' only survivng grandson, but disowned in AD 6 and exiled does not appear at all.

J69   An impostor claiming to be the son of Octavia

Even the deified Augustus, despite the unparalleled sanctity attached to him when he was ruler of the world, experienced this sort of outrage. An impostor emerged who had the nerve to pretend that he was born of the womb of Octavia, the emperor's most revered and honoured sister. He claimed to have been exposed at birth on the orders of his mother because of his extreme physical disability and to have been preserved by the man to whom he was entrusted for this purpose and brought up as his own son, while the man's own son was substituted for him. His intention seems to have been to contaminate that most sacred household and the memory of its true blood-line while at the same time defiling its integrity with the filthy contagion of a false connection. But while his ship was heading in full sail upon the winds of brazen audacity towards its outrageous destination, by order of Augustus he was assigned to the oar of a galley slave on a state trireme.

[Valerius Maximus, 9.15.2]

This story is not mentioned elsewhere.

SECTION K

ROME AND ITALY

Augustus' building works in Rome occupy three sections of his account of his achievements and expenses (*RG* 19–21). They also prompted his famous remark that he had found Rome made of brick and left it made of marble, quoted by Suetonius, *Augustus* 28.3 and by Dio 56.30 as his dying words, though Dio interprets them metaphorically as meaning the strength of the empire. For Augustan Rome, the literary, epigraphic and numismatic record can be supplemented in many cases by the archaeological remains. This section therefore includes archaeological notes extracted, by kind permission of the author and of OUP, from A. Claridge, *Rome: an Oxford Archaeological Guide*, (Oxford 1998).

General descriptions of Rome, and its organisation (K1–K12)

Most Augustan authors were Romans, writing for Romans, with therefore little reason to give a general description of their own city. Strabo's account of Rome (**K4**) is of great interest in so far as it shows us what a visitor to the capital of the empire found impressive. This is sometimes quite strikingly different from what we might expect.

K1   The eternal city
Piso built himself a house with meticulous craftsmanship from foundations to rooftop. Augustus commented: "You have given me the utmost pleasure by building it like that. It is like a sign that Rome will be the Eternal City."

[Plutarch, *Sayings of Kings and Commanders, Moralia* 207.15]

K2   A grudging compliment
Timagenes, who hated Rome's success, used to say that the only reason he regretted the fires which broke out in the city was that he knew that even better buildings would arise than those which had been destroyed.

[Younger Seneca, *Moral Epistles (to Lucilius)* 91.13]

On Timagenes see **P20**.

K3   General description of the architectural wonders of Rome, c. AD 77
[101] This seems an appropriate moment to turn to the wonders of our own city, to analyse the rich lessons of the last 800 years, and to demonstrate that in architecture as well we have conquered the world….[102] Even if we omit for the moment the Circus Maximus, built by the Dictator, Caesar, 600 metres long and 200 metres wide, with buildings of some 3 acres apiece, plus seating for 250,000, we must surely include the following in our catalogue of outstanding architectural works: for sheer magnificence there is the Basilica of Paullus, so famed for its Phrygian columns, the Forum of the Deified Augustus, and the Emperor Vespasian's Temple of Peace, the loveliest buildings the world has ever seen. Then there is the roof of the Ballot Office, built by Agrippa, though in Rome the architect Valerius of Ostia had already roofed a whole theatre for the Games of Libo. [103] Are we to admire the pyramids of the kings when the Dictator, Caesar, paid out 100,000,000 sesterces simply to purchase the land on which his forum was built? And if anyone is impressed by extravagance in an era of miserliness such as ours, then consider the house bought for 14,800,000 sesterces which was occupied by Clodius, who was assassinated by Milo. [104] I find all this no less remarkable than the crazed extravagance of kings, and for this reason I see Milo's own debts of some 70,000,000

sesterces as an extraordinary perversion of the human spirit. But then those were the days when old men still wondered at the vast scale of the Rampart, the substructures of the Capitol, and most remarkable of all, the Great Sewers of the city – which had involved tunnelling through our hills and, as I have explained in the preceding pages, turning Rome into a city supported on arches beneath which ships could sail, as happened in the aedileship of Marcus Agrippa which followed his consulship.

[Pliny, *Natural History* 36.101–104]

Basilica of Paullus: see **K15**.

Forum of Augustus: see **K17 – K28**.

Temple of Peace: dedicated by Vespasian in AD 75, built from the spoils from the Jewish War. The description of Rome must thus have been written between AD 75 and Pliny's death in the eruption of Vesuvius in AD 79.

The Ballot Office (Diribitorium): completed by Agrippa in 7 BC. Dio 55.8.4 describes it as the largest building with a single roof. He adds that the roof was destroyed in a fire in AD 80 (the year after Pliny's death) and could not be reconstructed.

Theatre for the Games of Libo: 63 BC, in a temporary theatre.

Forum of Caesar (forum Iulium): started by Julius Caesar in 54 BC, finished by Octavian in 29 BC.

Clodius…Milo: Publius Clodius Pulcher and Titus Annius Milo were bitter enemies as populist politicians and leaders of armed gangs in Rome in the 50s BC. Clodius was killed in a fight between the gangs in January 52 BC.

Great Sewer (Cloaca maxima): the culmination of Pliny's catalogue, he goes on to devote two sections in praise of its strength of construction 'standing well nigh indestructible for 700 years since the time of Tarquinius Priscus [*c*. 616–578 BC]'. Livy, who attributes it to Tarquinius Superbus [*c*. 534–510 BC] agrees with Pliny's assessment, writing that it had scarcely been matched by the new magnificence of his day (1.56).

aedileship of Agrippa: 33 BC. See **T8, T9** and **K54** . He had the sewers cleared, and sailed through to inspect them (Dio 49.43.1).

K4   The Campus Martius

In fact, the citizens of ancient Rome did not set a very high priority on the issue of its beautification, since they had other more important matters pressing for their attention. Later generations, however, and especially the present one including my own contemporaries, have more than made up for this and filled the city with many lovely buildings. In fact Pompey, the deified (Julius) Caesar, and Augustus, together with his children, friends, wife, and sister, have surpassed all others in the enthusiasm which they have shown for the building programme and the expenditure they have lavished upon it. The Campus Martius holds the majority of such buildings and as a result has enhanced its natural beauty with the glorious edifices which are their legacy to posterity. Indeed, the size of the Campus is almost unbelievable, offering as it does adequate space simultaneously for both chariot-racing and other equestrian activities, and for the vast number of people taking exercise, whether with ball-games, hoops, or bouts of wrestling. The sculptures which adorn the area, the ground which is grassy throughout the year, and the hill-tops (its crowning glory) rising beyond the river and stretching down to the main channel like the painted backdrop of a stage-set, all these provide a spectacle from which one can hardly turn away one's eyes. Nearby there is a second campus, surrounded by innumerable *stoas*, sacred groves, three theatres, an amphitheatre, and a packed succession of rich temples, all contriving to suggest, as it were, that the rest of the city was nothing more than a minor side-show.

[Strabo, *Geography* 5.3.8]

Strabo says little about the fora, but a great deal about the landscape, a focus which is in keeping with his descriptions of other cities. This passage is continued in **K29**.

Campus Martius: the 'Field of Mars' was a large flood-plain to the North of Rome enclosed by a bend of the Tiber and the Pincian, Quirinal and Capitoline hills. In the republic, the area was public land, outside the city wall and used for military training (hence its name) and election assemblies.

Second campus: it is not clear what area Strabo refers to here: the three theatres: of Pompey; Balbus (**K5**, **K51**) and Marcellus (**K52**, **K53**) and the Amphitheatre of Statilius Taurus (**K5**) are in the main Campus Martius.

K5   The Re-building of Rome

Even under the principate public-spirited generosity was still fashionable, and even Augustus had allowed Statilius Taurus, Marcius Philippus, and Cornelius Balbus to apply the spoils of war and their own superfluous wealth to the adornment of the city and for the admiration of posterity.

[Tacitus, *Annals* 3.72]

The context is the decision by Tiberius in AD 22 to allow Marcus Aemilius Lepidus to rebuild the *Basilica Aemilia*. The monuments are among those mentioned by Suet. *Aug*. 29.4: the Temple of Heracles and the Muses by Marcius Philippus (29 BC), Theatre of Cornelius Balbus (13 BC), Amphitheatre of Statilius Taurus (29 BC). Marcius Philippus was the son of Octavian's step-father, Philippus. For Statilius Taurus, see **K7** and **T16**; for Cornelius Balbus see **K51** and **M25**.

K6   Augustus' building regulations for Rome

Caesar Augustus took a particular interest in the constant deterioration of the fabric of the city from fire, collapse, and the fashion for renovation, mentioned above. To control the damage by fire he formed a fire brigade recruited from freedmen to bring help where needed; to reduce the danger of collapse he placed restrictions on the height of all new building, and a limit of seventy feet on the height of all buildings fronting onto the public streets.

[Strabo, *Geography* 5.3.7]

These measures highlight some of the dangers of living in the crowded capital and support Augustus' view of himself as concerned with the needs of the populace at large (compare Suet. *Aug*. 30; and Tac. *Ann*. 15.43 for Nero's similar measures after the great fire in Rome of AD 64).

K7   The post of city prefect (*praefectus urbi*)

[10] But Piso's particular distinction was that as city prefect he tactfully exercised the power of an office which had only recently been made permanent and which commanded only sullen obedience.

> *[Tacitus then gives an account of the origins of the post under the kings to administer the city in the temporary absence of kings and, later, magistrates.]*

[11] During the civil wars Augustus gave Cilnius Maecenas, a member of the equestrian order, total control over the administration of Rome and Italy. Later, when he became absolute ruler, the sheer size of the population and the ponderous inflexibility of legal remedies forced him to appoint a man of consular rank to control the slave population and the more disorderly elements of the populace, whose unruly tendencies yield only to the threat of force. Messala Corvinus was the first to hold this office, which he surrendered within a few days because he claimed that he did not know how to exercise its powers. Then Statilius Taurus had a distinguished tenure, despite his advanced old age. Finally Calpurnius Piso held the post for some twenty years with no less distinction, which by senatorial decree earned him a state funeral.

[Tacitus, *Annals* 6.10–11]

(Lucius) Calpurnius Piso (the *Pontifex*): he was consul in 15 BC and another distinguished soldier (see Vell. 2.98.1–3). He was appointed in AD 12, a date confirmed by the claim in Suet. *Tib*. 42.1 that he was appointed

by Tiberius, his drinking companion (see **K8**). His death in AD 32 prompts Tacitus' review of the office.

Maecenas: for his charge of the City see **R4** and Dio 49.16.2; 55.7.1.

(M. Valerius) Messala Corvinus: a prominent politician. On his resignation of this post see **P7** and **P8**.

(Titus) Statilius Taurus: next to Agrippa as a general trusted by Augustus; consul in 37 and 26 BC; prefect in 16 BC.

K8   Lucius Piso, city prefect

Lucius Piso, the city prefect, was drunk from the very moment he was appointed. He would spend most of the night at parties and then sleep till about midday. That was his morning routine. Nevertheless he discharged his duties, which included the security of the city, most conscientiously. The deified Augustus entrusted him with secret instructions when he put him in command of Thrace – which he conquered. Tiberius did likewise when he departed for Campania, leaving behind him in Rome a large number of suspicious activities and much unpopularity.

[Younger Seneca, *Moral Epistles (to Lucilius)* 83.14]

Piso: see above. He commanded Thrace around 14 –11 BC, see **D7**, Velleius 2.98.1–3 and note (Section **E**).

K9   Inscribed markers delimiting the banks of the Tiber

Gaius Marcius Censorinus, son of Lucius, grandson of Lucius, and Gaius Asinius Gallus, son of Gaius, consuls, in accordance with a decree of the Senate, set the limits. The next marker is 120 feet away in a straight line.

[*CIL* VI 31541 = *ILS* 5923]

It was in Augustus' interests to tackle the problem of maintaining Rome's urban infrastructure, which had become too complex a problem for the aediles (junior magistrates) to cope with on their own. Although Suet. *Aug*. 37 states that one of the new senatorial jobs created by Augustus was that of curator of the banks and channel of the Tiber (a problem with its flooding), this marker shows that only the consuls of 8 BC took charge of the task of defining the river's banks. The name of Asinius Gallus is erased but re-inscribed in all four surviving examples of this marker (he fell from favour in AD 30 under Tiberius). A further inscription (*ILS* 5924) shows that Augustus himself completed the task in the following year.

K10   Augustus' enlargement of the *pomerium*

Claudius also extended the *pomerium*, the sacred boundary of Rome, following ancient tradition whereby those who have expanded the empire are accorded the privilege of also extending the boundary of Rome. Yet no Roman general, with the exception of Lucius Sulla and the deified Augustus, had ever exercised this right, however great the nations they had conquered.

[Tacitus, *Annals* 12.23]

Pomerium: Claudius' extension of AD 49, a 'feel-good' measure connected with his conquest of southern Britain, was evidently criticised.

Lucius Sulla: the dictator of 82–81 BC had not added to the Empire, but may have extended the boundaries of Italy.

Augustus: Tacitus may be mistaken: Augustus says nothing of this in his *Res Gestae*; nor does the '*Lex de Imperio Vespasiani*' (**H52**).

K11   Honorific dedication by a section of the urban populace of Rome to
Gaius Caesar

The urban citizen populace who live in the 1[3]ᵗʰ region of the City… of wards [… to Gaius] Caesar, [son of Augustus] leader of the youth, priest, consul [designate], by public subscription.

[EJ 63a = *CIL* VI 899 + 39207]

Augustus' reorganisation of the city of Rome in 7 BC into 14 regions and 265 wards (Suet. *Aug.* 30.1) created new groupings of people with a collective social identity, who worshipped his divine spirit at their crossroads and co-operated to set up monuments like this one in honour of members of the imperial family.

K12   Famine in Rome, around AD 6

Famine in Rome reached such proportions that five *modii* [of corn] were selling at 27 and a half *denarii*.

[Jerome, *Chronicle,* AD 5]

Rome's large population and the importing of much of the grain supply from Egypt meant Rome was often in danger of famine. Augustus boasts of 12 distributions of corn carried out at his own expense (*RG* 15.1). Tiberius was commissioned to reorganise the grain supply in 23–22 BC (see Velleius 2.94.3 and note (Section E)). The usual price of corn in the empire was around one quarter of that quoted by Jerome for AD 5. Dio (55.26) reports severe famine in AD 6 (no doubt the same famine: Jerome's dates are very unreliable): measures taken included corn-doles paid for by Augustus, the appointment of ex-consuls to supervise distribution and the temporary removal from Rome of large households, foreigners and gladiators. This is almost certainly the famine described by Suetonius, *Augustus* 42.3.

Buildings of Rome (K13–K53)

These are arranged alphabetically, by their names in English.

Ara Pacis Augustae (Altar of Augustan Peace)

Archaeological note: Reconstructed in 1938 from hundreds of fragments, the altar is the most famous example of Augustan monumental sculpture in Rome. It consists of an altar proper, surrounded by a high enclosure, all made of white Italian (Luna) marble and elaborately carved in relief by some of the best sculptors of the day. It was decreed by the Senate on 4 July 13 BC to celebrate Augustus' return after 3 years' absence in Spain and Gaul (**C20**). The work took 3? years, and was dedicated on 30 January 9 BC (**C12, C40**). *Pax*, the goddess of Peace, was almost unknown before 13 BC but central to Augustus' later political ideology, and the word soon became synonymous with the Roman Empire at large, which was often simply called *Pax Romana.*

The altar platform, (39 x 35 feet) is built of tufa and travertine blocks capped with marble. Around the edge of the platform, with a wide doorway in the middle, rises the enclosure wall, which was composed of two courses of tall rectangular slabs (some weighing over ten tons) with a narrower horizontal course between them. The upper cornice is entirely reconstructed and has accordingly been left plain, but it ought to be richly ornamented and, according to the coin images, surmounted by large flame-like palmettes at the four corners. Otherwise the reconstruction is fairly reliable; the missing parts are integrated in plaster, where possible, using casts taken from the surviving marble parts. The great unknown, as always, is the original colour; all the reliefs will have been enhanced with brightly painted detail and have to be thought of in both dimensions.

The enclosure was carved inside and out, in imitation of a light columnal palisade. On the exterior, delicately wrought acanthus plants, the indispensable ingredients of Augustan imagery, extend up the columns and fill the lower zone, where their complex symmetrical scrolls are entwined with vines and ivy and pairs of alighting swans. In the upper zones, above a crossbar decorated with a Greek meander motif, are sculptured panel paintings. On the Field of Mars side, they refer to the mythical founders of Rome, Romulus and Aeneas. What little survives of that to the left of the door shows Mars on the left, Faustulus the shepherd on the right; between them is a fragment with a bird perched in a fig-tree – presumably that which grew at the entrance to the *Lupercal*, the cave where the wolf suckled Romulus and Remus. The right-hand relief shows Aeneas (with his mantle over his head) sacrificing to the Penates (household gods he had brought from Troy) who are sitting in their temple at Lavinium (top left). Below, two attendants bring the white sow who had farrowed thirty piglets, and the other offerings for the sacrifice. Leaning on a staff behind Aeneas is his son Ascanius – Iulus (the ancestor of the Julian clan).

The side of the enclosure which was turned towards the *Via Flaminia* was the altar's principal public face. In the panel relief on the right the goddess *Roma* was seated on a pile of armour between *Honos* and *Virtus*, the personifications of bravery in battle and its due reward, both particularly associated with Augustus. The relief on the left (restored in 1784) shows another seated female who ought to be *Pax*, though her iconography is much discussed. With the two children in her lap she strongly resembles *Venus Genetrix*, mother of the Julian family, while the figures of the Sky and Sea to either side suggest that she may represent Land (*Terra*) or Mother Earth (*Tellus*), or Italy, or Empire. The answer is probably that she is all these things, that Pax was a multiple concept, and portraying her for the first time was a considerable challenge.

It is the processional frieze carved in the upper register on two sides for which the altar is most famous nowadays. Along each side, some forty or fifty figures, executed at three-quarters life-size, move slowly in a public parade. The most important figures appear on one side: the front third of the procession, at the left end, is very fragmentary but clearly contained heralds and attendants, signifying the presence of priests and magistrates, perhaps also senators. In the middle third comes first Augustus, with the *rex sacrorum* (a high priest) close behind him, then the next four figures wearing leather helmets with spikes on top are the major *flamines* (chief priests) of the four major state cults: Mars, Quirinus, Divus Julius (in the background), and Jupiter (the one with the stick). Their *lictor* (attendant) follows, with his axe over his shoulder. After him is Agrippa. Both he and Augustus have their togas drawn up over their heads in their capacity as presiding magistrates and are distinguished by their greater height. The child with the torque round his neck could be any one of the many foreign hostage-princes being educated in Rome. The veiled lady is probably Livia, followed by various other members of the imperial family, with their children and servants. Everyone is dressed in his best, the men and boys in the new Augustan official form of the toga, and high-laced patrician boots, the women in the all-enveloping mantle and stola. The precise identities of the figures have evoked much scholarly concern, but many of the images, and indeed the whole procession, could be purely symbolic. On the opposite frieze, the same occasion is viewed from the other side: more magistrates and attendants in company with the ordinary citizens of Rome. The figure in the centre and another towards the front carry a box of incense and flask of wine. Those offerings, and the general air of informality, with people chattering to each other, the laurel wreaths on their heads and twigs of laurel in their hands are most suited to a *supplicatio* or festive thanksgiving, either for Augustus' return, or, more generally, for the Augustan peace.

K13 Ovid celebrates the dedication of the altar

Unaided to Peace's Altar has my song guided my footsteps;
From the month's ending this will be the day penultimate.   710
Come Peace, your comely tresses decked with laurel leaves
Of Actium, come and over all the globe sustain your gentle sway.
As long as Rome lacks enemies and her generals a source of triumphs,
So long will you to generals afford a glory greater than any war.
Let Roman soldiery bear arms only to curb the arms of enemies;   715
And for no cause save only ceremony let savage war-horns sound.
Let the wide world's shores from first to last be fearful of the sons
Of great Aeneas. Where they fear too little, let them feel love.
Come priests, add incense to the flames of peace; come, pour wine
Upon the victim's pure white head and let it fall. Pray to the gods,   720
Who hearken always to our pious prayers, that Caesar's house,
The guarantor of peace, in peace may live for ever.

[Ovid, *Fasti* 1.709–722]

This passage of Ovid's *Fasti*, celebrates the dedication of the altar on 30 January 9 BC (see **C12, C40** for the date on the official calendars) and makes the encomiastic link between dynastic continuity and world peace.

K14 Arch of Augustus in the Forum, *aureus*, 18–17 BC

Obv.:   Bare head of Augustus right.

S P Q R IMP CAESARI AVG COS XI TR POT VI (Senate and People of Rome to Imperator Caesar Augustus, consul for the 11th time, in the 6th year of his tribunician power).

Rev.:   Triple arch; Augustus in four-horsed chariot in centre; either side, figures holding up military standards, the right-hand figure also holding a bow.

CIVIB ET SIGN MILIT A PARTH RECVP (citizens and standards having been recovered from the Parthians)

[*RIC* Augustus 131, *BMC* Augustus 427]

In 20 BC Augustus achieved a diplomatic victory over the Parthians and retrieved the lost legionary standards (see **N41–N42**). This event was celebrated in Rome as a great success. Dio (54.8.3) mentions that, among other honours, a triumphal arch was erected. This seems to be depicted on this coin, but Roman coins sometimes depicted buildings that were never actually built, or not yet finished (cf. **K19**). The footings of a three-way arch, of Augustan date, between the Temple of Castor and the Temple of Divus Julius may possibly have belonged to this arch, but more probably belonged to that built in 29 BC to celebrate Octavian's triple triumph (**H17**).

Basilica Aemilia-Paulli and Portico of Gaius and Lucius in the Forum

We know from various literary sources that the original basilica was started in 55 BC by Lucius Aemilius Paullus and finished by his son in 34 BC. When this basilica and a row of shops in front of it burnt down twenty years later, the two elements were rebuilt in tandem (Dio 54.24.2–3). The shops were transformed into a grand two-storey portico, probably that dedicated in 2 BC in the names of Augustus' grandsons and heirs-apparent, Gaius and Lucius Caesar (Suet. *Aug*. 29). The reconstructed basilica, although actually paid for by Augustus and other friends, was dedicated in the name of an Aemilius Paullus (Dio 54.24.3).

The frieze of the lower order was carved with episodes from the legendary history of Rome. Somewhere at the same level stood statues of barbarians, larger than life-size and carved alternately in Numidian yellow and Phrygian purple marble. These were the columns that particularly impressed Pliny (**K3**), but we do not know whether they belonged to Augustus' building or a rebuilding in AD 22 by Marcus Aemilius Lepidus (Tac. *Ann*. 3.72).

K15   Dedication to Lucius Caesar by the Senate, 3 BC

To Lucius Caesar, son of Augustus, grandson of the deified, leader of the youth, consul designate even though only 14 years old, augur. The Senate (set this up).

[EJ 65]

This huge monumental inscription engraved upon three marble blocks in beautiful lettering was found on the northern side of the forum, by the basilica Aemilia-Paulli, so it may have belonged to the 'portico of Gaius and Lucius'. It charts the meteoric rise of Augustus' adopted son in public life, and the senate's apparent enthusiasm to celebrate a career that broke the usual age boundaries for holding magisterial office. On Gaius and Lucius, see **J56–J65**.

K16   Equestrian statue of Octavian in the Forum, *denarius*, 43 BC

Obv.: Bearded head of Octavian right.

C CAESAR III VIR R P C (Gaius Caesar, Triumvir for the establishment of
the Commonwealth)

Rev.: Equestrian statue of Octavian right, raising right hand.

S C ([Erected] by decree of the Senate)

[*RRC* 490/3, *BMCRR* Gaul 63]

This coin was made in late 43 BC after the formation of the triumvirate in the autumn, around the time of
Octavian's 20th birthday. The design on the reverse shows the honorific golden equestrian statue of him
which had been erected by a vote of the Senate in January of the same year. It stood on the Rostra, the
speaker's platform in the Roman Forum, one of the most prominent sites in the city.

Forum of Augustus / Temple of Mars Ultor (K17–K28)

The temple, dedicated to the war-god Mars Ultor (the 'Avenger'), had been vowed by Octavian in 42 BC at
the battle of Philippi. It was consciously related in design to the Temple of Venus in Caesar's Forum, but
one and a half times larger, and the front steps were normal (though flanked by fountains like the Venus
temple). The exterior order, all in white Italian (Luna) marble (as were the steps, the facing of the podium
and the *cella* walls and the pediment), was canonical Corinthian, the columns 17.8m high, eight across the
front and eight down the sides. In the front porch and the *cella* the floor was paved in Numidian yellow,
Phrygian purple and 'Lucullan' red/black marbles. Inside the *cella* the walls had Phrygian purple pilasters
framing statue niches behind a row of six freestanding columns down either side. In the apse, approached
by five steps, veneered in Egyptian alabaster and flanked by the legionary standards lost and then regained
in the wars against Parthia (Iraq), stood the cult statue of Mars. The temple was the ceremonial focus of
military politics and foreign policy: Augustus decreed that the Senate should meet in it when considering
wars and claims for triumphs (the space was as large as the Senate House proper); military commanders
setting off for the provinces officially took their leave there; it was the setting for the ceremony in which
high-born Roman boys assumed the *toga virilis* (adult toga), coming of military age.

The porticoes down the long sides of the forum were intended as venues for courts of justice, especially
the public prosecutors. Made longer by curving them into two great exhedras, and paved with Italian grey,
Numidian yellow, and 'Lucullan' red/black marbles, they had numerous statue niches built into their walls,
providing for an ever-expanding gallery of Rome's great and good. The larger central niche of the exhedra
was occupied on one side by a group showing Aeneas, ancestor of the Julian family, fleeing Troy with his
father and son, and on the other side by Romulus, founder of Rome, with a spear and the *spolia opima* 'spoils
of honour' he had won by killing the enemy general in battle. Each was flanked by statues of their respective
descendants: Julio-Claudians on one side, Great Men of the Republic (*summi viri*) on the other. Inscriptions
on the statue plinths gave the names and distinctions of each person, and a marble panel on the wall beneath
the niche carried a brief eulogy of their deeds (**K20–K25**). Some of the original series portrayed
personifications of the peoples conquered by Augustus, and the provinces of the Empire later donated others
– the inscribed base of one from Spain declared that it had used 100 pounds of gold (**K28**).

Suetonius, *Augustus* 29 gives the reasons for the building of forum and temple and its use. Dio 55.10
provides an account of dedication of forum and temple, as more briefly does Velleius 2.100.2.

K17   Architectural procrastination

An unusual number of those prosecuted in the courts by Cassius Severus seemed to be
winning their acquittal. When, therefore, his architect working on the Forum of
Augustus kept putting off the completion date, Augustus remarked with a laugh that
"I rather wish that Cassius would prosecute my forum – it would let me win my freedom
also!"

[Macrobius, *Saturnalia* 2.4.9]

K18   Ovid, *Fasti*: Mars comes to see his temple

But why do Orion and the other stars make haste to flee   545
From the heavens? Why does the night abbreviate her journey?
Why does fair daylight, heralded by Lucifer, the Morning Star, uplift

More quickly than its wont his sunbeams out of the liquid sea?
Am I mistaken, do I hear the sound of weapons? Ay, a crash there was
Of weaponry, for Mars is on his way; and as he comes he signals war.   550
The Avenger God himself descends from heaven to take his due
Meed of honour and in Augustus' forum to behold his temple.
Vast is the god and vast his temple too. For meet and right it is
That thus should Mars reside within his own offspring's city.
It is a shrine full worthy of the spoils he gained from the Giants.   555
How right it is that here Mars, the Marcher, launches his campaigns,
Whether an impious enemy assaults us from eastern kingdoms
Or from the realms of sunset and must be brought to heel.
The potentate of weaponry beholds the lofty temple's pediments
And indicates approval that the unconquered gods should hold   560
The highest places. On the doors he sees weapons of every shape,
Arms of the nations conquered by his troops. Here on one side
He sees Aeneas bent beneath the weight of his beloved burden.
And countless other ancestors of Julius' mighty line.
There on the other side he sees Romulus, whose shoulders bear   565
A conquered general's arms, and all the catalogue of famous deeds
Inscribed beneath each hero in due order. With Augustus' name he sees
The temple adorned, the work yet mightier for the name of Caesar.
He vowed it long ago, when as a youth at duty's holy call
He took up arms. For from great deeds must such a principate begin.   570
With arms outstretched, his loyal soldiers ranged to one side
While on the other stood the conspirators, he spoke these words:
"If he that is my father and the priest of Vesta is my just cause
For waging war, if now I seek vengeance for twin divinities,
Mars, stand to my side and satiate my sword with blood   575
Of scoundrels. Grant that your favour bless my better cause. Then,
If I am victor, you shall receive a temple and be called Avenger."
Such was his vow and joyous he returned, his enemies destroyed.
Nor is he satisfied but once to win for Mars the Avenger's name:
A hunter, hot on the trail, he tracks the standards seized by Parthia.   580
A nation they were, made safe by rolling plains, horses and archers
And the protecting rivers by whose flood all passage is denied.
The deaths of Crassus, father and son, had fired that nation's spirit
When all were lost together – soldiers, and standards, and their general.
Those Roman standards, symbols of pride in war, a Parthian bore;   585
The Roman eagle found a Parthian foe for standard-bearer.
Such was the shame that still had lingered now, had not the arms,
The mighty arms of Caesar proved Italy's guardians.
The ancient blight of shame, our century's disgrace, he wiped away;
The standards were retrieved and once more recognised their own.   590
What profit was there, Parthian, in arrows discharged backward,
Parthian fashion? What help your landscape for defence? What use
Your fiery horses? Our eagles you restore; your conquered bows surrender.
Gone are the symbols of our great disgrace – no longer yours.
Rightly to him, our double Avenger, are temple and title given;   595

Honour well merited is the discharge due for debts by honour sworn.
Quirites, Citizens of Rome, to the Circus come and celebrate the games
With due solemnity! The stage is not the proper place for heroes' gods.

[Ovid, *Fasti* 5. 545–598]

This passage marks the *Ludi Martiales*, the Games of Mars, on May 12, but also celebrates the temple of Mars Ultor ('the Avenger'). It has been suggested that this entry actually records the dedication of that temple and of the accompanying Forum of Augustus in 2 BC, usually held to have occurred on 1 August, and the detailed description of temple and forum fits this theory; alternatively, the poet may have transferred the material here since the book on August itself was never in fact written.

K19 *Aureus, c.* 18 BC of Temple of Mars?

Obv.: Bare head of Augustus right.

AVGVSTVS

Rev.: Circular, domed temple containing figure of god Mars holding legionary standard.

MARTIS VLTORIS ([Temple] of Mars the Avenger)

[*RIC* Augustus 28, *BMC* Augustus 315]

In 20 BC Augustus achieved a diplomatic victory over the Parthians and retrieved the lost legionary standards. This event was celebrated in Rome as a great success. Dio (54.8.3) mentions that, among other honours, a triumphal arch was erected and a temple dedicated to Mars the Avenger on the Capitol where the standards were to be kept. Both seem to be clearly depicted on coins. But we cannot easily identify Augustus' Parthian arch in the Forum (see **K14**), while the Temple of Mars the Avenger which was eventually dedicated in 2 BC was located not on the Capitol but as the centrepiece of the new Forum of Augustus. A large part of it still stands. It may well be that these coins depict structures that were decreed by the senate and people but never built, or were deliberately declined by the emperor. Modesty in accepting honours was an important aspect of Augustus' cleverly conceived imperial persona. It made the reality of monarchy easier for the Romans to bear.

Elogia from the Forum of Augustus, 2 BC, Rome (K20–K25)

Augustus declared that the statues of great Romans general on display in his Forum were intended to provide a yardstick against which his own achievements were to be judged and to inspire others to emulation too (Suet. *Aug.* 31.5). The following honorands can be identified from inscriptions found in the area of the Forum of Augustus: Alban Kings – Aeneas, Aeneas Silvius, ?Alba Silvius, the son of Silvius, Proca Silvius; Julii, Marcelli and Drusi – Gaius Julius Caesar Strabo, Gaius Julius Caesar (father of the dictator), Marcus Claudius Marcellus, Nero Claudius Drusus Germanicus; Republican heroes – Aulus Postumius Regillensis, ?Lucius Albinius, Appius Claudius Caecus, Gaius Duilius, Quintus Fabius Maximus, Lucius Cornelius Scipio Asiaticus, Quintus Metellus Numidicus, Gaius Marius, Lucius Cornelius Sulla Felix. In addition to the fragmentary remains of inscriptions found in the area of the Forum of Augustus itself, presumed copies of individual *elogia* have also been found in various Italian towns (including Arretium, Pompeii, and Lavinium). These are not all exactly contemporary with Augustus' forum (for example, the Pompeian examples may be Tiberian in date, and those at Lavinium were probably early 2nd century AD, but illustrate its continuing influence upon art and architecture. Similarly, the forum at Emerita (Merida, Spain) imitated the caryatids and medallions of Rome. Literary sources add the names of two other republican heroes commemorated. For the *elogium* of Drusus, see **J44**.

Bibliography: A. Degrassi, ed. *Inscriptiones Italiae* 13.3 *Elogia* (Rome 1937).

K20   *Elogium* of Aeneas (Forum of Augustus)
Aeneas, son of Venus, king of the Latins, ruled for 3 years.

[*Inscr. It.* 13.3.1]

K21   *Elogium* of Romulus, (Pompeii Forum)
Romulus, son of Mars, founded the city of Rome and reigned for 38 years. He was the first general to dedicate *spolia opima* (Spoils of Honour) to Jupiter Feretrius, having slain the enemy's general, Acro king of the Caeninenses, and, having been received among the company of the gods, was called Quirinus.

[*Inscr. It.* 13.3.86]

Elogia of Romulus and Aeneas were found in the Forum at Pompeii, and are generally thought to have been displayed on the façade of Eumachia's Building, dedicated to Augustan Concord. The *elogium* of Aeneas from Pompeii is far longer than that from the forum of Augustus (**K20**). For Romulus and the *spolia opima*, see **P3**.

K22   Statue of M. Valerius Corvinus in the Forum of Augustus
The deified Augustus had a statue erected to this Corvinus in his forum. On the head of the statue is the figure of a raven.

[Aulus Gellius, *Attic Nights* 9.11.10]

Gellius recounted the famous story of Valerius acquiring his *cognomen* (nickname) after a raven (*corvus*) helped him win a single combat with a Gallic champion in the 4th century BC. Livy 7.26 presents the story of Valerius Corvus, mentioned in lists of Roman heroes by Propertius (**G31** line 64) and Ovid (*Fasti* 1.602).

K23   *Elogium* of Aemilius Paulus (Arretium)
Lucius Aemilius Paulus, son of Lucius, twice consul, censor, interrex, praetor, aedile; after the Ligurians had been subdued in his first consulship he celebrated a triumph; he was made consul for a second time by the people so that he might wage war with king Perseus; he destroyed the king's forces in the ten days in which he reached Macedonia, and he captured the king with his children.

[*Inscr. It.* 13.3.81]

Lucius Aemilius Paulus was consul in 182 and 181 BC. His victory at the battle of Pydna in 168 BC ended the Third Macedonian War.

K24   *Elogium* of Publius Cornelius Scipio Aemilianus Africanus
Varro writes that Scipio Aemilianus was presented with the siege crown in Africa when Manilius was consul [149 BC] for having led three cohorts to rescue three others. The deified Augustus inscribed this story under Scipio's statue in the forum of Augustus.

[Pliny, *Natural History* 22.13]

*For the continuation of this passage, the award to Augustus of the siege crown, see **H14**.*

K25   *Elogium* of Marius (Forum of Augustus)
Gaius Marius, son of Gaius, consul seven times, praetor, tribune of the people [...] without drawing lots, as consul he waged war with Jugurtha, king of Numidia, captured him, and celebrating a triumph during his second consulship ordered him to be led before his chariot. He was appointed consul for the 3rd time in his absence. When consul for the 4th time he destroyed the army of the Teutones. As consul for the 5th time he routed the Cimbri, and celebrated his second triumph over them and the Teutones. When the state was in turmoil from the rebellious acts of the people's tribune and of the praetor who had seized the Capitol by force, he liberated it when consul for the 6th time. After his 70th year he was expelled from his country by civil arms, but when

restored by arms he was made consul for the 7th time. Out of the spoils of war against the Cimbri and Teutones he built the temple to Honour and Courage as victor. In triumphal clothing, with patrician sandals [......]

[*Inscr. It.* 13.3.17]

Gaius Marius (c. 157 – 86 BC): as his *elogium* shows, one of the leading generals and politicians of his period, but one of the most turbulent. He is mentioned as a Roman hero by Virgil, *Georgics* 2.168 (**G10**).

K26   Statues of Alexander the Great

It is also said that the tent of Alexander the Great was usually supported by statues, two of which have been dedicated in front of the Temple of Mars Ultor, and two in front of the *Regia* (Palace).

[Pliny, *Natural History* 34.48]

K27   Paintings of Alexander the Great by Apelles in the Forum of Augustus

At Rome Apelles' *Castor and Pollux with Victory* and *Alexander the Great* are much admired; likewise his portrait of *War Manacled,* with Alexander riding in triumph in his chariot. The deified Augustus, with remarkable self-restraint, set up both these paintings in the most crowded area of his forum, but in both cases the deified Claudius decided it would be more appropriate to remove Alexander's face and replace it with a likeness of Augustus.

[Pliny, *Natural History* 35.93–94]

Augustus liked to compare himself with Alexander the Great (see Index of Persons, Alexander).

K28   Base of a golden statue honouring Augustus, post-2 BC, Forum of Augustus

To Imperator Caesar Augustus, Father of the Fatherland. Further Hispania, Baetica, set this up because through his goodwill and constant care the province has been pacified. 100 pounds of gold.

[EJ 42 = *ILS* 103]

The dedication of the Forum of Augustus in 2 BC coincided with the award to Augustus of the title of *pater patriae*, which he regarded as the pinnacle of his achievements, according to the *Res Gestae* 35.1. Accordingly, statues set up in the complex laid special emphasis upon his new title, and celebrated him as the most significant extender of Rome's empire. This statue base dedicated by Baetica (also stressing his new title) may have supported a golden statue of the province personified or of Augustus himself, and may be related to Velleius' comment (2.39.2) that Augustus' forum gleamed with the inscriptions of the Spanish provinces and other peoples.

Mausoleum of Augustus

Among Octavian's earliest building projects, completed during his sixth consulship in 28 BC, the Mausoleum was, and remained, the largest tomb in the Roman world. In ground plan, the outer diameter measured c.89m and the outermost wall was around 12m high. Inside there are further five concentric concrete walls. The burial chamber consists of a circular hall around a central concrete pillar. The walls contained rectangular recesses for cinerary urns. The central pillar contains a square inner chamber, where Augustus' own urn may have been deposited. An epitaph for Octavia and Marcellus (**J32**) was found in the mausoleum.

   Given the ruinous state of the structure at its core, the original elevation and external appearance of the building are uncertain. Strabo's description (**K29**) suggests a simple mound while the relative strength of the fourth wall has suggested a stepped profile, with a second drum emerging from the first. A simple earth mound recalls the shape of a tumulus of Etruscan type. However, the name *mausoleum* was used of it from the start; this, and a stepped profile of more or less monumental architectural character, might imply a straightforward rival to the great dynastic tombs of the Hellenistic kings and specifically the tomb of King Mausolus of Caria at Halicarnassus, one of the seven wonders of the ancient world. Whichever type of reconstruction is favoured, the overall height is usually reckoned to have been about half the diameter, i.e. 40–45m.

   Two bronze plaques bearing the text of his *Res Gestae* were affixed to either side of the entrance to the mausoleum in AD 14.

K29   Strabo's description of the Mausoleum of Augustus

*(This passage continues **K4**)*

For all these reasons the Romans regard this area as their holiest ground and here they have built the tombs of all their most distinguished men and women. Most remarkable of all is the so-called Mausoleum, a huge mound set on a lofty plinth of white marble near the river, thickly shaded by a covering of evergreen trees right up to the summit. On the top is a bronze statue of Caesar Augustus while below the mound are the tombs of Augustus himself, his close relatives and family. Behind it there is a sacred precinct, very large and with wonderful promenades, while in the centre of the campus there is an enclosure, a wall (also of white marble) surrounding the site of his funeral-pyre. The wall is itself surrounded by iron railings and within the enclosure is a plantation of black poplars. In fact, anyone on his way to the Old Forum who saw such a succession of forums with their basilicas and stoas, and then the Capitol with all its works of art, together with those on the Palatine and in Livia's Promenade, might easily forget all the other wonders elsewhere in the city, such is the effect that Rome has upon the sightseer.

[Strabo, *Geography*, 5.3.8]

Portico of Livia

Vedius Pollio, a notoriously extravagant and cruel friend of Augustus (see **H40**) bequeathed his palace to Augustus in 15 BC (Dio 54.23.1–6). Augustus tore it down, in pointed moral disapproval of such luxurious residences, building instead the public portico named after his wife. Ovid also alludes to the construction by Livia of the Temple of Concord, expressing the harmony of her marriage to Augustus. Presumably the temple was within or part of the portico. The portico's size (around 115m x 75m) can be established from fragments of the Marble Plan of Rome, but no remains have been unearthed.

K30   Ovid, *Fasti* on the Portico of Livia

No less glorious was the gift which Livia gave to her beloved
Husband – a temple devoted to your name, Concordia.
Learn then, you coming generations: there, where now stands
The colonnade of Livia, once there stood a mighty palace.   640
Vast as a city was that single edifice, awesome its dimensions;
Such that many a city wall would hold a lesser space in its embrace.
Razed to the ground it was, though not for any treasonable crime.
Rather, the sheer extravagance was deemed inimical to the nation's health.
Such was the mighty work Caesar endured to overturn; and such   645
Was the wealth which Caesar as heir was willing to destroy.
Such is the conduct of a worthy censor; such the example set,
When the law's champion practises in deed according as he preaches.

[Ovid, *Fasti* 6. 637–648]

Portico of Octavia

The portico of Octavia, named in honour of his sister, was built by Augustus in about 27–25 BC, replacing an earlier portico of Metellus. The portico was a huge rectangular colonnade (120m x 140m) enclosing important temples to Jupiter and Juno and also incorporating a library in honour of Marcellus (see **K52**), schools and meeting rooms, and displaying quantities of antique Greek statuary and paintings. Part of the ceremonial gateway survives in a reconstruction of AD 203 after a fire; though little else survives, the portico is shown on one of the surviving fragments of a marble plan of the city drawn around AD 203–211.

K31 The Lysippus statues within the Portico of Octavia

This is the Metellus Macedonicus who had built the portico around the two temples without inscriptions which are now surrounded by the portico of Octavia. He brought from Macedonia the group of equestrian statues which faces the temples and even today forms the chief decoration of the place. The story about the creation of the group is that Alexander the Great ordered Lysippus, the most eminent sculptor of works of this kind, to make statues of the horsemen of his squadron who had fallen at the River Granicus, and to place his own statue amongst them.

[Velleius 1.11.3–4]

(Quintus Caecilius) Metellus Macedonicus: commander in Macedonia 148–146 BC.
The bronze statue group consisting of portraits of all 25 of Alexander's 'Companions' to die at the battle of Granicus in 334 BC was originally set up at Dion in Macedonia (Arrian, *Anabasis* 1.16.4). Pliny (*NH* 34.64) praises the lifelike quality of the group.

K32 Works of art in Octavia's buildings

[15] There is a tradition that Pheidias himself worked in marble, and that at Rome the outstandingly beautiful *Venus* in Octavia's Buildings is by him…[22] There is also a *Cupid* by Praxiteles, mentioned by Cicero in his denunciation of Verres as "a major tourist attraction at Thespiae", and which now stands in Octavia's Public Rooms.

[Pliny, *Natural History* 36.15 and 36.22]

Pheidias: Athenian sculptor, active 465–425 BC, most famous for the statue of Zeus at Olympia and the statues of Athena on the Acropolis and in the Parthenon.
Praxiteles: Athenian sculptor, active 375–330 BC.

The Senate House (*Curia Iulia*)

The Senate House, *Curia Iulia*, was begun by Julius Caesar and dedicated by Octavian in 29 BC (Dio 51.22.1). Augustus mentions the Senate House first of all his building works (*RG* 19.1 and at 34.1).

K33 Senate House, *denarius* of 34–28 BC

Obv.: Bare head of Octavian right.
No legend
Rev.: Front view of temple-like building: three windows in upper storey; colonnade with four columns on lower level; Victory on globe standing on apex; figures of warriors facing inwards on either angle.
IMP CAESAR (Imperator Caesar) inscribed on architrave.

[*RIC* Augustus 266, *BMC* Augustus 631]

This coin belongs to a series which was issued in the years around the Battle of Actium. The exact date is uncertain. The existing Senate House dates from the late third century AD, but it looks substantially the same as the building shown here. The statue of Victory on the top is probably meant to be the one that was placed inside the building by Octavian in commemoration of his victory over Cleopatra (see **C29**). Thus even the Senate House became a permanent monument to the emperor's rescuing of the Romans from foreign invasion.

K34   Paintings in the Senate House

[27] In addition, he placed two paintings in a wall of the new Senate House, which he was dedicating in the Place of Assembly – one showed *Nemea* seated upon a lion, holding a palm branch in her hand, and an old man with a staff standing nearby, above whose head was a picture of a two-horse chariot. It was entitled '*Encaustic,* by Nikias', this being his own technical term for the process. [28] The other painting is much admired. It shows a young man and his aged father, capturing the similarity between the two without concealing their difference in age. Above them swoops an eagle with a snake in its talons. Philochares claims that this is his work, and from this one painting alone one can get some sense of the extraordinary power of art, since thanks to Philochares two totally obscure men, Glaucio and his son Aristippus, are still after so many centuries the focus of the gaze of the Roman People's Senate.

[Pliny, *Natural History* 35.27–28]

Nemea: one of the four most important sets of games was held at Nemea. The painting by Nikias (active in 332 BC) celebrated a victory in the chariot race at these games.

Sundial of Augustus (*Horologium Augusti*)

Two obelisks were removed by Augustus from Heliopolis after his annexation of Egypt. One was set up on the eastern end of the central barrier in the Circus Maximus, and is now in Piazza del Popolo. The other (now in Piazza di Montecitorio) acted as the pointer for the giant sundial on the Campus Martius, dedicated in 10 BC, the twentieth anniversary of the conquest of Egypt. Pliny describes the sundial below (**K36**).

K35   Inscription on Sundial of Augustus (*Horologium Augusti*)

Imperator Caesar Augustus, son of the deified, chief priest, hailed *imperator* 12 times, consul 11 times, holding tribunician power for the 14th time, gave this as a gift to the Sun, once Egypt had been reduced to the power of the Roman people.

[EJ 14 = *ILS* 91]

K36   Pliny's description of the obelisks

[71] The obelisk which the deified Augustus set up in the Circus Maximus was carved by King Psemetnepserphreus, whose reign coincided with the time when Pythagoras was in Egypt. Without its base, which was cut from the same stone, it measures 85 feet 9 inches. The obelisk in the Campus Martius, which is 9 feet shorter, was carved by Sesothis....

[72] The deified Augustus found a remarkably ingenious use for the obelisk in the Campus Martius as a means of recording the sun's shadow and thus calculating the length of days and nights. He laid down a paved area equivalent in length to the shadow of the obelisk itself at noon on the final day of the winter solstice. On this at regular intervals, which were marked by bronze inserts in the pavement, he recorded the daily reduction in the shadow and then its increase once more. It is a device that is well worth studying and was designed by the brilliant mathematician, Facundus Novius. He also added a golden ball to the top of the obelisk, so as to enhance the shadow cast by the apex, which would have otherwise have appeared imprecisely defined. They say that he discovered this concept by analogy with the shadow cast by a human head.

[Pliny, *Natural History* 36.71–2]

Pliny's information is rather confused: the Circus Maximus obelisk commemorates Seti I and Ramses II (1348–1282 BC); the Campus Martius obelisk commemorates Psammetichus II, whose reign, 594–589 BC was before the time of Pythagoras (born mid-fifth century BC).

Temple of Apollo on the Palatine

The temple was vowed in 36 BC after Agrippa's defeat of Sextus Pompey and the deposition of Lepidus (**K37** and Dio 49.15.5) and dedicated on 9 October 28 BC (see **C34**). Its podium measured approximately 24 x 45m, but almost all the tufa blocks which faced it have been quarried away. To judge from fragments of the one remaining capital, the columns of solid white Italian marble were almost 15m high. It is not certain whether the temple faced out from the hill or the street leading up to the entrance to Augustus' house. The portico and library have not been identified with certainty on the ground. Two Danaids in black Greek marble and one in red Greek marble (presumably some of the Danaid statues mentioned by Propertius) were found in the ruins of the podium.

Suetonius (*Aug.* 29.1) mentions it as one of Augustus' three most important buildings; Augustus mentions it second of his building works (*RG* 19.1); Propertius celebrates the portico (**G19**) and the temple (**G39**); Virgil makes Aeneas predict its building (**K37b** in Addenda). See also notes on Horace, *Carmen Saeculare* (**L28**).

K37 Octavian vows the Temple to Apollo

Then Caesar returned victorious to Rome and announced that he intended to set aside for public use several houses which his agents had purchased so that the area around his house would be less crowded. He further promised the building of the Temple of Apollo and a portico around it, which he constructed without sparing any expense.

[Velleius 2.81.3]

K38 Statuary on the Temple of Apollo

[13] In Rome statues [by Bupalus and Athenis] are to be seen on the Palatine on the pediment of the temple of Apollo and on almost every building put up by the deified Augustus.

[32] There is at Rome a *Diana* by Timotheus in the Temple of Apollo on the Palatine, for which Avianius Evander sculpted a replacement head.

[Pliny, *Natural History* 36.13 and 36.32]

Bupalus and Athenis: flourished c. 540–537 BC (Pliny *NH* 36.11).
Timotheus: Greek sculptor, active 400–350 BC, worked on the Mausoleum at Halicarnassus (Pliny *NH* 36.30–31).

Temple of Castor and Pollux in the Forum

The surviving structure was a rebuild contemporary with the rest of the major Augustan monuments on the Forum. Tiberius dedicated it in AD 6, in his own name and that of his brother Drusus. All the marble revetment and the tufa blocks have been removed from the outside of the podium, leaving only the concrete core, but it once measured 32 x 50m and was 7m high. The temple proper in white Italian marble was peripteral (free-standing columns all round) with 8 columns at the front and back and eleven down the sides. The Corinthian columns were 14.8m high.

The Temple of Castor and Pollux is a clear and interesting case of Augustus 'privatising' a cult festival, by giving a long-established festival a new date and meaning specific to the imperial family. Livy records that the Temple was dedicated on 15 July, 484 BC and a festival celebrating Castor and Pollux and their intervention in the battle of Lake Regillus was held on this date into the imperial period. The original temple was rebuilt in 117 BC. Tiberius' temple replaced this one which may have been damaged in a forum fire of 14 BC or 9 BC. This time Castor and Pollux receive an association with the imperial family – Tiberius and Drusus, and a new dedication date is commemorated. It is possible that before their deaths an association with Gaius and Lucius Caesar was intended (they would have been 24 and 21 at the time the temple was eventually dedicated). Ovid (**K39**) marks the dedication of the temple on 27 January (AD 7) as do the official calendars (see **C11**).

K39   Ovid, *Fasti*: The dedication of the Temple of Castor and Pollux

But on the sixth day before the approaching Kalends,
A temple was dedicated to the heavenly twins, Leda's sons:
Heavenly brothers honoured by brothers from a race of gods
With a temple placed by Juturna's Lake.

[Ovid, *Fasti*, 1.705–708]

Brothers from a race of gods: on the dedicatory inscription, Tiberius used not his family name, 'Claudius' but 'Claudianus' to show that he had been adopted by another family, namely Augustus' (Dio 55.27). Thus Ovid can describe Tiberius and Drusus as coming from a race including Venus, Divus Julius and perhaps hint at Augustus' eventual deification.

Temple of *Concordia Augusta* (Augustan Concord)

A Temple of Concord of the fourth century BC celebrated the reconciliation of upper and lower classes in Rome. Restored in 121 BC, this conventional rectangular temple burnt down in 9 BC. The new Temple of Concord, 'Concord in the Imperial Family' was dedicated by Tiberius on 16 January AD 10 (**K41, C9**). Both the layout and symbolism of the new temple were completely different. The new temple was laid out with the *cella* crossways, the entrance on the long side through a narrower porch at the top of a tall flight of steps, to either side of which stood statues of Hercules and Mercury, symbolising respectively the security and prosperity of the Augustan regime. Inlaid in bronze on the threshold was Mercury's wand (*caduceus*), an emblem of peace. On the apex of the pediment, statues of three female deities, presumably Concord herself, with either *Pax* (Peace) and *Salus* (Health) – or *Securitas* (Security) and *Fortuna* (Good Fortune). Beside them stood two soldiers holding spears, Tiberius and his brother Drusus, in whose name the temple was dedicated (Dio 56.25), paid for by their share of the booty from their German triumph in 7 BC, represented by the figures of Victory at the outer angles.

The *cella*, a vast hall of 45 x 23m and often used for Senate meetings, was designed to display a fine collection of Greek works of art, including a statue of Vesta which Tiberius forced the people of Paros to sell to him (Dio 55.9.6).

K40   Temple of *Concordia Augusta*: *sestertius*, AD 35–36

Obv.:   Temple, showing statue of Concordia seated in the centre; statues of Hercules on the right and Mercury to the left stand either side of the stairway; statues of various gods and goddess above.
          No legend.

Rev.:   No pictorial design.
          S C (by decree of the Senate); TI CAESAR DIVI AVG F AVGVST P M TR POT XXXVII (Tiberius Caesar Augustus, son of the Deified Augustus, *Pontifex Maximus* in the 37th year of his tribunician power)

[*RIC* Tiberius 61, *BMC* Tiberius 116]

K41   Ovid, *Fasti*: the dedication of the Temple of *Concordia Augusta*

You shall keep good watch, Concord, over the Latin crowd,
Now that consecrated hands have dedicated you.   640

Furius, conqueror of the Etruscan people, had vowed to build
The ancient temple, and kept his vow.
The cause then was that the plebs had taken up weapons and split
From the nobility, and Rome feared her own strength.
The recent cause was better: Germany bowed her head,   645
With dishevelled locks, to your authority, revered general.
So you have offered spoils from a defeated race
And made a temple to the goddess whom you yourself worship,
A goddess established by the actions of your mother, and the altar she dedicated;
She who alone has been found worthy to share the bed of mighty Jupiter.   650

[Ovid, *Fasti* 1.639–650]

649   Livia had established a sanctuary of *Concordia* in the *Porticus Liviae*, see **K30**.

K42   Stone elephants in the Temple of *Concordia Augusta*

Augustus dedicated four amazing elephants made of obsidian in the Temple of
Concord.

[Pliny, *Natural History* 36.196]

obsidian: a dark, glassy stone.
Pliny also mentions by name and artist 4 separate statue groups and 3 paintings displayed in the temple.

Temple of Divus Julius

Today only part of the concrete infill survives of the podium, the front part of which, 3.5m above the Forum,
formed a second tribunal, the *rostra Iulia*, to match that at the other end, and was decorated with the symbols
of Octavian's own victory – the prows (*rostra*) of the ships captured at Actium. The temple itself marked
the spot where Caesar's body was cremated.

K43   Ovid, *Fasti*: the Ides of March

I was inclined to make no mention of the swords that slew our first citizen,
When from within her holy hearth Vesta gave utterance as follows:
"Let there be no doubts, but tell this tale. He was my priest, and those
Whose hands contrived his death at me raised sacrilegious weaponry.   700
For I myself it was snatched him away leaving behind a naked effigy.
Great Caesar did not die by swords; what fell was Caesar's shadow".
Thus, set in the heavens, Caesar indeed beheld the halls of Jupiter,
While in our mighty Forum here he dwells in his own dedicated temple.
But as for those who dared this dreadful deed, forbidden by all   705
The powers of heaven, all those who stained by sacrilege that head
Pontifical, in well-deserved death they all lie still. Be you my witnesses,
Philippi, and you whose scattered bones lie whitening the earth.
This was the work of Caesar, this his duty's call, this the first task
By righteous arms to seek his father's just revenge.   710

[Ovid, *Fasti* 3. 697–710]

This passage marks the Ides of March and Julius Caesar's assassination on that day in 44 BC. The extract's
opening line makes clear that the murder of the 'first citizen' (which would apply more naturally to Augustus
than Julius) is a delicate topic for Augustus, who survived several conspiracies. The goddess Vesta here
presents a positive version of Caesar's death in which he is not truly murdered but saved for divinity; her
stress on Augustus' revenge on his adoptive father's killers (especially at the battle of Philippi in 42 BC)
matches its prominence in Augustus' own autobiography (*Res Gestae* 2).

697   The ides of March is not commemorated in the official calendars, though the dedication of the
       Temple is (**C26**).
699   Julius Caesar was *pontifex maximus*.

K44   Pliny on 'Julius Caesar's comet'

[93] The only place in the whole world where a comet has a temple as its centre of
worship is in Rome. The deified Augustus personally felt that this comet had been
highly propitious to him, appearing as it did at the very start of his reign not long after
the death of his father Julius Caesar and at the games which, as a member of the priestly
college which he founded, he was celebrating in honour of Venus the Universal Mother.

[Pliny, *Natural History* 2.93]

For the continuation of this passage, see **H3**. The games were in honour of Venus Genetrix.

K45   Temple of Divus Julius, *aureus*, 36 BC

Obv.:   Bare head of Octavian right, bearded.
          IMP CAESAR DIVI F III VIR ITER R P C (Imperator Caesar, Son of the
          Deified, Triumvir for the establishment of the Commonwealth for a second
          time)
Rev.:   Temple with four columns; within stands a veiled figure holding augur's staff (*lituus*); DIVO
          IVLIO (To the Deified Julius) inscribed on temple, with a star in the pediment above.
          COS ITER ET TER DESIG (Consul for the second time and consul designate
          for the third time)

[*RRC* 540, *BMCRR* Africa 32]

When this coin was struck, the Temple of the Deified Julius depicted on the reverse was still under
construction in the Forum, on the spot where his body had been cremated. The star in the pediment is the
famous *sidus Iulium* (Julian star), mentioned above, **K44**. Octavian deftly took advantage of the popular
mood and caused a star to be placed on all Caesar's statues. It became a potent symbol of his own divine
parentage. The temple was dedicated in 29 BC (Dio 51.22; **C26**).

K46   Apelles' *Venus* dedicated by Augustus in the Temple of Divus Julius

Apelles' *Venus Rising from the Sea*, known to us as the *Anadyomene*, was dedicated
by the deified Augustus in the temple of his father Caesar.

[Pliny, *Natural History* 35.91]

Apelles of Cos was probably the most famous of Greek painters, active around 332 BC. The information
above comes from Pliny's detailed account of Apelles' career (*Natural History*, 35.79–97).

The Temple of Janus

This was one of Augustus' great symbolic revivals, to which he devotes a whole paragraph of his *Res Gestae*
(13), and which was celebrated by the poets: see Virgil, *Aeneid* 1.293–296 (**G36**) and Horace, *Odes* 4.15.8–9

(**G45**). Augustus' closures, celebrated at *RG* 13, belong to January 29 BC (end of the Civil Wars), 25 BC (end of wars in Spain), and at an unknown date claimed by Orosius 6.22 for 2 BC, when Christ was born. See R. Syme, *Roman Papers* 6 (Oxford, 1991) 441–50, arguing for 8–7 BC, with reopening in 2 BC (conflict with Parthia), the year after Augustus reached sixty. Dio (54.36.2) mentions another closure, voted by the senate in 11 BC, but overtaken by a Dacian attack.

K47   The founding of the Temple of Janus

[1] When Numa Pompilius [715–672 BC] had obtained the kingship, he prepared to establish in the young city, whose birth had been attended by violent warfare, a new order founded upon equity, legality and morality. [2] He understood that for such principles to become accepted, peaceful conditions were essential, since warfare made men savage, and it was necessary for his people's ferocity to be moderated by an enforced period of rest from fighting. So at the base of the Argiletum he built a temple to Janus, to serve as a kind of barometer of war. When the temple doors were open, it showed that the state was under arms; when closed, that all the surrounding peoples were subdued. [3] Only twice since the reign of Numa has it been closed: once in the consulship of Titus Manlius at the end of the First Punic War [235 BC]; and secondly, as we have seen in our own generation by the gods' grace, after the battle of Actium, when Caesar Augustus brought peace to the whole world, by land and sea.

[Livy, 1.19.1–3]

Livy must have written (or finally revised) this passage between 27 BC (when Octavian took the title Augustus) and 25 BC, when he closed the gates of the Temple of Janus for a second time.

K48   Ovid, *Fasti*: the Temple of Janus

"Why do you hide in peacetime, but when war's afoot
Unbolt your doors?" I asked. Janus without delay gave me the cause.
"My door stands open wide, its bolts withdrawn, that when
My people sally forth to war, wide open lies their homeward road.   280
In peace I bar my doors that peace may not depart;"

[Ovid, *Fasti* 1.277–281]

K49   Opening of the Temple of Janus late in Augustus' reign.

(Orosius is explicitly quoting Tacitus' Histories*)*

When Augustus was very old, the doors of the Temple of Janus were opened once again, since fresh conquests were sought along the outer boundaries of the world, often profitably, but sometimes at considerable cost. And so it went on until the reign of Vespasian.

[Orosius 7.3.7 = Tacitus, *Histories* fragment 4]

K50   Temple of Jupiter Tonans, *aureus*, c.19 BC

Obv.:   Bare head of Augustus right.
         CAESAR AVGVSTVS
Rev.:   Temple with six columns, pediment on podium with three steps; inside temple, a naked statue of
         Jupiter holds a thunderbolt in left hand and sceptre in right.
         [I]OV TON ([Temple of] Jupiter the Thunderer)

                                                                    [*RIC* Augustus 63a / *BMC* Augustus 362]

Suetonius mentions the temple of Jupiter Tonans on the Capitol as one of three of Augustus' most significant
works (Suet. *Aug*. 29.1) and it is also mentioned at *RG* 19.2. and its dedication is celebrated on calendars
(**C30**). Its building was apparently prompted by a lucky escape on a night march in Spain in 26 BC. A bolt
of lightning struck and killed the slave lighting Augustus' way (Suet. *Aug*. 29.3). The walls of the temple
were made of solid marble according to Pliny, *NH* 36.50. The depiction of the temple on the coin, as was
usual, shows the columns of the temple moved aside to show the cult statue of Jupiter. Pliny, *NH* 34.79
mentions the statue as a highly praised work by Leochares, a Hellenistic sculptor who worked on the
Mausoleum at Halicarnassus. Nothing survives of the temple.

K51   Theatre of Balbus

[59] The ancient authorities believed that onyx is only to be found in the mountains of
Arabia and nowhere else.... [60] So when Cornelius Balbus put up four small onyx
columns in his theatre, it was seen as something of a marvel.

                                                                    [Pliny, *Natural History* 36.59–60]

Cornelius Balbus triumphed in 19 BC, see **N2f, N9**. He built his theatre in Rome in 13 BC.

Theatre of Marcellus

The theatre was first planned by Julius Caesar but left unfinished at his death. Augustus took over the project
and completed it in the name of Marcellus who was to have been his heir, but died in 23 BC. The Centennial
Games of 17 BC were partly staged there, but its formal inauguration did not take place until 13 or 11 BC.
It was capable of holding 20,500 people. The lower archways led to the lowest tiers of seating and to staircases
which led to the middle tiers and a high-level corridor, behind the upper arcade, from which further
stairs led to the highest tiers. The façade is constructed entirely of travertine and embellished by framing
each arcade in an architectural order of semicolumns: Doric on the ground floor, the more delicate Ionic on
the next level up. There must have been an attic (third) level, probably a plain wall without arcades and
simply decorated with flat pilasters in keeping with the fact that the uppermost seating will have been of
wood.

K52   Theatre of Marcellus to honour his memory

It was to honour his memory that his mother Octavia dedicated the library and Caesar
the theatre, both of which bear his name.

                                                                    [Plutarch, *Marcellus* 30]

For the library in the Portico of Octavia, see **K31**.

K53   Beast hunts at the opening of the Theatre of Marcellus

In the consulship of Quintus Tubero and Paullus Fabius Maximus at the dedication of
the Theatre of Marcellus on 4 May [11 BC], Augustus was the first in the whole of Rome
to show a tame tiger in a cage, though the deified Claudius showed four at once.

                                                                    [Pliny, *Natural History* 8.65]

Aqueducts of Rome (K54–K63)

We know a great deal about Roman aqueducts in the time of Augustus, largely through the work of Sextus
Julius Frontinus who lived from about AD 30 to AD 104, and was given important positions by the emperors
Vespasian, Domitian, Nerva and Trajan, including three consulships. In AD 97, Nerva appointed him
Aqueducts Commissioner, and while in this post, he wrote a book about the history, administration and
maintenance of the aqueducts for which he was responsible (*de aquis urbis Romae* – The Aqueducts of

Rome). This book includes a wealth of technical information, facts and figures about the system in his day as well as exact quotations of earlier statutes. On the aqueduct at Venafrum, see **K71**–**K72**.

K54 The aqueducts built by Agrippa

[9] Later, in the consulship of Lucius Volcacius and (for the second time) the emperor Caesar Augustus, [33 BC], Marcus Agrippa, now aedile following his first consulship, tapped the waters of a new spring situated at the twelfth milestone from the city on the *Via Latina*, on a side road about two miles to the right as you go away from Rome. He also took a secondary supply from the *Aqua Tepula*. The new aqueduct was named the *Aqua Iulia* (Julian aqueduct) by its constructor, though the name Tepula was also retained because of the shared distribution. The channel of the *Aqua Iulia* ran for a distance of some fifteen and a half miles. In all some seven miles was built above ground. Of this, at the end closest to the city and beginning at the seventh milestone, some half a mile is built on substructures, while the remaining six and a half miles is built on arches. ... In that same year Agrippa repaired the almost totally dilapidated channels of the *Aqua Appia*, the *Aqua Anio*, and the *Aqua Marcia*, and took considerable pains to supply the city with a number of new fountains.

[10] Twelve years after building the *Aqua Iulia*, and having been three times consul himself, Agrippa also built the *Aqua Virgo* (Maiden aqueduct), bringing it to Rome from its source on the estate of Lucullus. This was during the consulship of Gaius Sentius and Quintus Lucretius [19 BC] and my researches show that the day on which it first flowed into the city was 9 June. It got its name, the *Virgo*, from the fact that a young girl showed a series of springs to a group of soldiers who were looking for water.... Its length is just over 14 miles and for nearly 13 miles of this it runs underground. Above ground it runs for a mile and a quarter, several different sections of which to a total of half a mile are built on a substructure, and three quarters of a mile on arches. The underground channels of the subsidiary sources extend to a total length of one and a half miles.

[Frontinus, *Aqueducts of Rome* 9–10]

The provision by Agrippa and Augustus of these new aqueducts, the *Aqua Iulia* and *Aqua Virgo*, increased Rome's supply by 70%, according to Frontinus' figures (*Aqueducts* 65–73). They supplied 35 new distribution chambers in 11 of the 14 regions in Rome. Of the new supplies, 20% went to imperial properties, 25% to private properties and 54% to public supplies, including storage cisterns, public buildings, ornamental fountains and water basins. Much of the water of the *Virgo* supplied the Baths of Agrippa and the water feature (*Euripus*) of the Gardens of Agrippa (*Aqueducts* 83–84).

K55 The *Aqua Alsietina*, built by Augustus.

I cannot really see why Augustus, that most rational of emperors, decided to take waters from the *Aqua Alsietina* – also known as the *Aqua Augusta*. They have nothing to commend them, being thoroughly unhealthy and for that reason no use for human consumption. It is possible that when he was starting on the construction of the *Naumachia*, he did not want to draw upon healthy water supplies and so brought the Alsietina's waters in their own dedicated channel. Any waters that were surplus to the requirements of the *Naumachia* he allocated to adjacent gardens and to private consumers for the purposes of irrigation. These waters are derived from Lake Alsietina, at a crossroads six and a half miles to the right of the 14th milestone on the *Via Claudia*. Its channel is just over 22 miles long, with 358 yards built on arches.

[Frontinus, *Aqueducts of Rome* 11]

Frontinus is surely right that the original point of the aqueduct was to supply the huge artificial lake (*naumachia*) built across the Tiber for naval displays (*Res Gestae* 23; Ovid, *Art of Love* 1.171–176 **G47**). Later the Alsietina was used primarily for the irrigation of suburban estates and, apparently, for driving water-mills.

K56   Supplements to the supply of the *Aqua Marcia*

To supplement the *Aqua Marcia* whenever drought made such help essential, Augustus also transferred additional supplies of the same high quality to its conduit by a subterranean channel, called the Augustan after its constructor. Its source lies further away than the springs of the *Aqua Marcia*, and its channel runs for about three-quarters of a mile to its junction with the *Aqua Marcia*.

[Frontinus, *Aqueducts of Rome* 12]

Frontinus does not say as much about this aqueduct as about those built by Agrippa and Augustus, but the supplement to the *Aqua Marcia* is mentioned at *RG* (20.2) along with other aqueduct restoration.

K57   *Aqua Marcia*, 5–4 BC, Rome

Imperator Caesar Augustus son of the deified Julius, chief priest, consul 12 times, in his 19th year of tribunician power, hailed *imperator* 14 times, repaired the channels of all the aqueducts.

[EJ 281 = *ILS* 98]

This inscription on an arch of the *aqua Marcia*, reused as a gateway in the later Aurelianic walls, is the earliest of three inscriptions commemorating the activities of emperors (also Titus and Caracalla) in maintaining the aqueduct.

K58   The *curator aquarum* – Aqueducts Commissioner

[98] Marcus Agrippa became the first permanent curator, so to speak, of his own public works and amenities, when he had completed his tenure of office as aedile – an office which he accepted even though he was already of consular rank. He now laid down the principles on which the waters should be allocated, insofar as supplies permitted, to public facilities, reservoirs, and private consumers. He also kept his own team of slaves to maintain the conduits, cisterns, and reservoirs. Augustus made this team public property after inheriting it from Agrippa in his will.

[99] After Agrippa, in the consulship of Quintus Aelius Tubero and Paulus Fabius Maximus [11 BC], resolutions of the senate were passed and a law promulgated to give these matters the proper regulation which they lacked, since they had hitherto depended entirely on the *ad hoc* decisions of individual officials. Augustus also published regulations for the water supply, based on Agrippa's records, laying down the rights of users and bringing the whole system under his own patronage. He established the meter-system of which I have written above, and appointed Messala Corvinus Commissioner for the control and supply of water, with two assistants Postumius Sulpicius, of praetorian rank, and Lucius Cominius, a junior senator. They were allowed to wear magistrates' insignia and their duties were defined by a resolution of the senate, as follows:

[100] "Whereas Quintus Aelius Tubero and Paulus Fabius Maximus, consuls, have tabled their report concerning the status of those who were appointed Aqueducts Commissioners by Caesar Augustus on the resolution of the senate; and

"Whereas they have sought to know the mind of the senate as to what action they wished to be taken in this matter;

"Be it resolved that this is the opinion of this order:

"That those who have responsibility for the public water supply, whensoever they have cause to go outside the city on their official occasions, shall be attended by two lictors and three public officials, one architect for each commissioner present, and the same number of secretaries, clerks, attendants, and heralds as is allocated to those who make public distribution of wheat among the people;

"That when for such and similar reasons they have business within the city they shall have use of all those same attendants, excepting only the lictors."

[Frontinus, *Aqueducts of Rome* 98–100]

The *curator aquarum* (Aqueducts Commissioner) is one of several administrative posts established by Augustus (see **T24–T25**). In this case, the formal creation of the post follows the death in 12 BC of Agrippa who, as Frontinus makes clear, had effectively held and established the post. The lictors were public assistants to magistrates: the number of lictors who accompanied a particular magistrate reflected the status of the office: a consul had twelve, a praetor six. The Aqueducts Commissioner thus appears as a minor magistrate, but the reality is clearly that the appointment was made by Augustus himself; that the first Commissioner effectively succeeded Agrippa, and that the man chosen, M. Valerius Messala Corvinus, was a very prominent and senior ex-consul (see Section **B**). The provision of lictors was abandoned by Frontinus' time (AD 97–c.104) but he remarked, 'For myself, when I am on my rounds inspecting aqueducts, my own integrity and the emperor's authority is a more than adequate substitute for the absent lictors.' (Frontinus, *Aqueducts* 101).

K59   The duties of Aqueducts Commissioner in granting supply

I shall now add details of the duties of the Aqueducts Commissioner in regard to the law and the resolutions of the senate which have a bearing on his statutory duties. The rights of private individuals to draw off water are governed by the following rules: no one may draw off water without authorisation from Caesar; no one may draw off water from the public supply without a licence; no-one may draw off more than the permitted quantity. In this way we seek to ensure that the additional supplies, which I have described, can be directed to new fountains and to new grants by the *princeps*. But in both cases the most stringent precautions need to be taken against fraud, which takes many different forms. Regular and thorough inspections of the channels must be made outside the city to keep a check on the licensed usage; similarly in the case of the public cisterns and fountains, in order to ensure that there is a constant flow of water by day and night. The Aqueducts Commissioner is required by senatorial decree to see that all this is done...

[Frontinus, *Aqueducts of Rome* 103]

K60   The right to draw water as a gift of the *princeps*

Anyone wishing to abstract water for his private use must seek permission and bring to the Aqueducts Commissioner a letter of authority from the *princeps*. It is then the duty of the Commissioner to give immediate effect to Caesar's grant....

[Frontinus, *Aqueducts of Rome* 105]

The most important point here is that the right to get water from the aqueducts was in the direct gift of the *princeps* to whom a direct application had to be made. Frontinus after this passage set out the exact procedures which had to be followed by the Commissioner, Deputy Commissioner and surveyors, and the relevant senatorial decree of 11 BC aimed at ensuring that the imperial ruling could not be by-passed.

K61   Water rights granted by Augustus not transferable

[107] The right to licensed water supplies does not pass by inheritance, purchase, or any form of new ownership of property. But it was a privilege granted to the public baths that water supplies, once granted by licence, should be theirs in perpetuity. The evidence for this is to be found in ancient senatorial resolutions, of which I give one example below. Today, however, every grant of water is renewed when the owner of the property changes.

[108] "Whereas the consuls, Quintus Aelius Tubero and Paulus Fabius Maximus,

have reported that it should be established what is the legal basis under which those licensed to draw water outside and within the city are entitled to do so; and

"Whereas they have sought to know the mind of the senate as to what action they wished to be taken in this matter;

"Be it resolved that the grant of a water supply shall extend only for such time as the same owner shall possess the title to the land for which such supply was received; exceptions to this rule shall apply to waters supplied to the public baths and supplies granted in the name of Augustus."

[Frontinus, *Aqueducts of Rome* 107–8]

K62   Special measures to ensure maintenance of the aqueducts, 11 BC

[124] I should imagine that no one can have the slightest doubt that those aqueducts closest to Rome, that is to say those within the seventh milestone, require the most careful maintenance as being built of worked stone. The reason is that these are the largest structures and each carries a number of conduits. If it ever proved necessary to interrupt these supplies, the greater part of the city would be deprived of water. But there is a further complication: almost all the conduits ran through the fields of private citizens, which raised problems of how best to make provision for future expenditure on repairs, unless some sort of legal framework was established to insure against this possibility. It was also essential to guarantee access from the owners for contractors seeking to make such repairs. As a result, the senate passed a resolution, as follows:

[125] "Whereas the consuls, Quintus Aelius Tubero and Paulus Fabius Maximus, have reported on the repair of the conduits, channels, and arches of those aqueducts known as the Julian, Marcian, Appian, Tepulan, and Anio; and

"Whereas they have sought to know the mind of the senate as to what action they wished to be taken in this matter;

"Be it resolved that whensoever repairs are necessary to those conduits, channels, and arches which Augustus Caesar promised the senate that he would repair at his own expense, at such time the earth, clay, stones, brickwork, sand, timber and other materials required for such works may legally be requisitioned, uplifted, and transferred from the nearest available source from which it may be so requisitioned, uplifted, and transferred, subject to due and fair compensation for their value to the private citizens concerned, which shall be assessed by an arbitrator of high public reputation; and for the purpose of all such transfer of materials and the making of all such repairs, as often as is required, all roads and cart-tracks through the lands of private citizens shall be open and available to the appointed contractors, subject to fair compensation for damage done to the owners' interests."

[Frontinus, *Aqueducts of Rome* 124–125]

repair at his own expense: aqueducts had previously been built or occasionally repaired under the supervision of censors, at public expense.

subject to due and fair compensation: this would fit in with his boast (*Res Gestae* 21.1) to have built his forum in Rome on land he purchased.

K63   The law against 'water-piracy'

The text of the law follows.

[129] Titus Quinctius Crispinus, the consul, put the following resolution to the People and the People passed this resolution in the Forum before the *rostra* of the

temple of the Deified Julius on the thirtieth day of June [9 BC]. The Sergian tribe voted first. On their behalf Sextus Varro, son of Lucius, cast the first vote.

"Whosoever, following the adoption of this statute, shall wilfully or with malice aforethought pierce or damage, or cause to be so pierced, damaged, or debased, any channel, conduit, arch, pipe, tube, cistern, or reservoir pertaining to the public waters which are delivered to this city; and

"Whosoever shall thereby prevent such waters or any portion thereof from proceeding, descending, flowing, reaching, or being conveyed to the city of Rome; and

"Whosoever shall prevent such waters being distributed, or allocated or discharged into cisterns or reservoirs in any part of the city of Rome or the areas, buildings, or localities as are presently or shall be in the future adjacent to the city, or in the gardens, holdings, or properties (to the owners of which gardens, holdings, or properties has been or shall in the future be given licence to abstract water);

All such persons shall be liable to a fine of 100,000 sesterces, payable to the Roman People.

[The law, quoted in full by Frontinus, continues along similar lines]

[Frontinus, *Aqueducts of Rome* 128–129]

Frontinus mentions the problems caused by people boring private holes in the conduits to steal water, praising and quoting a law passed in 9 BC laying down stringent penalties for this. Unlike a *senatus consultum* (senatorial decree), a law (*lex*) was brought directly before the people, for them to vote upon.

Italy (K64–K73)

It is clear from a later period at Pompeii that neither the power of Rome nor the emperors prevented a vigorous and competitive system of local government. The same was true of other communities under Augustus, even though they might increasingly try to associate their community with Rome and especially the emperor, as many of the examples below show. For other examples of this, see the introduction to (Section C), the Calendars, many from communities outside Rome, and also the Pisan decrees **J61**, **J64**), lamenting the deaths of Gaius and Lucius.

K64   Augustus' division of Italy into 11 regions

I now propose to give you a round tour of Italy and its cities. By way of preface I should point out that I intend to follow the example of the deified Augustus when he divided the whole of Italy into eleven regions, but to deal with them in the order suggested by the coastline. In a somewhat hasty survey such as this it is impossible to stick to any strict sequence of neighbouring cities, so when it comes to my account of the hinterland I shall follow Augustus' practice of using alphabetical order, including a summary of the colonies which he recorded in his list.

[Pliny, *Natural History* 3.46]

K65   The regions of Italy

[49] The Ligurian coastline is the ninth under the Augustan dispositions... [50] Next to it is the seventh region, which includes Etruria... [62] The distance (to Naples) by sea from Cerceii is 78 miles. This region, starting from the Tiber, is the first region of Italy following Augustus' division... [97] The town of Metapontum (is) where the third region of Italy ends... [99] The second region lies next to it and includes the Hirpini, Calabria, Apulia, and the Salentini... [106] Next comes the fourth region, which includes the bravest of the tribes of Italy, the Frentani, the Marrucini, the Paeligni, the

Marsi etc... [110] The fifth region is Picenum, which was once the most densely populated... [112] The sixth region is Umbria, including the Gallic lands on this side of Ariminum... [115] The eighth region is bounded by Ariminum, the river Po, and the Appennines... [123] The eleventh region derives its name from the river Po and is called the Transpadane. Though it is an entirely inland region, the river carries to it along its generous stream all forms of maritime produce... [126]... Then comes (Venetia), the tenth region of Italy, lying along the Adriatic sea.

[Pliny, *Natural History* 3. Various]

The regions seem to have served mainly as administrative units for the census. They seem to have cut across previous ethnic and cultural boundaries and are seen as evidence of increased unity within Italy: (*CAH* X² pages 430–431).

K66   Vedius Pollio at Beneventum, pre-15 BC
Publius Veidius Pollio, son of Publius, (built the) *Caesareum* for Imperator Caesar Augustus and the colony of Beneventum.

[*ILS* 109 = *CIL* IX 1556]

Vedius Pollio was a friend of Augustus. Son of a freedman, he attained equestrian status. He was notorious for his wealth and cruelty (see **H40**, **K30** and Dio 54.23.1–6). Beneventum (modern Benevento) in southern Italy was perhaps his home town. He died in 15 BC. Only this building inscription survives so it is not clear what type of building the *Caesareum* was. The inscription spells his name differently from literary sources.

K67   Building of an amphitheatre at Luceria, 27/2 BC
Marcus Vecilius Campus, son of Marcus, grandson of Lucius, prefect of engineers, military tribune, joint chief magistrate with judicial powers, priest, saw to the construction of the amphitheatre on his private land and the enclosure wall surrounding it at his own expense in honour of Imperator Caesar Augustus and of the colony of Luceria.

[EJ 236 = *AE* 1938.110]

This inscription survives in two copies at modern Lucera (North Puglia), engraved upon limestone architraves above impressive entranceways into the amphitheatre. The doorways are flanked by Ionic columns and topped by pediments, each decorated with a sculpted shield and spear. The enclosure wall mentioned served to mark off an area around the outside of the amphitheatre, presumably to help with crowd control. The construction of the amphitheatre would have required considerable financial commitment from this private benefactor.

Bibliography: M. Buonocore, ed. *Epigrafia anfiteatrale dell'Occidente Romano* III no.73 (Rome 1992) – for photographs.

K68   Arch at Ariminum, commemorating the *via Flaminia*, 27 BC
The [Roman] Senate and People, [to Imperator Caesar Augustus, son of the deified, hailed *imperator* seven times], consul seven times and designated for the 8th, to commemorate his building of the *via Flaminia* [and the rest] of the most frequented roads in Italy on his initiative and at his expense.

[EJ 286 = *ILS* 84]

The end of the 209 mile long *via Flaminia* from Rome to Ariminum (modern Rimini) was marked by an honorific arch bearing this inscription. The road was originally built by C. Flaminius, when censor in 220 BC. Augustus' pride in his restoration of the *via Flaminia*, emerges from *Res Gestae* 20.5. He did not himself repair the other roads, but instructed other triumphal generals to use their booty for this purpose (Suetonius, *Augustus* 30.1). For example, C. Calvisius Sabinus (consul 39 BC, triumph 28 BC) and M. Valerius Messalla Corvinus (consul 31 BC, triumph 27 BC) each restored part of the *via Latina*. See **K68b** in Addenda.

K69 Repair of roads commemorated, *denarius*, 17 BC

Obv.: Bare head of Augustus left.
S P Q R IMP CAESARI (Senate and People of Rome to Imperator Caesar)

Rev.: Two arches on a viaduct each surmounted by an equestrian statue and a trophy of arms.
QVOD VIAE MVNITAE SVNT (Because the roads have been repaired)

[*RIC* Augustus 142, *BMC* Augustus 435]

Roads were very important to the Romans. Road-building was a prestigious activity symbolic of Roman triumph over the physical landscape and its conquered inhabitants. It is thus no surprise that the structure depicted on this coin commemorating Augustus' road-building looks like a military monument.

K70 Milestone on the *via Aemilia*, 2–1 BC

Imperator Caesar Augustus, chief priest, consul 13 times, in his 22nd year of tribunician power, saw to the building of the *via Aemilia* from Ariminum to the river Trebia. 79.

[EJ 288 = *ILS* 9371]

This milestone was extracted from a river near Bononia (modern Bologna). The milestone's distance along the road from Ariminum (modern Rimini) is recorded by the number, 79. The *via Aemilia* ran 176 miles from Ariminum to Placentia (modern Piacenza) and was originally built by M. Aemilius Lepidus (consul 187 BC).

K71 Augustus' edict on the aqueduct of Venafrum, 18–11 BC

Edict of Imperator Caesar [Augustus …(6 lines missing)…….] in the name of the people of Venafrum […… may it be lawful] and permitted. [9] Whatever channels, conduits, sluices, springs and [….] have been made, built, or constructed above or below the level for the purpose of bringing or repairing a water-supply, or whatever other structure has been made above or below the level for the purpose of bringing or repairing a water-supply, in whatever condition any of these things has been made, it is my wish that they exist and keep that same condition, and that it is my wish to re-make, replace, restore or repair once and more often in this condition, to place pipes, conduits, and tubes, to create an opening, or to do whatever else will be necessary for the purpose of bringing a water-supply, while whatever place or piece of land in the estate, which [is or] is said [to be] belonging to Quintus Sirinius son of Lucius, of the Terentina tribe, and in the estate which is or is said to be of Lucius Pompeius Sulla son of Marcus of the Terentina tribe, has been enclosed by a wall, through which place or beneath which place the conduits of that water-supply reach, let neither that wall nor part of that wall be destroyed or removed for any other reason than for the purpose of repairing or inspecting the conduits: [20] and let there [not be anything belonging to a private individual] there to hinder this water-supply from being able to proceed, flow, or be brought [………….] it is my wish that on the right and on the left around that channel and around those structures [which] have been made for the purpose of bringing [this] water-supply, eight feet of land be empty, through which place it may be lawful and permitted for the people of Venafrum or for someone who in the name of the people of Venafrum [.....], to travel {for the purpose of} bringing this water-supply or of making or repairing the structures of this water-supply, if this is done in good faith, and to convey, bring, or carry whatever of these things will be necessary for the purpose of making or repairing, so that it shall be as near as possible, and that whatever is taken away from there, be deposited as equally as possible for eight feet on the right and on the left, provided that indemnity regarding these things is guaranteed on oath. [30] And it is my wish that the colonists of Venafrum have the right and power over all these things in this way, provided that no owner of any piece of land or place, through which piece of land or place this water-supply usually proceeds, flows, or is brought, have his access barred on account of this structure; nor on account of this structure should he be any the less able to cross, transfer, or divert directly from one part of his land into another; nor let it be permitted to any of those, through whose land this water-supply is brought, to taint, divert, or misappropriate that aqueduct or to do anything to hinder this water-supply from being able directly to be brought and to flow into the town of Venafrum.

[37] Whatever water proceeds, flows, or is brought into the town of Venafrum, it is my wish that the joint chief magistrate or joint chief magistrates, prefect or prefects of that colony have the right and power to distribute and allot this water for the purpose of selling it, or to impose and settle a tax upon it, by decree of the majority of the town councillors, provided that the decree is made thus, when among the town councillors no less than two-thirds of them are present, and to proclaim a law concerning this by decree of the town councillors, provided that the decree is made just as has been written above; provided that this water, which will be distributed and allotted in this way, or about which a decree will be issued in this way, is not brought other than in lead pipes up to 50 feet from the channel; nor let these pipes or channels be placed or put except underground, which ground will have the status of the course of a public road, or of a boundary; nor let this water be brought through a private place against the wish of whoever owns that place. [49] And it is my wish that whatever law the joint chief magistrates or prefects proclaim by decree of the town councillors, for protecting the water-supply or structures, which have been or will be made for the purpose of this aqueduct or its use, provided it is made in accordance with what has been written above, be valid and authoritative [...(11 lines missing)......... [62]..] which to a colonist or inhabitant [...........] it is my wish that the person to whom the business is given by a decree of the town councillors in the way which has been dealt with above, when going to law, be legally investigated, then, the person who is deciding lawsuits between citizens and non-citizens, should allow legal proceedings before assessors for 10,000 sesterces for each matter, and by serving summons to up to 10 witnesses; provided that the rejection of assessors is carried out between the one who is going to law and the one with whom the lawsuit is conducted, just as [is in accordance with the law], which has been passed concerning private lawsuits, it will be permitted and proper.

[EJ 282 = *ILS* 5743]

Venafrum is in Campania, near Cassino, between Rome and Naples. Compare **K61–K63** on laws and decrees on the aqueducts in Rome. The passage is revealing of the extreme detail and complexity of imperial administration carried out directly in the name of Augustus. In Italy, as in Rome (**K60**), he is presented as being ultimately responsible for the supply of water.

K72   Inscribed markers for the Venafrum aqueduct

By command of Imperator Caesar Augustus around that channel which was made for the purpose of bringing the water-supply, eight feet of land on the right and left has been left empty.

[EJ 283 = *ILS* 5744]

Six stone markers bearing this inscription have been found alongside the course of the Venafrum aqueduct, which can be traced for 14 miles. The inscriptions echo lines 21–23 of the edict above.

K73   An outstanding benefactor at Herculaneum

Seeing as Marcus Ofillius Celer, joint chief magistrate for the second time, made the statement that it was conducive to the town's dignity to act in response to the public service of Marcus Nonius Balbus, they decreed on this matter as follows: Marcus Nonius Balbus, for as long as he lived here, displayed a father's spirit together with the utmost generosity to individuals and everyone alike. Therefore it pleases the town councillors that an equestrian statue be set up to him in the most frequented place out of public funds and that it be inscribed: 'To Marcus Nonius Balbus, son of Marcus, of the Menenia tribe, praetor with proconsular power, patron. The whole governing body of the people of Herculaneum (set this up) on account of his public service'; and also in the same place, where his ashes have been gathered together, that a marble altar be made and set up and publicly inscribed: 'To Marcus Nonius Balbus, son of Marcus'; and that a procession proceed from this place at the festival of the dead, and that one day be added in his honour to the athletic games, which had usually occurred, and that when shows are performed in the theatre his seat be placed there. They decreed.

[*AE* 1976.144]

Herculaneum, on the Bay of Naples, was destroyed by the eruption of Mt. Vesuvius in AD 79. In the Augustan period, the senator Marcus Nonius Balbus was an exceedingly generous benefactor to the town, rebuilding the town's basilica, gates, and defensive wall, and he received outstanding honours in recognition of this fact. His father (of the same name) and other members of his family bathed in his reflected glory. Outside the Suburban Baths were a statue of him (set up by one of his freedmen) and his funerary altar, upon which this inscription was engraved. It records the town council's decree passed after his death regarding his posthumous honours. These are unusually lavish for someone who was not a member of the imperial family, and reflect the influence of Greek hero cult. He was also honoured by many statues set up during his lifetime not just by the people of Herculaneum, but also by various Cretan communities, since he had served as governor of Crete and Cyrene.

SECTION L

RELIGION

> I have been chief priest, augur, one of the Fifteen for conducting sacred rites, one of the Seven in charge
> of feasts, Arval brother, member of the fraternity of Titus, and fetial priest. [*Res Gestae*, 7.3]

Thus Augustus recorded his membership of no fewer than seven priestly colleges. In doing so, he proclaimed his great piety, but also illustrated several themes of religion under Augustus: first, the importance he placed on traditional state religion; second, his deliberate revival of archaic religious practices; third, his innovative use of religion to enhance his own prestige, since, although priesthoods were held by members of the Roman political class, it was very unusual to hold more than one. The context of the *Res Gestae* illustrates another vital aspect of religion under Augustus. The best known copy of the inscription comes from a Temple to Rome and Augustus and the 'title' of the inscription is *Res Gestae Divi Augusti* – 'The Achievements of the Deified Augustus (see Introduction to Section A). Augustus may have shunned direct worship of himself during his lifetime, but many indirect ways were found, and deification after his death was a foregone conclusion.

Tradition and Revival (L1–L7)

L1   Symbols of four priesthoods held by Augustus, *denarius* of 16 BC

Obv.:   Bust of Venus right.
          C ANTISTIVS VETVS III VIR (name and title of moneyer)
Rev.:   Above left and right: ladle (*simpulum*), augur's wand (*lituus*); below left and right: tripod and
          sacrificial bowl (*patera*).
          COS / IMP CAESAR AVGV / XI (Imperator Caesar Augustus, consul for the
          eleventh time)

                                                                [*RIC* Augustus 367, *BMC* Augustus 98]

The aura of sacredness surrounding the person of Augustus is a frequent theme on the coinage. The obverse here depicts the goddess Venus, the divine ancestor of the Julian clan to which Augustus belonged by adoption. The reverse shows the symbols of the four great Roman priesthoods: a ladle (for pouring offerings of wine) for the *pontifices* (priests with general oversight of the state cults); a wand for the augurs (diviners); a tripod for the *quindecimviri sacris faciundis* ('The fifteen for performing rituals' who also kept and consulted the Sibylline books and were given charge of the Centennial Games); and a sacrificial bowl for the *septemviri epulones* (a seven-man board chiefly responsible for the feast (*epulum*) held at some games). Together, these motifs refer not just to these prestigious priesthoods but more particularly to Augustus, who was the first Roman ever to belong to all four priesthoods at once (*RG* 7.3). Augustus was made a *pontifex* in 47 BC, and *pontifex maximus*, in 12 BC; his coinage shows that he became *augur* c.42 BC, *quindecimvir* c.37 BC and *septemvir* by 16 BC.

The other three minor priesthoods held by Augustus (see introduction) were revived from obscurity by Augustus (there were others to which he did not belong in person). The *fratres arvales* (arval priests) were responsible for the cult of Dea Dia at a sanctuary five miles south-west of Rome, where extensive inscribed records have been found for the imperial period. The *fetiales* were responsible for the ritual aspects of declarations of war and treaties; Octavian performed the ritual declaration of war against Cleopatra in person in 32 BC (Dio 50.4.5). The duties of a *sodalis Titius* (member of the Titius college) are obscure. See further Beard, North and Price, *Religions of Rome* 1998: 1.186–96, and *OCD²* articles on individual priesthoods.

L2   Augustus associated with the *Salii*, *denarius* of 17 BC

Obv.:   Bare head of Augustus right.
AVGVSTVS TR POT (Augustus, tribunician power)

Rev.:   Priest's hat (*apex*) between two sacred shields (*ancilia*).
P STOLO III VIR (name and title of moneyer)

[*RIC* Augustus 343, *BMC* Augustus 74]

Symbols of traditional Roman religious ritual and practice, such as those depicted on the reverse of this coin, played a large part in decorative art in the Augustan period, representing the new atmosphere of piety and observance which Augustus himself encouraged among the Roman people. The *apex* was a conical felt cap worn by the *Salii*, a group of priests connected with the war-god Mars. They carried the *ancilia*, sacred shields, in procession on certain appointed days in March and October relating to the traditional beginning and ending of the military campaigning season. These motifs refer to war, religion, and Roman antiquity, three favourite themes of the new Roman self-image which was being created under Augustus. Augustus boasts at *RG* 10.1 that his name was included in the hymn of the *Salii* by decree of the senate (in 29 BC: Dio 51.20.1).

L3   Religious reforms
(Tiberius said that) Augustus had adapted for modern usage some of the cruder practices of antiquity.

[Tacitus, *Annals* 4.16]

Suetonius *Augustus*, 31.1–4, gives details of Augustus' revivals.

L4   Augustus' restoration of temples
At February's beginning, so they say, our Saviour Juno, neighbour   55
To Phrygia's Mother Goddess, was honoured with new temples.
Where are they now, those temples which on Kalends long ago
Were consecrated to her? Fallen they lie, victims of time's long march.
It was our blessed leader's care and providence that all the rest should
Never be suffered likewise to decay crumbling to ruination.   60
Beneath his care our temples do not feel the searing touch of age; and so
He binds by ties of obligation not just mankind but all the gods as well.
O holy one, builder of temples and re-builder too, this is my prayer:
May all the gods repay your care by mutual benefaction, and grant
You years in heaven to match the years on earth you gave to them.   65
May they for ever at your doors take post as guardian sentries.

[Ovid, *Fasti* 2. 55–66]

This passage celebrates Augustus' extensive restoration of decaying temples, of which he claimed to have repaired 82 in one year, 28 BC (*Res Gestae* 20.4) Livy described Augustus as 'the founder and restorer of all our temples' (**P4** section 7).

L5   Sibylline oracles

At the same time Tiberius reminded Caninius, that because this famous name had
become attached to so many spurious collections of oracles, Augustus had ordained a
set day during which they were to be delivered to the City Praetor, and that no private
citizen should thereafter be permitted to retain them in his possession.

[Tacitus, *Annals* 6.12]

Lucius Caninius Gallus: consul in 2 BC. In AD 33, as *quindecimvir* he had proposed adding to the official
corpus of Sibylline oracles (prophecies consulted in times of crisis). For Augustus' precaution against
unauthorised and potentially inflammatory oracles, see Suet. *Aug*. 31.1. Such precautions are a sign of the
lasting discontent that underlay society in ancient Rome.

L6   Augustus' dedication to the public *Lares*, 4 BC, Roman Forum

Sacred to the public *Lares*. Imperator Caesar Augustus, chief priest, holding tribunician
power for the 19th time, set this up from the offering of money which the people
collected for him on 1 January in his absence, during the consulship of Gaius Calvisius
Sabinus and Lucius Passienus Rufus.

[EJ 41 = *ILS* 99]

Lares were protecting spirits of a place, in this public context, guardians of the state. From Suetonius,
Augustus 57.1, we learn that people from all levels of society brought gifts to the Capitol for Augustus on
1 January each year, even when he himself was absent from Rome. The start of each new year was also
marked by sacrifices on behalf of Augustus and his family by the Arval priests on the Capitol. This inscribed
base shows that Augustus made a point of using the proceeds of the popular collection for dedicating a public
religious monument in the centre of Rome. The words 'from the offering of money which the people' are
inscribed in slightly larger letters than the rest of the text.

L7   Records of the Arval priesthood, AD 14, Rome

[… seeing as Gnaeus Cornelius] Lentulus, son of Gnaeus, augur, president in place of
[…], referred [to] the Arval priests for discussion – that a tree [in the grove] of the Dea
Dia had fallen down because of old age – seeing as he asked them what they wished
to be done concerning this matter, they decreed on this matter as follows: [since a tree]
in the grove of the Dea Dia had fallen down because of old age, it should be destroyed
for a sacrifice [in the grove], and none of its [wood] should be taken away.

[7] [The following were present]: Lucius Domitius Ahenobarbus, son of Gnaeus,
Lucius Calpurnius [Piso] priest, Paullus Fabius Maximus, son of Quintus.

[9] Under the same consuls, on 14 May in the *Regia*, [Gnaeus Cornelius] Lentulus,
son of Gnaeus, augur, president, co-opted Drusus Caesar, son of Tiberius, grandson of
Augustus, as an Arval [priest] in place of Lucius [Aemilius] Paullus and summoned
him to the rites. [The following were present:] Gnaeus Pompeius, son of Quintus,
Lucius Domitius Ahenobarbus, [Lucius Calpurnius] Piso priest, [Titus] Quinctius
Crispinus [Valerianus]; [Imperator Caesar] Augustus, Tiberius Caesar, son of
Augustus, Germanicus [Caesar, son of Tiberius], Paullus Fabius Maximus co-opted
by written notice.

[18] Under the [same] consuls, on 15 December in the *Regia*, [Gnaeus Cornelius]
Lentulus, son of Gnaeus, augur, president, [coopted] as Arval priest Gnaeus Pompeius,
augur, in place of Gnaeus [Pompeius, son of Quintus] and {….name erased … } in
place of Imperator [Caesar] Augustus [and] summoned them to the rites.

[The following were present; Drusus] Caesar, son of Tiberius, Lucius Piso priest,
Titus Quinctius [Crispinus Valerianus], Marcus Cornutus; [Tiberius Caesar] Augustus
[son of the deified Augustus] co-opted by written notice.

[*CIL* VI 2023a]

This is an extract from the detailed inscribed records of their activities kept by the Arval brothers (an archaic priesthood revived by Augustus). They worshipped the obscure Dea Dia in a sacred grove just outside Rome, at modern Magliana. Increasingly, their activities focused on honouring the emperor and his family, celebrating imperial anniversaries. The 12 members of the college were important senators at Rome, including members of the imperial family, and held position for life, being replaced by co-option on death. The first part of this text records how a dead tree, as the goddess' property, has to be destroyed within the grove to avoid profanation. The other fragments record the replacement of deceased Arval brothers, Augustus being replaced by someone whose name was subsequently erased – perhaps Gnaeus Calpurnius Piso, condemned in AD 20 under Tiberius. The *Regia* was the palace of the old kings of Rome in the forum. Bibliography: J. Scheid, *Commentarii fratrum arvalium qui supersunt* (Rome 1998) no.2 [for updated text and commentary].

Emperor-Worship (L8–L19)

L8   Capricorn and globe symbolising Augustus' fate, *aureus, c.* 18 BC

Obv.:   Bare head of Augustus right.
          No legend.
Rev.:   Capricorn to left, holding globe and rudder in front paws, with horn of plenty (*cornucopia*) behind.
          AVGVSTVS

[*RIC* Augustus 127, *BMC* Augustus 344]

Augustus' birthday fell on 23 September (**C33**). But the zodiacal sign widely associated with him was Capricorn (a goat-fish in antiquity, rather than just a goat as it is usually depicted nowadays), which is nine months too early. It probably stands for the date of his conception in December 64 BC, when his mother had reportedly been 'visited' by a snake in the Temple of Apollo. The suggestion of divine parentage is here combined with symbols of world-rule, the globe and the ship's rudder (for orderly government), and prosperity (the horn of plenty). The design designates Augustus as the man foreordained by the gods to rule the world in peace and harmony. The reference point of all these tightly packed symbols is explained by the simple legend consisting of Augustus' name.

L9   Altar of Fortuna Redux, *aureus, c.* 19 BC

Obv.:   Augustus, laureate, right.

No legend.

Rev: Rectangular altar inscribed:

FORT RED / CAES AVG / S P Q R ([Altar of] Fortuna the Home-bringer, the Senate and People of Rome [dedicated it] to Caesar Augustus)

[*RIC* Augustus 53a, *BMC* Augustus 358]

When in 19 BC Augustus returned to Rome after a three-year absence in the East, an altar was dedicated to Fortune the Home-Bringer (*Redux*) near the Porta Capena, the gate through which he had re-entered the city on 12 October (**C35**). At this altar the *pontifices* and Vestals celebrated the rites of a new festival, the *Augustalia*, founded to commemorate the date (*RG* 11). The festivities on this occasion were exceptionally elaborate because of the diplomatic victory recently won over the Parthians (**N42**), and because Augustus' prolonged absence since 22 BC had caused significant political tension within Rome itself (Dio 54.10.1–3 quoted in note on **C35**). These events show how the emperor became the focus of religious attention, even having religious festivals named after him, like a god.

L10   Public vows for Augustus' safety, *denarius*, 16 BC

Obv.:   Inscription within oak-wreath.

I O M / S P Q R V S / PR S IMP CAE / QVOD PER EV / R P IN AMP / ATQ TRAN / S E (To Jupiter Greatest and Best the Senate and People of Rome took vows for the safety of Imperator Caesar because through him the State is in a more expansive and peaceful condition)

Rev.:   Pillar inscribed IMP / CAES / AVGV / COMM / CONS (to Imperator Caesar Augustus by common consensus)

S C / L MESCINIVS RVFVS IIIVIR (By decree of the Senate, Lucius Mescinius, member of the Board of Three in charge of the Mint)

[*RIC* Augustus 358, *BMC* Augustus 92]

Some coins of Augustus, such as this one, are decorated not with symbols but with abbreviated versions of honorary inscriptions which probably appeared in full on actual monuments in the city of Rome. These legends refer to vows of gratitude taken by the senate and people in honour of Augustus' achievements in foreign ('more expansive') and domestic ('more peaceful') policy. This is paralleled in the *Res Gestae* where Augustus claimed that he had put an end to all internal wars (*RG* 34.1) and extended the boundaries of all the provinces (*RG* 26.1). The reference to 'common consensus' on the reverse legend also echoes *RG* 34.1 where Augustus himself claimed that he 'possessed control of everything by universal consensus'. There was no room for dissenting voices in Augustus' new world.

L11   Votive games celebrating Augustus' return, 13 BC, Rome

[Publius Quinctilius] Varus, [son] of Sextus, [priest?], consul, arranged [votive games to Jupiter Best and Greatest] on behalf of the return of [Imperator Caesar] Augustus, son of the Deified, [with his colleague Tiberius Claudius] Nero. In accordance with a senatorial decree.

[EJ 36 = *ILS* 88]

This base commemorates games organised by Quinctilius Varus and Tiberius to celebrate Augustus' return to Rome from Spain and Gaul. The altar of Augustan peace (**K13**) was also dedicated to mark this occasion and Horace *Odes* 4.2 (**G41**) looks forward to this return. Similar bases also record votive games in honour of Augustus' returns to Rome in 8 BC and 7 BC, given by the consuls of the year.

L12 The introduction of the cult of the Augustan *Lares* at Rome, ?7 BC

To the Augustan *Lares*: the priestly attendants who on 1 August first took up post: Antigonus, the slave of Marcus Iunius Eros, Anteros, the slave of Decimus Poblicius Barna, Eros, the slave of Aulus Poblicius Dama, Iucundus, the slave of Marcus Plotius Anteros.

[EJ 139 = *ILS* 3612]

As part of his reorganisation of the city of Rome into administrative districts, Augustus introduced the cult of his own *lares* (protecting spirits) into the pre-existing *lares*-cult at crossroads. The priests of these cults were generally freedmen, and their attendants were usually slaves, with the result that Augustus fostered loyalty towards himself from even the lowest sections of society. This inscription appears to have been set up by the first such set of attendants to hold post, probably in 7 BC.

L13 Worship of the *genius* (divine spirit) of Augustus

To the *Lares Compitales* cross-roads are dear; to dogs no less. 140
The *Lares* hunt down thieves; Diana's hound-packs likewise.
Sleepless the *Lares* watch by night; sleepless too the dogs.
I sought the twin statues of those twin divinities and found
Nothing; perished they were by the power of time's decay.
Rome has a thousand twin *Lares* now, and a leader's *Genius*, whose gift 145
Bestowed them. Every district now pays honour to its three divinities.
I ramble. For to this theme Augustus' month lays claim. My song
Must needs return to hymn the *Bona Dea*, our Good Goddess.
A pinnacle there is of natural rock from which derives its name,
The Crag, they call it. Of Mount Aventine it forms a goodly part. 150
Here Remus took his futile stance while to his brother's gaze
The birds of Palatine vouchsafed the earlier omens. There
On that gently sloping ridge the Senators established
A temple that abominates the gaze of men. An heiress
Of the ancient name of Clausus made the dedication, a maid 155
Whose body never had experienced sexual intercourse.
Livia restored that shrine, that she might never fail to imitate
Her husband and in all ways to follow him.

[Ovid, *Fasti* 5.140–158]

This passage marks the setting up of images of the *Lares Compitales* (the paired gods of hearth and home) and of the divine spirit (*genius*) of Augustus in each of the 265 smallest administrative units (*vici*) of Rome, showing one possibility for indirect cult of the living Augustus (who refused direct emperor-worship at Rome). It also celebrates the restoration of the shrine of the *Bona Dea* (Good Goddess) by Livia, Augustus' consort, descended like the shrine's founder from Clausus (155).

L14 The Temple of Augustus at Fanum

The two middle columns of the basilica (at the Julian Colony at Fanum) are omitted, so as not to obstruct the view of the front of the Temple of Augustus which stands at the mid-point of the side wall of the basilica facing the centre of the forum and the Temple of Jupiter.

[Vitruvius, *On Architecture* 5.1.7]

Vitruvius describes his design for the basilica at Fanum Fortunae (Fano) in Umbria, which takes special account of the Temple of Augustus. Vitruvius published his work at the start of Augustus' principate (see **R22**).

L15   Temple of Augustus at Puteoli

[Lucius] Calpurnius, son of Lucius, built this temple to Augustus with its ornaments at his own expense.

[EJ 110 = *CIL* X 1613]

Puteoli (modern Pozzuoli on the Bay of Naples) was Rome's main harbour in this period. The temple referred to here was transformed into the church of S. Procolo in the 11th century. This inscription no longer survives, but was seen and recorded in the 16th century on the façade of the church. Its interpretation is consequently controversial, with some scholars suggesting that the inscription was misread, that the temple was actually the town's *Capitolium*, and that instead of recording a temple to Augustus, the inscription recorded a building of Calpurnius, an *Augustalis*. If the temple was to Augustus, it must have been built during his life, otherwise it would have been dedicated to the 'Deified Augustus'.

L16   Temple of Augustus at Pergamum

The deified Augustus did not prevent the building of a temple at Pergamum to himself and the City of Rome.

[Tacitus, *Annals* 4.37]

Did not prevent: this formula is accurate: according to Dio 51.20.6–9, the inhabitants of Asia and Bithynia-Pontus (no doubt to win the favour of the new master of the East) approached Octavian with their request to put up temples to him; he insisted that Rome was included, and that Roman citizens should have their own temples to Julius Caesar in Ephesus and Nicaea. So he showed favour, ensuring the gratitude of his subjects, without conceding too much. For a priest of this temple, see **M85**. Another temple to Rome and Augustus was built at Lugdunum, the capital of the new province of Lugdunensis, **M18–M20**. Augustus was honoured as a god at Myra in Lycia (**M82**).

L17   Altar to the *numen* of Augustus, AD 12–13, Narbonne

[On the front]

During the consulship of Titus Statilius Taurus and Lucius Cassius Longinus on 22 September, a vow was undertaken by the commoners of Narbo in perpetuity:

[7] May it be good, favourable and prosperous for Imperator Caesar Augustus, son of the Deified, Father of the Fatherland, chief priest, in his 34th year of tribunician power, for his wife, children and family, and for the senate and Roman people and for the colonists and inhabitants of the Julian Ancestral Colony of Narbo Martius, who have bound themselves to worship his divinity for ever. [12] The people of Narbo have set up an altar at Narbo in the forum, at which, each year on 23 September, on which day the good fortune of the age brought him forth as governor of the world, three Roman equestrians from the commoners and three freedmen are to sacrifice a victim each and are to supply at their own expense to colonists and inhabitants on this day incense and wine for worshipping his divinity; [20] and on 24 September they are also to supply incense and wine to colonists and inhabitants; also on 1 January they are to supply incense and wine to colonists and inhabitants; also on 7 January, on which day he first entered upon his rule over the world, they are to worship with incense and wine and sacrifice a victim each and supply incense and wine to colonists and inhabitants on this day; [29] and on 31 May, because on this day in the consulship of Titus Statilius Taurus and Manlius Aemilius Lepidus he brought the commoners' judgements into harmony with the town's councillors, they are to sacrifice a victim each and supply incense and wine to colonists and inhabitants for worshipping his divinity. And one of these three Roman equestrians [or three] freedmen ....

[On the right side]

The commoners of Narbo have dedicated an altar of the divinity of Augustus {(2 lines erased)} according to the regulations which have been written below:

[5] Divinity of Caesar Augustus, Father of the Fatherland, when I give and dedicate to you today this altar, I shall give and dedicate it by these regulations and in these regions, which here today I shall declare openly, as the lowest soil is of this altar and inscriptions: if anyone will wish to clean, decorate or restore it, let what may be done for its benefit, be permitted by both human and divine law; [14] or if anyone will carry out a rite with a sacrificial victim, who does not hold up the entrails in front of him, nevertheless as far as this is concerned let it be done validly; if anyone will wish to give a gift to this altar and to enrich it, let it be permitted, and let the same law exist for this gift as for the altar; let the other laws governing this altar and inscriptions be the same as those for the altar of Diana on the Aventine. [22] By these laws and in these regions, just as I have declared, I give and dedicate this altar to you in the interests of Imperator Caesar Augustus, Father of the Fatherland, chief priest, in his 35th year of tribunician power, of his wife, children and family, of the senate and Roman people, and of the colonists and inhabitants of the Julian Ancestral Colony of Narbo Martius, who have bound themselves to worship his divinity in perpetuity, so that you may willingly be propitious.

[EJ 100 = *ILS* 112]

The inscriptions on this altar from Narbo (modern Narbonne, southern France) date to AD 11 and 12–13, but were reinscribed in the second century AD, showing that the altar's cult continued to be relevant. It is noteworthy that the altar is being established on the initiative of the commoners. The deity invoked is the divinity (*numen*) of Augustus, rather than Augustus himself, who is himself listed as one of the beneficiaries of the cult. Narbo was the first Roman colony in Gaul, and under Augustus became provincial capital of Gallia Narbonensis. Cult at the altar is to be performed by six men, probably the town's *seviri Augustales*, on various significant days: Augustus' birthday, 23 September; New Year's Day, 1 January; the day on which he first took up the consulship, 7 January (see also the calendar entries for these days in Section **C**). This arrangement ensures that these six men, who would not otherwise be liable for public expenditure because of not belonging to the town council, are obliged to act as the town's benefactors.

The first inscription suggests that the setting up of the altar was prompted at least partly by Augustus' intercession in legal disputes between the commoners of Narbo and the town's councillors.

The second inscription provides further evidence for the populist character of this altar, since the law of the altar of Diana on the Aventine at Rome is taken as its model. This temple of Diana had long been associated with plebeian interests, and it continued to have such connotations under Tiberius (see the enigmatic inscription about Sejanus, EJ 53 = LACTOR 8, no. 13).

L18   Augustus unimpressed by a 'miracle'

When the people of Tarraco reported that a palm tree had grown on an altar to him, Augustus replied, "That shows how often you light a fire there."

[Quintilian, *The Orator's Education*, 6.3.77]

Despite this dry response, the city of Tarraco (Tarragona, Spain) later minted coins showing the altar with its miraculous palm tree, pictured in Zanker, *Power of Images* (fig. 237).

L19   Bilingual dedication to Julia and Venus Genetrix, Lesbos

[Latin] To Julia, daughter of Caesar.   To Venus the Ancestress.

[Greek] To Julia, daughter of Caesar.   To Aphrodite the Ancestress.

[EJ 63 = *IG* XII.2 537]

This pair of similar bilingual inscriptions honoured Julia and Venus Genetrix in juxtaposition. It is unclear to what sort of monument they belonged originally since the inscriptions were found reused in a church on the Greek island of Lesbos (modern Lesvos).

Julia's son, Gaius Caesar, was identified as Ares in Athens (**M84**).

The **Ludi Saeculares** *(Centennial Games)* **(L20–L28)**

The *Ludi Saeculares* (Centennial Games) were celebrated to mark the beginning of a new era (or *saeculum*) every 110 years; their celebration in 17 BC was designed to usher in just such a new age. Augustus' Julian laws of the previous year promoting the family are conspicuously present in the background to the games: people otherwise barred from this sort of public occasion by the *lex Iulia de maritandis ordinibus* are specifically included, and Horace's hymn also alludes to these laws. The family is also emphasised by the prominent roles in the celebrations assigned to mothers of households, and to boys and girls with both parents living. Augustus' own family is mentioned by name in the prayers. The Ilithyiae, Deities of Childbirth, receive sacrifices. Alongside this emphasis upon the family, the games also stressed the divine favour enjoyed by the Roman people, and the expansion of Roman rule.

The games were authorised by the Sibylline books (whose guidance in performing the rituals is referred to in the inscription), which had recently been transferred from the temple of Jupiter Best and Greatest to that of Palatine Apollo, and were conducted under the auspices of the priestly college of the Fifteen in charge of sacrifices (which actually had at least 20 members), in accordance with senatorial directions, and also seemingly under instruction by a letter from Augustus himself. The fact that Augustus was not yet *pontifex maximus* must have influenced the decision to celebrate these games in such style, since, because they fell beyond the remit of the *pontifex maximus*, they allowed Augustus and Agrippa, as members of the priestly college of the Fifteen and holders of tribunician power, to take centre stage. Various sources combine to give us a very detailed picture of the festival: Censorinus was a Roman grammarian of the third century AD. His work *On the birthday* preserves much information from earlier sources about time and its divisions.

L20   Censorinus' definition of a *saeculum*

A *saeculum* is the longest span of human life from birth to death.

[Censorinus 17.2]

L21   A *saeculum* variously reckoned as 100 or 110 years

[17.7] Some people think that for the Romans a *saeculum* is marked by *ludi saeculares*. But even if these can be relied on, then the length of a Roman *saeculum* is uncertain. For the proper intervals of time after which those games should recur are unknown as regards the past, and it is not even known how long they should be. [17.8] They were established to occur every hundred years according to Antias and other historians; and Varro, in his first book about the origins of theatrical shows, wrote 'when there were many portents, and the wall and tower between the Colline and Esquiline Gates had been struck by lightning, the Board of Fifteen consulted the Sibylline books and announced that for three nights on the Campus Martius there should be Tarentine games in honour of Father Dis and Proserpina and that black animals should be sacrificed and that the games should happen every hundred years.' [17.9] Similarly, in book 136, Livy writes: 'in the same year, Caesar held *ludi saeculares* with great pomp: the custom is that these are held every hundred years to mark the end of a *saeculum*.' However both the writings of the Board of Fifteen and the edicts of the Deified Augustus seem to show they are repeated every hundred and ten years. This was how Horace in his song which was sung at the *ludi saeculares* denoted the time:

> So that the sure cycle of eleven decades
> May bring back the singing and the games,
> Thronged thrice in bright day, thrice
> In welcome night.

[17.10] This disagreement over the time shall be found to go back a long way if we look back over the annals of history.

[Censorinus 17.7–10]

Varro: the greatest of all Roman scholars, Marcus Terentius Varro (116–27 BC), wrote a huge range of works, most of them, including the one quoted here, lost.

Board of Fifteen: see **L1**, also Syme, *Augustan Aristocracy* pages 47–49.

Sibylline books: a collection of prophecies in Greek verse, traditionally consulted for advice in times of crisis. Augustus took steps to control possession of these books (see above, **L5**).

Horace: for the whole poem, see **L28**.

L22 The dates of the first five *ludi saeculares*

(This passage continues L21)

The first *ludi saeculares* were established after the expulsion of the kings by Valerius Publicola 245 years after the foundation of Rome (Antias gives the consuls as Publius Valerius and Spurius Lucretius); in the writings of the Board of Fifteen it was in 299 AUC, when Marcus Valerius and Spurius Verginius were consuls.

(Antias makes the second games) when Marcus Valerius Corvus and Gaius Poetilius were consuls, 408 years after the foundation of Rome, and indeed the writings of the Board of Fifteen make it in 410 AUC, when Gaius Marcius Rutilus and Titus Manlius Imperiosus were consuls.

The third games were, according to Antias and Livy, when Publius Claudius Pulcher and Lucius Iunius Pullus were consuls, in 505 AUC, but according to the writings of the Board of Fifteen in 518 AUC, when Publius Cornelius Lentulus and Gaius Licinius Varus were consuls.

[17.11] Three different opinions are found about the fourth games: Antias, Varro and Livy write that they were held when Lucius Marcius Censorinus and Manius Manilius were consuls, 605 years after the foundation of Rome, but Piso the Censor, Gnaeus Gellius, and also Cassius Hemina who was alive at that time state that it was three years later, when Gnaeus Cornelius Lentulus and Lucius Mummius were consuls, in 608 AUC. In the writings of the Board of Fifteen, the games are recorded in 628 AUC when Marcus Aemilius Lepidus and Lucius Aurelius Orestes were consuls.

The fifth were held by Caesar Augustus and Agrippa in 737 AUC when Gaius Furnius and Gaius Iunius Silanus were consuls.

[Censorinus 17.10 – 17.11]

Valerius Publicola: Valerius Maximus, writing under Tiberius, gives a story of the origin of the games (Valerius Maximus 2.4.5). A father's search for a cure for his three sick children led him to the discovery of an altar to Dis buried in the Campus Martius at an area known locally as Tarentum. Publicola apparently then publicly carried out the same rites as the father. This story is very difficult to reconcile with Varro's account, and the idea of *ludi saeculares* in around 509 BC is almost certainly a fiction designed to exalt the history of the games by linking them to Rome's first consul, Publicola.

AUC: Romans dated events in their history either by reference to the consuls of the year or by years *ab urbe condita* (from the foundation of the city: so, in our scheme, 1 AUC = 753 BC). All dates in this passage are given under the Roman system. Their equivalents are given in the table below.

Third games: Zosimus (see **L23**) gives an account of the reasons for these games and dates them to 502 AUC = 252 BC.

Fourth games: these are the only games to be roughly datable with any certainty. Livy, *Summary* 49 notes the celebration of these games in 605 AUC = 149 BC, one hundred years after the previous games. The combined evidence of 3 contemporary historians, including L. Calpurnius Piso Frugi (tribune 149 BC, consul 133 BC) should suffice to make the dates given (149 or 146 BC) accurate, at least to within a few years. The consequence was that the next games should have been held in Octavian's youth (around the 40's or early 30's BC); for Augustus to be able to celebrate them at any point (even in his long reign) required imaginative arithmetic and a creative approach to historical tradition.

737 AUC: it seems strange that Augustus did not celebrate the games a year later in 738 AUC = 16 BC, which would have been an exact 110 years since the official date of the previous games (see table below).

The dates given by Censorinus for the five *ludi saeculares* may be tabulated as follows. In each case the dates given by historians (Antias, Livy, Varro etc.) are given in one column, while those given by the Board of Fifteen appear in another. The *saeculum* figure represents the number of years since the previous games reported by the respective sources.

Ludi Saeculares	Historians		Board of Fifteen	
	Date of Games	*Saeculum*	**Date of Games**	*Saeculum*
1	245 AUC = 509 BC	–	299 AUC = 455 BC	–
2	408 AUC = 346 BC	163 years	410 AUC = 344 BC	111 years
3	505 AUC = 249 BC	97 years	518 AUC = 236 BC	108 years
4	605/8 AUC = 149/6 BC	100/103 years	628 AUC = 126 BC	110 years
5	737 AUC = 17 BC	132/129 years	737 AUC = 17 BC	109 years

Zosimus on the *ludi saeculares*

Zosimus was a pagan Greek historian who wrote a history of the Roman Empire from Augustus to AD 410. His source for this digression on the *ludi saeculares* was a work *On the Long-Lived* by Phlegon of Tralles, a freedman of the emperor Hadrian, whose work also preserves the Sibylline oracle quoted by Zosimus.

L23   Augustus' revival of the *ludi saeculares*

[1] After this, in the 502nd year from the foundation of the city, when wars and pestilence had been raging, the senate decided to seek an escape from such afflictions by resort to the Sibylline Oracles. So they instructed the Board of Ten appointed for this purpose to consult the oracles. The prophecies indicated that the evils would cease if they sacrificed to Hades and Persephone, and once they had sought from them also the proper location, sacrifices were offered to Hades and Persephone as instructed … during the fourth consulship of Marcus Popilius. [2] Once the ceremonies were over and they had achieved release from the afflictions which threatened them, they once again buried the altar, which stood in a remote corner of the Campus Martius. This particular ceremony fell into disuse for a time, but after suffering a number of setbacks Octavius Augustus revived the festival, whose last celebration had occurred during the consulship of Lucius Censorinus and Marcus Manilius. Ateius Capito gave a detailed exposition of the rites and the times when the sacrifice should be held and the procession organised, as laid down by the researches of the Board of Fifteen charged with the preservation of the Sibylline Oracles.

[Zosimus 2.4.1–2]

502nd year: this date would be 252 BC.
Hades and Persephone: Zosimus, writing in Greek, gives the Greek version of names of gods.
fourth consulship of Marcus Popilius: this was in 348 BC.
Ateius Capito: a prominent lawyer, see **T21**.

L24   Zosimus' description of the *ludi saeculares*

[1] I shall now give an approximate description of the form taken by the festival. Heralds go about the city summoning all to witness the spectacle, which they have never seen before and will never see again. During the summer season, a little before the start of the ceremonies, the Board of Fifteen take their seats upon a platform set up on the Capitol and in the temple on the Palatine and distribute to the people symbols of purification: these consist of torches together with sulphur and bitumen. Slaves may not participate in this ritual, only free men. [2] When all the people have gathered both

at the stipulated locations and also in the temple of Artemis built on the Aventine Hill, each man brings an offering of corn, barley and beans. Then in honour of the Fates they celebrate an all-night festival with due solemnity for […] nights. When the time of the festival arrives, which is celebrated for three days and three nights on the Campus Martius, they dedicate their offerings on the banks of the river Tiber in the Tarentum district. They make their sacrifices to the gods Zeus, Hera, Apollo, Leto, and Artemis, and also to the Fates, the Ilithyiae (goddesses of childbirth), Demeter, Hades, and Persephone. [3] On the first night of the festival at the second hour on three altars set up on the banks of the river the Emperor, assisted by the Board of Fifteen, sacrifices three lambs. Having sprinkled the altars with their blood, he offers them as a burnt sacrifice. Elsewhere, they set up a kind of theatrical stage set, and there they light torches and fires, a newly commissioned hymn is chanted, and sacred ceremonies conducted. [4] Those conducting these ceremonies are rewarded with the first-fruits of the crops, corn, barley, and beans, which – as I have explained – have already been distributed among the whole populace. On the next day they go up to the Capitol and once they have conducted the traditional sacrifices there, they proceed to the prepared theatre. There they conduct ceremonies in honour of Apollo and Artemis. On the following morning, at the hour laid down by the oracle, leading Roman matrons gather on the Capitol and offer prayers and sing hymns to the god, as the ritual requires. [5] On the third day in the temple of Apollo on the Palatine twenty-seven young men of noble birth together with the same number of maidens, all of excellent standing (defined as having both parents still alive), sing hymns and paeans in both Greek and Latin for the safety of all cities under Roman rule. Other ceremonies are also conducted in accordance with the divine ordinances and for as long as these continue to be celebrated the Roman Empire will endure unharmed.

[Zosimus 2.5.1–5]

[1]   *Heralds*: portrayed on coinage of 17 BC (see Zanker, *Power of Images*, fig. 132b). Suetonius (*Claudius* 21.2) tells us that when Claudius, under a different reckoning, gave Centennial Games in AD 47, only 63 years after Augustus' games, the solemn invitation of the herald to 'games which no-one has ever seen before or will ever see again' was greeted with derision.
      distribute…symbols of purification: portrayed on coinage of 16 BC (see **L26**). The inscribed edict, lines 29–36 (**L27e**), confirms the Capitol and Palatine as the location for ritual purification.

[2]   *temple of Artemis*: The edict, lines 29–36 (**L27e**), mentions corn being offered at the Temple of Diana on the Aventine.

L25   The Sibylline oracles concerning the *ludi saeculares*

(This passage continues L24)

In order to ensure that we can realise the truth of all the activities I have recorded, I shall set out the Sibyl's oracles, which have already been reported to me by other sources.

[6.1]   But whensoe'er the longest span of life for mortal man
         Comes round again, accomplishing a cycle of one hundred years
         And ten, remember then, O Roman, nor ever let it slip your memory,
         Remember all these things: to the immortal gods make sacrifice
         Upon the plain beside the mighty waters of the Tiber, there   5
         Where the channel is most narrow, when night spreads o'er the earth
         And sun has veiled his light, there make your sacrifice of lambs and goats
         With fleece of darkened hue unto the Fates, the sources of all life;

Conciliate with sacrifices, too, the Ilithyiae, goddesses of childbirth,
As heaven's law demands; then to the Earth let there be sacrificed   10
A sow, black, and full pregnant with her young. Let there be brought
Unto the altars of great Jupiter bulls of the purest white in their entirety,
By day and not by night, since for the gods of heaven it is the day
That is the right and proper time to offer up a sacrifice. So must you
Also sacrifice by day. Then from your hands let Juno's shrine receive   15
The finest carcass of a heifer. Phoebus Apollo, too, Latona's son,
Whom otherwise men call The Sun, let him receive like offerings as these.
Let Latin hymns be sung by boys and girls to fill the Immortals' shrine.
Separately let maidens constitute a choir, separately the boys, the flower
Of burgeoning manhood – but all must of living parents be the offspring,   20
All must be scions of the loftiest lineage. Those that upon this day
Are bound in marriage, let them at Juno's far-famed altar
Take their place and on their knees make supplication to her divinity.
Then to each man and woman, women especially, let there be given
Perfumes to purge away their sins. Let all bring forth from their homes   25
Whatever it is right for mortal men to offer to the gods as first-fruits
From their own source of livelihood, gifts of propitiation to the kindly gods
And to all the blessed ones, offspring of Uranus. Let all such offerings
Remain in that place, piled up as treasure, that from their store
For men and women seated in that spot you may make due provision.   30
Constantly, day and night, tight-packed let mighty crowds assemble
Close to the thrones reserved there for the gods. Let them commingle
Earnest prayer with laughter. All these things remember for ever
And store up in your heart all these ordinances. Then shall this land,
The land of Italy and all its peoples too, accept upon their necks   35
Thy yoke, and live beneath thy sway for ever more.

[Zosimus 2.5.5 – 2.6.1]

L26 Augustus distributes *suffimenta* for the *ludi saeculares, aureus,* 16 BC

Obv.:   Head of Augustus right, wearing laurel wreath.
IMP CAESAR TR POT IIX (Imperator Caesar, eighth year of the tribunician
power)

Rev.:   Augustus, wearing toga and seated on stool resting on a platform, distributes *suffimenta* taken from
a box at his feet to two figures standing before him, also in togas.
L MESCINIVS (name of moneyer), LVD S on platform (Centennial Games), AVG
SVF P below (Augustus gave *suffimenta* to the People)

[*BMC* Augustus 85]

Augustus is depicted distributing *suffimenta,* purificatory incense-cakes made from sulphur and tar, to the people, represented here by two figures properly attired as citizens in their togas. The distribution of *suffimenta* by the Fifteen is mentioned by Zosimus (**L24**) and by the official inscription (**L27e, L27i**) This scene stresses Augustus' religious piety and his personal involvement in the proceedings.

Ludi saeculares inscriptions (L27a – L27t)

We have a dossier of documents relating to the production of the Centennial Games in 17 BC, preserved as fragments of a tall marble inscription (c.4m. high), substantial chunks of which were found beside the Tiber, probably near the place (the sanctuary known as the Tarentum) where it was originally displayed, and where the core rites were celebrated. It is presumably the marble *stele* prescribed by the Senate in its decree (**L27h**). It contains a degree of repetition since it first of all sets out how the celebrations are to be performed, and then records how they have duly been performed. Two fragments were published only in 1985.

L27a   Senatorial decrees of 18 and 17 BC concerning the *ludi saeculares*

………….. [Seeing as Publius Lentulus and Gnaeus Lentulus,] consuls, raised the matter of the allocation of money for the Centennial Games, about which a decree had recently been passed that they should be held [in the following year], seeing as they asked them what they wished to be done concerning this matter, they decreed on this matter as follows: since it is not found in the ancient books for how much money [we] are accustomed [to award the contract for] the Centennial [Games], let it be based for the Fifteen in charge of sacrifices upon the sum which has been established by way of funding for the colleges of priests and recently [for the augurs for the games] which they performed on behalf of Caesar's welfare, so that the consuls instruct the praetors in charge of the treasury that they see to the giving and allocation of that money.

[In the following] year, in the consulship of Gaius Silanus and Gaius Furnius, on 17 February, a senatorial decree was passed that the things which [are] necessary [for] the centennial sacrifice should be contracted according to the words which have been written below.

[On 17 February in the] Julian [senate house]. The following were present at the drafting: Marcus Junius Silanus son of Marcus, of the Sabatine tribe, Gnaeus Cornelius Lentulus [son of Lucius]……….. –rinus, Gaius Asinius Pollio, son of Gnaeus, of the Arnensis tribe, Lucius Vinicius [son of ?, of the Poblilia tribe]…….. the Centennial Games……..

[*AE* 1988.20]

L27b   Senatorial decree; prayer by the Fifteen; ?letter from Augustus.

Seventeen lines of text too fragmentary to translate, but sufficient for the following summary:

Four lines of a fragmentary decree deal with the financing of the games. It is followed by a prayer of the Fifteen, led by Augustus, to all the immortal gods, including by name Apollo, Latona, Diana, Hercules, and Jupiter the Stayer. The Capitoline triad of Jupiter, Juno and Minerva presumably headed this list, although their names are not preserved. The prayer, ten lines long, appears to request success at home and abroad for the Roman people. The last three lines of this fragment contain another document, perhaps part of the instructions, which follow.

[*AE* 1988.21]

L27c   Instructions setting out how the celebrations should be carried out, (?between 17 February and 24 March)

Twenty-three lines of fragmentary text, summarised as follows:

The Fifteen are instructed how to celebrate the games. This includes details of what activities are to be performed by whom, where, and on what days. The fragmentary details (mentioning, for example, offerings, sacrifices, and the centennial hymn) correspond to the much better preserved record of the celebrations which follows later.

[*CIL* VI 32323, lines 1–23]

L27d   Edict of the Fifteen, ?24 March

On the same day an edict was enacted with the following words: [how the citizens ought to celebrate] the centennial sacrifice and games which [recur in the 110th year, about this matter] which [we openly proclaimed] in a public assembly according to our ancestors' custom and precedent, [......] so that, if anyone had been absent from the public assembly or had not [understood] properly, they might learn what each of them [ought to do] and on what day.

[*CIL* VI 32323, lines 24–28]

L27e   Discussion and edict of the Fifteen on purification and offerings, ?between 18 February and 24 March

Under the same consuls, and the same officials of the Fifteen in charge of sacrifices, [the matter was brought] to the college .... that means of purification be given and corn be received, that the college.... [decides that on the Capitol in front of the temple of] greatest [Jupiter] and in front of the temple of Jupiter the Thunderer and [... on the Palatine in front of the temple] of Apollo and in its portico, and that corn [should be received] in the places [specified above and at the temple of Diana on the Aventine and] in its portico ...Moreover they decreed that to individuals at the platforms [the Fifteen...] they should receive two portions of corn each and also ...[...] they should all assemble then ...

[*CIL* VI 32323, lines 29–36]

L27f   Two edicts of the Fifteen, 25 March

Under the same consuls on 25 March in front of the temple [...] concerning this matter the following action was decided upon [...]

Games, festivals, and ritual banquets throughout [three nights and the same number of days... which] have been decreed [by] the college, these [will be celebrated... from the night] on which the day dawns 1 June... to 3 June because each ...

Also concerning this matter it was decided that [...] M. Agrippa, L. Censorinus [...] M. Lollius, L. Arruntius [...] the edict was enacted [...]

So that with less trouble [...] 28 May materials for fumigation [...] 29 or 30 or [31 May...]

[*CIL* VI 32323, lines 37–49]

L27g   Senatorial decrees on spectators at the Centennial Games, 23 May

On 23 May in the [Julian] enclosure [... the following were present at the drafting....] Aemilius Lepidus, Lucius Cestius, Lucius Petronius Rufus [....]

Seeing as Gaius Silanus, consul, made this statement: the Centennial Games after many [years] will occur [in the current year, through the agency of Imperator Caesar] Augustus and Marcus Agrippa, holders of tribunician power; [because it is agreed that as many people as possible watch] these games on account of religion and also because [no one will be present a second time] at such a spectacle, [it seems right ... that it is to be permitted] for those who are not yet married [to attend with impunity on the days of these games. Seeing as he asked them what they wished to be done concerning this matter, they decreed on this matter as follows: that, since those games] have been established for the sake of religion, and since no mortal [is permitted to watch them] more than once, it is to be permitted to those who [are subject to] the law on the marrying [of the orders] to watch with impunity [...the games] that the Fifteen in charge of sacrifices exhibit.

[*CIL* VI 32323, lines 50–57]

L27h   Senatorial decrees on public record of the Centennial Games, 23 May

On the same day, in the same place, the same men were present at the drafting, and a senatorial decree was passed.

Seeing as Gaius Silanus, consul, made this statement: it is conducive towards preserving the memory of such a great [religious ceremony that a public record of the] Centennial [Games] be inscribed upon a bronze pillar and one of marble, [and both set up for the future memory of the event] in that place, where the games are to be held. Seeing as he asked them what they wished to be done concerning this matter, they decreed on this matter as follows: that either or both consuls [are to set up] for the [future memory of the event one pillar] of bronze and another of marble, on which a public record [of these games has been inscribed, in that place, and that the same men] are to contract out this task and give instructions to the praetors in charge of the [treasury, to pay] the contractors the [amount for which the contract is made].

[*CIL* VI 32323, lines 58–63 = EJ 30A–B]

L27i   Edict of the Fifteen, 24 May

Another considerably damaged part of the inscription, which can be summarised as follows:

The Fifteen issue an edict concerning the distribution of materials for purificatory fumigation apparently to all citizens and their wives on 26–28 May, prior to their participation in various ceremonies on the Capitol; the edict then deals with the involvement of women in holding ritual banquets also on the Capitol, and their ritual fumigation; a specific role is assigned to the mothers of households on 29 and 30 May. They announce their intention to hold centennial Latin games on 1 June during the night, and arrange for the involvement of trumpeters in the ceremonies, seemingly to draw people's attention to what is happening.

[*CIL* VI 32323, lines 64–89]

(At roughly this point, the inscription shifts to recording what actually happened)

L27j   Night of 31 May: Augustus sacrifices to the Fates

[90] On the following night on the field by the Tiber [Imperator Caesar Augustus sacrificed nine ewe-lambs to the Fates] consumed whole according to the Argive rite, and in the same [rite nine nanny-goats, and he prayed as follows:]

"Fates! As [is written] with regard to you in those books, [accordingly so that anything and everything may be better for the Roman people, the Quirites, to you let there be a sacrifice with nine] ewe-lambs and nine nanny-goats: [I ask and pray that you increase the authority and majesty of the Roman people, the Quirites] in war and at home; [that the Latin name always remain subject, and that you bestow everlasting safety,] victory, and good health [on the Roman people, the Quirites; that you favour the Roman people, the Quirites, and the legions of the Roman people, the Quirites; that you keep safe the] state of the Roman people, the Quirites; [that you be] willingly [well-disposed to the Roman people,] the Quirites, to the college of the Fifteen, [to me, my family and household, and that] you accept [this] sacrifice of nine ewe-lambs and nine [nanny-]goats to be sacrificed whole: in accordance with these things, be honoured with this ewe-lamb, and become willingly well-disposed to the Roman people, the Quirites, to the college of the Fifteen, to me, my family and household."

[*CIL* VI 32323, lines 90–99]

L27k   Night of 31 May: theatrical shows and sacred banquets

[100] Once the sacrifice had been completed, games at night were begun on a stage to which there was no theatre attached and no seats set up, and 110 married women, to

whom notice had been given by an announcement of the Fifteen, held a ritual banquet, with two seats set up for Juno and Diana.

[*CIL* VI 32323, lines 100–102]

L27l 1 June: Augustus and Agrippa sacrifice to Jupiter

On 1 June, on the Capitol, Imperator Caesar Augustus sacrificed a suitable bull to Jupiter Best and Greatest, and at the same place Marcus Agrippa sacrificed a second, and then they prayed as follows:

"Jupiter Best and Greatest! As is written with regard to you in those books, [accordingly] so that anything and everything may be better for the Roman people, the Quirites, to you let there be a sacrifice with this fine bull: I ask and pray you; the rest as above."

At the *atalla* were present Caesar, Agrippa, Scaevola, Sentius, Lollius, Asinius Gallus, Rebilus.

[*CIL* VI 32323, lines 103–107]

L27m 1 June: games and sacred banquets; edict suspending mourning

Then the Latin games were begun in the wooden theatre, which had been set up on the field next to the Tiber, and in the same way the mothers of households held a ritual banquet, nor were those games interrupted which had begun by night; and an edict was published.

[110] The Fifteen in charge of sacrifices proclaim:

"Since, in accordance with custom that is sound and likewise observed by frequent examples, whenever there has been a rightful reason for public joy, it has been resolved that the mourning-period of married women be reduced, and that this be revived and carefully observed at the time of rites and games that are so solemn seems to be conducive both to the gods' honour and to the memory of their worship: we have decided that it is our duty to give notice to women by an edict to reduce their mourning-period."

[*CIL* VI 32323, lines 108–114]

L27n Night of 1 June: Augustus sacrifices and prays to the Goddesses of Childbirth

Then at night by the Tiber, Imperator Caesar Augustus performed a sacrifice to the *Ilithyiae* (Goddesses of Childbirth) with nine pancakes, nine round-cakes, and nine Greek-style cakes; he prayed as follows:

"*Ilithyia* (Goddess of Childbirth)! As is written with regard to you in those books, [accordingly so that anything] and everything [may be better] for the Roman people, the Quirites, to you let there be a sacrifice with nine pancakes, nine round-cakes, and nine Greek-style cakes: I ask [and pray you; the rest as above].'

[*CIL* VI 32323, lines 115–118]

L27o 2 June: Agrippa sacrifices to Juno; mothers pray to Juno

On 2 June, on the Capitol, Marcus Agrippa sacrificed a cow to queen Juno [according to the Argive rite?] and he prayed as follows:

[121] "Queen Juno! As is written with regard to you in those books, [accordingly so that anything] and everything [may be better for the Roman people, the Quirites,] to you let there be a sacrifice with a fine cow: I ask and pray you; [the rest as above].

Then to the 110 married mothers of households, to whom notice [had been given ..., Marcus Agrippa?] dictated with these words:

"Queen Juno, if whatever there is which [may be better for the Roman people, the Quirites ...] married [mothers of households] resting on their knees [pray that] you... [increase the authority] and majesty of the Roman people, the Quirites, [in war and at home; that the Latin name always remain subject, and that you bestow] everlasting [safety,] victory, [and good health on the Roman people, the Quirites; that you favour the Roman people, the Quirites, and the legions of the Roman people,] the Quirites; [that you keep safe] the state [of the Roman people, the Quirites; that you be willingly well-disposed to the Roman people,] the Quirites, to the college of the Fifteen, to us, [our families and households. These things we, 110] married [mothers of households of the Roman people,] the Quirites, [resting] on our knees [ask and pray.]"

[132] At the *atalla* were present Marcus Agrippa [.............]

[*CIL* VI 32323, lines 119–132]

L27p   Games, night-time sacrifices and sacred banquet

Games, as on the previous day, were performed.[...?]

Then, at night by the Tiber, Caesar Augustus [sacrificed a pregnant sow... to Mother Earth] and he prayed [as follows]:

"Mother Earth! As [is written] with regard to you in those [books, accordingly so that anything and everything may be better for the Roman people, the Quirites, let there be a sacrifice] to you of a suitable pregnant sow: [I ask and pray you;] the rest [as above]."

The married women held a ritual banquet [on this day in the same way as on the previous day.]

[*CIL* VI 32323, lines 133–138]

L27q   3 June: Augustus and Agrippa sacrifice to Apollo and Diana

On 3 June, on the Palatine, Imperator Caesar Augustus and Marcus Agrippa performed a sacrifice [to Apollo and Diana] with [nine pancakes], nine round-cakes, and nine Greek-style cakes, and they prayed as follows:

[141] "Apollo! As is written with regard to you in those books, accordingly so that anything and everything may be better for the Roman people, the Quirites, to you let there be a sacrifice with nine round-cakes, nine pancakes, and nine Greek-style cakes: I ask and pray you; the rest as above."

"Apollo, as I have prayed to you with the gift of round-cakes and with a fitting prayer, accordingly with this, be honoured with these cakes on offer, become willingly well-disposed."

The same for the Greek-style cakes.

With the same words, Diana.

[*CIL* VI 32323, lines 139–146]

L27r   3 June: Horace's hymn sung

Once the sacrifice had been performed, 27 boys, with fathers and mothers living, to whom notice had been given, and the same number of girls sang the hymn; in the same way on the Capitol.

Quintus Horatius Flaccus composed the hymn.

[150] The Fifteen were present: Imperator Caesar, Marcus Agrippa, Quintus Lepidus, Potitus Messalla, Gaius Stolo, Gaius Scaevola, Gaius Sosius, Gaius Norbanus, Marcus Cocceius, Marcus Lollius, Gaius Sentius, Marcus Strigo, Lucius

Arruntius, Gaius Asinius, Marcus Marcellus, Decimus Laelius, Quintus Tubero, Gaius Rebilus, Messalla Messallinus.

[*CIL* VI 32323, lines 147–152]

L27s   3 June: Games, chariot-races take place; additional shows promised

Once the stage-games had been completed ... next to that place, where the sacrifice had been performed on earlier nights and where a theatre and stage were put in place, turning-posts were set up and chariots were started off and Potitus Messalla sent out acrobat-riders. An edict was published as follows:

The Fifteen in charge of sacrifices proclaim:

"The games, which, lasting seven days, we have added at our expense to the solemn games, we begin on 5 June in the form of Latin games in the wooden theatre which is by the Tiber at the 2nd hour, Greek musical games in the theatre of Pompey at the 3rd hour, and Greek city-games in the theatre [which is] in the circus Flaminius at the 4th hour."

[*CIL* VI 32323, lines 153–158]

L27t   5–12 June: additional games held

After a day's break, which was 4 [June ....,] on 5 June, [Latin] games were begun [..... in] the wooden theatre, Greek musical games [in Pompey's theatre, and Greek city-games in the theatre which is in the circus Flaminius.]

[162] On 11 June an edict was published [as follows: the Fifteen in charge of sacrifices proclaim:] "On 12 June we will present a beast hunt [.......]"

On 12 June, in an exhibition procession boys [.....], Marcus Agrippa [sent out] chariots [....]

[*CIL* VI 32323, lines 159–165]

L27u   Conclusion

All these things were accomplished by the Fifteen [in charge of sacrifices: Imperator Caesar Augustus, Marcus Agrippa...] Gnaeus Pompeius, Gaius Stolo, Gaius S[....]{name erased ?Gaius Asinius Gallus}, Marcus Marcellus....

[*CIL* VI 32323, lines 166–168]

The celebration combined elements old and new: the prayer to subject the Latin name alludes to Rome's early expansion into Latium; important novelties are the way in which the Palatine triad (Apollo, Diana, and Latona) are presented as parallel to the traditional Capitoline triad of Jupiter, Juno, and Minerva, and the emphasis upon family and fertility.

We can see how the Fifteen are concerned to secure the involvement of as many of the citizen populace as possible in the ceremonies, both actively in being purified and making offerings, and also as spectators of the shows. The central rituals of the festival were sacrifices to deities on the Field of Mars next to the Tiber, in a place known as 'Tarentum', where there was a sanctuary to the gods of the underworld, and ritual banquets by 110 married women. These rituals, lasting three nights and days, were markedly archaic and Greek in tone. After these celebrations, various spectacles were performed, such as the singing of Horace's Centennial Hymn by a chorus of children in honour of the Capitoline and Palatine triads, and different types of shows in various theatres, including the new theatre of Marcellus (here called the theatre in the Circus Flaminius, not yet officially dedicated). Finally, the Fifteen paid for an extra seven days of further spectacles, including Latin and Greek shows, a beast hunt, chariot-racing, and a procession of boys (probably the 'Troy Games').

The language used is very precise (such as distinguishing between three different kinds of cake-offerings), often archaic, and sometimes unparalleled, for example the word *atalla* – perhaps a type of sacrificial bowl). Bibliography: M. Beard, J. North, S. Price, *Religions of Rome* I (CUP 1998) 201–6; D. Feeney, *Literature and Religion at Rome* (CUP 1998) 28–38: The whole text is collated and re-edited in B. Schnegg-Köhler,

Die augusteischen Säkularspiele (Munich 2002). Syme, *Augustan Aristocracy* 48–49 gives brief notes on the quindecimvirs.

L28 Horace, *Carmen Saeculare* (Centennial Hymn)

Horace's poem was written for performance during the *Ludi Saeculares* (Centennial Games) by a chorus of 27 boys and 27 girls. The festival was created and presented as a celebration of Augustus' setting of Rome to rights, and of his ushering in of a new age (see note on page 266), and this is duly reflected in Horace's poem. Particular achievements commemorated include the marriage law and foreign triumphs, especially the Parthian settlement of 20 BC. The whole games placed Augustus at centre stage of state religion, though he ostentatiously refused to become *pontifex maximus* until 12 BC (RG 10). Indeed it is no coincidence that these games were celebrated at this time (see **L21–L23** for evident fabrication of the date) since they did not fall under the remit of the *pontifex maximus*, but of the college of quindecemvirs of which Augustus was president. The hymn, performed in the vicinity of Augustus' home on the Palatine, at Apollo's temple, similarly places Augustus at the centre of state religion, giving the greatest prominence to Apollo and his twin sister, Diana. By comparison, the Capitoline triad (Jupiter, Juno, Minerva) is mentioned less frequently and less explicitly (and see note on line 5, below).

> Phoebus and thou, Diana, ruler of the woods,
> Bright glory of heaven, for ever worshipped and
> To be worshipped, grant us our supplications
>   At this holy time,
>
> When the Sibylline verses commanded   5
> That chosen maidens and innocent boys should chant
> To the gods who delight in Rome's seven hills
>   A hymn of praise.
>
> Bountiful Sun, who in your gleaming chariot send forth
> The day and conceal it, and are daily re-born, unchanging   10
> Yet ever new, may you behold nothing greater than
>   The City of Rome.
>
> Gently bringing on childbirth aright in fullness
> Of time, Ilithyia, protect mothers, whether
> You choose to be honoured as Lucina   15
>   Or as Genitalis.
>
> Goddess, grant to us offspring and prosper
> The Fathers' decrees on women's wedlock,
> Prosper the marriage law, that it may be
>   Fruitful of children,   20
>
> So that the sure cycle of eleven decades
> May bring back the singing and the games,
> Thronged thrice in bright day, thrice
>   In welcome night.
>
> You Fates, ever truthful to tell what has once   25
> Been ordained – and may the fixed bound of events
> Confirm it – add to our blessings already received
>   A destiny blessed.
>
> Prolific in crops and herds, may the Earth
> Grant Ceres her wheaten crown.   30
> May the rains and Jupiter's breezes bring
>   Nurture to the new-born.

Lay your arrows aside, O kindly and gentle Apollo,
And hearken now to the suppliant boys;
O twin-horned queen of the stars, Moon,   35
    Hear the girls.

If Rome is your work, if through you the Trojan squadrons
Gained the Etruscan shore, as a remnant
Commanded to move their homes and city as the course
    To salvation;   40

If for them, unscathed through the conflagration of Troy,
Chaste Aeneas, his country's survivor, built
The path to freedom, destined to give them more than
    They had left behind,

Then, O Gods, grant virtuous ways to youth ready to   45
Learn and tranquillity to gentle elders, and, Gods,
Grant to Romulus' people, prosperity, posterity
    And every glory,

And fulfil whatever by sacrifice of white oxen
He entreats, the glorious offspring of Anchises   50
And Venus, vanquisher of those who take up arms,
    Mild to the fallen foe.

Now the Mede fears the forces strong by land
And sea and the Alban axes; now
The Scythians, so recently arrogant, and the Indians   55
    Seek responses.

Now Faith, Peace, Honour, old-fashioned Modesty,
And Virtue so long neglected dare to return,
And now once more appears blest Plenty
    With horn overflowing.   60

Phoebus, the seer, resplendent with his
Gleaming bow, and beloved of the Muses
Nine, whose health-giving art relieves the
    Body's weary limbs –

If he beholds with favour the Palatine's altars,   65
Then he prolongs the Roman state and happy
Latium for another cycle and an ever
    More blessed age.

And Diana, who holds the Aventine and the Algidus,
Pays heed to the prayers of the fifteen men   70
And to the supplications of these boys turns
    Kindly ears.

Homeward we bear this our sure and certain hope
That such is Jupiter's will, the will of all gods,
We, a chorus, skilled to proclaim the praises   75
    Of Phoebus and Diana.

1 The hymn begins and ends with Phoebus Apollo and Diana, the twin children of Latona. Apollo was the god perhaps most closely associated with Augustus, appropriated to celebrate his victory at Actium (the site of a temple to Apollo, extended by Augustus after his victory: **H9–11**). The hymn was first sung on the Palatine at the Temple of Apollo (**K37–38**) which was next to Augustus' own house, and only then was repeated on the Capitol, the traditional centre of Roman religion. Diana is regularly worshipped in conjunction with her twin brother, as well as in her own right, as, for example in the Homeric *Hymn to Apollo* 3.15; at Pompeii, where the temple to Apollo contained paired statues of both; and on the Palatine as part of the temple of Apollo, see **J7, K37b, K38, K74**.

5 *Sibylline verses*: see **L25**. Augustus edited these ancient and important texts and transferred them from the Capitol to gilded cases under the pedestal of Apollo's statue in the Palatine temple (Suet. *Aug*. 31.1, wrongly connecting it with Augustus becoming *pontifex maximus* in 12 BC, since the transfer is referred to by Virgil (died 19 BC), *Aeneid* 6.69–71 = **K37b** in Addenda, page 415).

13 *Ilithyia*: goddess of childbirth. Augustus sacrificed to her on the night of June 1, see **L27n**. Her prominence reflects Augustan concern with family values, but also the fact that, at the time of the games, Julia was heavily pregnant with Lucius Caesar, adopted by Augustus, together with Gaius, later in the year.

17–20 Horace refers to Augustus' marriage law, the *Lex Iulia de maritandis ordinibus* carried through the assembly by Augustus with the senate's approval in 18 BC (see note on page 354–5).

21 *Eleven decades*: see Censorinus, **L21** above, quoting this verse.

25 *Fates*: sacrifices to the Fates began the festival (**L27j**).

28–31 A representation of this theme is depicted on the East side of the Altar of Augustan Peace (see Zanker 172–6: 'the stanza … reads like a poetic paraphrase of the relief'). Compare also Horace, *Epistles* 1.12.28–9 (**G34**), published a couple of years before.

41–8 The story of Aeneas' founding of Rome was of great interest to writers of the Augustan age, told by Livy (1.1–2), Dionysius of Halicarnassus, as well as in Virgil's *Aeneid*.

42 chaste: Horace avoids Virgil's usual description of Aeneas as '*pius*', using instead '*castus*'.

49 *White oxen*: the inscriptions show that only Jupiter and Juno received sacrifice of oxen during the festival (**L27l, L27o**). Thus the gods invoked in lines 45–6, and the 'you' of line 37, though not explicitly named, are the king and queen of the gods.

50–1 *Offspring of Anchises and Venus*: Augustus.

51–2 *Vanquisher ... mild ...*: cf. **RG** 3.2; Virgil, *Aeneid* 6.853.

53–6 Horace refers to the Parthian (= Median) settlement of 20 BC (lines 53–4), also celebrated on a contemporary gold coin (**K14**), and the reception of embassies from the remote Scythians and Indians (see **N1, N39–40** and in *Aeneid* 6.795–800 = **G37**).

54 *Alban axes*: the axes included in the *fasces* outside Rome, and so a symbol of Roman power (see on Virgil, *Aeneid* 6.818); 'Alban' stands for Roman, by virtue of Rome's supposed foundation from Alba Longa.

59 *Plenty*: a cornucopia (horn of plenty) also appears on a contemporary gold coin (**L8**)

69 *Aventine ... Algidus*: Diana had temples on the Aventine Hill in Rome (rebuilt by Lucius Cornificius, supporter of Octavian and consul 35 BC – Suet. *Aug*. 29.1) and at Algidus, the east end of the Alban Hills south of Rome.

SECTION M

THE ADMINISTRATION OF EMPIRE

General description (M1–M5)

M1   Administration greater than conquest

When he was told that Alexander had completed most of his conquests by the age of thirty-two and had no idea what he was to do with the rest of his life, Augustus remarked how surprised he was that Alexander did not think that the administration of his empire was a greater task than its mere conquest.

[Plutarch, *Sayings of Kings and Commanders, Moralia* 207.8]

Alexander died at 33: Octavian was 32 when he entered Alexandria, ending the civil war.

M2   Imperial/Public provinces

Government of the provinces has been apportioned in different ways at different times. Current arrangements are those laid down by Caesar Augustus. For when his country entrusted him with the pre-eminent position in its governance and he became supreme ruler for life in war and in peace, he divided the whole empire into two parts. One he assigned to himself, the other to the people of Rome. For himself he took all those areas that still needed a military garrison – in effect those that were barbaric, or bordering on tribes not yet brought to heel, or infertile and difficult to cultivate and therefore inevitably prone to break loose and revolt, because whatever else they lack there is never a shortage of military strongholds. All the rest he assigned to the Roman people – all those that were peaceful or easily manageable without recourse to arms. Each of the two parts he divided into a number of provinces, designated 'Caesar's' or 'the People's.' To his own provinces Caesar despatches legates and procurators, settling the provincial boundaries and organising their administration in different ways at different times according to circumstances; to their provinces the People send out either praetors or proconsuls, and these too are variously divided according to the requirements of the moment.

To begin with Caesar organised the People's domain by creating two consular provinces: first, Libya, or as much of it as was under Roman control and outside the realm of Juba originally, and now of his son, Ptolemy; secondly, Asia, consisting of all the territory lying this side of the river Halys, and the Taurus mountains, apart from Galatia and the tribes formerly ruled by Amyntas, together with Bithynia and the Propontis. He then established ten praetorial provinces: in Europe and its neighbouring islands there were Further Spain (so called), the area around the rivers Baetis and Anas; Narbonitis, in Gallia Celtica; thirdly, Sardo and Cyrnus (Sardinia and Corsica); then, fourth, Sicily; fifth, Illyria, as far as Epirus, and sixth, Macedonia; seventh, Achaea, as far as Thessaly, Aetolia, Acarnania, and some of the Epirote tribes along the borders of Macedonia; eighth, Crete, together with Cyrenaica; ninth, Cyprus; and tenth, Bithynia, together with the Propontis and certain parts of Pontus.

All the other provinces are Caesar's. To some of them he sends out as governors men of consular rank, to others praetorians, and to some equestrians. Kings, dynasts, and decarchs are all part of Caesar's portion – and always have been.

[Strabo, *Geography* 17.3.25]

This passage relates to Augustus' settlement of 28/27 BC (see **H18–H25**, especially **H19** which this passage continues). The most important distinction for Strabo is whether a province is under imperial control or not, although in fact this passage provides excellent evidence for the richly variegated nature of the empire, with many different types of administration.

Legates and procurators: they enjoyed no independent authority, but had to do everything according to orders. *Legati Augusti propraetore* (legates of Augustus with praetorian status) were senators and administered the more important areas; *procurators,* usually equestrians, administered the more minor provinces.

Praetors or proconsuls: under the republic, the most important provinces were governed by proconsuls (men who had previously been consul (chief magistrate): other provinces were governed by ex-praetors. Both types of governors enjoyed independent and supreme authority (civil, military and legal) within their province in the republic and technically continued to do so under Augustus.

According to the requirements of the moment: reinforces this idea of flexibility and adaptability, which underlay the success of the empire.

M3   Military commands in Africa

Under the reign of the deified Augustus and of Tiberius, the legion and auxiliaries stationed in the province of Africa to guard the boundaries of our empire were under the control of the proconsul.

[Tacitus, *Histories* 4.48]

Control of the proconsul: he had independent military command; hence Tiberius rebuked a governor for not giving his own military decorations (Tac. *Ann*. 3.21.3) and allowed the last known salutation as *imperator* to a private individual here (**N3**). Yet he interfered in the selection of a governor in AD 21 (Tac. *Ann*. 3.32.3; 35).

M4   Dedication to Mars Augustus, AD 6–7, Lepcis Magna (North Africa)

Sacred to Mars Augustus. Because, under the auspices of Imperator Caesar Augustus, chief priest, father of his country, and under the command of Cossus Lentulus, consul, one of the Fifteen in charge of sacrifices, proconsul, the province of Africa was liberated from the Gaetulian war. The town of Lepcis set this up.

[EJ 43 = *AE* 1940.68]

Rome waged war against the Gaetulians from AD 3–6, after they had rebelled against the 'friendly king' Juba II. (See **N10, M31, M32**). This inscribed limestone panel commemorates the success of Cossus Cornelius Lentulus (consul 1 BC, proconsul of Africa c. AD 6), to celebrate which his son added 'Gaetulicus' to his name, and he himself was awarded triumphal decorations (*ornamenta triumphalia*), see Vell. 2.116.2. It also illustrates the subordinate position of military commanders to Augustus: even though Africa is a 'public' province, the military success of its governor (who was not directly appointed by Augustus, unlike in 'imperial' provinces) is represented as accomplished under Augustus' auspices.

M5   Travels to the provinces

Drusus pointed out that rulers often had to visit the outer reaches of their empires, and that the deified Augustus himself had often travelled to the West and the East accompanied by his wife, Livia.

[Tacitus, *Annals* 3.34]

Accompanied by his wife: Livia seems to be in Gaul in 22/21 BC (**P11**), and Greece from Plutarch, *Moralia* 385f.

EGYPT (M6–M14)

On the conquest of Egypt see **N31–N32**. Quite exceptionally, but perhaps at first only as a stop-gap measure, Augustus/Octavian when he left Egypt in 30 BC entrusted its administration to an equestrian, who had to be given special powers. Despite Gallus' disgrace (see **P5–P6**) the equestrian prefectship becomes firmly established. Other unusual administrative arrangements in Egypt (**M9, M13**) derive largely from the Roman practice of adopting and adapting pre-existing systems of government. Tacitus and Strabo (**M8, M9**) stress the strong military presence here, as in other imperial provinces.

M6   Government of Egypt (1) – senators barred from Egypt

Augustus had forbidden senators and the more high ranking Roman equestrians to enter Egypt without his express permission. This was one of the secrets of his successful despotism. He made of it a special administrative area, so as to ensure that no one should get control of that province and starve Italy into surrender (however small their forces), since it had the capacity to resist the most formidable armies because it held the keys to control of both land and sea.

[Tacitus, *Annals* 2.59]

M7   Government of Egypt (2)

For the deified Augustus had decreed that legal proceedings should be held before the Prefects of Egypt, even though they were only members of the equestrian order, and that their decisions should be regarded as no less valid than those of the Roman (senatorial) magistrates.

[Tacitus, *Annals* 12.60]

M8   Government of Egypt (3)

Ever since the time of the deified Augustus and down to this day members of the equestrian order have governed Egypt with what was effectively sovereign power over the country and the forces by which it was garrisoned. This was a matter of policy and designed to keep close to home the control of a province which was relatively inaccessible, highly productive of cereals, and prone to violent disorder by reason of a general licentiousness and religious superstition combined with ignorance of the rule of law and civil administration.

[Tacitus, *Histories* 1.11]

Cereals: Josephus, *Jewish War* 2.386, asserts that Egypt provided Rome with one third of her annual grain supply.

Violent disorder: see e.g. H. Musurillo, ed., *The Acts of the Pagan Martyrs* (Oxford, 1954); Philo, *Embassy to Gaius*; Josephus, *Jewish War* 2.487–98; Claudius' letter to the Alexandrians, in LACTOR 8, no.27.

M9   Government of Egypt (4)

Egypt is now a province. It brings in significant revenues to the treasury and is ruled by the most reliable administrators, sent out there as governors from time to time. The Prefect Governor has the status of a king, and his immediate subordinate is the Legal Administrator, who is responsible for the majority of lawsuits. A third official, the so-called *Idiologus*, or Procurator, investigates all property to which no-one has legal title and property whose title ought to fall to Caesar. They are accompanied by Caesar's freedmen and stewards, to whom matters of varying degrees of importance are delegated. There are also three legions of soldiers, one based in the city itself, the other two in the country at large. As well as these, there are nine Roman cohorts, three in the city, three based in Syene on the borders of Ethiopia as a garrison for the region, and three elsewhere. There are also three cavalry detachments, similarly deployed at key locations.

Of the local officials in the city, one is the Interpreter, who wears purple, has hereditary privileges and looks after the interest of the city; another is the Recorder; another the Chief Justice; the fourth the Night Commander. These offices existed also under the kings.

[Strabo, *Geography* 17.1.12]

legions: the early imperial garrison of Egypt was three legions, reduced to two before AD 23 (**N52**).

M10   The Vatican obelisk, c.30 BC

By command of Imperator Caesar son of the Deified. Gaius Cornelius Gallus, son of
Gnaeus, prefect of the engineers of Caesar, son of the Deified, established Forum Julium.

[EJ 374 = *AE* 1964.255 + *AE* 1968.521]

This inscription has been dimly detected despite having been erased from the base of the obelisk brought to Rome
by Caligula for the Vatican Circus. It relates to the obelisk's location in Egypt, where it appears to have been set
up in 'Forum Julium'. Its interpretation is controversial, since Gallus' expected title, prefect of Egypt, does not
appear, but instead he is called 'prefect of engineers'. It has been suggested that this may be because Gallus set
up the obelisk in the earliest days of Rome's conquest of Egypt, before he had become prefect of Egypt.

M11   Strabo on Cornelius Gallus

Cornelius Gallus was Caesar's first appointment as prefect of the country. He attacked
the city of Heroon which had revolted and captured it with only a small force, and
broke up unrest in the Thebaid arising from the tribute.

[Strabo, *Geography* 17.1.53]

M12   Jerome's Chronicle, 27 BC

Thebes in Egypt razed to the ground.
Cornelius Gallus, poet from Forum Julii, whom we have mentioned earlier as first ruler
of Egypt, died by his own hand aged 43.

[Jerome, *Chronicle* 27 BC]

Thebes was destroyed as part of Cornelius Gallus' suppression of a revolt in the Thebaid (area around
Thebes), see **M11**. The revolt is more likely to have been a few years before Gallus' death.
Forum Julii: Jerome probably meant to designate modern Fréjus (Gaul) as Gallus' birthplace, but a Forum
Julium in Egypt is also linked to Gallus (**M10**) and confusion is possible.

M13   Private dedication to the imperial family and prefect of Egypt, 4 BC, Pelusium

On behalf of Imperator Caesar Augustus, son of the god, and Livia, wife of Augustus,
and Gaius Caesar and Lucius Caesar, sons of the Imperator, and Julia, daughter of the
Imperator, and Gaius Turranius, prefect of Egypt, Quintus Corvius Flaccus, son of
Quintus, having been *epistrategos* of the Thebaid, whilst judge in Pelusium, dedicated
a throne and altar in the 26th year of Caesar and the 13th day of the month Tybi.

[Greek: EJ 62 = *IGRRP* I.1109]

The post of *epistrategos* was held by a Roman of equestrian rank in charge of one of the three administrative
districts in Egypt. The dating system uses the Egyptian calendar to refer to the month, but specifies the year
by reference to Augustus' reign, dating it from his conquest of Egypt in 30 BC. Pelusium was on the coast,
at the most easterly point of the Nile delta.

M14   Embassy from Alexandria in AD 13

[...] Year 42 of Caesar, 4th of [...], ninth hour. Augustus took his seat in the Temple of
Apollo in the Roman library and gave audience to the envoys of the Alexandrians.
Sitting with him were Tiberius Caesar and Drusus Caesar, Valerius Messalinus
Corvinus, [...] Capito [...four other names, including Marcus Avidius Orgolianus].
Alexander handed over the decrees and spoke:

[Another 21 lines of fragmentary text can be partially read: Alexander conveyed the good wishes of the
Alexandrians to Augustus, and mentioned Livia and Tiberius. Augustus looked at the decree. A second
speaker, Timoxenus, introduced the request of the embassy, describing the Alexandrians as suppliants of
Augustus, but pointing out that the city enthusiastically worships the Fortune of Augustus. Then the papyrus
breaks off.]

[Greek: EJ 379: *Papyrus from Oxyrhynchus* 2435 (Reverse)]

The embassy is dated (like **M13**) by reference to Augustus' reign over Egypt. The council of Augustus described here fits in very well with the situation described by Dio 56.28.2–3 for AD 13: Augustus then rarely visited the Senate house, but decisions made by him in consultation with Tiberius, his adopted children and a group of senators were to be treated as approved by the senate.

The reading of A.K. Bowman, *Journal of Roman Studies* 1976 is given here, adding the name of Ateius Capito.

GAUL (M15–M22)

From 121 BC, the area from the Mediterranean to Lake Geneva had been 'The Province' of Rome. Julius Caesar captured the rest of Gaul (modern France and Belgium) between 58 and 50 BC. Augustus divided this area, known as *Gallia Comata* ('Long-haired Gaul') and organised as a single province since its conquest, into Aquitania, Belgica and Lugdunensis, known collectively as *Galliae Tres* (Three Gauls). 'The province' also known as *Gallia Transalpina* became known under Augustus as Narbonensis after the provincial capital, Narbo. The sources below show a variety of ways in which Gaul was administered and 'Romanised'. For Gaul see also Shield of Virtue at Arles: **H24**; Altar at Narbonne: **L17**.

M15   Administration of Gaul

Augustus Caesar divided Gaul into four parts: he assigned the Celts to the province of Narbonensis, Aquitania he designated as Julius Caesar had done, but with the addition of fourteen tribes living between the rivers Garumna (Garonne) and Liger (Loire). The rest he divided in two: the area up to the upper parts of the Rhine he included within Lugdunensis; the rest within Belgica.

[Strabo, *Geography* 4.1.1]

M16   Census in Gaul, 27 BC

While he held an Assembly at Narbo, a census was carried out in *Galliae Tres* (Three Gauls), which his father, Caesar, had conquered.

[Summary of Livy 134]

M17   Roman mint moved to Lugdunum (Lyons), *aureus*, 15–12 BC

Obv.:   Bare head of Augustus right.
   AVGVSTVS DIVI F (Augustus, son of the Deified)
Rev.:   Butting bull facing right.
   IMP X (hailed as victorious commander for the tenth time)

[*RIC* Augustus 166a, *BMC* Augustus 450]

In around 15 BC Augustus opened a mint for the production of most of the empire's gold and silver coins at Lugdunum (Lyons), in central Gaul, where this coin was made. The reasons for the shift away from Rome are not known. Some think that it was a move by Augustus to take personal control of the precious-metal coinage, while leaving the base-metal coins to the Senate. It is just as likely that he thought that a mint located closer to the northern frontier and to Spain, the empire's main source of gold and silver, would make paying the army on the Rhine and Danube an easier task. Bronze coins were also issued at Lugdunum.

M18 Temple and altar to Augustus at Lugdunum

The temple dedicated to Caesar Augustus by the union of all the Celtic people is situated in front of this city at the confluence of the two rivers. In it there is a remarkable altar inscribed with the names of their tribes, sixty in number, together with a representative image for each tribe, plus another large altar.

[Strabo, *Geography*, 4.3.2]

The Pan-Gallic altar (to Augustus and Rome) at Lugdunum (Lyons) became the focus for the emperor cult in Gaul and the site of an annual festival on 1 August for representatives from 60 states around Gaul. The altar is pictured on coins from the Lyons mint (**M20**).

M19 Revolt over the census, and Pan-Gallic altar at Lugdunum, 12 BC

The states of Germany on both sides of the Rhine were attacked by Drusus, and a revolt which arose in Gaul over the census was settled. An altar to the god Caesar was dedicated at the confluence of the Arar and the Rhône, with an Aeduan named Gaius Julius Vercondaridubnus being instituted as its priest.

[Summary of Livy 139]

Dio 54.32.1 alludes to the revolt and the altar.

M20 Lugdunum Mint Coin: altar, *sestertius*, AD 9–14

Obv.: Head of Augustus right, wearing laurel wreath.
　　　　CAESAR AVGVSTVS DIVI F PATER PATRIAE (Caesar Augustus, Son of the Deified, Father of the Fatherland)
Rev.: Altar decorated with two statues.
　　　　ROM ET AVG (To Rome and Augustus)

[*RIC* Augustus 231a, *BMC* Augustus 565]

On the altar, see **M18, M21**. On the mint at Lugdunum, see **M17**.

M21 Priest of Augustus at Three Gauls Sanctuary, Cahors

To Marcus Lucterius Leo, son of Lucterius Senecianus, who has executed all official posts in his country, priest of the altar of Augustus between the confluence of the Arar and Rhône rivers. The community of the Cadurci set this up at public expense on account of his services.

[EJ 120 = *ILS* 7041]

The identity of this priest of the cult of Augustus at the sanctuary of the Three Gauls in Lugdunum at the confluence of the Saône and Rhône rivers is noteworthy, since one of his ancestors, Lucterius Cadurcus, had been a fierce opponent of Julius Caesar, together with Vercingetorix in 52 BC (Caesar, *Gallic War* 7.5–8, 8.30–35, 44). He is thus a good illustration of how emperor-worship helped assimilate members of the local élite into Roman power structures. This inscription was found near the site of Divona Cadurcorum (modern Cahors, SW France), 200 miles from Lugdunum (Lyons) across the Massif Central.

M22 Dedicatory inscription on the 'Maison Carrée', Nîmes, AD 2/5

[line 1] To Gaius Caesar, son of Augustus, consul. To Lucius Caesar, son of Augustus, consul designate

[line 2] Leaders of the younger generation.

[EJ 75]

With some ingenuity, two different inscriptions have been reconstructed purely from the holes left by the original bronze lettering on the front frieze and architrave of the Maison Carrée, one of the best preserved Roman temples, in the forum at Nemausus (Nîmes, Southern France). As such, they are rather speculative, but a recent re-examination of the building rejects the first inscription, a dedication to Agrippa, and instead suggests that the building was only ever dedicated to Gaius and Lucius. It is thought that line 1 of the inscription was created in AD 2–3, and line 2 in AD 4–5. The temple is thought to have housed cult related to the imperial family. For photos of the temple, see the on-line LACTOR.

Bibliography: R. Amy and P. Gros, *La Maison Carrée de Nîmes* (Paris 1979)

SPAIN (M23–M28)

Though Roman rule had long been established in parts of the Iberian peninsula, others were only finally subdued under Augustus (see **N47–N49**). As in Gaul, Augustus reorganised the area, establishing a system of provincial administration which stayed in place far beyond his own principate. Strabo (**M23**) provides a valuable analysis of how the different levels of Roman administration in an area were managed. Note how peaceful and comfortable it is made to sound – Strabo was clearly not a critic of Roman rule, even though he came from an area which had lost its freedom. On Spain see also the statue base from Forum of Augustus: **K28**.

M23 Administration of Spain

At the present time, when provinces have been allocated, some to the people and senate, the others to the emperor, Baetica belongs to the people and a proconsul is sent as governor, with a legate and a quaestor under him. The eastern boundary of Baetica has been set near Castulo. The rest of Iberia is Caesar's: he sends out two legates, one of consular, the other of praetorian rank. The praetorian legate is accompanied by a legate responsible for administering justice to the Lusitanians who inhabit the area adjacent to Baetica as far as the River Durius and its tributaries. This area is now known in its own right as Lusitania. Here is the city of Emerita Augusta. The rest of Caesar's territory, comprising the greatest part of Iberia is governed by the consular legate who has a significant army consisting of three legions. He also has three legates, one of whom, with two of the legions, guards the whole area to the north of the Durius. ... The next area as far as the Pyrenees is guarded by the second legate with the other legion. The third legate oversees the interior and preserves the interests of those now described as 'toga-wearing' or, as it were, pacified and converted to a civilised way of life, Italian outlook and style of dress. These are the Celtiberians and those living near the river Iberus on both sides up to the regions next to the Mediterranean. The governor himself winters administering justice on the Mediterranean coast, especially in New Carthage and Tarraco, while in summer, he tours, always overseeing matters that need correcting. There are also procurators of Caesar, men of equestrian rank who distribute payment to the soldiers.

[Strabo, *Geography* 3.4.20]

provinces: on the division of the empire into imperial/public provinces, and the officials in charge, see **M2**.

known in its own right as Lusitania: Spain had previously been divided into two provinces, known as Hispania Citerior and Hispania Ulterior (Nearer and Further Spain). From about 13 BC, Hispania Ulterior was divided into Baetica and Lusitania.

Emerita Augusta: see **M26**.

The rest of Caesar's territory: that is Hispania Citerior, also known as Tarraconensis.

Iberus: now R. Ebro; Tarraco (modern Tarragona); New Carthage (modern Cartagena).

M24 'Romanisation' of Baetica

The Turdetanians, however, and especially those around the River Baetis, have changed over completely to the Roman way of life, and do not remember their own language any more. Most have become Latins and have received Roman colonists, so they are not far off all being Romans. The present jointly-founded cities Pax Augusta in the Celtic area, Emerita Augusta in the land of the Turdulians, and Caesaraugusta in the area of the Celtiberi as well as some other settlements show clearly the change in civic life.

[Strabo, *Geography* 3.2.15]

Strabo here provides useful contemporary evidence on the striking way in which the lifestyle of people across the Roman world gradually evolved to incorporate 'Roman' elements. The loss of native languages is revealing. This level of 'Romanisation' no doubt explains why Baetica was designated a 'Public' province. *Become Latins*: 'Latin rights' were conferred on many provincial communities in the Late Republic and under Augustus. Chief magistrates of such communities automatically became Roman citizens, with associated tax and legal privileges. Ordinary members of such communities gained commercial privileges and could settle in Rome as Roman citizens.

M25 Cornelius Balbus, from Cadiz in Baetica

All these fell to Roman arms and earned a triumph for Cornelius Balbus – his award of a foreigner's triumphal chariot being a unique honour – together with a grant of full citizen rights. For though he was born in Cadiz, he and his great-uncle Balbus were both accorded Roman citizenship.

[Pliny, *Natural History* 5.36]

Lucius Cornelius Balbus and his uncle or great-uncle of the same name showed the élite of the provinces that with luck and skill they could become part of the élite of Rome itself. Balbus senior received Roman citizenship in 72 BC and became Rome's first foreign-born consul in 40 BC. Balbus junior served under Julius Caesar: though not a consul, he was awarded consular rank by Augustus and made proconsul of Africa (21–20 BC), campaigning against the Garamantes (see **N9** for the rest of this passage) and being awarded a triumph (**N2f**).

M26 Dedicatory inscription in the theatre, 16/15 BC, Mérida

Marcus Agrippa, son of Lucius, thrice consul, thrice holder of tribunician power.

[EJ 74 = *ILS* 130]

Emerita in Lusitania (modern Mérida, Spain) was founded by Augustus as a veteran colony in 25 BC, following the Cantabrian wars. Agrippa had actually left the area well before 16/15 BC, the year to which this dedicatory inscription is dated by reference to his tribunician power. Although he may well have sponsored the building of the theatre before his departure, the colonists may have had their own reason for dating the theatre's construction so precisely. The dedication of the theatre may have coincided with the town's promotion to capital of the new province of Lusitania during the reorganisation of the Spanish provinces 16–13 BC (**M23**).

M27 Edicts of Augustus, 15 BC, north-west Spain

Imperator Caesar Augustus, son of the deified, in his 8th year of tribunician power, and as proconsul proclaims:

"I have learned from all of my deputies who have been in charge of the province across the Duero river that the fortress-dwelling Paemeiobrigenses, who belong to the Susarri people, remained loyal when all the rest were in revolt. Therefore I present them all with perpetual exemption from obligations; and as for the lands and boundaries which they possessed when my deputy Lucius Sestius Quirinalis governed this province, I order them to possess these lands without any dispute.

To the advantage of the fortress-dwelling Paemeiobrigenses, who belong to the Susarri people, to whom I had previously given exemption from all demands, I put back in their place the fortress-dwelling Aiiobrigiaecini, who belong to the Gigurri people, with the consent of the community itself; and I order the fortress-dwelling Aiiobrigiaecini to perform every public obligation with the Susarri."

Decided at Narbo Martius on 14 and 15 February, in the consulship of Marcus Drusus Libo and Lucius Calpurnius Piso.

[G. Alföldy, *ZPE* 131 (2000) 177ff]

This bronze tablet, containing two edicts issued at Narbonne, was found in 1999 in north-west Spain. In them, Augustus proposes measures for dealing with the aftermath of his military campaign in Cantabria, rewarding a people who had been loyal to Rome in the period 26–22 BC. They concern minor peoples in north-west Spain, rural populations with a fortified centre. He exempts the Paemeiobrigenses (in the area of modern Bembibre) from obligations to Rome (providing taxation and manpower), which he transfers onto the Aiiobrigiaecini. These peoples lived in an area between Lusitania (roughly Portugal) to the south and Asturia to the north, by the river Durius (modern Duero).

Presumably, this bronze was originally displayed in such a centre; the text contains several striking errors and peculiar abbreviations, suggesting that it was a copy at second, or even third, remove from the original. The word 'province' is here used (in its original sense, which was changing only under Augustus) to denote an area of military activity rather than an administrative geographical district. The preamble mentions only Augustus' tribunician power and proconsulship (this latter is most unusual), in virtue of whose powers he could issue these edicts, rather than listing all his imperial titles in general. Lucius Sestius Quirinalis is the suffect consul of 23 BC, known to have dedicated victory altars to Augustus at the end of the world on the Atlantic coast.

M28   Local bronze coin showing Augustus and Rome, Italica, 27 BC–AD 14

Obv.:   Bare head of Augustus right.
      PERM AVG MVNIC ITALIC (with the permission of Augustus, town of Italica)
Rev.:   Personified figure of Rome holding shield and spear.
      ROMA (Rome)

[*RPC* 1, no. 61]

This coin was made in the Roman town of Italica in Baetica (modern Santiponce, near Seville, Spain). In the reign of Augustus, towns and cities all over the Roman Empire made their own base-metal coinage for low-value transactions. They were not generally supplied with imperial Roman bronze coins. Nevertheless they often used very Roman-looking designs. The head of the new emperor was used everywhere from Spain to Asia Minor (**M58**) by communities seeking to show off their new-found Roman-ness.

Some coins, such as this one, proclaim that they were issued 'with the permission of Augustus'. Whether such permission was really necessary, or rather spontaneously sought and advertised by cities seeking some indication of imperial favour, is unclear.

FRIENDLY KINGDOMS (M29–M34)

From quite early in the development of the Roman empire, Rome seems to have realised that friendly relationships with kings whose territories lay on the margins of the empire could be established to mutual advantage: the king could expect Roman military support against internal and external enemies; Rome might call on troops in return, and was spared the trouble of garrisoning and administering a province, though the kingdom might later become formally part of the empire, when a king died or when a region became easier and more profitable to govern directly. Friendly kings might be rewarded by having their territories extended, or punished by having them removed. See also on Judaea (**M35–M46**).

M29   Rome's method of rule
Of the whole territory subject to the Romans, part is ruled by kings, part they call provinces and hold themselves, and send out prefects and tax-collectors. There are also free cities, some of which came over to the Romans as friends from the start, while the Romans themselves have made others free as a mark of honour. There are also some dynasts, tribal leaders and priests subject to them. These live according to the customs of their ancestors.

[Strabo, *Geography* 17.3.24]

M30   Rough Cilicia better as a client kingdom
The region (Rough Cilicia) was naturally suited to brigandage and piracy..., and with a view to all that it was thought that the district should be subject to kings rather than Roman governors who were sent out to administer justice and could not be everywhere at once, nor with an armed force. And so Archelaus in addition to Cappadocia took Rough Cilicia.

[Strabo, *Geography* 14.5.6]

Rough Cilicia (*Cilicia Tracheia*, the mountainous area of modern Turkey directly opposite Cyprus) was granted to Amyntas, King of Galatia, after his help for Octavian at Actium. After Amyntas' death in 25 BC, it was given to Archelaus, King of Cappadocia (reigned 36 BC–AD 17) who also received Lesser Armenia in 20 BC (see **J37**).

M31   Juba given Mauretania to rule
Shortly before my own time the kings of the house of Bogud and Bocchus, who were well-disposed towards Rome, ruled Mauretania. When they died, Juba succeeded to the throne, having been given the kingdom to add to his father's dominions by Caesar Augustus.

[Strabo, *Geography* 17.3.7]

M32   Juba's rule over Libya
The current situation is that Mauretania and a significant part of the rest of Libya has been turned over to Juba because of his friendship and goodwill towards Rome.

[Strabo, *Geography* 6.4.2]

The brothers Bogud and Bocchus II succeeded their father Bocchus I as Kings of Mauretania (modern Morocco and West Algeria). They both supported Julius Caesar in the Civil War against Pompey. Under the triumvirate, Bogud supported Antony, but was expelled by Bocchus II who supported Octavian and was rewarded with the kingdom (Dio 48.45.3). Bocchus died in 33 BC and his kingdom became a direct dependency of Rome (Dio 49.43.7). Mauretania was added to Juba's kingdom of Numidia (East Algeria) in 25 BC. Juba (II) was brought up in Italy and received Roman citizenship from Octavian. With the addition of Mauretania to his own kingdom of Numidia, he ruled over most of North Africa. Juba helped provide local information for Gaius' expedition to the East (**N45**).

M33   Arch of Cottius, 9–8 BC, Segusio
To Imperator Caesar Augustus, son of the deified, chief priest, in his 15th year of tribunician power, hailed *imperator* 13 times. Marcus Julius Cottius, son of King

Donnus, prefect of the communities which are listed below – Segovii, Segusini, Belaci, Caturiges, Medulli, Tebavii, Adanates, Savincates, Ecdinii, Veaminii, Venisami, Iemerii, Vesubianii, Quadiates – and the communities which have been subject to this prefect (set this up).

[EJ 166 = *ILS* 94]

This is a large bronze inscription on the arch at modern Susa in the Alps. Cottius inherited his father's kingdom as prefect under Augustus, to rule over the Alpine area in the interests of Rome. Six of the tribes listed here are included amongst the conquered peoples inscribed upon Augustus' victory monument at La Turbie (see **N16**).

M34   The Kingdom of Thrace

Rhoemetalces (I) had been the ruler of the whole of that kingdom, but on his death Augustus divided it between his brother Rhescuporis and his son Cotys (IV).

[Tacitus, *Annals* 2.64]

Rhoemetalces (I): (ruled 31 BC – AD 13) a member of a nexus of dependent monarchs also linked to the Pontic dynasty (see **J37**). On Roman campaigns to support him, see **N50–N52**. He provided cavalry for Rome after the Pannonian revolt (Velleius 2.112.4). He ruled all southern Thrace after 11 BC, but the division between his successors gave the preferable coast to one, the mountains to the other. Claudius annexed the kingdom in AD 46 and entrusted it to equestrian governors.

JUDAEA (M35–M52)

We have a great deal of information about Judaea, largely because of the historian Josephus, a Jewish priest of royal descent, born in Jerusalem in AD 37 who was given Roman citizenship by Vespasian and spent the second half of his life in Rome, writing historical works in Greek on Jewish subjects.

M35   Judaea under Augustus: an overview

The kingdom had been handed over to Herod by Mark Antony and later the victorious Augustus extended his dominion. After Herod's death a usurper named Simon had seized the throne, pre-empting the emperor's decision and was duly punished by the current governor of Syria, Quinctilius Varus, who then brought the Jewish nation under tighter control, with the kingdom divided into three and ruled by Herod's three sons.

[Tacitus, *Histories* 5.9]

Herod (the Great): appointed king in 40 BC, he went over to Octavian, and ruled until his death in 4 BC.
Extended his dominion: M.Grant, *The Jews in the Roman World* (London, 1974) 94, provides a map.
Simon: a slave of Herod (Josephus, *Jewish War* 2.57–9). On Herod's succession, see **M42–M44**.
(Publius) Quinctilius Varus: consul 13 BC, governor of Syria 7/6–5/4 BC, killed in Germany AD 9.
Three sons: Herod, Antipas, and Philip; Tacitus omits the eldest, Archelaus, deposed in AD 6.

M36   Herod confirmed as King of Judaea by Octavian after Actium

[387] However, the king decided to meet the danger face to face. So he sailed off to Rhodes, where Caesar was then quartered, and sought an audience with him, dispensing with his diadem and approaching as humbly as any private citizen and dressed accordingly, for all his regal spirit. He spoke bluntly, making no attempt to conceal the truth.

[388] "Caesar," he said, "I was made a king by Antony and I acknowledge that in return I have proved myself in every way a very useful ally to him. I make no secret of the fact that, had I not been detained in Arabia, you would certainly have found me under arms and in my place supporting him. As far as my resources would permit, I supplied him with auxiliary troops and thousands of measures of corn. Not even after

the disaster at Actium did I abandon the man who had been so generous to me. [389] Rather, when I found I was no further use to him as an ally, I became his most loyal adviser and insisted that there was only one solution for the disastrous errors he had made, and that was the death of Cleopatra. If he would eliminate her, I promised him money, fortified strong points for his protection, an army, and my personal support in the war against you. [390] But his own infatuation with Cleopatra together with the god who gave you victory stopped his ears. With his defeat I must accept my own; and with his death I surrender my diadem of kingship. I have come to you pinning my hope of safety on my record of loyalty and in the expectation that I shall be judged, not by whose friend I was but rather by what kind of friend I proved."

[391] Caesar replied: "Your safety is guaranteed; your reign is now more secure than ever. Such a model of true friendship deserves to be the ruler of many. Strive to remain loyal to those whose fortunes have prospered more than Antony's, for I have the most glorious expectations for one endowed with such admirable qualities as yourself. In fact Antony did us a favour in listening to Cleopatra rather than to you, since the reward for his folly is that we have gained your allegiance. [392] Indeed, in the matter of favours it appears that you have already made a very good start. I have had a despatch from Quintus Didius, who tells me that you sent him troops to help him against the gladiators. So now I am issuing a decree of confirmation of your kingship and I shall endeavour in due course to add further favours, so that you will never regret the loss of Antony."

[393] With these expressions of goodwill to the king, he placed the diadem on his head and made his gift public by the issue of a decree which lavished praise and compliments upon him.

[Josephus, *Jewish War* 1.387–393]

[388] Antony's army at Actium did include forces of other friendly kings, listed by Plutarch (*Antony* 61) who also includes troops sent by Herod in Antony's army. Amyntas, King of Galatia, deserted to Octavian just before the battle with his force of horsemen of Celtic ancestry (Plutarch, *Antony* 63, Velleius 2.84.2, and Horace *Epode* 9.17–18 – **G5**). Amyntas was rewarded by the addition of Isauria and Rough Cilicia to his kingdom, but on his death in 25 BC, most of his kingdom was annexed into the province of Galatia (Dio 53.26.3, **N1**).

[389] Cleopatra makes the obvious scapegoat for Herod, but she had also actively supported Herod's mother-in-law, Alexandra, against him (Josephus, *Jewish Antiquities* 15.62–67).

[392] Quintus Didius was probably governor of Syria in 30 BC. After Actium a group of gladiators in Cyzicus (Turkey) tried to march to Egypt to help Antony and Cleopatra (Dio 51.7).

M37 Augustus adds territories to Herod's kingdom (30 BC)

And when he reached Egypt, after the deaths of Antony and Cleopatra, he not only heaped fresh honours upon him but also transferred to his kingdom the territory which had been annexed by Cleopatra, together with Gadara, Hippos, Samaria, and the coastal areas of Gaza, Anthedon, Joppa, and Strato's Tower (later Caesarea).

[Josephus, *Jewish War* 1.396]

Annexed by Cleopatra: Antony had notoriously given Cleopatra parts of Roman territory including Judaea (Plutarch, *Antony* 36; Dio 49.32.5).

M38 Augustus adds territories to Herod's kingdom (c.23 BC)

[342] It was at this point, with the foundations of the city of Sebaste already laid, that Herod decided to send his sons Alexander and Aristobulus to Rome, so that they might be introduced to Caesar. [343] On arrival at Rome they stayed as guests at the house of Pollio, one of Herod's most enthusiastic supporters, and they were even invited to stay

with Caesar himself. He welcomed the boys with every sign of goodwill and gave Herod the right to confirm whichever of them he wished as heir to his kingdom. He also granted him the kingdoms of Trachonitis, Batanaea, and Auranitis which he had taken over under the following circumstances.

[344] A certain Zenodorus had taken a lease on the estates of Lysanias but had found the revenues unsatisfactory. However, he had a number of bands of brigands in Trachonitis, and he used these to enhance his income. For the men living in that area lived miserable lives and launched regular raids upon the territory of the people of Damascus. So far from putting a stop to their activities, Zenodorus took a cut of their profits. [345] In their desperate plight the people of the region appealed to Varro, who was governor at the time, begging him to write to Caesar about the depredations of Zenodorus. When Caesar got these reports he wrote back instructing Varro to drive out the brigands and allocate the territory to Herod, in the hope that under his administration the people of Trachonitis would now cease to be a plague to their neighbours.

[Josephus, *Jewish Antiquities* 15. 342–345]

Lysanias: had been king of Ituraea (modern Lebanon). He was executed by Antony in 34 BC and his land given to Cleopatra. The territory reverted to Zenodorus, possibly a son of Lysanias, in 30 BC.

M39   Herod's buildings in Jerusalem in honour of Augustus
His own palace, was built in the upper city and consisted of two enormous and extraordinarily beautiful houses with which not even the Temple could stand comparison. These he named after his friends, calling one the Caesareum and the other the Agrippeum.

[Josephus, *Jewish War* 1.402]

M40   Jewish – Arab conflict in around 9 BC
[279] Herod was infuriated by their activities and demanded the surrender of these terrorists together with the repayment of the debt of sixty talents which he had lent to Obadas through Syllaeus, since it had now reached the stipulated date for repayment. [280] But Syllaeus had already demoted Obadas and himself taken over the conduct of all policy. He categorically denied the existence of any terrorists in Arabia and procrastinated over the repayment of the money demanded. The matter was referred for arbitration to the Governors of Syria, Saturninus and Volumnius, [281] and it was finally agreed through their good offices that Herod should be repaid within thirty days and that fugitives from their respective kingdoms should be returned. In Herod's kingdom not a single Arab wanted for crime or any other reason was discovered, whereas the Arabs were found to have been harbouring terrorists in their lands. [282] When the agreed date for repayment of the loan arrived, Syllaeus set out for Rome without honouring his undertakings. Herod therefore sought to recover both the debt and the terrorists who had taken shelter in Arab territory. [283] Once Saturninus' and Volumnius' officials had given him permission to go in hot pursuit of the offenders, he led an expeditionary force into Arabia covering seven days' march in three days. When he reached the fortress where the terrorists were quartered, he captured them all in his first assault and razed the fortress (called Rhaepta) to the ground. But he made no attacks on the other inhabitants of the area.

[Josephus, *Jewish Antiquities* 16. 279–283]

Syllaeus: Nabatea was an Arab kingdom dependent on Rome, to the south-east of Judaea. Though a kingdom, real power was apparently in the hands of the chief minister, Syllaeus. He was an enemy of Herod, who had refused to let him marry his sister, Salome. Syllaeus had helped (or, according to Strabo, hindered) the Roman expedition to Arabia c. 25 BC, see **N18, N22.**

Governors...Saturninus and Volumnius: C. Sentius Saturninus (consul 19 BC) was actually the legate of Augustus in Syria; Volumnius was procurator (mainly responsible for collecting tax): both were answerable directly to the *princeps*.

M41   Augustus furious at Herod leading an army outside his own kingdom, c. 9 BC

[When somewhat exaggerated news of the events described in **M40** above reached Syllaeus already in Rome and in attendance at the court, he appealed to Caesar Augustus...]

[289] Caesar was irritated by Syllaeus' account and proceeded to interrogate those of Herod's friends who were in Rome, together with his own officials who had returned from Syria. He asked only one question: did Herod lead his army out of his own territory? [290] Since they were compelled to answer that single question and Caesar, as a result, heard nothing of the causes or extent of Herod's actions, he became even more incensed and wrote a savage reprimand to Herod to the effect that he had always hitherto regarded him as a friend, but would now treat him as a subject.

[Josephus, *Jewish Antiquities* 16. 289–290]

HEROD'S SUCCESSION (M42–M44)

Herod died in 4 BC: bitter family rivalries and intrigues during his lifetime were inevitable, given that he had 10 wives. He had executed two sons in 7 BC and his eldest just before his death (better to be Herod's pig than his son, Augustus joked). He also changed his will shortly before his death. It was no surprise therefore that the succession was disputed, by two of his sons by Malthace, Antipas and Archelaus or that a Jewish revolt against Rome occurred while Augustus was trying to resolve the succession. Quinctilius Varus, governor (legate of Augustus) of Syria, had left one of the three legions stationed in Syria under Sabinus in Jerusalem. According to Josephus, Sabinus' failure to control Passover crowds resulted in violence and the looting of the Temple treasury, in turn prompting a revolt (Josephus, *Jewish War* 2.40–54).

M42   Rival successors to Herod petition Augustus (4 BC)

[20] Meanwhile another rival claimant to the throne, Antipas, set out for Rome asserting that the terms of the original will, in which he had been nominated as king, should have greater force than the codicil ... [22] At Rome all his relatives who loathed Archelaus transferred their support to him. For every one of them the prime consideration was their desire for self-government under the administration of a Roman governor. Failing that, they wanted Antipas as King ... [25] Caesar pondered the claims of both parties in private, taking account also of the size of Herod's kingdom and extent of its revenues, not to mention his large number of children, and re-reading the various despatches on the subject sent to him by Varus and Sabinus. Then he called together a council of leading Romans, including for the first time Gaius, the son of Agrippa and Julia, whom he had adopted, and canvassed their opinions.

[Josephus, *Jewish War* 2. 20, 22, 25]

(Publius Quinctilius) Varus: consul in 13 BC, married to a daughter of Agrippa, then Marcella, great-niece of Augustus. In 4 BC he was governor (legate of Augustus) of Syria.

Sabinus: procurator of Syria, sent to Judaea to control the country while Herod's will was resolved.

council: on this council (*consilium*) see F. Millar, *The Emperor in the Roman World* (London 1992) p. 268.

M43   Jewish Revolt (4 BC)

[66] Varus received the news of the revolt from Sabinus and his officers, and being anxious for the safety of the whole legion, rushed urgently to its relief. [67] Taking with him the two remaining legions and their four associated auxiliary cavalry wings, he

set out for Ptolemais after issuing orders for the auxiliary troops of the kings and chieftains to assemble there. On his way through Berytus (Beirut) he also acquired an additional 1,500 heavy infantry from that city. [68] The rest of his army joined him at Ptolemais, including Aretas, an Arab whose hatred of Herod had inspired him to bring a considerable force of foot soldiers and cavalry. Varus immediately sent a section of the army into the area of Galilee neighbouring on Ptolemais under the command of his friend, Gaius. He routed the opposition, captured and burnt the city of Sepphoris, and sold the inhabitants into slavery. [69] Varus himself, with the bulk of the army, marched into Samaria, sparing its capital city once he discovered that it had taken no part in the insurrection, before camping near a small village called Arous. This had been part of Ptolemy's dominions and for that reason had been sacked by the Arabs as part of their vendetta against even the friends of Herod. [70] After that he moved on to another fortified village called Sappho, which he also sacked, together with all the other villages nearby which he happened to come across. Conflagration and slaughter raged everywhere and there was no holding out against the devastation caused by Aretas' Arabs. [71] Enraged by the deaths of Arius and his men, Varus even gave orders for Emmaus to be burnt to the ground, though its inhabitants had fled.

[72] After that he headed for Jerusalem and he had only to be seen with his army for the Jewish forces to scatter. [73] The insurgents fled into the hill country, but the people of the city welcomed him and disclaimed all responsibility for the revolt, insisting that they had themselves given the insurgents no encouragement and had only granted them admittance to the city because at festival time they had no option but to allow the crowds to enter. Indeed their experience had been closer, they said, to that of being besieged with Romans than of conniving with the insurgents who besieged them. [74] Varus had previously been formally welcomed before the city by Joseph (Herod's nephew), together with Gratus and Rufus, leading the royal army, the citizens of Sebaste, and the soldiers of the legionary garrison in their traditional military uniform. Sabinus himself, however, had not dared to face Varus and had already left the city and departed for the coast. [75] Varus now sent a detachment of his army into the countryside to hunt down the leaders of the revolt and a large number were captured. He imprisoned the less obvious troublemakers, but crucified about two thousand of the most guilty elements.

[76] Then came the news that about ten thousand armed insurgents remained under arms in the area of Idumaea. Varus had by now realised that the Arabs were not behaving as allies should, but were simply fighting to pay off old scores, and out of their loathing for Herod were inflicting more destruction on the country than he would have wished. So he dismissed them all and with his own legions hurried to meet the rebels. [77] On the advice of Achiab they surrendered without a fight. So Varus exonerated the majority, but sent the ringleaders to stand trial before Caesar. [78] Caesar pardoned most of them, but ordered some members of the royal family to be punished, including a number who were related to Herod himself, on the grounds that they had rebelled against a king who was of their own blood. [79] Having thus sorted out the situation in Jerusalem, Varus returned to Antioch leaving the same legion as before to garrison the city.

[Josephus, *Jewish War* 2.66–79]

M44   Herod's kingdom divided up on his death (4 BC)

[317] Caesar heard submissions from both sides and then dissolved his council. His decision came a few days later: he refused to appoint Archelaus as king, but instead made him the ethnarch of half the kingdom which had been subject to Herod, promising

to reward him with the title of king if he could prove that he measured up to the responsibility. [318] He divided the rest of the kingdom into two parts, giving one to each of Herod's two sons, Philip and Antipas, Antipas being the one who had disputed his right to the whole kingdom with his brother Archelaus.

[Josephus, *Jewish Antiquities* 17. 317–318]

Josephus gives details (not included here) of which areas and cities were to pay taxes to which ethnarch (tribal ruler).

M45   The end of Archelaus' ethnarchy (AD 6)

And so Archelaus took over his ethnarchy, but he could not forget his long-standing feuds and continued to treat with great cruelty not only the Jews but also the Samaritans. As a result they both sent embassies to Caesar to denounce him, and in the ninth year of his rule he was exiled to the city of Vienna (Vienne) in Gaul and his property confiscated to the imperial treasury.

[Josephus, *Jewish War* 2. 111]

M46   Judaea designated a province, with an equestrian governor

Archelaus' territory was now designated a province and Coponius, a Roman of the equestrian order, was sent out as procurator, with Caesar's authority to exercise full powers, including capital punishment.

[Josephus, *Jewish War* 2.117]

M47   Quirinius made governor of Syria, AD 6, to conduct a census

[1] Quirinius was a Roman senator. He had successfully discharged all the offices of the *cursus honorum* and reached the consulship. With a distinguished record matched by few, he arrived in Syria having been appointed governor and *juridicus* of that nation by Caesar, and with a commission to take a census of all property. [2] Coponius, an equestrian, was sent with him as a colleague to act as governor of Judaea with a grant of absolute powers. Quirinius also paid a visit to Judaea, which had been made part of his province of Syria, in order to make an assessment of property and to sell off the estate of Archelaus.

[Josephus, *Jewish Antiquities* 18. 1–2]

M48   The nativity story, AD 6?

In those days a decree went out from Caesar Augustus that all the world should be enrolled. This was the first enrolment, when Quirinius was governor of Syria.

[Luke, 2.1 (*RSV*)]

Publius Sulpicius Quirinius was governor (legate of Augustus) of Syria only from AD 6.

M49   A distinguished equestrian involved in Quirinius' census

Quintus Aemilius Secundus, son of Quintus, of the Palatina tribe, in the camp of the deified Augustus, under Publius Sulpicius Quirinius, governor for Caesar of Syria, decorated with honours, prefect of the 1st Augustan cohort, prefect of the 2nd naval cohort. Also, by command of Quirinius, I conducted the census of the community of Apamea of 117,000 citizen men; and also sent by Quirinius against the Ituraeans on Mount Lebanon, I captured their fortress; and before military service I was prefect of engineers, transferred by two consuls to the treasury; and in the colony I was quaestor, twice aedile, twice chief magistrate, and priest. Buried there are Quintus Aemilius Secundus, son of Quintus, of the Palatina tribe, and Aemilia Chia, freedwoman. This monument will not further pass to the heir.

[EJ 231 = *ILS* 2683]

The origin of this tombstone is not known. The colony of Berytus (modern Beirut), perhaps the colony where Aemilius was quaestor etc. was founded c.15 BC to help quieten down the area of Mount Lebanon.

M50   A consular career from Tibur

[....] king; when it had been brought into the power of [Imperator Caesar] Augustus and the Roman people, the senate [decreed] two days of thanksgiving [to the immortal gods] because of the successful [completion] of affairs [and] triumphal decorations for him; as proconsul he governed the province of Asia; [as deputy] of the deified Augustus with praetorian powers [he governed] Syria and Phoenicia for a second time.

[EJ 199 = *ILS* 918]

This large, but fragmentary career-inscription was found at Tibur (modern Tivoli). Once thought to record the career of Sulpicius Quirinius (consul 12 BC), well-known as the instigator of Augustus' census in Judaea in Luke's Gospel, it is more likely to be that of L. Calpurnius Piso (consul 15 BC).
Bibliography: R. Syme, 'The Titulus Tiburtinus', in *Roman Papers* III, ed. A.R. Birley (Oxford 1984) 869–84.

M51   Bronze coin from Judaea, AD 9

Obv.:   ear of barley.
          KAICAPOC ([coin] of Caesar)
Rev.:   palm tree.
          L ΛΘ (dating formula = AD 9)

[*RPC* 1, no. 4955]

After the deposition of Archelaus, Roman prefects issued coins on the local standard in the name of the emperor, but which mostly avoided designs likely to upset Jewish religious sensibilities.

M52   Salome bequeaths land to Livia

[31] Soon afterwards Coponius went back to Rome and Marcus Ambibulus was appointed as his successor in office. In his time King Herod's sister, Salome, died bequeathing to Julia (Livia, Augustus' wife) Jamnia and all its associated lands, Phasaelis, which lies in the plain, and Archelais, an area where the date palm grows prolifically producing fruit of the highest quality.

[Josephus, *Jewish Antiquities* 18.31]

THE GREEK EAST (M53–M68)

Many cities and states of the Greek East had constitutions dating back around 500 years. The Romans had long recognised that in many cases these cities could be left to govern themselves, though obviously they reserved the right to interfere on major issues. See **M29** for Strabo's comments on free cities.

M53 & M54   Senatorial decrees on a treaty with Mytilene, 25 BC

Decrees of the senate concerning the treaty. In the consulship of [Imperator Caesar] Augustus for the 9th time and Marcus Silanus [....] by command of Marcus Silanus in accordance with a decree of the senate [......] June in the Julian Senate house the following were present at the drafting: [Paulus Aemilius] Lepidus son of Lucius of the Palatina tribe, Gaius Asinius Pollio [son of Gnaeus...], Lucius Sempronius Atratinus son of Lucius of the Falerna tribe, Marcus Terentius Varro son of Marcus of the Papiria tribe, Gaius Junius Silanus [.....], Quintus Acutius [...] son of Quintus.

Concerning the matters about which Marcus Silanus [made] this statement: a letter [had been sent] to Imperator Caesar Augustus his fellow consul, [and a reply had come, that] if it were pleasing to the senate [for there to be a treaty] with [the Mytileneans, the conduct] of this matter [would be entrusted to Silanus] himself; concerning this matter the following [was decreed: that Marcus Silanus] consul, if it seems good to him, [should see to the arrangement of] a treaty [with the Mytileneans and anything else] that seems to accord with the [public interest and] his own [integrity]. Decreed.

29 June [in...., the following] were present [at the drafting]: Gaius Norbanus [Flaccus son of] Gaius [.....], son of Appius of the Palatina tribe [......], Censorinus [.....], Marcus Valerius [.....] son of [.......], son of [.....] of the Clustumina tribe [...., Marcus Terentius] Varro [son of Marcus] of the Papiria tribe, Gaius [.....].

Concerning the matters about which Marcus [Silanus made this statement, that he had obeyed everything in the] decree [of the senate] given to him, [namely that if it seems good to him,] he should see to the arrangement of [a treaty] with the Mytileneans [and anything else that seems to accord with the public] interest and [his own] integrity; that it remained for the [consequences of this matter to be dealt with], concerning which [the following was decreed: that Marcus Silanus] consul, if it seems good to him, should see to [the treaty being sent to the Mytileneans], as established, [and this treaty and the decrees of the senate] concerning this matter being inscribed [on a bronze tablet ...] and [set up] in public. [Decreed.]

In the consulship of [Imperator Caesar] Augustus for the 9th time and Marcus Silanus [........ *about 30 lines missing*]

M54   The treaty with Mytilene

Let the Mytilenaeans keep the rule [and dominion which they have had up to now (?)] in such a way as power is exercised according to the best right and the best law]. Let [the Mytilenaeans] not allow the enemies [of the Romans to pass through their own] dominions with public [consent so as] to wage war on the Romans or on those ruled by [them or on the allies of the Romans], nor [help] them [with weapons, funds or ships]. Let the Romans [not allow] the enemies [of the Mytilenaeans to pass through their own] country and their own dominions [with public consent] so as [to wage war] on the Mytilenaeans [or on those ruled by them or on the allies] of the Mytilenaeans, nor help [them] with weapons, funds or ships.

If anyone should begin a war [against the Mytilenaeans or] against the Romans [and] the [allies of the Romans, let the Romans help the Mytilenaeans, and the Mytilenaeans help the Romans and the allies] of the Romans [.........] and let it be steadfast. [Let there be] peace [for all time .... *only tiny fragments survive from here*]

[Greek: EJ 307 = *IG* XII.2.35]

These decrees are inscribed upon fragments of marble blocks, found reused on the old acropolis of Mytilene (the main city on the Greek island of Lesbos), from a large monument honouring Potamon, son of Lesbonax, a famous orator and benefactor during the second half of the 1st century BC. On its base were inscribed a number of texts relating to his benefactions to the town, including a letter brought back by Potamon from Julius Caesar, in which he accepted Mytilene's offers of peace and alliance, and honorific decrees voted by Mytilene for Potamon. Therefore it seems a fair assumption that Potamon was also involved as an envoy in 25 BC, probably together with the poet Crinagoras of Mytilene. Mytilene is confirmed as an ally of Rome and a free, rather than subject, city.

The decrees illustrate the functioning of the senate in Augustus' absence. At this time, Augustus was in Spain waging war against the Cantabrians. Consequently, his fellow-consul has convened the senate, raised the issue, and recommended consulting Augustus by letter.

Bibliography: R.K. Sherk, *Roman Documents from the Greek East* (John Hopkins Press, 1969) no.26

M55 Cyzicus deprived of freedom; Samos granted freedom

[22 BC] Augustus deprived the people of Cyzicus of their freedom.

[17 BC] Augustus gave the Samians their freedom.

[Jerome, *Chronicle* 22 BC, 17 BC]

Cyzicus: a Greek city on the Sea of Marmara. Dio explains that the people of Cyzicus had scourged and killed some Roman citizens during an internal dispute (54.7.6, under 20 BC): Augustus restored their freedom in 15 BC (Dio 54.23.7).

Samos: Aegean island and its main city. Augustus spending the winter of 21/20 BC there on his way to Syria provides a likely occasion for this grant (Jerome's dates are often approximate).

M56 Letter of a proconsul to Chios, c. AD 4/5?, Chios

[.............] by [......] of Staphylos of the existing circumstances? to the Chian envoys, when they read aloud the letter of Antistius Vetus, the proconsul before me, a most distinguished man, following my general intention of observing the writings of the proconsuls before me, I considered it sensible to regard as well the letter of Vetus concerning these things; but later, when I met in turn both parties in the dispute about their claims, I heard them in full and in accordance with my custom I requested more carefully written memoranda from both parties. When I received [these] and reached the appropriate place, I found a sealed copy of (by the dates) the oldest senatorial decree, issued when Lucius Sulla was consul for the 2nd time, in which the senate replied to the Chians who had testified in how many cases they dealt with Mithridates in behaving uprightly on behalf of the Romans and suffered at his hands. The senate specially confirmed that they use the laws, customs and rights which they held at the time when they entered into friendship with Rome, so that they might be subject to no instruction whatever of magistrates or of pro-magistrates, and all Romans among them obey Chian laws. I also found a letter of Imperator Augustus son of a god when consul for the 8th time which he wrote to the Chians [...] concerning the free city [...]

[Greek: EJ 317 = *SEG* XXII 507]

This inscription was found in the city of Chios (on the Aegean island of the same name). It shows the proconsul writing this letter (the immediate successor to C. Antistius Vetus, consul in 6 BC, governor of Asia c. AD 2/3 or 3/4) being duly cautious before intervening in a dispute in a free city. He cites precedent dating from Sulla's 2nd consulship in 80 BC and Augustus' 8th consulship in 26 BC.

Bibliography: R.K. Sherk, *Roman Documents from the Greek East* (John Hopkins Press, 1969) no.70 (updated text)

M57 The empire: loyalty to Rome

Then the delegations from Aphrodisias and Stratonicea cited decrees, the former a decree of Julius Caesar praising their long-standing loyalty to his cause, the latter a recent declaration by the deified Augustus in which he commended their unwavering loyalty towards Rome in the face of the Parthian invasions.

[Tacitus, *Annals* 3.62]

In AD 22 a host of delegations from the Greek cities sought confirmation of their temple charters.

Aphrodisias: For the grant of Julius Caesar and good relations with his heir Octavian, see the famous archive engraved on a monumental wall in the city: J. M. Reynolds, *Aphrodisias and Rome* (London, 1982) 38–106 nos. 6–13, with Caesar's decree confirmed in 39 BC (no. 8f.).

Stratonicea: The grant (dating from 40 BC) is also mentioned on an inscription (*CIG* 2715).

M58 *c.* AD 5, Local bronze coin of Hierapolis (Asia Minor), showing Augustus

Obv.:   Bare head of Augustus right.
ΣΕΒΑΣΤΟΣ (Augustus)

Rev.:   lyre.
ΙΟΛΛΑΣ ΙΟΛΛΟΥ ΓΡΑΜΜΑΤΕΥΣ ΙΕΡΑΠΟΛΙΤΩΝ (Iollas son of Iollas, secretary, [coin] of the people of Hierapolis).

[*RPC* 1, no. 2954]

Hierapolis (modern Pamukkale, W. Turkey) was one of the many city communities in western Asia Minor in the wealthy Roman province of Asia that made bronze coins in its own name but with the image of Augustus. The Greek inscription reveals that the person in charge of the coinage was a local official, a *grammateus*, or secretary. This kind of arrangement is characteristic of the style of Roman imperial rule. Most of the local administration was delegated to local communities which were largely self-governing. The imperial state mostly reserved for itself only major issues of foreign and defence policy though, if called in to adjudicate, governors and emperors could become closely involved in relatively minor matters, including coin-production (see **M28**).

M59 Letter of Agrippa to the Council of Elders at Argos, 17–16 BC?

Of the elders.

Agrippa greets the elders of the Argives descended from Danaus and Hypermestra. I am fully aware of my responsibility for the continuation of your organisation and for the preservation of its ancient reputation, and I have given back to you many of the rights which had been lost, and for the future I am [eager] to take thought for you and [...]

[Greek: EJ 308]

This inscribed plaque was found at Argos. It probably dates from the period when Agrippa was present in the Greek East, 17–13 BC, possibly in connection with a visit by him to Argos in 16/15 BC. It shows Rome's interest in fostering the long existing associations of elders in Greek cities, which had been involved in local religious activities, possibly shifting their focus onto emperor-worship, so as to become an eastern equivalent to the institution of *Augustales* in the West. Danaus was the mythical king of Argos, whose daughter Hypermestra was the only one of fifty not to murder her husband as ordered by him.

Bibliography: R.K. Sherk, *Roman Documents from the Greek East* (John Hopkins Press, 1969) no.63.

M60   Edicts of Augustus 7–6 BC, Cyrene

[Edict 1] Imperator Caesar Augustus, chief priest, in his 17th year of tribunician power, *imperator* 14 times, proclaims: since I find that 215 Romans in all from every age-group in the province of Cyrene have a census rating of 2,500 *denarii* or more, from whom jurors are drawn, and that among them there are some cliques, and since embassies from the province's cities have complained bitterly that these have been oppressing the Hellenes in lawsuits involving the death-penalty, with the same individuals prosecuting and bearing witness for each other in turn, [10] and since I myself too have learnt that some innocent people have been crushed in this way and have been carried off to the ultimate punishment, until the senate deliberates about this matter or I myself find some better solution, the governors of the province of Crete and Cyrene, in my opinion, will be acting honestly and appropriately if they appoint in the province of Cyrene the same number of Hellenic jurors as of Romans from the highest census ratings, nobody less than 25 years old, whether Roman or Hellene, and if indeed there is an abundance of such men, nobody with a census rating and property less than 7,500 *denarii*; or if the number of jurors who need to be appointed cannot be met in this way, let them appoint people with half, and not less, of this census rating as jurors in trials of Hellenes involving the death-penalty. [21] And a Hellene who is on trial, one day before the prosecutor begins to speak, is to be given the power over whether he wants all his jurors to be Romans or half to be Hellenes. If he has selected half Hellenes, then once the balls have been weighed and names written on them, let there be drawn from the one urn the names of the Romans and from the other those of Hellenes, until up to 25 of each race have been selected, of whom the prosecutor may reject up to one from each race if he wishes, and the defendant three in all, provided he rejects neither Romans nor Hellenes exclusively; then all the rest should depart for the voting and give their votes separately, the Romans casting their votes into one voting-urn, and the Hellenes separately into another. [31] Then once the tallying of votes on both sides has been done separately, the governor is to declare publicly what is the judgement of the majority of all jurors. And since for the most part the relatives of the deceased do not leave unjust deaths unavenged, and since it is likely that Hellenic prosecutors on behalf of the dead who are kinsmen or fellow-citizens will not be lacking who will exact punishment from the guilty, all who are the governors of Crete and Cyrene, in my opinion, will be acting justly and appropriately, if in the province of Cyrene they do not allow a Roman to prosecute a Hellene for the killing of a Hellenic man or woman, except if someone not honoured with Roman citizenship brings an action for the death of one of his relatives or fellow-citizens.

[Edict 2] Imperator Caesar Augustus, chief priest, in his 17th year of tribunician power proclaims: there ought not to be ill-will and censure against Publius Sextius Scaeva, because he saw to Aulus Stlaccius Maximus son of Lucius and Lucius Stlaccius Macedo son of Lucius and Publius Lacutanius Phileros freedman of Publius, being sent bound to me from the province of Cyrene, when these men said that they knew and wanted to declare something that was connected with my safety and the public interest; for Sextius did this properly and carefully. Further, since they know nothing of matters connected with me and the public interest, but said that they had fabricated this in the province, and made it clear to me that they had lied, I am releasing them from custody with their freedom. But I am preventing from leaving without my command Aulus Stlaccius Maximus, whom the Cyrenians' envoys accuse of having removed statues from public places, including one underneath which the city had inscribed my name, until I decide about this matter.

[**Edict 3**] Imperator Caesar Augustus, chief priest, in his 17th year of tribunician power proclaims: I command those from the province of Cyrene who have been honoured with Roman citizenship to perform their public duties in turn no less than the body of the Hellenes, except for those to whom exemption from tax together with citizenship has been given by law or by senatorial decree or by decree of my father or of myself. And as for those same men, to whom exemption from tax has been given, I wish that they be exempt for the property they possessed at that time, but that they pay dues for all the property acquired after that point.

[**Edict 4**] Imperator Caesar Augustus, chief priest, in his 17th year of tribunician power, proclaims: whatever disputes occur between Hellenes in the province of Cyrene, with the exception of those on trial for life, for whom whoever is in charge of the province ought himself to pass judgement and determine or to provide a panel of jurors, for all the other cases I wish that Hellenic jurors be given, unless someone being investigated or called to account wants to have jurors who are Roman citizens. But between those to whom as a result of this decree of mine Hellenic jurors will be given, I do not wish any juror to be given from the home city of the prosecutor or investigator or whoever is being investigated or called to account.

[Greek: EJ 311 = *SEG* IX.8]

Cyrene was a city on the North African coast immediately south of mainland Greece, colonised by Greeks c. 630 BC. The surrounding territory was also known as Cyrene.

This series of four edicts by Augustus (7/6 BC) and a senatorial decree (4 BC – **M78**), itself introduced by a fifth edict, appear on a large marble slab, over 2 metres high, found reused as a bench in the *agora* of Cyrene. The first four edicts are separated by a blank line from the fifth edict and decree. Some parts of the text are of disputed meaning, especially in edict 3 and 5, but together they give an illuminating picture of the parts played by Augustus and the Senate in provincial administration. Cyrene was governed jointly with Crete as a 'public' province, but clearly Augustus was prepared to intervene in such a province. Edicts 1–4 relate to the affairs of Cyrene, 1–2 dealing with embassies sent from there to Rome, and 3–4 tackling the question of citizen status and judicial liability.

Edict 1 represents Augustus' response to an embassy from Cyrene, which has approached him directly, rather than the Senate. Augustus courteously presents his statement as advice, but it was in effect a command (a good example of Augustus' exercise of *auctoritas* (authority) rather than *potestas* (power) see *RG* 34.3).

Edict 2: Publius Sextius Scaeva is governor of Crete and Cyrene.

Bibliography: B. Levick, *The government of the Roman empire* (Croom Helm, 1985) nos 46, 58, 84; R.K. Sherk, *Roman Documents from the Greek East* (John Hopkins Press, 1969) no.31

JEWISH RIGHTS (M61–M67)

Josephus preserves a series of documents (**M62–M67**) relating to the treatment of Jews and rights granted them by Augustus. The Jews of Cyrene obviously preserved the documents as a guarantee of their rights. For us they provide valuable evidence of the way Augustus' rule was administered on a 'petition and response' model, which remained true for subsequent emperors. They also show how decisions were conveyed from one level of government to another.

M61   Jews complain about persecution to Augustus

[160] The Jews of Asia and those living in Libya in the areas about Cyrene were suffering at the hands of the city authorities in those areas. Even though their kings had previously granted them equality of civic rights, they were now being abused by the Greeks, who were going so far as to confiscate their temple monies and discriminate against them in private disputes. [161] Their sufferings were acute and they could see no end to the malevolence of the Greeks. So they sent a delegation to Caesar to register a complaint about this state of affairs. He confirmed their already existing right of equality of taxation and wrote letters to this effect to the local officials. I record below copies of those documents as evidence of the goodwill which from the beginning our rulers have displayed towards us.

[Josephus, *Jewish Antiquities* 16. 160–161]

M62   Augustus' decree on the Jews

[162] *The decree:* "Caesar Augustus, chief priest, [in the .... year] of his tribunician power decrees as follows: Whereas the Jewish nation has proved itself a friend to the Roman people not only at the present time but also in times past, and especially in the time of my father the Emperor Caesar, and whereas their High Priest Hyrcanus has proved himself likewise, [163] it has been decided by myself and my sworn council in accordance with the will of the Roman people: that the Jews shall be permitted the use of their own customs following their ancestral law and in accordance with their usage in the time of Hyrcanus, High Priest of the Most High God; that their sacred monies shall be declared inviolable and may be sent up to Jerusalem and handed over to the Treasurers in Jerusalem; that they shall not be liable for bail to appear in court on the Sabbath or on the day of preparation for the Sabbath after the ninth hour; [164] that if anyone is convicted of stealing their holy books or sacred monies, whether from a synagogue or other place of assembly, such person shall be deemed guilty of sacrilege and his property be forfeit to the public Treasury of the Romans; [165] that the resolution which they passed in my honour for the gracious favour which I show to all men, and in honour of Gaius Marcius Censorinus, shall be publicly displayed together with this decree in the most conspicuous location assigned to me by the League of Asian States in Ancyra; that if anyone breaks any of the aforementioned ordinances, he shall suffer condign punishment."

This decree was inscribed on a pillar in the Temple of Caesar.

[Josephus, *Jewish Antiquities* 16. 162–165]

M63   Augustus' letter to the Governor of Cyrene

[166] "Caesar to Norbanus Flaccus, greetings:

The Jews, whatever their numbers, who in accordance with their ancient custom have collected sacred monies to send up to Jerusalem may continue to do so without let or hindrance."

So much for Caesar's instructions.

[Josephus, *Jewish Antiquities* 16. 166]

M64   Agrippa's letter to Ephesus

[167] But Agrippa also wrote personally on the Jews' behalf, as follows:

"Agrippa to the magistrates, council, and people of Ephesus, greetings.

My policy is that in accordance with their ancient traditions the Jews of Asia should be made responsible for the care and protection of the sacred monies which they collect for delivery to the temple in Jerusalem. [168] Anyone who steals these sacred monies from the Jews and then takes refuge in a place of asylum is to be forcibly removed and handed over to the Jews, on the same principle as that which allows the forcible removal of those guilty of other forms of sacrilege. I have also written to the praetor, Silanus, instructing him that no one is to compel a Jew to give bail for appearance in court on the Sabbath."

[Josephus, *Jewish Antiquities* 16. 167–168]

M65   Agrippa's letter to Cyrene

[169] "Marcus Agrippa to the magistrates, council, and people of Cyrene, greetings. Augustus has already sent letters to Flavius, who was praetor of Libya at the time, and to the other officials of the province concerning the Jews in Cyrene. He gave instructions that they should be allowed to send their sacred monies up to Jerusalem without let or hindrance, in accordance with their ancestral custom. [170] It has come to my notice that they are now being harassed by certain common informers and prevented from despatching these monies, on the pretext that they are in default of tax payments, which are not in fact owing. My instructions are, therefore, that these monies are to be restored and the Jews are not to be molested in any way whatsoever. And if sacred monies have been confiscated from any of their cities, those responsible for the administration of such matters are to see to it that proper reparation is made to the Jews of those cities."

[Josephus, *Jewish Antiquities* 16. 169–170]

M66   Governor's letter to Sardis

[171] "Gaius Norbanus Flaccus, proconsul, to the magistrates and council of Sardis, greetings.

Caesar has written to me with instructions that the Jews shall not be prevented from collecting monies according to their ancestral custom, however great the sums, and sending them up to Jerusalem. I am writing to you therefore to make it absolutely clear that this is Caesar's policy, and mine."

[Josephus, *Jewish Antiquities* 16. 171]

M67   Governor's letter to Ephesus

[172] The proconsul Julius Antonius wrote in exactly similar terms.

"To the magistrates, council and people of Ephesus, greetings.

On 13 February, when I was in Ephesus on my judicial circuit, the Jews residing in the province of Asia reminded me that Caesar Augustus and Agrippa had agreed that they should be allowed to follow their own traditional customs and bring [to Jersualem] first-fruit offerings, collected of their own free will from their own resources and out of respect for their God, and that for this purpose they should be allowed to travel as a group without let or hindrance. [173] They asked me to confirm the rights granted to them by Augustus and Agrippa by a similar declaration of policy. I wish it to be clearly understood that I am allowing them to enjoy the same privileges as were accorded to them by Augustus and Agrippa to live according to their ancestral customs without let or hindrance."

[Josephus, *Jewish Antiquities* 16. 172–173]

M68   Petitioning of Octavian abroad by Fishermen (29 BC)

Once, when we put into Gyaros in the Cyclades, I came across a tiny fishing village. As we were setting sail, we took on board one of their number who had been elected by them as their spokesman to take a petition to Caesar, who at that time was in Corinth, on his way home to celebrate his triumph for the victory at Actium. In the course of the journey, the fisherman explained to those who enquired that he had been sent to petition for some mitigation of tax. For his community were required to pay one hundred and fifty drachmas, when they could barely raise one hundred.

[Strabo, *Geography* 10.5.3]

This story provides a very good illustration of how the Roman empire worked on a 'petition and response' model, see **M60**. Note that the emperor might not be in Rome itself, and could therefore be hard to find. It is interesting that this tax burden, which was considered excessive, could be up for negotiation.

Romanisation and the Building of New Cities (M69–M75)

As in the new provinces of Gaul and Spain, Romanisation took place elsewhere in the empire, even where the introduction of Roman culture seemed and was entirely out of keeping with local culture (**M69, M70, M75**). On the building of new cities named in honour of Augustus, see also sources on Nikopolis (**H10 & H11**) and compare the founding of new colonies in the West, for example **M24** and **M26** above.

M69   Roman sport and leisure brought to Jerusalem by Herod

[268] First of all Herod established a quadrennial athletic festival in honour of Caesar. He also built a theatre in Jerusalem, together with a vast amphitheatre out in the plain, both buildings being remarkable for their extravagance, but entirely alien to Jewish culture, since the Jews have no tradition of using such buildings or putting on such spectacles. [269] Nevertheless, Herod celebrated this quadrennial festival in the most ostentatiously spectacular fashion, sending out notices to all the surrounding peoples and inviting competitors from the whole nation.

[Josephus, *Jewish Antiquities* 15. 268–269]

M70   Augustus honoured in the theatre in Jerusalem

[272] All round the theatre were set up inscriptions in honour of Caesar, and the trophies he had won in his wars against various nations, all of them made from refined gold and silver.

[Josephus, *Jewish Antiquities* 15. 272]

M71   Bilingual dedication of theatre, AD 1–2, Lepcis Magna, Tripolitania

When Caesar Augustus, son of the Deified, was chief priest, in his 24th year of tribunician power, consul 13 times, and Father of the Fatherland, Annobal Rufus, embellisher of his country, lover of concord, priest, chief magistrate (*sufes*), prefect of religious rites, son of Himilco Tapapius, supervised its construction with his own money and also dedicated it.

[Latin and Neo-Punic: EJ 346 = *IRT* 321–23]

Lepcis was an important Punic harbour-town on the north coast of modern Libya, deriving its wealth from exporting olive oil. It was in this period an autonomous 'free town', but members of the local élite began to sponsor the construction of Roman-style buildings from c.8 BC. The theatre is a conspicuous example of this. Its dedicatory inscription survives in three copies, two of which survive *in situ* on the lintels above doorways into the *orchestra*, engraved in both Latin and Neo-Punic. The Neo-Punic texts are not literal translations from the Latin. The post of *sufes* was annual chief magistrate. A series of statues of members of the imperial family were set up in a temple in the forum.

M72   The *via Sebaste* in Pisidia, (Galatia) 6 BC

Imperator Caesar Augustus, son of the Deified, chief priest, consul 11 times and designated for the 12th, hailed *imperator* 15 times, in his 18th year of tribunician power, built the *via Sebaste*, under the supervision of Cornutus Aquila, his propraetorian legate.

[EJ 294 = *ILS* 5828]

Together with the establishment of Roman colonies, the building of the *via Sebaste* (Augustan Road) played an important part in bringing the mountainous district of Pisidia (in the new province of Galatia) under Roman control. It was 6–8m wide, sufficient to carry wheeled traffic. Sebastos was the Greek equivalent of Augustus. Cornutus Arruntius Aquila was governor of Galatia.

M73   Cities of Caesarea in friendly kingdoms

So greatly was he loved, even by foreigners, that kings who were friends of Rome founded cities in his honour, which they named 'Caesarea', for example King Juba in Mauretania and the now very famous city in Palestine.

[Eutropius, *Brief History* 7.10]

'Each of the Kings who was a friend and ally of Augustus founded cities in his own territory called 'Caesarea'.' (Suetonius, *Augustus* 60.1). By Palestine, Eutropius means Judaea.

M74   Herod builds new cities (Sebaste in Samaria and Caesarea Maritima)

[403] But it was not just by buildings that he recorded for posterity the names and memory of his friends. His desire to honour them extended to whole cities. In the district of Samaria, for example, he founded a city with the most splendid perimeter walls some two and a half miles long. There he settled some six thousand colonists and allocated to them some of the most fertile land. In the centre of the city he built a vast temple, with a huge precinct some two hundred and seventy-five metres in length, dedicated to Caesar. He called the city Sebaste (*Greek equivalent of Augusta*) and gave it a special constitution of its own. [404] Later in addition, when he received further allocations of territory from Caesar, there too Herod built in his honour a temple of white marble beside the sources of the river Jordan at a place called Paneion ... [407] In short, it is impossible to name any single suitable site within his kingdom which he left without some visible mark of honour to Caesar. And once he had filled his own kingdom with temples, he lavished upon the whole province similar honorific memorials, setting up monuments to Caesar in many cities.

[414] On a hill facing the mouth of the harbour (of Caesarea) stood the vast and singularly beautiful temple of Caesar. Inside were two statues, one a colossal statue of Caesar, modelled on the statue of Zeus at Olympia and in no way inferior to it; the other a statue of Rome, modelled upon and matching that of Hera at Argos. Herod dedicated the city as a whole to the province, the harbour to the merchants who plied those waters, and to Caesar the honour of founding it. Hence the name of the city, Caesarea ... [416] He also rebuilt Anthedon, a coastal city which had been destroyed during the war, and named it Agrippeium. So close was his friendship with this same Agrippa, that he even carved his name over the gateway which he had built in the Temple [in Jerusalem].

[Josephus, *Jewish War* 1. 403–407, 414, 416]

M75   Caesarea

[136] At about this time Herod's building of Caesarea Sebaste was complete ... [137] ... This was the immediate occasion for elaborate celebrations, with a huge festival of dedication and the most extravagant ceremonials. He had already announced that there

would be a music festival and athletic contests, and had also organised large numbers of gladiators and wild beasts, together with horse racing and other costly extravaganzas of the kind found in Rome and elsewhere. [138] He also arranged that it should be celebrated every four years and even dedicated the festival to Caesar. Never one to miss an opportunity for self-glorification, Caesar enhanced his prestige by despatching at his own expense all the paraphernalia necessary for such a festival. [139] His wife, Julia (Livia), also personally contributed from her own resources many of her most valuable treasures, so that the total contribution amounted to at least 500 talents' worth.

[Josephus, *Jewish Antiquities* 16. 136–139]

Controls on Provincial Governors (M76–M79)

Tacitus, *Annals* 1.2.2 (Section **F**) provides a brief but damning indictment of what provinces had suffered from governors under the republic. It had been widely accepted under the republic that a praetor or consul might recoup his electoral expenses by profits made as a provincial governor. Repeated legislation had been ineffective. The principate may well have improved the situation, by reducing electoral competition, as may Augustus' powers to remove senators and the possibility of provincials appealing to the emperor.

M76   Tyrannical behaviour...

Not so long ago, when Volesus was proconsul of Asia under the divine Augustus, he executed three hundred people in one day by chopping their heads off. As he swaggered through those corpses with the arrogant demeanour of one who had performed some conspicuously great feat, he announced in Greek: "Now that's the act of a real king"...

[Younger Seneca, *Concerning Anger* 2.5.5]

M77   ... punished

In order that what he was proposing in the case of Silanus might seem more acceptable by citing a precedent, Tiberius ordered the reading of a letter of Augustus and a decree passed by the senate concerning Volesus Messala, who had also been a proconsul of Asia.

[Tacitus, *Annals* 3.68]

The context of the passage is the trial in AD 22 of Gaius Junius Silanus for extortion while governor of Asia. Silanus was outlawed and exiled to Kynthos (an island in the Cyclades). Lucius Valerius Messala Volesus, consul in AD 5, must have been similarly punished for his crimes in Asia.

M78   Senatorial decree on extortion, Cyrene, 4 BC

Imperator Caesar Augustus, chief priest, in his 19th year of tribunician power, proclaims: I decided to send to the provinces a decree of the senate ratified in the consulship of Gaius Calvisius and Lucius Passienus when I was present and named jointly as its author, and relating to the safety of the allies of the Roman people, so that it may be known to everyone whom we look after, and to append it to my edict, from which it will be clear to all who live in the provinces how much attention we – the senate and I – are paying that none of our subjects suffer any mistreatment or extortion.

Decree of the senate.

Gaius Calvisius Sabinus and Lucius Passienus Rufus, consuls, made this statement, 'about the matters which Imperator Caesar Augustus, our leader, in accordance with the opinion of a council which he had chosen by lot from the senate, wished us to refer to the senate, relating to the safety of the allies of the Roman people.' On this matter the senate decreed: [90] our ancestors ordained by law legal proceedings for the recovery of money, so that in cases when they have been wronged the allies may more easily be able to bring a prosecution and recover money if robbed of it. But the nature of such courts is sometimes most burdensome and unpleasant for those for whose benefit the law was written, given that the provinces are too far from Rome for witnesses to be dragged when they are poor and perhaps also weak because of illness or old age. In view of these circumstances, the senate wishes, if, after this decree of the senate has been produced, any of the allies, either publicly or as individuals, wish to reclaim money exacted, apart from investigating on a capital charge the person who has seized it, and if they report the situation in person to one of the magistrates who has the power to convene the senate, that the magistrate bring these men before the senate as quickly as possible and give them whichever public advocate they themselves ask for, who will speak before the senate on their behalf. [103] But if someone has been excused from this public duty in accordance with the laws he need not act as advocate, if unwilling. In order that <there might be jurors?> for these trials to be heard for those bringing charges in the senate, the magistrate, who gives them access to the senate, on the same day when no fewer than 200 of the senate is present, is to draw by lot four out of all those of consular status either in Rome itself or within 20 miles of the city. Similarly three out of all those of praetorian status who are in Rome itself or within 20 miles of the city. Similarly two out of all the rest of those of senatorial status or who have permission to give an opinion in the senate, who at that time are either in Rome or nearer than 20 miles of the city. [112] But let him not draw by lot anyone who is 70 years old or more, or who has been appointed to some magistracy or public office, or is president of a court, or supervisor of corn-distribution, or whom ill-health hinders from performing this public duty, having declined the office by oath openly before the senate and having presented three senators who have taken an oath relating to this, or someone who by kinship or by marriage is related to the defendant, so as not to be compelled against his will to be a witness in a public court by the Julian law on trials, or someone whom the man being called to account swears before the senate is a personal enemy, provided he does not exclude by oath more than three. [119] The magistrate who carries out the drawing of lots is to see to it that within two days those pursuing their money and the person from whom they are pursuing it reject, by turns, jurors from the nine drawn by lot in the way described, until five remain. [123] If any of these jurors should die before the case is judged, or if any other reason prevents him from making his judgement, and his excuse is sanctioned, once five senators have taken an oath, then let the magistrate in the presence of the jurors and of those pursuing their money and of the man from whom they are pursuing it, select by lot from these men those who are of the same rank, and have held the same magistracies, as that man, to replace whom he is being selected by lot, happened to have held, provided that he does not select by lot a man whom this decree of the senate does not allow to be selected for the trial of the one who is being called to account. The chosen jurors must hear only about these things and decide about the things for which the person is being called to account as having purloined publicly or privately; they must order to be returned as large a sum of money as the investigators show to have been taken from them publicly or privately, provided that the jurors give their decision within 30 days. Those who are obliged to decide about these matters and deliver their opinion, until they decide and deliver their opinion, may disregard all public duties except for public sacred ones. And the senate wishes that the magistrate who has carried out the drawing of lots (or, if he cannot, the senior consul) direct this arbitration and give permission for summoning witnesses who are in Italy, provided that he allow the summoning of no more than five for someone pursuing a private case, and no more than ten for someone pursuing a public case. [142] Likewise the senate wishes that jurors who are selected by lot in accordance with this decree each declare openly his own opinion, and whatever the majority declare is to stand.

[Greek: EJ 311 = *SEG* 9.8]

For the first four Cyrene edicts, see **M60**. This, the fifth edict, introduces a senatorial decree relating to the whole empire dealing with the procedure for accusing governors of illegal acquisitions. It is based upon the recommendations of the council of senators which Augustus had established in order to organise the Senate's agenda in advance of its meetings (compare Dio 53.21.4 and Suetonius, *Augustus* 35.3).

M79   Governors called to account
Some of those in charge of provinces under Tiberius and his father Caesar had turned their public commission and duty to protect into exercise of power and tyranny for their own benefit, and had filled their territories with an intolerable burden of bribe-taking, robbery, injustice, the expulsion and banishment of people who had done nothing wrong and the execution without trial of the leading citizens. But when they returned to Rome at the end of their time of office, the emperors required an account and audit of what they had done, especially when aggrieved cities sent ambassadors. For on these occasions, they themselves acted as impartial judges, listening equally to prosecution and defence: they thought it right not to prejudge anyone as guilty before the trial, but gave judgement without hostility or favour, but in accordance with the absolute truth and what they thought was just.

[Philo, *Speech against Flaccus* 105–106]

Philo led a Jewish embassy to Gaius in AD 39/40 when an old man and so can be assumed to have lived through much of Augustus' reign. It does, however, also suit his case to present previous emperors as punishing wrong-doing of governors: Philo is asking for the same just treatment to be shown to Avilius Flaccus, prefect of Egypt AD 32–38, for his persecution of the Jews of Alexandria.

Honours (M80–M85)
M80 shows a community adopting a Roman consul as their patron. On a grander scale, cities around the empire might well wish to show their loyalty to the *princeps*, or a member of his family (especially if they had previously backed the wrong side). For other dedications and honours from around the empire included in other sections, see **J38, J39** (Tiberius); **H34** (Augustus).

M80   Patronal tablet, 12 BC, Africa
In the consulship of Publius Sulpicius Quirinius and Gaius Valgius, the senate and people of the tax-paying communities in the district of Gurza made a pact of hospitality with Lucius Domitius Ahenobarbus, son of Gnaeus, grandson of Lucius, proconsul, and co-opted both himself and his descendants as patron for themselves and their descendants, and he received them and their descendants into his good faith and clientship. The following saw to this being done: Ammicar, son of Milchato, from Cynasyne, Boncar, son of Azzrubal, from Aethogursa, and Muthunbal, son of Sapho, from Uzita.

[EJ 355 = *ILS* 6095]

This bronze tablet is a typical example of the official co-option of a prominent Roman (Domitius Ahenobarbus, consul 16 BC) as patron of a provincial community.

M81 Honours for the imperial family, 17–12 BC, Thespiae
The people (honour) Agrippina, daughter of Marcus Agrippa.
The people (honour) Marcus Agrippa, son of Lucius. To the Muses.

The people (honour) Lucius Caesar.
The people (honour) Gaius Caesar.
The people (honour) Julia, daughter of Imperator Caesar Augustus, wife of Marcus
   Agrippa. To the Muses.
The people (honour) [Livia,] wife of [Imperator] Caesar [Augustus]. [To the Muses].

[Greek: EJ 76]

Thespiae was a city in south-central Boeotia (Greece), and held an important festival for the Muses. These two stone blocks once belonged to a large base supporting statues of Agrippa and Julia, and smaller ones of their children. The statues were set up in the sanctuary of the Muses, where the Thespians had also previously dedicated a statue of Augustus to the Muses. The dedication can be dated to between the birth of Lucius Caesar and the death of Agrippa.

M82 Honours for Augustus and Agrippa in Myra, Lycia
The people of Myra (honour) the god Augustus Caesar, son of a god, *imperator* of land and sea, benefactor and saviour of the whole world.
The people of Myra (honour) Marcus Agrippa, benefactor and saviour of their race.

[Greek: EJ 72 = *IGRRP* III 719]

Myra was an important city in Lycia (south-west Turkey).

M83 Honours to Agrippa and his sons, Mytilene (after 2 BC)
To Gaius Caesar and Lucius Caesar, sons of Augustus, son of the god Caesar, leaders of the younger generation.
To Marcus Agrippa saviour god and founder of the city and to his son Marcus Agrippa the grandson of Augustus.

[Greek: EJ 67 = *IG* XII 2, 168]

This marble base from Mytilene on the Greek island of Lesbos honours Marcus Agrippa and his three sons, but treats Agrippa Postumus separately from Gaius and Lucius. Marcus Agrippa had made Lesbos his headquarters while in charge of the eastern half of the empire 23–21 BC (Dio 53.32.1), though the reference to Gaius and Lucius as 'leaders of the younger generation' dates the text to after 2 BC. The translation does not represent that the text itself is extremely poorly cut, being full of mistakes.

M84 Dedication to Gaius Caesar, ?AD 2, Athens
The people (honour) Gaius Caesar, son of Augustus, new Ares.

[Greek: EJ 64 = *IG*² II.3.3250]

The prominence of the Roman imperial family in prestigious areas of Athens is illustrated by this dedication to Gaius from the Theatre of Dionysus on the slopes of the Acropolis. It may date from AD 2, acknowledging Gaius as a new war-god in the light of his recent success in Armenia. The Athenians may have been inspired to honour Gaius in the wake of his visiting the city during his tour of duty in the East. It is also tempting to make a link with the temple to Ares dating from this same period in the Agora just to the north of Agrippa's Odeion. It is a temple originally built in the 5th century BC somewhere in the Attic countryside, but dismantled and reconstructed in the Agora. During the 1st century BC, Athens had suffered at hands of Romans, having repeatedly backed the wrong side (Mithridates, then Brutus and Cassius, finally Antony), so perhaps their monuments in honour of members of the imperial family partly reflect their anxiety to get it right this time.

M85   Documents in honour of Menogenes, an envoy to Rome

A tall pedimented marble plaque (2.24m high), found near the temple of Artemis at Sardis, contains 12 documents in honour of a local citizen, Menogenes. Document 1 (see **J56**) records Menogenes acting as envoy to convey the city's congratulations to Augustus on the coming-of-age of Gaius Caesar. Document 2 (about 1 July, 5 BC is a copy of a letter of Augustus acknowledging the embassy, and Menogenes' role.]

Document 2: about 1 July, 5 BC

[22] Imperator Caesar Augustus, son of a god, chief priest, in his 19th year of tribunician power, sends greetings to the magistrates and council of the Sardians. Your envoys Iollas son of Metrodoros and Menogenes son of Isidoros the son of Menogenes had a meeting with me in Rome and handed over your decree through which by revealing your resolutions concerning yourselves you also join in rejoicing at the coming-of-age of the elder of my sons. And so I commend you for showing zeal in proving yourselves to be grateful towards me and all my kin in return for the benefactions you have received from me.

[Greek: EJ 99 = *IGRRP* 4.1756, lines 22–27]

[**Summary of documents 3–6**: honours to Menogenes following his successful return from his embassy to Rome from the council (no.3: about 1 September 5 BC), from council and people (no.4: about October 5 BC), and from elders (nos 5–6: about 1 September and October 5 BC).]

Document 7: early August, 4 BC

[75] Charinos son of Charinos, from Pergamon, the chief priest of the goddess Rome and of Imperator Caesar Augustus son of a god, greets the magistrates, council and people of the Sardians: when the electoral assembly had been convened and the 150 men from the cities had assembled, they were all eager to honour the annual public advocate of the Assembly of the Hellenes in Asia, Menogenes son of Isidoros son of Menogenes your citizen, because of his evident goodwill towards Asia and because of having completed his term of office honestly and profitably, with a painted gilded statue in armour which is to be placed in whichever city of Asia he should desire, and beneath it is to be inscribed: 'The Hellenes in Asia honoured Menogenes son of Isidoros son of Menogenes from Sardis, public advocate, having completed his term of office honestly and profitably for Asia.' Because of this we have also written to you concerning his honours so that you may know of them.

[Greek: EJ 99 = *IGRRP* 4.1756, lines 75–82]

[**Summary of Documents 8–12**: all honouring Menogenes. Letter of Demetrios, high priest of Rome and Augustus (no.8: Aug/Sept 3 BC); two decrees of the Hellenes of Asia (nos 9–10: end of 3/ early 2 BC & Oct-Dec 2 BC); two decrees of the council of Sardis (nos 11–12: both Aug/Sept 1 BC).]

SECTION N

WAR AND EXPANSION

'The achievements of the deified Augustus by which he subjected the world to the empire of the Roman people' forms the first part of the 'heading' of the *Res Gestae*. Claims of Rome's right to world domination can be found in Augustan literature and iconography. Certainly the period of Octavian/ Augustus saw a huge increase in the size of the Roman Empire. Augustus list his conquests in *Res Gestae* 26–32; Suetonius, *Augustus* 20–21 provides a similar list, and see **N1** below. Whether there was any fixed plan of military expansion is more difficult to determine. Augustus' will advised against further expansion of the empire (Dio 56.33). For a narrative account of Augustan expansion see *CAH* X² pages 147–197.

This section arranges material alphabetically by area. It includes areas which were certainly not brought within the Roman Empire by Augustus, but which are mentioned by him and by the poets.

N1 Eutropius' fourth-century perspective

Never before Augustus had Rome so flourished. For, with the exception of the civil wars, in which he was unbeaten, he added to the Roman empire Egypt, Cantabria, Dalmatia (which had often previously been beaten but was only then completely subdued), Pannonia, Aquitania, Illyricum, Raetia, the Vindelici and Salassi in the Alps, all the states on the Black Sea coast, the most notable of these being Bosphorus and Panticapaeum. He also defeated the Dacians in battles. He cut down huge numbers of Germans, and even moved them to beyond the Elbe which is in Barbarian land far beyond the Rhine. But he conducted this war through Drusus, his step-son, and similarly, through Tiberius, his other step-son, the Pannonian War in which he transferred 40,000 prisoners from Germany and located them across the bank of the Rhine in Gaul. He recovered Armenia from the Parthians. The Persians gave him hostages for the first time and returned the Roman standards which they had taken after the defeat of Crassus.

The Scythians and Indians, whose name had previously been unknown in Rome, sent him envoys and gifts. Galatia was also made a province under him: this had previously been a kingdom; Marcus Lollius as propraetor was its first governor. Many kings came from their kingdoms to do him homage and rushed to his carriage or horse, in Roman togas.

[Eutropius, *Brief History* 7.9–10]

The *Fasti Triumphales* (List of Triumphs) (N2)

A triumph was a spectacular parade through Rome, celebrated by a military commander (*triumphator*) who had won a major victory. The day was a public holiday. Something of the meaning and atmosphere can perhaps be captured by the tradition of a slave standing behind the *triumphator* to repeat to him the words 'Remember you are mortal.' Its award, properly by decree of the senate and vote of the people was the height of a Roman's ambition. Many examples can be cited of its lure affecting military objectives and the governing of provinces; and of the awarding of a triumph being a matter of political intrigue. Under the late republic and triumvirate, triumphs proliferated (14 between 43 and 33 BC), but they quickly die out under the principate, except for members of the imperial family. Reasons are easily found: jealousy of such honours on the part of a *princeps* notoriously not a natural general; a reduction in the number of areas of 'independent command' ('public' provinces), after the reorganisation of the provinces in 27 BC (see **M2–M4**); the well-publicised refusal of Augustus and Agrippa to celebrate triumphs (*RG* 4.1; Dio 54.11.6, 54.24.8). Instead, triumphal ornaments were awarded (see note on Vell. 2.104.2).

Two lists of triumphs survive at least in part from Rome, the *fasti triumphales Barberini* and the *fasti triumphales Capitolini*. The *Capitolini* list was found in the forum in 1546. The original location of the *Fasti Barberini* is unknown. The two lists seem to provide between them a complete list of triumphs celebrated in the age of Augustus.

N2a   29 BC   Imp. Caesar over the Dalmatians. 13 August.
          Imp. Caesar over Egypt. 15 August.

Octavian actually celebrated a 'triple triumph' – three full triumphs on consecutive days (**H16**). The *fasti triumphales Barberini* omit the middle triumph, that celebrated for Actium.

N2b   28 BC   C. Calvisius Sabinus over Spain. 26 May.
          C. Carrinas over the Gauls. 30 June.
          L. Autronius Paetus, proconsul, over Africa. 16 August.

Gaius Calvisius Sabinus: a loyal supporter of Julius Caesar and his heir. He was consul in 39 BC and commanded Octavian's fleet against Sextus Pompey in 39–38 BC, and spoke against Antony in the senate in 32 BC (Plutarch, *Antony* 58). Proconsul of Spain in 29/28 BC, he followed Octavian/Augustus' call to those who had won triumphs to restore roads (Suet. *Aug.* 30.1; Dio 53.22.1), by using his spoils to restore the *via Latina* as shown by a milestone.

Gaius Carrinas: suffect consul in 43 BC, legate of Octavian in Further Spain, legionary commander against Sextus Pompey in 36 BC and proconsul in Gaul. Dio (51.21.6) gives his victories as being against the Morini and Suebi, though he also (wrongly) suggests that his triumph was celebrated jointly with the first of Octavian's triple triumph.

Lucius Autronius Paetus: consul in 33 BC.

N2c   27 BC   M. Licinius Crassus, proconsul, over Thrace and the Getae. 2 July.
          M. Valerius Messalla Corvinus, proconsul, over Gaul. 25 September.

Marcus Licinius Crassus: consul in 30 BC (see **Section B**); as proconsul of Macedonia, he conducted campaigns in 29 and 28 BC. (Dio 51.23–27), during which he killed Deldo, king of the Bastarnae. He claimed the *spolia opima*, see **P3–P4**.

Marcus Valerius Messalla Corvinus: consul in 31 BC (see **Section B**), governed Gaul, 28–27 BC, conquering the Aquitani. Like Calvisius he also helped restore the *via Latina* as encouraged by Augustus, a deed celebrated by the poet Tibullus (1.7.57–62 = **K68b** in Addenda).

N2d   26 BC   Sextus Appuleius, proconsul, over Spain. 26 January.

Sextus Appuleius: the elder son of Augustus' step-sister Octavia. Governor (proconsul) of Nearer Spain in 28 BC. His command, and campaigns for which he triumphed thus pre-dated the settlement of 28/27 BC, after which generals in Spain, a province of Augustus were acting under his *imperium* and therefore not eligible for triumphs.

N2e   21 BC   L. Sempronius Atratinus, proconsul, over Africa. 28 September.

Lucius Sempronius Atratinus: noted as an orator. At some point between 38 and 34 BC in command of Antony's fleet. Consul 34 BC, taking over from Antony on 1 Jan. The date or circumstances of his defection to Octavian are not recorded, but he left Augustus as his heir (see **T35**). Proconsular governors of Africa, a 'public province' under the settlement of 28/27 BC commanded their own legion and thus remained eligible for triumphs (See **M2–M4**).

N2f   19 BC   L. Cornelius Balbus, proconsul, over Africa. 27 March.

Lucius Cornelius Balbus: see **M25** and **N9** for his campaigns. He built a theatre in Rome. (**K51**) presumably with the spoils of his campaign and prompted by an instruction from Augustus (Dio 54.18.2).

Triumphs of Tiberius: these are not recorded on the *Fasti Triumphales*, but are mentioned by Suetonius, *Tib.*9.2 and 17.1–2; Vell. 2.122.1; Dio 55.6.5, 55.8.2, 56.17.1.

N3   Exceptional Honours for Generals (being hailed *imperator*)
Even Augustus had granted to a few of his generals the distinction (of being hailed as *imperator* by their legions), but Tiberius' grant to Blaesus was the last example of this honour.

[Tacitus, *Annals* 3.74]

The context is Tiberius' grant of this distinction to Quintus Junius Blaesus in AD 22. Being hailed as '*imperator*' was traditionally the first step to being granted a triumph. Other *triumphators* under Augustus were presumably allowed the title '*imperator*'. According to Dio 51.25.2, Marcus Licinius Crassus (**N2c**) was not, but it still appears on inscriptions (*ILS* 8810).

N4   *Denarius, 32–29* BC

Obv: Female bust, possibly Venus.

Rev: Octavian in military dress.
        CAESAR DIVI F (Caesar, Son of the Deified)

[*RIC* Augustus 251 / *BMC* Augustus 609]

The importance of the army to Octavian's position, as well as his continued desire to expand the territory of the Roman world, is reflected in the imagery of the coinage. Although this coin seems to allude specifically to the Battle of Actium, it is symptomatic of a wider tendency for coins to depict Octavian/Augustus in military guise. In this case Octavian is shown leading the troops into battle, a design linked with an obverse that seems to depict Venus (ancestress of the family of Julius Caesar). After this time military scenes, often connected with the celebration of victories, are frequently used on the coinage of Augustus.

N5   *Denarius, 29–27* BC

Obv: Victory, standing right, on prow, holding wreath and palm.

Rev: Octavian standing in ornamented quadriga, holding branch.
        IMP CAESAR (Imperator Caesar)

[*RIC* Augustus 264 / *BMC* Augustus 617]

This coin contains many allusions to the themes of warfare and military success. The obverse depicts Victory standing on the prow of a ship – a reference to the naval victory at Actium. The reverse shows Octavian standing in a triumphal *quadriga* (four-horse chariot), a common scene from the celebration of a triumph. This coin specifically commemorates the triple triumph of Octavian in 29 BC (see **H16** and **N2 introduction**).

N6   Cistophorus (3 denarii) of Ephesus, 28 BC

Obv: Octavian, laureate, right.

IMP CAESAR DIVI F COS VI LIBERTATIS P R VINDEX (Imperator Caesar, Son of the Deified, Consul for the sixth time, Defender of the Liberty of the People of Rome)

Rev: *Pax* holding caduceus. Snake emerging from *cista mystica* (basket used in cult of Dionysus) to right.

PAX (Peace)

[*RIC* Augustus 476 / *BMC* Augustus 691]

This coin from the mint of Ephesus, in the Roman province of Asia Minor, illustrates the seemingly contradictory link between war and peace as ideals of the Augustan period. Despite the obvious Roman ideology of world conquest and the prevalence of military imagery, *pax* ('peace' or sometimes 'pacification') was a concept at the heart of the Augustan ethos, as shown by the *Ara Pacis* (see **K13**) and the Temple of Janus (**K47–K49**). The reverse of this coin depicts and names the Roman goddess *Pax*, while the obverse affords Augustus the honorary title '*Defender of the Liberty of the People of Rome*'. The implication here is that through war and his campaigns against Antony, Augustus was able to free the East, and restore peace and stable government.

N7   The use of geography

My original contention – that the majority of geographical studies have a practical application to political science – seems to be particularly true under modern conditions. The supreme test of military leadership lies in the ability to control the land and the sea and to unite nations and cities under a single authority and system of administration. Obviously, therefore, the whole corpus of geographical studies has a bearing on the art of military leadership, since its subject matter covers all land and sea, both inside and beyond the inhabited world. Geographical analysis is of critical importance to such men, since they need to know the precise truth about such matters and whether it is based on first-hand knowledge or guesswork. For they will discharge all their duties much more efficiently if they know the size of a given country, its orientation, and its particular characteristics, whether of climate or terrain.

[Strabo, *Geography* 1.1.16]

The claim that geography should be useful, especially to those with an empire to conquer and rule, might seem obvious. However, the Hellenistic period had seen a great flourishing of rather abstract and theoretical geography through the works of Eratosthenes, Hipparchus and others, with mathematical calculations of the earth's circumference and discussions of relative lines of latitude. However, Caesar's commentaries had shown the importance of practical geography in military campaigns, and Strabo himself explicitly links the growth in geographical knowledge to the conquests of Alexander, Mithridates, the Parthians, and the Romans (1.2.1). Agrippa's commentary and map (**N8**) may provide further evidence that practical knowledge of the world was important for the ruling Romans. However, one may question the true utility of Strabo's account for anyone wishing to travel around the world he describes. Instead he provides a fascinating guide to the general nature of the peoples and places of the empire.

N8   M. Agrippa's *commentarii*

[Agrippa's *Geographical Commentary* does not survive, but Pliny's Index to *Natural History* cites Agrippa prominently as a source for information in books 3–6 where Pliny discusses geography. Pliny also refers to him specifically in his text as his source for information on the following:]

3.8	origin of settlements on coast of Baetica	5.9	the Atlantic? coast of Africa
3.16	dimensions of Baetica	5.40	length of (Med) coast of Africa
3.86	circumference of Sicily	5.102	Lycia
4.77	circumference of the Black Sea	6.3	Black Sea
4.78	distance from Byzantium to the Danube	6.39	Caspian sea area
4.81	area from Danube to Ocean	6.57	India measurement
4.83	the North coast of the Black Sea	6.136–7	Media, Parthia, Mesopotamia,
4.91	Sarmatia, Scythia, Taurica		orientation and size
4.98	Germany, Raetia, Noricum	6.196	Length of Ethiopia
4.105	coastline of Gaul		

AFRICA (N9–N10)

Various campaigns against tribes to the south of the Roman province of Africa are known, probably as deterrents or reactions to incursions threatening the dependent kings of the area or the province of Africa. Governors of this 'public' province could still hope for triumphs, and two were gained at the start of the period by Atratinus in 21 BC and Balbus in 19 BC (**N2e, N2f**) but later Passienus Rufus in AD 2 and Cossus in AD 6 receive only triumphal ornaments (Vell. 2.116.2, **N10**).

N9   Balbus' campaigns against the Garamantes in the Sahara desert

Beyond the Black Mountain lies the desert and then the Garamantean town of Thelgae, together with Debris (where there are springs which pour out boiling water from midday to midnight and then for the same number of hours ice-cold water till midday), and Garama, the world-famous capital of the Garamantes. All these fell to Roman arms and earned a triumph for Cornelius Balbus, his award of a foreigner's triumphal chariot being a unique honour, together with a grant of full citizen rights. For though he was born in Cadiz, he and his great-uncle Balbus were both accorded Roman citizenship. It is a remarkable fact that our sources have handed down to us the names of the captured cities already described above; but they also state that as well as Cydamum and Garama, the names and effigies of all the other tribes and cities which he defeated were carried in his triumph.

[Pliny, *Natural History* 5.36]

Pliny goes on to give a specific list of 25 fortified towns, tribes and places captured by Balbus. On Balbus, see **M23**, on his triumph in 19 BC, **N2f**.

N10   Gaetulian war

During this period too, in Africa, Cossus, a general of Caesar, confined within narrower boundaries the Musolani and Gaetulians who had been wandering freely, and forced them, through fear, to keep away from Roman frontiers.

[Orosius, *Against the Pagans* 6.21.18]

This was in AD 6 (Dio 55.28.3–4). See also a dedication to Mars Augustus (**M4**). Cossus Cornelius Lentulus received triumphal decorations only, and a *cognomen* 'Gaetulicus' (Vell. 2.116.2 – Section **E**).

The ALPS (Noricum, Raetia) (N11–N17)

Part of the Alps remained under the control of King Cottius (see **M33**). Varro campaigned against an Alpine tribe, the Salassi, in 25 BC, founding a veteran colony of Augusta Praetoria (Aosta). Tiberius and Nero Drusus pacified the area in campaigns of 15–14 BC. *Res Gestae* 26.3 records the pacification of the region. Horace, *Odes* 4.4 and 4.14 (**G42, G44**) celebrate the campaign.

N11   Alpine tribes subdued by Augustus

Beyond Lake Como, situated at the foot of the Alps, lie the lands of the Raeti and Vennones sloping towards the east and on the other side, the Lepontii, Tridentini, Stoni and other small tribes which previously kept a hold on Italy through their banditry and inaccessibility. But now some have been completely destroyed, others so completely subdued that the mountain passes through their territory, formerly few and treacherous, are now numerous, safe from harm from local people and as easily passable as building technique allows. For Augustus not only eliminated banditry but built roads whever possible.

[Strabo, *Geography* 4.6.6]

N12   The Alpine Salassi

This Alpine tribe possessed gold mines and controlled their territory, at least through brigandage, even at the time of Julius Caesar and the triumvirate. Later, however, Augustus completely overthrew them, and sold them all as booty at Eporedia, a colony which the Romans had established as a garrison against the Salassi, but which could only offer slight resistance until the tribe had been wiped out. 8,000 fighting men were captured and 36,000 other people, but Terentius Varro, the general who overthrew them, sold them all as war-booty. Caesar sent 3,000 Romans to found the city of Augusta at the site where Varro had set up camp, and now the whole area, up to the highest mountain-passes is at peace.

[Strabo, *Geography* 4.6.7]

Dio 53.25.2–5 gives a slightly longer account of the campaign, mentioned in the summary of Livy 135 (**D4**). The claim to be suppressing brigands and pirates and to be civilising the world had been made by Roman commanders throughout the whole of the first century BC, but Augustus used such claims to support the important notion of the *pax Augusta* (Augustan Peace: see *RG* 26.3).

Salassi: mentioned on the Alpine triumphal arch, Pliny *NH* 3.136, below.

Augusta: Augusta Praetoria, now Aosta, see **N13**.

Terentius Varro: it is not clear whether this is the same Terentius Varro as named on the consul list for 23 BC or the governor of Syria (**M38**) or neither.

N13   Augustus honoured at new colony of Augusta Praetoria, 23–20 BC

To Imperator Caesar Augustus, son of the Deified, consul for the 11th time, hailed as victorious general 8 times, holder of tribunician power. The Salassi locals, who at the start settled themselves into the colony, (set this up) to their patron.

[EJ 338 = *ILS* 6753]

The colony of Augusta Praetoria Salassorum (modern Aosta) in the Alpine region of north-west Italy was founded by Terentius Varro c.25 BC. The local inhabitants (the Salassi) were forcibly evicted from the best land in the area, which was distributed to 3,000 veterans, including members of the praetorian guard (**N12** and Dio 53.25). The colony was on a strategically significant site, controlling the River Duria, the lower stretches of which were rich in gold; it also straddled the Great and Little St Bernard passes. This inscription shows how the Salassi evidently thought that it was in their interests to embrace this new state of affairs.

N14   Pacification of the Alpine tribes.

Tiberius and his brother Drusus put an end to their free incursions in a single summer campaign so that there has now been peace and regular payment of tribute for thirty-three years.

[Strabo, *Geography* 4.6.9]

Dio's account of the campaigns of 15–14 BC at 54.22.

N15 Augustus receiving triumphal branches, *aureus*, 15–12 BC

Obv: Augustus, head bare, left
AVGVSTVS DIVI F (Augustus, son of the Deified)

Rev: Augustus seated on platform, receiving branches from two men in military dress
IMP X (Hailed *imperator* (victorious general) for the tenth time)

[*RIC* Augustus 164b / *BMC* Augustus 447]

This coin, issued between 15 and 12 BC in Lyons, has a clear image of Augustus' military success. The figure seated on the platform is identified as Augustus, while the two figures in military dress handing triumphal branches to the *princeps* are normally identified as Tiberius and Drusus. The date of this coin therefore suggests the commemoration of the conquest of Raetia by the stepsons of Augustus in 15 BC. The title IMP(erator) is used here in its more traditional sense of a commander saluted by his troops. However it is the *princeps*, rather than his generals as was traditional, who receives this accolade. It was vital that Augustus was seen as the supreme commander of the troops.

N16 Triumphal monument to Alpine victories 7–6 BC

[136] This seems an appropriate moment to record the inscription from the triumphal monument for our Alpine victories, which runs as follows:

> *To Imperator Caesar Augustus, son of the Deified, Pontifex Maximus, hailed as victorious general 14 times, in his 17th year of tribunician power, the Senate and People of Rome (set up this monument) in commemoration of the fact that by his leadership and under his auspices all the tribes of the Alps stretching from the Adriatic to the Mediterranean were brought under the power of the Roman People. The following Alpine tribes were defeated: the Triumpilini, Camunni, Venostes,* [137] *Vennonetes, Isarchi, Breuni, Genaunes, Focunates, four tribes of the Vindelici, the Cosuanetes, Rucinates, Licates, Catenates, Ambisontes, Rugusci, Suanetes, Calucones, Brixentes, Leponti, Uberi, Nantuates, Seduni, Varagri, Salassi, Acitavones, Medulli, Ucenni, Caturiges, Brigiani, Sobionti, Brodionti, Nemaloni, Edenates, Vesubiani, Veamini, Gallitae, Triullati, Ecdini, Vergunni, Eguituri, Nematuri, Oratelli, Nerusi, Velauni, Suetri.*

[138] I have not included the fifteen non-belligerent states of the Cottiani, nor those that were controlled by the Italian municipalities under the *Lex Pompeia*.

[Pliny, *Natural History* 3.136–138]

Part of the inscription (*CIL* 5.7817) from the monument, at modern La Turbie (overlooking Monaco) has also been found and the monument has been reconstructed.

Cottiani: the peoples ruled by the friendly king, Cottius – **M33**.

N17   An equestrian procurator.
Q. Octavius Sagitta, procurator of Caesar Augustus in Vindelicia and Raetia and the
Poenine valley for four years.

[EJ 224 = *ILS* 9007]

Despite its conquest, the area was not made into a formal province by Augustus. Instead it was ruled by an
equestrian procurator, responsible to Augustus himself.

ARABIA (N18–N22)

Aelius Gallus' expedition to Arabia took place in 26–25 or 25–24 BC. Strabo, who describes Aelius Gallus as 'my
friend and comrade' (2.5.12), thus provides excellent evidence for the aims of the expedition, the wealth of an
area often known as *Arabia Felix* ('Fortunate Arabia'). He also provides much detail about the expedition itself.

N18   Aims of the expedition against Arabia
The recent Roman campaign against the Arabs, led in my own time by Aelius Gallus, has
given us a great deal of information about the distinctive characteristics of the region.
Augustus Caesar sent him out to secure intelligence about the local tribesmen and the
topographical features of the area, and of Ethiopia as well, since he realised that the
Trogodyte country adjacent to Egypt also borders closely on Arabia, since the Arabian gulf
separating the Arabs from the Trogodytes is extremely narrow. His strategy was to either
win over the Arabs to an alliance or to conquer them. But there was an additional
consideration: from time immemorial it was rumoured that the area was very rich and that
they traded spices and precious stones for gold and silver, but never parted with the proceeds
of their trading to outsiders. It was Augustus' hope either to acquire wealthy allies or to
conquer wealthy enemies. His expectation of assistance from the Nabataeans encouraged
him further, since they were allies and had promised to help him in every way they could.
       Therefore Gallus launched the expedition. But the Nabataean viceroy, Syllaeus,
deceived him: for though he promised to guide him on the route, to supply everything,
and to collaborate with him, he acted treacherously throughout ...

[Strabo, *Geography* 16.4.22]

N19   Expedition into Arabia
Aelius Gallus, of the equestrian order, is the only one so far to have led Roman armies
into this area. For Augustus' son, Gaius Caesar, contented himself with viewing Arabia
from afar. But Gallus actually destroyed certain strongholds not hitherto mentioned by
our previous authorities. They were: Negrana, Nestus, Nesca, Magusus, Caminacus,
Lambaetia, as well as Mariba (with its 6 mile circumference, already described) and
Caripeta, which was as far as he went.

[Pliny, *Natural History* 6.160]

The advance to Mariba is mentioned in the *Res Gestae* (26.5). Despite Pliny's positive report, the expedition
failed, perhaps because of heat and disease (Dio 53.29), perhaps because of the treachery of Syllaeus, the
Nabataean, as Strabo states.

N20   Herod sends troops for the expedition
It was at about that time that Herod sent to Caesar a supporting force of some 500
picked members of his bodyguard. These Aelius Gallus took with him on his expedition
to the Red Sea and they proved extremely useful to him.

[Josephus, *Jewish Antiquities* 15.317]

N21 Hollow military successes in Arabia

The next country he marched through belonged to Nomads and most of it was truly desert: it was called Ararene and its king was Sabos. He spent fifty days passing through this country without roads, reaching a city called Negranoi, and a fertile and peaceful country. The king had fled and so the city was captured in the first attack. From here he reached the river in six days. Here the barbarians joined battle, and about ten thousand of them fell, but only two Romans: they were naive in their use of weapons, being utterly unwarlike, with bows, spears, swords and slings, but mostly double-edged axes. Immediately afterwards, he took a city called Asca, which had been abandoned by its king. From there he went to the city of Athrula, and after taking it without resistance, established a garrison, prepared for supplies of corn and dates for the march and advanced to the city of Marsiaba, belonging to the Rhammanitae tribe, who were subjects of Ilasaros. For six days he attacked and besieged the city, but gave up for lack of water. He was only two days' march from the country which produced spices, according to what he heard from prisoners, but had wasted six months' time on his journey, through being badly guided.

[Strabo, *Geography* 16.4.24]

Augustus, *Res Gestae* 26.5, manages to give these hollow military successes a positive spin, with the failure to capture Marsiaba being reported as 'penetrated as far as Mariba'.

Athrula: near the modern border between Saudi Arabia and Yemen. The tombstone of a cavalryman, Publius Cornelius, who must have been from Gallus' expedition, has been found there (see G.W. Bowersock, *Roman Arabia*, (Harvard 1983) pages 148–153).

N22 Failure of the expedition

The whole journey took him less than sixty days on the way back, although the outward journey had taken six months. Then he took his army across to Myus Harbour within eleven days, then to Coptus, and landed at Alexandria with those who had been able to survive. He had lost the others, not through enemy action, but disease, exhaustion, starvation and the harsh terrain: only seven men had been killed in action. For these reasons, this expedition did not provide great benefit towards knowledge of the region, though it did contribute a little. But the man to blame for what happened, Syllaeus, paid the penalty at Rome: though he pretended friendship, he was convicted for his treachery in the expedition and other wrongdoing, and was beheaded.

[Strabo, *Geography* 16.4.24]

Disease: Dio's account of the expedition concentrates on describing the disease (53.29.3–8).

Syllaeus: chief minister of the dependent kingdom of Nabataea in Arabia. Strabo consistently blames Syllaeus for deliberately misleading Gallus, though the motive he ascribes – that Syllaeus wished to become ruler of the area once the Romans had destroyed the local tribes but had been 'wiped out by starvation, exhaustion, disease and whatever else he treacherously contrived' – seems far-fetched. Though Strabo implies that Syllaeus was executed as a direct result of the failed expedition, Josephus' accounts of Herod's reign show that he was still chief minister of Nabataea and even a guest of Augustus in Rome in the first decade BC, though executed around 7 BC, see **M40–M41**.

ARMENIA (N23–N25)

Armenia Major was not of much value to Rome, but became a prize in the propaganda struggle between Rome and Parthia (*RG* 27.2). The Romans kept hostages to deploy against incumbent Parthian and Armenian monarchs or to fill gaps.

N23   Relations with Armenia up to around 1 BC

(This passage continues N46 and is continued in N25)

The Armenians had no love for Rome, thanks to the treachery of Mark Antony who had seduced their king, Artavasdes (I), with the promise of friendship, but then imprisoned and finally executed him. Mindful of his father's experience, his son, Artaxias (II), remained hostile to Rome and protected himself and his kingdom by alliance with the powerful Arsacids. But thanks to the treachery of his relatives he was assassinated and Tigranes (II) was appointed by Augustus as the new ruler of Armenia and introduced to his kingdom under escort by Tiberius Nero. He did not last long. His children's reign was similarly brief, though in the custom of foreign nations brother and sister shared a marriage bed as well as their kingdom.

[Tacitus, *Annals* 2.3]

Tacitus is explaining the background to hostilities between Rome and Parthia in AD 16.

Artavasdes (I): he had not proved a reliable ally to Mark Antony in his Parthian expedition.

Artaxias (II): his replacement by his brother Tigranes (II) took place in 19 BC. Roman coins announced the capture of Armenia see **N24**.

Tigranes (II): he died before 6 BC. Tacitus underestimates the length of his reign.

His children's reign: Erato, with her brother-husband, Tigranes (III) had taken the throne after the death of their father Tigranes (II). They were deposed and returned in about 1 BC until his death during Gaius' mission, when she abdicated.

N24   Capture of Armenia, *aureus* of 20 BC or 19–18 BC

Obv: Augustus, head bare, right
Rev: Victory, right, cutting the throat of bull
            ARMENIA CAPTA (Armenia captured)

[*RIC* Augustus 514 / *BMC* Augustus 671]

In the *Res Gestae* (*RG* 27), Augustus boasts that he could have established a province of Armenia after its king Artaxes had been killed, but chose instead to establish a client kingdom. The imagery used on the coinage which marked this event also clearly suggests the subjugation of Armenia, while the legend '*ARMENIA CAPTA*', together with the depiction of Victory slitting the throat of a bull, reflects the inequality of the client kingdom and Rome, reflected in the *Res Gestae* and other sources.

N25   Rome and Armenia, around 1 BC to AD 16.

(This passage continues N23)

[4] Augustus then proceeded to appoint Artavasdes (II) to the throne, but he was deposed with disastrous results for Rome. Gaius Caesar was given the task of settling the Armenian problem and he appointed Ariobarzanes as the new king. A Mede by origin, his splendid appearance and admirable character won the approval of the

Armenians, but after his accidental death they refused to accept his son and experimented instead with the rule of a woman, called Erato. They soon got rid of her and were now disorganised and bewildered, in a state of anarchy rather than liberty. As a result they readily accepted the exiled Vonones as their king.

[Tacitus, *Annals* 2.4]

Artavasdes (II): he held Armenia in the period of Erato's exile, some time between 6 and 1 BC.

Gaius Caesar: Augustus' grandson and adopted son was sent out in 1 BC to restore Roman influence. He made an accord with Parthia but was fatally wounded in the disturbances in Armenia (see **J59**).

Vonones (I): eldest son of Phraates IV, king of Parthia. He had been in Roman custody since 10 BC and was deployed as king in AD 6 after unrest in Parthia, but dethroned in AD 12 (see **N46**). He found the throne of Armenia vacant and occupied it between AD 12 and 15/16.

The BALKANS (Illyricum (Dalmatia/Pannonia)) (N26–N28)

Under Augustus the area was known as Illyricum (as at *RG* 30.1). At some point Illyricum was divided into two provinces, Dalmatia and Pannonia, but our sources use the names so flexibly that the division cannot be dated.

Octavian had instigated a campaign in Illyricum between 35–33 BC which enhanced his dubious military reputation and provided him with one of his three triumphs of August 29 BC. He later produced memoirs of the campaign.

In 27 BC Roman control was mainly confined to the Adriatic seaboard, but it was extended to the Danube by the conquests of 13–8 BC. The Pannonian revolt of AD 6–9 posed a serious threat to Rome's stability, but was crushed and Augustus was able to set in place the military commands on which the two provinces of Dalmatia and Pannonia were established.

'The sources are more interested in Germany and tell us little about these campaigns. Dio, our main source, presents them merely as crushing revolts: he appears to have thought that all Illyricum had been conquered by Augustus' campaigns of 35–33 BC.' (J. Rich, *Dio* page 210). The main sources are:

War in Pannonia under Tiberius: 13–9 BC: Vell. 2.96.2–3; Dio 54.31.2–4; 54.34.3–4; 54.36.3; 55.2.4
The revolt of AD 6–9: Vell. 2.114.4–117.1; Dio 55.28–31; Dio 56.11–17.

N26   Summary of Livy, book 141 (10 BC)

Drusus' brother, Nero, subdued the Dalmatians and the Pannonians.

[Summary of Livy 141]

N27   A distinguished career at Alexandria Troas (Asia Minor), c. AD 14

To Gaius Fabricius Tuscus, son of Gaius, of the Aniensis tribe, joint chief magistrate, augur, prefect of the Apulan cohort and of the works which have been executed in the colony by Augustus' command; military tribune of the 3rd Legion Cyrenaica for 8 years, tribune of the levy of freeborn men which Augustus and Tiberius Caesar carried out at Rome; prefect of engineers for 4 years, prefect of the praetorian cavalry wing for 4 years; he was presented with the untipped spear and golden crown by Germanicus Caesar, commander in the German war. By decree of the town councillors.

[EJ 368 = *AE* 1973.501]

The use of Latin on this stone plaque found at modern Tuzla, Turkey points to its original location as the colony of Alexandria Troas. The town's council honours a local man who has held local magistracies, as well as completing a distinguished military career, which culminated in his being granted military decorations by Germanicus c.AD 14. He may be identical with the author mentioned by Pliny the Elder as being a source for some of his *Natural History*. The inscription illustrates the atmosphere of crisis at Rome around AD 6 following the Pannonian revolt, since the act of holding a levy of soldiers at Rome is highly unusual (compare Dio 55.31.1). Usually troops were recruited from volunteers rather than being conscripted.

N28   Freedmen enlisted

In both Germany and Illyricum Augustus Caesar enlisted several cohorts of freedmen, whom he nicknamed his 'volunteers'.

[Macrobius, *Saturnalia* 1.11.32]

Dio (56.23) tells us that emergency measures, including conscription of freeborn Romans and enrolment of freedmen followed news of the Varus disaster of AD 9. Velleius (2.111.1) and Dio (55.31.1) tell us that freedmen were enlisted following the revolt in Illyricum, AD 6.

BRITAIN (N29–N30)

Britain is regularly mentioned by the poets of the period (see **G3, G27, G44,** Propertius 2.6). Public opinion may have expected an invasion by Augustus. According to Dio, Augustus projected expeditions to Britain in 34, 27 and 26 BC (Dio 49.38.2; 53.22.5; 53.25.2), but nothing came of it.

   Strabo's comments on the lack of profit to be gained from annexing Britain as a province might be seen as serious economic analysis, but may simply provide an excuse for the failure of Rome to conquer the island. This would be in line with Strabo's presentation of Rome and its imperialistic project which is surprisingly sympathetic given that Strabo himself came from the margins of the empire and from a family which had been in favour with the local ruling dynasty before Rome took control.

N29   No profit in invading Britain

As far as strict military requirements go, there would be no great advantage in researching the truth about such far distant countries and their inhabitants, especially if they inhabit islands which are incapable of offering us profit or injury thanks to their inaccessibility. Take Britain, for example. The Romans could have annexed it to their empire; but they regarded it with contempt, since they realised that it posed no threat to them whatsoever (lacking as they did the military resources to cross the channel and attack us), and that if they did capture it they would derive no advantage from doing so. For it is quite clear that Rome now gets more from customs dues than any direct taxation could possibly bring in, once you deduct the cost of a military garrison and revenue collection. The same practical considerations apply even more in the case of the other islands around Britain.

[Strabo, *Geography* 2.5.8]

it posed no threat: Julius Caesar claimed British reinforcements being sent over to Gaul as the pretext for his expeditions to Britain in 55 and 54 BC (Caesar, *Gallic War* 4.20.1).

N30   Taxation from Britain

Julius Caesar won two or three victories over the Britons, even though he only shipped two legions from his army across the channel. He also brought back hostages, slaves, and a massive collection of other booty. But now some of the tribal chieftains there have won the friendship of Augustus Caesar by sending embassies and paying homage to him. They have even dedicated offerings to him on the Capitol and have almost managed to make the whole island a sort of Roman enclave. They are so tolerant of the heavy taxes imposed on their exports to Celtic lands and the imports from those same lands (ivory chains, necklaces, red-amber gems, glass vessels, and similar frippery) that the island has no need of a garrison. The minimum requirement for such an exercise would be one legion and supporting cavalry just to collect the tribute, so that the cost of the army would equal the income accruing from the revenues. Inevitably, the revenue brought in by the taxation would consequently be diminished and the risks of confrontation increased if we decided to use force.

[Strabo, *Geography* 4.5.3]

Julius Caesar: his accounts of his expeditions of 55 and 54 BC are Caesar, *Gallic Wars* 4.20–38, 5.1–23.
tribal chieftains: *Res Gestae* (32.1) names Dumnobellaunus and Tincommius.

EGYPT (N31–N32)

Egypt was acquired directly as a result of Octavian's defeat of Antony and Cleopatra VII, last Ptolemaic queen of Egypt. The Civil Wars had highlighted the danger presented by Egyptian independence. Only the establishment of direct Roman control could ensure that the power and wealth of Egypt were never again used against Rome. Thereafter Augustus' main concern was the administration of the large and important province, see **M6–M14**, but he also ensured that his annexation of this large, famous, ancient and wealthy kingdom was not forgotten, by coinage and the striking symbolism of transporting obelisks to Rome.

N31 Capture of Egypt, *denarius* of 27 BC

Obv: Augustus, head bare, right
   CAESAR DIVI F COS VII (Caesar, Son of the Deified, Consul for the seventh time)
Rev: Crocodile, right
   AEGVPTO CAPTA (Egypt captured)

[*RIC* Augustus 544 / *BMC* Augustus 655]

The importance of the capture and annexation of Egypt cannot be overestimated. The achievement was celebrated on both gold and silver coinage, such as on this *denarius* of Augustus dating to 27 BC. This coin shows a beautifully rendered crocodile, symbolic of Egypt and the announcement 'EGYPT CAPTURED'. '*Capta* type' coins are a common form of commemoration of military success.

N32 Obelisks

[69] Above all else, there was the added difficulty of transporting obelisks to Rome – so much so that the ships which carried them became a focus of public attention. [70] To celebrate such a remarkable event, the deified Augustus dedicated the first ship to transport an obelisk in a permanent dock at Puteoli. It was later destroyed by a fire.

[Pliny, *Natural History* 36.69–70]

On Augustus' inventive use of the obelisks, see **K35–K36**. Egyptian obelisks now also decorate Thames Embankment, London, and Central Park, New York.

ETHIOPIA (N33–N35)

Soon after the annexation of Egypt, Roman thoughts turned towards expansion towards the south. Cornelius Gallus had already commemorated his excursions into Ethiopia (**P5**) by Spring 29 BC. Petronius campaigned in 25 or 24 BC and put down a revolt in around 22 BC (Dio 54.5.4–6) after which stable relations seem to have been maintained with Roman power extending to Napata (*RG* 26.5) well into modern Sudan. Modern Ethiopia lies south-east of the area the Romans called Ethiopia.

N33   The Ethiopians

The Ethiopians stretching towards the south and Meroe are not numerous nor populous, inhabiting the long, narrow, winding stretch of river land I have previously described. Nor are they well prepared for war or any other way of life. And now the whole country is similarly disposed, as evidenced by the fact that the country is sufficiently garrisoned by the Romans with three cohorts, not even at full strength. But when the Ethiopians dared to attack them, they endangered their own country.

[Strabo, *Geography* 17.1.53]

The Ethiopians may have learnt that an expedition was planned against them and tried to pre-empt it, perhaps when Rome was engaged on the expedition to Arabia.

N34   Petronius' expedition to Ethiopia (25/24 BC)

The Ethiopians, made over-confident by the fact that part of the force in Egypt had been detached to campaign with Aelius Gallus against the Arabs, attacked the Thebaid and the garrison of three cohorts at Syene and, taking them by surprise, overran Syene, Elephantine and Philae, enslaved the inhabitants and pulled down statues of Caesar. Petronius set out with fewer than ten thousand infantry and eight hundred cavalry against thirty thousand. He first forced them to flee to Pselchis, a city in Ethiopia … From Pselchis he went to Premnis, a fortified city … he attacked and captured the fortress at the first onset, and next set out for Napata. This was the royal residence of Candace, and her son was there: she herself was residing in a place nearby. She sent an embassy to treat for friendship and the return of the prisoners from Syene and the statues, but Petronius attacked and captured Napata, after her son had fled, and razed it to the ground. Having enslaved the inhabitants, he turned back with his plunder, judging that the regions further south would be hard to cross. But he fortified Premnis more strongly, put a garrison in place with two years' supply for four hundred men, then departed for Alexandria.

[Strabo, *Geography* 17.1.54]

Dio 54.5.4–6 gives a similar, but briefer account. Pliny (*NH* 6.181) mentions some other towns being captured.

Syene, Elephantine, Philae: important settlements all in the area of the modern Aswan Dam.

statues of Caesar: a bronze head of Augustus was found at Meroe, the capital of Ethiopia, in front of some sort of victory monument.

Premnis: actually Primis. A Roman garrison has been excavated there, modern Qasr Ibrim on the Nile on the Egypt-Sudan border.

N35   Ethiopian revolt and peace settlement, c. 21 BC

Meanwhile Candace advanced against the garrison with many thousands of men. Petronius, however, went to relieve it and got to the fortress first. After making it secure in various ways, he told the ambassadors to go to Caesar: they replied that they did not know who Caesar was or where they would have to go to find him, so he gave them escorts. They went to Samos, where Caesar was staying, on his way to Syria, after sending Tiberius to Armenia. The ambassadors achieved everything they asked, and Caesar also remitted the tribute which he had imposed.

[Strabo, *Geography* 17.1.54]

Strabo implies that Candace's attack occurred while Petronius was returning from his campaign above, but the embassy to Augustus shows that this campaign must be a few years later as Augustus spent the winter of 21/20 BC on Samos.

GERMANY (N36–N38)
Germany was the scene of the most difficult, prolonged and ultimately unsuccessful campaigns of Augustus' reign. The most detailed account of the various campaigns is given by Velleius, 2.97.1–4; 2.104–114 and then on the Varus disaster, 2.117–122. The major events in Germany seem to be:

Defeat of Lollius (16 BC): Vell. 2.97.1; Dio 54.20.4–6; Tac. 1.10.4; Suet. *Aug.* 23.1.

Preparation for invasion (16–13 BC).

Drusus' invasions of Germany (every year 12–9 BC): Dio 54.32–33; 54.36.3; 55,1.2–5; Vell. 2.97.2–3; Livy 139–142.

Tiberius invades Germany (8 BC): Dio 55.6.1–3; Vell. 2.97.4.

Peace 8 BC – AD 1.

Revolt (AD 1) crushed by M. Vinicius (AD 1–3): Vell. 2.104.2 and Tiberius (AD 4–5) Vell. 2.104.3–114.

Varus disaster (AD 9): Suet. *Aug.* 23; Vell. 2.117–122.

N36   The geography of Germany
[98] Along the whole seaboard as far as the Scaldis, a German river, the land is occupied by tribes with territories of indeterminate extent – our sources differ widely on the subject. The Greek authorities, and some of our Roman ones, state that the German coastline measures 2,300 miles; Agrippa claims that together with Raetia and Noricum its length is 631 miles and its breadth 228 miles, though Raetia alone is almost wider than that. But of course it was only conquered at about the time of his death, while the exploration of Germany went on for many years after and is still incomplete. [99] As far as one can guess, its coastline will turn out to be little short of what the Greeks assert and its length about that suggested by Agrippa.

[Pliny, *Natural History* 4.98–99]

Scaldis: modern river Schelde, on which Antwerp (Belgium) now stands.

Germany's length: the distance from the coast of Germany to the Italian Alps is around 580 miles.

its breadth: Romans probably regarded Germany as being bounded by the Rhine to the west and the Elbe to the east. The distance between these two rivers which run roughly parallel varies between about 200 and 300 miles. Agrippa's figures can thus be seen to have been impressively accurate, unlike the figure quoted for the coastline.

N37   Exploration of the North Sea
Most of the northern ocean was explored under the auspices of the deified Augustus, when our fleet sailed round Germany as far as the Cimbric promontory. From there, having been confronted by a vast sea of which they had also heard reports, they sailed on to the lands of the Scythians, an area of excessive cold and damp.

[Pliny, *Natural History* 2.167]

Cimbric promontory: modern Denmark. The fleet was sent under Tiberius in AD 5. Augustus mentions this expedition in *Res Gestae* 26.4.

Scythians: Scythia referred sometimes to the area which we might term modern Russia, but it was often used much more generally to refer to 'the North', when the earth was divided up schematically into four regions – the West (Celts), the South (Ethiopians), the East (Indians), the North (Scythians).

N38   Tombstone of a soldier killed in the Varus disaster
To Marcus Caelius, son of Titus, of the Lemonia tribe, from Bononia, [centurion] of the 18th legion. In his 53rd year, he fell in the Varian war. It will be permitted to bury the bones [of his freedmen]. Publius Caelius, son of Titus, of the Lemonia tribe, his brother set this up.

(*Portrait bust*) Marcus Caelius Privatus, freedman of Marcus.

(*Portrait bust*) Marcus Caelius Thiaminus, freedman of Marcus.

[EJ 45 = *ILS* 2244]

This tombstone, found at Castra Vetera, Lower Germania (modern Xanten, Germany) commemorating one of the soldiers (from Bononia, modern Bologna) massacred by the Germans in the Varus disaster of AD 9 is dominated by a depiction of the deceased wearing his military decorations and holding his staff of office as centurion. He is flanked on either side by portrait busts of his two freedmen, bearing their names in small letters. As so often with inscriptions, parts of the text crucial for our understanding have disappeared, so it is unclear how his official rank is referred to, and whose bones are mentioned, but it is likely that permission is being granted to bury his freedmen here.

INDIA (N39–N40)

What prompted Indian rulers to seek Roman friendship is unknown, but the embassies to Augustus were the first Roman diplomatic contacts with India and were of great value to the regime. India is mentioned in the context of world conquest at *RG* 31.1 and by Horace *Odes* 4.14.41 (**G44**); Propertius 2.10.16 (**G17**) and 3.4.1 (**G30**); Virgil *Aeneid* 6.795 (**G37**).

N39   Indian envoys reach Augustus

Meanwhile, envoys from India and Scythia, having crossed the whole world, finally found Augustus at Tarraco in Further Spain. This represented the end of their quest which reflected on Augustus the glory of Alexander the Great.

[Orosius, *History* 6.21.19]

The embassy is also mentioned by Suetonius, *Augustus* 21.3. Augustus was in Spain 27–24 BC.
Alexander the Great's conquests had actually reached as far as India.

N40   A second Indian embassy to Augustus

This may be an appropriate point at which to add the report of Nicolaus of Damascus. He says that at Antioch, near Daphne, he happened upon a group of Indians, an embassy on its way to Caesar Augustus. Judging by the letter they carried, there had clearly been more of them originally, but only the three whom he claimed to have seen had actually survived, the rest having died mainly as a result of the arduous journey. Their letter, written in Greek on vellum, made it clear that it had been written by Porus, overlord of six hundred lesser kings, who nevertheless set great store by winning the friendship of Augustus. He said that he was ready to grant him safe conduct through his domains, wherever he wished to go, and assured him of his co-operation whenever appropriate. Such, says Nicolaus, were the contents of the letter; as for the accompanying gifts for Caesar, they were carried by eight slaves, sprinkled with perfumes and naked except for their loincloths. The gifts included the Hermes, a dwarf deprived of his arms since birth, whom I myself have seen with my own eyes, huge vipers, a snake some five metres long, a river tortoise of some three cubits, and a partridge bigger than a vulture.

[Strabo, *Geography* 15.1.72–3]

Nicolaus of Damascus wrote a universal history in 144 books at the time of Augustus, which now exists only in a very fragmentary form. Nicolaus was friend and historian of Herod the Great and tutor to the children of Antony and Cleopatra. Dio (54.9.8–10) also includes some details of this embassy. This embassy reached Augustus in Syria in 20 BC.

PARTHIA (IRAQ) (N41–N46)

Roman and Parthian claims to control the eastern end of Asia Minor had come into conflict in the mid-first century BC. The Arsacid dynasty had scored signal victories (as against Marcus Crassus and Mark Antony, 53 and 36 BC), but Augustus recovered by diplomacy the standards that the Romans had lost (20 BC) and succeeded in making a Roman nominee king of Armenia Major, which Parthian monarchs needed for ambitious members of the royal family. The Parthian kingdom was unstable and claimants to the throne, the sons of the king's various wives and concubines, numerous. After a down-turn in relations, Gaius Caesar was sent out in 1 BC to restore Roman influence. Crinagoras wrote a poem on his departure (**G48**). His mission culminated in an accord with Parthia in AD 2, but he was fatally wounded in the disturbances in Armenia (AD 3). See Velleius 2.101–102; Dio 55.10.20–1; **J59–J61.**

N41   Ovid on Roman standards lost by Crassus in 53 BC

Crassus by the Euphrates lost his standards, son, and soldiery, and then   465
Himself his last surrender made to death. "Tell me, O Parthian",
The goddess said, "Why do you gloat? Those standards you'll return.
And for the death of Crassus will arise an Avenger seeking retribution."

[Ovid, *Fasti* 6. 465–468]

The coincidence on 9 June of the Vestalia, the festival of Vesta, with the anniversary of the battle of Carrhae in 53 BC allows Vesta to prophesy that Crassus' defeat by the Parthians will be avenged: this is likely to allude to Gaius' expedition of 1 BC (cf. on *Ars Amatoria* 1.177–216, **G47**).

N42   Parthian standards recovered, *denarius* of 18 BC

Obv: Head of Liber, wearing ivy-wreath, right.

TVRPILIANVS III VIR ((P Petronius) Turpilianus, moneyer)

Rev: Trousered Parthian, kneeling right, holding out a standard.

CAESAR AVGVSTVS SIGN RECE (Caesar Augustus, Receiver of the standards)

[*RIC* Augustus 287 / *BMC* Augustus 10]

The significance of the return of the Roman standards is clear from the numerous coin issues that commemorate the event (see also **K14**), but also from the fact that this same scene was chosen as the centre-piece of the cuirass of the *princeps*, as depicted on the famous *Prima Porta* statue of Augustus. Although there was no military campaign, it was represented as a military victory: 'Phraates accepted the Roman *imperium* on his knees' (Horace, *Epist.* 1.12.27–28 **G34**). The reverse of this coin beautifully demonstrates the Roman perception of this episode.

N43   Phraates IV sends his children to Rome

(This passage is continued in N46)

Even though he had defeated Rome's armies and generals, Phraates (IV) had always shown the utmost respect for Augustus himself and had sent him several of his children as a means of cementing their friendship – though his motives were not so much fear of Rome as distrust of the loyalty of his own people.

[Tacitus, *Annals* 2.1]

Tacitus is explaining the background to hostilities between Rome and Parthia in AD 16. Phraates IV was king of Parthia 38 BC – 2 BC. He defeated Antony's invasion in 36 BC. A rival for the throne took Phraates' son to Rome, but Augustus returned the prince in 24 BC (Dio 53.33.2). Strabo (**N44**) names four sons, two of whom died in Rome as shown by their funerary inscriptions, **N44b** in Addenda, page 415.

N44   Phraates' Children in Rome

Orodes' successor, Phraates (IV), was so eager to maintain friendly relations with Caesar Augustus, that he even returned the standards which the Parthians had dedicated as trophies in celebration of their victory over the Romans. He also invited Titius, the current governor of Syria, to a conference at which he handed over to him as hostages four of his legitimate sons, Seraspadanes, Rhodaspes, Phraates, and Vonones, together with the wives of two of them and four of their sons. His real motive was fear of conspiracy and assassination attempts on his own life, since he realised that no one could get the better of him unless he gained the support of a member of the Arsacid dynasty, since they enjoyed huge popularity among the Parthians.

[Strabo, *Geography* 16.1.28]

N45   Preparations for Gaius' expedition to the East

Charax is a fortified township situated deep within the Persian Gulf… I am not unaware of the fact that it was the birthplace of Dionysius, our most modern authority on the geography of the world. The deified Augustus sent him to the east to compile a detailed report on every aspect of the area, at the time when his eldest son (Gaius) was about to lead an expedition into Armenia to challenge the Parthians and Arabians. But I hold to the opinion stated in the introduction to this work that every author is at his most thorough when describing his own country. However, in this section, I have decided to follow the reports of the Roman armies, and of King Juba in his despatches to the above-mentioned Gaius Caesar on the subject of this same expedition to Arabia.

[Pliny, *Natural History* 6.141]

Dionysius of Charax is unknown, but Isidorus of Charax wrote on routes across the desert to Syria, regularly cited by Pliny for distances and seems also to have written more generally on geography. This passage like N7 and N8 shows the military importance of geographical information.

Juba: Juba the Younger (II) is known to have written a history and description of Africa.

N46   Vonones appointed Parthian King

(This passage continues N43 and is continued in N23)

[2] After the death of Phraates and his successors in a series of bloody civil wars, a delegation came to Rome from the leading Parthians to invite Vonones, as the eldest son of Phraates, to succeed to the throne. Augustus took this as a significant compliment to himself and showered him with gifts. The barbarians gave him a delighted welcome, as usually happens with new rulers. But their delight was soon replaced by a sense of shame that Parthia could have sunk so low as to have asked for a king from a foreign power; that their king was the product of an alien culture and therefore tainted; and that the throne of the Arsacid dynasty was now merely one of Rome's provinces, the property of the Roman people to be disposed of as they wished. The glory of those who had slain Marcus Crassus and driven out Mark Antony would count for nothing, if the Parthians were to be ruled by a slave of Augustus who had learned over many years to tolerate slavery.

[3] So they sent for another member of the Arsacid blood-line, Artabanus (III), who had grown to manhood among the Dahae. After an initial defeat he re-grouped his forces and seized power. The defeated Vonones took refuge in Armenia, a buffer kingdom between the two great powers of Rome and Parthia, whose throne was currently vacant.

[Tacitus, *Annals* 2.2–3]

Vonones (I): eldest son of Phraates IV, king of Parthia. He had been in Roman custody since 10 BC.

Artabanus (III): his maternal relatives, the Dahae, were a tribe with a suitably warlike reputation. He defeated Vonones in AD 12 and kept his throne until about AD 38.

SPAIN (N47–N49)

Parts of Spain had been ruled by Rome from 218 BC, but other parts remained as theatres of war, with 6 triumphs claimed between 36 and 26 BC. Augustus set out finally to pacify Spain in person in 26 BC, claiming success the following year by closing the gates of the Temple of Janus, symbolising peace. In reality resistance was only crushed finally by Agrippa in 19 BC. Velleius 2.90.2–3 (Section **E**) gives a very brief summary of the two hundred years of fighting in Spain.

N47   Spain finally subdued by Augustus

The nature of its geography and inhabitants means that in Spain, more than in Italy or any other part of the world, it is harder to hold onto captured territory. Therefore, the first province to be entered by the Romans, at least on the mainland, was the last of all to be completely subdued – only in our lifetime, under the leadership and auspices of Augustus Caesar.

[Livy, 28.12.12]

N48   Cantabrian War

Since it was announced that the rebellion was rather serious, Caesar undertook an expedition himself rather than entrusting it to someone else. He came to Segisama himself, positioned his camp and then, dividing his army into three sections, he encompassed the whole of Cantabria and surrounded the fierce people like wild beasts caught in a trap. Nor was there any respite on the side of the Ocean since the fleet was attacking the enemy in the rear. The first battle against the Cantabrians was fought under the walls of Bergida. They quickly fled from there to the heights of Mount Vindius, believing that the Ocean's waters would reach them there sooner than Roman arms. Thirdly the town of Aracelium was eventually taken after stout resistance. Finally there was the siege of Mount Medullus. When it was surrounded by a continuous ditch of eighteen miles and the Romans were advancing on all sides, the barbarians, seeing that their last hour had come, struggled to hasten their deaths by fire and sword and a banquet of poison which there is commonly extracted from the yew tree. So most saved themselves from captivity which seemed worse than death to those never before conquered. Caesar received reports of these operations carried out by his legates, Antistius and Furnius, and by Agrippa, while wintering on the coast at Tarraco. He was soon there himself to bring some of the enemy down from the mountains, to secure the obedience of others by taking hostages and to sell some into slavery, by right of conquest. His achievement seemed to the senate to deserve a laurel crown and triumphal chariot; but so great was Caesar that he despised the glorification of a triumph.

[Florus, *Summary of Wars: Cantabrian and Asturian War* 2.33.48–53]

(Gaius) Antistius (Vetus): consul 30 BC. *(Gaius) Furnius*: later governor of Tarraconensis c.22–19 BC.

despised…a triumph: Augustus however accepted the privilege of wearing triumphal dress on the first day of every year and ceremonially closed the gates of the Temple of Janus (Dio 53.26.5). Augustus' autobiography closed with the successful end of the Cantabrian campaign (Suet. *Aug*. 85.1). His return was celebrated by Horace (**G29**).

N49   Cantabrian revolt, 19 BC

An attempt by the Cantabri to revolt was crushed.

[Jerome, *Chronicle* 20 BC]

Dio (54.11.2–5) dates this revolt to 19 BC. His account mentions 'many reverses' and that 'Agrippa lost many of his soldiers'.

THRACE (N50–N51)

Major campaigns were conducted in Thrace by M. Licinius Crassus in 29–27 BC and by L. Piso around 14–11 BC. In between two other governors of Macedonia had intervened: M. Lollius 19–18 BC and L. Tarius

Rufus 17 BC. In each case the campaigns were in support of the Thracian King Rhoemetalces. On the division of his kingdom after his death, see **M34**.

N50 Crassus' campaigns 29–27 BC

[134] Also recorded are the wars waged by Marcus Crassus against the Bastarnae, the Moesians, and other tribes. [135] This is the record of the wars waged by Marcus Crassus against the Thracians.

[Livy, Summary 134–5]

For Crassus' campaigns against the Bastarnae (a tribe on the north of the Black Sea) and his claim for 'Spoils of Honour', see **P3–P4**.

N51 The Thracians were brought to heel by Lucius Piso.

[Livy, Summary 140]

N52 Troop dispositions

[4] Tiberius gave a brief survey of the number of legions deployed and the provinces which they guarded. I think it would be useful if I did the same, so as to make clear the extent of Rome's military manpower at that time, the number of her client kings, and the significantly smaller size of her empire under Augustus.

[5] Two fleets, based on Misenum and Ravenna, guarded the twin coastlines of the Italian peninsula. The adjacent coastline of Southern Gaul was defended by warships captured by the victorious Augustus at the battle of Actium and despatched with a full complement of crews to the town of Forum Julii (Fréjus). But our main strength lay on the Rhine, where eight legions provided defence against Gauls and Germans alike. Three more legions held down the recently conquered provinces of Spain. King Juba ruled Mauretania, transferred to him by gift of the Roman People, while the rest of Africa and Egypt were each garrisoned by another two legions. Beyond Egypt, from the borders of Syria all the way to the river Euphrates, a whole vast swathe of territory was controlled by four legions, while along its boundaries a number of client kings (Iberian, Albanian, and others) were afforded protection from external threats by the formidable power of Rome. Rhoemetalces (II) and the children of Cotys (IV) held Thrace; four legions defended the banks of the Danube, two in Pannonia and two in Moesia. Two more, located behind the forward provinces, provided a strategic reserve from their bases in Dalmatia, whence they were close enough to be able to be summoned to Italy if support was suddenly needed there. But of course Rome also had its own garrison, the three urban and nine praetorian cohorts, recruited mainly from Etruria, Umbria, ancient Latium, and the old Roman settlements. Then in the provinces at key locations and of comparable strength there were allied warships, cavalry squadrons, and light infantry. But details are unreliable, since their locations varied according to circumstance and their numbers were increased or sometimes reduced accordingly.

[Tacitus, *Annals* 4.4–5]

Tacitus gives this review under the year AD 23, though implying in [4] that any difference lay between his own day and Augustus, rather than between AD 14 and AD 23. Compare figure 2, page 20.

The smaller size of her empire under Augustus: This tells against the idea that Roman imperialism waned after the beginning of the Principate. Tacitus wrote his *Annals* under Trajan. Suetonius, *Augustus* 49 gives a briefer account of the army under Augustus.

Recently conquered provinces of Spain: see **N47–N49**.

King Juba: on this client king, see **M31–M32**.

Rhoemetalces (II) and the children of Cotys (IV): see **M34**.

Etruria, Umbria, ancient Latium: The recruiting grounds of the élite praetorians had been those of the legions under the Republic: Italians were privileged.

SECTION P

CONSPIRACIES, SCANDALS, FREE SPEECH

Of Suetonius' twelve Caesars, only Augustus, Tiberius, Vespasian and Titus died natural deaths. Julius Caesar died at the hands of 'liberators' including Brutus, 'the noblest Roman of them all'. Augustus' successors died because of the ambition of others, or their own intolerable megalomania. Suetonius lists a series of revolts and conspiracies against Augustus (*Aug.* 19.1). Many of the scandals and conspiracies of Augustus' reign are by their very nature and their failure obscure to us.

Conspiracies and Scandals (P1–P8)

P1   Augustus' misfortunes

[147] The whole world would account the deified Augustus one of the happiest of men. Yet if one studies it carefully, his life will be found to contain considerable variations in the cycle of human fortune ...

[149] There were so many mutinies in his armies, so many bouts of life-threatening illness, Marcellus' suspect ambitions, the disgrace of Agrippa's banishment, the fact that he was so often a target for assassination, and the accusation that he murdered his own children. He knew much sorrow, not only the sorrow of bereavement, but also at his daughter Julia's adultery, and the revelation that she had plotted parricide; there was the insulting withdrawal from public life of his step-son Nero; another adulterous affair, this time involving his granddaughter Julia. Add to these a long list of setbacks – shortage of funds for the armies, the rebellion in Illyricum, the need to enlist slaves, shortage of manpower, plague in Rome, famine in Italy, and his decision to commit suicide which, after four days of starvation, brought him near to death. [150] Then came the disaster to Varus' legions with the disgrace it brought to his own reputation, the enforced rejection of Agrippa Postumus after his adoption as heir, and the loneliness he felt after Agrippa was exiled, the suspicion aroused against Fabius of betraying state secrets; and then, towards the end of his life, the machinations of his wife and Tiberius. In short, whether this god has acquired or earned his place in heaven I know not – but he died with his enemy's own son nominated as his heir.

[Pliny, *Natural History*, 7.147–150]

Pliny's preceding chapters had illustrated the fickleness of fortune: he proves his point (with some exaggeration) by showing that even Augustus suffered many misfortunes. Sections 147 and 148 include a list of misfortunes from the start of his adult life to the Battle of Actium.

P2   Marcus Lepidus' plot to assassinate Octavian (30 BC)

Maecenas prosecuted the son of Lepidus [the triumvir] for plotting against Caesar, and also the boy's mother for complicity: Lepidus himself he overlooked as being unimportant. Maecenas sent the son to Caesar at Actium.

[Appian, *Civil Wars* 4.50]

The fullest account of this plot to assassinate Octavian on his return to Rome after Actium is given by Velleius (2.88 Section **E**). It is also included in the brief summary of Livy book 133 (**D2**).

Marcus Licinius Crassus and the *spolia opima* (29 BC) (P3–P4)

Marcus Licinius Crassus was a supporter of Sextus Pompey, then Mark Antony, before his defection to Octavian. He was rewarded with the consulship in 30 BC (see Section **B**). Appointed proconsul of Macedonia, he conducted successful campaigns against the Bastarnae, and killed their king, Deldo, with his own hands (Dio 51.23–24). He claimed the rarest of military distinctions, the *spolia opima*, the spoils offered by a

Roman general who had killed an enemy leader in single combat. The tradition had apparently been established by Romulus (see **K21**), and there had only been two further recorded instances of this award in Roman history. From Octavian's point of view, the timing could hardly have been worse: he had recently rebuilt the Temple of Jupiter Feretrius, where the spoils would be deposited, as part of his association of himself with Rome's first founder, Romulus. Further, Licinius' claim would potentially overshadow Octavian's triple triumph of August 29 BC. Licinius' claim was denied. Livy's account of one of the winners of *spolia opima*, Aulus Cornelius Cossus reveal to us Octavian's own involvement, and the spurious grounds on which Licinius' claim was disallowed. The episode must however have highlighted the question of Octavian's constitutional position, whether he was technically commander-in-chief of all Roman armies (see Syme, *Roman Revolution* 308–309). It also indicates a step in the jealous monopoly of military honours under the principate.

P3   Temple of Jupiter Feretrius

As a result of this (friendship between Atticus and Octavian), it happened that when the temple of Jupiter Feretrius which had been built by Romulus on the Capitol was found to be in danger of collapse, having lost its roof and suffered from severe neglect over many years, Caesar followed Atticus' advice and decided to have it repaired.

[Nepos, *Life of Atticus* 20.3]

One of the first steps in Octavian's association of himself with Romulus was his restoration of this temple on the Capitol (**A19.2**). According to Nepos' account, this was prompted by the advice of Pomponius Atticus (110–32 BC), multi-millionaire, friend and correspondent of most important politicians of his age, father-in-law of Agrippa and historian. The meaning of the temple's cult title, Feretrius, was obscure to the Romans.

P4   Aulus Cornelius Cossus and the Spoils of Honour

[5] I follow all previous authorities in recording that it was Aulus Cornelius Cossus who, as a military tribune, first laid up those symbols of success, the 'Spoils of Honour' (*spolia opima*) in the temple of Jupiter Feretrius. [6] But this account poses its own problems: first, the term is properly applied only to those 'Spoils of Honour' which an army commander seizes from his opposite number. Secondly, we acknowledge only one man as 'army commander' – the one under whose auspices the war is conducted. However, the inscription on the actual 'Spoils' has suggested to those same authorities, and myself, that Cossus captured the 'Spoils' while holding office as consul. [7] I have since learned that Augustus Caesar, the founder and restorer of all our temples, claims to have entered the temple of Jupiter Feretrius, which he had rescued from long years of dilapidation, and there personally read the inscription on the linen corslet. As a result I have felt it tantamount to sacrilege to deny Cossus his Spoils by refusing to accept the evidence of his key witness, Caesar, the man who actually rebuilt the temple. [8] In this matter each must reach his own conclusions as to how such an error could have led to Aulus Cornelius Cossus being recorded as consul some ten years later, and then only jointly with Titus Quinctius Poenus. This error occurs both in the ancient annals, the Magistrates' archives, and in the linen-scroll records stored in the temple of Moneta, which are repeatedly cited by Macer Licinius as his authorities....

[11] Be that as it may, it seems to me that speculation in any direction is entirely futile. The fact remains that the man who fought the battle dedicated his new-won 'Spoils' in that sacred spot before Jupiter, to whom he paid his vows, and beneath the gaze of Romulus himself. We can hardly discount as false the evidence of such powerful witnesses to the fact that Aulus Cornelius Cossus describes himself as 'consul'.

[Livy 4.20. 5–8, 11]

[8] If Cossus was only military tribune at the time, and consul only ten years later, as all Livy's sources clearly show, then there clearly was a precedent for the *spolia opima* being awarded to a commander other than the supreme commander.

Gaius Cornelius Gallus, prefect of Egypt (27/6 BC) (P5–P6)

The fall of this prominent poet and politician, the first prefect of Egypt, is mysterious. Various reasons and criticisms of his behaviour are offered by our sources: an ungrateful and malevolent nature leading to his exclusion from Augustus' house and imperial provinces, followed by (unspecified) accusations (Suet. *Aug.* 66.2); arrogance, idle gossip against Augustus, many reprehensible actions including setting up statues of himself all over Egypt and inscribing a list of his achievements on pyramids; public loss of the emperor's favour followed by numerous indictments and condemnation by the senate (Dio 53.23). For more on the episode, see Syme, *RR* 309–310; L. J. Daly in C. Deroux (ed.) *Studies in Latin Literature and Roman History 1* (1979).

P5   Gallus monument

Gaius Cornelius Gallus, son of Gnaeus, Roman equestrian, and, after kings had been utterly defeated by Caesar son of the Deified, the first prefect of Alexandria and Egypt; [twice] victorious in battles of the Thebaid revolt during the 15 days in which he conquered the enemy; sacker of five cities – Boresis, Coptus, Ceramice, Great Diospolis, Ophieon; once the leaders of these revolts had been intercepted, he led his army [across] beyond the Nile's cataract, into an area where [weapons] had never [before] been advanced either by the Roman People nor by the kings of Egypt; the Thebaid, which had been the common fear of all the kings, was subdued; envoys of the Ethiopian king were given an audience at Philae, the king received under his protection, a ruler established over Ethiopian Triacontaschoenos; he gave this as a gift to the ancestral gods and to the Nile, his helper.

[EJ 21 = *ILS* 8995]

A rose-coloured granite stele, from Philae (by the modern Aswan Dam in Upper Egypt), depicting a man on horseback striking down his enemy. Three texts appear on the monument, in Latin, Greek, and hieroglyphics. The Greek text contains minor variations upon the Latin, but the hieroglyphic text is not a translation, instead presenting Gallus' victories in the language customarily used by the Egyptians to praise their kings. Gallus was the first prefect of the new province of Egypt following the defeat of Antony and Cleopatra. There is some dispute whether he was chosen partly in virtue of his equestrian status, or whether he was simply the best man for the job on the spot. The boastful tone of this monument has been thought to be indicative of why he fell from favour.

P6   Gallus welcomes a disgraced freedman

Quintus Caecilius Epirota was a native of Tusculum and a freedman of Atticus, the Roman equestrian with whom Cicero corresponded. While tutor to his patron's daughter, who was married to Marcus Agrippa, he was suspected of misdemeanour and dismissed. Thereupon he took himself off to Cornelius Gallus and lived with him on the most amicable terms. This was one of the most serious charges laid against Gallus himself by Augustus. Later, following Gallus' conviction and death, he started a school.

[Suetonius, *Grammarians* 16]

Cicero: Marcus Tullius Cicero, 106–43 BC, orator, politician and writer.
Atticus: see note on **P3** above. His daughter, Caecilia Attica, married Agrippa in 37 BC.

Valerius Messala Corvinus, City Prefect (*praefectus urbi*) (P7–P8)

Marcus Valerius Messala Corvinus fought against the Triumvirs at Philippi in 42 BC, but joined Octavian, held the consulship in 31 BC (see Section **B**, 31 BC), and celebrated a triumph (see **N2c**). In 26 BC he was appointed to the new post of City Prefect, only to resign, claiming that the position was unconstitutional. See **K7** and Syme, *RR* 211–212.

P7   Messala Corvinus resigns after 6 days as City Prefect

Messala Corvinus, made the first Prefect of the City, resigned his office six days later, arguing that its powers were inappropriate for a citizen.

[Jerome, *Chronicle* 26 BC]

P8   Messalla's saying

I can only resort to the saying of Messalla Corvinus, that most skilful speaker, 'The power of my position shames me'.

[Younger Seneca, *Pumpkinification of Claudius* 10.2]

In Seneca's satire, the writer is making Augustus say that he regrets establishing the principate now that he sees what Claudius has done as *princeps*. The quotation from Messalla would apply perfectly to his rejection of the post of *praefectus urbi*.

Conspiracy of Fannius Caepio and Varro Murena (23/22 BC) (P9–P10)

There is no agreement in ancient sources or modern writers about either the date or the people involved in this conspiracy, let alone details or motives: Dio (54.3) links it to the trial of the otherwise unknown Marcus Primus, governor of Macedonia; Velleius' brief narrative (2.91.2) raises as many questions as it answers; Tacitus (*Annals*, 1.10.4 = Section **F**) is even briefer. It is not clear whether the elected consul of 23 BC was somehow involved (see note on Section **B**, 23 BC). For a brief discussion of the problems of the conspiracy see the note on Velleius 2.91.2 (Section **E**) and, with further bibliography, J.W.Rich, *Dio* pages 174–176.

P9   Slave of Caepio, would-be assassin of Augustus

Caepio had also planned to assassinate Augustus but his plot was discovered and he was condemned. A slave concealed him in a chest and transported him by night first to the Tiber, thence to Ostia, and finally to his father's country house in the Laurentum district. When they were later shipwrecked off Cumae, he kept him hidden in Naples, and when captured by a centurion could not be persuaded by bribes or threats to betray the fugitive.

[Macrobius, *Saturnalia* 1.11.21]

Caepio's father freed this slave but ostentatiously crucified another who had betrayed Caepio. Augustus condoned these actions (Dio 54.3.6–7).

P10   Tiberius prosecutes Caepio

He (Tiberius) brought a prosecution for high treason against Fannius Caepio, who had conspired against Augustus with Varro Murena, and secured his condemnation.

[Suetonius, *Tiberius* 8.1]

Suetonius mentions the conspiracy briefly elsewhere (Suet. *Aug.* 19.1; 56.4) and adds (Suet. *Aug.* 66.3) that Maecenas, the brother-in-law of Murena, confided the discovery of the plot to his wife, to Augustus' annoyance.

Egnatius Rufus (19 BC)

On this conspiracy, see Velleius 2.91–2.93 (Section **E**) and Dio 53.24.4–6. The conspiracy is also mentioned without details at Tacitus, *Annals* 1.10.4 (Section **F**); **P11**; Suet. *Aug.* 19.1.

P11   Cinna's plot to assassinate Augustus (16 BC)

[9.2] But when he was in his forties and staying in Gaul, evidence was laid before him that Lucius Cinna, not one of our most sparkling intellects, was plotting against him. He was told when, where, and how he planned to make the attempt. One of the conspirators passed on the information. [9.3] Augustus decided that he must punish him and called a meeting of his council of friends. It cost him a night's sleep as he pondered the implications of condemning a young nobleman of impeccable reputation (apart from this one act), who was also the grandson of Gnaeus Pompey. By this stage of his career he was incapable of killing even one man. Yet this was the same Caesar to whom Mark Antony in earlier days had dictated the terms of the proscriptions over dinner.

[9.4] As he agonised over the decision, he gave vent to many different and self-contradictory comments ... [9.6] In the end it was his wife, Livia, who interrupted him.

"Will you listen to a woman's advice?" she said. "Do what the doctors do. When conventional remedies fail, they try their opposites. Severity has got you nowhere. Lepidus followed Salvidienus; Murena followed Lepidus. Caepio followed Murena; Egnatius followed Caepio – quite apart from all the others whose reckless audacity scarcely merits mention. Now is the time for an experiment: see if clemency gets you any further. Pardon Lucius Cinna. He has been arrested. He cannot harm you further; but he could do wonders for your reputation."

[9.7] Enchanted to have found himself such an excellent source of advice, he thanked his wife and gave immediate orders countermanding the invitation to his friends to attend the Council. Instead he summoned Cinna into his presence alone, ordered everyone else out of the room, and gave instructions for a second chair to be brought for him. "First of all," he said, "I want no interruptions while I am speaking; no protests at my words. You will be given ample time to speak in due course. [9.8] When I found you in my enemies' camp, an opponent not so much by choice as by birth, I spared your life and let you keep all your family estates. Today you are so successful and so rich that your conquerors are envious of the man they conquered. You were a candidate for the priesthood. I passed over many whose fathers had fought by my side to give it to you. Though I have done you such favours, you have decided to murder me."

[9.9] At this Cinna exclaimed that such madness was utterly alien to his thoughts. "You are breaking our bargain, Cinna," replied Augustus. "We agreed: no interruptions. I say again, you are preparing my assassination." He then listed the place, the accomplices, the date, and the plan for the assassination, and the name of the one who would wield the dagger …

[9.11] I do not want to fill up the bulk of this book repeating the whole of the speech which, by common consent, is said to have gone on for more than two hours. This was the only punishment which Augustus intended to impose, and he wanted to make the most of it. "It is your life, Cinna," he said, "which I am giving back to you for the second time. Last time your were my military opponent; now you are a conspirator and a parricide. But let this day mark the beginning of our friendship. Let us do battle once more: but this time to see which of us will show the greater good faith – I in my gift of life to you; you in your debt for your life to me". [9.12] After that he even gave Cinna a consulship, complaining only that he had not had the courage to stand as a candidate. He found him a truly loyal and close friend, and became his only heir. He was never again the target of a plot from any source.

[Younger Seneca, *Concerning Clemency* 1.9.2 – 1.9.12]

Two books of *Concerning Clemency* survive, the most explicitly political of Seneca's dialogues. It is addressed to Nero and combines praise of the *princeps* for his natural clemency with a strong exhortation to continue on this course, in order to achieve both security for himself (as Augustus achieved by his reaction to Lucius Cinna's plot) and popularity with his subjects. The date of the treatise is given by 1.9.1 (**H7**): Nero's nineteenth year ran from 15 December AD 55 to 14 December AD 56. Seneca remarks previously that Augustus could only really be regarded as a clement leader from his time as *princeps* (**H7–H8**). Other passages from *Concerning Clemency* are **H48** and **P15**.

The story about Gnaeus Cornelius Cinna (Seneca erroneously calls him Lucius) belongs to Augustus' visit to Gaul in 16 BC, when he was in his late forties: it is repeated by Dio (55.14–22), who changes the date to AD 4, probably misled by Seneca's mention of Cinna's consulship coming 'after that'.

Adultery by Augustus' daughter and granddaughter (P12–P16)

In 2 BC Augustus tried his daughter Julia and her lovers under his own adultery law and banished her to the island of Pandataria. Though political motives can be adduced for his suddenly taking notice of her activities, they were an embarrassment to the author of laws protecting the institution of marriage and making adultery a criminal offence (see **S10–S27**), and who was legally responsible for the conduct of his family. On Julia, see **J48–J54**; on the scandal and Julia's lovers see also Velleius 2.100.4 (Section **E**).

P12   Elder Julia tried and banished, 2 BC

The deified Augustus sent his own daughter into exile. Her promiscuity put her beyond the reach of any formal indictment and brought the scandals of the imperial household into the public domain. It was said that she had made herself available to armies of adulterers, that she had wandered the streets of the city in nocturnal orgies, that the Forum and the Rostrum from which her own father had moved the law against adultery had been a favourite spot for her lecheries, that she went daily to the statue of Marsyas and there, abandoning adultery for prostitution, insisted on her right to every form of lascivious behaviour, even with unknown lovers. These were scandals which any *princeps* had a duty not only to punish but also to conceal, since there are some deeds whose sheer obscenity infects those who seek to punish them. But he could not contain his anger and he made them all public. As time went by, however, his anger turned to shame and he came to lament the fact that he had not concealed her deeds and avoided public comment, having remained in ignorance of them for so long that comment could only bring disgrace.

[Younger Seneca, *On Benefits* 6.32]

Seneca is arguing above that even the most powerful people can be done a favour in the form of good and frank advice such as Augustus might have received from Maecenas and Agrippa had they still been alive in 2 BC.

P13   Iullus Antonius executed for adultery, his son exiled

That year [AD 25] saw also the death of Lucius Antonius, scion of a famous but ill-fated family. His father, Iullus Antonius, had been executed for adultery with Julia, and he himself was still little more than a boy when Augustus (his great-uncle) banished him to the state of Massilia (Marseilles), disguising what was effectively a sentence of exile under the pretext of furthering his academic studies.

[Tacitus, *Annals* 4.44]

Iullus Antonius (43 BC – 2 BC) was the son of Mark Antony and his first wife, Fulvia. Brought up by Octavia, in 21 BC he married Marcella the elder daughter of Octavia and C. Claudius Marcellus. Horace praises him in *Odes* 4.2 (**G41**), probably written in 16 BC.

P14   A freedman tortured to give evidence of an affair of Elder Julia

Aesopus, a freedman of Demosthenes, was well aware of his patron's adulterous relationship with Julia. Though subjected to protracted torture he steadfastly refused to betray him until Demosthenes himself confessed, when convicted on the evidence of others who were aware of his activities.

[Macrobius, *Saturnalia* 1.11.17]

Augustus' law on adultery allowed the torture of slaves for evidence, see **S21**.

P15   Augustus' clemency to Julia's lovers

[3] We see him as a god, and not because we are instructed to do so. We acknowledge that Augustus was a good *princeps*, that he well deserved the title of Father of his Fatherland, for one reason only – that he did not seek to avenge with cruelty the insults to himself which other rulers often find even more offensive than actual injuries; that he smiled at insults; that he seemed to be the victim of punishment even when he was

imposing it; that so far from killing all those who were convicted of adultery with his daughter, Julia, he exiled them for their own safety and issued them with personal letters of recommendation. [4] That is real clemency – not just to grant a man his life, but to guarantee it personally when you know that there will be many who are angry on your behalf and eager to earn your favour by spilling your enemy's blood.

[Younger Seneca, *Concerning Clemency* 1.10.3 – 1.10.4]

On the context of this passage, see **P11** above. On punishment for adultery, see **S26, S27**.

he exiled them: Sempronius Gracchus, one of Elder Julia's lovers, was exiled to an African island, Cercina (see **J48**): for Augustus' clemency to a lover of Younger Julia, see below, **P16**.

P16   Punishments for adultery with members of Augustus' family

Augustus' consistent good fortune in his public life was offset by the failings within his own household. The scandalous conduct of his daughter and granddaughter led to their banishment from Rome and the execution or exile of their lovers. For though adultery is a common enough failing among men and women, Augustus branded it as sacrilege and high treason, and in so doing exceeded the bounds of traditional tolerance and his own legislation. The fates of others I shall deal with in the context of their times, provided that I live long enough to complete my present labours and take on a further project. As for Decimus Silanus, the only punishment inflicted on him for his adultery with the emperor's granddaughter was that he forfeited the friendship of the emperor. But he had the good sense to realise that this meant exile.

[Tacitus, *Annals* 3.24]

His daughter and granddaughter: the exiling of the two Julias took place in 2 BC and AD 8. Augustus put his family so high that seducing its female members was deemed to constitute 'diminishing the majesty of the Roman people' – effectively treason. See Velleius 2.100.2–5 (Section **E**) and Dio 55.10.12–16.
Decimus (Junius) Silanus: he had an influential brother, Gaius, to plead for him, and was allowed to return after 15 years.

P17   Lollius struck off list of Gaius Caesar's friends, AD 2

Marcus Lollius was disgraced for taking bribes from all the kings of the East and struck off the list of his friends by Augustus Caesar's son, Gaius. He poisoned himself.

[Pliny, *Natural History* 9.118]

Lollius: consul 21 BC (see Section **B** and note). He was an enemy of Tiberius (Suet. *Tiberius* 12–13) and may have fallen victim to court intrigue, though, as Pliny noted in the previous section (9.117), the wealth of his granddaughter was fabulous. Velleius, loyal to Tiberius, celebrates Lollius' death, 2.102.1 (Section **E**).

P18   Fabius excluded from Augustus' friendship, commits suicide, AD 14

Fulvius, the friend of Caesar Augustus, who was then an old man, heard him lamenting the desolation of his house, since two of his grandsons were dead and the last one was in exile as the result of slander, and he had been forced to bring in his wife's son as imperial successor, though he pitied his grandson and wanted to recall him from exile. Fulvius told his own wife what he had heard. She told Livia and Livia bitterly rebuked Caesar for not sending for his grandson if that had long been his decision, rather than making her subject to the hatred and hostility of the future emperor. So when Fulvius made his usual visit early next morning, and said, 'Good morning, Caesar,' Caesar replied, 'Good-bye, Fulvius.' He understood and returned straight home, and calling for his wife, said, 'Caesar has discovered that I have not kept his confidence: and therefore I intend to kill myself.'

[Plutarch, *Moralia* 508A–B (*On Talkativeness*)]

Plutarch here is making a moral point about the dangers of gossip rather than writing history: Fulvius is not otherwise known, and Plutarch probably means Fabius, that is Paullus Fabius Maximus, a prominent and loyal supporter of Augustus. Tacitus tells a similar, though briefer story, about Fabius at *Annals* 1.5.1–2 (Section **F**) and Pliny mentions him as betraying state secrets (**P1**).

Free Speech (P19–P24)

P19   A stubbornly republican lawyer

[1] In one of the letters of Ateius Capito we are told that Antistius Labeo was supremely learned in the laws and traditions of the Roman People as well as in civil jurisprudence. [2] 'But', he goes on, 'his almost crazy love of freedom became for him an obsession, to such an extent that even when the deified Augustus was *princeps* and exercising absolute power in the state, he refused to regard any regulation as secure and legally binding, unless he could find sanction and precedent for it in the corpus of ancient Roman law.'

[Aulus Gellius, *Attic Nights* 13.12.1–2]

See **T21** for another view of the two most distinguished, but opposed, Augustan lawyers.

P20   Augustus' tolerance

[4] The deified Augustus has many memorable deeds and sayings to his credit, and they demonstrate clearly that he was never a slave to anger. The historian Timagenes had made many caustic comments about Augustus himself, his wife, and his household, which have passed into common currency – not surprisingly, since wit that is a little *risqué* tends to go the rounds and be regularly repeated. [5] Indeed, Caesar advised him many times to moderate his language, but when he persisted, he banned him from the palace. After that Timagenes lodged with Asinius Pollio and grew old in his household, becoming a sort of national institution. The fact that he was banned from the palace by Caesar closed no other doors to him. [6] He gave public readings of his histories, which he compiled in the years that followed these events and those books which contained the record of the achievements of Caesar Augustus he consigned to the flames and burned. He kept up his vendetta against Caesar, but no one was afraid to be his friend, nor did anyone treat him like a leper, accursed of heaven. In fact, though he had fallen from a great height, in Pollio he found a real bosom friend. [7] Caesar put up with all this with great patience, as I have said, showing no sign of irritation even that Timagenes had laid violent hands on his reputation and achievements. He never remonstrated with Pollio, his enemy's host. [8] The only comment he allowed himself was to remark to Asinius Pollio: "So you've become a tiger-keeper, then!", and when Pollio began to offer excuses, he silenced him. "Enjoy it, my dear Pollio, enjoy it." Pollio then said that if Caesar required it, he would order Timagenes out of the house at once. Caesar replied: "Do you seriously imagine that I would do such a thing, when it was I that originally made you friends again?" There was a time when Pollio had had a grudge against Timagenes, and his only reason for abandoning it had been that Caesar had started one instead …

[Younger Seneca, *Concerning Anger* 3.23.4–8]

Seneca's long treatise *Concerning Anger*, written under Claudius and addressed to Seneca's elder brother Annaeus Novatus, presents the Stoic view that anger is a completely destructive emotion that should be rooted out of the soul. The example illustrates Augustus' own tolerance of free speech and unwillingness to be provoked to anger.

Timagenes was a Greek historian, well known for free speech. See Index of Persons, Timagenes.

(Gaius) Asinius Pollio: a Caesarian commander, he was consul in 40 BC, then retired to devote himself to history-writing; he was frequently credited with free speech.

P21   Augustus' relationship with writers

Livy's reputation for eloquence and objectivity as an historian made him the greatest
of the great. Indeed his praise of Gnaeus Pompeius was so lavish that Augustus
nicknamed him *Pompeianus*. But this never did any damage to their friendship. As for
men such as Scipio, Afranius, and even Cassius and Brutus, whom I have just
mentioned, none of them is described by Titus Livius as 'brigand' or 'parricide' as is
the modern fashion; he regularly refers to them as men of distinction. The writings of
Asinius Pollio make similarly complimentary references to those same figures. As for
Messala Corvinus, he refers to Cassius as his 'victorious general' (*imperator*). Yet both
he and Pollio were allowed to live out their lives in honourable prosperity.

[Tacitus, *Annals*, 4.34]

In AD 25, the historian Cremutius Cordus was prosecuted for praising Brutus in his *History*. Tacitus gives
him a speech in his own defence in which he points out that Augustus could call Livy '*Pompeianus*'
(Pompey's man) without even any damage to their friendship. Cordus' defence did not prevent his work
being burned in AD 25; he starved himself to death.

(*Q. Metellus*) *Scipio*: a connexion of the generals of the third and second centuries BC, he was Pompey the
Great's father-in-law and shared his consulship in 52 BC.

(*Lucius*) *Afranius*: Consul 60 BC, he became legate of Pompey in Spain. Both Afranius and Scipio died after
being defeated by Caesar at Thapsus in Africa, in 46 BC.

(*Gaius*) *Asinius Pollio*: see on **P20** above.

(*Marcus*) *Valerius Messala Corvinus*: see on **P7, P8** above.

P22   A slave's service to his master

Under the deified Augustus free speech did not yet endanger a man but it could cause
trouble for him. Rufus, a man of senatorial rank, once in a dinner party conversation
said that he hoped Caesar would not return safe from the expedition which he was then
preparing, adding that all bulls and calves shared his aspirations. There were some
people present who listened carefully to what he said. At daybreak the next morning
the slave who had stood at his feet during dinner told him what he had said while under
the influence of drink. He urged him to catch Caesar and volunteer information against
himself. He took the slave's advice and went to meet Caesar on his way down to the
Forum. He swore that he had been off his head the previous day, prayed that his words
might fall upon his own head and those of his sons, and begged Caesar to forgive him
and let him return to his good graces. Caesar said that he would, whereupon he declared
that no one would believe that he had returned to favour unless he made him a gift. He
then asked for a sum of money that was not to be sneezed at even by one who was
already a favourite. This he was given, with Caesar's added comment that "For my
own sake I must now make sure that I am never angry with you." In this Caesar behaved
admirably, both in pardoning him and in combining generosity with clemency. Anyone
hearing this tale is bound to praise Caesar – but he will praise the slave first. You will
hardly be surprised to hear that in return for his actions he received his manumission.
But it cost his master nothing – Caesar had already financed his freedom.

[Younger Seneca, *On Benefits* 3.27]

In book 3 of *On Benefits* Seneca considers whether or not slaves can confer benefits deserving gratitude and
concludes that service given by a slave beyond his legal obligation and out of goodwill counts.

P23   The Treason Law applied to libel

Tiberius had revived the *lex maiestatis* (the Law of Treason), a statute familiar also to
our ancestors under the same name. But its applications were different, and included
any act of public misconduct damaging to the majesty of the Roman people, such as

betrayal of an army or incitement to popular sedition. Actions were required as evidence of guilt; words were disregarded. Augustus was the first to bring written libel within the scope of this law, provoked by the unrestrained defamation of men and women of distinction in the satirical writings of Cassius Severus.

[Tacitus, *Annals* 1.72]

Tiberius had revived the lex maiestatis: The law, originally passed by the demagogue Appuleius Saturninus in 103 BC, had been in operation two years before Augustus' death (Dio 56.27.1). In his turbulent last decade Augustus' regime became more autocratic.

Cassius Severus: a bold orator of no family who had attacked among others the Vitellii (Suet. *Vitellius* 2.1): convicted of treason under Augustus, he was banished to Crete and his writings were burnt (Tac. *Ann.* 4.21.5).

P24   Literary censorship

[5] So uninhibited were his speeches that he went beyond the bounds of legitimate free expression, and earned the nickname Rabienus from his habit of savaging all and sundry, whatever their status. Despite his faults, his was a larger than life personality, overwhelming – rather like his genius ... He was the first target and victim of a novel form of punishment devised by his enemies, who contrived to have all his books burned. It was an unusual and unprecedented departure for punishment to be imposed upon literature ...

[7] As for the man who had thus denounced the writings of Labienus, his own writings were consigned to the bonfire in his lifetime; but the fact that this happened to him made it a good example not a bad one. Labienus found this insult unendurable. He had no desire to outlive the products of his genius, so he had himself carried to the tombs of his ancestors and immured there, doubtless for fear that the fires which had been applied to the source of his reputation might be denied to his own body. Thus he not only put an end to his life but also conducted his own interment.

[8] I remember how on one occasion, when he was giving a reading from his history, he rolled up a large part of the scroll and declared, "the sections which I am passing over will be read after my death." They must have contained some formidably honest opinions to have made even a Labienus frightened to publish them. A neat saying of Cassius Severus, Labienus' most hated opponent, did the rounds at that time when Labienus' books were being burned by senatorial decree. "Now they will have to burn me alive, as well; I know those books by heart." Let me tell you of an elegant little book which you should get from your friend, Gallio, who read to us a reply to Labienus on behalf of Maecenas' freedman, Bathyllus.

[Elder Seneca, *Controversies* 10 preface 5–8]

The Elder Seneca (around 50 BC – AD 40) is writing about the orator and writer Titus Labienus. The pun, '*Rabienus*' is almost the same in Latin as English: Labienus' invective was rabid. (Latin *rabies* = madness). *Cassius Severus*: see on **P23**. He would seem the most likely person to have denounced the writings of Labienus. Dio mentions the burning of libellous material and punishment of the authors as happening late in Augustus' reign. (Dio 56.27 – under AD 13). The emperor Gaius (AD 37–41) allowed Labienus' works, along with Cassius Severus', to be republished (Suetonius, *Gaius* 16.1).
Bathyllus: an actor and well-known favourite of Maecenas (**R23**).

Ovid's exile

The most famous example of the loss of free speech under Augustus is the case of Ovid, banished in AD 8 from Rome to Tomis on the Black Sea (modern Romania), for 'a poem and a misjudgement' (*Tristia* 2.207), that is the writing of his *Art of Love* and perhaps for something relating to the scandal involving the Younger Julia (see **P16**). See introduction to Ovid (Section **G**, **G56** and **G47**).

SECTION R

MAECENAS AND THE ARTS

Maecenas (R1–R13)

R1   Patron of Virgil
Let there be Maecenases and there shall be no lack of Virgils.

[Martial, 8.55.5]

The poet Martial (around AD 41–104) no doubt wished there were a patron similar to Maecenas in his day.

R2   Patron of Horace
Maecenas, descendant of ancient kings, my safeguard and sweet glory.

[Horace, *Odes* 1.1.1–2]

Horace dedicated his first three books of *Odes* to Maecenas. Virgil did likewise with his *Georgics*. From the poetry in Section **G**, see also Horace, *Epode* 7 (**G3**); *Satires* 1.5.27–33 (**G4**); *Epode* 9 (**G5**); *Satires* 2.6 (**G7**); Propertius 2.1 (**G15**). For an overall assessment of Maecenas and his role, see Dio's obituary (55.7).

R3   Profited from the proscriptions
Some of the possessions of Favonius had come to belong to Maecenas.

[Commentator on Juvenal, *Satires* 5.3]

This chance piece of information (Juvenal's poem mentions neither Favonius nor Maecenas) confirms what would anyway have been suspected, that part of Maecenas' vast wealth came from those, like Marcus Favonius, proscribed by the triumvirs.

R4   Maecenas in command of Rome and Italy
During the civil wars Augustus gave Cilnius Maecenas, a member of the equestrian order, total control over the administration of Rome and Italy.

[Tacitus, *Annals* 6.11]

Tacitus tells us this in the context of explaining the post of City Prefect, see **K7**. For Maecenas' charge of the city, see Velleius 2.88.2–3 (Section **E**); Dio 49.16.2 and 55.7.1.
The family name 'Cilnius', would link him with an ancient Etruscan family, but it was probably the name of his mother's family rather than his father's.

R5   Maecenas' signet-ring
Maecenas used a frog, which proved to be a source of considerable anxiety, since it usually brought demands for subscription-money for Augustus.

[Pliny, *Natural History* 37.10]

For Augustus' signet ring, a sphinx, see **H1**: Augustus will have needed a great deal of subscription-money to fund his campaigns while triumvir.

R6   Maecenas and Agrippa irreplaceable as advisers
[2] He would often exclaim that these things would not have happened if Maecenas or Agrippa had been alive. Though he had thousands to command, such was the irreparable loss of these two men. [3] Yet when legions were destroyed, others were immediately enlisted; when a fleet was wrecked, a new one put to sea in a few days; when fire devastated public buildings, bigger and better ones arose upon their ruins. But nothing could fill the gap in his life left by the deaths of Maecenas and Agrippa.

Inevitably the question must be asked – must we seriously imagine that there were no other comparable figures whom he could have recruited in their place? Or was it a flaw in his own make-up that he preferred to repine than to replace? [4] There is no reason to think that Agrippa and Maecenas made a habit of telling him the truth. Had they lived they would have dissembled with the best of them. It is more that the very nature of a royal temperament is to glory in what is lost in order to demean what still remains and to attribute the virtues of honesty to those from whom there is no longer any danger of receiving it.

[Seneca, *On Benefits 6.32.2–4*]

Seneca is arguing that even the most powerful people can be done a favour in the form of good and frank advice. Maecenas and Agrippa were both dead in 2 BC when Augustus tried his daughter Julia and her lovers under his own adultery law and banished her to the island of Pandataria. Seneca's cynical assessment of the real freedom enjoyed by Augustus' advisers no doubt springs from his own experiences as adviser to Nero. The start of this passage, outlining Augustus' reaction to discovering his daughter's behaviour and his subsequent regret, is given in **P12**.

R7   The retirements of Maecenas and Agrippa

(The context is the speech of Seneca asking Nero to allow him to withdraw from public life)

[53.3] "Augustus, your own great-great-grandfather, allowed Marcus Agrippa to retire to the peace and seclusion of Mytilene, and granted Gaius Maecenas what was tantamount to retirement abroad within the confines of Rome itself. Of these, one had been his comrade in arms; the other had borne the tremendous burden of civil administration at home. They were both richly rewarded, but no more than they deserved for their outstanding services."

[55.2] Nero replied: "My great-great-grandfather Augustus did indeed allow Agrippa and Maecenas to claim rest from their labours, but he did so at an age when his prestige could guarantee the permanence of such and similar concessions. Certainly he never revoked the rewards he had heaped on either of them."

[Tacitus, *Annals* 14.53 & 55]

Marcus Agrippa: Agrippa never retired but died (12 BC) in harness. His residence in Mytilene (23–22 BC), presented as a retirement by Velleius (2.93.2) and Suetonius (*Augustus* 66.3), actually gave him speedy access to the Syrian and Balkan armies in case Augustus had trouble at Rome. Tacitus allows Seneca to strengthen his own argument for retirement, but as Nero points out in his reply, the ages of the two emperors were very different: Augustus was 40 in 23 BC, Nero only 24 at the date of this passage (AD 62).

Gaius Maecenas: Tacitus, *Annals* 3.30 (**R27**) claims that he lost the friendship of Augustus.

comrade in arms: in particular, Agrippa had fought at Naulochus (36 BC), in the Balkans (35–34 BC), and at Actium (31 BC).

R8   Maecenas' effeminacy

[114.4] All this is even more true of a man's natural abilities, which are inseparable from his character. Abilities are shaped by character, controlled by it, and guided by its rules. There is no need for me to describe how Maecenas lived – it is too well known already: his way of walking, his prissy mannerisms, his ostentation, his shamelessness in the indulgence of his vices. As you would expect, therefore, his speech was as sloppy as his untidy habits of dress; no less striking than the failings which marked his words were those which could be seen in his behaviour, his associates, his household, and his wife. He really would have been an outstanding figure, if he had applied his talents in a more disciplined fashion, if he had not deliberately made himself hard to understand, and cultivated an ambiguity of expression. So you will see that his eloquence is that of a drunkard – convoluted, rambling, and wholly undisciplined.

[Younger Seneca, *Moral Epistles (to Lucilius)* 114.4]

Seneca's moral epistle (not a real letter, but one of a series of moral essays in letter form, written around AD 62–65) maintains that style of writing reflects the character of the writer.

R9   Maecenas' poetry
(This passage continues R8)

[114.5] Consider the following expression; could anything be more clumsy?

"A river bank with long-haired woods above"

What about this?

"The river's channel let them plough with skiffs, where
Churning the shoals their wake creates a wave-garden"?

What would you think of someone who

"Crimps his effeminate curls and with his lips
Whispers sweet nothings and begins to sigh,
Just as the woodland tyrants are adored
With humbled necks"?

Consider this,

"A faction irredeemable, they rummage through our banquets
With wine-flasks tempting our homes, till duping them with hope
They exact the penalty of death"?

Or this,

"Genius, that scarce bears witness to his own festivities"

Or this,

"Thin filament of wax and crepitating grain"

Or again,

"The hearth with clothes mother and wife adorn."

[114.6] The moment you read this, would it not strike you that this was the style of the man who was always striding about the city with his tunic in a mess? After all, even if he was required to sign documents when standing in for Caesar in his absence, he was slovenly about his appearance. Such writing must seem typical of the man who would appear at the tribunal to give judgement, or at the rostrum to make a speech, or at any other public gathering, with his head wrapped in a cloak right up to the ears just like a rich man's runaway slaves in a theatrical farce; typical of the man who at the very height of the civil wars, when there was panic in the city and everyone armed to the teeth, appeared in public escorted by two eunuchs, rather more manly than himself; typical of the man who only had one wife, but was endlessly remarried.

[114.7] These lines, so sloppily constructed, carelessly expressed, and composed in defiance of all convention, are clear proof that his character was equally strange, depraved, and eccentric. He is much admired for his moderation, since he was sparing of the sword and disinclined to shed blood. Only in the licentiousness of his daily life did he show what he was capable of. But he rather damaged the effect of the praise that was his due by the affected extravagance of his oratory. [114.8] It is clear that he was not mild, but effeminate. All those circumlocutions, that distorted vocabulary, those extraordinary sentiments which often suggest great thoughts are in the making until some feeble sentiment emerges – all these prove the point conclusively. Extreme success had gone to his head. All these faults are partly characteristic of the man, partly due to the climate of the times.

[Younger Seneca, *Moral Epistles (to Lucilius)* 114.5–8]

[5] Augustus parodied Maecenas' affected speech, according to Suetonius, *Augustus* 86.2.
[6] *endlessly remarried*: Maecenas' wife, Terentia, was notoriously unfaithful (see **R8**).

R10   Maecenas' prose style

Augustus knew that his friend Maecenas wrote in a rather sloppy, affected, and degenerate style, so he often used to write to him in a similarly artificial manner. By contrast with the disciplined restraint which he usually exhibited in his communications, his private correspondence with Maecenas was filled with a stream of light-hearted expressions such as these: "Farewell my ebony of Medullia, my Etrurian ivory, my Arretine silphium-juice, my Adriatic diamond, pearl of the Tiber, Cilnian emerald, Iguvine jasper, Porsenna's beryl, carbuncle of Hadria – or, not to put too fine a point upon it, you Poultice for randy wives."

[Macrobius, *Saturnalia* 2.4.12]

Suetonius also records Augustus parodying Maecenas' prose style (Suetonius, *Augustus* 86.2).

R11   Comparing Maecenas and Regulus

Do you then count Maecenas more fortunate than Regulus, when he was driven to distraction by love and heartbroken by the daily repulses of his bad-tempered wife, and driven to seek sleep's consolation through the gentle echoes of sweet music's distant harmonies?

[Younger Seneca, *Concerning Providence* 3.10]

In this work Seneca defends the gods for allowing the good to suffer. One of his arguments is that the virtuous man can suffer nothing that is truly bad, because virtue is the only good and vice the only evil. Regulus' noble suffering is contrasted with the contemptible softness of Maecenas. On Regulus, see the note on **G23**, line 37ff. Maecenas' beautiful wife Terentia was believed to be one of Augustus' paramours (Dio 54.19.3; 55.7.5; Suetonius, *Augustus* 69.2). On Maecenas' passion for the actor Bathyllus, see **R23**.

R12   Augustus' birthday presents from Maecenas

Every year on his birthday he would receive from his lifelong friend, Maecenas, a drinking cup as a gift.

[Plutarch, *Moralia* 207.6]

R13   Auditorium of Maecenas

The building is the only one of a much larger residential complex of the *horti Maecenatis* (Gardens of Maecenas) which Maecenas began to build on a run-down area of the Esquiline in the 30s BC. His *horti* and this building cut right across part of the old city wall. Maecenas spent most of the last fifteen years of his life in semi-retirement in his *horti*. On his death, he left them to Augustus.

'Auditorium' is the name given to the room by its excavators in 1874, who saw the seven concentric steps in the rounded, apsidal end as seats of a miniature theatre, where members of Maecenas' celebrated literary circle (Virgil, Horace, Propertius and others) would recite their latest works. Alternatively, given that the holes around the second step down from the top seem to have carried water-pipes, the installation could have formed a cascade (though what happened to the water once it reached the bottom of the steps is not clear). Either way, the room was essentially a setting for dinner parties: the couches would be arranged in front of the apse, facing the transept at the other end, where entertainments would be staged. This end was originally either open, or with a wide door, giving access to a front terrace, from where there will have been a view to the Alban hills in the distance. All trace of the roof has gone: it was probably of wood, not concrete.

Lives of Horace and Virgil (R14–R15)

R14   Life of Horace

This biography, transmitted with the poems of Horace, is generally thought to be derived from the life of Horace composed a century after the poet's death by Suetonius for his work *On The Lives of Famous Men* (c. AD 90–120?), some other parts of which survive. Most of its information is extracted from the poems, but sometimes offers independent evidence. It is particularly informative on the relationship between the poet, Maecenas and Augustus: the poem 'Horace, I love you' and the citations from Augustus' letters occur only here, and are likely to derive from Suetonius' own researches in the imperial archives.

Note: The paragraph numbers given here are not standard (there are none), but are included for ease of reference.

[1] Quintus Horatius Flaccus came from Venusia and claimed to be the son of a freedman debt collector, though popular belief has it that he was a dealer in salt fish. The evidence for this is that in a quarrel by way of abuse someone claimed to have seen his father "always wiping his nose on his arm". He served as a military tribune in the Philippi campaigns of the civil war, having been recruited by Marcus Brutus, one of the army commanders. His side lost, but he gained his pardon and took a position as clerk to the quaestor. He ingratiated himself first with Maecenas, then with Augustus, and finally became an important figure in both their circles of friends. There is clear evidence of Maecenas' affection for him in the well known epigram:

> "Horace, I love you more than my own belly.
> Were it not so, you'd see your bosom friend
> As skinny as Ninnius"

but even more so in his final testament, where he appended the following exhortation to Augustus, "Look after Horatius Flaccus as you looked after me."

[2] Augustus offered him the post of correspondence secretary, as is evidenced by the following note to Maecenas: "Before, I used to be able to write my own letters to friends, but now I am so pre-occupied and in such poor health that I want to rob you of our friend, Horace. So he will come from feasting at your table, that home for parasites, to enjoy my royal fare instead – and help me with my correspondence."

Horace refused the invitation, but even so Augustus did not hold it against him, nor did he allow his friendship towards him to cool in any way.

[3] Some of his letters still survive and I quote from one or two of them to prove the point. "Claim any rights you like when you are in my house, as if we shared it. It will be entirely proper; you will not be out of order. After all, that is the way I wanted it to be between us, if only your health had permitted". Again, "You are always in my thoughts; how much so you can learn also from our friend, Septimius. I happened to mention you in his presence. You may have been so proud as to spurn my friendship, but that was no reason for me to reciprocate." There are other additional light-hearted remarks. He calls him, for instance, "an unadulterated prick" and "that delightful little manikin", and one way and another he made him a rich man by his generosity.

[4] As for his writings, Augustus so admired them and was so certain that they would live for ever that he not only commissioned him to write the *Carmen Saeculare*, (Centennial Hymn), but also badgered him into celebrating the victory of his stepsons, Tiberius and Drusus, over the Vindelici. This forced Horace to add a fourth volume to his three books of *Odes* many years after their first publication. Furthermore, after reading several of his *Conversation Pieces* (Satires), Augustus complained that he personally did not get a mention. "You must realise that I am cross with you that in all your many pieces of this kind you carefully avoid having a *Conversation* with me. I suppose you are afraid that it will ruin your reputation with posterity to be seen to have been a friend of mine." This drove Horace to respond with the poem addressed to him in person, which begins,

> Caesar, upon your shoulders all alone you bear the burden
> Of so many and such cares: with arms you guard our state,
> With morals enhance it, and with laws improve it. Too much
> Would I offend against the public good were I to steal your time
> With my too lengthy conversation. ......

[5] Horace was a fat little man – he says so himself in his *Satires*, and Augustus confirms the fact in the following letter: "Onysius has brought me your slim volume. Small though it is, I shall accept it in the spirit in which it was sent, as making amends in full. But it seems to me that you are frightened to let your books become bigger than yourself. Yet it is only height you lack, not circumference. So feel free to squeeze your creations into a small pot, provided that it encompasses no less than your own *embonpoint*."

[6] The tradition is that he was extraordinarily lecherous. It is said that he had a mirrored bedroom in which he so arranged his prostitutes that wherever he looked he could watch his own 'performance'. He spent most of his time in rural retreat on his Sabine or Tiburtine estates, and his house can still be seen near the little grove of Tiburnus. I have acquired some elegies attributed to him and also a letter in prose, which purports to be a commendation of himself to Maecenas. I suspect, however, that both are forgeries. The elegies are vulgar and the letter is also incoherent – certainly not one of his characteristic vices.

[7] He was born on 8 December, in the consulship of Lucius Cotta and Lucius Torquatus [65 BC], and died at the age of fifty-seven on 27 November, in the consulship of Gaius Marcius Censorinus and Gaius Asinius Gallus [8 BC], fifty-nine days after the death of Maecenas. He made Augustus his heir by open declaration, since the violent onset of his illness prevented him from signing and sealing the testamentary documents. He was buried and his body lies at the edge of the Esquiline close to the tomb of Maecenas.

[Suetonius, *On Famous Men, Horace*]

[4] *Carmen Saeculare*: see **L28**.
Victory of Tiberius and Drusus: *Odes* 4.4 and 4.14 (**G42** and **G44**).
the poem addressed to him: *Epistles* 2.1 (**G46**).

R15   Life of Virgil

This biography is associated with the second-century Virgilian commentator Aelius Donatus, though much of it may be older (it too may well owe something to the lost life by Suetonius; note the similar use of Augustus' letters at 31). As for the life of Horace, its information is largely extracted from the poems, not always reliably (for example, the biographical conjecture based on *Eclogue* 5 (Daphnis, 14) is improbable), and the otherwise unsubstantiated information given here needs to be treated sceptically Virgil's exceptional status leads already in this biography to the kind of fantastic exaggerations which in the Middle Ages characterised him as a magical figure. The most obviously fantastical chapters of this biography are here omitted (for examples stories about his birth, 2–5).

[1] Publius Vergilius Maro was of humble parentage, especially on his father's side. Some say he was a working potter, though most people say he was the paid assistant to a summoner named Magus. Tradition has it that in time he became Magus' son-in-law, thanks to his own hard work, and then managed to expand the value of their small estate to a remarkable extent by buying up woodland and keeping bees.

[2] Virgil was born in the consulship of Gnaeus Pompeius Magnus (Pompey the Great) and Marcus Licinius Crassus [70 BC] on 15 October in a district not far from Mantua known as Andes …

[6] He spent his early years in Cremona until he took the *toga virilis* on his fifteenth birthday, in the year when the two men in whose consulship he had been born were once again consuls, and on the very day on which the poet Lucretius died. [7] But then he moved from Cremona to Mediolanum, and thence to Rome shortly afterwards. [8]

He was tall and heavily built, dark-skinned and of rustic appearance. His health was indifferent: he suffered frequently from gastric pains, throat infections, and severe headaches, frequently also vomiting blood ...

[11] In all other aspects of his life it is generally agreed that he was blameless in thought and word – so much so that in Naples he earned the popular nickname "*Parthenias*, the Virgin", and if he was ever seen publicly in Rome – which he very rarely visited – he would slip into the nearest house to avoid those who followed him and pointed him out. [12] Augustus once offered him the property of someone who had been exiled, but he could not bring himself to accept it. [13] He had about ten million sesterces of his own, thanks to the generosity of his friends, and a house in Rome on the Esquiline near to the gardens of Maecenas; but he usually preferred his rural retreats in Campania and Sicily.

[14] He was already grown up when he lost his parents, his father being already blind, and two of his own brothers, Silo, who died while still a boy, and Flaccus, who was fully grown and whom he laments as Daphnis in the *Eclogues*. [15] He studied medicine among other things and more particularly mathematics. Only once did he plead a case in court, and never again; he was a very hesitant speaker according to Melissus, and sounded almost as if he were uneducated ...

[19] Soon after he began to write the *Annals of Rome*, but defeated by the scope of the subject he turned to the *Eclogues*. His primary motivation was to honour the memory of Asinius Pollio, Alfenus Varus, and Cornelius Gallus, who had exempted his property from confiscation during the redistribution of the Transpadane lands among their veterans ordered by the Triumvirate after their victory at Philippi. [20] Then he wrote the *Georgics* in honour of Maecenas, who had helped to protect him, at a time when he was still comparatively unknown, from the violence of one of the veterans, with whom he had got into a legal dispute about his farm and was nearly murdered by him. [21] Finally he started upon his *Aeneid*. The theme is complex and elaborate, and the poem is modelled upon Homer's twin epics, being derived from the shared heritage of Greek and Latin heroes and history. But it also contained an account of the origins of Rome and the family of Augustus, which was a theme especially dear to the poet's heart. [22] While he was writing the *Georgics,* tradition tells us that it was his daily practice to dictate a very large number of verses in the morning and then to spend the rest of the day reducing them to a tiny number, neatly observing that his method of composition owed much to the habits of a mother bear, who licked her cubs into shape. [23] As for the *Aeneid*, he first wrote a prose version and divided it into twelve books; he then proceeded to compose his verses at random, at whatever point the fancy took him, and in no particular order. [24] To avoid losing the flow of inspiration, he would leave certain sections unfinished and others 'shored up', so to speak, with makeweight words or phrases. These he light-heartedly called his 'scaffolding poles', which he inserted to support the edifice until the more permanent columns became available. [25] He completed his *Eclogues* in three years, the *Georgics* in seven, and the *Aeneid* in eleven. [26] The publication of the *Eclogues* met with such success that they were often performed as recitations on the stage by singers. [27] Virgil read his *Georgics* to Augustus over a span of four successive days on the way back from his victory at Actium, while he was staying at Atella in order to let his throat heal, with Maecenas taking over the reading whenever he became too hoarse. [28] His voice was melodious and extraordinarily pleasant to listen to and Seneca tells us [29] that the poet Julius Montanus used to say that he would have stolen some of Virgil's lines if

he could have also stolen his voice, expression, and power of delivery. When Virgil was reading they sounded wonderful; but with any other reader the same lines sounded feeble and lacking in effect. [30] Such was the fame of the *Aeneid* that almost before it was begun the poet Propertius felt able to make the following proclamation:

> "Give way, writers of Rome; you Greeks, depart this earth;
> That which is greater than the *Iliad* is brought to birth"

[31] Meanwhile Augustus who chanced to be be absent campaigning in Cantabria used to demand with supplications and even light-hearted threats in his letters that Virgil should send him "something from the *Aeneid*, either" – as he himself put it – "a first *essai*, or any *soupçon* that he pleased as an *hors d'oeuvre*". [32] But it was only after many years, when the poem was at last assuming its final shape, that Virgil read him three complete books, the second, fourth, and sixth. This last had such a remarkable effect upon Octavia, who attended the readings, that she is said to have fainted away when he reached the lines about her son, "You shall be Marcellus", and could scarcely be revived. [33] He gave readings also to a number of others, but only to small groups and usually of those passages about which he felt some doubt, so that he could assess their impact on his audience. [34] They say that Eros, his secretary and freedman, in his extreme old age used to tell the story of how during a public reading Virgil once completed two of his half-lines off the top of his head. He reached the two words "Misenus, son of Aeolus" and added "than whom was none more skilled"; then in the next line to the phrase "to stir the hearts of men" he casually tossed off the similarly inspired words "and fire them up with trumpet call to arms". He immediately told Eros to add both phrases to the manuscript.

[35] At the age of fifty-one, intending to put the finishing touches to his *Aeneid*, he decided to retire to Greece and Asia and for three years to concentrate solely on polishing the text, so that he would then be free to devote the rest of his life to philosophy. But while *en route* he happened to meet Augustus at Athens on his way back to Rome from the East, and decided not to be parted from him and even to make the journey home in his company. But while he was exploring the neighbouring town of Megara under a ferocious sun, he caught a fever and made matters worse by refusing to delay his departure by sea. As a result by the time he reached Brundisium he was significantly worse and died there a few days later on 21 September, in the year of the consulship of Gnaeus Sentius and Quintus Lucretius [19 BC]. [36] His remains were taken to Naples and laid in a tomb on the *Via Puteolana*, just short of the second milestone. On it is inscribed his own epitaph, which reads as follows:

> "Mantua gave me birth; Calabria death; and now for evermore
> In Naples' arms I lie, who sang of shepherds, warriors, and country lore".

[37] He named Valerius Proculus, his half-brother, heir to half his estate, Augustus to a quarter, Maecenas to a twelfth, with Lucius Varius and Plotius Tucca as residuary legatees. These two last edited the *Aeneid* for publication after his death on Caesar's instructions. [38] Sulpicius of Carthage has left us a few lines on the subject, which read as follows:

> "Virgil in raging flames commanded that they be destroyed,
> Those songs which told the tale of Phrygia's hero prince.
> Tucca and Varius refused; great Caesar too pronounced
> His veto, and thereby salvaged the story of our Latin folk;

> So nearly a second time by fire was luckless Pergamum sacked;
> So nearly a second time upon the funeral pyre was Troy destroyed."

[39] Before leaving Italy Virgil had made a pact with Varius that if anything happened to him he would burn the *Aeneid*. He insisted vigorously that he would do no such thing. As a result, during his last illness Virgil asked repeatedly for his papers so that he could burn them himself. But when no one brought them to him he gave no specific instructions as to their disposal, [40] but bequeathed all his manuscripts jointly to Varius and Tucca (mentioned above) on condition that they would publish nothing which he himself would not have published. [41] With Augustus' encouragement, however, Varius did publish the poem with just a few superficial alterations and without attempting even to complete the unfinished lines.

[46] Asconius Pedianus, in his work *Against Virgil's Critics,* gives us a rather limited number of the complaints laid against him, and those mostly concerned with history and his many alleged borrowings from Homer. He tells us that Virgil's defence against the charge was to ask why his critics did not try the same trick. They would very soon discover that it was easier to steal a club from Hercules than a line from Homer. But he also tells us that Virgil's planned retirement was to enable him to refine his text to satisfy his detractors.

[Donatus, *Life of Virgil*]

[19] *Asinius Pollio*: politician, historian, patron of arts: see Index of Persons.
      Alfenus Varus: consul 39 BC, lawyer.
      Cornelius Gallus: politician, poet, first Prefect of Egypt see **P5**.
[30] *Propertius*: 2.34.65–66.
[32] *Octavia*: on her grief for her son, Marcellus see **J25**; on the line, *Aeneid* 6.883 see **G37**.
[34] *two of his half-lines*: *Aeneid* 6.164 and 6.165

Culture and the Arts (R16–R27)

R16   Gaius Maecenas Melissus

Gaius Melissus was a freeborn native of Spoletium who, because of a quarrel between his parents, had been exposed to die. He was lovingly and diligently reared and given an advanced education, before being handed on as an expert in grammar to Maecenas as a gift from the man who reared him. He found himself welcomed as a friend and treated as such, with the result that, though his mother gave evidence that he was freeborn, he remained a freedman, preferring his present situation to his original true status. For this reason he was quickly given his freedom and even won the approval of Augustus, who appointed him to the task of organising the library in the Portico of Octavia.

[Suetonius, *Grammarians* 21]

Portico of Octavia: see **K31**.

R17   Head of the Palatine Library

Gaius Julius Hyginus, a freedman of Augustus and a native of Spain (though some think he came from Alexandria and had been brought to Rome by Caesar as a boy after its capture) ... was head of the Palatine Library, but that did not prevent him taking large numbers of pupils. He was a very close friend of the poet, Ovid, and of the historian and ex-consul, Clodius Licinius, who tells us that he died in considerable poverty and was supported throughout his lifetime by his own generosity.

[Suetonius, *Grammarians* 20]

R18   Asinius Pollio's Library at Rome

In Rome Asinius Pollio was the originator of this new fashion [the habit of placing bronze busts of authors in libraries], since he was the first to establish a library and thus make the works of human genius public property.

[Pliny, *Natural History* 35.10]

Gaius Asinius Pollio was consul in 40 BC, patron of Virgil and of the arts generally. His library was built from booty from his campaign in Illyria for which he celebrated a triumph in 39 BC. He then retired from politics (though Tacitus makes later lawyers describe him as 'crammed with the spoils of the war between Antony and Augustus (Tac. *Ann.* 11.7)) but continued to be celebrated in the Augustan period for his artistic patronage, his history of the period 60–42 BC, and his refusal to flatter Augustus.

R19   Asinius Pollio's sculpture collection

[33] Being a man of strong enthusiasms, Asinius Pollio was naturally eager for his collection to attract public attention. It included Arcesilaus' *Centaurs Ridden By Nymphs*, Cleomenes' *Muses of Thespiae*, Heniochus' *Ocean and Jupiter*, the *Nymphs of the Appian Spring* by Stephanus, *Hermes with Eros*, a double bust by Tauriscus (of Tralles – not the famous engraver), [34] *Jupiter God of Hospitality* by Papylus, the follower of Praxiteles, and a group composition by Apollonius and Tauriscus jointly, carved from a single block of stone and brought to Rome from Rhodes, showing *Zethus and Amphion with Dirce* roped to the bull ... In the same collection *Father Liber* by Eutychides is widely admired, as is the *Apollo* by Philiscus of Rhodes in the Temple of Apollo, close to Octavia's Portico, and likewise the *Latona*, the *Diana*, the *Nine Muses*, and another nude *Apollo*.

[Pliny, *Natural History* 36.33–34]

This and other references in Pliny *NH* 36.22–23 allow 11 statue groups to be identified in Pollio's collection. The majority seem to have been marble statues of the first century BC.

R20   Greek intellectuals in Rome

Xenarchus, whose lectures I once attended, did not spend very long in his home town but, having chosen the life of a teacher, lived in Alexandria, Athens, and finally Rome. He became a friend of Areius and later of Caesar Augustus, and until a ripe old age was held in the highest esteem.

[Strabo, *Geography* 14.5.4]

Strabo and other intellectuals and writers who came from the Greek East had at their disposal some of the best teachers in the world. Strabo gives us a strong sense of the flourishing cultural life of the cities of Asia Minor, many of whose most talented citizens were attracted to Rome and to the imperial court.

R21   Studius' landscape painting

Within the Augustan period I must also allow a well-earned accolade to Studius, who was the first to introduce the delightful vogue for wall-painting. He decorated walls with scenes of country houses, porticoes, and ornamental gardens, groves and woodlands, hills and lakes, channels, streams, and coastlines, or any other scene that takes your fancy, together with scenes of country walks or sea voyages, paying visits to country estates, whether on horseback or by carriage, scenes of fishing, fowling, or hunting, and even the grape harvest. One can find in his *oeuvre* splendid villas approached across the marshes, women carried on men's shoulders for a bet and, as they are carried along, shrieking with terror when they stumble, and many other exquisitely humorous drawings of the same kind. He also introduced the practice of painting in open air galleries views of maritime cities. The effect was delightful; the cost minimal.

[Pliny, *Natural History* 35.116–117]

Paintings of ornamental gardens may still be seen today in the 'Auditorium of Maecenas' (**R13**) and the House of Livia on the Palatine. Examples of the other types of wall painting can be seen at Pompeii.

R22   Preface to Vitruvius, *On Architecture*

[1] When, Imperator Caesar, your divine mind and genius won dominion over the whole world and all Rome's enemies were laid low by your unconquerable valour, her citizens exalted by the triumph of your victory, and all the conquered nations hearkened to your word, then indeed were the Senate and People of Rome set free from fear at last to be guided and governed by your wisdom and counsel. Amid such vast pre-occupations I did not dare to publish my treatise *On Architecture*, for all the profound research that underpinned its findings, for I was afraid that I might irritate by such an interruption at an inappropriate time.

[2] But then I came to realise that you have regard not only for the well-being of all our citizens and the governance of our state, but also for the opportunity this affords for the construction of public buildings. As a result not only has our state been enlarged by the addition of new provinces, but the prestige of our empire has derived extraordinary distinction from its public buildings. So I perceived that it would be a neglect of duty if I failed to bring this material to your notice at the first opportunity, particularly since I was originally an adviser in such matters to your father, whose great qualities I much admired. Now that the conclave of heaven has granted him a place amid the homes of the immortals and his imperial power has been transferred to you, my devotion to his cause remained loyal to his memory and has made me support you.

Initially, therefore, along with Marcus Aurelius, Publius Minidius, and Gnaeus Cornelius, I was made an overseer of artillery, responsible for the construction and repair of catapults, missile launchers, and heavy artillery. Promotion followed for all of us, and after first appointing me Inspector, with your sister's encouragement, you have continued to retain me in that office.

[3] I am bound to you by a debt of obligation in that to the end of my life I need have no fear of poverty. And so, having seen how you have already built much and are continuing to do so, I have embarked upon this treatise which is dedicated to you. For the future, too, I am confident that your concern for buildings public and private is such that you will bequeath to posterity an architectural legacy proportionate to the greatness of your other achievements. I have set for myself precise terms of reference and my aim is to ensure that by reference to this work you may be fully informed about buildings already completed and those planned for the future. Within these books I have set out a comprehensive account of the science of architecture.

[Vitruvius, *On Architecture* Preface 1.1–3]

Despite this dedication to Augustus, there is a marked lack of reference to important buildings of Augustus' reign, or even to buildings in Rome, in the rest of Vitruvius' work.

R23   Augustus and Maecenas at games

The Augustan Games (*Ludi Augustales*), then instituted for the first time, were marred by quarrels arising from the rivalry of the performers. Augustus had been inclined to tolerate such shows as a way of indulging Maecenas' grand passion for the actor

Bathyllus. But he was not personally averse to such amusements, since he believed that to participate in popular entertainment was a mark of political sensitivity.

[Tacitus, *Annals* 1.54]

Ludi Augustales: see above, on Tacitus, *Annals* 1.15.2 (Section **F**).
To participate in popular entertainment: Suet. *Aug*. 45.1 says that Julius Caesar lost popularity because he read papers at the games; Tiberius was a poor attender, see the next passage.

R24   Augustus' attendance at the games
Various explanations were offered for Tiberius' absence from the games, such as his dislike of crowds, his depressive temperament, and his fear of unfavourable comparison with Augustus' more genial demeanour at such gatherings.

[Tacitus, *Annals* 1.76]

The games were given in AD 15 by Drusus and Germanicus. On this occasion Tiberius may have been trying not to upstage his sons.

R25   Exotic animals displayed at games by Augustus
[64] Scaurus in his aedileship was the first to display 150 panthers at once; Pompey the Great then produced 410, followed by the deified Augustus with 420.

[Pliny, *Natural History* 8.64]

R26   A naval display
A naval battle was staged on the lake itself, in imitation of the battle once more modestly staged by Augustus with lighter ships and fewer combatants on his artificial lake beyond the Tiber.

[Tacitus, *Annals* 12.56]

The show Tacitus is describing was staged by Claudius in AD 52. Augustus mentioned his naval battle at *RG* 23; Tacitus, *Annals* 14.15 refers to 'a grove which Augustus had planted round the naval lagoon.'

R27   Maecenas' 'successor', Sallustius Crispus
At the end of the year two famous men, Lucius Volusius and Sallustius Crispus died. Crispus had been born an equestrian, but Gaius Sallustius, the outstanding historian of Rome, had adopted his sister's grandson into his family. So he had ready access to gaining high office. Instead he followed Maecenas in being without senatorial status, yet surpassing in power many who had celebrated triumphs or held the consulship. His culture and elegance set him far from what was traditionally expected and his affluence and resources came dangerously close to decadence. Yet he had a vigour of spirit equal to huge undertakings, all the keener for his appearance of lethargy and indolence. Therefore he was second only to Maecenas while he was alive; then the man most often entrusted with secret business of the emperors, complicit in the killing of Agrippa Postumus; but as time passed, his friendship with Tiberius became impressive rather than influential. The same had happened with Maecenas. Influence is, by definition, rarely permanent. Or else both sides get fed up when one has nothing left to grant, the other has nothing left to ask for.

[Tacitus, *Annals* 3.30]

At the end of the year: Sallustius Crispus died in AD 20.
Gaius Sallustius: the historian, better known as Sallust.
Agrippa Postumus: see especially Tacitus, *Annals* 1.6 (Section **F**).

THE SOCIAL LEGISLATION OF AUGUSTUS

Introductory Note

The civil wars of the latter half of the first century BC had inflicted terrible damage upon the fabric of Roman society. The ranks of the senatorial and equestrian orders, the Roman governing classes, were severely depleted by death and by ruin of family fortunes. There was also perceived, though possibly with some exaggeration, to be a collapse in morality, in respect both for traditional Roman virtues and family values, and for the previously accepted hierarchy of society. During the principate of Augustus an attempt was made to restore public stability, by a number of laws directed towards particular aspects of society. These attempted to encourage marriage and the production of legitimate children, to control the transmission of wealth, and hence of social status, through inheritance, to control admission to Roman citizenship, in particular by imposing restrictions on manumission, i.e., the freeing of slaves; and to demarcate the social orders more clearly and introduce greater orderliness into public conduct.

Notes on Legal Sources and Authors

Celsus (Publius Iuventius Celsus), praetor AD 106 or 107, consul twice, the second time in 129, governor of Thrace and later Asia, and a member of Hadrian's *consilium*, was a distinguished jurist and author of numerous legal works, especially the *Digesta*, in 39 books, which are frequently cited in Justinian's *Digest*.

Collatio legum Mosaicarum et Romanarum (*Comparison of the Jewish and Roman Laws*): this work, probably dating from the early fourth century AD, is a collection of excerpts from classical juristic works and imperial constitutions; at the head of each title is a passage, in Latin, from Old Testament Jewish law.

Digest: this was one of three works commissioned by the emperor Justinian at his accession in AD 527 in order to restate the whole body of existing Roman law in a consistent and convenient form. The *Digest* was compiled from the works of the major jurists, especially the five great jurists (Papinian, Paul, Ulpian, Modestinus and Gaius) declared as authoritative by the Law of Citations (AD 426) of Theodosius and Valentinian, and including other jurists cited by them. This makes the work particularly valuable for ancient historians, even though the extent to which the texts of the original works were revised over the centuries, and possibly also by the compilers themselves, cannot be determined with certainty. Nevertheless the *Digest* preserves some details, even sometimes the actual wording, of many earlier Roman laws, and interpretations of them.

Fragmenta Vaticana: the so-called 'Vatican Fragments' are the fragments of a juristic collection found in the Vatican in 1821 in a palimpsest manuscript originally written in the fourth or fifth century AD. The juristic works mainly used seem to be those of Papinian, Paul and Ulpian, though it is evident that the texts used had been much altered in post-classical times.

Gaius was a famous Roman jurist of the latter half of the second century AD, whose gentile name and cognomen are unknown. He wrote several commentaries on legal topics, and his best-known work, the *Institutes*, a highly influential introductory handbook for law students, was the basis for the imperial *Institutiones* published in the reign of Justinian. He was one of the five 'canonical' jurists named in the original version of the Law of Citations (AD 426), all of whom are cited frequently in the *Digest*.

Law of Citations: see '*Digest*'

Modestinus (Herennius Modestinus), a lawyer of the first half of the third century AD, was a pupil of Ulpian. Among his numerous works was *De Excusationibus* (On Excuses) on exemption from the duty of being *tutor* or *curator*, which is unusual for being written in Greek. Modestinus himself had some connections with the East and is known to have spent some time in Dalmatia. Since the *Constitutio Antoniniana* of AD 212 had made all free inhabitants Roman citizens, there was a pressing need for works to assist Greek speakers to become familiar with Roman law.

Papinian (Aemilius Papinianus), a close associate of the emperor Septimius Severus, worked for a few years at the end of the second century in the emperor's office for petitions (*a libellis*) after being assistant to a praetorian prefect, and was praetorian prefect himself from AD 205. He was considered the foremost among the five jurists declared authoritative in the Law of Citations.

Paul (Julius Paulus) practised as advocate and teacher in Rome, before entering imperial service under the Severi, becoming assistant to Papinian as praetorian prefect and possibly head of the records office (*a memoria*). He was a member of Septimius Severus' *consilium* and later that of Severus Alexander. He wrote over 300 books, although the influential *Sententiae* ('Opinions'), an elementary summary of the *Digest* in 5 books, popular with practising lawyers, may have been compiled later from his writings.

Scaevola (Quintus Cervidius Scaevola) was a late second century jurist, who died about AD 175. Some of his works were not published until long after his death, well into the third century.

Ulpian (Domitius Ulpianus), another of the original five jurists cited in the Law of Citations, worked from AD 202–209 drafting constitutions and replies to petitions for Septimius Severus, holding the office from AD 205 of secretary for petitions (*a libellis*). Between AD 213 and 217 he composed over two hundred books on Roman law and several on the duties of public officials. The *Regulae* ('Rules') attributed to him are probably a later work based on other jurists; a number of other works were also falsely credited to him. His works were the most widely used of any Roman lawyer's, and supply more than two-fifths of the contents of the *Digest*.

Marriage

There were two main laws, the *lex Julia de maritandis ordinibus*, ('Julian law on marrying categories') of 18 BC, and the *lex Papia Poppaea* issued in AD 9. We do not have anything resembling a complete text of either law. Ancient sources on the laws are scrappy and disjointed, and it is impossible to distinguish exactly which provisions belonged to which law. Even in Roman legal writings, they are commonly lumped together as the *lex Julia et Papia*. Our legal sources such as Ulpian and Paul belong mainly to the Severan period (late 2nd – early 3rd century AD). There are many modern discussions of the law; see especially S.M. Treggiari, *Roman Marriage* (Oxford 1991) 60–80.

Suetonius (*Augustus* 34.1) remarks that Augustus found difficulty in implementing his marriage law of 18 BC, the *lex Julia,* because of its unpopularity and persistent attempts to evade or circumvent it. He was therefore obliged to have a second law issued, *lex Papia Poppaea* (named after the consuls, both incidentally bachelors, who formally introduced it). This law mitigated some of the earlier law's severity, and at the same time closed some loopholes for evasion. For instance, according to Dio (54.16) men had been securing the benefits of the law, without hindrance to their bachelor life-styles, by getting betrothed to infant girls, who would not be legally eligible for marriage until the age of 12; betrothals were now limited to two years.

Marriage and the production of children were encouraged by various rewards and penalties. Most of these were of appeal mainly to wealthier Romans, especially those with political ambitions. Evidence from Egypt suggests that poorer people may have been exempt. According to the *Gnomon of the Idios Logos* (a legal handbook used by the emperor's fiscal official in Egypt), unmarried and childless men owning less than 100,000 sesterces, and women less than 50,000, could inherit. Rewards included accelerated promotion in their political careers for men, and for women an increase in the independent control which they could exercise over their own property. Paradoxically, these incentives were also likely to encourage divorce, if a marriage was unproductive, to enable remarriage. Freed slaves were also given various inducements to conform to the traditional Roman values of marriage and parenthood. Restrictions were introduced on permissible marriages, particularly on marriage to members of senatorial families. By another *lex Julia*, also enacted in 18 BC, adultery became for the first time a criminal offence and was severely penalised. Under the marriage laws, those who failed to marry and have children were penalised, both men and women, by restriction on their ability to inherit from any persons other than close relations (in practice, up to second cousins). This law in particular displays the marks of careful legal thought. Existing Roman law from the Republic had attempted in various ways to resist the dissipation of fortunes by wills away from families of the deceased; now, in the absence of beneficiaries capable of inheriting, these fortunes would simply pass to the state. For upper-class Romans, inability to benefit from inherited wealth would mean, literally, social degradation; under Augustus, membership of the senatorial and equestrian orders became dependent upon financial qualification. The laws therefore created strong incentives to comply.

Marriage Restrictions (S1–S2)

Some of these were introduced to further the distinction of ranks in society, and some for moral reasons; the latter are discussed below. Notice that more attention is paid to the marriage of senators and their male descendants. Women took their status from their husbands.

S1 Marriage restrictions laid down by the Julian law on marrying categories

The *lex Julia* provides as follows: 'A senator, his son, or his grandson or great-grandson through the male line shall not knowingly or with fraudulent intent become betrothed to or marry a freedwoman, or a woman who is or has been, or whose father or mother has been, an actress.

'Nor shall a senator's daughter or his granddaughter or great-granddaughter through the male line knowingly or fraudulently become betrothed to or marry a freedman, or any man who is or has been, or whose father or mother has been, an actor.'

This section prevents a senator from marrying a freedwoman or a woman whose father or mother have been actors; likewise, a freedman marrying a senator's daughter. There is no bar to marrying someone either of whose grandparents has been an actor. It makes no difference whether the daughter is in power (*patria potestas*) or not;

however, Octavenus says that father and mother are to be regarded as the lawful parents, even if the child is illegitimate. Nor does it make any difference whether the father is a biological or an adoptive one.

Does it matter if he was an actor before he adopted? Or if a natural father was one, before his daughter's birth? And if a man of this unacceptable status adopted a daughter, then emancipated her, does that make her (the daughter) ineligible for marriage? Or if a natural father of this status died? Pomponius rightly takes the view that application of the law in such a case would be contrary to the meaning of the statute, and that such people should not be classed together with the rest.

If the father or mother of a freeborn woman became actors after [her marriage], it would be grossly unfair to divorce her, since the marriage was quite properly contracted, and perhaps may already have produced children. Obviously, if the wife herself takes up acting, she has to be divorced.

Senators are also barred from marrying any women that other freeborn men are forbidden to marry.

[*Digest* 23.2.44 = Paul, *On the* lex Julia et Papia, Book 1]

In the extract above quoted from Paul's commentary on the law, Paul, like a typically thorough lawyer, after quoting a section of the law, goes on to discuss how it is to be applied in a variety of problematic cases, and quotes a number of previous legal opinions. The last sentence probably derives from Ulpian's interpretation of the law. It presumably refers to the ban introduced by the Julian law on adultery (see below) on convicted adulteresses marrying freeborn men, as well as other later legislation, for which, however, we have no reliable evidence. From Dio (60.24.3) it appears that a ban on marriage by serving soldiers existed by the time of Claudius, though we do not know whether this also was part of the *lex Julia*. The purpose of the law may have been partly the preservation of military discipline, but it was also perhaps intended to keep Roman women in Italy available for marriage and the production of legitimate citizen children.

S2   Marriage restrictions laid down by the Papius-Poppaeus law

The *lex Papia* provides that all freeborn persons except senators and their children can marry freedwomen.

[*Digest* 23.2.23 (Celsus *Digest* Book 30)]

The passage of this law cited by Celsus, along with Dio 54.16.2, has in the past been mistakenly taken to show a change from the previous situation. However, there is no reason to believe that marriages between freeborn and freed were illegal under the Republic. A freed slave could marry a free Roman, although among the élite, who attached great importance to family and connections when choosing marriage partners, such a match would probably be regarded as socially undesirable.

S3   Marriage: rewards and penalties in public life

For instance, the seventh chapter of the *lex Julia* assigns priority in taking the *fasces* (symbols of magisterial authority) not to the elder consul, but to the one who has more children, either in his legal control (*potestas* – literally 'power'), or dead in warfare. If both have the same number of children, the one who is married or counts as married takes precedence. If both are married and have the same number of children, the one who entered on office first and is older, takes the *fasces* first.

[Gellius, *Attic Nights* 2.15.4]

Marriage: rewards and penalties through legislation on ability to inherit (S4–S5)

Gaius' *Institutes*, a legal handbook written towards the middle of the second century AD, briefly states the main categories of those whose ability to receive inheritances was restricted. The unmarried (*caelibes*) and married but childless (*orbi*) were able to receive bequests only from close relatives, that is, up to the sixth degree (descendants of a common great-great-great-great-grandparent). No surviving ancient text actually says this, but it is implied in Ulpian *Regulae* 16.1 (on inheritance between husband and wife) and *Fragmenta Vaticana* 216–7 (on exemptions from acting as *tutor*). The *lex Papia* later allowed *orbi* to take half from relatives up to the third degree (those descended from a common great-grandparent), if made heirs in their wills (Ulpian *Regulae* 18). The degrees of relationship, up to the seventh, and the nearer relationships embraced within them are enumerated in *Digest* 38.10.

Marriage and the production of children progressively increased their ability to benefit from the wills of outsiders (including spouses, if not blood relatives). Account was taken of the high level of child mortality.

Men and women were expected to marry and begin to have children within specified age limits, covering the years when producing children was a possibility; the unmarried had limited rights of inheritance. The lower age limit was, realistically, set several years above the minimum legal age for marriage (12 for girls, 14 or the assumption of the *toga virilis*, usually a year or two later, for boys). In practice, Romans usually entered their first marriages some time later. Women were allowed a period of grace before remarriage after divorce or the death of their husbands. Originally, in archaic Rome, early remarriage was banned on religious grounds, but there were obvious practical implications as well; there is a good deal of legal discussion about determination of the paternity of children born earlier. The period set by the *lex Julia* was found to be inadvisably short, and lengthened by the *lex Papia*. A tax of 5 per cent on inheritances was introduced; the revenue went to the upkeep of the armed forces.

The so-called *Liber singularis regularum*, ('Rules, in One Book') sometimes referred to as the *Tituli Ulpiani* or *Regulae*, is probably not by Ulpian, but is likely to be the work of an unknown lawyer of the third and fourth century, based on Gaius' *Institutes* and other sources. To retain the benefit of marriage, a widow or divorced woman was required to remarry within a specified period (14). The rubric to the previous section of this work (13) reads 'On unmarried and childless men, and widowers with children' (*de caelibe, orbo et solitario patre*) but the text following does not provide any information on how a widower with children was penalised. 'Pernicianum' (16) is possibly an error for 'Persicianum' after Paullus Fabius Persicus, consul AD 34. Those whose '*ius antiquum*' (18) was recognised could inherit whether they had children or not, so long as they were named as heirs in the will.

S4   Restrictions on inheritance imposed on unmarried and childless people

[111] Moreover, unmarried people (*caelibes*), who are forbidden by the *lex Julia* to receive inheritances and legacies, and also the childless (*orbi*) whom the *lex Papia* forbids to receive more than half of an inheritance or of legacies…

[286a] In addition, the childless, who under the *lex Papia* lose half of inheritances and legacies, on the grounds that they have no children, were formerly considered to be able to benefit in full from trusts. Later, however, by the *senatusconsultum Pegasianum* [c. AD 73], they have been banned from receiving gifts under trusts, as well as inheritances and legacies. These are transferred to those in the will who have children, or if no one has children, to the people, just as in the case of inheritances and legacies which lapse for the same or a similar cause.

[Gaius, *Institutes* 2.111, 286a]

S5   Privileges on ability to inherit dependent on family status

[14] *On the penalty of the* lex Julia

The *lex Julia* allows women a period of grace of one year after the death of a husband, six months after divorce, but the *lex Papia* allows two years from his death, a year and six months from divorce.

[15] *On tenths*

[15.1] Husband and wife can inherit one tenth from each other, on grounds of marriage. But if they have surviving children from another marriage, in addition to the tenth they receive on grounds of marriage they receive an additional tenth for each child. [15.2] Also, a daughter or son of both of them who dies after naming day adds one tenth; two dying after naming day add two tenths. [15.3] In addition to the tenths they may receive the usufruct of one third of the deceased's property, and actual ownership when they have children. [15.4] Moreover, a woman may inherit, in addition to the tenth, a dowry left to her as a legacy.

[16] *Inheritance between husband and wife*
[16.1] Sometimes husband and wife can receive the full benefit from each other, for instance, if both or either is not yet at the age at which the law requires children, that is if the man is less than 25 or the woman than 20. The same applies, under the *lex Papia*, if both have been married until the upper age limit, that is, 60 for men, 50 for women, and also if the married couple are blood relatives, up to the sixth degree. It also applies, if the husband is absent, during the duration of, and for one year after, his absence. They are free to make wills in each other's favour if they have received the right of children from the emperor, or if they have together a (living) son or daughter, or if they have lost a son aged 14 or a daughter aged 12, or two three years old, or three after their naming days. However a child of any age, under a year and a half below puberty, gives full capacity to benefit. In addition, if the wife gives birth within ten months of the death of her husband, she benefits in full from him.
[16.2] Sometimes they receive nothing from each other, that is if they have contracted a marriage contrary to the *lex Julia et Papia Poppaea*, for instance, if someone has married a woman of ill repute or a senator has married a freedwoman.
[16.3] Those who have failed to comply with either law before the age of 60 or 50, even though the law no longer applies to them after those ages, will nevertheless be subject in perpetuity to its penalties, under the *senatusconsultum Pernicianum*. However, by a *senatusconsultum* passed under Claudius, if a man over 60 has married a woman under 50, he will be regarded as having married before the age of 60.
[16.4] But if a woman over 50 marries a man under 60, it is called an 'unequal' marriage, and under the *senatusconsultum Calvisianum* (possibly AD 44 or 53) it does not enable her to benefit from inheritances, legacies and dowries. As a result, at her death the dowry will pass to the state...

[18] *Those who have ancient entitlement to lapsed estates*
In addition, the *lex Papia* gives ancient entitlement (*ius antiquum*) to children and relatives of the testator, up to the third degree. Anything which someone does not receive under the will, belongs to these people, if they have been instituted as heirs, either in whole or in part, as the case may be.

[Ulpian (*On Rules, in One Book*) 14–16, 18]

Tax on inheritance with exemptions for families

In AD 5, Augustus introduced a law, or possibly re-enacted one previously repealed, the *Lex Julia de vicesima hereditatum* (AD 5). This established a 5 per cent tax on inheritances by will; the revenues were allocated to a newly-established treasury, the *aerarium militare*, used for funding the army's retirement gratuities. This law did not form part of the marriage legislation, but is clearly related to it in intent. By exempting close relatives from paying the tax, it encouraged marriage and the production of children. The exemption appears to have extended only as far as the second degree of relationship – that is, including, as well as one's own children, brothers and sisters, grandparents and grandchildren. Perhaps also half-brothers and half-sisters by the same mother but different fathers (cognates – see introduction to **S6** for meaning of this term) were included. (Because of changes in the praetor's edict between 71 and 66 BC, legitimate children already had primary rights of intestate inheritance from their mothers). The law applied only to legitimate children.

The range of exemption contrasts with the six degrees exempted from penalties under the marriage laws. However, this is understandable if one looks at other likely aims of the two. After the upheavals of the late Republic, there was a pressing need not only to replenish the citizen stock in general, but in particular the wealthy, i.e., the governing élite. Unless the marriage laws allowed exemption within a wide range of unmarried and childless relatives, it was likely that too many estates would simply go to the Treasury, making it difficult to maintain a class from whom senators could be drawn. The tax, however, was intended to produce revenue for the Treasury; too many exemptions would be counter-productive.

Dio's account of the law (55.25.5–6) which he dates to AD 5, is incorrect in saying that the tax did not originally apply to the poor; they did not receive exemption until the reign of Trajan (Pliny, *Panegyricus* 40).

Guardianship (*tutela*) (S6–S7)

All orphaned minors, irrespective of sex, were required to have a *tutor* (financial guardian); adult women continued to have one, though one with more limited functions. For details of Roman guardianship, see R. Saller, *Patriarchy, Property and Death in the Roman Family* (1994) 181–9 and J.F. Gardner, *Women in Roman Law and Society* (1986) 14–22.

S6   Men's exemption from being *tutor*

Property belonging to fatherless children was administered by a *tutor*, either the nearest male agnate, if there was one, or one appointed by the father's will or by a magistrate. Agnates were relatives in the male line of descent, being related through an original *paterfamilias* (patriarch): relatives through females, i.e., by blood only, not by descent from the same *familia*, were cognates. Being the *tutor* of a minor was particularly burdensome, since it carried responsibility for managing the child's property. Only men could be *tutor*s. Under the marriage laws, certain (male) cognates (but not agnates), were exempted from being required to act as *tutor*s. A manuscript found in the Vatican in 1821 contained the fragments of a collection of juristic writings, and imperial constitutions, since known as the 'Vatican Fragments'. The juristic texts are drawn apparently from the works of the early third-century jurists Papinian, Paul and Ulpian. The fragments quoted are from a work of Ulpian on the functions of the *praetor tutelaris*, the praetor responsible for appointing *tutor*s.

It is possible that the parts relating to blood relatives, i.e. cognates, applied also to inheritance, but (as implied by Ulpian *Regulae* 16.1) to cognates only, not to relatives by marriage.

[216] Exempted under the *lex Julia* are cognates in the sixth degree, and in the seventh the son of a male or female cousin – and also a daughter, by legal interpretation, and anyone in the *potestas* of any of these, or woman married to them, or those married to our female relatives in this degree, or, among those in our *potestas* related to them by that degree of relationship which does not exceed the specified degree. [217] Likewise the cognates of those married to us, up to the same degree, or our relatives through our wives are excepted.

[*Fragmenta Vaticana* 216, 217]

S7   Women exempted from legal guardianship through the *ius liberorum* (having three children)

Males, once they reached adulthood, were no longer required to have a *tutor* (legal guardian or tutor); adult women, however, still had to have one, whose function was not to administer their property but to give or withhold authorisation for certain legal transactions affecting it. In practice, this presented little real hindrance to most women's financial independence, since a *tutor* could be legally prevented from unreasonable opposition. However, the assent of a *tutor legitimus* (nearest male agnate or, for a freedwoman, her patron) could not be compelled. For some women, therefore, freedom from this restraint had some value.

Gaius explains the nature of *tutela*, and its various types. The changes made by the marriage legislation are explained in 194–5. An 'Atilian' *tutor* was one appointed, as provided by the *lex Atilia* (c. 210 BC), by the urban praetor at Rome (in the provinces, this was done, as provided in a law of the 1st century BC, by the governor). A nominal guardian, *tutor fiduciarius*, was one appointed after the woman underwent a fictitious sale (*coemptio*); this was a way of changing *tutor*es. The sale was effected by the procedure known as mancipation (*mancipatio*), hence 'remancipated'.

[144] Parents are allowed to appoint by their will tutors to children whom they have in their *potestas* (legal control). Tutors are assigned to males below the age of puberty, and to women of any age, even if they are married. For the early lawyers wanted women, even

if adult, to have tutors, because of their instability of judgement. [145] So if a man has appointed in his will a tutor to his son and daughter, and both reach puberty, the son ceases to have a tutor. However, the daughter nevertheless remains under guardianship, for it is only by the *lex Julia et Papia Poppaea* that women are freed from guardianship by the right of children (*iure liberorum*)... [190] Now, there seems to be virtually no persuasive argument why women of full age should be under guardianship. The reason is commonly thought to be that because of the unreliability of their judgement they are often taken in, and that it would be fair for them to be controlled by the authority of tutors, but that argument seems to be specious rather than true. Grown-up women conduct their dealings personally, and in certain cases the tutor's authorisation is interposed merely as a formality, and often he is actually compelled by the praetor to give it against his will... [194] Freeborn women are released from guardianship by the right of three children. Freedwomen, on the other hand, [are released] by right of four, if they are in the *tutela legitima* (legal guardianship) of their patron or his children, whereas others, if they have a different kind of tutor, such as Atilian or nominal, are released by three. [195] A freedwoman can have a different sort of tutor in various ways, if, for instance, she was manumitted by a woman; then she ought to request a tutor under the Atilian law [c. 210 BC] or in the provinces under the *lex Julia et Titia* [1st century BC]. [195b] Again, if she was manumitted by a man and with his authorisation underwent a *coemptio* (fictitious sale), then was 'remancipated' and manumitted again, she ceases to have her patron as guardian, and begins to have as guardian her (new) manumitter, who is called a nominal tutor. [195c] Likewise, a freedwoman has to request a tutor under the same laws if her patron has died leaving no male descendant in the family.

[Gaius, *Institutes* 1.144–5, 190, 194–195c]

S8   Freedmen and freedwomen with children exempted from certain inheritance laws

Gaius outlines the history of the rules governing patron's rights of inheritance from their freedmen, up to and including the *lex Papia Poppaea*. The change to the inheritance rules in the interest of patrons gave prosperous freedmen (42) a strong incentive to produce children. This indicates that one should distrust Suetonius' assertion (*Aug*. 40.3) that the motive for limiting manumissions was to preserve the Roman people from 'pollution' by foreign or servile blood. On the other hand, the more numerous the freed slave's legitimate freeborn heirs, the less each one's share, so decreasing their chances of upward social mobility. Whether or not this was part of the intended result, it would help to preserve the social differentiation which Augustus tried to encourage.

  Freedwomen also had some encouragement to produce freeborn, legitimate children (43), although their chances were slim of having enough children to qualify for the benefit. Under the *lex Aelia Sentia* (see II below) they could only exceptionally be freed under the age of 30. All adult women were required to have the authorisation of a male tutor for certain legal transactions involving property. For most women, this was in practice little hindrance to their financial independence. However, a freedwoman's tutor was her patron, and therefore was a *tutor legitimus*, and he could not be compelled to authorise a will which was not in his interest. As shown above, women freed by women (who could not be tutors) were in a better position.

Manus (41) means much the same as *potestas*, but is applied only to wives; by the time of Augustus, marriage accompanied by the wife's entry into her husband's legal control (*manus*) had become very uncommon.

[39] Now let us consider the estates of freedmen. [40] At one time a freedman could pass over his patron in his will without penalty; for the law of the Twelve Tables [451–450 BC] called the patron to the inheritance of his freedman if he had died intestate and left no direct heir. If he had died intestate and left an heir at civil law, the patron had no claim to his estate. And if it was one of his own biological children whom he had left as heir

at civil law, there appeared to be no ground for objection; but if his heir was an adopted son or daughter, or a wife who was in his *manus* (legal control), then it was obviously unfair that there should be no claim left for the patron.

[41] Therefore later on [late 2nd century BC?] this legal inequity was corrected by the praetor's edict. For if the freedman makes a will, he is required to make it so as to leave his patron one half of his estate, and if he leaves him nothing or less than half, then the patron can claim possession of half, contrary to the will. If he dies leaving as heir at civil law an adoptive son or a wife in his legal control (*manus*) or a daughter-in-law who had been in his son's *manus*, then equally the patron can claim half against these heirs too. However, natural children enable the freedman to exclude his patron, not only those children whom he has in his legal control (*potestas*) at the time of his death but also those emancipated or given in adoption – provided that they are appointed heirs to some part of the estate in the will, or that, if passed over, they apply under the edict for possession contrary to the will. For children who have been specifically disinherited do not exclude the patron.

[42] Later under the *lex Papia* the rights of patrons were increased in regard to wealthier freedmen. For it is provided by that law that from the estate of a freedman who leaves more than 100,000 sesterces and has fewer than three children, whether he has made a will or died intestate, an appropriate share is owed to the patron. Therefore, if the freedman has left one son or one daughter, as heir, accordingly a half is due to the patron, as if he had died without children, or if he has left two children, one-third; if he has left three, the patron is excluded.

[43] As for the estates of their freedwomen, patrons were not injured by the ancient law, since a freedwoman, being under the statutory guardianship (*legitima tutela*) of her patron, could not make a will except with his authorisation. Therefore, if he had given authorisation for her to make a will, then either he had to blame himself if he was not left as her heir, or if he was then he got the inheritance. But if he had not given authorisation, and she died without a will, then again he got the inheritance, since a woman cannot have heirs at civil law, for earlier there was no heir or claimant to possession who could exclude the patron. Later, however, freedwomen were being liberated from the *tutela* of their patrons by the right of four children, and in that way were allowed also to make a will without the tutor's authorisation. Accordingly, the *lex Papia* provided that an appropriate share was due to the patron in proportion to the number of children the woman had at the time of her death. So, from the property of a woman who left all four children surviving her, one-fifth was due to the patron; but if she outlived all her children, the whole inheritance belonged to the patron.

[Gaius, *Institutes* 3.39–43]

S9   Attempts in AD 20 to relax the Papius-Poppaeus law

There followed a proposal to relax the provisions of the *Lex Papia Poppaea,* which Augustus had sanctioned in his old age to reinforce the Julian Legislation (*Leges Juliae*) with more severe penalties for celibacy, and as a means of increasing revenue to the Treasury. But it had failed to counter the current fashion for the childless state by encouraging marriage or the desire to raise a family. Meanwhile the numbers of those threatened by the law was steadily increasing, since every household was vulnerable to the contrived denunciations of informers. Hitherto their own misdemeanours had been their only source of danger; now it was the law itself.

[Tacitus, *Annals* 3.25]

The Lex Julia – Exacting punishment for adultery (S10–S29)

Augustus' law of 18 BC on adultery, the *lex Julia de adulteriis coercendis* (Julian law on restraining adulteries) made adultery for the first time a criminal offence, along with *stuprum* (unlawful sex), which also included homosexual relations, punishable by the loss of half the man's property. The law is discussed in J.F. Gardner *Women in Roman Law and Society* (Routledge 1986) 121–132 and S.M. Treggiari *Roman Marriage* (OUP 1991) 277–298. *Digest* 48.5 *Ad Legem Juliam de Adulteriis Coercendis* consists mainly of later legal interpretations of the law; only five chapters are directly cited. The *Mosaicarum et Romanarum Legum Collatio* (Comparison of Roman and Jewish Laws), a fragmentary collection of excerpts from classical juristic writing, with some biblical texts apparently inserted later, contains some citations of the law by the jurist Paul. Five chapters of the law can be identified; the origin of other parts of the law is uncertain.

Chapter 1 of the law on adultery: *stuprum* (unlawful sex) and adultery (S10–S12)

Stuprum (see Gardner, *Women in Roman Law and Society* 121–5) was distinguished from adultery, which applied specifically to relations with married women. *Stuprum* appears to have covered both sex with 'marriageable' (i.e. not acknowledged concubines or women whom senators were banned from marrying), but unmarried, women and homosexual relations, at least with boys. The *lex Julia* did not apply to slaves.

S10   Encouraging adultery made illegal (Adultery law, chapter 1)

These words of the law 'let no one hereafter knowingly and with evil intent commit *stuprum* or adultery' apply both to someone who encourages *stuprum* or adultery and to someone who commits it.

[*Digest* 48.5.13.12 (Ulpian, *On Adulteries* Book 1)]

S11   A definition of *stuprum* and adultery (Adultery law, chapter 1)

The law refers to *stuprum* and adultery without distinction, and with rather a misuse of terms. Strictly, adultery is committed with a married woman; the term derives from children conceived by another (*alter*). *Stuprum*, however, is committed against a virgin or a *vidua* (widow/unmarried woman); the Greeks call it 'corruption'.

[*Digest* 48.5.6.1 (Papinian, *On Adulterers*, Book 1)]

S12   Another definition of *stuprum* and adultery (Adultery law, chapter 1)

Stuprum is committed by someone who keeps a free woman for a (sexual) relationship, not marriage – except, of course, a concubine. [1] Adultery is committed with a married woman; *stuprum* is committed with a *vidua*, or a virgin or a boy.

[*Digest* 48.5.35(34) (Modestinus, *On Rules*, Book 1)]

Chapter 2 of the law on adultery: a father's right to kill, and a husband's (S13–S17)

If the woman's *paterfamilias* was still alive, the law allowed him to kill the woman, and her lover as well, if actually caught in the act in his or his son-in-law's house (a circumstance surely seldom likely to arise). However, he must kill both at once, and immediately. Later juristic discussions of the *lex Julia* agree that the law based this right on the legal rather than the biological relationship. This was because the Roman father's legal authority over those in his *potestas* laid upon him a public duty; he was legally responsible for their conduct.

Husbands, however, were liable to be prosecuted for homicide if they killed their wives. They could kill with impunity only adulterers caught in the matrimonial home, and belonging to certain low-grade categories of men, including those subject to *infamia* (see Paul, *Sententiae* 2.26.4 and *Collatio* 4.3.2, below). From the late second century AD they were required to report afterwards to the local judicial officials. Moreover, husbands were required to divorce their wives, and could be prosecuted for pimping (*lenocinium*) if they did not, or if they were found guilty of abetting the adultery (see below).

S13 A father allowed to kill an adulterer if he also kills his daughter
(Adultery law, chapter 2)

[3] In the second chapter, if a father, in [the case of] a daughter in his *potestas*, or one who with his consent, when she was in his *potestas*, has come into the control (*manus*) of her husband, catches an adulterer in his own or his son-in-law's house, or if his son-in-law calls him in, (then) the law allows that father with impunity to kill the adulterer, provided that he kills his daughter at the same time. [6] But if he does not kill his daughter, but only the adulterer, then he is charged with homicide.

[*Collatio* 4.2.3, 6 (Paul, *On Adulterers*, in one book)]

S14 The right allowed to both natural and adoptive fathers (Adultery law, chapter 2)

In the second chapter of the *lex Julia* on adulteries it is permitted to a father, whether adoptive or natural, to kill with his own hand an adulterer caught with his daughter, whatever her rank, in his own or his son-in-law's house.

[Paul, *Sententiae* 2.26.1]

S15 The right only applicable to the head of a family (Adultery law, chapter 2)

[21.20] A father is given the right of killing an adulterer along with a daughter *whom he has in his power*; therefore no other class of father, including a father who is a son-in-power, may do this lawfully.

[23 (22) Preface] In this law a biological father is not distinguished from an adoptive father.

[*Digest* 21 (20) & 23 (22) preface (Papinian, *On Adulteries* Book 1 and *On Adulterers* Book 1)]

S16 A husband only allowed to kill an adulterer of low status (Adultery law, chapter 2)

[4] A husband can kill only those caught in adultery who are subject to *infamia* and those who sell their bodies for a living, also slaves – but not his wife, whom he is forbidden to kill.

[Paul, *Sententiae* 2.26.4]

S17 Further definition of those who count as 'low status' (Adultery law, chapter 2)

[1] Now, certain persons are enumerated, whom a husband is allowed to kill when he has caught his wife in adultery, though he may not kill his wife. [2] Therefore according to the laws a husband, even one who is a son-in-power, is allowed to kill an adulterer caught in his house, if he is a slave, or someone who has taken the gladiator's oath, or one who has hired out his services to engage in combat with wild animals. [3] He may also kill someone caught in adultery who has previously been convicted in a criminal court, or a freedman, whether his own or his father's, and whether of citizen or Latin status. [4] He is also allowed to kill the freedman of one of his parents or children if the person caught is a *dediticius*.

[*Collatio* 4.3.1–4 (Paul, *On Adulterers*, in one book)]

dediticius: see **S36**.

S18 A husband's right to detain an adulterer (Adultery law, chapter 5)

In the fifth chapter of the *lex Julia* it is provided that a husband may detain an adulterer caught in the act for twenty hours, in order to call the neighbours to witness.

[Paul, *Sententiae* 2.26.3]

S19   A husband's right to detain an adulterer (Adultery law, chapter 5)

[Preface] In the fifth chapter of the *lex Julia*, it is laid down as follows: 'A husband who has caught a man committing adultery with his wife, and either is not willing or not allowed to kill him, may lawfully and with impunity detain him for a period not exceeding twenty hours, day and night, in order to obtain witness to the fact. [5] 'In order to obtain witness to the fact' is intended to allow the bringing in of witnesses who will give testimony for the accuser that the man was caught in adultery.

[*Digest* 48.5. 26(25) preface 5 (Ulpian, *On Adulteries*, Book 2)]

S20   Reason for exemption from prosecution (Adultery law, chapter 7)

[1] In the seventh chapter of the *lex Julia* it is laid down as follows: 'No one is to place on the list of the accused a man who, without trying to evade prosecution, is at the time absent on public business; for it was not considered right that someone absent on public business should be on the list of those charged, while he is engaged in public work. [2] It was necessary to add: 'Without attempting to evade prosecution': but if someone has arranged to be absent on public business, with the intention of avoiding prosecution, this device is to do him no good.

[*Digest* 48.5.16(15).1,2 (Ulpian, *On Adulteries*, Book 2)]

S21   Evidence from slaves (Adultery law, chapter 9)

In cases under the law of adultery, the accuser could demand that evidence was taken from slaves themselves accused of adultery (**1, 14**), or belonging to someone who had been accused (**11** and compare **P14**). Slaves had not the free man's right to give evidence in court. Their evidence was admissible only if taken under torture. Efforts were made to ensure truthful testimony under torture. An accused man's slaves were valued before being tortured, and twice the value paid to the owners or parties concerned (later compensated for loss in value, if there was an acquittal). In chapters 2–4 'the person whom the matter concerns' is interpreted as including not only the slave's owner, but also anyone having bought him in good faith from a third party, someone holding him as a pledge, a usufructuary (someone having, by legal agreement, the use of the slave), who shared with the owner, and joint owners, who shared the money among them.

[Preface] If an accuser demands, whether he has wished to be present or not, that a slave accused of adultery be interrogated, the judges are to order the slave to be valued. Once they have valued him, they shall order the man who has named the slave in his accusation to hand over that amount of money, and as much again, to the person whom the matter concerns. [1] Let us consider to whom the money is to be paid, since the law specifies 'to the person whom the matter concerns' ... [11] The law orders that those slaves who have been subjected to interrogation are to be made public property ... The reason for making them public property is so that they may tell the truth without any fear and not hold out under questioning, from apprehension at returning into the possession of the accused ... [14] The accuser's slaves also, if they are questioned under torture, are made public property. It is right that his slaves also should cease to belong to him, in case they should tell lies.

[*Digest* 48.5.28(27) preface-1, 11, 14 (Ulpian, *On Adulteries* Book 3)]

Other provisions of the law on adultery affecting husbands and fathers (S22–S25)

A husband was required to divorce his adulterous wife and to prosecute her and her lover for the crime of adultery. He had priority over all other accusers, even the woman's father, for a period of sixty days; the father came next after him. The act of divorce must be witnessed by seven Roman citizens, unlike normal divorces, for which no witnesses at all were required. If the husband did not divorce his wife and prosecute within the time limit, he was himself liable for prosecution for a new crime, introduced under the *lex Julia*, the crime of *lenocinium* (pimping). He was also liable if he did not take action against her lover, and especially if it could be shown that he had done a deal with the adulterer instead, or profited financially in some way from the adultery – if, for instance, he had taken money either beforehand, to turn a blind eye, or afterwards, to refrain from taking action against the guilty party.

S22   Husband and father have first right to bring an action for divorce

It is permitted to a husband first, or to a father who has a daughter-in-power, to bring an accusation within sixty days of the divorce, and no one else is allowed to bring action within that period; after that time, the wishes of neither are taken into account.

[*Digest* 48.5.15(14).2 (Scaevola, *Rules*, Book 4)]

S23   Time limit set for husband or father to prosecute

If a husband takes precedence and starts a prosecution, time does not run out for the father, because he cannot initiate a prosecution, but until one of them takes the initiative, time runs out for both. When, however, the husband begins action, the remaining time does not run for the one who cannot do so. The same applies whether a start is made with the adulterer or the adulterous woman; for the time ceases to run out for the accuser against the party against whom he has not begun an action. The rule applies both to husbands and to fathers.

[*Digest* 48.5.4.pr (Ulpian, *Disputations*, Book 8)]

S24   Husband himself liable for prosecution if he does not divorce an adulterous wife

The crime of *lenocinium* (pimping) is laid down by the Julian law on adulterers, since a penalty is appointed for the husband who has received anything from the adultery of his wife, and likewise in the one who, after his wife has been caught in adultery, retains her.

[*Digest* 48.5.2.2 (Ulpian, *Disputations*, Book 8)]

S25   A prosecution for adultery not liable to the charge of false accusation

Someone who accuses by the right of a husband or a father is not liable to the penalty for false accusation (*calumnia*) if he loses.

[*Collatio* 4.4.1 (Paul, *On Adulterers*, in one Book)]

Penalties for adulterers (S26–S27)

The penalties for convicted adulterers were heavy: banishment to an island and loss of a large part of their property. Conviction for adultery also carried the more widely applicable penalty of disgrace (*infamia*), which included various restrictions upon the individual's legal capacity (described in J.F. Gardner *Being a Roman Citizen* (London 1993) 110–126).

In addition, the adulterous woman may have been banned from marriage except to ex-slaves. A passage from a fragmentary text falsely believed to be an epitome of a work by Ulpian (*Rules* 13.2) apparently asserts that the *lex Julia* forbade marriage between not only senators (as with any woman convicted of a criminal offence), but *any* freeborn persons and a list of categories of women – including bawds (*lenae*) and women convicted in a criminal prosecution, as well as prostitutes, actresses, etc. The list also includes convicted adulteresses. However, the text is corrupt and not supported by other evidence, and any ban on adulterous women is more likely to have been introduced by the law on adultery. The most we can say is that the Julian adultery law probably barred adulterous women from subsequent marriage with freeborn men. This would be a particularly severe penalty for adulteresses of high rank, since, as already mentioned, family connections were of importance in the choice of marriage partners; freedmen had no legal relatives.

S26 Punishments for adulterers

It has been decided that women convicted of adultery are to be punished by loss of half their dowry and one third of their property and banishment to an island, and adulterous men by banishment to an island and loss of half their property, with the proviso that they are banished to different islands.

[Paul, *Sententiae* 2.26.14]

S27 Convicted adulterers subject to *infamia* (legal disgrace)

[10] The senate decreed that it was not seemly for any senator to marry or retain as wife a woman condemned in a criminal trial, where anyone could bring a charge, except someone who was legally barred from making an accusation in such a court. [11] If any woman was publicly convicted of false accusation or collusion, she is not regarded as convicted of a criminal offence. [12] Someone caught in adultery is as if convicted of a criminal offence. If she is proved to be guilty of adultery, she will suffer disgrace not only because she was caught in adultery but also because she has a criminal conviction. But if she was not caught, but only convicted, then she is disgraced because of the conviction.

[*Digest* 23.2.43.10–12 (Ulpian, *Lex Julia et Papia*, Book 1)]

Effectiveness of the law? (S28–S29)

Augustus apparently considered adultery a matter of public concern. This was presumably his justification for what constituted a startling departure from the Roman tradition of respect for the privacy of the marital relationship, and for the right of the *paterfamilias* to control matters within his own household. The penalties instituted by the law both for the adulterers themselves and for complaisant husbands were extremely severe, but whether they really acted effectively even as a deterrent is doubtful. How rife adultery (as distinct from the suspicion of it) actually was in Roman society cannot be judged from the rhetorical and often light-hearted treatment of the subject by moralising and satirical writers of Augustus' own time and later; they treat it as something not generally taken seriously, even by husbands. The husband who accepts his own cuckolding, whether from venial motives or from indifference, is a stock figure in their works, as in the sample below from Horace. These, of course, are not the only possible explanations of the behaviour of husbands who chose not to invoke the full rigour of the law against straying wives and their lovers, but rather to maintain the marriage.

Indeed, the law itself made it difficult to prevent a husband from forgiving his wife, instead of divorcing her and denouncing her and her lover. No one else could bring an accusation, not even the woman's father, until the husband had failed to do so within the sixty days of grace that were allowed him. Even then a charge of adultery could not be brought against the woman or her lover, nor could one of *lenocinium* (pimping) be brought against the husband, unless it was possible for an outsider to obtain positive proof that there had actually been any adultery. Moreover, a charge of *lenocinium* would have to be proved against the husband before proceedings could be brought against the other two. An accuser would have to be confident of being able to prove his case, or else he would lay himself open to a charge of *calumnia*, false accusation.

This in effect left open the possibility of reconciliation between husband and wife, and the survival of the marriage. It would be going beyond our evidence to suggest that this was any part of the original intent of the legislator. However, indications, admittedly from a rather later period, i.e., the beginning of the third century AD, are that by that time at least there was an element of public opinion in favour of letting sleeping dogs lie, where possible.

Ulpian, who worked as legal secretary to the emperor Septimius Severus in the first decade of the third century, drafting replies to petitions, shows awareness of this built-in restraint upon the invocation of the law by outsiders, and in effect expresses his approval of it. According to Dio (77.16), even the emperor Septimius was not disposed to pursue the matter energetically. Of the legislation with which Dio credits him, we have direct evidence only of a modification to the *lex Julia,* extending its scope to engaged couples as well as married (*Digest* 48.5.14(13).3). In a surviving rescript of AD 199 (*Codex Justinianus* 9.9.2) he pointed out that a husband was not open to a charge of *lenocinium* if the wife's adultery was merely suspected. The emperor's short-lived interest in enforcing the law appears to have waned on discovering the impracticality of doing so; many people brought charges but were unwilling to follow them up by prosecuting.

S28   A poet's view

Soon she looks for lovers at her husband's parties. She is not choosy about whom she picks to give forbidden pleasures, hastily, away from the lamplight; no, she stands up openly when called for, though her husband is well aware of it, whether she is invited by a travelling salesman or the master of a Spanish ship.

[Horace, *Odes* 3.6.25–32]

S29   Difficult for an outsider to bring a charge of adultery

While a marriage lasts, a woman cannot be charged with adultery by anyone allowed to make an accusation, except for her husband; for if a wife has her husband's approval and the marriage is peaceful then no one else ought to disturb and upset her and her marriage, unless he shall first have accused her husband of pimping (*lenocinium*).

[*Digest* 48.5.27(26) preface (Ulpian, *Disputations*, Book 3)]

S30   Sumptuary legislation

[14] Finally, there was the Julian law which was laid before the People while Augustus was emperor. Under this there were fixed limits to expenditure on feasts and banquets: two hundred sesterces on ordinary working days; three hundred on the Kalends, Nones and Ides, and certain other festivals; but for weddings and their associated banquets, one thousand sesterces.

[15] Capito Ateius says that there was still another decree – I can't remember for certain whether of the deified Augustus or of Tiberius Caesar – under which for a certain number of high days and holy days the permitted expenditure for banquets was raised from three hundred to two thousand sesterces, so that at least some limits should be imposed upon the flooding tide of extravagance.

[Gellius, *Attic Nights* 2. 24.14–15]

Romans of the Augustan period seem to have believed that one ingredient of traditional Roman virtue and morality was thrift or modesty of life-style, with wealth and luxury damaging the state (see Livy, **D1** chapter 11). From 161 BC, sumptuary legislation limited the amount of money that could be spent on a feast, the kind of food that could be served and the number of guests. Suetonius describes Augustus' own frugal eating habits (*Aug.* 76) and his dinner parties, 'no great extravagance, but in very good taste' (*Aug.* 74). For his ostentatious destruction of a huge villa bequeathed to him, see **K30**.

Immediately before this passage Gellius has discussed various sumptuary laws including the *lex Fannia* of 161 BC, through 4 other laws to Augustan times.

Manumission – Augustan Legislation (S31–S36)

At the end of the Republic there were two main types of formal manumission which made the freed slave a Roman citizen. A third type, by enrolment in the census, is also mentioned in our sources, but was rarely used in the Republic, being inconvenient in practice, and fell into disuse under the Empire, because of the increasing infrequency of censuses from the late Republic onwards, and their final disappearance. The two main methods in use were by will and 'by the rod' (*vindicta*).

Vindicta took the form of a collusive lawsuit before a magistrate with the appropriate authority, normally a praetor or provincial governor. A third party claimed on behalf of the slave that he was wrongfully held in slavery, and touched the slave with a rod (*vindicta*) as he did so. The owner did not oppose the claim, and the magistrate declared the slave free. An owner could declare in his will that certain slaves were to be free; this took effect after the owner's death, when the heirs implemented the will. Those not set free simply passed to new ownership along with the rest of the estate. So-called 'informal manumission', i.e, manumission by any other means, such as a statement before friends, or a letter, had no legal validity, though by the end of the Republic the slave in question was treated as free, though not a Roman citizen – in fact, without any specifically defined status.

During the reign of Augustus two laws were passed which made significant changes in the rules concerning the freeing of slaves. The *lex Fufia Caninia* (2 BC) limited the proportion and maximum numbers of his slaves whom an owner could set free in his will. The *lex Aelia Sentia* (AD 4) applied to manumissions by an owner during his lifetime, and appears to have attempted to introduce some control upon the quality of the individuals who were to be introduced to the body of Roman citizens by release.

However, it appears that a patron could not rely on receiving respect and deference from his ex-slave. A clause of the law gave to patrons for the first time the possibility of taking legal action against those ex-slaves who, far from showing them respect, treated them with active disrespect or even resorted to violence. An ex-slave could be sued on grounds of ingratitude – the *accusatio liberti ingrati* ('accusation against an ungrateful slave'). Nothing is known about the original content of this clause – what behaviour was held to constitute 'ingratitude' or what penalties were prescribed. Our legal texts date from much later in the Empire, and it is evident that there were many later modifications. This later evidence shows no general agreement on what counted as an offence, suggesting that the original law did not specify particular behaviour, and the punishment to be imposed is left to the discretion of the magistrate hearing the case.

There is a large modern bibliography on the manumission laws. There are useful discussions in K.R. Bradley, *Slaves and Masters in the Roman Empire* (Oxford 1984) chapter 3, A. Watson, *Roman Slave Law* (Baltimore, 1987) pp.28–32 (and see also pp.35–39 on the clauses of the marriage laws affecting freed slaves) and J.F. Gardner, *Being a Roman Citizen* (London 1993) chapter 2.

S31   A contemporary rhetorical account of the dangers of manumission

Dionysius of Halicarnassus, who taught Greek at Rome 30 BC – 8 BC, comments in his account of the early history of Rome on the undesirable reasons for which, he alleges, slaves were being freed in his time. He alleges that criminals and accomplices of criminal owners were being manumitted; also that some owners wishing to exploit the corn dole, or to make a show at their funerals, were manumitting large numbers. His account is rhetorical, and he does not suggest that such motives were the norm, nor does he suggest the abolition of manumission altogether – perhaps because the numbers of slaves could make this socially dangerous. He also suggests that there was a considerable body of Roman public opinion in favour of introducing some controls on the freeing of slaves.

There can be no truth, however, in Suetonius' assertion (*Augustus* 40) that Augustus' motive for the laws was racial, to keep the supposedly pure Roman stock from corruption by foreign or slave blood. It was already far too late for that, since new citizens had been being admitted into the Roman people, both from among slaves and free, throughout Rome's long history, and did not cease to be so. Moreover, several of the provisions of the Augustan laws on marriage, summarised below, actually encouraged ex-slaves to produce citizen children, as did one provision of the *lex Aelia Sentia* itself.

[4] [In the past] most slaves got their freedom because of good conduct, and this was the best way of release from their masters, but a few paid a sum of money which they had earned by decent honest work.

But in our times things are not like that. Things are in such a state of confusion and what was fine in the Roman state has become so dishonoured and debased that some who have made money by robbery and burglary and prostitution buy their freedom with this money and immediately are Romans. [5] Others, who have conspired with and abetted their owners in poisonings, murders and crimes against the gods or the people receive from them this reward. Some are freed so that they can receive the corn dole issued every month and any other charitable handout from the government to needy citizens and pass it to those who freed them, and others because of their owners' frivolity and desire for worthless popularity. [6] Now, I know of some who have allowed all their slaves to be freed after their death, so that they could have a good reputation when they were dead, and at their funerals their biers might be followed by many people with felt caps on their heads. Among those in the funeral procession were some who, as those in the know could tell you, had only recently come out of prison, who had committed crimes for which they ought to have died a thousand times. However, most people when they look at these ineradicable stains on the community are distressed and disapprove of the custom, considering it unfitting that a foremost state, one fit to rule the whole world, should make such people citizens.

[Dionysius of Halicarnassus, *Roman Antiquities* 4.24.4–6]

S32   The *lex Fufia Caninia* on manumission, 2 BC

Gaius' account of the context of the laws contains some interesting information. Manumission by will was not abolished totally, and there was no restriction on the number who could be set free in an owner's lifetime. Even households possessing as few as 2 slaves were affected by the *lex Fufia*, but the upper limit of 'not more than 500 slaves' suggests that many rich owners might be expected to have many more, employed in various types of work, domestic, agricultural and commercial. As Gaius tells us elsewhere (1.46), the law itself and subsequent senatorial decrees prevented attempts at evasion of the restrictions.

Having so many slaves was a potential danger to their owner during his lifetime. In AD 10, the Senate thought it desirable to pass a decree, the *senatusconsultum Silanianum* (*Digest* 29.5), that if an owner was killed, all the slaves in the house at the time were to be interrogated under torture and then executed. Their fears were not unfounded. There are accounts in the younger Pliny, *Letters* 3.14 and 8.14 and Tacitus, *Annals* 14.42–5, of owners being attacked and even killed, or at least of this being suspected, by their slaves.

Even the few slaves in small households who could be freed by will could cumulatively make a large number, which might be thought to threaten the stability of Roman society. Ex-slaves entered Roman society with no legally recognised family connections. Their patrons were the nearest equivalent who could provide some sort of social control, since their freedmen were expected to show them some degree of respect and deference. However, if owners died without children, there was no one to inherit their patronal rights over the freed slaves. It is possible that a further reason for restricting the number of manumissions was to limit the number of such unattached freedmen.

[42] Furthermore, by the *lex Fufia Caninia* a fixed limitation has been set on the setting free of slaves by will. [43] For someone who owns more than 2 and not more than 10 slaves is allowed to free up to half of that number; someone who has more than 10 and not more than 30 is allowed to free up to one-third of that number. But someone who has more than 31 and not more than 100 is granted the power to free up to a quarter. Finally, someone who has more than 100 and not more than 500 is allowed to free no more than one-fifth, nor is anyone with more than 500 allowed to free a greater number. The law prescribes that no one may manumit more than 100. But if someone has only one or two slaves altogether, the law does not apply; there is no restraint on his power to set them free. [44] But the law does not apply at all to owners manumitting otherwise than by will. And therefore those who manumit by the rod (*vindicta*) or by the census or among friends may set their entire slave household free, provided there is no other barrier to their freedom.

[Gaius, *Institutes* 1.42–44]

Lex Aelia Sentia on manumission, AD 4 (S33–S36)

An important aim of the lex *Aelia Sentia* seems to have been to ensure that those slaves freed were of good character, deserved their freedom, and were acceptable as members of the Roman citizen body. Age-limits were set both for owners and slaves, and various grades of freedom, short of full Roman citizenship, were created; these will be discussed below.

S33   Age limits set by the *Lex Aelia Sentia* on manumission

The purpose of the age limits was apparently to ensure on one hand that the owner was sufficiently mature and experienced not to be subject to undue influence from his slave, and on the other that the slave had given meritorious service over a long enough period to be thought to have deserved freedom. Exceptions were also made for a number of other reasons; however, a case must be made for these before a tribunal of Roman citizens. One reason was close personal association between master and slave, such as a nurse or child-minder, or actual biological relationship. It was taken for granted that (male) owners or their sons might have sexual relations with female slaves, who might then produce children. These children would be born as slaves; alternatively, the owner might be a freed slave who had managed to buy and then manumit his blood relative. Personal trust was another acceptable reason, shown by the intention to put the ex-slave in charge of managing his patron's property, or even (among lower-class owners, at least) of marrying her.

[17] A slave in whom the following three conditions are combined becomes a Roman

citizen: (i) he is more than 30 years old, (ii) he is his master's property by full legal right of ownership and (iii) he is freed in a legally right and proper manner, that is, by the rod or the census or by will. But if any of these conditions is not met, he will be a Latin. [18] As for the requirement about the age of the slave, that was introduced by the *lex Aelia Sentia*. That law prevented slaves from becoming Roman citizens upon being freed unless they had been manumitted by the rod after a tribunal had determined that there was just cause for manumission. [19] Just cause exists if, for instance, someone frees before a tribunal his son or daughter, or his natural brother or sister, or a foster-child or a child-minder or a slave intended to become his business agent (procurator) or a slave woman freed for the purpose of marriage. [20] In the city of Rome a tribunal is constituted of five senators and five Roman equestrians, whereas in the provinces it consists of 20 local judges (*recuperatores*), and is held on the last day of the assizes. At Rome, however, manumissions before the tribunal take place on certain fixed days. [21] Additionally, a slave set free under the age of 30 can become a Roman citizen if he was both freed and made heir under the will of an insolvent owner, and no other heir excludes him.

[36] However, not everyone who wishes to manumit is permitted to do so. [37] If a man sets a slave free in order to defraud a creditor or a patron, his act is without effect, since the *lex Aelia Sentia* prevents the setting free. [38] Likewise, under the same law an owner under the age of 20 is not allowed to manumit otherwise than by *vindicta* and with just cause for manumission proved before a tribunal. [39] There is just cause for manumission if someone manumits his father or mother or his child-minder or foster-brother, and also those reasons may be adduced which were set forth above in relation to slaves under the age of 30. Likewise conversely the reasons we have given in the case of an owner under 20 may be applied to a slave under the age of 30. [40] Consequently, because of this restriction on manumissions by owners under the age of 20, someone aged 14, even though he has the capacity to make a will and to appoint an heir in it, cannot, if he is under the age of 20, give a slave his freedom (in his will).

[Gaius, *Institutes* 1.17–21, 36–40]

'Latins' under the *Lex Aelia Sentia* on manumission (S34–S35)

Although Gaius talks of 'Latins' when discussing the *lex Julia*, the initial position under the law was that slaves not properly manumitted simply because the conditions of age were not fulfilled, but without any other known shortcomings, were left in a state of *de facto* freedom. A law of uncertain date, the *lex Junia*, passed under either Augustus or Tiberius, regularised the situation by giving them a chance of becoming Roman citizens. The term 'Latin' seems to have been applied because of a similarity to the right of *conubium* (intermarriage) with Romans that Latins had in the early Republic. This, however, merely meant that Latin men could have legitimate children by Roman women; it was not in itself a way of access to Roman citizenship. 'Junian' Latins could become citizens if they showed their willingness to conform to Roman values by settling down in a marital relationship with a Roman or Latin woman (though not a Latin woman with a Roman man), starting a family, and having a child who reached a year old. Both the birth and survival to the age of one year had to be duly attested before a magistrate, and citizenship could be applied for. This was known as *anniculi probatio* (proof of a one-year-old). We have one clearly attested example in L. Venidius Ennychus; two wooden tablets from Herculaneum dated AD 60 and 62 record his making of the necessary declarations. He even succeeded in becoming a member of the *Augustales* in Herculaneum. He appears in a marble inscription recording the members (*Année Epigraphique* 1978.119, originally published by G. Guadagno, *Cronache Ercolanesi* 7, 1977, 114–123); it consists of three lists. The first lists freeborn citizens, designated as 'son of'; the third lists freedmen, described as 'freedman of'. The members in the second list, in which Venidius appears, have no designation at all. They are not freedmen of anyone, since they were not properly manumitted by their owners, but they are not theirs (although when they die their property goes to the ex-owner or his heirs).

However, as Weaver points out in an article, in practice it would not be easy for many Junians to manage to reach a magistrate and make the necessary declarations in order to establish *anniculi probatio* and gain citizenship. See P.R.C. Weaver 'Where have all the Junian Latins gone?' *Chiron 20* (1990) 275–305, especially pages 275–283, 302–4. Since 'Junian' Latins, like Roman citizens, used the *tria nomina*, the three names, this created possibilities of confusion over the legal status of individuals living in Roman communities, some of which, as evidence from private law shows, were becoming realised by the end of the first century AD. However, since, with the disappearance of the citizen voting assemblies, citizen status among civilians in the lower orders became mainly of private importance, the state did not actively pursue the matter.

S34   Manumitted slaves given the status of 'Junian Latins' under the *Lex Aelia Sentia*

[22] These people are called Junian Latins, 'Latins' because they are given a status like that of Latin colonists, and 'Junian' because by the *lex Junia* they received freedom, when previously they were held to be slaves. [23] However, under the *lex Junia* they are unable either to make wills themselves or to receive bequests under the wills of others, or to be appointed as guardians under a will. [24] In saying that they cannot receive bequests by will, we mean to say that they cannot receive anything either as inheritance or as legacy. They can, however, benefit from a trust … [28] Latins, however, achieve Roman citizenship in many ways. [29] It was provided in the first place by the *lex Aelia Sentia* that if those who were freed under the age of 30 and became Latins took as wives women who were Romans or 'colonial' Latins or of the same condition as themselves, calling to witness the fact no fewer than seven adult Roman citizens, and if they bore a child, and that child became one year old – then they could, under the provisions of that law, go before the praetor, or in the provinces before the governor, and present proof that they had taken a wife in accord with the *lex Aelia Sentia* and had by her a child aged one year. And if the official before whom the case was proved pronounced that it was so, then the Latin himself and his wife, if of the same status as himself, and his child, if also of the same status, were decreed to be Roman citizens.

[Gaius, *Institutes* 1. 22–24, 28–9]

S35   A freedman gains citizenship through 'proof of a one year old' under the *Lex Aelia Sentia*

[5] In the consulship of [Gaius Vellei]us Paterculus and Marcus Manilius Vopiscus [AD 60] on 24 July Lucius Venidius Ennychus testified that a daughter had been born to him from his wife Acte.

[89] (*The text is very fragmentary, but may be restored from what remains*) [Magistrate's name finds] that of those from [the number of freedmen who by the Lex] Aelia Sentia have proved cause [… of Lucius Venidius] Ennychus and Livia [Acte his wife], because [they have] declared that a daughter [born to them] is one year old, which is the [point to be established], their [claim is established] and they are [Roman] citizens. The day before the Kalends of [(month)] in the consulship of Publius Marius and Lucius Asinius Gallus [AD 62].

[*Tabulae Herculanenses* 5 and 89]

S36   *Dediticii: Lex Aelia Sentia* prohibits certain slaves from being manumitted

Augustus' anxiety to keep undesirables from becoming citizens is shown by the creating of a category known as *dediticii*, a term originally applied to surrendered opponents in war. Certain slaves, even though correctly manumitted according to Roman law, were nevertheless not admitted to Roman citizenship – indeed they were permanently excluded. Unlike Junian Latins, they were given no opportunity of becoming citizens –

their exclusion was permanent. These were slaves who had criminal convictions, or had been submitted by their owners to certain demeaning forms of punishment, or set to employments which, for a free Roman, brought *infamia*. These undesirables were not thought fit to mix with the people of the city of Rome itself or even to come within 100 miles of the city. If any were caught breaking the ban, they were sold into slavery and, if re-manumitted, they were made public slaves.

[13] Under the *lex Aelia Sentia* it is provided that slaves who have been put in bonds by their owners as punishment, or branded, or who on account of some wrongdoing have been put to the question under torture and convicted, and those who have been handed over to fight in armed combat or against wild beasts, or put into a troupe of gladiators or into prison – those slaves, if they are later manumitted by the same owner or by someone else shall be free and of the same status as surrendered foreigners (*dediticii*). [14] 'Surrendered foreigners' is the term used of those who formerly took up arms and fought against the Roman people, and surrendered after being defeated. [15] Slaves, accordingly, disgraced in this way, when they are set free, by whatever means and at whatever age, and even if they were the full legal property of their owners, we shall never call either Roman citizens or Latins, but in all cases they are ranked as *dediticii*.

[25] Those classed as *dediticii* cannot in any circumstances benefit under a will, any more than can any foreigner; moreover, the prevailing opinion is that neither can they make wills themselves. [26] So the worst category of freedom is that of those classed as *dediticii*, and by no law or senatorial decree or imperial constitution are they allowed access to Roman citizenship. [27] What is more, they are banned from living inside the city of Rome or within the hundredth milestone from Rome; and if any of them break this prohibition, they and their property are to be sold at public auction, on condition that they are not to be held slave either in Rome or within the hundredth milestone from Rome, and they are never to be set free. If they are set free, then it is ordered that they are to be slaves of the Roman people. These regulations are in the *lex Aelia Sentia*.

[Gaius, *Institutes* 1.13–15, 25–27]

Freed slaves in the Augustan Marriage Laws – a summary

Certain clauses in the *Lex Julia de maritandis ordinibus* (18 BC) and the *Lex Papia Poppaea* (AD 9) concerned freed slaves. For convenience, these are summarised here:

Marriage

Senators and their families are not to marry freed persons.
A freedwoman married to her patron is unable to divorce him without his consent.
A married freedwoman with a male patron cannot be required to provide *operae* (services specified as a condition of freedom).

Children and Inheritance

Four children are required (compared with three for freeborn) for a freedwoman to have the privileges of *ius liberorum* (if she had a male patron or his male children as *tutor*); three if she had a female patron, or had made *coemptio* (i.e., passed out of his *tutela*) with the patron's consent.

Patrons may claim a proportion of estates worth over 100,000 sesterces left by freedmen; this is reduced for each legitimate child of the freedman – three children exclude the patron (four for a freedwoman).

A freedwoman can make a will without her patron's consent only if she has at least four children; and a patron (or patroness, with *ius liberorum*) can still claim a proportion of the estate. The will can be set aside in the patron's favour if there are no surviving children.

SECTION T

AUGUSTAN SOCIETY

Social Order

It was regarded as a necessary part of the programme of restoration of stability to Roman society after the disruption of the civil wars that the hierarchy of Roman society should be demarcated more clearly, in particular by marking off clearly the two upper orders, the senators and equestrians (*equites*). Senators, as we have seen, were fenced off from certain lower ranks of society by a ban on intermarriage. Fixed property levels were set for membership of each order, whose members were expected to wear the dress appropriate to their rank (see below) on public occasions.

Senatorial status

Two passages of Dio describe Augustus' reforms to senatorial status in 18 BC (Dio 54.17.3) and 13 BC (Dio 54.26.3–5 and 54.26.8). Suetonius differs from Dio on the changes of 18 BC. According to Suetonius, *Augustus* 41.1, the figures were eight hundred thousand and one million two hundred thousand. However, Suetonius is the only source for the former, and the latter may be a confusion with the occasion in AD 4, reported by Dio 55.13.6, when Augustus not only subsidised some poor senators and *equites* to the requisite property levels, but raised some eighty to one million two hundred thousand.

The *vigintiviri* ('twenty men'), whose functions were assigned in 13 BC to men with the equestrian census, were made up of several groups of minor magistrates. Three were responsible for implementing capital sentences, three had charge of the mint, four were responsible for street cleaning, and ten were assigned to the centumviral courts. These four small boards, and some others, had existed under the Republic, but Augustus dropped the others, and formed the four into one board of twenty. The vigintivirate was regarded as the first step in a public career, before entering the Senate.

T1   The *Lex Saenia* on patricians

At this time the emperor Claudius granted patrician status to all senators who were members of Rome's most ancient families or of particularly distinguished ancestry. There were now few survivors of what Romulus had called the 'Greater Families' and Lucius Junius Brutus the 'Lesser Families' of Rome. Few even survived from those who had been promoted to replace them by Julius Caesar under the *Lex Cassia* and the emperor Augustus under the *Lex Saenia*.

[Tacitus, *Annals* 11.25]

According to Augustus' own account of his achievements (*Res Gestae* 8.1) he also increased the number of patricians. This was done in 30 BC by a *lex Saenia* and Julius Caesar had done the same c. 45 BC by a *lex Cassia*, from which Augustus' own father benefited (Suetonius, *Augustus* 2); Claudius found it necessary to repeat the process in AD 48, acting as censor. New patricians were as liable to die out as the old: they were vulnerable to imperial suspicion; and the cost of maintaining their position made them limit the size of their families to a dangerous extent. Claudius did not pass a law but was acting as censor in AD 48. It was important for the prestige of the senate and the credibility of the emperor to sustain both its numbers (in AD 48 even by provincials) and traditional rankings. Patricians had once formed the entire senate; they were divided into four 'greater' families and a number of 'lesser', allegedly so called by Rome's first founder (c. 753 BC) and, according to Tacitus, by the founder of the Republic (c. 509). Patricians were also required to fill the Roman priesthoods.

Marcus Vipsanius Agrippa (T2–T14)

Marcus Vipsanius Agrippa (c.63–12 BC) was the constant friend and supporter of Augustus. He accompanied him to Rome from Apollonia after news of Julius Caesar's assassination, and led his military campaigns for the next twenty-five years. As well as Augustus' supporter, he was his likely successor, son-in-law, and eventually almost an equal partner in power.

For praise of Agrippa in poetry, see Horace, *Odes* 1.6 (**G22**); *Epistles* 1.12 (**G34**); and Virgil, *Aeneid* 8.682–685 (**G38**). Dio 54.28–29 gives an obituary as well as details of his death and funeral.

T2   Agrippa hides his obscure family name 'Vipsanius'

[12] In this particular rhetorical exercise Latro said something more damaging to himself than to his declamation. He was making a display speech, with Caesar Augustus in the audience together with Marcus Agrippa, whose sons – Augustus' grandsons – Caesar was thought at the time to be about to adopt. Marcus Agrippa was not by birth a *nobilis*, but had been raised to that status. [13] The topic set for the declamation was "Adoption", and at the point where Latro took the role of the young man he said, "And now, look at him, from the lowest of the low he is being grafted onto the nobility by adoption" – and so on to the same effect. Maecenas nodded to Latro to indicate that Caesar was in a hurry and that he should now bring his declamation to a close. Some people thought that he did this out of sheer spite, and that his purpose was not to prevent Caesar hearing what was said, but to ensure that he noticed it. But under the deified Augustus freedom reigned to such an extent that for all Agrippa's extraordinary influence many were prepared to sneer openly at his low birth. Originally he was called Vipsanius Agrippa, but he had abandoned the name Vipsanius as being evidence of his father's humble origins, and was known simply as Marcus Agrippa. Once, when he was appearing for the defence, a prosecutor addressed him with the words, "Agrippa, Marcus, and what's that other name?" – meaning Vipsanius of course.

[Elder Seneca, *Controversies* 2.4.12–13]

at the time: Gaius and Lucius Caesar were adopted in 17 BC.
not a nobilis*:* The term *nobilis* was applied to someone descended from a consul.
Vipsanius: Vipsanius was Agrippa's family name. It has not been found on any inscriptions, even though these invariably give a person's official name including the family name.
Maecenas: In contrast with Agrippa, Maecenas' ancestry was extremely aristocratic. See **R2**.

T3   Character of Agrippa

He was a man of the highest character, unconquerable by hard work, lack of sleep or danger. He gave his obedience willingly, but to one man only, but was eager to command others. In all he did, he would brook no delays, but no sooner had he made a decision than he acted upon it.

[Velleius, 2.79.1]

Velleius gives this assessment of Agrippa in the context of his preparing a fleet for Octavian's campaign against Sextus Pompey in 38–36 BC.

T4   Agrippa's guiding proverb

Marcus Agrippa was a man of formidable personality, the only one of those whom our civil wars brought to fame and power of whom it could be said that his success redounded to the state's advantage. He used to say that he owed much to the proverb "United we stand; divided we fall." He maintained that thanks to this he had become the best of brothers and the best of friends.

[Younger Seneca, *Moral Epistles (to Lucilius)* 94.46]

United we stand … the equivalent Roman expression was quoted if not coined by the historian Sallust.
best of friends: his friendship with Augustus is given by Valerius Maximus as the last word in friendship (Valerius Maximus, 4.7.7).

T5   Agrippa's artistic taste

It was Caesar, the Dictator, who gave particular public prestige to painting, by placing before the temple of Venus, the Universal Mother, pictures of Ajax and Medea. This was later reinforced by Marcus Agrippa, even though in matters of taste he was of more rustic severity than refined sensibility. Yet there is still extant a magnificent speech of his, which would have done credit to the greatest of Romans, in which he discusses the possibility of making all paintings and statues public property. This would certainly be preferable to driving them all into exile in the country houses of the rich. Yet for all his severity, he was not above purchasing from the people of Cyzicus two paintings of Ajax and Venus for the sum of 1,200,000 sesterces. Furthermore, in the hottest room of his own baths he had inserted small paintings into the marble facing, though they were removed not long ago, during repairs.

[Pliny, *Natural History* 35.26]

T6   His birth and ill-fortune: the bad luck of Agrippa

[45] To be born feet first is abnormal, and for this reason they call such babies 'Agrippas' – 'awkward deliveries'. This is how Marcus Agrippa is said to have been born, though he is almost unique among all those delivered in this way in being blessed by good fortune. Yet he, too, seems to have paid the price for his ill-omened manner of birth. For he endured a miserable boyhood because of his bad feet, he spent his whole life in warfare and for that reason was always liable to meet an untimely end, while all his offspring proved a disaster to the earth, especially the two Agrippinas, who gave birth to Gaius and Domitius Nero, both of whom scarred the entire human race with suffering. [46] His life, furthermore, was short since he was carried off at the age of fifty while enduring torments because of his wife's adulterous affairs and his own tedious servitude to his father-in-law, Augustus.

[Pliny, *Natural History* 7.45–46]

T7   His first marriage

This sort of conduct led to Marcus Vipsanius Agrippa choosing an alliance with his family and marrying the daughter of an equestrian in preference to a woman of a nobler family. As the intimate friend of the young Caesar, his own influence and the power of Caesar allowed him a free choice. And the person who arranged the marriage was, we must admit, Mark Antony, the triumvir.

[Nepos, *Life of Atticus* 12.1]

This passage comes from the biography of Titus Pomponius Atticus (110–32 BC), an extremely well-connected multi-millionaire, friend and correspondent of all the most important politicians of his age. His daughter, Caecilia Attica, was born in 51 BC. The marriage to Agrippa took place in 37 BC and produced at least one daughter, Vipsania, Tiberius' first wife. In 28 BC, Agrippa married Marcella, elder niece of Augustus: this marriage produced a further daughter, also Vipsania, who married P. Quinctilius Varus. Finally he married Augustus' daughter, Julia in 21 BC, and had five children by her.

T8   Pliny on Agrippa's water works of 33 BC

During his aedileship Agrippa added to the existing aqueducts the *Aqua Virgo,* as well as combining or repairing the channels of the others. He also added some 700 reservoirs, 500 fountains, and 130 cisterns, a number of which were elaborately decorated. Upon these works, and all within the space of a single year, he set up 300 statues of bronze or marble and 400 marble columns. In his account of his own aedileship he himself adds that he held games lasting for 59 days and kept some 170 public baths open free of charge.

[Pliny, *Natural History* 36.121]

Pliny wrongly gives the *Aqua Virgo* rather than the *Aqua Julia* as built during Agrippa's aedileship. Agrippa's aedileship, held most unusually after he had been consul, was undertaken to carry out public programmes to increase Octavian's popularity in the run-up to the Battle of Actium. For more examples of his water works see **K54, K58**.

T9   Agrippa's provision for Rome's water-supply
So great is the supply of water coming into the city through the aqueduct system that whole rivers may be said to flow through the city and its sewers; in fact almost every house has its own cisterns, pipes, and fountains in abundance. This was Marcus Agrippa's primary concern, though he adorned the city with many other structures as well.

[Strabo, *Geography* 5.3.8]

T10   Agrippa's map of the world
Agrippa was a meticulous worker, particularly in the pains he took with this particular project, since he was planning to set before the eyes of Rome a map of the whole world. It is, therefore, impossible to believe that he and his co-worker, the deified Augustus, made a mistake. For the portico containing the map was started by Agrippa's sister, but completed by Augustus according to the designs and writings of Marcus Agrippa.

[Pliny, *Natural History* 3.17]

Pliny is defending the figure he quotes for the area of Baetica given by Agrippa. For Agrippa's geographical work, see **N8**.

T11   Agrippa's Pantheon
Diogenes of Athens was responsible for the decoration of Agrippa's Pantheon. His *Caryatids* on the columns of this temple command an admiration that is almost unique, as do also his statues on the pediments, though because of their height they are less familiar to the general public.

[Pliny, *Natural History* 36.38–39]

Caryatids, as on the Erechtheion on Athens' Acropolis, are columns carved in the form of women.

T12   Colossal statue of Agrippa on the Acropolis at Athens
The People (dedicated this statue of) Marcus Agrippa, son of Lucius, three times consul, their benefactor.

[*IG* II² 4122]

This inscription appears on a huge base (16.75 m. high) of Hymettan marble located in front of the Propylaea, where it visually balances the Temple of Athene Nike. It probably dates some time after 23 BC, when Agrippa was active in the Greek East. The base supported a colossal statue of Agrippa in a 4-horse chariot. The text is inscribed over an earlier inscription, which has been erased, suggesting that Agrippa may have supplanted statues honouring two Hellenistic kings, Eumenes II of Pergamon and his brother Attalos II. Agrippa also built an Odeion (covered theatre) in the *agora* (forum) and possibly also relocated the Temple of Ares there.

T13   Agrippa and Augustus, *aureus* of 13 BC

Obv: Augustus, head bare, right.
CAESAR AVGVSTVS
Rev: Agrippa, wearing naval crown, right.
M AGRIPPA PLATORINVS III VIR (Marcus Agrippa, Platorinus, moneyer)

[*RIC* Augustus 409 / *BMC* Augustus 110]

The depiction of Agrippa on the coinage in conjunction with the portrait of Augustus is highly significant. The same honour was afforded to Gaius and Lucius, but not to Marcellus, nor to Tiberius until AD 13. Agrippa also appears with Augustus on a *denarius* of 13 BC, showing both men as tribunes (**H27**). On this coin he wears the naval crown, a gold crown, decorated with miniature ships' beaks, awarded for Agrippa's naval victory over Sextus Pompeius in 36 BC. Agrippa is also described wearing the naval crown in Virgil's description of the shield of Aeneas (*Aeneid* 8.684 = **G38**).

T14   Augustus' funeral oration in praise of Agrippa, 12 BC (*laudatio Agrippae*)

[…] The tribunician power was granted to you for a period of five years in accordance with a senatorial decree, when the Lentuli were consuls, and granted again for another Olympiad when Tiberius Nero and Quinctilius Varus your sons-in-law were consuls. And it was ratified by law that to whatever provinces the public affairs of Rome might drag you, no-one's power there should be greater than yours. You were raised to the highest position with our support and through your own virtues by the agreement of all men.

[EJ 366, with addition of *ZPE* 52 (1983) 61–62]

A small papyrus fragment, from the Fayum (modern El Faiyum) in Egypt, preserves a snatch of Augustus' funeral eulogy for Agrippa, translated into Greek. It illustrates how Agrippa was recognised as Augustus' main collaborator, and his gradual accumulation of powers. In 18 BC (during the consulship of Publius Cornelius Lentulus Marcellinus and Gnaeus Cornelius Lentulus), he was granted tribunician power for 5 years (a power only previously granted to Augustus), and his proconsular authority was renewed, probably also for 5 years. In 13 BC (during the consulship of Tiberius and Varus), his authority in the provinces was given precedence over all others' (*imperium maius*).

Senators (T15–T29)

T15   Tomb of Lucius Munatius Plancus, post-22 BC, near Caieta, Latium
Lucius Munatius Plancus, son of Lucius, grandson of Lucius, great-grandson of Lucius, consul, censor, hailed *imperator* twice, one of the seven in charge of feasts, celebrated a triumph over the Raetians, built the temple of Saturn from the booty, distributed lands in Italy at Beneventum, founded colonies of Lugdunum and Raurica in Gaul.

[EJ 187 = *ILS* 886]

The inscription appears on an imposing funerary monument at modern Gaeta, in Lazio. It summarises Plancus' distinguished career: consul in 42 and censor in 22 BC, he celebrated a triumph on 29 December 43 BC, and commemorated this by restoring the temple of Saturn. He was in charge of distributing land at

Beneventum for veteran soldiers of the triumvirs in 42 BC. He founded Lugdunum (modern Lyons) and Raurica (modern Augst, near Basle, Switzerland) when he was governor (proconsul) of Gallia Comata in 43 BC. In 27 BC, he proposed the name 'Augustus'.

T16   Honours for Titus Statilius Taurus, 26–16 BC, Spain

To Titus Statilius Taurus, hailed as *imperator* three times, twice consul, patron.

[*ILS* 893 = *CIL* 2.3556]

This column-like base from Ilici (modern Elche) in the Spanish province of Tarraconensis was set up in honour of Statilius Taurus, consul in 37 and 26 BC. He was first hailed as *imperator* for success in Africa, for which he celebrated a triumph in 34 BC, to commemorate which he built his amphitheatre in the Campus Martius; he was hailed *imperator* twice more, perhaps for victories in Dalmatia (32 BC) and Spain (29 BC). For Velleius' judgement on him as closest to Augustus after Agrippa, see note on his consulship in 26 BC (Section **B**).

T17   Consulships (1) – Tarius Rufus

Lucius Tarius Rufus, a man of the humblest origins, earned a consulship by his dedication as a soldier. He was in every other way a man of old-fashioned parsimony, but in his desire to make a great impression he spent every penny of his capital, to the tune of some 100 million sesterces accumulated through the generosity of the deified Augustus, on buying up agricultural land in Picenum and farming it himself.

[Pliny, *Natural History* 18.36]

Tarius Rufus was suffect consul in 16 BC, see Section **B**. The sum given in the text is enormous, but not (quite) impossible: (see *Res Gestae* 16–17 for vast sums spent by Augustus on rewarding veterans.) When he put his son on trial for attempted patricide, he asked Augustus to be a member of his *consilium* (advisory panel). See also **H48**, which implies that Augustus would have been an heir.

Picenum is the area across the Apennines from Rome, on the Adriatic coast.

T18   Gnaeus Cornelius Lentulus: his ingratitude to Augustus

[1] Gnaeus Lentulus, the augur, whose fabulous wealth made him a household word until the imperial freedmen made him look poor, could look at a bank balance of some four hundred million sesterces. And 'look at' is the appropriate description, because that is all he could do. He was devoid of intelligence and a coward morally and physically. [2] Though avaricious in the extreme he found it easier to issue cash than conversation, such was his total poverty of language. He owed all his success to the deified Augustus, to whose resources he added only his own poverty crippled by the burden of a noble lineage. Yet when he became our leading citizen in wealth and influence, he was always complaining about Augustus and how he had distracted him from his intellectual pursuits, observing that all the riches heaped upon him were as nothing compared to the losses he had suffered from abandoning his practice of oratory.

[Younger Seneca, *On Benefits* 2.27.1–2]

Seneca uses the attitude of Lentulus to the *princeps*' generosity to illustrate how not to receive favours. He compares Lentulus' wealth to that of the imperial freedmen who, particularly under Claudius and Nero, were resented by the governing class for the fabulous wealth they amassed through proximity to the *princeps*. Lentulus held the consulship in 14 BC and is said by Suetonius, *Tiberius* 49 to have been hounded to death so Tiberius could get his fortune.

T19   Consulships (2) – Quirinius

At about the same time Tiberius moved a motion in the Senate that the death of Sulpicius Quirinius should be honoured with a state funeral. Quirinius had no connection with the ancient patrician family of the Sulpicii, but was a native of the township of Lanuvium. He had proved an indefatigable soldier and given distinguished service to Augustus, for which he received the consulship. He had then been awarded triumphal honours for his Cilician campaign, where he sacked a number of fortresses of the Homonadenses, before being appointed adviser to Gaius Caesar on his appointment as Governor of Armenia. He had also been assiduous in paying his respects to Tiberius during his retirement in Rhodes, a fact which he then revealed to the senate for the first time, praising Quirinius' loyalty to himself while at the same time denouncing Marcus Lollius as the source of Gaius Caesar's disgraceful quarrelsomeness.

Others had less happy memories of Quirinius. As I have already stated, he had endangered the life of Aemilia Lepida, and to them he was a horrid old man with far too much power.

[Tacitus, *Annals* 3.48]

(*Publius*) *Sulpicius Quirinius*: his first known military service had been against African tribesmen (Florus 2.31); he reached the consulship in 12 BC. He went on to govern Galatia and subdue the tribe of the Homonadenses in the south of the province ('*Cilicia*'), capturing 44 fortresses (Pliny, *Natural History* 5.94). Quirinius succeeded the disgraced M. Lollius as adviser to Gaius Caesar. (AD 2–4; compare Suet. *Tib*. 12. 1; for Tiberius' need of friends, see **J37**). Quirinius had gone on to govern Syria (**M47–M49**).

Aemilia Lepida: In AD 20 Quirinius had accused his former wife of poisoning and pretending that her child was his. In spite of demonstrations against him in the theatre (Tac. *Ann*. 3.22f.), Lepida was exiled.

T20   Cinna given the consulship

*(For the context, Cinna pardoned for plotting to assassinate Augustus, see **P11**)*

After that he even gave Cinna a consulship, complaining only that he had not had the courage to stand as a candidate. He found him a truly loyal and close friend, and became his only heir.

[Younger Seneca, *On Clemency* 1.9.12]

T21   Consulships (3) – Ateius Capito

The year saw the deaths of a number of men of very great distinction, including Gaius Ateius Capito, of whom mention has already been made above. His distinction as a lawyer had won him a pre-eminent position in Roman public life, even though his grandfather had been a mere centurion in Sulla's army, and his father a praetor. Augustus gave him accelerated promotion to the consulship, so that the distinction of this high office would establish his precedence over another outstanding lawyer, Marcus Antistius Labeo. These two men were both adornments of their generation: but Labeo won the higher reputation by his integrity and robust independence of thought, while Capito gained greater approval from the ruling house for his obsequiousness. Labeo never rose beyond the praetorship, and this injustice enhanced his general reputation; Capito gained a consulship and with it the hatred that derives from envy.

[Tacitus, *Annals* 3.75]

The year: the context is the obituary section for the year AD 22.

Gaius Ateius Capito: suffect consul in AD 5; played an important part in the *ludi saeculares* in 17 BC, see **L23**. Member of Augustus' council (**M14**); jurist (**P19, S30**); water commissioner (**T24**).

Marcus Antistius Labeo: for an anecdote about his reactionary republicanism, see **P19**.

The careers of both men illustrate the principle that politicians were advanced, not only for distinction of birth or military achievements, but for civil attainments (Tac, *Ann*. 4.6.2).

T22   An Augustan consul

At the end of the year, Poppaeus Sabinus died. A man of humble origins, he had obtained the consulship and an honorary triumph through the friendship of emperors, and had been placed in charge of important provinces for twenty-four years not in recognition of any special talent, but because he was just equal to the job.

[Tacitus, *Annals* 6.39]

Gaius Poppaeus Sabinus was governor of Moesia AD 12–35.

T23   A senator from Histonium (on the Adriatic coast of Italy, directly east of Rome)

Publius Paquius Scaeva, son of Scaeva and Flavia, grandson of Consus and Didia, great-grandson of Barbus and Dirutia; quaestor; member of the board of ten for adjudicating legal disputes by decree of the senate after his quaestorship; member of the board of four for sentencing by decree of the senate after his quaestorship and membership of the board of ten for adjudicating disputes; tribune of the people; curule aedile; judge of inquiry; praetor of the treasury; governed the province of Cyprus as proconsul; curator of roads outside Rome by decree of the senate for five years; proconsul for a second time, without drawing lots, by authority of Augustus Caesar and, by decree of the senate, sent to settle affairs in the province of Cyprus for the future; fetial priest; cousin and husband of Flavia, daughter of Consus, granddaughter of Scapula, great-granddaughter of Barbus; he lies buried with her.

Flavia, daughter of Consus and Sinnia, granddaughter of Scapula and Sinnia, great-granddaughter of Barbus and Dirutia; cousin and wife of Publius Paquius Scaeva, son of Scaeva, grandson of Consus, great-grandson of Barbus; she lies buried with him.

[EJ 197 = *ILS* 915]

Paquius Scaeva was a *novus homo* (the first member of his family to be a senator). This explains the pride shown in listing all his minor offices on his tombstone. T.P. Wiseman, *New Men in the Roman Senate* (Oxford 1971) describes him as 'the prime example of untiring civil service.'

T24   The post of Aqueducts Commissioner

Since I have carried my discussion on to the introduction of Commissioners, it will not be out of place to add the names of those who followed Messala in this post up to my own appointment. Messala was succeeded by Ateius Capito in the consulship of Asinius Pollio and Gaius Antistius Vetus [AD 13] …

[Frontinus, *Aqueducts of Rome* 102]

T25   Part-time judicial duties of the Commissioners of Aqueducts, Roads and Corn

And moreover, inasmuch as the Commissioners of Roads and of Corn Distribution discharge their public duties for one fourth part of each year, so too the Aqueducts Commissioners shall make available such and similar periods for private and public adjudication.

[Frontinus, *Aqueducts of Rome* 101]

This forms part of a senatorial decree of 11 BC quoted by Frontinus about the Aqueducts Commissioners (see **K58**). Commissioners of Roads and of Corn Distribution were boards of ex-praetors established in 20 BC and 22 BC respectively. These new posts are mentioned by Suetonius, *Augustus* 37 and dated by Dio 54.1.4 and 54.8.4.

Augustus' gifts to senators (T26–T27)

Augustus established the sum of one million sesterces as the qualification for men who embarked on a senatorial career (Dio 54.17.3, under 18 BC, noting Augustus' gifts). This may have proved a great obstacle to senatorial families, especially those with several sons (in **T27**, Hortalus is asking Tiberius in AD 16 for further financial support for his four sons). Augustus boasts of his own generosity in bailing out impoverished senators (and thus allowing them to continue as senators) in appendix 4 of his *Res Gestae* (Section **A**). Suetonius, *Augustus* 41 also mentions this.

T26   Augustus' large gifts to senators (1)

Augustus had actually paid off the debts of a senator friend of his unasked, to the tune of about four million sesterces. In return by way of thanks for his generosity he got the following note: "Nothing for me, then?"

[Macrobius, *Saturnalia* 2.4.23]

T27   Augustus' large gift to senators (2)

Marcus Hortalus was the grandson of the orator Quintus Hortensius and was persuaded by Augustus with a generous gift of a million sesterces to marry and raise children to ensure that his distinguished family should not die out.

[Tacitus, *Annals* 2.37]

T28   Moneyer's coin (1): *sestertius*, c. 22 BC

Obv: oak wreath between laurel branches.
        OB CIVIS SERVATOS (for saving the citizens)
Rev: large letters S C (Decree of the Senate)
        C GALLVS C F LVPERCVS III VIR A A A F F S C (Gaius Gallus Lupercus, son of Gaius, moneyer responsible for the casting and striking of bronze, silver and gold)

[*RIC* Augustus 377 / *BMC* Augustus 171]

T29   Moneyer's coin (2), *aureus*, c. 18 BC

Obv: Augustus, laureate, right.

CAESAR AVGVSTVS

Rev: open flower showing petals and stamen.

L AQVILLIVS FLORVS IIIVIR (L Aquillius Florus, moneyer)

[*RIC* Augustus 308 / *BMC* Augustus 45]

Almost all the coins issued by the Mint of Rome during the Augustan period carry the names of the magistrates responsible for their production, as they had done during the latter part of the Roman Republic. The magistrates responsible for coin issue were known as *tresviri aere argento auro flando feriundo* (magistrate of the college of three responsible for the casting and striking of bronze, silver and gold). Under the reformed *cursus honorum* the position was occupied by young men as one of their first magisterial roles. During the Republic the coinage produced under the authority of these officials often carried designs of personal significance – imagery relating to their family history. Although the magistrate's names were reintroduced onto coinage in about 23 BC, the gold and silver coins continued to be dominated by the complex Augustan imagery that had developed during the last few decades, while the bronze coinage included simple images such as Augustus' *corona civica* (civic crown – see **H20**) and the letters SC (*senatus consultum*). Only a handful of coins included personal reverse types, and these were often just simple puns on the name of the magistrate concerned (such as the 'floral' coin of the moneyer Florus above). This trend was short-lived at the Mint of Rome and such officials do not seem to have been appointed at the other mints.

Equestrian Status (T30–T33)

Much is obscure about the nature and purpose of Augustus' reforms; for a discussion see F. Millar *The Emperor in the Roman World* (2nd edition, London 1992) 279–284. Several of Augustus' changes were clearly intended to increase the prestige and dignity of the order by reviving some of its Republican associations, although it is not known whether entry depended upon a formal grant from the emperor.

Although there is no direct evidence for the level at which the equestrian property qualification was now set, it is accepted that this was 400,000 sesterces under the Empire. Augustus seems, initially at least, to have refrained from applying this too strictly, in view of the financial hardship suffered by many because of the civil wars. Clearly birth as well was held to count (Suetonius, *Augustus* 40.1). The privilege of viewing from the front 14 rows of the theatre dated back to a *lex Roscia* of 67 BC.

In the early Republic the *equites* were a military force of cavalry for the defence of the state. Eighteen centuries (groups of 100 men) received from the censors the 'public horse', and were given an allowance for its upkeep. Later their function was purely civil, and denoted a select group who had priority in voting in the *comitia centuriata* (voting assembly).

Augustus revived, at least symbolically, their dignity by holding a public parade of *equites* on horseback. He also revived, on at least one occasion, a serious moral censorship of this body which Suetonius' account (*Augustus* 38–40) implies had become somewhat disorderly and disregarded by the late Republic (see Ovid, *Tristia* 2.89–96 = **G56** and **T31–T32**).

He also appears, although the evidence on this is somewhat confused, to have made some effort to prevent *equites* from appearing in discreditable types of public performances (Dio 54.2.5). Tiberius in AD 11 rescinded a ban previously imposed on *equites* from appearing as gladiators, since it had proved ineffective (Dio 56.25.7–8); according to Suetonius (*Augustus* 43.3), their appearance in both theatrical and gladiatorial performances had at some time been banned by the senate. Augustus himself in 22 BC extended a previous ban on sons of senators to those *equites* who were grandsons of senators (Dio 54.2.5).

T30   Equestrians

[30] When the deified Augustus laid down the regulations for judicial panels, most of the judges belonged to the class entitled to wear only the iron ring; as a result they were called Justices rather than equestrians. The title 'equestrian' remained the prerogative of those in the troop of *equites equo publico* (equestrians with a public horse). Originally, also, there were only four panels of Justices, with barely a thousand names in each, since the provinces had not yet been allowed the privilege of judicial service. And it remains a regulation to this day that no newly admitted citizen shall be allowed to serve as a justice on those panels. [31] As for the panels themselves, they were distinguished by a series of different titles, such as the Tribunes of the Treasury,

Tribunes of the Select, and Tribunes of the Justices. There were also the so-called Nine Hundred, chosen from the whole body to act as guardians of the ballot boxes in the elections. Yet even this order (of Justices) jealously guarded its sub-divisions, with one member claiming the title of Tribune of the Nine Hundred, another Tribune of the Select, and another the title of Tribune. [32] Finally in the ninth year of Tiberius' rule as *princeps*, the equestrian order was brought into a single unified body.

[Pliny, *Natural History* 33.30–32]

Pliny the Elder was himself a member of the equestrian order.

Within the general status of equestrian, Augustus seems to have revived special categories of equestrian: the *equites equo publico*, whose title means 'equestrians with a horse supplied by the state', but who at this date were not actually provided with a horse. Another select group within the equestrian class were the 'Justices'. Both honours were probably in the gift of the *princeps* and subject to his scrutiny.

T31 Getting the facts straight

Augustus' admirable restraint in his role as censor was also widely applauded. A Roman equestrian was being taken to task by him for the way in which he had dissipated his wealth. But he proved in open court that he had in fact increased it. So he then charged him with failure to obey the laws governing matrimonial obligations (and the avoidance of celibacy). The equestrian stated that he had a wife and three children and then added the following comment: "Next time, Caesar, when you find yourself investigating the affairs of honourable gentlemen, may I suggest you employ honourable investigators."

[Macrobius, *Saturnalia* 2.4.25]

On the laws governing matrimonial obligations, see **S5–S6**: on dishonourable investigators, see **S9**.

T32 Not the emperor's business

A Roman equestrian, when Augustus criticised him for having squandered his inheritance, justified himself by saying, "I thought it was mine."

[Quintilian, *The Orator's Education* 6.3.74]

Status Distinctions in Public

As part of his programme to restabilise Roman society after the upheavals of the civil wars, Augustus attempted in various ways to encourage orderly behaviour and recognition of rank and status in public places, especially the forum and the theatre.

This, rather than antiquarianism, was the reason for the dress code required by Augustus in the Forum, namely the wearing of the toga, rather than appearing *pullatus* (Suetonius, *Augustus* 40.5). The toga was the distinctive garment of the Roman citizen, and marked them off both from free non-Romans and from slaves. There was no officially-prescribed garment for slaves, and their everyday working garb, usually a tunic with a mantle as required, both dark (*pullus*) in colour, would often differ little, if at all, from the clothes ordinarily worn by free men (though both, obviously, might vary according to the owner's wealth). *Pullatus* therefore meant something like 'casually dressed'. The toga, and the tunic generally worn with it, had in their design indications of the status of the wearer. The tunic worn by senators (*tunica laticlavia*) had a broad stripe of purple running down the front, that of *equites* a narrow one (*tunica angusticlavia*). A toga with a purple border (*toga praetexta*) was worn by consuls, praetors, curule aediles and the higher orders of priests, and also by freeborn boys until they reached adulthood, when they replaced it with a plain one.

In the *lex Julia theatralis* of c. 22 BC, the regulations on seating arrangements introduced by Augustus (Suetonius, *Augustus* 44) made rank and status evident. They also showed a concern for public decency and morality, especially in the separation of young boys from the spectators at large, and the exclusion or restriction of women from viewing certain types of spectacle. Married men, who had thereby complied with the basic expectation of the marriage laws, were also singled out for special placing. A detailed discussion of this law and its probable working in practice may be found in Elizabeth Rawson, *Roman Culture and Society* (Oxford, 1991) 508–545.

T33   Proper behaviour in the theatre

A Roman equestrian was drinking at a performance: Augustus sent him a message to say, "If I want lunch, I go home." "You would," said the equestrian, "since you don't need to worry about losing your seat."

[Quintilian, *The Orator's Education*, 6.3.63]

The Emperor as Heir (T34–T36)

The standard practice of giving friends and allies legacies under the republic continued under the empire. 'Augustus expected the kindness he showed to his friends to be reciprocated even at their death, for although he did not hunt legacies and could not bear to accept legacies from people he did not know, he weighed up without generosity friends' death-bed tributes. He could not hide his disappointment if they were ungenerous or failed to honour him in their words; nor his delight if he was gratefully and duly honoured.' (Suetonius, *Augustus* 66.4) This concern was practical as well as sentiment, since he wrote in his will (written in AD 13) that he had received legacies totalling 1,400,000,000 sesterces over the previous 20 years and spent almost all of this on the state (Suetonius, *Augustus* 101.3).

T34   Surprising heirs: Augustus expected to inherit money from his protégés

Titus Marius of Urbinum deserved vilification. Rising from the lowest ranks to the highest military honours thanks to the generous patronage of the deified Augustus, he became a rich man through the abundant profits of his position. Not only did he declare at various intervals of his life that he would leave his fortune to the man to whom he owed it all, but even on the day before he died he said the same thing to Augustus himself. In the event, however, he failed even to mention Augustus in his will.

[Valerius Maximus, 7.8.6]

T35   The orator Atratinus makes Augustus his heir

Atratinus, regarded as a famous orator, chose to end his life in his baths, when seriously ill, leaving Augustus as his heir.

[Jerome, *Chronicle* 21 BC]

On Lucius Sempronius Atratinus, see **N2e**.

T36   Herod's legacy to Augustus

To Caesar he left ten million pieces of silver coin, and also vessels of silver and gold and some very valuable garments. To Julia, the wife of Caesar and to some others he left five million pieces of silver.

[Josephus, *Jewish Antiquities* 17.190]

Josephus laters tells us that Augustus gave the money back to Herod's children, keeping only the vessels as mementoes (Josephus, *Jewish Antiquities* 17.323). Herod's sister, Salome, left land to Livia. (**M52**).

Individuals (T37–T42)

T37   'Laudatio Turiae', 8/2 BC, Rome

This huge funerary inscription, preserved in only a fragmentary state, reads as if recording the eulogy declaimed for a deceased noblewoman by her husband. Her identity is unknown, although she has been identified in the past as Turia, wife of Quintus Lucretius Vespillo. The inscription commemorates her extraordinary feats during the triumviral period, when her parents were murdered and her husband exiled, but also presents her as the ideal virtuous wife, who possessed the moral values promoted under Augustus. Bibliography: E. Wistrand, *The so-called Laudatio Turiae* (Lund 1976) with text, translation and commentaries [some of his supplements are adopted below].

[Heading in larger letters]

[…………..] of my wife.

[Left-hand column]

T37a *Murder of her parents*

[…………..] by the uprightness of your character […….…] you remained [………..]

[3] Suddenly [before our wedding-]day you were bereft of both of your parents, when they were murdered together in the solitude [of the countryside]. That the death of your parents [did not remain unavenged was primarily through your efforts], since I had gone away to Macedonia, and your sister's husband [Cluvius] to the province of Africa.

[7] You performed your filial duty with such great energy, by petitioning ceaselessly, and by pursuing justice, that we would not [have achieved] anything more had we been present. [But] you share these merits with that most virtuous lady [your sister].

[10] While you were doing this, once punishment [had been exacted] from the guilty, you immediately [betook] yourself out of your father's home in order to protect [your virtue] into [my] mother's home, [where] you awaited my arrival.

T37b *Dispute over her father's will*

[13] Then both of you were harassed to agree that your [father's] will, in which we were heirs, [be declared] invalid, on the grounds that a *coemptio* had been made with his wife: in this way, you, together with all your father's [property], inevitably reverted [to] the guardianship of those who were pursuing the matter: your sister would be entirely lacking a share [in that inheritance], because she had been transferred into Cluvius' power. I have found out, even though I was absent, how you responded, and [with what] resolution you resisted them.

[18] You protected our common cause with the truth: the will was not invalid, so that [both of us] would keep the inheritance rather than you alone possessing all the property, and you were firm in your [opinion] that you would defend your father's written word in such a way, that you asserted that, if you did not prevail, you would share it with your sister: nor would you become subject to the status of legal guardianship, for which there was [legally no right against you], for there was no proof that your family belonged to any clan which [might by law force] you to do this: for even if your father's will had been invalid, those who were putting forward the claim [did not have] the right to do this, since they were not of the same clan.

[25] They yielded to your steadfastness and did not pursue the matter any further: once this was done, you successfully completed by yourself the defence which you had undertaken [of respect towards your father], affection to your sister, and loyalty to me.

Coemptio: involved a wife becoming absolutely subject to her husband's control.

T37c *A wife's virtues*

[27] Rare are the marriages which last long enough to be ended by death, not cut short by divorce: [for it befell] us, that it was extended into its 41st year without animosity. If only our long-continued [marriage] had undergone [its final] change through my lot, as it was fairer that I as the older partner yield to fate.

[30] Why [should I mention] your domestic virtues of modesty, obedience, affability, forbearance, [diligence] with your wool-working, [religion] without superstition, adornment that did not seek attention, and modest dress? [Why should I

speak of your love for your relatives] and loyalty to your family, since you honoured my mother just as much as your own parents, and saw to providing [the same tranquillity] for her as for your own parents, and you had the other countless attributes common [to all] married women who cultivate a worthy reputation? They are your own virtues which I proclaim, and it has been the lot of very few women to show their excellence by enduring such things which fortune has ensured are rare [for women].

[37] We preserved with equal care all your inheritance received from your parents: for you were not concerned with acquiring what you handed over to me in its entirety. We shared the duties in such a way that I protected your fortune, whilst you looked after mine. I shall omit [many things] about this aspect so that I do not associate your own achievements with me: let it suffice that I have said something about [your] feelings.

[42] You offered your generosity both to very many friends and especially to [your] beloved [family]. One might name [with praise] other women, but you have had only one most like [yourself........], your sister; for you brought up your kinswomen [worthy of such a thing.........] in your homes with us. So that those same women might be able to attain [a marriage worthy of] your [family], you provided dowries: by common consent, Gaius Cluvius and I took upon ourselves these dowries [which had been settled by you] and, though approving [your generosity], we substituted our own private property and gave [our own estates] as dowries, so that you did not let your own patrimony suffer diminution. [I have mentioned] this not in order to advertise our merits, [but so that it might be known that] we [considered it] a matter of honour [that those plans] of yours, which you had developed out of loving generosity, be carried out through our agency. [Several other favours] of yours ought to be passed over [...(several lines missing)...]

[Right-hand column]

T37d *Her husband exiled under the Triumvirate*

[2a] You provided support for my flight [by selling] your ornaments, when you [took] all the gold and pearls from your body and handed them over to me and then you enriched me in my absence with slaves, money, and income, [having cunningly deceived] my enemies' guards.

[6a] [You pleaded for my life in my absence], something which your courage encouraged you to try. The clemency [your words won] from those against whom you argued protected [me]. [And yet always] your words were uttered with strength of spirit.

[9a] [Meanwhile when a band of] men [collected] by Milo, whose house [I had acquired] through purchase [when he was] in exile, was about to burst in [and plunder], seizing the opportunity of the civil war you [successfully repulsed them and] defended our home.

[...(12 lines missing)...] that I was restored to my country by him, for unless you had provided something for him to save, [in taking care of my safety] he would have promised his help to no avail. In this way I owe my life no less to your loyalty [than to Caesar].

[4] Why should I now unearth our more private and hidden plans [and our secret conversations]: how, when provoked by sudden news to face present and imminent [dangers] I was preserved by your advice; how you did not allow me hastily [to test providence] too rashly in my boldness and how, once I was thinking on a more modest scale, [you devised] for me a trusty place of refuge and you [chose] as allies in your plans for saving me your [sister] and her husband Gaius Cluvius, with all of you sharing the same danger? [I would not finish], if I were to try to embark on this topic. It is enough for me and for you that [I hid] safely.

T37e *Her husband restored by Augustus, despite Lepidus*

[11] And yet I shall confess that the bitterest experience in my life was felt on your behalf, after [I had now been restored] as a citizen to my country through the favour and judgement of the absent Caesar Augustus, [when] Marcus Lepidus, his colleague who was present, was accosted [by you] about my recall [and] you, prostrate on the ground [at his] feet, not only were not raised up, but were dragged away and manhandled like [a slave], your body covered in bruises. Yet with a most steadfast [spirit you kept reminding him] of Caesar's edict with his congratulation on my recall, and, despite having heard insulting words and having received cruel wounds, you openly [declared these things] so that the instigator of my dangers might become known. [Soon this affair] damaged him.

[19] What could have been more effective than this courage? To provide for Caesar an [opportunity] for clemency [and together with] protecting my life to stigmatise [Lepidus'] relentless cruelty by [your outstanding] endurance.

[22] But why say more? Let me be thrifty with my speech, which must and can [be brief, so that] by dwelling on your greatest achievements I do not treat them unworthily, since [in view of the magnitude] of your services [towards me] I shall display before everyone's eyes an inscription [recording the saving of my life].

T37f *Lack of children*

[25] Once peace had been established in the world and the state set to rights, then peaceful [and happy] times befell us. We wanted children, whom [fate] had [begrudged] us for a considerable time. If Fortune had been willing to continue serving our interests as usual, [what] would [either] of us have lacked? Going [otherwise], our hopes were fading. What you planned [because of this and what] you tried to embark upon, would perhaps seem [remarkable and admirable] in some women: but in you they are nothing to wonder at when compared with [the rest of your] virtues, [and I shall now pass over them].

[31] Distrusting your ability to bear children [and] grieving at my being childless, so that I should not lose hope of having children by keeping you [in marriage] and become [unhappy] because of this, you spoke out about a divorce. You proposed that you would [hand over] an empty house to the fertility of another woman, with [no other] intention than that you yourself should seek out and provide a worthy match for me on the basis of our well-known unanimity, and you asserted that you would treat future children as [shared] and as if your own, and that you would not divide our property, [which] had [up to then] been shared, but that [it] would remain [under my control] and, if I wanted, under your administration: that [you] would possess [nothing separate], and that you [would offer me from henceforth] the services and affection of a sister or mother-in-law.

[40] I must confess that I was so inflamed, that I took leave of my senses, that I was so [horrified] at your intentions, that only with difficulty did I regain my composure. To think that divorce between us was being contemplated [before] it had been decreed by fate; to think that [you] could imagine some reason why [you should cease] to be my wife [while I was alive], when you had remained most faithful when I had been almost exiled from life.

[44] What desire or necessity for having children could I have had that was so great [that on this account] I should set aside my good faith, and exchange certainty for uncertainty? But why say more? [You remained with me as wife]; for I could not have yielded to you without disgrace to myself and unhappiness to us both.

[48] But in your case, what is more remarkable than that [you took pains] to meet my needs, so that, when I could not have children from you, I might nevertheless have children by your agency, and so that you, distrusting your ability to produce a child, might prepare for me fertility by marriage with another?

T37g *Her death: her husband's grief*

[51] If only our marriage [could have] continued, the life-span of both of us permitting, [until] you had performed the last rites for me, once I, as the older, had been carried out for burial, which would have been fairer, and I would have died leaving you as the survivor, a daughter for me in place of my childlessness.

[54] You were fated to predecease me. You bequeathed grief to me in my longing for you, and you did not leave children [to comfort me in my unhappiness]. I too shall redirect my feelings according to your judgements, [and I shall follow your instructions].

[56] Let all your thoughts and precepts take second place to your praises, so that they may be [a consolation] to me so that I do not [excessively] miss what I have consecrated to immortality so that it is remembered [for ever].

[58] I shall not lack the fruits of your life. Strengthened [in spirit] by your reputation [and] instructed by your deeds, I shall resist fortune, which has not snatched everything away from me, [since] it has allowed me to exalt your memory with praises. But whatever tranquillity I had, I have lost [with you], [since I regard] you as my guardian and champion in the face of dangers, and I am overcome by my disaster and I cannot keep to my promise.

[63] Natural grief wrenches away the strength of my self-possession: I am being drowned in sorrow and I cannot remain steadfastly [unmoved by grief or pain]: thinking again about my previous misfortunes and about future happenings I collapse [without hope]: bereft of such great and such effective defences, as I contemplate your reputation, I seem not so much destined for enduring bravely as for loss and sorrow.

[67] The conclusion of this speech will be that you deserved everything but that I did not manage [to provide] you with everything. I have regarded your last instructions as law: what I shall be able to do besides, I shall do.

[69] I ask your departed spirit to grant you peace and to watch over you in this way.

[EJ 357 = *ILS* 8393 (for complete text)]

The husband appears to suggest he planned to adopt his wife at his death (right column, 52–53), just as Augustus did Livia in AD 14.

T38　Funerary inscription, near Corfinium (Italy)

[………….wife] of …… Niger, married for 39 years to a single husband, reached her last day amid the greatest unanimity, left three surviving children by him: one son who has performed the highest municipal offices through the judgements of Augustus Caesar; a second son who has performed the highest offices of equestrian rank in the military service also of Caesar Augustus and who is now destined for higher rank; and a most respected daughter who has married a most upright man; and from her daughter, two [grandchildren] [……..]

[EJ 359 = *ILS* 2682]

This funerary inscription to a woman whose name has not been preserved illustrates the importance of the family under Augustus. She is praised as having been married to a single husband (*univira*), an ideal promoted against the background of Augustus' marriage legislation. Even Livia (whose marriage to Augustus was her second) was hailed as *univira* by Horace (*Odes* 3.14.5 = **G29**). This tombstone goes on to record the achievements of her two sons and daughter (three children being the requisite number to entitle her to certain legal privileges, see **S4**, **S5**, **S7**). The virtue of unanimity (*concordia*) was also one espoused by the imperial family, with Tiberius rebuilding the temple of Concord in the forum (**K40–K41**) and Livia building another in her portico (**K30**).

T39   Tombstone of a new Roman citizen, Noricum

Gaius Julius Vepo, individually presented with Roman citizenship and with exemption (from public burdens) by the deified Augustus, made (this) for himself and for his wife, Boniata daughter of Antonius, and for their family, in their lifetime.

[*ILS* 1977 = *CIL* 3.5232]

This is a fine marble funerary monument from Celeia in Noricum (modern Celje in Slovenia).

Licinus, freedman of Augustus (Gaius Julius Licinus) (T40–T42)

Licinus is mentioned by name as one of many freedmen Augustus honoured by a close working relationship (Suet. *Aug.* 67.1). Other writers treat him as an early example of greed and abuse of power shown by imperial freedmen. Certainly he seems to have been exceptionally honoured in being made procurator of Gaul, responsible for all revenue and expenditure. He remains the only known example of a freedman procurator: Dio's account of his blatant embezzlement (Dio 54.21.3–8) perhaps explains why.

T40   Licinus' wealth

Licinus was taken prisoner as a boy in Germany... Julius Caesar employed him to run his accounts and not long after freed him. Then, when put in charge of administration of the Gauls by Augustus he robbed them and when faced with burning resentment, constructed a basilica in the name of Gaius Julius. He died under Tiberius. So he was as rich as if he had swallowed the wealth of Crassus, and he was said to possess estates too wide for a falcon to fly across.

[Scholiast on Juvenal, *Satires* 1.109]

T41   Licinus in Gaul

Licinus reigned for many years in Lugdunum.

[Younger Seneca, *Apocolocyntosis* ('Pumpkinification of Claudius') 6]

Seneca's satirical work mentions Lugdunum as Claudius' birthplace. Claudius' freedmen were notorious. The Gauls complained to Augustus about Licinus' depredations in 15 BC (Dio 54.21). Seneca's comment on his long tenure is likely to be comic exaggeration. Licinus was a target of Seneca elsewhere (Seneca, *Letters* 119.9 and 120.19).

T42   Augustus cheats Licinus

Whenever Augustus was launching out on some new public works, his freedman Licinus used to make a substantial contribution towards the costs. Following his normal practice he once gave Augustus a banker's draft for a hundred thousand sesterces, but in this case part of the linear superscription above the figure extended beyond the final letters specifying the actual sum, leaving an empty space below. This was too good an opportunity to miss and Caesar in his own hand added a second C to the original, carefully filling the empty space with matching handwriting. As a result he got double the sum. The freedman pretended not to have noticed, but the next time some public building works were undertaken he gently chided Caesar for his action by handing him a draft couched in the following terms: "Sir, I am contributing towards the costs of this new work – whatever figure you choose to insert this time."

[Macrobius, *Saturnalia* 2.4.24]

_____   _____
H̄SC̄   converted to H̄SC̄C̄, 'HS' being the abbreviation for 'sesterces'.

CONCORDANCE
(By document number)

A: LITERARY SOURCES

Antipater			124–125	K62
47	G48		128–129	K63
Appian		**Gaius**		
Civil Wars 4.50	P2	*Institutes*		
Censorinus			1.13–15	S36
17.2	L20		1.17–21	S33
17.7–10	L21		1.22–24	S34
17.10–11	L22		1.25–27	S36
22	H36		1.28–29	S34
Collatio			1.36–40	S33
4.2.3,6	S13		1.42–44	S32
4.3.1–4	S17		1.144–5	S7
4.4.1	S25		1.190, 194–195c	S7
Crinagoras			2.111.286a	S4
27	G40		3.39–44	S8
29	G20	**Gellius**		
Digest of Roman Law		*Attic Nights*		
21 (20) & 23 (22) pr	S15		2.15.4	S3
23.2.23	S2		2. 24.14–15	S30
23.2.43.10–12	S27		9.11.10	K22
23.2.44	S1		10.11.5	J11
48.5.2.2	S24		13.12.1–2	P19
48.5.6.1	S11		15.7.3	J57
48.5.35 (34)	S12	**Horace**		
48.5.4 pr	S23	*Carmen Saeculare*	L28
48.5.13.12	S10	*Epistles*		
48.5.15(14).2	S22		1.12	G34
48.5.16 (15).1,2	S20		1.16.27–9	G35
48.5.26 (25) pr 5	S19		2.1.1–4, 245–70	G46
48.5.27(26) pr	S29	*Epodes* 7	G3
48.5.28 (27) pr 1,11,14	S21	*Epodes* 9	G5
Dionysius of Halikarnassos		*Odes*		
Roman Antiquities 4.24	S31		1.1.1–2	R2
Donatus			1.2	G21
Life of Virgil	R15		1.6.	G22
Eutropius			1.12	G23
7.9–10	N1		1.37	G24
7.10	M73		2.7.	G25
Florus			3.3	G26
2.32.42–44	J59		3.5	G27
2.33.48–53	N48		3.6	G28
Frontinus			3.6.25–32	S28
Aqueducts			3.14	G29
9–10	K54		4.2	G41
11	K55		4.4	G42
12	K56		4.5	G43
98–100	K58		4.14	G44
101	T25		4.15	G45
102	T24	*Satires*		
103	K59		1.5.27–33	G4
105	K60		2.1.1–20	G6
107–8	K61		2.6. 29–59	G7

Jerome			1.12.35	H35
Chronicle			2.4.1	J13
27 BC	M12		2.4.2	J14
26 BC	P7		2.4.7	J15
22 BC	M55		2.4.9	K17
21 BC	T35		2.4.11	J16
20 BC	N49		2.4.12	R11
17 BC	M55		2.4.13	J17
AD 5	K12		2.4.18	H43
Josephus			2.4.19	J18
Jewish Antiquities			2.4.20	J19
15.268–269	M69		2.4.23	T26
15.272	M70		2.4.24	T42
15.317	N19		2.4.25	T31
16.136–139	M75		2.4.27	H45
16.160–1	M61		2.4.29	H15
16.62–165	M62		2.5.2	J50
16.166	M63		2.5.3–4	J51
16.167–8	M64		2.5.8	J52
16.169–170	M65	**Martial**		
16.171	M66		8.55.5	R1
16.172–3	M67	**Nepos**		
16.279–283	M40		*Life of Atticus*	
16.289–290	M41		12.1	T7
17.190	T36		19.4	J35
17.299–301	M44		20.3	P3
18.1–2	M47	**Orosius**		
18.31	M52		6.21.18	N10
Jewish War			6.21.19	N39
1.386–393	M36		7.3.7	K49
1.396	M37	**Ovid**		
1.398–400	M38		*Ars Amatoria*, 1.1–228	G47
1.401–402	M39		*Fasti*	
1.401–7, 414–6	M74		1.1–14	G49
2.20, 22, 25	M42		1.277–288	K48
2.66–79	M43		1.529–536	G50
2.111	M45		1.587–616	H23
2.117	M46		1.639–650	K41
Livy			1.705–708	K39
preface	D1		1.709–722	K13
1.19.1–3	K47		2.3–18	G51
4.20. 5–8, 11	P4		2.55–66	L4
28.12.12	N47		2.119–144	H38
Summary 134–142	D2–9		3.415–428	H30
134	H22		3.697–710	K43
134	M16		4.625–628	H4
134–5	N50		4.673–676	H5
135	H16		4.857–862	G52
139	M19		4.949–954	H31
140	N51		5.129–158	L13
141	N26		5.545–598	K18
Luke (St.)			6.465–468	N41
Gospel, 2.1	M48		6.637–648	K30
Macrobius			*Metamorphoses*	
Saturnalia			1.199–205	G53
1.11.17	P14		1.557–566	G54
1.11.21	P9		15.817–879	G55
1.11.32	N28			

B: COINS

BMC Augustus			
10	N42	(70	T13)
45	T29	81	J41
71	J4		
74	L2	*RIC* Augustus	
85	L26	28	K19
92	L10	42b	H25
98	L1	53a	L9
110	T13	63a	K50
115	H27	127	L8
126	H32	131	K14
171	T28	142	K69
275	J24	164b	N15
315	K19	166a	M17
335	H25	205	J58
344	L8	225	J41
358	L9	231a	M20
362	K50	251	N4
427	K14	264	N5
435	K69	266	K33
447	N15	277	H21
450	M17	287	N42
506	J41	308	T29
513	J58	338	J4
565	M20	343	L2
609	N4	358	L10
617	N5	367	L1
631	K33	377	T28
655	N31	407	H27
656	H21	409	T13
671	N24	413	H33
691	N6	419	H32
		471	J24
		476	N6
BMC Tiberius		514	N24
116	K40	544	N31

BM CM		*RIC* Tiberius	
1995.4–1.1	H18	61	K40

BMCRR		*RPC*	
Africa 32	K45	61	M28
Gaul 63	K16	1141	J67
Gaul 74	H2	2496	J27
		2954	M58
EJ		4955	M51
15	N31		
(18	N6)	*RRC*	
26	N42	490/2	H2
35	L10	490/3	K16
66	J58	540	K45

C: INSCRIPTIONS

Index of Persons

The following usual and ancient abbreviations for *praenomina* (first names) are used:

A.	Aulus		M'.	Manius
C.	Gaius		P.	Publius
Cn.	Gnaeus		Q.	Quintus
D.	Decimus		Sex.	Sextus
L.	Lucius		T.	Titus
M.	Marcus			

Other abbreviations:

Aug Augustus
cos consul
cos suf suffect consul
XVvir *quindecimvir* ('member of the board of fifteen')

Ancient authors were inconsistent in how they referred to Romans. So too is normal modern usage. Well known figures are referred to by their usual names, other Romans by their family names. Consuls for the period 31 BC–AD 14 are listed in Section **B**.

Sex. Aelius Catus (cos AD 4)
Aelius Gallus (second prefect of Egypt)
    Arab expedition: N18–N22; N34
L. Aelius Lamia (cos AD 3): E116.3
Q. Aelius Tubero (cos 11 BC): L27r
    aqueducts: K58; K61; K62
M. Aemilius Lepidus (triumvir): F1.1; T37e
    pontifex maximus: A10.2; H29;
    army defects to Oct: C40; E88.1; F2.1; F10.3;
    insignificant: F8.4; P2
M. Aemilius Lepidus (son of triumvir)
    conspirator: D2; E88; P2; P11
M. Aemilius Lepidus (cos AD 6)
    career and possible emperor: E114.5; F13.2
    military command & honours: E115.2–3
M' Aemilius Lepidus (cos AD 11)
Paullus Aemilius Lepidus (censor 22 BC)
    character: E95.3
    senate 'committee': M53
Q. Aemilius Lepidus (cos 21 BC): L27r
L. Aemilius Paullus (cos 182–1, 168 BC)
    victory at Pydna: G37.837
    elogium: K23
L. Aemilius Paullus (cos AD 1)
    arval brethren: L7
Mamercus Aemilius Scaurus: F13.4
Q. Aemilius Secundus: M49
M. Agrippa (cos II 28 BC, cos III 27 BC)
    at Actium: G38
    aedileship: K3; K54; K58; T8
    buildings: K3; K54; M26; T8; T9; T10; T11
    census with Aug.: A8.1
    centennial games: A22.2; L22; L27
    character: T2–T6
    death: D5; E96.1; F3.3; T14
    Herod's friend: M39; M74
    honours: E88.2; T13
    letters to provinces: M59; M64; M65; M67
    marriages: E93.2; F3.1; P6; T7

poetry: G22; G34;
    Spain subdued: E90.1
    statues: M81; M82; M83; T12
    tribunician power: E90.1; H26; H27; T13; T14
    water commissioner: K58
    withdraws from public life: E93.2; P1; R7
Agrippa Postumus (grandson of Aug)
    adoption: E104.1
    banishment: F3.4; P1
    character: E112.7; F4.3
    coinage: J67
    death: F6.1–2; J48; R27
    visited by Aug? F5.1–2
Agrippina (granddaughter of Aug)
    marriage to Germanicus: J26
    statue: M81
Alexander the Great of Macedon (356–323 BC)
    H1; J20; K26; K27; K31; M1; N40
Alexander (son of Herod the Great): M38
P. Alfenus Varus (cos AD 2)
Amyntas (friendly king of Galatia): M2
    at Actium: G5.17–18
C. Antistius Vetus (cos 30 BC)
    governor of 'Nearer' Spain: E90.4; N48
C. Antistius Vetus (cos suf 6 BC)
    governor of Asia: M56
    moneyer: L1
Iullus Antonius (cos 10 BC)
    career and marriage: E100.4
    addressed by Horace: G41
    adultery and suicide: E.100.4; F10.4; P13
M. Antonius (Mark Antony) F1.2
    birthday: C6
    corrupted by vice: F9.4
    defeat at Actium: D2; G38; H11
    defeated by Parthians: E91.1; N46
    plunder restored by Aug.: A24.1; H12
    Herod: M35–M36
    treaties with Oct: F10.3; G4

Index of Places

Index of Themes

Family Tree 1 [31 BC]

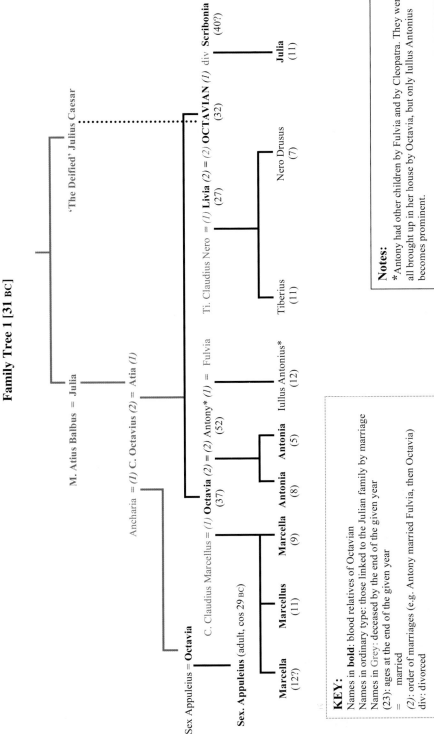

KEY:
Names in **bold**: blood relatives of Octavian
Names in ordinary type: those linked to the Julian family by marriage
Names in Grey: deceased by the end of the given year
(23): ages at the end of the given year
= married
(2): order of marriages (e.g. Antony married Fulvia, then Octavia)
div: divorced

_____ : relationships

·········· : adoption

Notes:
*Antony had other children by Fulvia and by Cleopatra. They were all brought up in her house by Octavia, but only Iullus Antonius becomes prominent.

Family Tree 2 [17 BC]

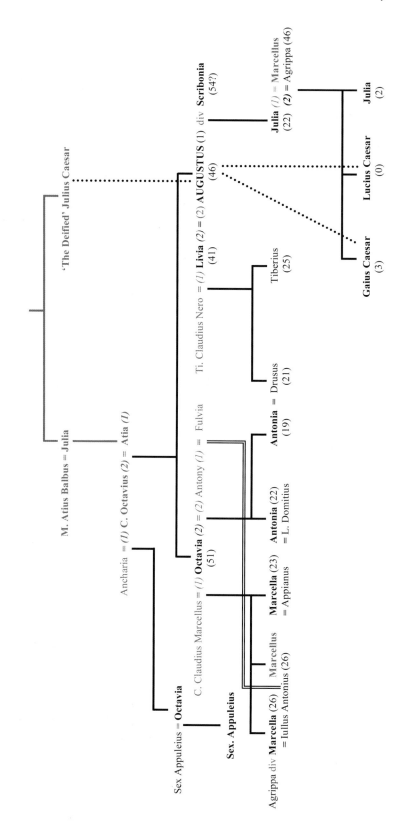

Family Tree 3 [AD 1]

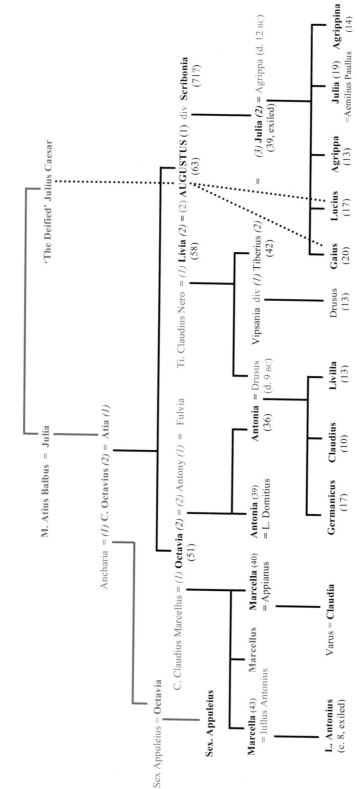

Family Tree 4 [AD 14]

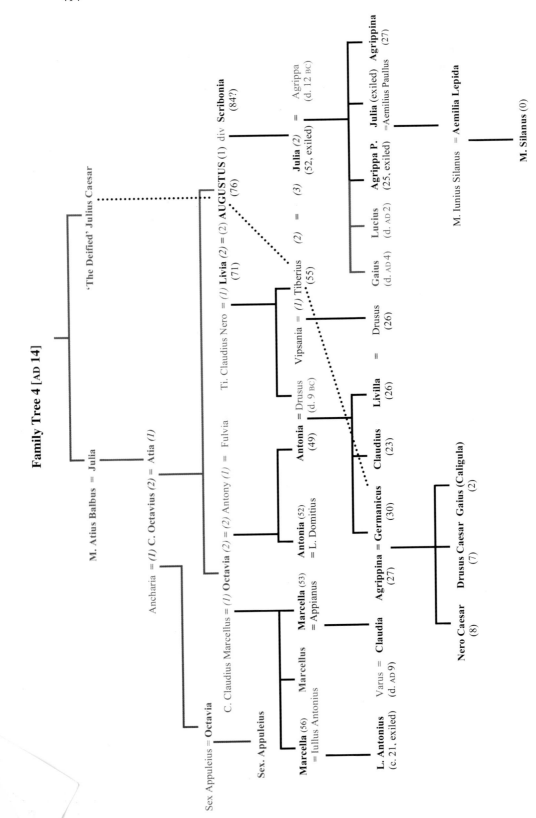

Addenda

K37b Aeneas' prayer to the Sibyl at Cumae

And you, most holy prophetess, who knows   65
What is to come, grant (for all I ask is owed to me by fate)
That the Trojans may settle in Latium, along with
Our far-travelled gods and the displaced powers of Troy.
Then will I build in solid marble a temple for Phoebus and Diana
And establish a festival in honour of Phoebus.   70
You too will find pride of place within our lands.

[Virgil, *Aeneid* 6.65–71]

69   Virgil portrays Aeneas as praying to establish the temple of Apollo dedicated by Augustus (see **A19.1, C34, G19, G39, K37–8**).

70   Games of Apollo were instituted in 212 BC, but Virgil's readers may have been meant to think of the prestigious Actian Games established by Augustus (**H11**) and the Centennial Games (**L20–28**) perhaps already being planned in Virgil's lifetime.

71   *Pride of place*: Augustus transferred the sibylline oracles from the Capitol to gilded cases under the pedestal of Apollo's statue in the Palatine temple (Suet, *Aug.* 31.1).

K68b Tibullus celebrates Messalla's road-building

The man kept away from home in Tusculum or ancient gleaming Alba
   should praise that monumental road.
For there, by your own generosity, hard gravel has been laid down
   and stone fitted skilfully together on top.
And the farmer shall sing your praises when he returns home from Rome,
   late at night, but confident in the surface beneath his feet.

[Tibullus, *Poems* 1.7.57–62]

For Messalla, prominent Roman aristocrat and supporter of the new regime, see Section **B**, 31 BC. He maintained a circle of poets under his patronage, amongst whom Tibullus was the most distinguished, who celebrated their patron's achievements. This poem celebrates his triumph (see **N2c**) and birthday. Messalla helped restore the *Via Latina* which led south-east from Rome to Casilinum (*c.* 135 miles).

N44b Funerary inscriptions, from Rome, of 2 sons of Phraates

Seraspadanes of Parthia, son of Phraates the Arsacid, King of Kings. Rhodaspes of Parthia, son of Phraates the Arsacid, King of Kings.

[EJ 183 = *ILS* 842]

N8b Portico of the Nations

For Augustus had built a portico in which he had arranged statues representing every nationality. This portico was known as the portico 'of the Nations'.

[Servius, *Commentary on Aeneid* 8.721]

For the context of the comment see **G38**.

No trace of this portico survives and only one other literary reference to it is known (Pliny 36.39, 'a statue of Hercules stands on the ground in front of the entrance to the Portico of the Nations'). Pliny shortly afterwards mentions that the Theatre of Pompey contained statues of 14 nations over which Pompey had triumphed: Augustus' portico was intended to show his world-conquest.